D1241512

Beowulf

Garland Reference Library of the Humanities (Vol. 20)

Beowulf

An Edition with Manuscript Spacing Notation and Graphotactic Analyses

Robert D. Stevick

Garland Publishing, Inc., New York & London

Copyright © 1975

by Robert D. Stevick

All Rights Reserved

2-6-76- BT6672

Library of Congress Cataloging in Publication Data

Beowulf.
    Beowulf : an edition with manuscript spacing notation
and graphotactic analyses.

    Bibliography: p.
    I. Stevick, Robert David, 1928-   ed.
PR1580.S8   1975   829'.3   75-1201
ISBN 0-8240-1090-6

Printed in the United States of America

Contents

PREFACE

This edition of Beowulf could not have been completed without assistance from both individuals and organizations. Preparation of the text and computer programming for the appendices was carried out with support of the Australian-American Educational Foundation, in the form of a research grant for work at the University of Sydney. That University, besides making available its facilities, also provided funds for computer time required in preliminary development of the computer programs. The Computing Centre of The University of New South Wales offered excellent cooperation through the various phases of programming trials, errors, and eventual successes. Dr. N. Solntseff (then at the University of N.S.W.) more than once came to the rescue when programming problems arose. Dr. John Jacobson (University of Washington) made valuable suggestions whenever called upon. Further research funds for computer time were provided by the University of Washington. Staff of the British Museum permitted me to examine the Beowulf manuscript for verification of certain facsimile readings for final assurance (if such were needed) of the reliability of the published facsimiles and textual commentaries. Assistance of many kinds came also from uncounted persons whom I thank here sincerely if only collectively. Such cooperation, I should like to think, is only natural among those who study Beowulf or, if they do not, those whose dedication to knowledge is in other ways of the highest order.

INTRODUCTION

Argument

I offer here an edition of <u>Beowulf</u> unique in representing not
only the text of alphabetic and other written symbols of the
late tenth century manuscript, but also the incidence and
measure of spacings between the symbols in lineal order.
Both the marks of writing and the spacings between them carry
linguistic information. Hence the text that follows will
facilitate study of aspects of the structure of Old English
not directly accessible through a text that transcribes only
the written symbols. The syntax, morphology, phonology, and
other features of the text have been analyzed on the evidence
of written symbols alone; the prosodic (or suprasegmental)
features, on the other hand, can be analyzed only with the
record provided by spacings varied in width and deployed by
other than lexical criteria. The spacing features also provide
extensive evidence for analysis of syllable structure in Old
English. With the extended linguistic information recoverable
from marks and spacings together, the present text will also
facilitate study of literary aspects of the great Anglo-Saxon
heroic poem, particularly its meter and style.

In addition to serving linguistic and literary purposes,
this edition should prove to have at least some small value to
other, more specialized areas of study. Attention to spacings
as well as to linguistic forms helps identify features of the
writing that have not before been noticed. Some have to do
with processes in the scribes' copying, such as the addition of
a letter at the end of a morphic set of letters after a succeeding set of letters already had been begun, or the first scribe's
apparently construing two morphemes, not one, when he wrote

icge (1107), a notable crux in the text. These features have relevance to textual criticism. Some other features of writing and spacing may provide the heuristics for further research into the history of the one extant text; at the least, something more about the scribes' _Vorlage_ may be discoverable with the help of this new text.

Some analysis of the relation of the manuscript's written symbols and spacings has already been carried out, particularly in my monograph _Suprasegmentals, Meter, and the Manuscript of Beowulf_. In that study I have tried to show that there is a clear set of correlations among linguistic, metrical, and graphic features of the manuscript text: specifically, patterns in the positions of spacing in letter-strings and the measure of spacings, on the one hand, correspond in complex but definite ways to features of syntax and meter, on the other. (The text in the present edition was prompted by the monograph, and not the other way around.) Other analysis of the relation of writing and spacing appears directly or indirectly in other sections of this Introduction as well as in the appendices to this edition. The appendices consist essentially of limited concordances of graphotactic features of the _Beowulf_ manuscript; occurrences of spacing within the representations of words have been isolated and sorted by various criteria, and the dominant patterns have been described in headnotes to the appendices. The extent of the analysis of the written symbols together with their spacings that has already been carried out argues for rather than against the potential value of this edition for linguistic and literary study of Old English. Because spacing features now appear to be as much an intentional part of the manuscript text as are the alphabetic and other symbols, and because they seem to have been "written" with considerable care and skill, their significance may be expected to be of very high order. The exhaustive study that these features require is feasible only with a text that incorporates them.

The potential value of this edition also derives from the fact that some other Anglo-Saxon manuscripts have linguistically significant positioning of spacings and variation in their measure. These do not include, unfortunately, the other three major poetic codices in Old English--The Vercelli Book, The Exeter Book, and The Junius Manuscript ("The Cædmon Manuscript"). But in "Scribal Notation of Prosodic Features in The Parker Chronicle, Anno 894 [893] " I have shown, for example, that parsing of a passage by principally graphotactic analysis yields a patterning congruent with that produced by parsing by traditional linguistic methods. The same kind of demonstration has been carried out by Virginia Joan Cyrus in The Tollemache Orosius: Text with Spacing Notation Edited for Computer Analysis. The British Museum MS. Royal 15B.xxii, a copy of Aelfric's Grammar, is almost a showpiece of spacing by linguistic principles; brief illustrative analysis is contained in Chapter 25 of my English and Its History. My own survey--only just underway--of Anglo-Saxon manuscripts has turned up still others in which spacing features yield to and extend linguistic analysis of Old English texts. Thus, the present edition may serve as a working model for transcribing the remaining texts: by this means a wealth of new linguistic data may be made available in easily and accurately manipulable form.

It will be clear already that this edition of Beowulf is intended for advanced students of the poem and its language, not for readers making first acquaintance with this earliest literary masterpiece in English. The appearance of the text implies the same specification of its intended users. Transcription of the written symbols and spacings does not require that the text be printed in all capital letters, and a more "natural" looking text can be produced in capital and lower case letters as in the manuscript, with notation of spacing given as superscript numerals. (The latter system is used for citation in my previous studies of Anglo-Saxon manuscripts.)

Instead of this form--

$DHAA 3 COOM 3 OF 1 MOORE/ 4 UNDER 3 MIST- 5 -HLEOTHUM// 3 (0710)
GRE-9-NDEL 6 GONGAN/ 3 GODES 5 YRRE 4 BAER//5   (0711)

--the text could have this form:

710 Ða[3] com[3] of[1] more[4] under[3] mist-[5]-hleopum[3]
711 gre[9]ndel[6] gongan[3] godes[5] yrre[4] bær[5] .

The mode of transcription adopted here seems to be the most
feasible one at present, however, if the edition is to be
immediately usable both by persons working directly from the
printed text and by persons utilizing electronic data processing
machines. (For the latter, the text can be made available on
magnetic tape.) Maximum utility of the text requires that it
conform to the limited character set in much of the standard
computing equipment and that the printing display all items of
the transcript in the lineal order of the punchcard and magnetic
tape records from which the text is produced. It may be noted
in passing that the editor has found neither of the two modes
of transcription to be more difficult than is the other to
read from the page.

Another departure from ordinary conventions of editing
is the use of hyphens and spaces in the transcription. Because
the spacings in the manuscript may or may not occur between
words, may or may not separate constituent morphemes of a word,
may or may not come between letters within a morpheme spelling,
practical considerations require that the linguistic nature of
the position of a manuscript spacing must be identified. By
rules given below, hyphens, spaces, and their combinations
provide notation for word boundaries, word-constituent morpheme
boundaries, and nonmorpheme boundaries at which spacing occurs
in the manuscript.

Transcription of Manuscript Data

Each line of the transcription contains exactly 80 characters (including blanks), the length of punchcards for electronic data processing machines; it was on punchcards that the text was initially keyboarded. The text consists of the manuscript features and editorial additions transcribed according to the following conventions.

A. Manuscript features

(1) The alphabetic symbols are transcribed in the order in which they appear in the manuscript. All letters shared by the conventional alphabets for Old English and Modern English are transcribed without change. For the others, these substitutions have been made:

ð (and Ð)	transcribed	DH
þ (and Þ)	"	TH
æ (and Æ)	"	AE.

(In the Old English of Beowulf, none of the character sequences dh, th, or ae occurs within a morpheme letter-string.) By convention, ⁊ 'wynn' is transliterated as W. The manuscript symbol ę is very rare in the text and for want of additional print characters is transcribed variously, according to the normal form of the word in which it occurs: in 1981 -ręced it is treated as if it were e, but in 2126 bęl it is treated as if it were æ.

(2) Other distinctive symbols in their contexts are represented as follows.

(a) The single point, usually raised in the first scribe's (S1's) copy but on the line in the second scribe's (S2's) copy, is transcribed as a full stop (a period); most marks of punctuation in the manuscript are of this kind. Multiple marks for pointing are transcribed in lineal sequence. The unique ⟨. . ,⟩ in line 91 is registered as ⟨. . ,⟩. The recurrent ⟨:-⟩ at the end of a section of the poem in S2's copy is registered as ⟨. . -⟩.

Scribal marks indicating where a correction is to be made, or where a superscript letter is to be read as a correction, and the like, are not transcribed; their significance is only that of changing written characters that are in error.

(b) The mark resembling an acute accent is transcribed as ⟨+⟩ adjacent to and preceding the first letter of the morph in which it occurs in the manuscript. In the manuscript the mark is generally centered over the vowel in the morphic string of letters. Thus, MS. ban is transcribed as +BAAN (the reduplication of A is explained below).

(c) Abbreviations in the manuscript are represented as follows:

Manuscript	ꝥ (for þæt)	transcribed	TH=
"	⁊ (for ond)	"	=AND
"	ꝣ (for eþel)	· "	.=EETHEL. (as at 913).

Manuscript ū, ī, etc. transcribed U=, I=, etc. (where the superior horizontal stroke signifies a following nasal consonant, e.g., MS. gū for gum (1486), dō/leasan for dōmleasan (2890), bear̄ for bearm (896))

| " | ḡ (for ge) | transcribed | G= (as at 2570) |
| " | æft͂ (for æfter) | " | AEFT= (as at 2060). |

The latter two of the list belong to the S2's copy; the few other abbreviations, e.g., M= representing men (3165), particularly on the last, and crowded, folio, are transcribed similarly.

(d) Capitalization is transcribed by ⟨$⟩ preceding and adjacent to the letter capitalized in the manuscript; ⟨$$⟩ signifies that all following letters in the text up to a hyphen, an asterisk, or a blank are capitalized in the manuscript.

(3) Spacing between letters not standing in normal

xiv

juxtaposition (with or without ligature) is transcribed with
numerals 1 through 7, the ascending order of numerals corresponding to increasing measure of space between successive
letters. Varied measure of spacing is illustrated in these two
examples:

289b   5 SEE 1 THE 2 WEEL 3 THENCEDH// 4

1545a   7 $OF- 1 -SAET 2 THAA 3 THONE 4 SELE- 1 -GYST/ 9

(See further comment below.) Measure of spacing that cannot
be determined, usually because of loss of or damage to portions
of the manuscript, is represented by the numeral 8; the same
numeral is also used when editorial emendation adds or deletes
word units. End of a manuscript line is represented by the
numeral 9. Both 8 and 9 thus represent indeterminate measure
of spacing between successive letters in contrast to the lineally
determinate spacing represented by the numerals 1 through 7.
Absence of spacing between letter strings representing types
of linguistic materials that elsewhere are commonly written
with intervening space is transcribed as 0 (zero); e.g.,
manuscript sepe appears as SEE 0 THE.

B. Editorial additions

All parts of the transcript not representing purely graphic
features of the manuscript are additions made according to the
following conventions.

(1) Identification of verse lines: each verse line
begins a line of transcription, starting in column 1 (of the 80-
column punchcards and the printed text); a verse line whose transcription requires more than 73 characters is divided at the
halfline position, the transcription of the b-verse (the
second halfline) beginning in column 11. A line is identified
for its place in the textual sequence by standard verse linecount given as a four-digit numeral enclosed in parentheses,
the serial identification occupying columns 75-80.

(2) End of an a-verse (a first halfline) is marked by a

xv

virgule, and end of a b-verse is marked by two virgules. These markings follow without space the last letter in the verse string and precede the spacing-notation numeral; if a mark of punctuation follows the verse, it is transcribed preceding the virgule(s) marking end-of-verse.

(3) Section numberings in the manuscript, occurring at the fitt divisions of the poem, consist of roman numerals with or without pointing; they are transcribed with the appropriate letters (and punctuation, if any) beginning in column 26; in columns 75-80 the identification is (FITT).

(4) Vowel length is represented by reduplication: a "long e" conventionally printed with editorial macron, ē, is transcribed EE, ǣ is transcribed AEAE, etc. The present edition follows the text of Friederich Klaeber's Beowulf and The Fight at Finnsburg (3rd edition, 1950), in distinguishing vowel length. It departs from Klaeber's text consistently in transcribing one form, however: the relative particle þe/ðe is given here only with short vowel, as THE / DHE. This is an expedient to avoid homographs with the second person pronoun form þē/ðē 'thee' transcribed as THEE / DHEE. In doubtful instances where, for example, Klaeber prints anrǣd in the text (1529, 1575), but gives "(ān-?)" in his Glossary, the form in the text (i.e., AN- 0 -RAEAED) is given here. Klaeber's sē has also been changed here to se (i.e., SE) twice (2646, 2733), and we should read wē (2654).

(5) Emendation of the manuscript text is registered by the conventions described next. The changes again are those adopted by Klaeber in Beowulf and The Fight at Finnsburg, with very few departures to correct minor errors or to provide readings determined by investigators whose work was not available to Klaeber; the latter have been gleaned from Kemp Malone's "Readings" given in his edition of The Nowell Codex (Volume 12 of Early English Manuscripts in Facsimile), cross-checked with Malone's "Readings from the Thorkelin Transcripts of Beowulf." Klaeber's text is in error in reading ða instead of þa (1288), maþelode instead of maðelode (1473).

(a) Deletion is marked by a pair of parentheses ⟨( )⟩ preceding the letter(s) omitted in the edited text; end of the deletion is a hyphen, a blank, or an asterisk. A manuscript reading not incorporated into Klaeber's text has no other editorial additions in the transcription; the principal instance is that there is no reduplication of vowel symbols.

(b) Addition to the manuscript reading is marked by an asterisk ⟨*⟩ preceding the letter(s) added in the edited text; end of the addition is a hyphen or a blank. Reduplication of vowel symbols and any other editorial addition may occur within any added string of symbols.

(c) Replacement of a manuscript reading is transcribed as a deletion and addition sequence. Manuscript sole (302) replaced by edited text sāle, for example, is transcribed ( )SOLE*SAALE.

(6) Restoration of manuscript readings that have not been preserved either in the manuscript in its present condition or in earlier transcriptions of it is transcribed here as replacement: the deletion symbol ⟨( )⟩ precedes a string of downward-pointing arrows ⟨↓⟩ , one such mark representing each illegible or lost letter, so far as this has been determined. Kemp Malone's "Readings" in his edition of The Nowell Codex serves as the usual authority for the number of letters to be restored; the restorations are those in Klaeber's text.

Illegible text that cannot be restored except by pure conjecture is transcribed as a string of downward-pointing arrows only; the transcription matches Klaeber's text.

(7) Morph boundaries are signified by a hyphen, a blank, or a combination of these symbols according to the following rules:

(a) Identification of morph boundaries.

(1) Any position in the manuscript text at which space is left between letter strings is regarded as a morph boundary. Space is defined here as any distance

xvii

between letters in the lineal sequence in the manuscript greater
than that for normal contiguity of letters in this noncursive
script. (Ligature is discussed in a later section of the
Introduction.) End of a manuscript line, as mentioned earlier,
is treated as spacing of a distinctive and indeterminate kind.

(2) Any position corresponding to a word
boundary (as defined by morphotactic and syntactic rules) is
regarded as a morph boundary.

(3) Any position corresponding to onset of
a root morpheme or a prebase morpheme is regarded as a morph
boundary. However, the onset of an inflectional suffix is not
so regarded for purposes of transcription, and neither is the
onset of a derivational suffix, with the exception of -līce.
Reasons for these rules are pragmatic. Roots and prebases are
usually set off from preceding morphs by spacing; see Appendices
II and III. On the other hand, suffixed morphemes almost never
are separated from preceding morphemes unless morpheme boundary
and syllable boundary are coincident —MAEAER-2-NE (mǣrne, 36),
but usually BEEA-2-GA (bēaga, 35), HREE-2-THIG (hrēþig, 94),
etc.; see Appendix I.

(b) Notation of morph boundaries.

Because the identification of morphs, for purposes of
transcription, proceeds from both graphic and linguistic
criteria, the types of morphs thus isolated are distinguished
in the notation.

(1) The boundary of a morph that is not
coincident with a morpheme or word boundary as stipulated in
(2) and (3) just above is marked by a hyphen attached to the
letter string with no blank intervening between the hyphen and
the numeral for the measure of spacing in the manuscript.
Single morpheme fela, for example, divided at the end of a
manuscript line is transcribed FE-9-LA.

(2) The boundary of a morph coincident with
the type of morpheme boundary stipulated in (3) above is marked

by a hyphen attached to the letter string and a blank intervening between the hyphen and the spacing numeral. Editorially
marked māpmgestrēona (1931) is transcribed 4 MAATHM- 3 -GE- 2
-STREEONA/ 4.

(3) The boundary of a morph that is
coincident with a word boundary, as stipulated above, is
marked by a blank (only) intervening between the letter string
and the spacing numeral. Thus, editorially marked gyf hēo gȳt
lyfað, constituting line 944b, is transcribed 4 GYF 9 HEEO 1
GYYT 3 LYFADH// 5.

A comprehensive illustration is drēam-healden/de. (1227)
transcribed as 6 DREEAM- 4 - HEAL-2-DEN-9-DE.// 7.

Again because both graphic and linguistic criteria are
employed for identification of morphs in the transcription,
the numeral 0 is utilized to register absence of manuscript
spacing at a linguistically defined morph boundary: in line
1277 occurs 4 =AND 0 GALG- 0 -MOOD/ 4. As the transcription
of the text will show, zero-spacing has pragmatic justification
in that the positions in which it occurs are similar to those
in which space occurs elsewhere--and usually normally--in the
manuscript. As the analyses in the appendices will confirm,
zero-spacing is an essential feature of the graphotactic
structure of the manuscript text.

Summary of the notation system for transcribing the
manuscript.

A	F	L	R	W
B	G	M	S	X
C	H	N	T	Y
D	I	O	U	
E	K	P	V	

Correspond to Anglo-Saxon
alphabetic symbols

(J, Q, Z are not used; W transliterates Anglo-Saxon ƿ 'wynn';
V occurs only in numerals.)

0 - 9   a numeral registers lineal measure of spacing
          between strings of letters; arabic numerals do
          not occur in the Anglo-Saxon text.

          (blank) represents word boundary and some morpheme
          boundaries; see B(7)(b), above.

+   (plus sign) represents "acute accent" in manuscript;
          see A(2)(b), above.

-         (hyphen) represents morph boundaries not coincident
          with word boundaries; see B(7)(b), above.

*   (asterisk) represents editorial addition to the
          manuscript text; see B(5)(b), above.

/   single virgule represents end of a first halfline
          of verse; a pair of virgules represents end of a
          second halfline of verse.

=   represents an abbreviation mark in the manuscript;
          see A(2)(c), above.

$ represents capitalization in the manuscript; see
          A(2)(d), above.

,   (comma) represents a similarly shaped mark of
          punctuation in the manuscript.

.   (period or full stop) represents the similarly
          shaped pointing in the manuscript.

↓   (downward-pointing arrow) represents an illegible
          or lost letter in the manuscript; see B(6), above.

( )   (open and close parentheses) in juxtaposition
          represent an emendation by which the manuscript
          text that follows is deleted in Klaeber's text,
          see B(5)(a), above; parentheses also enclose
          numerals designating verse linecount at the end
          of each line of transcription.

Measurement of Spacing in the Manuscript

Determination of the measure of spacings is a task for human
investigators--and practiced ones--alone. It cannot be carried
out by technological devices and cannot be entrusted to inex-
perienced assistants. Because transcription of spacings is the
most distinctive facet of this edition, a somewhat detailed
sketch of the problems and procedures in determining measure
of spacing should be set down, if only that they will be on
record.

The text initially was transcribed from beginning to end
with a gap left at every point in the sequence of letters where
spacing was left in the manuscript; a gap was also left between
words and before each root or prebase morpheme. Verseline
numbering and markings for ends of a-verses and b-verses were
added. Subsequently, the spacings in the manuscript were
assessed and numeral notation added to the transcript.
Separate readings of the manuscript--one for the written
symbols, the other for the spacings--in some ways simplified
the task of transcription (though it did increase the time
required for it); more importantly, it made possible a rate of
notation and concentration on spacings that such a task requires
for close discrimination, on the one hand, and alertness to
contextual variations, on the other. The separate readings
also served to keep linguistic expectations about spacings
from distorting assessment of their sizes: the task was to
record the measure of spacing accurately on graphic principles
rather than linguistic or metrical ones.

The contextual variations and the graphic principles are
the factors that rule out mechanical means to determine
spacings. They do not, however, lessen the rigor with which
measure of spacing can be determined. There are long stretches
of manuscript text in the hands of both scribes in which a
millimeter scale yields approximately the notation that appears

in this edition. Most of the text copied by S2, in fact, has
spacing whose measure in millimeters corresponds very closely
to that of the notation, for measures 2 through 7; about one
and a half millemeters counts as 1, and one millimeter, the
distance between letters in normal juxtaposition, counts as 0.
There are many places in the text copied by S1, on the other
hand, where a millimeter scale does not approximate the
notation given here. Change in size of spacings relative to
a fixed scale is illustrated very clearly in the manuscript
text for line 1210 where, in the middle of a word in the middle
of a verse, the scribe changed (or sharpened) his pen, with
immediate change in size of both letters and spacings; between
verses 1422 and 1423, at a change from one page to the next, is
another conspicuous change in relative size of letters and
spacings. The manuscript page containing verses 805-827,
copied by S1, has generally more than usual distance between
nonspaced letters, making assessment of minimal spacings
especially difficult. At any point in the text, therefore,
spacing notation is determined by the width of the space
relative to the size of letters and spaces in the immediate
context.

Determining measure of spacing poses no problems, however,
in most of the text. For the transcript that follows, it was
not practical to omit numeral notation for spacing even in
instances where measure of spacing may be questionable:
computer processing of the text would not succeed if any
feature were left unspecified (or if multiply-defined); also,
an editor's decisions on problematic instances--even when any
one may be only a best guess--may be expected to be recorded
in full. The question marks beside readings in the worksheets
for the transcription cannot practically be included in the
final text. Specific problems in determining measure of
spacing nevertheless deserve full description, and it is to
describing them that most of this section is devoted.

Wherever manuscript copy is illegible, the numeral 8

xxii

ndicates that the measure of spacing cannot be determined;
t stands at word boundaries and at certain morpheme boundaries
as described earlier), but any other potential position of
pacing is not noted. The form seoðð̄an (1875) ends a manu-
cript line; emendation, adding nō after seoðð̄an, poses the
roblem of where to put "8" to signify indeterminate spacing
nd where to put "9" to signify end of manuscript line. The
cribal addition of superscript c above a space in ge-hwylcre
805) poses a similar problem. Where the text is completely
bscure, as in line 2229, only two spacing facts are noted--
hat end of a manuscript line occurs (signified by the numeral
) and a word boundary at the halfline point is marked
signified by the numeral 8). A few spacings in the scribes'
opy therefore inevitably will not have been recorded in this
ext.

   With the rare occurrences of runic symbols, as ⟨◊⟩ (913),
nd roman numerals, as ·xv̄· (207), spacing has also been
egarded as indeterminate, since these are in morphographic
ather than alphabetic writing: following spacing has the
otation "8".

   Corrections in the manuscript--additions or changes after
urther text has been copied--often affect the spacing between
onsecutive morphs. In line 90, a 3 "was squeezed in" later,
s Malone notes, to change sæde to sægde. Before and after
he 3 was added there was no spacing within the word. In line
285 the scribe erased the last stroke of an m to make the first
 in bunden after the word was written; the resultant gap is
ot counted as spacing in the transcript. In line 1951 an n
pparently has been added by the same scribal hand to fill a
-space in syðð̄an well. Because this position can only have
een a word boundary for the scribe, yet because the source of
he error can only be conjectured, the indeterminateness of
he significance of the (now) 0-spacing is registered, with
8" standing for the measure. On the same manuscript page,
he later addition (apparently by another hand) of s in

xxiii

<u>on-hōhsnod</u>[e] (1944), fills a small space originally left
between <u>h</u> and <u>n</u>. In the transcription no notation of the
original spacing is given. The reasons are these. The
transcription would be greatly complicated in recording
spacing both before and after the change, and it would not
provide uniquely defined data for that portion of the manuscript text. Again the reasons for the original spacing and
the omission of the <u>s</u> (as well as reason for omitting the
inflectional -<u>e</u>, if that emendation is correct) can only be
conjectured; but since the spacing was small and presumably
not at a word or morpheme boundary, the expedient was not to
record the original spacing. Fine as the distinctions between
these two examples may be, the basis of discrimination is clear
enough to be applied consistently to several other problematic
portions of the manuscript text. The effect on analysis of
spacing of the manuscript will be very small indeed.

In certain instances, where earlier editors have not noted
corrections in the manuscript but where the present editor
infers from spacing characteristics that the text has been
changed, the spacing that stands after the putative correction
is recorded. In line 1604 the final <u>n</u> in <u>wine-drihten</u> seems
to have been added after the next word was begun, and leaves
only a 1-space. The compound noun ends a verse line, a
position which on this manuscript page most often has a 4-space
or 5-space (or larger); except in this line the only lesser
spaces in that position are 3-spaces. Without the <u>n</u>, the line
would end with a 5-space. In addition, all other instances of
<u>en</u> (e.g., in <u>þeoden</u>, 1598) on the manuscript page have ligature
<u>en</u> (as is also normal elsewhere), with a rising final stroke
(the tongue) of the <u>e</u>; in the instance of <u>-drihten</u> the <u>e</u> has
a flatly horizontal stroke, as is normal for nonligature <u>e</u>.
The <u>n</u>, too, is differently shaped, most noticeably in the mark
joining the two short downstrokes. We may conjecture that the
scribe misconstrued syntax (and consequently meter), writing
<u>selfne</u> and probably also <u>gesāwon þā</u> before he realized his
error: he easily corrected the form but had no practical way

o restore the spacing. Whatever the cause of error and process
f correction may have been, the spacing is erratic. But in
his kind of matter it has seemed best to record only the
esultant spacing. The reasoning behind this editorial
rinciple is that an attempt to isolate every addition made by
 scribe where space had been left cannot at this stage be
ubjected to any clear control, and the matter is best left to
ubsequent studies of the manuscript. There are two good
easons to suspect that s is a later addition in folces hyrde,
n line 2981: lack of spacing between words with the morpho-
ogical features and syllable structure of these two is
ontrary to S2's normal copy, and the resultant string of
leven letters without spacing is probably unique (count of
etters between spaces not yet having been carried out). The
anuscript copy of these words is badly torn; since evidence
f letter shape cannot be brought to bear, the inference of
orrection by adding s should be registered here, not in the
ext itself. Finally, when only spacing criteria support
udgment that a correction has been made, it is certainly
 referable--at this stage in the study of graphotactics of
nglo-Saxon manuscripts--to record spacing as the scribes
inally left it. Thus, I infer that the g was added to hrēmig,
ine 1882, and d was added to aged (emended to āgend), line
883--both corrections in a single line of the manuscript.
hile other evidence is not conclusive (from scrutiny of the
acsimiles), the spacing in both instances strongly suggests
hanges after succeeding letters were written. The tran-
cription nevertheless lists a 1-space after each of these
orms.

Apart from change in size of writing, illegible text, and
pecial symbols, the chief problems in determining measure of
pacing arise from individual characteristics of the hand-
riting styles of the scribes, particularly the style of S1.

Although S1 and S2 wrote some parts of the copy in

xxv

which millimeter measure approximates the notation for spacing,
differences in their handwriting habits requires one thorough-
going difference in the mode of determining measure of their
spacings. Both the spacings and the letter shapes and sizes
show less variation in S2's copy than in S1's. The thickness
of vertical strokes of S2's pen also makes the distance between
successive letters less readily perceptible as white space;
especially the space between letters with adjacent straight
vertical strokes appears to be less than the space occurring
when, say, d̲ or ð̲ stand on the left, or when æ̲ stands on the
right. Whatever the shape of a letter, at whatever point he
began it, a string of letters that are normally juxtaposed will
have equal distances between them when measured at mid-height
nearest points. Thus, since S2 was so regular in moving his
hand to the right for successive nonspaced letters, distance
between nearest points of spaced letters provides the most
accurate determination for measure of spacing for his copy.
S1's writing is of a different character. Besides the sudden
changes in size of letters and spaces noted above, there are
less conspicuous variations, such as the larger writing (and
spacing) in the last half dozen lines of Fitt XXIII (lines
1645-50) and the first several lines of the succeeding fitt.
More important is the fact that, apart from variation in size
of his writing, S1 shapes several of his letters so that a
final stroke toward the right may vary greatly in length.
Unlike S2, S1 does not confine the right edge of his letters
thus keeping all instances of a given letter to a uniform
width; and since he normally begins a succeeding letter so as
not to have it touch the preceding one (apart from letters
joined by ligature), there are hundreds of instances in his
copy in which white space is noticeable between adjacent downstrokes of two letters, and only normal distance for
juxtaposed letters in the noncursive script between the
rightmost flourish of the first letter and the nearest point
of the next one. Only on the basis of extensive comparisons
does it become clear that significant measure of space between

uccessive letters for S1 is to be made between the "body" of
he letters--the visually prominent adjacent portions of the
etters. With S1, perceptual sameness or difference is the
asis for determining measure of spacing; with S2, measure by
fixed scale (locally adjusted) is the firmer basis for
etermining measure. Despite these differences between the
cribes' individual styles, their principles of spacing are
losely similar. Even so, the styles are different and
nalysis of the text consequently should be done separately
or each scribe's copy.

Some details of the problem in measuring S1's spacing
onclude this section. For reasons already given, S2's copy
an usually be measured in a fairly mechanical and straight-
orward way, but S1's cannot. Whether the area between letters
s to be regarded as a spacing is the major problem in terms
f number of instances encountered. It arises from the
ombination of two factors. One is that S1 varied the length
f the final stroke of many of his letters, as mentioned above.
he other is that his range of spacings includes a very slight
isplacement of a letter to the right of where it would stand
f in normal juxtaposition to its predecessor; this 1-spacing
s clearly within his set of spacing habits, as countless
nambiguous examples show. Some ostensible instances turn out
ot to be problems at all, when another criterion may take
recedence. Such an instance is presence or absence of ligature
oining certain pairs of letters. A specially compact example
s in line 1864a, transcribed GE 1 WIDH 4 FEEOND 4 GE O WIDH 4
REEOND/ 9, where the sequence of e and w (MS. ɤ) are joined in
he second occurrence, but are slightly separated in the first.
questionable case is recede, line 728. By comparison with
eced, line 770, its lack of ligature suggests the tran-
cription should read RE-1-CED; the shape of the c is also
nusual, however, contributing to the decision not to regard
he sequence as spaced. But absence of ligature between e and
indicates that ge-man, line 265, is GE- 1 -MAN, hē ne is HEE

1 NE in line 1082, mǣ-ned is MAEAE-1-NED in line 857, etc.

The genuinely problematic instances nearly all involve the letter following close on an ɪ or r̲, æ, a̲, or long s̲, the letter preceding d̲ or ð̲, or the position between doubled nn, tt, or gg. Lines 1425-27 provide another compact example, in which transcription is given as CYNNES (1425), CUN-1-NIAN (1426), ON 1 NAES (1427); CUN-1-NIAN (1444) on the same manuscript page may be added. A 1-space is clearly present in all but the first form; the gap between n̲'s in cynnes seems not to be spacing, but there is room for doubt. Likewise, sinnigne, line 1379, is doubtful and perhaps should read SIN-1-NIG-1-NE. Space does not seem to be left between n̲'s in manna cynnes, line 701, or manna, 789; it is commonly left between n̲'s within a form, as Appendix I will show; in 1725 the scribe clearly wrote MAN-2-NA and elsewhere MAN-1-NA and the like in many cases.

The shape and process of forming ɪ in S1's hand led to the decision that spacing was not intended after ɪ in dēofla (756), -fultuma (1455), -hleopum (710), bolgen- (709), -hwylc (874), gyldenne and lēane (1021), scyldinga (1069); the instance of maþelode (1383) is a specially good example, when compared with golde (1382) and eald- (1381).

The shape and process of forming r in S1's hand led to the decision that spacing was intended after r in spræc (1168, 1171), even though this form elsewhere, as in 1215 and 1698, is not internally spaced. Compared with mēaras (865), faran, in the same line, reads as FAR-1-AN. A pair FOR-1-HT and FER-1-HDHE occur in 754.

No space seems to be intended between t's in ge-mētte (757) or flette (1025). Sufficient contrast of distance between g's leads to transcription of HIG 3 WIG-1-GE 4 (1770) but WIIG- 0 -GE- 5 -WEORTHAD (1783).

No space seems to be intended after æ in sǣlum (1170): the final, horizontal stroke of the æ is long, but the ɪ picks up to the left of the end of that stroke, presumably indicating specifically that the gap is not spacing. The two 1-spaces in hæleþa (1852), HAEL-1-E-1-THA, are judged by the shape of the tail of the l, and by the apparent retouching of the tongue of the e by the scribe, presumably to minimize a space before the following þ; compare mē þīn, separated by a 2-space in the next line. The transcription, in regard to spacing, is occasionally only a best guess: hyrde (931), bearnum and brōþrum (1074), monnes and cynnes (1729), gēata (1856) are the principal examples.

Special problems arise when several successive letters must be judged to have spacing or not to have it. Letters are more generously spaced in hafelan (1614), hreþre (1745), prōwade (1589), and strǣle (1746); the greater distance between them may be attributable to their occurring at the ends of manuscript lines, though the stretching of a string of letters in that position occurs only once each few hundred lines, on the average. At the beginning of a manuscript line hafelan (1780) is also stretched out. The following are some of the few forms that occur mid-line in the manuscript and have been interpreted as having spacing of successive letters:

hæleþa (611)	transcribed HAE-1-L-1-E-1-THA
hroden (emended roden) (1151)	transcribed R-1-O-1-DEN
frēond-laþu (1192)	transcribed FREEOND- 3 -L-1-A-1-THU
-fremmanne (174)	transcribed FREM-2-MAN-1-N-1-E

At the end of a manuscript line heorote (1267) seems to be HEOR-1-O-1-TE. But in several instances it is not easy to decide whether the scribe intended spacing or not. To give but one more example, healfre (1087) has been judged not to have internal spacing: if one follows the procedure by which the letters a, l, f have been formed, reasons for the judgment should be apparent. Genuine doubt remains about the transcription of a few instances of spacing of successive letters, such as that of fāhne (716), and those listed together first in this paragraph.

Lest the length of the foregoing review of problems in
determining measure of spacing give the wrong impression, this
much may be said. Since nearly all the spacings in the hands
of both scribes can be recognized and measured, the
indeterminate and ambiguous instances merely reduce the
exactness of statistical analysis that may be performed on the
data that constitute the text. The manuscript of Beowulf was
copied by human scribes and has been transcribed here by a
human editor: the text has only the precision of patterns that
people, not machines, ordinarly produce with practice and care.

Manuscript Punctuation

Transcription of pointing in the manuscript has also been
carried out with care. It may turn out that pointing was as
accurately copied by the scribes as was the text of alphabetic
symbols. Certainly there is reason to suppose that its
purpose is not limited to the function Malone conjectures.
"In our codex, as elsewhere," he says "pointing marks
separation. The scribe might punctuate if he wished to
separate one word or word-group from another, or from its
context, by a visible sign. Usually he left such separations
to take care of themselves, or provided for them in his
spacings, but now and again he marked them with points" (The
Nowell Codex, p. 29). In the case of certain numerals, such
as ·xv̄· (207), and fitt numbers, and in the case of runic symbols
as ·ᛞ· (520, 913, 1702), pairs of points distinguish nonalphabetic (or nonphonological) writing. The point between
anrǣd and naes (1575) may well be to separate the forms: they
had been written in near contiguity, naes having been
written originally nes, the e later altered to æ; the two forms
also span a halfline boundary in a context in which 3- to
5-spaces are the norm. Perhaps the scribe, in a moment of in-
attention or hesitation, took the second form to be a suffix

when he wrote it first; when he saw his error, he changed the
vowel symbol and inserted a point to signal separation of the
forms. The point is transcribed in this edition. Another
point (which Zupitza explains as having the same function as
the one in 1575) occurs in 273 between wē and sōplīce; this
point is not transcribed here: no other type of correction
is evident in the manuscript, it occurs in the middle of a
halfline--a rare position for unquestioned points--and it is
not raised, as is normal in the writing of S1. Its reason
for being is obscure. Similarly, the point between þ and gē
in 338 is not transcribed: it seems to be accidental. In 494
what may be a point between nytte and behēold is not transcribed. Zupitza does not register it; Malone thinks it is
mistakenly set before instead of after behēold, as may well be
the case. Another reason to doubt its authenticity as a point
is that, despite the long tongue of the e in nytte, the mark is
not centered, as is normally the case for points. The non-
centered mark in 927 (displaced left instead of right) has been
transcribed, however, since its characteristics are otherwise
normal. Finally, the mark between grunde and tēah in 553 has
been transcribed as a point, but with doubts as to its being
intentional punctuation: it is not raised, it occurs within a
halfline, and it does not accompany correction of letters.

Except in very few instances, the pointing is transcribed on
the authority of Malone. He gives only counts of points on any
manuscript page (not a full list of their specific positions),
but generally his readings of the pointing are clear. If
Malone is doubtful about the presence of a point, even when one
is listed by Zupitza, it has been omitted in the present text;
two exceptions are those at the ends of lines 1029 and 1904.

The original pointing of the manuscript is especially
difficult to determine with a degree of accuracy approaching
that of the alphabetic text. It seems unlikely that any more
than Malone has found can ever be determined, or with any more

assurance, by examination of the manuscript and collation with earlier transcripts of it. If anything more is to be learned about the pointing, it will probably be discovered through theory-based predictions based on distributional patterns' nearly intact in the unquestioned occurrences of points. The alphabetic text has errors, though it is certainly not a careless copy; most errors are patent and have been corrected by sound and usually straightforward editorial techniques. The spacing, as it now appears, is sytematically varied, consistent with linguistic and metrical principles. There are several reasons to believe the pointing may also be dependable as a record of deliberate composition of the text. Most points were placed where they occur as part of the original copying: they are usually centered in spacings of regular widths. Clearly, they are not consistently placed to mark sentence ends, and they do not occur often enough to be simply line-end markers, or halfline markers as in the Junius manuscript of the "Caedmonian" poems. More significantly, the scribes may be inferred to have taken the trouble in certain instances to be sure a point was not obscured. The right margin of the recto of most folios is lost or damaged, hence the occurrence of points at ends of lines cannot be fully recovered. There are a few instances, however, that may be significant. A prime example is the point terminating line 451. The final word, sorgian is divided at the end of the manuscript line, with only the last two letters carried over to the beginning of the next, followed by a point within a 7-space. If the line ending with sorgí- had been extended as far to the right as were the second and fourth lines following it, the last two letters could have been written on the same line; the point could then have been placed close to the final n on the same line, hardly exceeding the margin. Just as one-syllable brēost two lines later is, by the scribal norms, an undividable string of letters, so apparently the point is neither expendable nor to be obscured. Similar instances of a point following the last syllable of a word that begins a new manuscript line occur at the ends of 317, 1227, and at the end of 1715a.

The Appended Analyses

Three analyses of the text, executed by a computer, are included in this edition as appendices. In each appendix the text has been analyzed in four blocks: lines 1-661, 662-1320, 1321-1939, these three comprising the copy of the first scribe, and lines 1940-3182 comprising the second scribe's copy. The initial reason for breaking the text into blocks was a limitation in storage capacity of the computing equipment on which analyses were first made. Division of the text into four parts has been retained because the partial lists seem to be of more convenient size for visual scanning than complete lists would be, without introducing loss or distortion of the general "picture" of the distribution characteristics of the spacing features.

Appendix I concerns spacings that occur at other than morpheme boundaries; the other two concern position and measure of spacing that separate root and prebase morphemes within words. Together they show the high degree of regularity with which each of the scribes adhered to some of his spacing principles; the principles have sufficient definition to warrant using them as the basis for re-examining some textual problems and exploring some further facets of the alphabetic text. Some, like the apparent adding of ᵹ to give hrēmiᵹ (1882), have already been mentioned. Others are here only briefly illustrated.

A very simple pair of examples may be found in gryre (1282) and scēata (752). Each word is divided at the end of a manuscript line, with the last two letters carried over to the next line. The scribe first wrote gryr; subsequently he wrote re

on the next line and scraped away (imperfectly) the r at the
end of gryr. The sufficiency of Malone's account of the error
occurring "by dittography" may be doubted. Rather, when S1 had
gotten as far as gryr, he decided not to complete the form,
since to do so would extend it beyond the ruled margin. His
principle for dividing words called for a full syllable (or
more) on the new line, hence the writing of re and the erasure.
At 752 S1 may be inferred to have followed the same process,
except that he neglected to erase the t of sceat. The error,
apparent on linguistic grounds, is readily explicable by the
scribe's principles of dividing strings of letters.

The manuscript reading merewioingas (2921) has been for a
long time, as Malone terms it, a "bone of contention." That
the scribe intended that reading (and not, say, merewicinga)
is the inference supported by spacing characteristics. There
are reasons to believe that the final s was added as a
correction by the scribe after he had written subsequent
letters. In the facsimile the s looks normal. Yet its
presence leaves the text without space between the compound
noun or name and the following word milts. The 0-space at the
boundary between forms of these types is contrary to the
scribe's writing habits; it is also contrary to the principle
of leaving space between verse halflines; and it produces a
string of ten letters unusual in both its length and structure.
Elsewhere in the scribe's copy, modification of already copied
text is in the nature of correction, and the correction
normally produces the reading accepted on modern editorial
principles.

In ways such as these it should be possible to resolve
some textual problems and reach still other decisions about
the accuracy of the text as transmitted. Beyond this, the
appendices should serve as a starting point for further study
of syllable structure, morphotactics, linguistic prosody, and
other features of Old English, as well as for refining our
understanding of Anglo-Saxon meter and style--as well as the
splendor--of Beowulf.

Further Research

There would be no point to publishing this edition if there were not many potential uses of the text, or if the author intended to retain sole proprietorship of the domain of graphotactics of the Beowulf manuscript along with other research areas related to the data recorded in the following pages. I believe that many uses can be made of this edition: accordingly, it is to enable further research of certain kinds that this work is now made available.

A new concordance to Beowulf in which vowel length is distinguished (unlike the concordance prepared by Bessinger and Smith) could be produced quickly and inexpensively and in any format desired. To eliminate notation of lineal spacing in the manuscript (the combination of hyphens, numerals, and blanks) requires only four subroutine computer instructions in SNOBOL4, for example; root and prebase morphemes can be kept as distinct units for concording, or all intraverbal notation can be removed leaving only words as units. An "off-the-shelf" computer concordance program could do the rest. Manuscript readings alongside emended forms can be retained, or by a simple subroutine of computer instructions either original reading or emendation can be deleted.

Metrical studies of various kinds may also be assisted by the text that has been prepared here. Vowel-length is coded in. So is linecount. Identification of a-verse and b-verse units can also be coded if it should be needed, and it can, of course, be retained in the virgule notation or changed to any other notation desired. Thus if, for example, one's research interest in metrics should call for isolation of verses (whether distinguishing a- and b-verses or not) according to presence of long vowels, number of long (or short) vowels, patterns of long and short vowels, frequency of recurrence of any of these factors, and so on—the data are recorded in a form usable either for

visual scanning and manual sorting or for electronic data
processing.

Some kinds of linguistic data are also accessible to
machine-assisted gathering and sorting. A count (and listing, if
wished) of occurrences of any grapheme or grapheme combination
can be made, should there be any reason for doing so. Thus,
consonant sequences (or "clusters") can be isolated, as can any
other phonotactic information. If a careful set of definitions
were constructed and spelling variants allowed for, inflectional
or derivational suffixes could be at least partially sifted and
sorted mechanically. Any of the prepositions or other particles,
in whatever kind of context desired, can similarly be extracted.
The occurrences of compounds--and their frequency and distribu-
tion--can also be isolated.

Many of these types of data, though, may be of less interest
to linguistic studies (since they have had a century's head
start) than they may be to studies in stylistics.

Still further types of research involving graphic features
of lineal spacing are in order and are now practical without
repetition of the very considerable labor required to record the
graphotactic features of the manuscript. Quite a number of
topics in graphotactics have been mentioned in earlier sections
of this Introduction and need not be repeated here. Suffice it
to say that they seem to be germane to linguistic studies as
well as to metrical studies.

Mention of the apparent relations of manuscript graphotactics to linguistic and metrical features of the text of Beowulf
calls in turn for at least brief commentary on the relation of
this edition to my earlier study, Suprasegmentals, Meter, and
the Manuscript of Beowulf. In simplest as well as most funda-
mental terms, this edition is subsequent to and independent of
that monograph. The earlier study convinced me that the incidence and measure of spacing between letter-strings was neither
arbitrary nor capricious (as it had seemed to earlier editors)
and that the only practical way to further the study of the text,

including its graphic spacing, was to prepare an edition incorporating the graphotactic information. That information had not had explicit recording in full. Further, because of the massive amount of that kind of information, the record of that information would remain limited in manipulability if it were not prepared in a format handleable by a computer. Thus, the edition was undertaken to provide a full and explicit transcription of both text and spacing in the unique, late tenth century copy of the poem.

An incidental relation of this edition to Suprasegmentals is that it may clarify and answer some of the queries, reservations, and objections raised by the earlier study. For instance, the principles for determining measure of spacing are explained here in detail not provided earlier: measurement from what to what, with regard or disregard for which features (e.g., hairline extensions of rightmost flourish of the pen) and in what context, by means of an arbitrary uniform scale (e.g., millimeter measure) or not—these and other matters will be clearer.

On the other hand, this edition will not in itself clarify or answer some other concerns. It could not in any case dispel the notion that the Suprasegmentals volume offered a theory of meter rather than only some deductions about the meter of Beowulf; a theory of meter is something quite different, and there is probably no better ostensive definition of such a theory than Thomas Cable's The Meter and Melody of Beowulf. Likewise, this edition may not cancel the impression of some that my earlier study recreated specifically the suprasegmental, or prosodic, features of Old English speech as used in verse, when it offered instead an hypothesis that correlation of graphotactic and syntactic features implied further correlation with linguistic prosodics, whatever the phonic and systemic details of the prosodic features of Old English might have been.

Yet this edition should help make some of the concerns resolvable. Ideally, it may even help make some issues inevitably resolvable, for it provides for the first time a complete, explicit record of the text including its graphotactic features: arguments based only on samples need no longer be offered. Further, if for instance one is convinced that the spacing--both where it is and how wide it is--gives guidance for reading the poem as it was read by the scribes who copied it, yet if one disregards fixed patterns such as those of spacing after a two-syllable first root of a compound noun, then one's interpretive performance mechanically based on spacing will be both odd and irrational for being too narrowly based. For this kind of error there is no longer excuse.

In brief, this new text of _Beowulf_ enlarges the resources of further research. It does this by recording additional data contained in the manuscript of the poem, by describing and illustrating some characteristic patterns of those data, and by offering the data in a format readable by both people and the computers they may use in their research. It is hoped and expected that full understanding and interpretation of the data can now the more easily and surely proceed.

List of Works Cited

J. B. Bessinger, Jr., and Philip H. Smith, Jr. (eds.),
A Concordance to Beowulf (Ithaca, 1969).

Thomas Cable, The Meter and Melody of Beowulf (Illinois
Studies in Language and Literature, 64, Urbana, 1974).

Virginia Joan Cyrus, The Tollemache Orosius: Text with
Spacing Notation Edited for Computer Analysis, University
of Washington, Dissertation, 1968.

Fr. Klaeber (ed.), Beowulf and the Fight at Finnsburg, 3rd
ed. (Boston, 1950).

Kemp Malone (ed.), The Nowell Codex: British Museum Cotton
Vitellius A. xv, Second MS (= Early English Manuscripts
in Facsimile, vol. XII (Copenhagen, 1963).

-----"Readings from the Thorkelin Transcripts of Beowulf,"
PMLA, 64 (1949), 1190-1218.

Robert D. Stevick, English and Its History: The Evolution
of a Language (Boston, 1968).

-----"Scribal Notation of Prosodic Features in The Parker
Chronicle, Anno 894 [893]," Journal of English Linguistics,
I (1967), 57-66.

-----Suprasegmentals, Meter, and the Manuscript of Beowulf
(The Hague, 1968).

Julius Zupitza (ed.), Beowulf: Reproduced from the Unique
Manuscript British Museum MS. Cotton Vitellius A. xv;
2nd ed. Norman Davis (Early English Text Society, 245,
London, 1959).

TEXT

BEOWULF

```
$$HWAET 3 $$WEE 2 $$GAAR- 1 -$$DE-9-NA/ 3 IN 0 GEEAR- 3 -DAGUM.// 6          (0001)

THEEOD- 2 -CYNINGA/ 9 THRYM 2 GE- 2 -FRUUNON// 4                              (0002)

HUU 0 DHAA 3 AETHE-2-LINGAS/ 3 ELLEN 9 FRE-2-ME-1-DON.// 6                    (0003)

$OFT 3 SCYLD 3 SCEEFING/ 3 SCEATHENA 9 THREEATUM// 4                          (0004)

MONEGU= 4 MAEAEGTHUM/ 4 MEODO- 3 -SETLA 9 OF- 2 -TEEAH// 3                    (0005)

EGSODE 3 ()EORL*EORLAS/ 3 SYDHDHAN 3 AEAEREST 3 WEARDH// 9                    (0006)

FEEA- 3 -SCEAFT 2 FUNDEN/ 5 HEE 2 THAES 3 FROOFRE 4 GE- 1 -BAAD// 9          (0007)

WEEOX 2 UNDER 3 WOLCNUM/ 3 WEORDH- 3 -MYNDUM 3 THAAH.// 9                     (0008)

ODH 2 TH= 3 HIM 2 AEAEG- 0 -HWYLC/ 4 ()THARA 3 YMB- 2 -SITTEN-1-DRA// 9      (0009)

OFER 2 HRON- 8 -RAADE/ 5 HYYRAN 2 SCOLDE// 3                                  (0010)

GOMBAN 9 GYLDAN/ 3 TH= 0 WAES 2 GOOD 2 CYNING.// 6                            (0011)

DHAEAEM 2 EAFERA 3 WAES/ 9 AEF-1-TER 3 CEN-1-NED// 2                          (0012)

GEONG 3 IN 1 GEARDUM/ 3 THONE 3 GOD 9 SENDE// 4                               (0013)

FOLCE 2 TOO 0 FROOFRE/ 4 FYREN- 2 -DHEARFE 3 ON- 9 -GEAT// 4                  (0014)

()TH=*THE 1 HIIE 3 AEAER 2 DRUGON/ 3 ALDOR- 8 -()++ASE*LEEASE.// 4           (0015)

LANGE 9 HWIILE/ 5 HIM 2 THAES 3 LIIF- 2 -FREEA// 4                            (0016)

WULDRES 3 WEALDEND/ 9 WOROLD- 2 -AARE 3 FOR- 2 -GEAF.// 6                     (0017)

BEEO- 0 -WULF 3 WAES 3 BREEME/ 9 BLAEAED 2 WIIDE 4 SPRANG// 4                 (0018)

SCYLDES 3 EAFERA/ 4 SCEDE- 9 -LANDUM 3 IN.// 7                                (0019)

$SWAA 2 SCEAL 8 ()++++++*GEONG 8 ()+UMA*GUMA/ 3 GOODE 9 GE- 2 -WYRCEAN// 3   (0020)

FROMUM 3 FEOH- 2 -GIFTUM./ 3 ON 1 FAEDER 9 ()++RME*BEARME// 5                 (0021)
```

END FOLIO 132R +

```
TH= 2 HINE 3 ON 1 YLDE/ 4 EFT 2 GE- 3 -WUNIGEN// 4                           (0022)

WIL- 9 -GE- 1 -SIITHAS/ 5 THONNE 4 WIIG 3 CUME.// 5                          (0023)

LEEODE 3 GE- 2 -LAEAESTEN/ 9 LOF- 2 -DAEAEDU= 3 SCEAL// 4                     (0024)

IN 1 MAEAEGTHA 4 GE- 2 -HWAEAERE/ 3 MAN 1 GE- 9 -THEEON.// 6                  (0025)

HIM 2 DHAA 3 SCYLD 3 GE- 2 -WAAT/ 4 TOO 1 GE- 3 -SCAEP- 2 -HWIILE// 9        (0026)

FELA- 4 -HROOR 3 FEERAN/ 3 ON 1 FREEAN 3 WAEAERE// 5                         (0027)

HII 2 HYNE 9 THAA 1 AET- 1 -BAEAERON/ 4 TOO 1 BRIMES 3 FARODHE// 4           (0028)

SWAEAESE 3 GE- 0 -SIITHAS/ 9 SWAA 2 HEE 3 SELFA 4 BAED// 4                    (0029)
```

```
THENDEN 3 WORDUM 3 WEEOLD/ 9 WINE 3 SCYLDINGA// 5          (0030)
LEEOF 3 LAND- 2 -FRUMA/ 5 LANGE 9 AAHTE// 5               (0031)
THAEAER 3 AET 2 HYYDHE 3 STOOD/ 4 HRINGED- 2 -STEFNA// 2  (0032)
IISIG 9 =AND 0 +UUT- 3 -FUUS/ 3 AETHELINGES 3 FAER.// 5   (0033)
AA- 0 -LEEDON 2 THAA/ 1 LEEOFNE 9 THEEODEN// 5           (0034)
BEEA-2-GA 3 BRYTTAN/ 3 ON 1 BEARM 3 SCIPES// 9           (0035)
MAEAER-2-NE 4 BE 2 MAES-1-TE/ 5 THAEAER 2 WAES 3 MAADMA 3 FELA// 9   (0036)
OF 1 FEOR- 4 -WEGUM/ 3 FRAETWA 2 GE- 0 -LAEAEDED.// 5     (0037)
$NE 2 HYYRDE 9 IC 2 CYYM- 1 -LIICOR/ 4 CEEOL 1 GE- 2 -GYRWAN// 4    (0038)
HILDE- 3 -WAEAEP-2-NUM/ 9 =AND 0 HEADHO- 3 -WAEAEDUM// 3  (0039)
BILLUM 2 =AND 0 BYR-1-NUM/ 4 HIM 2 ON 2 BEAR-9-ME 4 LAEG// 4   (0040)
MAADMA 3 MAENIGO/ 4 THAA 2 HIM 3 MID 3 SCOL-9-DON// 3     (0041)
ON 1 FLOOD-1-ES 2 AEAEHT/ 4 FEOR 3 GE- 2 -WIITAN.// 5    (0042)
$NALAES 9 HII 2 HINE 4 LAEAESSAN/ 3 LAACUM 3 TEEODAN// 3  (0043)
THEEOJ- 2 -GE- 1 -STREEO-9-NUM/ 3 THON 8 THAA 8 DYDON// 3  (0044)
THE 3 HINE 3 AET 1 FRUM- 2 -SCEAFTE/ 9 FORDH 2 ON- 0 -SENDON// 4   (0045)
AEAEN-1-NE 3 OFER 3 YYDHE/ 4 UMBOR- 3 -WE-9-SENDE// 5     (0046)
```

END FOLIO 132V +

```
THAA 0 GYYT 4 HIIE 3 HIM 3 AA- 0 -SETTON/ 4 SEGEN 3 ()GEL*GYL-9-DENNE// 5 (0047)
HEEAH 1 OFER 2 HEEAFOD/ 5 LEETON 3 HOLM 2 BERAN// 9      (0048)
GEEA-1-FON 2 ON 1 GAAR- 2 -SECG/ 4 HIM 3 WAES 2 GEOOMOR 4 SEFA// 9  (0049)
MURNENDE 5 MOOD/ 3 MEN 2 NE 3 CUNNON.// 5               (0050)
SECGAN 2 TOO 9 SOODHE/ 4 SELE- 4 -RAEAE-1-DEN-1-()NE*DE// 4   (0051)
HAELEDH 3 UNDER 4 HEOFENU=/ 9                            (0052)
     HWAA 4 THAEAEM 3 HLAESTE 3 ON- 2 -FEENG.// 9       (0052)
```

.I.   (FITT)

```
$$DHAA 2 WAES 2 ON 1 BURGUM/ 4 BEED- 0 -WULF 3 SCY-1-L-2-DINGA// 3  (0053)
LEEOF 9 LEEOD- 2 -CYNING/ 4 LONGE 4 THRAAGE// 4          (0054)
FOLCUM 3 GE- 0 -FRAEAE-9-GE/ 4 FAEDER 3 ELLOR 4 HWEARF// 5  (0055)
ALDOR 3 OF 1 EAR-2-DE/ 9 OTH 2 TH= 2 HIM 3 EFT 2 ON- 1 -WOOC// 4   (0056)
HEEAH 2 HEALF- 3 -DENE/ 4 HEEOLD 9 THEN-1-DEN 4 LIFDE// 4  (0057)
```

2

GAMOL 2 =AND 0 GUUTH- 2 -REEOUW/ 4 GLAEDE 3 SCYL-9-DINGAS// 4   (0058)

DHAEAEM 2 FEEOWER 3 BEARN/ 3 FORDH- 4 -GE- 0 -RIIMED// 2   (0059)

IN 9 WOROLD 3 WOOCUN/ 4 WEORO-2-DA 4 ()RAESWA*RAEAESWAN// 5   (0060)

HEORO- 2 -GAAR. 3 =AND 9 HROODH- 3 -GAAR/ 4 =AND 1 HAALGA 3 TIL// 5   (0061)

HYYR-2-DE 4 IC 3 TH= 8 ,,,/ 8 ,,,-8-ELAN 3 CWEEN.// 9   (0062)

HEADHO- 3 -SCILFINGAS/ 5 HEALS- 2 -GE- 1 -BEDDA// 4   (0063)

THAA 1 WAES 3 HROODH- 9 -GAARE/ 5 HERE- 3 -SPEED 2 GYFEN// 3   (0064)

WIIGES 3 WEORDH- 3 -MYND./ 3 TH= 9 HIM 3 HIS 2 WINE- 2 -MAAGAS// 4   (0065)

GEORNE 4 HYYR-2-DON/ 3 ODHDH 3 TH= 9 SEED 2 GEO-2-GODH 3 GE- 0 -WEEOX// 5 (0066)

MAGO- 2 -DRIHT 4 MICEL/ 3 HI= 9 ON 2 MOOD 4 BE- 1 -ARN// 4   (0067)

TH= 2 HEAL- 3 -RECED/ 4 HAATAN 2 WOLDE.// 9   (0068)

END FOLIO 133R *

MEDO- 8 -AERN 4 MICEL/ 3 MEN 1 GE- 0 -WYRCEAN// 5   (0069)

()THONE*THONNE 2 YLDO 9 BEARN/ 3 AEAEFRE 3 GE- 2 -FRUUNON.// 3   (0070)

=AND 0 THAEAER 2 ON 2 IN-1-NAN/ 4 EALL 9 GE- 2 -DAEAELAN// 3   (0071)

GEONGUM 3 =AND 0 EAL-2-DUM/ 3 SWYLC 3 HIM 3 GOD 9 SEAL-2-DE// 5   (0072)

BUUTON 2 FOLC- 3 -SCARE/ 4 =AND 0 FEORUM 2 GUMENA.// 9   (0073)

DHAA 1 IC 3 WIIDE 5 GE- 1 -FRAEGN/ 4 WEORC 2 GE- 1 -BAN-1-NAN// 3   (0074)

MANIGRE 9 MAEAEGTHE/ 4 GEOND 3 THIS-2-NE 2 MIDDAN- 3 -GEARD// 3   (0075)

FOLC- 3 -STE-9-DE 4 FRAET-1-WAN/ 4 HIM 3 ON 1 FYRSTE 4 GE- 1 -LOMP// 3   (0076)

AEAEDRE 9 MID 2 YLDUM./ 4 TH= 2 HIT 3 WEARDH 3 EAL- 3 -GEARO// 4   (0077)

HEAL- 4 -AER-9-NA 4 MAEAEST/ 4 SCOOP 2 HIM 3 HEORT 2 NAMAN// 3   (0078)

SEE 1 THE 2 HIS 9 WORDES 4 GE- 1 -WEALD/ 3 WIIDE 3 HAEFDE.// 7   (0079)

SHEE 1 BEEOT 3 NE 9 AA- 0 -LEEH/ 5 BEEAGAS 3 DAEAEL-1-DE// 5   (0080)

SINC 2 AET 0 SYMLE/ 4 SELE 9 HLIIFA-2-DE.// 5   (0081)

HEEAH 2 =AND 1 HORN- 3 -GEEAP/ 4 HEADHO- 3 -WYLMA 9 BAAD// 5   (0082)

LAADHAN 3 LIIGES/ 3 NE 1 WAES 3 HIT 3 LENGE 3 THAA 0 GEEN// 9   (0083)

TH= 0 SE 2 ()SECG*ECG- 3 -HETE/ 4 AATHUM- 2 -()SWERIAN*SWEEORAN// 3   (0084)

AEFTER 3 WAEL- 2 -NII-9-DHE/ 4 WAECNAN 2 SCOLDE.// 6   (0085)

WHAA 2 SE 2 ELLEN- 3 -GAEAEST/ 4 EAR-9-FODH- 2 -LIICE// 6   (0086)

THRAAGE 3 GE- 2 -THOLODE/ 4 SEE 1 THE 3 IN 1 THYYSTRU= 9 BAAD// 4   (0087)

TH= 2 HEE 3 DOOGORA 3 GE- 2 -HWAAM/ 4 DREEAM 3 GE- 1 -HYYR-9-DE.// 6   (0088)

3

HLUUDNE 4 IN 2 HEALLE/ 5 THAEAER 2 WAES 4 HEAR-2-PAN 9 SWEEG// 4   (0089)

SWUTOL 4 SANG 3 SCOPES/ 3 SAEGDE 3 SEE 2 THE 2 CUJTHE// 9   (0090)

FRUM- 3 -SCEAFT 4 FIIRA/ 3 FEOR-1-RAN 3 REGCAN..,// 9   (0091)

END FOLIO 133V ✝

CWAEDH 5 TH= 1 SE 2 AEL- 0 -MIHTIGA/ 4 EORDHAN 3 WORHTE// 9   (0092)

WLITE- 4 -BEORHTNE 5 WANG/ 4 SWAA 3 WAETER 4 BE- 9 -BUUGEDH// 4   (0093)

GE- 0 -SET-1-TE 5 SIGE- 6 -HREE-2-THIG/ 4 SUN-1-NAN 9 =AND 0 MOONAN// 3   (0094)

LEEOMAN 3 TOO 4 LEEOHTE/ 5 LAND- 2 -BUUEN-9-DUM// 3   (0095)

=AND 0 GE- 4 -FRAET-1-WADE/ 5 FOLDAN 3 SCEEA-2-TAS// 9   (0096)

LEOMUM 3 =AND 0 LEEAFUM/ 4 LIIF 2 EEAC 3 GE- 1 -SCEOOP// 4   (0097)

CYN-9-NA 3 GE- 2 -HWYLCUM/ 3 THAARA 3 DHE 2 CWICE 4 HWYRFATH.// 9   (0098)

$SWAA 0 DHAA 4 DRIHT- 3 -GUMAN/ 3 DREEAMUM 3 LIFDON// 9   (0099)

EEADIG- 2 -LIICE/ 4 ODH 0 DHAET 2 ✝AAN 2 ON- 1 -GAN// 3   (0100)

FYRE-1-NE 4 FREM-9-MAN/ 3 FEEOND 3 ON 2 HELLE// 3   (0101)

WAES 3 SE 0 GRIM-2-MA 3 GAEAEST/ 9 GREN-1-DEL 5 HAATEN// 2   (0102)

MAEAERE 3 MEARC- 3 -STAPA/ 9 SEE 1 THE 4 MOORAS 3 HEEOLD// 3   (0103)

FEN 2 =AND 0 FAESTEN/ 3 FIIFEL- 2 -CYN-9-NES 3 EARD// 3   (0104)

WON- 2 -SAEAELII 3 WER/ 4 WEAR-1-DO-1-DE 3 HWIILE// 9   (0105)

SITHDHAN 4 HIM 3 SCYP-1-()PEN✝PEND/ 3 FOR- 2 -SCRIFEN 3 HAEFDE// 9   (0106)

IN 1 CAAINES 3 CYN-1-NE/ 5 THONE 3 CWEALM 3 GE- 2 -WRAEC// 9   (0107)

EECE 2 DRIHTEN/ 4 THAES 3 THE 2 HEE 4 AABEL 3 SLOOG.// 5   (0108)

$NE 0 GE- 9 -FEAH 5 HEE 3 THAEAERE 3 FAEAEHDHE/ 5   (0109)

AC 2 HEE 3 HINE 4 FEOR 9 FOR- 2 -WRAEC// 3   (0109)

METOD 2 FOR 3 THYY 1 MAANE/ 4 MAN- 1 -CYNNE 9 FRAM// 4   (0110)

THANON 2 UN- 1 -TYYDRAS/ 3 EALLE 4 ON- 2 -WOOCON// 9   (0111)

EOTENAS 3 =AND 0 YLFE/ 5 =AND 0 ORC- 0 -NEEAS// 3   (0112)

SWYLCE 5 GII-9-GANTAS/ 8 THAA 1 WIDH 3 GODE 4 WUN-1-NON// 5   (0113)

✝ END FOLIO 134R

LANGE 3 THRAAGE/ 9 HEE 8 HIM 3 DHAES 4 LEEAN 2 FOR- 4 -GEALD.// 9   (0114)

.II.   (FITT)

4

SGE- 8 -WAAT 3 DHAA 2 NEEOSIAN/ 4 SYTHOHAN 3 NIHT 3 BE- 1 -COOM// 9   (0115)

HEEAN 3 HUUSES/ 5 HUU 2 HIT 4 HRING- 3 -DENE// 3   (0116)

AEFTER 9 BEEOR- 2 -THEGE/ 3 GE- 1 -+BUUN 4 HAEFDON.// 7   (0117)

BFAND 3 THAA 0 DHAEAER 9 IN-1-NE/ 4 AETHELINGA 2 GE- 1 -DRIHT// 4   (0118)

SWEFAN 2 AEFTER 9 SYMBLE/ 4 SORGE 3 NE 1 CUUDHON// 3   (0119)

WON- 0 -SCEAFT 3 WERA/ 9 WIHT 3 UN- 2 -HAEAELO// 3   (0120)

GRIM 2 =AND 0 GRAEAE-2-DIG/ 3 GEARO 2 SOONA 9 WAES// 3   (0121)

REEOC 2 =AND 0 REETHE/ 4 =AND 0 ON 2 RAESTE 4 GE- 0 -NAM// 3   (0122)

THRIITIG 9 THEGNA/ 4 THANON 2 EFT 1 GE- 1 -+WAAT// 6   (0123)

HUUDHE 4 HREE-1-MIG/ 9 TOO 1 HAAM 2 FARAN// 3   (0124)

MID 3 THAEAERE 4 WAEL- 2 -FYLLE/ 3 WIICA 9 NEEOSAN.// 6   (0125)

DHAA 0 WAES 3 ON 0 UUHTAN/ 3 MID 2 AEAER- 2 -DAEGE// 9   (0126)

GRENDLES 3 GUUDH- 2 -CRAEFT/ 4 GUMUM 3 UN- 1 -DYRNE// 9   (0127)

THAA 1 WAES 3 AEFTER 2 WISTE/ 3 +WOOP 2 UP 1 AA- 0 -HAFEN// 2   (0128)

MICEL 9 MORGEN- 2 -SWEEG/ 3 MAEAERE 5 THEEODEN// 2   (0129)

AETHELING 3 AEAER- 0 -GOOD/ 9 UN- 2 -BLIIDHE 3 SAET// 4   (0130)

THOLODE 4 DHRYYDH- 2 -SWYYDH/ 3 THEGN- 1 -SORGE 9 DREEAH// 3   (0131)

SYDH-3-THAN 3 HIIE 5 THAES 3 LAADHAN/ 3 LAAST 2 SCEEA-9-WE-1-DON// 3   (0132)

WERGAN 3 GAASTES/ 4 WAES 3 TH= 2 GE- 3 -WIN 2 TOO 9 STRANG// 5   (0133)

LAADH 3 =AND 0 LONG- 1 -SUM/ 3 NAES 3 HIT 2 LENGRA 9 FYRST// 3   (0134)

                    END FOLIO 134V +

AC 1 YMB 3 AANE 2 NIHT/ 4 EFT 8 GE- 8 -FREMEDE// 9   (0135)

MORDH- 4 -BEALA 3 MAARE/ 5 =AND 0 NOO 2 MEARN 3 FORE// 9   (0136)

FAEAEHDHE 5 =AND 0 FYRENE/ 4 WAES 2 TOO 0 FAEST 3 ON 1 THAAM// 2   (0137)

THAA 9 WAES 3 EEADH- 2 -FYNDE/ 5 THE 2 HIM 3 ELLES 4 HWAEAER// 2   (0138)

GE- 0 -RUUM- 9 -LIICOR/ 3 RAESTE 8 *SOOHTE// 5   (0139)

BED 2 AEFTER 5 BUURUM/ 3 DHAA 1 HIM 9 GE- 2 -BEEACNOD 3 WAES// 3   (0140)

GE- 0 -SAEGD 4 SOODH- 3 -LIICE/ 5 SWEOTO-9-LAN 3 TAAC-1-NE// 6   (0141)

HEAL- 4 -DHEGNES 5 HETE/ 4 HEEOLD 2 HY-9-NE 4 SYDH-2-THAN// 3   (0142)

FYR 3 =AND 0 FAESTOR/ 3 SEE 1 THAEAEM 3 FEEONDE 9 AET- 2 -WAND.// 6   (0143)

BSWAA 2 RIIXODE/ 4 =AND 0 WIDH 2 RIHTE 5 WAN// 9   (0144)

AANA 3 WIDH 3 EALLUM/ 3 ODH 4 TH= 1 IIDEL 4 STOOD// 3   (0145)

5

HUUSA 3 SEELEST/ 9 WAES 2 SEEO 3 HWIIL 3 MICEL// 4   (0146)

().XII.*TWELF 2 WINTRA 4 TIID/ 2 TORN 1 GE- 9 -THOLODE// 4   (0147)

WINE 3 ()SCYLDENDA*SCYLDINGA/ 3 WEEANA 3 GE- 2 -HWELCNE// 9   (0148)

SIIDRA 2 SORGA/ 4 FOR- 0 -DHAAM 8 *SECGUM 3 WEARDH// 3   (0149)

YLDA 3 BEARNUM/ 9 UN- 0 -DYRNE 4 CUUDH// 2   (0150)

GYDDU= 3 GEODMORE/ 5 THAET-1-TE 3 GREN-9-DEL 4 WAN// 3   (0151)

HWIILE 3 WIDH 3 HROOTH- 2 -GAAR/ 5 HETE- 4 -NIIDH-1-AS 9 WAEG// 4   (0152)

FYRENE 4 =AND 0 FAEAEHDHE/ 4 FELA 3 MISSEERA// 3   (0153)

SIN- 1 -GAA-9-LE 4 SAECE/ 4 SIBBE 2 NE 1 WOLDE// 4   (0154)

WIDH 4 MAN-1-NA 3 HWONE/ 9 MAEGENES 4 DENIGA// 2   (0155)

FEORH- 3 -BEALO 3 FEOR-1-RAN/ 9 FEEA 4 THINGIAN// 3   (0156)

NEE 2 THAEAER 3 NAEAENIG 3 WITENA/ 3 WEENAN 9 THORFTE// 5   (0157)

()BEOR*BEORH-2-TRE 5 BOOTE/ 5 TOO 1 ()BANU=*BANAN 3 FOLMU=.// 9   (0158)

END FOLIO 135R +

()++*AC 8 ()++*SE 8 AEAEG- 0 -LAEAECA/ 8 EEHTENDE 3 WAES// 3   (0159)

DEORC 2 DEEATH- 2 -SCUA/ 9 DUGUTHE 4 =AND 0 GEO-1-GO-1-THE// 4   (0160)

SEOMA-1-DE 4 =AND 0 SYRE-2-DE/ 9 SIN- 1 -NIHTE 3 HEEOLD// 3   (0161)

MISTI-1-GE 3 MOORAS/ 3 MEN 2 NE 9 CUN-1-NON// 3   (0162)

HWYDER 4 HEL- 2 -RUUNAN/ 3 HWYRFTUM 9 SCRII-2-THADH// 4   (0163)

SWAA 2 FELA 3 FYRENA/ 4 FEEOND 2 MAN- 1 -CYN-9-NES// 2   (0164)

ATOL 3 AAN- 0 -GENGEA/ 3 OFT 3 GE- 1 -FRE-1-MEDE.// 9   (0165)

HEARDRA 5 HYYNDHA/ 4 HEOROT 2 EAR-2-DODE// 4   (0166)

SINC- 9 -FAAGE 4 SEL/ 3 SWEAR-2-TUM 2 NIH-1-TUM// 3   (0167)

NOO 1 HEE 2 THONE 9 GIF- 3 -STOOL/ 3 GREETAN 2 MOOSTE// 4   (0168)

MAATHDHUM 2 FOR 1 METO-9-DE/ 4 NEE 1 HIS 1 MYNE 3 WISSE// 4   (0169)

TH= 0 WAES 2 WRAEAEC 2 MICEL/ 9 WINE 2 SCYL-2-DINGA// 3   (0170)

MOODES 4 BREC-1-DHA/ 3 MONIG 2 OFT 9 GE- 0 -SAET// 4   (0171)

RIICE 4 TOO 1 RUUNE/ 4 RAEAED 1 EAHTEDON// 2   (0172)

HWAET 9 SWIIDH- 3 -FERHDHUM/ 4 SEELEST 3 WAEAERE// 4   (0173)

WIDH 2 FAEAER- 2 -GRYRU=/ 9 TOO 0 GE- 3 -FREM-2-MAN-1-N-1-E.// 7   (0174)

$HWIILUM 4 HIIE 2 GE- 1 -HEE-9-TON/ 3   (0175)

        AET 3 ()HRAERG*HAERG- 3 -TRAFUM// 2   (0175)

6

WIIG- 2 -WEOR-1-THUNGA/ 9 WORDUM 3 BAEAEDON// 4   (0176)

TH= 2 HIM 2 GAAST- 4 -BONA/ 3 GEEO-1-CE 9 GE- 1 -FRE-2-ME-2-DE.// 5   (0177)

WIDH 3 THEEDD- 3 -THREEAUM/ 2 SWYLC 3 WAES 9 THEEAW 2 HYRA.// 5   (0178)

HAEAETHENRA 4 HYHT/ 3 HELLE 2 GE- 1 -MUN-9-DON// 4   (0179)

IN 1 MODD- 2 -SEFAN/ 3 METOD 4 HIIE 2 NE 2 CUUTHON// 9   (0180)

DAEAE-1-DA 3 DEEMEND/ 3 NE 1 WISTON 3 HIIE 4 DRIHTEN 3 GOD.// 9   (0181)

                        END FOLIO 135V ✦

NEE 8 HIIE 8 HUURU 3 HEO-2-FENA 4 HELM/ 3 HERIAN 8 NE 9 CUUTHON// 3   (0182)

WUL-1-DRES 3 WAL-1-DEND/ 3 WAA 2 BIDH 3 THAEAEM 2 DHE 9 SCEAL// 5   (0183)

THURH 3 SLIIDHNE 4 NIIDH/ 3 SAAWLE 5 BE- 0 -SCUUFAN// 9   (0184)

IN 0 FYYRES 3 FAETHM/ 3 FROOFRE 3 NE 1 WEENAN// 3   (0185)

WIHTE 2 GE- 9 -WENDAN/ 3 WEEL 3 BIDH 3 THAEAEM 2 THE 1 MOOT// 3   (0186)

AEFTER 3 DEEADH- 9 -DAEGE/ 3 DRIHTEN 3 SEECEAN.// 2   (0187)

=AND 0 TOO 0 FAEDER 3 FAETHMUM/ 9 FREODHO 4 WILNIAN.// 9   (0188)

                        .III.   (FITT)

$SWAA 0 DHAA 3 MAEAEL- 3 -CEARE/ 4 MA-1-GA 3 HEALF- 1 -DENES// 3   (0189)

SIN- 0 -GAA-9-LA 4 SEEADH/ 3 NE 2 MIHTE 4 SNOTOR 5 HAELEDH// 4   (0190)

WEEAN 2 ON- 9 -WENDAN/ 3 WAES 3 TH= 1 GE- 1 -WIN 2 TOO 2 SWYYDH// 4   (0191)

LAATH 2 =AND 0 LONG- 2 -SUM/ 2 THE 9 ON 0 DHAA 1 LEEODE 5 BE- 1 -COOM// 3 (0192)

NYYD- 2 -WRACU 3 NIITH- 1 -GRIM/ 3 NIHT- 9 -BEALWA 4 MAEAEST// 4   (0193)

TH= 0 FRAM 3 HAAM 2 GE- 2 -FRAEGN/ 4 HIGE- 1 -LAA-9-CES 4 THEGN// 3   (0194)

GOOD 1 MID 1 GEEATUM/ 3 GRENDLES 3 DAEAE-1-DA// 9   (0195)

SEE 0 WAES 2 MON- 0 -CYN-2-NES/ 5 MAEGENES 4 STRENGEST// 3   (0196)

ON 9 THAEAEM 3 DAEGE/ 5 THYSSES 4 LIIFES// 4   (0197)

AETHELE 3 =AND 1 EEACEN/ 3 HEET 9 HIM 3 YYDH- 2 -LIDAN// 3   (0198)

GOODNE 3 GE- 1 -GYR-1-WAN/ 3 CWAEDH 3 HEE 1 GUUDH- 9 -CYNING// 4   (0199)

OFER 3 SWAN- 3 -RAADE/ 4 SEECEAN 3 WOL-2-DE// 4   (0200)

MAEAER-9-NE 4 THEEODEN/ 4 THAA 2 HIM 2 WAES 3 MAN-2-NA 3 THEARF// 4   (0201)

DHONE 9 SIIDH- 2 -FAET 2 HIM/ 3 SNOTERE 4 CEOR-1-LAS// 4   (0202)

LYYT- 3 -HWOON 2 LOOGON./ 9 THEEAH 8 HEE 2 HIM 2 LEEOF 2 WAEAERE// 5   (0203)

        END FOLIO 136R ✦

                        7

HWETTON 3 HIGE- 8 -ROOFNE/ 9 HAEAEL 3 SCEEA-2-WE-2-DON// 4   (0204)

HAEFDE 3 SE 1 GOODA/ 4 GEEA-1-TA 3 LEEODA// 9   (0205)

CEM-2-PAN 3 GE- 1 -CORONE/ 5 THAARA 3 THE 4 HEE 2 CEENOSTE// 9   (0206)

FINDAN 3 MIHTE/ 4 ().XV.NA*FIIF-8-*TYYNA 8 SUM// 4   (0207)

SUND- 3 -WUDU 3 SOOHTE/ 9 SECG 3 WIISADE// 6   (0208)

LAGU- 2 -CRAEFTIG 2 MON/ 3 LAND- 2 -GE- 0 -MYR-9-CU// 4   (0209)

FYRST 3 FORDH 3 GE- 1 -+WAAT/ 3 FLOTA 3 WAES 2 ON 1 YYDHUM.// 9   (0210)

+BAAT 3 UNDER 4 BEORGE/ 5 BEORNAS 3 GEARWE// 4   `   (0211)

ON 9 STEFN 3 STIGON/ 3 STREEAMAS 4 WUNDON// 3   (0212)

SUND 2 WIDH 2 SAN-9-DE/ 5 SECGAS 4 BAEAERON// 3   (0213)

ON 2 BEARM 3 NACAN/ 4 BEOR-1-HTE 9 FRAETWE// 5   (0214)

GUUDH- 2 -SEARO 2 GEA-1-TOLIIC/ 3 GUMAN 2 UUT 1 SCU-9-FON// 3   (0215)

WERAS 3 ON 1 WIL- 2 -SIIDH/ 3 WUDU 2 BUN-1-DEN-1-NE.// 6   (0216)

GE- 1 -WAAT 9 THAA 2 OFER 4 WAEAEG- 3 -HOLM/ 3   (0217)

            WIN-1-DE 2 GE- 1 -FYYSED// 4   (0217)

FLOTA 2 FAA-9-MII- 4 -HEALS/ 3 FUGLE 2 GE- 1 -LIICOST// 3   (0218)

ODH 3 TH= 2 YMB 3 AAN- 2 -TIID/ 9 OOTHRES 4 DOOGORES// 4   (0219)

WUNDEN- 2 -STEFNA/ 4 GE- 0 -WADEN 2 HAEFDE// 9   (0220)

TH= 0 DHAA 2 LIIDHENDE/ 5 LAND 1 GE- 1 -SAAWON// 5   (0221)

BRIM- 3 -CLIFU 3 BLIICAN/ 9 BEORGAS 3 STEEAPE.// 4   (0222)

SIIDE 2 SAEAE- 2 -NAESSAS/ 4 THAA 0 WAES 3 SUND 9 LIDEN// 4   (0223)

EOLETES 2 AET 2 ENDE/ 5 THANON 2 UP 1 HRADHE// 4   (0224)

WE-9-DERA 5 LEEODE/ 4 ON 1 WANG 2 STIGON.// 3   (0225)

SAEAE- 2 -WUDU 2 SAEAELDON/ 9 SYRCAN 5 HRY-1-SE-1-DON.// 4   (0226)

GUUDH- 2 -GE- 1 -WAEAE-2-DO/ 3 GODE 3 THAN-9-CEDON// 4   (0227)

THAES 4 THE 2 HIM 4 YYTH- 0 -LAADE/ 4 EEADHE 3 WUR-3-DON.// 9   (0228)

                    END FOLIO 136V +

THAA 8 OF 0 WEALLE 4 GE- 1 -SEAH/ 3 WEARD 2 SCILDINGA// 3   (0229)

SEE 1 THE 8 HOLM- 9 -CLIFU/ 5 HEALDAN 3 SCOLDE// 4   (0230)

BERAN 2 OFER 3 BOLCAN/ 9 BEOR-1-HTE 3 RANDAS// 3   (0231)

FYRD- 2 -SEARU 3 FUUS- 2 -LICU/ 1 HINE 9 FYR- 2 -WYT 3 BRAEC// 3   (0232)

                            8

MOOD-' 1 -GE- 2 -HYG-1-DUM/ 2 HWAET 3 THAA 1 MEN 9 WAEAERON.// 5   (0233)

$GE- 0 -WAAT 3 HIM 2 THAA 0 TOO 1 WARODHE/ 4 WICGE 3 RIIDAN// 9   (0234)

THEGN 3 HROODH- 2 -GAARES/ 4 THRYM-1-MUM 3 CWEHTE// 4   (0235)

MAEGEN- 9 -WUDU 2 MUNDUM/ 3 METHEL- 3 -WORDUM 2 FRAEGN.// 4   (0236)

HWAET 9 SYNDON 2 GEE/ 4 SEARO- 3 -HAEBBENDRA// 4   (0237)

BYRNUM 3 WERE-9-DE/ 4 THE 2 THUS 3 BRONT-1-NE 4 CEEOL// 3   (0238)

OFER 2 LAGU- 2 -STRAEAETE/ 9 LAEAEDAN 2 CWOO-1-MON// 3   (0239)

HIDER 3 OFER 3 HOLMAS/ 4 *HWAET 8 *IC 8 ()LE*HWIILE 2 WAES// 9   (0240)

ENDE- 4 -SAEAETA/ 2 AEAEG- 1 -WEARDE 4 HEEOLD// 2   (0241)

THE 2 ON 2 LAND 1 DENA/ 9 LAADHRA 2 NAEAENIG// 4   (0242)

MID 1 SCIP- 3 -HERGE/ 4 SCEDH-2-THAN 3 NE 9 MEA-1-H-1-TE// 4   (0243)

NOO 1 HEER 2 CUUDH- 2 -LIICOR/ 4 CUMAN 3 ON- 2 -GUNNON.// 9   (0244)

LIND- 4 -HAE-1-BBENDE/ 5 NEE 0 GEE 4 LEEAFNES- 3 -WORD// 3   (0245)

GUUDH- 9 -FREM-1-MEN-1-DRA/ 5 GEARWE 3 NE 1 WISSON// 3   (0246)

MAAGA 2 GE- 9 -MEE-1-DU/ 3 NAEAEFRE 4 IC 2 MAARAN 3 GE- 0 -SEAH// 3   (0247)

EORLA 2 OFER 9 EORTHAN/ 3 DHON-1-NE 2 IS 2 EEOWER 2 SUM// 3   (0248)

SECG 8 ON 1 SEAR-1-WUM/ 9 NIS 3 TH= 1 SELD- 3 -GUMA// 4   (0249)

WAEAEPNUM 3 GE- 1 -WEORDHAD/ 3   (0250)

          ()NAEFRE*NAEFNE 9 HIM 3 HIS 3 WLITE 3 LEEOGE// 5   (0250)

AEAEN- 2 -LIIC 3 AN- 1 -SYYN/ 3 NUU 9 IC 2 EEOWER 3 SCEAL// 3   (0251)

FRUM- 2 -CYN 2 WITAN/ 3 AEAER 0 GEE 4 FYR 9 HEONAN// 5   (0252)

                    END FOLIO 137R +

LEEAS- 3 -SCEEA-2-WERAS/ 4 ON 1 LAND 2 DENA// 9   (0253)

FUR-1-THUR 2 FEER-1-AN/ 3 NUU 1 GEE 3 FEOR- 6 -BUUEND// 3   (0254)

MERE- 9 -LIIDHENDE/ 5 ()MINE*MIINNE 4 GE- 1 -HYYRADH// 5   (0255)

AAN- 3 -FEALDNE 3 GE- 9 -THOOHT/ 5 OFOST 4 IS 2 SEELEST// 5   (0256)

TOO 0 GE- 3 -CYYDHAN-1-NE/ 9 HWANON 4 EEJWRE 3 CYME 4 SYNDON.// 9   (0257)

                    .IIII.   (FITT)

$HIM 2 SE 2 YLDESTA/ 5 =AND- 0 -SWARODE// 5   (0258)

WERODES 3 WIISA/ 9 WORD- 4 -HORD 2 ON- 1 -LEEAC// 4   (0259)

WEE 0 SYND 5 GUM- 1 -CYNNES/ 9 GEEATA 4 LEEODE// 5   (0260)

                         9

=AND 0 HIGE- 2 -LAACES/ 5 HEORDH- 2 -GE- 1 -NEEATAS.// 9   (0261)

WAES 2 MIIN 2 FAEDER/ 4 FOL-1-CUM 3 GE- 2 -CYYTHED// 3   (0262)

AETHELE 9 ORD- 2 -FRUMA/ 5 ECG- 8 -THEEOW 3 HAATEN.// 4   (0263)

GE- 1 -+BAAD 3 WINTRA 9 WORN/ 3 AEAER 0 HEE 3 ON 1 WEG 3 HWURFE.// 5   (0264)

GAMOL 4 OF 0 GEAR-9-DUM/ 5 HINE 3 GEAR-3-WE 4 GE- 1 -MAN// 3   (0265)

WITENA 3 WEEL- 9 -HWYLC/ 4 WIIDE 2 GEOND 3 EORTHAN.// 5   (0266)

WEE 1 THURH 3 HOLDNE 9 HIGE/ 4 HLAAFORD 4 ()HLAFORD 8 THIINNE// 4   (0267)

SUNU 1 HEALF- 9 -DENES/ 4 SEECEAN 4 CWCOMON// 4   (0268)

LEEOD- 3 -GE- 2 -BYRGEAN/ 9 WES 4 THUU 0 UUS 4 LAARE-2-NA 3 GOOD.// 5   (0269)

HABBADH 3 WEE 2 TOO 2 THAEAEM 9 MAEAERAN/ 3 MICEL 3 AEAEREN-2-DE// 4   (0270)

DENIGA 3 FREEAN./ 5 NE 9 SCEAL 3 THAEAER 3 DYR-2-NE 4 SUM// 3   (0271)

WESAN 3 THAES 4 IC 9 WEENE/ 5 THUU 0 WAAST 4 GIF 3 HIT 2 IS// 3   (0272)

SWAA 3 WEE 1 SOOTH- 1 -LIICE/ 9 SECGAN 4 HYYRDON// 5   (0273)

END FOLIO 137V +

TH= 1 MID 2 SCYLDINGUM/ 4 SCEADHONA 9 IC 2 NAAT 4 HWYLC.// 5   (0274)

DEEOGOL 4 DAEAED- 3 -HATA/ 3 DEOR-1-CUM 9 NIHT-1-UM// 4   (0275)

EEAWEDH 3 THURH 3 EG-1-SAN/ 3 UN- 1 -CUUDHNE 4 NIIDH// 9   (0276)

HYYNDHU 4 =AND 0 HRAA- 2 -FYL/ 5 IC 1 THAES 4 HROODH- 2 -GAAR 4 MAEG// 3   (0277)

THURH 9 RUUM-1-NE 5 SEFAN/ 3 RAEAED 2 GE- 0 -LAEAERAN.// 5   (0278)

HUU 2 HEE 3 FROOD. 8 =AND 9 GOOD/ 3 FEEOND 3 OFER- 3 -SWYYDHETH// 4   (0279)

GYF 3 HIM 3 ED- 0 -()WENDAN*WENDEN/ 9 AEAEF-1-RE 3 SCOL-2-DE.// 5   (0280)

BEA-1-LUWA 5 BISIGU/ 4 BOOT 3 EFT 9 CUM-1-AN// 4   (0281)

=AND 0 THAA 2 CEAR- 4 -WYLMAS/ 4 COOLRAN 3 WURDHATH.// 9   (0282)

ODHDHE 3 AA 0 SYTHDHAN/ 3 EARFODH- 4 -THRAAGE// 5   (0283)

THREEA- 3 -NYYD 9 THOLADH/ 5 THEN-2-DEN 3 THAEAER 3 WUNADH// 3   (0284)

ON 1 HEEAH- 3 -STE-2-DE/ 9 HUUSA 4 SEE-2-LEST.// 5   (0285)

WEARD 3 MATHELODE/ 4 DHAEAER 1 ON 2 WICGE 9 SAET// 4   (0286)

OM-1-BE-1-HT 3 UN- 1 -FORHT/ 3 AEAEG- 2 -HWAE-8-T4RES 3 SCEAL// 9   (0287)

SCEARP 4 SCYLD- 3 -WIGA/ 3 GE- 0 -SCAAD 3 WITAN// 4   (0288)

WOR-2-DA 9 =AND 0 WOR-2-CA/ 5 SEE 1 THE 2 WEEL 3 THENCEDH// 4   (0289)

IC 2 TH= 1 GE- 2 -HYYRE/ 3 THAET 9 THIS 2 IS 3 HOLD 1 WEOROD// 3   (0290)

FREEAN 2 SCYL-1-DINGA/ 3 GE- 0 -WIITATH 9 FORDH 4 BERAN// 4   (0291)

10

AEAEPEN 2 =AND 0 GE- 1 -WAEAE-1-DU/ 3 IC 0 EEOW 2 WIISIGE.// 9   (0292)

HWYLCE 4 IC 1 MAGU- 4 -THEGNAS/ 4 MIINE 4 HAATE// 4   (0293)

IDH 9 FEEONDA 4 GE- 2 -HWONE/ 4 FLOTAN 3 EEOWERNE// 5   (0294)

IIW- 9 -TYR-2-WYD-2-NE/ 5 NACAN 3 ON 1 SANDE// 6   (0295)

ARUM 2 HEAL-9-DAN/ 4 JTH 0 DHAET 2 EFT 3 BYREDH// 4   (0296)

FER 3 LAGU- 3 -STREEA-9-MAS/ 8 LEEOF-1-NE 4 MA-1-N-2-NAN// 3   (0297)

   END FOLIO 138R +

UDU 2 WUNDEN- 4 -HALS/ 9 TOO 8 WEDER- 5 -MEARCE// 6   (0298)

OOD- 2 -FREM-3-MEN-1-DRA/ 9 SWYLCUM 3 GIFE-1-THE 5 BIDH// 4   (0299)

H= 2 THONE 5 HILDE- 4 -RAEAES/ 9 +HAAL 2 GE- 2 -DIIGEDH.// 6   (0300)

E- 1 -WITON 3 HIM 3 THAA 1 FEERAN/ 4 FLOTA 9 STILLE 4 +BAAD// 3   (0301)

EOMODE 5 ON 0 ()SOLE*SAALE/ 4 SIID- 1 -FAE-1-TH-1-MED 9 SCIP// 3   (0302)

N 1 ANCRE 5 FAEST/ 5 EOFOR- 3 -LIIC 3 SCIO-1-NON// 9   (0303)

FER 2 HLEEOR- 5 -()BERAN*BERGAN/ 5 GE- 3 -HRO-1-DEN 3 GOL-1-DE// 3   (0304)

AAH 3 =AND 8 FYYR- 4 -HEARD/ 4 FERH- 2 -WEAR-1-DE 5 HEEOLD// 5   (0305)

UUTH- 0 -MOOD 9 ()GRUMMON*GRIM-1-MON/ 4 GUMAN 3 OONETTON// 3   (0306)

IGON 2 AET- 9 -SOM-1-NE/ 4   (0307)

   OTH 1 TH= 2 HYY 3 ()AEL*SAEL 0 TIM-1-BRED.// 4   (0307)

EATO- 0 -LIIC 3 =AND 9 GOLD- 2 -FAAH/ 3 ON- 0 -GYTON 3 MIHTON.// 5   (0308)

H= 1 WAES 3 FORE- 9 -MAEAEROST/ 5 FOLD- 3 -BUUENDUM// 4   (0309)

RECE-1-DA 5 UNDER 9 RODERUM/ 3 ON 1 THAEAEM 3 SE 1 RIICA 3 BAAD.// 5   (0310)

IIXTE 4 SE 9 LEEOMA/ 5 OFER 3 LANDA 3 FE-1-LA.// 7   (0311)

IM 3 THAA 2 HILDE- 9 -DEEOR/ 3 ()OF*HOF 1 MOODIGRA// 4   (0312)

ORHT 4 GE- 1 -TAEAEHTE/ 4 THAET 9 HIIE 5 HIM 2 TOO 1 MIHTON// 4   (0313)

EG-1-NUM 3 GAN-1-GAN/ 9 GUUDH- 3 -BEORNA 3 SUM// 4   (0314)

ICG 2 GE- 2 -WENDE/ 5 WORD 9 AEFTER 4 CWAEDH.// 4   (0315)

AAEAEL 1 IS 2 MEE 1 TOO 2 FEERAN/ 3 FAEDER 9 AL- 0 -WALDA// 4   (0316)

IO 2 AAR- 2 -STAFUM/ 4 EEOW-3-IC 1 GE- 3 -HEAL-9-DE.// 6   (0317)

IIDHA 5 GE- 1 -SUNDE/ 5 IC 1 TOO 3 SAEAE 3 WILLE// 5   (0318)

IDH 9 WRAADH 5 WEROD/ 3 WEAR-1-DE 6 HEAL-1-DAN.// 9   (0319)

   + END FOLIO 138V

                              11

$STRAEAET 3 WAES 3 STAAN- 3 -FAAH/ 4 STIIG 4 WIISODE// 4   (0320)

GUMUM 9 AET- 1 -GAE-1-OERE/ 6 GUUDH- 4 -BYRNE 5 SCAAN// 4   (0321)

HEARD 9 HOND- 3 -LOCEN/ 6 HRING- 3 -IIREN 3 SCIIR// 4   (0322)

SONG 3 IN D SEAR-9-WUM/ 3 THAA 2 HIIE 3 TOO 0 SELE 5 FURDHUM// 4   (0323)

IN 2 HYRA 3 GRY-9-RE- 3 -GEAT-2-WUM/ 4 GANGAN 3 CWOO-1-MON// 4   (0324)

SETTON 9 SAEAE- 0 -MEE-1-THE/ 4 SIIDE 4 SCYL-1-OAS// 3   (0325)

RONDAS 3 REGN- 2 -HEARDE/ 9 WIDH 3 THAES 3 RE-1-CE-1-DES 3 WEAL.// 5   (0326)

BUGON 3 THAA 0 TOO 2 BENCE/ 9 BYRNAN 5 HRING-2-DON// 4   (0327)

GUUDH- 3 -SEARO 3 GUMENA/ 9 GAARAS 3 STOODON// 3   (0328)

SAEAE- 1 -MAN-2-NA 4 SEARO/ 3 SAMOD 9 AET- 2 -GAE-1-OERE// 5   (0329)

AESC- 3 -HOLT 3 UFAN 2 GRAEAEG/ 4 WAES 0 SE 9 IIREN- 3 -THREEAT// 4   (0330)

WAEAEPNUM 3 GE- 1 -WUR-2-THAD/ 4 THAA 0 DHAEAER 9 WLONC 2 HAELEDH// 4   (0331)

OORET- 3 -MECGAS/ 4 AEFTER 4 ()HAELE-9-THUM*AETHELUM 3 FRAEGN.// 5   (0332)

HWANON 4 FERIGEADH 4 GEE/ 4 FAEAET-9-TE 3 SCYLDAS// 4   (0333)

GRAEAEGE 4 SYR-1-CAN/ 3 =AND 0 GRIIM- 3 -HELMAS// 9   (0334)

HERE- 4 -SCEAFTA 5 HEEAP/ 3 IC 1 EOM 3 HROODH- 2 -GAARES// 9   (0335)

+AAR 3 =AND 0 OM- 2 -BIHT./ 5 NE 1 SEAH 2 IC 3 EL- 1 -THEEODIGE// 5   (0336)

THUS 9 MANIGE 5 MEN/ 3 MOODIG- 0 -LIICRAN.// 4   (0337)

WEEN 1 IC 2 TH= 2 GEE 0 FOR 9 WLEN-1-CO/ 3   (0338)

          NALLES 3 FOR 2 WRAEC- 3 -SIIDHUM.// 4   (0338)

AC 1 FOR 2 HIGE- 9 -THRYM-8-MUM/ 5 HROODH- 2 -GAAR 3 SOOHTON.// 5   (0339)

          + END FOLIO 139R

HIM 2 THAA 3 ELLEN- 9 -ROOF/ 2 AND- 2 -SWARODE// 4   (0340)

WLANC 2 WEDERA 3 LEEOD./ 4 WORD 9 AEFTER 3 SPRAEC// 4   (0341)

HEARD 2 UNDER 3 HELME/ 5 WEE 0 SYNT 9 HIGE- 2 -LAACES.// 5   (0342)

BEEOD- 3 -GE- 1 -NEEATAS/ 5 BEEO- 0 -WULF 3 IS 9 MIIN 2 NAMA// 5   (0343)

WILLE 2 IC 2 AA- 0 -SECGAN/ 4 SUNU 4 HEALF- 9 -DENES// 4   (0344)

MAEAERUM 3 THEEODNE/ 5 MIIN 2 AEAEREN-1-DE.// 9   (0345)

ALDRE 5 THIINUM/ 4 GIF 2 HEE 1 UUS 3 GE- 2 -UN-1-NAN 3 WILE// 9   (0346)

TH= 1 WEE 4 HINE 5 SWAA 3 GOODNE/ 5 GREETAN 3 MOOTON.// 9   (0347)

12

ULF- 1 -GAAR 5 MATHELODE/ 5 TH= 1 WAES 3 WENDLA 3 LEEOD// 9   (0348)

WAES 4 HIS 3 MOOD- 0 -SEFA/ 4 MANEGUM 2 GE- 1 -CYYDHED.// 9   (0349)

IIG 2 =AND 0 WIIS- 4 -DOOM/ 3 IC 2 THAES 3 WINE 5 DENIGA// 4   (0350)

REEAN 9 SCIL-2-DINGA/ 5 FRIINAN 3 WILLE// 6   (0351)

EEAGA 4 BRYT-9-TAN/ 4 SWAA 3 THUU 2 BEE-1-NA 5 EART// 6   (0352)

HEEO-1-DEN 2 MAEAER-9-NE/ 6 YMB 4 THIIN-1-NE 6 SIIDH.// 5   (0353)

AND 0 THEE 3 THAA 4 =AND- 0 -SWARE/ 9 AEAEDRE 5 GE- 2 -CYYDHAN// 4 (0354)

HE 0 MEE 3 SE 1 GOODA/ 4 AA- 0 -GIFAN 9 THEN-1-CEDH.// 7   (0355)

WEAR= 2 THAA 3 HRAED- 2 -LIICE/ 6 THAEAER 3 HROODH- 9 -GAAR 4 SAET// 4 (0356)

ALD 1 =AND 0 ()UN*AN- 2 -+HAAR/ 5 MID 3 HIS 4 EORLA 9 GE- 2 -DRIHT.// 5 (0357)

EODE 3 ELLEN- 3 -ROOF/ 4 TH= 2 HEE 1 FOR 4 EAX-9-LUM 3 GE- 1 -STOOD// 4 (0358)

DENIGA 3 FREEAN/ 4 CUUTHE 4 HEE 9 DUGUDHE 5 THEEAW.// 6   (0359)

WULF- 0 -GAAR 5 MADHELODE/ 9 TOO 1 HIS 3 WINE- 3 -DRIHT-2-NE// 6   (0360)

END FOLIO 139V +

WEER 3 SYNDON 3 GE- 0 -FERE-9-DE/ 4 FEORRAN 3 CUMENE// 4   (0361)

DFER 4 GEO-1-FENES 4 BE- 9 -GANG/ 4 GEEATA 3 LEEODE// 6   (0362)

THONE 4 YLDESTAN/ 2 OORET- 9 -MECGAS.// 7   (0363)

BEEO- 0 -WULF 5 NEM-1-NADH/ 5 HYY 1 BEENAN 9 SYNT// 4   (0364)

TH= 2 HIIE 5 THEEODEN 3 MIIN/ 3 WIDH 4 THEE 1 MOOTON// 9   (0365)

WORDUM 4 WRIXLAN/ 4 NOO 0 DHUU 3 HIM 4 WEAR-1-NE 9 GE- 2 -TEEDH// 5 (0366)

DHIINRA 5 GEGN- 3 -CWIDA/ 6 GLAED- 0 -MAN 9 HROODH- 3 -GAAR// 6   (0367)

HYY 2 ON 1 WIIG- 5 -GE- 3 -TAAWUM/ 4 WYRDHE 9 THIN-1-C-1-EADH.// 5 (0368)

EORLA 4 GE- 3 -AEHTLAN/ 5 HUURU 2 SE 9 AL-1-DOR 4 DEEAH// 4   (0369)

SEE 2 THAEAEM 5 HEADHO- 4 -RINCUM/ 9 HIDER 4 WIISADE.// 9   (0370)

.VI.   (FITT)

SHROODH- 2 -GAAR 5 MA-2-THE-1-LODE/ 6 HELM 3 SCYL-1-DINGA// 9   (0371)

IC 3 WINE 5 CUUDHE/ 5 CNIHT- 5 -WESENDE// 6   (0372)

WAES 3 HIS 9 EALD- 1 -FAE-2-DER/ 5 ECG- 3 -THEEO 3 HAATEN// 4   (0373)

DHAEAEM 2 TOO 2 HAA= 9 FOR- 3 -GEAF/ 5 HREE-1-THEL 5 GEEA-1-TA// 4 (0374)

AANGAN 3 DOHTOR/ 9 IS 3 HIS 3 ()EAFORAN*EAFORA 4 NUU// 5   (0375)

HEARD 4 HEER 3 CUMEN/ 9 SOOHTE 5 HOL-2-DNE 4 WINE.// 7   (0376)

13

DHONNE 5 SAEGDON 2 TH=/ 9 SAEAE- 0 -LIITHENDE// 6   (0377)

THAA 0 DHE 4 GIF- 3 -SCEATTAS/ 5 GEEA-1-TA 9 FYRE-3-DON// 5   (0378)

THYDER 4 TOO 2 THAN-1-CE/ 4 TH= 2 HEE 4 ().XXX-9-()TIGES*THRIITIGES// 4   (0379)

END FOLIO 140R +

MANNA 3 MAEGEN- 2 -CRAEFT/ 3 ON 1 HIS 8 MUND- 9 -GRIPE// 5   (0380)

HEA-1-THO- 2 -ROOF 3 HAEBBE/ 4 HINE 4 HAALIG 2 GOD// 9   (0381)

FOR 3 AAR- 2 -STAFUM/ 3 UUS 2 ON- 1 -SENDE// 4   (0382)

TOO 1 WEST- 3 -DENU=/ 9 THAES 1 IC 1 WEEN 4 HAEBBE.// 6   (0383)

WIDH 3 GRENDLES 4 GRYRE/ 9 IC 8 THAEAEM 3 GOODAN 2 SCEAL// 3   (0384)

FOR 1 HIS 2 MOOD- 3 -THRAE-2-CE/ 9 MAAD-1-MAS 5 BEEO-1-DAN// 4   (0385)

BEEO 0 DHUU 2 ON 1 OFESTE/ 6 +HAAT 9 IN 0 +GAAN// 3   (0386)

SEEON 2 SIBBE- 4 -GE- 2 -DRIHT/ 3 SAMOD 3 AET- 9 -GAEDERE.// 6   (0387)

GE- 0 -SAGA 3 HIM 2 EEAC 3 WORDUM/ 3   (0388)

     TH= 2 HIIE 9 SINT 3 WIL- 0 -CUMAN// 4   (0388)

DENIGA 3 LEEODUM/ 3 *THAA 8 *TOO 8 *DURA 8 *EEODE// 8   (0389)

*WIID- 8 -*CUUDH 8 *HAELEDH/ 8 WORD 1 IN-9-NE 1 AA- 0 -BEEAD.// 5   (0390)

EEOW 2 HEET 2 SECGAN/ 4 SIGE- 2 -DRIHTEN 9 MIIN// 3   (0391)

ALDOR 3 EEAST- 2 -DENA/ TH= 2 HEE 1 EEOWER 3 AETHELU 9 CAN// 4   (0392)

=AND 0 GEE 3 HIM 2 SYNDON/ 4 OFER 3 SAEAE- 4 -WYLMAS// 9   (0393)

HEARD- 3 -HICGENDE/ 6 HIDER 3 WIL- 0 -CUMAN// 4   (0394)

NUU 0 GEE 9 MOOTON 3 GAN-1-GAN/ 4   (0395)

     IN 1 EEOWRUM 4 GUUDH- 3 -()GEA*GE- 8 -TAA-9-WUM// 4   (0395)

UNDER 3 HERE- 4 -GRIIMAN/ 5 HROODH- 2 -GAAR 3 GE- 9 -SEEON// 4   (0396)

LAEAETADH 4 HILDE- 4 -BORD/ 4 HEER 3 ON- 1 -BIID-8-AN// 9   (0397)

WUDU 2 WAEL- 4 -SCEAF-1-TAS/ 4 WORDA 3 GE- 1 -THINGES.// 9   (0398)

AA- 0 -RAAS 4 THAA 1 SE 2 RIICA/ 5 YMB 3 HINE 3 RINC 2 MA-9-NIG// 5   (0399)

THRYYDH- 1 -LIIC 4 THEGNA 3 HEEAP/ 4 SUME 3 THAEAER 9 BIDON// 5   (0400)

HEADH0- 3 -REEAF 5 HEEOL-1-DON/ 3   (0401)

     SWAA 3 HIM 2 SE 9 HEAR-2-DA 4 3E- 3 -BEEAD.// 5   (0401)

     END FOLIO 140V +

SNYRE-2-DON 5 AET- 2 -SOMNE/ 8 THAA 9 SECG 2 WIISODE// 5   (0402)

14

N-4-DER 4 HEORO-1-TES 4 HROOF/ 4 *HEATHO- 8 -*RINC 8 *EEODE// 8   (0403)

EARD 9 UNDER 3 HELME/ 5   (0404)

    TH= 2 HEE 2 ON 1 ()HEODHE*HEORDHE 4 GE- 0 -STOOD.// 5   (0404)

EEO- 9 -WULF 2 MADHELODE/ 5 ON 2 HIM 3 BYRNE 4 SCAAN// 3   (0405)

EARO- 9 -NET 2 SEOWED/ 4 SMITHES 3 OR- 2 -THANCUM// 1   (0406)

AES 8 THUU 2 HROODH- 9 -GAAR 3 HAAL/ 4 IC 1 EOM 3 HIGE- 4 -LAACES// 4   (0407)

AEAEG 1 =AND 0 MAGO- 9 -DHEGN./ 5 HAEBBE 3 IC 2 MAEAERDHA 3 FELA// 3   (0408)

A- 1 -GUN-1-NEN 9 ON 1 GEOGOTHE/ 6 MEE 3 WEARDH 4 GRENDLES 5 THING.// 2   (0409)

A 9 MIIN-1-RE 4 EETHEL- 3 -TYRF/ 5 UN- 0 -DYR-1-NE 4 CUUDH// 4   (0410)

CGADH 9 SAEAE- 1 -LIIDHEND/ 5 TH= 2 THAES 3 SELE 4 STANDE// 5   (0411)

CED 3 SEELESTA/ 9 RINCA 4 GE- 2 -HWYL-1-CUM// 5   (0412)

DEL 4 =AND 0 UN- 2 -NYT/ 4 SYDHDHAN 9 AEAEFEN- 4 -LEEOHT// 4   (0413)

DER 4 HEOFENES 5 HAADOR/ 4 BE- 9 -HOLEN 3 WEOR-1-THEDH.// 7   (0414)

AA 1 MEE 2 TH= 3 GE- 0 -LAEAER-1-DON/ 4 LEEODE 9 MIINE// 5   (0415)

AA 0 SEELESTAN/ 3 SNOTERE 4 CEORLAS.// 4   (0416)

EEO-9-DEN 5 HROODH- 3 -GAAR/ 5 TH= 1 IC 1 THEE 1 SOOHTE// 5   (0417)

R- 3 -THAN 3 HIIE 9 MAEGENES 5 CRAEFT/ 5 ()MINE*MIINNE 4 CUUTHON.// 4   (0418)

LFE 3 OFER- 9 -SAAWON/ 4 DHAA 0 IC 2 OF 1 SEAR-1-WUM 4 CWOOM.// 5   (0419)

AH 3 FROM 9 FEEONDUM/ 5 THAEAER 1 IC 1 FIIFE 3 GE- 0 -BAND// 5   (0420)

DH-1-DE 4 EO-9-TENA 4 CYN/ 3 =AND 1 ON 2 YYDHUM 4 SLOOG.// 4   (0421)

CERAS 9 NIHTES/ 5 NEARO- 3 -THEARFE 3 DREEAH// 4   (0422)

AEC. 9 WEDERA 4 NIIDH/ 4 WEEAN 3 AAHSODON// 5   (0423)

    + END FOLIO 141R

R- 3 -GRAND 8 GRA-9-MUM/ 5 =AND 0 NUU 2 WIDH 5 GREN-2-DEL 6 SCEAL// 8   (0424)

DH 4 THAA= 9 AAG- 0 -LAEAECAN/ 4 AANA 2 GE- 3 -HEEGAN.// 5   (0425)

ING 4 WIDH 3 THYRSE/ 9 IC 8 THEE 0 NUU 0 DHAA// 5   (0426)

EGO 3 BEORHT- 4 -DENA/ 4 BIDDAN 2 WILLE// 9   (0427)

-8-DOR 4 SCYL-3-DINGA/ 4 AANRA 4 BEENE.// 6   (0428)

E 0 DHUU 2 MEE 9 NE 2 FOR- 1 -WYR-2-NE/ 7 WIIGEN-2-DRA 5 HLEEO// 4   (0429)

EO- 0 -WINE 9 FOL-1-CA/ 4 NUU 1 IC 4 THUS 4 FEOR-2-RAN 4 COOM.// 5   (0430)

E 0 IC 1 MUOTE 9 AANA/ 4 *=AND 8 MIINRA 4 EORLA 4 GE- 1 -DRYHT.// 4   (0431)

AND 0 THES 2 HEAR-9-DA 5 HEEAP/ 5 HEOROT 4 FAEAELSIAN// 6   (0432)

15

HAEBBE 2 IC 1 EEAC 9 GE- 0 -AAHSOD/ 5 TH= 0 SE 3 AEAEG- 0 -LAEAECA// 4   (043

FOR 2 HIS 4 WON- 4 -HYYDUM/ 9 WAEAEP-1-NA 4 NE 1 REC-2-CEDH.// 7   (043▮

IC 1 TH= 3 THONNE 5 FOR- 2 -HICGE/ 9   (0439

    SWAA 2 MEE 4 HIGE- 1 -LAAC 3 SIIE// 4   (0439

MIIN 2 MON- 3 -DRIHTEN/ 9 MOODES 4 BLIIDHE.// 7   (043▮

TH= 1 IC 1 SWEORD 4 BERE/ 5 OTHDHE 3 SIIDNE 9 SCYLD// 4   (043▮

GEOLO- 2 -RAND 3 TOO 1 GUUTHE./ 6 AC 2 IC 1 MID 9 GRAAPE 4 SCEAL// 4   (043▮

FOON 2 WIDH 3 FEEONDE/ 6 =AND 1 YMB 9 FEORH 5 SACAN// 5   (043

LAADH 3 WIDH 4 LAATHUM/ 4 DHAEAER 3 GE- 0 -LYY-9-FAN 3 SCEAL// 5   (044

DRYHTNES 4 DUOME/ 6 SEE 1 THE 5 HINE 9 DEEADH 4 NIMEDH.// 6   (044▮

WEEN 3 IC 3 TH= 2 HEE 3 WILLE/ 5 GIF 3 HEE 9 WEAL-3-DAN 4 +MOOT// 5   (044

IN 1 THAEAEM 3 GUUDH- 4 -SELE/ 5 GEEO-9-TENA 5 LEEODE// 5   (044

ETAN 3 UN- 0 -FOR-3-HTE/ 1 SWAA 4 HEE 9 OFT 4 DYDE// 5   (044▮

    END FOLIO 141V +

MAEGEN 4 HREEDH- 3 -MAN-1-NA/ 4 NAA 8 THUU 9 MIIN-4-NE 3 THEARFT// 5   (044

HAFA-1-LAN 4 HYYDAN./ 3 AC 2 HEE 9 MEE 4 HABBAN 3 WILE// 6   (044

()DEORE*DREEORE 4 FAAHNE/ 5 GIF 2 MEC 9 DEEADH 3 NIMEDH.// 7   (044▮

BYREDH 4 BLOODIG 3 WAEL/ 4 BYRGEAN 9 THEN-1-CEDH// 4   (044

ETEDH 2 +AN- 0 -GEN-1-GA/ 4 UN- 1 -MURN- 0 -LIICE// 9   (044▮

MEAR-1-CADH 4 MOOR- 3 -HOPU/ 3   (045

    NOO 0 DHUU 4 YMB 3 MIINES 9 NE 3 THEARFT// 5   (045▮

LIICES 3 FEORME/ 6 LENG 3 SORGI-9-AN.// 7   (045▮

$ON- 1 -SEND 5 HIGE- 1 -LAACE/ 5 GIF 1 MEC 4 HILD 9 NIME// 7   (045▮

BEA-1-DU- 3 -SCRUUDA 5 BETST/ 3 TH= 0 MIINE 3 BREEOST 9 WEREDH// 7   (045

HRAEGLA 3 SEELEST/ 4 TH= 1 IS 5 HRAEAED-1-LAN 3 LAAF// 9   (045▮

WEELANDES 4 GE- 2 -WEORC/ 4 GAEAEDH 2 AA 0 WYRD 2 SWAA 1 HIIO 2 SCEL.// 9 (045▮

    .VII.   (FIT

$HROODH- 4 -GAAR 5 MA-1-THELODE/ 6 HELM 3 SCYL-2-DINGA// 9   (045

()FERE*FOR 5 ()FYHTUM*GE- 8 -*WYRHTUM 4 THUU/ 0   (045

    WINE 4 MIIN 2 BEEO- 1 -WULF.// 3   (045

=AND 9 FOR 3 AAR- 2 -STAFUM/ 4 UUS-2-IC 0 SOOHTEST// 5   (045

16

E- 2 -SLOOH 9 THIIN 2 FAE-1-DER/ 4 FAEAEHDHE 4 MAEAESTE.// 7   (0459)

ARTH 6 HEE 9 HEA-2-THO- 2 -LAAFE/ 6 TOO 2 HAND- 3 -BONAN// 3   (0460)

O 1 WILFINGU=./ 9 DHAA 1 HINE 6 ()GARA*WEDERA 2 CYN// 3   (0461)

R 2 HERE- 5 -BROOGAN/ 9 HABBAN 3 NE 0 MIHTE.// 7   (0462)

ANOV 3 HEE 0 GE- 3 -SOOHTE/ 9 SUUDH- 3 -DENA 4 FOLC// 4   (0463)

ER 3 YYDHA 3 GE- 2 -WEALC/ 5 AAR- 9 -SCYL-8-DINGA// 6   (0464)

END FOLIO 142R ✝

AA 1 IC 2 FUR-2-THUM 3 WEEOLD/ 3 FOL-1-CE 4 DE-9-()NINGA*NIGA// 4   (0465)

NO 0 ON 3 GEO-1-GODHE 5 HEEOLD/ 4 ()GIM*GIN-2-()ME*NE 0 RIICE// 9   (0466)

RO- 5 -BURH 4 HAELETHA./ 7 DHAA 0 WAES 5 HERE- 2 -GAAR 9 DEEAD// 3   (0467)

IN 1 YLDRA 3 MAEAEG/ 3 UN- 0 -LIFIGENDE// 5   (0468)

ARN 9 HEALF- 1 -DENES/ 5 SEE 0 WAES 4 3ETERA 4 DHON= 2 IC// 3   (0469)

DHD4AN 9 THAA 1 FAEAEHDHE/ 5 FEEO 2 THINGO-1-DE.// 7   (0470)

NDE 3 IC 2 WYLFINGU=/ 9 OFER 3 WAETERE3 5 HRYCG// 4   (0471)

LDE 3 MAAD-1-MAS/ 3 HEE 9 MEE 2 AATHAS 4 SWOOR.// 7   (0472)

ORH 2 IS 0 MEE 1 TOO 2 SECGANNE/ 9 ON 0 SEFAN 2 MIINUM// 3   (0473)

ME-2-NA 3 AEAENGUM/ 3 HWAET 9 MEE 1 GRENDEL 5 HAFADH.// 6   (0474)

YNDHO 3 ON 2 HEOROTE/ 9 MID 3 HIS 3 HETE- 4 -THANCUM// 4   (0475)

EAE3- 4 -NIIDHA 1 GE- 0 -FREMED/ 9 IS 1 MIIN 3 FLET- 1 -WEROD// 4   (0476)

IG- 2 -HEEAP 4 GE- 0 -WANOD/ 3 HIIE 9 WYRD 3 FOR- 3 -SWEEOP// 4   (0477)

1 3R-2-END-1-LES 3 GRYRE/ 4 GOD 9 EEATHE 4 MAEG// 5   (0478)

JNE 3 DOL- 4 -()SCADHAN*SCEADHAN/ 3 DAEAE-2-DA 2 GE- 9 -THWAEAEFAN.// 7   (0479)

JL 3 OFT 2 GE- 0 -BEEOTEDON/ 4 BEEO-1-RE 9 DRUNC-1-NE// 6   (0480)

ER 3 EALO- 3 -WAEAEGE/ 4 OORET- 2 -MECGAS// 9   (0481)

E 2 HIIE 4 IN 0 BEEOR- 1 -SELE/ 7 BIIDAN 3 WOL-2-DAN// 3   (0482)

END-9-LES 4 GUUTHE/ 6 MID 2 GRYRUM 4 ECGA.// 7   (0483)

JN= 2 WAES 9 THEEOS 3 MEDO- 8 -HEAL/ 4 ON 2 MORGEN- 3 -TIID// 3   (0484)

HT- 9 -SELE 5 DREEOR- 3 -FAAH/ 6 THON= 3 DAEG 3 LIIXTE.// 4   (0485)

, 9 BENC- 3 -THELU/ 4 BLOODE 4 BE- 1 -STYYMED// 4   (0486)

✝ END FOLIO 142V

LL 4 HEORU- 9 -DREEORE/ 5 AAHTE 3 IC 2 HOLDRA 4 THYY 0 LAEAES// 4   (0487)

17

DEEOR-1-RE 9 DUGUDHE/ 6 THE 1 THAA 3 DEEADH 2 FOR- 1 -NAM// 4   (0488)

SITE 2 NUU 0 TOO 9 SYMLE/ 3 =AND 0 ON- 2 -SAEAEL 3 MEOTO// 2   (0489)

SIGE- 3 -HREEDH 2 SECGU=/ 9 SWAA 4 THIIN 2 SEFA 5 HWET-1-TE.// 7   (0490)

THAA 0 WAES 3 GEEAT- 9 -MAECGUM/ 3 GEADOR 3 AET- 0 -SOM-2-NE// 5   (0491)

ON 2 BEEOR- 9 -SELE/ 7 BENC 1 GE- 1 -RYYMED// 4   (0492)

THAEAER 2 SWIIDH- 3 -FERHTHE/ 9 SITTAN 3 EEODON// 4   (0493)

THRYYDHUM 4 DEALLE/ 5 THEGN 9 NYTTE 5 BE- 2 -HEEOLD// 4   (0494)

SEE 0 THE 3 ON 3 HANDA 4 BAER/ 9 HRODEN 4 EALO- 3 -WAEAEGE// 4   (0495)

SCENCTE 5 SCIIR 3 WERED/ 9 SCOP 2 HWIILUM 3 SANG// 5   (0496)

HAADOR 4 ON 2 HEO-1-ROTE/ 9 THAEAER 3 WAES 4 HAELEDHA 4 DREEAM// 3   (0497)

DUGUDH 3 UN- 2 -LYYTEL/ 9 DENA 4 =AND 0 WE-2-DERA.// 9   (0498)

                                .VIII.   (FITT)

()$$HUN*$$UN- 2 -FERDH 4 MATHELODE/ 5 ECG- 0 -LAAFES 4 BE-9-ARN// 5   (0499)

THE 1 AET 2 FOOTUM 4 SAET/ 3 FREEAN 4 SCYLDI-9-NGA.// 7   (0500)

ON- 1 -BAND 3 BEADU- 3 -RUUNE/ 5 WAES 2 HIM 9 BEEO- 2 -WULFES 5 SIIDH// 4 (0501)

MOOD-1-GES 3 MERE- 4 -FARAN/ 9 MICEL 4 AEF- 1 -THUNCA.// 5   (0502)

FOR- 3 -THON 3 THE 1 HEE 1 NE 9 UUTHE/ 5 TH= 1 AEAENIG 4 OODHER 5 MAN// 8 (0503)

AEAEFRE 9 MAEAER-1-DHA 4 THON 2 MAA/ 5 MIDDAN- 4 -GEARDES.// 4   (0504)

        + END FOLIO 143R

GE- 9 -()HEDDE*HEEDE 4 UN-1-DER 3 HEOFENUM/ 4 THON= 3 HEE 1 SYLFA// 9   (0505)

EART 5 THUU 0 SE 3 BEEO- 2 -WULF/ 4 SEE 1 THE 4 WIDH 4 BRECAN 9 WUNNE// 5 (0506)

ON 0 SIIONE 3 +SAEAE/ 5 YMB 3 SUND 3 FLITE// 9   (0507)

DHAEAER 2 GIT 4 FOR 3 WLENCE/ 5 WADA 3 CUN-1-NE-2-DON// 9   (0508)

=AND 8 FOR 3 DOL- 3 -GILPE/ 5 ON 0 DEEOP 3 WAETER// 4   (0509)

ALDRU= 9 NEETHDON/ 4 NEE 2 INC 4 AEAENIG 4 MON// 4   (0510)

NEE 1 LEEOF 9 NEE 3 LAADH/ 4 BE- 2 -LEEAN 2 MIHTE// 5   (0511)

SOR-2-H- 1 -FULL-1-NE 9 SIIDH/ 5 THAA 0 GIT 4 ON 1 SUND 3 REEON.// 6   (0512)

THAEAER 2 GIT 2 EEA-9-GOR- 4 -STREEAM/ 3 EAR-2-MUM 4 THEHTON// 4   (0513)

MAEAE-9-TON 4 MERE- 3 -STRAEAE-3-TA/ 4 MUNDUM 4 BRUG-9-DON// 4   (0514)

GLI-2-DON 3 OFER 3 GAAR- 4 -SECG/ 4 GEOFON 2 YYTHU= 9 WEEOL// 3   (0515)

WINTRYS 5 ()WYLM*WYLMUM/ 5 GIT 1 ON 1 WAETERES 2 AEAEHT// 9   (0516)

                                  18

SEOFON 2 NIHT 5 SWUNCON/ 6 HEE 1 THEE 3 AET 2 SUNDE 9 OFER- 2 -FLAAT.// 5 (0517)

HAEFDE 3 MAARE 3 MAEGEN/ 4 THAA 9 HINE 3 ON 1 MOR-1-GEN- 4 -TIID// 3   (0518)

ON 1 HEA-2-THO- 1 -RAEAEMES/ 9 HOLM 2 UP 1 AET- 2 -BAER.// 5   (0519)

OHANON 5 HEE 0 GE- 4 -SOOHTE/ 9 SWAEAESNE 8 .=EETHEL.// 8   (0520)

EEOF 4 HIS 3 LEEODUM/ 4 LOND 9 BRONDINGA// 5   (0521)

REODHO- 3 -BUR-1-H 4 FAEGERE/ 9 THAEAER 4 HEE 4 FOLC 4 AAHTE// 5   (0522)

URH 3 =AND 1 BEEAGAS./ 9 BEEOT 2 EAL 0 WIDH 4 THEE// 5   (0523)

        END FOLIO 143V ✝

SUNU 3 BEEAN- 0 -STAANES/ 5 SOODHE 9 GE- 1 -LAEAESTE.// 7   (0524)

HON= 2 WEENE 3 IC 1 TOO 1 THEE/ 5 WYRSAN 8 GE- 9 -THINGEA// 6   (0525)

HEEA+ 1 THUU 2 HEADHO- 3 -RAEAESA/ 5 GE- 3 -HWAEAER 9 DOHTE// 5   (0526)

RIMRE 5 GUUDHE/ 5 GIF 3 THUU 2 GRENDLES 9 DEARST// 4   (0527)

IHT- 3 -LONGNE 3 FYRST/ 4 NEE-1-AN 3 BIIDAN.// 9   (0528)

EEO- 1 -WULF 4 MATHELODE/ 6 BEARN 2 ECG- 1 -THEEOWES// 9   (0529)

WAET 3 THUU 1 WORN 3 FELA/ 5 WINE 3 MIIN 3 ()HUN*UN- 2 -FERDH// 9   (0530)

EEORE 5 DRUNCEN/ 4 YMB 3 BRECAN 2 SPRAEAECE// 9   (0531)

AEGDEST 5 FROM 2 HIS 4 SIIDHE/ 5 SOODH 2 IC 1 TALIGE// 9   (0532)

H= 1 IC 2 MERE- 4 -STRENGO/ 4 MAARAN 3 AAHTE// 4   (0533)

AR-9-FETHO 4 ON 3 YYTHUM/ 4 DHONNE 3 AEAENIG 3 OOTHER 3 MAN.// 9   (0534)

IT 2 TH= 2 GE- 2 -CWAEAEDON/ 3 CNIHT- 4 -WESENDE// 5   (0535)

AND 0 GE- 9 -BEEO-1-TE-1-DON/ 3 WAEAERON 3 BEEGEN 3 THAA 0 GIIT// 4   (0536)

)O*ON 0 GEOGODH- 9 -FEEORE/ 5 TH= 0 WIT 3 ON 2 +GAAR- 0 -SECG 4 UUT// 1   (0537)

LDRUM 9 NEEDH-2-DON/ 3 =AND 0 TH= 2 GE- 1 -AEF-1-NDON 3 SWAA.// 7   (0538)

AEF-1-DON 2 SWURD 9 NACOD/ 4 THAA 0 WIT 3 ON 0 SUND 2 REEON// 5   (0539)

EARD 2 ON 9 HANDA/ 4 WIT 2 UNC 3 WIDH 3 HRON- 3 -FIXAS// 4   (0540)

ERIAN 9 THOOHTON./ 5 NOO 3 HEE 3 WIHT 4 FRAM 2 MEE// 5   (0541)

LOOD- 2 -YYTHU= 9 FEOR/ 3 FLEEOTAN 4 MEAHTE// 6   (0542)

RA-2-THOR 3 ON 1 HOL-9-ME/ 4 NOO 2 IC 2 FRAM 4 HIM 1 WOLDE.// 7   (0543)

HAA 1 WIT 4 AET- 9 -SOMNE/ 5 ON 0 +SAEAE 4 WAEAERON// 3   (0544)

        ✝ END FOLIO 144R

IIF 1 NIHTA 3 FYRST/ 9 OTH 1 TH= 1 UNC 3 FLOOD 3 TOO- 1 -DRAAF// 5   (0545)

WADO 2 WEALL-1-ENDE/ 9 WE-1-DERA 4 CEAL-1-DOST// 5   (0546)

NIIPENDE 5 NIHT./ 4 =AND 0 NORTHAN- 9 -WIND// 4   (0547)

HEADHO- 3 -GRIM 3 =OND- 1 -HWEARF/ 5 HREEO 3 WAEAERON 9 YYTHA// 4   (0548)

WAES 1 MERE- 3 -FIXA/ 3 MOOD 2 ON- 3 -HREERED.// 4   (0549)

THAEAER 9 MEE 3 WIDH 3 LAADHUM/ 4 LIIC- 3 -SYRCE 4 MIIN// 4   (0550)

HEARD 1 HOND- 9 -LOCEN/ 4 HELPE 3 GE- 2 -FREME-2-DE// 5   (0551)

BEA-1-DO- 4 -HRAEGL 9 BROO-1-DEN/ 2 ON 3 BREEOSTUM 3 LAEG// 4   (0552)

GOLDE 3 GE- 2 -GYR-9-WED/ 3 MEE 0 TOO 3 GRUNDE. 2 TEEAH// 4   (0553)

FAAH 3 FEEOND- 0 -SCADHA/ 9 FAESTE 4 HAEFDE.// 5   (0554)

GRIM 2 ON 1 GRAAPE/ 9 HWAETHRE 4 MEE 3 GYFE-1-THE 4 WEARDH// 5   (0555)

TH= 2 IC 2 AAG- 0 -LAEAECAN/ 9 ORDE 3 GE- 0 -RAEAEHTE// 6   (0556)

HILDE- 3 -BILLE/ 4 HEATHO- 3 -RAEAES 9 FOR- 2 -NAM// 4   (0557)

MIHTIG 3 MERE- 3 -DEEOR/ 2 THURH 2 MIINE 9 HAND// 9   (0558)

                    .VIIII.   (FITT)

$SWAA 3 MEC 3 GE- 3 -LOOME/ 5 LAADH- 2 -GE- 3 -TEEO-1-NAN// 4   (0559)

THREEATE-9-DON 4 THEARLE/ 4 IC 1 HIM 3 THEENO-1-DE// 4   (0560)

DEEO-1-RAN 2 SWEOR-9-DE/ 5 SWAA 2 HIT 3 GE- 2 -DEEFE 5 WAES// 4   (0561)

NAES 4 HIIE 4 DHAEAERE 9 FYLLE/ 5 GE- 1 -FEEAN 3 HAEFDON// 4   (0562)

MAAN- 2 -FOR- 2 -DAEAEDLAN/ 9 TH= 2 HIIE 3 MEE 2 THEEGON// 4   (0563)

SYMBEL 5 YMB- 3 -SAEAETON/ 4 +SAEAE- 9 -GRUNDE 5 NEEAH.// 5   (0564)

AC 2 ON 2 MER-2-GEN-2-NE/ 4 MEECU= 9 WUN-1-DE// 6   (0565)

                  END FOLIO 144V +

BE 2 YYDH- 2 -LAAFE/ 5 UP-1-PE 3 LAEAEGON// 3   (0566)

()SWEDDU=*SWEORDU= 9 AA- 0 -SWEFEDE/ 5 TH= 2 SYDH-2-THAN 4 NAA// 4   (0567)

YMB 2 BRONT-8-NE 9 FORD/ 5 BRIM- 3 -LIIDHENDE// 5   (0568)

LAADE 4 NE 1 LET-1-TON/ 8 LEEOHT 9 EEASTAN 3 COOM// 4   (0569)

BEORHT 4 BEEACEN 3 GO-1-DES/ 4 BRIMU 9 SWATHREDON// 4   (0570)

TH= 0 IC 1 SAEAE- 2 -NAESSAS/ 3 GE- 2 -SEEON 3 MIHTE// 9   (0571)

WINDIGE 3 WEALLAS/ 4 WYRD 2 OFT 1 NEREDH// 4   (0572)

UN- 0 -FAEAEGNE 9 EORL/ 4 THON-1-NE 3 HIS 3 ELLEN 2 DEEAH.// 6   (0573)

HWAETHERE 3 MEE 0 GE- 9 -SAEAELDE/ 5   (0574)

                        20

```
TH= 0 IC 1 MID 2 SWEORDE 4 OF- 2 -SLOOH// 4                          (0574)

NICERAS 9 NIGENE / 4 NOO 2 IC 1 ON 1 NIHT 2 GE- 0 -FRAEGN// 4        (0575)

UNDER 2 HEO-9-FONES 5 HWEALF/ 4 HEARDRAN 2 FEOHTAN// 3               (0576)

NEE 2 ON 1 EEG- 9 -STREEAMUM/ 3 EARMRAN 3 MANNON.// 5                (0577)

(I)HWATHERE*HWAETHERE 9 IC 0 FAARA 4 FENG/ 3 FEEORE 3 GE- 0 -OIIGOE// 5  (0578)

SIITHES 3 WEERIG/ 9 OHAA 0 MEC 3 +SAEAE 3 OTH- 2 -BAER// 4           (0579)

FLOOD 2 AEFTER 4 FAR-1-ODHE/ 4 ON 9 FIN-1-NA 3 LAND.// 5             (0580)

(I)WUDU*WADU 3 WEALLEN-1-DU/ 3 NOO 1 IC 2 WIHT 2 FRA= 9 THEE// 4     (0581)

SWYLCRA 3 SEARO- 3 -NIIDHA/ 3 SECGAN 4 HYYRDE// 9                    (0582)

BILLA 5 BRODGAN/ 4 BRECA 4 NAEAEFRE 3 GIIT// 3                       (0583)

AET 0 HEADHO- 9 -LAACE./ 6 NEE 0 GE- 3 -HWAE-2-THER 4 INCER// 2      (0584)

SWAA 3 DEEOR- 0 -LIICE/ 9 DAEAED 3 GE- 0 -FREMEDE// 4                (0585)

FAAGUM 2 SWEOR-1-DUM/ 3 NOO 0 IC 9 THAES 3 *FELA 8 GYLPE// 5         (0586)

THEEAH 3 DHUU 2 THIINUM 4 BROODH-2-RUM/ 3 TOO 9 BANAN 4 WURDE// 6    (0587)

HEEAFOD- 3 -MAEAEGUM/ 4 THAES 3 THUU 0 IN 9 HELLE 4 SCEALT// 3       (0588)

                            END FOLIO 145R +


WERHDHO 3 DREEO-1-GAN/ 3 THEEAH 2 THIIN 9 WIT 8 DUGE.// 7            (0589)

SECGE 3 IC 2 THEE 0 TOO 3 SOODHE/ 4 SUNU 3 ECG- 9 -LAAFES// 6        (0590)

TH= 1 NAEAEFRE 4 ()GRE*GREN-8-DEL 4 SWAA 2 FELA/ 3                   (0591)

           GRYRE 9 GE- 0 -FREME-2-DE// 5                             (0591)

ATOL 3 AEAEG- 0 -LAEAECA/ 3 EAL-1-DRE 9 THIINUM// 5                  (0592)

HYYNDHO 3 ON 2 HEO-1-ROTE/ 5 GIF 3 THIIN 2 HIGE 9 WAEAERE// 5        (0593)

SEFA 2 SWAA 4 SEARO- 2 -GRIM/ 2 SWAA 2 THUU 2 SELF 9 TALAST.// 6     (0594)

AC 2 HEE 4 HAFADH 3 ON- 1 -FUN-1-DEN/ 4                              (0595)

           TH= 2 HEE 9 THAA 2 FAEAEHDHE 5 NE 1 THEARF// 5            (0595)

ATOLE 4 ECG- 3 -THRAECE/ 9 EEOWER 3 LEEODE// 5                       (0596)

SWIIDHE 4 ON- 1 -SITTAN/ 4 SIGE- 9 -SCYL-1-DINGA// 5                 (0597)

NYMEDH 4 NYYD- 3 -BAADE/ 4 NAEAE-2-NEGU= 9 AARADH.// 5               (0598)

LEEODE 3 DENIGA/ 4 AC 1 HEE 2 LUST 2 WIGEDH// 9                      (0599)

SWEFEDH 4 OND 3 ()SENDETH*SNEEDETH./ 6 SECCE 3 NE 3 WEENETH// 9      (0600)

TOO 1 GAAR- 3 -DENUM/ 4 AC 2 IC 1 HIM 3 GEEATA 3 SCEAL// 9           (0601)

AFODH 3 =AND 1 ELLEN/ 4 UN- 1 -GEAARA 4 NUU// 3                      (0602)
```

21

GUUTHE 3 GE- 9 -BEEODAN/ 4 GAEAETH 3 EFT 8 SEE 1 THE 4 +MOOT.// 7   (0603)

TOO 1 MEDO 9 MOODIG/ 5 SITHTHAN 4 MORGEN- 3 -LEEOHT// 4   (0604)

OFER 3 YLDA 4 BEARN/ 4 OOTHRES 4 DOOGO-1-RES// 4   (0605)

SUNNE 9 SWEGL- 5 -WERED/ 3 SUJTHAN 4 SCIINEDH.// 7   (0606)

THAA 2 WAES 9 ON 2 SAALUM/ 4 SINCES 5 BRYT-1-TA// 5   (0607)

GAMOL- 9 -FEAX 4 =AND 0 GUUDH- 3 -ROOF/ 5   (0608)

      GEEO-1-CE 5 GE- 3 -LYYF-1-DE// 9   (0608)

           END FOLIO 145V +

BREGO 5 BEOR-2-HT- 5 -DENA/ 4 GE- 1 -HYYRDE 4 ON 8 BEEO- 9 -WULFE// 5   (0609)

FOL-1-CES 5 HYRDE/ 5 FAEST- 4 -RAEAEDNE 3 GE- 3 -THOOHT// 5   (0610)

DHAEAER 3 WAES 5 HAE-1-L-1-E-1-THA 4 HLEAHTOR/ 9 HLYN 2 SWYN-1-SODE// 5   (0611)

WORD 2 WAEAER-1-ON 3 WYN- 0 -SUME/ 9 EEODE 4 WEALH- 1 -THEEOW 8 FORDH// 4 (0612)

CWEEN 3 HROODH- 2 -GAARES/ 9 CYN-1-NA 3 GE- 0 -MYNDIG// 5   (0613)

GREETTE 4 GOLD- 2 -HRO-9-DEN/ 3 GUMAN 3 ON 2 HEALLE.// 5   (0614)

=AND 0 THAA 2 FREEO- 0 -LIIC 9 WIIF/ 5 FUL 1 GE- 1 -SEALDE// 5   (0615)

AEAEREST 2 EEAST- 3 -DENA/ 9 EETHEL- 3 -WEARDE// 6   (0616)

BAED 2 HINE 4 BLIIDHNE/ 4 AET 2 THAEAERE 9 BEEOR- 3 -THEGE// 7   (0617)

LEEODJM 4 LEEOFNE/ 5 HEE 2 ON 2 LUST 9 GE- 3 -THEAH// 5   (0618)

SYMBEL 4 =AND 0 SELE- 2 -FUL/ 4 SIGE- 2 -ROOF 9 KYNING// 4   (0619)

YMB- 2 -EEODE 5 THAA/ 1 IDES 4 HELMINGA// 9   (0620)

DUGU-2-THE 3 =AND 0 GEO-1-GO-1-THE/ 5 DAEAEL 3 AEAEG- 0 -HWYLCNE// 9   (0621)

SINC- 2 -FATO 3 SAELDE/ 5 OTH 1 TH= 2 SAEAEL 3 AA- 0 -LAMP// 3   (0622)

THAET 9 HIIO 2 BEEO- 0 -WULFE/ 5 BEEAG- 4 -HRODEN 3 CWEEN// 3   (0623)

MODDE 9 GE- 2 -THUNGEN/ 4 ME-1-DO- 2 -FUL 4 AET- 2 -BAER.// 7   (0624)

GREETTE 9 GEEA-1-TA 4 LEEOD/ 3 GODE 3 THANCODE// 6   (0625)

WIIS- 3 -FAEST 9 WOR-2-DUM/ 4   (0626)

      THAES 4 DHE 3 HIRE 4 SE 2 WILLA 4 GE- 1 -LAMP// 9   (0626)

TH= 2 HEEO 3 ON 1 AEAENIGNE/ 2 EORL 3 GE- 0 -LYYFDE// 5   (0627)

FYRENA 9 FROOF-1-RE/ 4 HEE 2 TH= 1 FUL 4 GE- 3 -THEAH// 5   (0628)

WAEL- 3 -REEOW 3 WIGA/ 9 AET 8 WEAL-1-H- 0 -THEEON.// 5   (0629)

      END FOLIO 146R +

```
=AND 0 THAA 1 GYDDODE/ 5 GUUTHE 3 GE- 8 -FYYSED.// 9                          (0630)

=EEO- 0 -WULF 1 MATHELODE/ 5 BEARN 3 ECG- 2 -THEEOWES.// 5                    (0631)

=C 2 THAET 9 HOGODE/ 5 THAA 0 IC 2 ON 2 HOLM 3 GE- 1 -STAAH.// 5              (0632)

=AEAE- 3 -BAAT 2 GE- 9 -SAET/ 4 MID 2 MIINRA 4 SECGA 3 GE- 1 -DRIHT// 5       (0633)

=H= 0 IC 2 AANUNGA/ 9 EEOWRA 3 LEEODA// 5                                     (0634)

=ILLAN 3 GE- 1 -WORHTE/ 5 OTHDHE 3 ON 1 WAEL 9 CRUNGE.// 5                    (0635)

=EEOND- 3 -GRAAPUM 4 FAEST/ 4 IC 0 GE- 3 -FREM-9-MAN 3 SCEAL// 5             (0636)

=OR-2-LIIC 3 ELLEN/ 4 OTHDHE 3 ENDE- 3 -DAEG// 4                             (0637)

=N 9 THISSE 4 MEODU- 3 -HEALLE/ 5 MIINNE 2 GE- 2 -BIIDAN.// 5                (0638)

=HAAM 2 WIIFE 9 THAA 2 WORD/ 3 WEEL 3 LIICODON// 4                           (0639)

=ILP- 2 -CWIDE 4 GEEATES/ 4 EEODE 9 GOLD- 4 -HRODEN.// 5                     (0640)

=REEO- 1 -LICU 3 FOLC- 3 -CWEEN/ 3 TOO 1 HIRE 9 FREEAN 4 SITTAN.// 7         (0641)

=THAA 0 WAES 3 EFT 3 SWAA 3 AEAER/ 3 IN-1-NE 3 ON 9 HEALLE// 6               (0642)

=HRYYDH- 3 -WORD 3 SPRECEN/ 4 DHEEOD 3 ON 1 SAEAELUM// 3                     (0643)

=IGE- 9 -FOL-2-CA 4 SWEEG/ 3 OTH 0 TH= 2 SEM-1-NINGA// 3                     (0644)

=UNU 3 HEALF- 3 -DENES/ 9 SEECEAN 3 WOL-1-DE// 5                             (0645)

=EAEFEN- 2 -RAES-1-TE./ 5 WISTE 4 THAEAEM 2 AAH- 0 -LAEAECAN// 9             (0646)

=OO 0 THAEAEM 4 HEEAH- 1 -SELE/ 5 HILDE 3 GE- 2 -THINGED.// 6                (0647)

=IDHDHAN 4 HIIE 9 SUNNAN 3 LEEOHT/ 4 GE- 2 -SEEON 3 MEAHTON// 4             (0648)

=TH 0 DHE 3 NII-9-PEN-1-DE/ 4 NIHT 4 OFER 4 EALLE// 4                        (0649)

=CADU- 4 -HELMA 3 GE- 9 -SCEAPU/ 4 SCRIIDHAN 3 CWOOMAN// 3                   (0650)

=AN 2 UNDER 4 WOLCNU=/ 9 WEROD 3 EALL 3 AA- 0 -RAAS.// 7                     (0651)

=GE- 8 -GREET-1-TE 3 THAA/ 2 GUMA 3 OOTHERNE// 9                            (0652)

=RCODH- 2 -GAAR 4 BEEO- 0 -WULF/ 5                                           (0653)

         =AND 0 HIM 3 HAEAEL 4 AA- 0 -BEEAD.// 3                             (0653)

=IIN- 1 -AERNES 9 GE- 0 -WEALD/ 4 =AND 0 TH= 2 WORD 2 AA- 0 -CWAEDH.// 6    (0654)

                 ✝ END FOLIO 146V


=NAEAEFRE 5 IC 2 AEAENEGU= 9 MEN/ 3 AEAER 3 AA- 0 -LYYFDE// 5               (0655)

=ITHDHAN 3 IC 3 HOND 3 =AND 0 ROND/ 3 HE-3-9-BAN 3 MIHTE// 6               (0656)

=HRYYTH- 3 -AERN 3 DENA/ 5 BUJTON 4 THEE 2 NUU 0 DHAA// 9                   (0657)

=AFA 3 NUU 2 =AND 0 GE- 3 -HEALD/ 5 HUUSA 4 SEELEST// 4                     (0658)

=E- 1 -MYNE 9 MAEAERTHO/ 5 MAEGEN- 2 -ELLEN 2 CYYDH// 4                     (0659)
```

WACA 3 WIDH 3 WRAATHUM/ 9 NE 3 BIDH 3 THEE 4 WILNA 3 +GAAD// 3   (0660)
GIF 2 THUU 1 TH= 2 ELLEN- 2 -WEORC/ 3 ALDRE 9 GE- 2 -DIIGEST.// 9   (0661)

                        .X.   (FITT)
$$DHAA 3 HIM 4 HROOTH- 1 -GAAR 5 GE- 0 -WAAT/ 5   (0662)
        MID 3 HIS 3 HAE-9-LETHA 4 GE- 1 -DRYHT// 5   (0662)
EODUR 4 SCYLDINGA/ 4 UUT 9 OF 2 HEALLE// 5   (0663)
WOL-1-DE 4 WIIG- 1 -FRUMA/ 4 WEAL-1-H- 2 -THEEO 3 SEE-9-CAN// 4   (0664)
CWEEN 3 TOO 0 GE- 2 -BEDDAN/ 5 HAEFDE 4 KYNING- 9 -WUL-1-DOR// 4   (0665)
GREND-1-LE 4 TOO- 3 -GEEANES/ 4 SWAA 1 GUMAN 9 GE- 1 -FRUNGON// 5   (0666)
SELE- 3 -WEARD 3 AA- 0 -SETED/ 3 SUNDOR- 3 -NYT-9-TE 5 BE- 1 -HEEOLD// 4 (0667)
YMB 3 ALDOR 3 DENA/ 3 EOTON- 2 -WEARD 9 AA- 0 -BEEAD// 4   (0668)
HUURU 1 GEEATA 5 LEEOD/ 3 GEORNE 4 TRUWODE// 9   (0669)
MOODGAN 3 MAEGNES/ 4 METODES 3 HYL-1-DO.// 6   (0670)
DHAA 1 HEE 0 HI= 9 OF 1 DYDE/ 5 IISERN- 4 -BYRNAN// 4   (0671)
HELM 2 OF 2 HAFE-1-LAN/ 9 SEALDE 4 HIS 4 HYRSTED 3 SWEORD// 3   (0672)
IIRENA 3 CYST/ 4 OM-9-BIHT- 5 -THEGNE// 5   (0673)
=AND 0 GE- 2 -HEAL-2-DAN 3 HEET/ 3 HILDE- 3 -GEATWE// 9   (0674)
GE- 2 -SPRAEC 3 THAA 0 SE 3 GOODA/ 4 GYLP- 3 -WORDA 4 SUM.// 4   (0675)
BEEO- 0 -WULF 9 GEEATA/ 4 AEAER 2 HEE 2 ON 2 BED 3 STIGE// 4   (0676)
        + END FOLIO 147R

NOO 1 IC 3 MEE 6 AN 9 HERE- 3 -WAESMUM/ 5 HNAA-1-GRAN 4 TALIGE// 5   (0677)
GUUTH- 3 -GE- 9 -WEORCA/ 4 THON-2-NE 5 GRENDEL 5 HINE// 4   (0678)
FOR- 2 -THAN 2 IC 9 HINE 5 SWEORDE/ 5 SWEBBAN 3 NELLE// 4   (0679)
ALDRE 3 BE- 2 -NEEO-9-TAN/ 3 THEEAH 3 IC 1 EAL 2 MAEGE// 5   (0680)
+NAAT 3 HEE 3 THAARA 3 GOODA/ 9   (0681)
        TH= 1 HEE 2 MEE 4 ON- 0 -GEEAN 3 SLEEA// 5   (0681)
RAND 3 GE- 1 -HEEAWE/ 3 THEEAH 9 DHE 3 HEE 1 ROOF 2 SIIE// 4   (0682)
NIITH- 2 -GE- 1 -WEORCA/ 3 AC 0 WIT 3 ON 2 NIHT 9 SCULON.// 4   (0683)
SECGE 3 OFER- 3 -SITTAN/ 4   (0684)
        GIF 2 ()HET*HEE 2 GE- 9 -SEE-1-CEAN 3 DEAR.// 7   (0684)
WIIG 3 OFER 3 WAEAEPEN/ 4 =AND 0 SITHDHAN 2 WIITIG 9 GOD// 3   (0685)

                        24

N 0 SWAA 3 HWAETHERE 0 HOND/ 6 HAALIG 4 DRYHTEN// 3   (0686)

AEAER-9-DHO 3 DEEME/ 5 SWAA 2 HIM 2 GE- 2 -MET 3 THINCE.// 7   (0687)

YLDE 9 HINE 4 THAA 3 HEA-1-THO- 4 -DEEOR/ 5   (0688)

      HLEEOR- 4 -BOLSTER 3 ON- 9 -FEENG// 6   (0688)

ORLES 3 AND- 1 -WLITAN/ 3 =AND 0 HINE 4 YMB 2 MONIG// 9   (0689)

NEL- 0 -LIIC 5 +SAEAE- 3 -RINC/ 4 SE-1-LE- 3 -RESTE 2 GE- 1 -BEEAH.// 6 (0690)

AEAENIG 9 HEORA 4 THOOHTE/ 4 TH= 1 HEE 3 THANON 3 SCOLDE// 5 (0691)

FT 3 EARD- 9 -LUFAN/ 4 AEAEFRE 3 GE- 1 -SEECEAN// 4   (0692)

OLC 2 OTHDHE 3 FREEC- 1 -BURH/ 9   (0693)

      THAEAER 3 HEE 3 AA- 0 -FEEDED 2 WAES.// 6   (0693)

C 3 HIIE 4 HAEFDON 3 GE- 0 -FRUUNEN/ 9   (0694)

      TH= 2 HIIE 3 AEAER 0 TOO 3 FELA 3 MICLES// 5   (0694)

N 1 THAEAEM 2 WIIN- 2 -SELE/ 9 WAEL- 3 -DEEADH 3 FOR- 1 -NAM// 3 (0695)

ENIGEA 4 LEEODE/ 4 AC 2 HIM 9 DRYHTEN 3 FOR- 3 -GEAF// 4   (0696)

IIG- 2 -SPEEDA 4 GE- 2 -WIOFU./ 9 WEDERA 5 LEEO-1-DUM// 5   (0697)

         END FOLIO 147V +

ROOFOR 3 =AND 0 FULTUM/ 8 TH= 8 HIIE 9 FEEOND 4 HEORA// 5   (0698)

HURH 3 AANES 4 CRAEFT/ 4 EALLE 9 OFER- 4 -COOMON// 4   (0699)

EL-2-FES 3 MIHTUM/ 3 SOODH 3 IS 1 GE- 2 -CYY-9-THED// 4   (0700)

H= 1 MIHTIG 4 GOD/ 2 MANNA 3 CYNNES// 4   (0701)

EEOLD 8 ()RIDE*WIIDE- 9 -FER-1-HDH/ 4 COOM 2 ON 2 WAN-1-RE 5 NIHT// 5 (0702)

CRIIDHAN 3 SCEA-9-DU- 4 -GENGA/ 5 SCEEO-1-TEND 4 SWAEAEFON// 4 (0703)

HAA 3 TH= 2 HORN- 9 -RECED/ 5 HEAL-3-DAN 3 SCOL-1-DON.// 6 (0704)

ALLE 5 BUUTON 2 AANU=/ 9 TH= 1 WAES 4 YLDUM 3 CUUTH// 5 (0705)

H= 1 HIIE 3 NE 1 MOOSTE/ 5 THAA 1 METOD 9 NOLDE.// 6   (0706)

E 3 ()SYN*SCYN- 2 -SCATHA/ 5 UNDER 4 SCEA-2-DU 4 BREG-9-DAN.// 5 (0707)

C 2 HEE 2 WAEC-1-CENDE/ 4 WRAATHUM 4 ON 0 ANDAN// 9   (0708)

AAD 4 BOLGEN- 3 -MOOD/ 4 BEADWA 5 GE- 1 -THINGES.// 9   (0709)

         .XI.   (FITT)

DHAA 3 COOM 3 OF 1 MOORE/ 4 UNDER 3 MIST- 5 -HLEOTHUM// 3 (0710)

RE-9-NDEL 6 GONGAN/ 3 GODES 5 YRRE 4 BAER// 5   (0711)

MYNTE 9 SE 2 MAAN- 3 -SCADHA/ 5 MAN-2-NA 4 CYN-1-NES// 6   (0712)

SUM-1-NE 3 BE- 9 -SYRWAN/ 4 IN 0 SELE 4 THAAM 2 HEEAN// 4   (0713)

WOOD 2 UND-1-ER 3 WOLC-9-NUM/ 5   (0714)

          TOO 1 THAES 4 THE 1 HEE 3 WIIN- 1 -RECED// 4   (0714)

GOLD- 2 -SELE 3 GUME-9-NA/ 4 GEAR-1-WOST 4 WISSE.// 7   (0715)

FAEAET-2-TUM 3 FAAHNE/ 5 NE 9 WAES 3 THAET 4 FOR-2-MA 4 SIIDH// 7   (0716)

TH= 1 HEE 4 HROOTH- 0 -GAARES/ 4 HA= 9 GE- 1 -SOOHTE.// 7   (0717)

NAEAEFRE 4 HEE 3 ON 1 ALDOR- 3 -DAGUM/ 2 AEAER 9 NEE 8 SITHDHAN// 4 (0718)

                    END FOLIO 148R ✝

HEAR-1-DRAN 5 HAEAELE/ 5 HEAL- 3 -DHEGNAS 9 FAND// 4   (0719)

COOM 3 THAA 2 TOO 0 RECEDE/ 4 RINC 3 SIIDHIAN// 3   (0720)

DREEA-9-MUM 5 BE- 0 -DAEAELED/ 4 DURU 1 SOONA 5 ON- 1 -ARN// 3   (0721)

FYYR- 9 -BENDUM 3 FAEST/ 5   (0722)

          SYTHDHAN 5 HEE 3 HIRE 4 FOLMUM 9 AET- 8 -HRAAN.// 7   (0722)

SON- 2 -BRAEAED 3 THAA 2 BEALO- 4 -HYYDIG/ 4   (0723)

          DHAA 9 HEE 8 GE- 8 -BOLGEN 3 WAES// 4   (0723)

RECEDES 2 MUUTHAN/ 2 RATHE 9 AEFTER 3 THON// 3   (0724)

ON 0 FAAGNE 5 FLOOR/ 4 FEEOND 2 TRED-9-DODE// 5   (0725)

EEODE 3 YRRE- 4 -MOOD/ 3 HIM 2 OF 1 EEAGUM 3 STOOD// 9   (0726)

LIGGE 3 GE- 0 -LIICOST/ 4 LEEOHT 1 UN- 0 -FAEAEGER.// 4   (0727)

GE- 0 -SEAH 2 HEE 9 IN 0 RECEDE/ 4 RINCA 3 MANIGE// 4   (0728)

SWEFAN 3 SIB-1-BE- 9 -GE- 2 -DRIHT/ 4 SAMOD 2 AET- 2 -GAEDERE// 5 (0729)

MA-1-GO- 2 -RIN-9-CA 3 HEEAP/ 5 THAA 0 HIS 3 MOOD 3 AA- 0 -HLOOG.// 5 (0730)

MYNTE 3 THAET 9 HEE 0 GE- 2 -DAEAELDE/ 5   (0731)

          AEAER 1 THON 2 DAEG 3 CWOOME.// 6   (0731)

ATOL 9 AAG- 0 -LAEAECA/ 5 AANRA 3 GE- 2 -HWYLCES// 5   (0732)

LIIF 1 WIDH 3 LIICE/ 4 THAA 9 HIM 2 AA- 0 -LUM-2-PEN 2 WAES// 4   (0733)

WIST- 3 -FYLLE 4 WEEN/ 0 NE 4 WAES 9 TH= 8 WYRD 4 THAA 1 GEEN.// 5 (0734)

TH= 2 HEE 3 MAA 2 MOOSTE/ 4 MAN-1-NA 9 CYN-1-NES// 5   (0735)

DHICGEAN 4 OFER 3 THAA 1 NIHT/ 5 THRYYOH- 2 -SWYYOH 9 BE- 3 -HEEOLD// 5 (0736)

MAEAEG 4 HIGE- 3 -LAACES/ 6 HUU 0 SE 1 MAAN- 9 -SCADHA// 5   (0737)

UNDER 3 FAEAER- 3 -GRIPUM/ 3 GE- 0 -FARAN 2 WOL-9-DE.// 6   (0738)

26

```
NEE 2 TH= 2 SE 3 AAG- 0 -LAEAECA/ 5 YLDAN 4 THOOHTE// 5              (0739)
AC 1 HEE 0 GE- 9 -FEENG 4 HRA-1-DHE/ 6 FOR-1-MAN 2 SIIDHE// 5         (0740)
              * END FOLIO 148V


SLAEAEPENONE 9 RINC/ 3 SLAAT 1 UN- 1 -WEAR-1-NUM// 5                  (0741)
+BAAT 3 BAAN- 1 -LOCAN/ 2 BLOOD 9 EEDRUM 3 DRANC// 5                  (0742)
SYN- 3 -SNAEAEDUM 3 SWEALH/ 4 SOONA 9 HAEFDE// 4                      (0743)
UN- 1 -LYFIGENDES/ 4 EAL 1 GE- 1 -FEORMOD.// 4                        (0744)
FEET 9 =AND 0 FOLMA/ 3 FORDH 2 NEEAR 3 AET- 0 -STOOP// 4              (0745)
NAM 2 THAA 2 MID 2 HAN-9-DA/ 3 HIGE- 3 -THIIHTIGNE// 4                (0746)
RINC 2 ON 0 RAESTE/ 8 RAEAEHTE 4 ON- 1 -GEEAN// 3                     (0747)
FEEOND 2 MID 1 FOLME/ 5 HEE 1 ON- 9 -FEENG 3 HRA-1-THE// 5            (0748)
IN-1-4IT- 3 -THANCU=/ 5 =AND 0 WIDH 3 EARM 2 GE- 9 -SAET// 5          (0749)
SOONA 4 TH= 0 ON- 0 -FUNDE/ 5 FYRENA 4 HYRDE// 4                      (0750)
TH= 2 HEE 9 NE 3 MEETTE/ 5 MIDDAN- 4 -GEAR-1-DES// 5                  (0751)
EOR-2-THAN 2 ()SCEAT*SCEEA-9-TA/ 4 ON 1 EL-1-RAN 4 MEN// 4            (0752)
MUND- 3 -GRIPE 4 MAARAN/ 9 HEE 1 ON 1 MOODE 4 WEARDH// 4              (0753)
FOR-1-HT 3 ON 0 FER-1-HDHE/ 4 NOO 1 THYY 9 AEAER 2 FRAM 2 MEAHTE// 5  (0754)
HYGE 3 WAES 3 HIM 3 HIN- 2 -FUUS/ 9 WOLDE 4 ON 3 HEOLSTER 5 FLEEON// 4 (0755)
SEECAN 4 DEEOFLA 9 GE- 2 -DRAEG/ 4                                    (0756)

        NE 1 WAES 3 HIS 4 DROHTODH 4 THAEAER// 4                      (0756)
SWYLCE 9 HEE 2 ON 2 EALDER- 4 -DAGUM/ 3 AEAER 2 GE- 0 -MEETTE.// 7    (0757)
GE- 9 -MUNDE 4 THAA 0 SE 1 GOODA/ 4 MAEAEG 3 HIGE- 2 -LAACES// 4      (0758)
AEAEFEN- 9 -SPRAEAECE/ 5 UP- 1 -LANG 3 AA- 0 -+STOOD// 3              (0759)
=AND 1 HIM 2 FAESTE 3 WIDH- 9 -FEENG/ 5 FINGRAS 4 BUR-1-STON// 4      (0760)
EOTEN 3 WAES 3 UUT- 9 -WEARD/ 3 EORL 1 FUR-1-THUR 4 STOOP// 3         (0761)
MYNTE 3 SE 1 MAEAERA./ 9 ()HWAER*THAEAER 8 HEE 3 MEAHTE 4 SWAA.// 5   (0762)
              END FOLIO 149R *


WIIDRE 4 GE- 2 -WINDAN/ 8 =AND 9 ON 2 WEG 4 THANON// 4                (0763)
FL-1-EEON 2 ON 0 FEN- 4 -HOPU/ 4 WISTE 9 HIS 3 FINGRA 4 GE- 0 -WEALD// 4 (0764)
ON 0 GRAMES 4 GRAAPUM/ 9 THAET 8 ()HE 8 WAES 4 GEEOCOR 5 SIIDH// 5    (0765)
TH= 1 SE 4 HEARM- 3 -SCA-9-THA/ 4 TOO 2 HEORUTE 5 AA- 0 -TEEAH.// 6   (0766)
                              27
```

DRYHT- 3 -SELE 9 DYNEDE/ 5 DENU= 3 EALLUM 2 WEARDH// 4   (0767)

CEASTER- 3 -BUU-9-ENDUM/ 4 CEENRA 4 GE- 1 -HWYLCUM// 4   (0768)

EORLUM 2 EALU- 9 -SCERWEN/ 3 YRRE 3 WAEAERON 2 BEEGEN.// 6   (0769)

REETHE 4 REN- 9 -WEAR-1-DAS/ 5 RECED 3 HLYNSODE// 6   (0770)

THAA 0 WAES 3 WUNDOR 9 MICEL/ 5 TH= 1 SE 2 WIIN- 1 -SELE.// 7   (0771)

WIDH- 3 -HAEFDE 5 HEA-1-THO- 9 -DEEORUM/ 4   (0772)

          THAT 3 HEE 2 ON 3 HRUUS-1-AN 4 NE 0 FEEOL// 4   (0772)

FAEAESER 9 FOLD- 4 -BOLD/ 4 AC 2 HEE 1 THAES 4 FAESTE 3 WAES.// 5   (0773)

IN-1-NAN 2 =AND 9 UUTAN/ 3 IIREN- 2 -BENDUM// 4   (0774)

SEAR-1-O- 3 -THONCUM 3 BE- 0 -SMI-9-THOD/ 4   (0775)

          THAEAER 3 FRAM 3 SYLLE 3 +AA- 3 -BEEAG.// 6   (0775)

MEDU- 3 -BENC 9 MONIG/ 3 MIINE 4 GE- 0 -FRAEAEGE// 5   (0776)

GOL-1-DE 4 GE- 1 -REGNAD/ 9 THAEAER 3 THAA 2 GRAMUM 4 WUN-1-NON// 5   (0777)

THAES 3 NE 2 WEENDON 9 AEAER/ 3 WITAN 3 SCYL-2-DINGA// 5   (0778)

TH= 1 HIT 3 AA 0 MID 3 GE- 0 -METE/ 9 MAN-1-NA 4 AEAENIG.// 7   (0779)

()HET*BET- 0 -LIIC 3 =AND 0 +BAAN- 3 -FAAG/ 4   (0780)

          TOO- 2 -BRE-9-CAN 3 MEAHTE// 5   (0780)

LIS-1-TUM 3 TOO- 0 -LUUCAN/ 4 NYM-1-THE 3 LIIGES 5 FAETHM// 4   (0781)

SWULGE 5 ON 1 SWA-1-THU-1-LE/ 6 SWEEG 9 UP 2 AA- 0 -STAAG.// 6   (0782)

                    END FOLIO 149V +

NIIWE 4 GE- 0 -NEAH-2-HE/ 5 NORDH- 3 -DENU= 2 STOOD// 9   (0783)

ATELIIC 4 EGESA/ 5 AANRA 4 GE- 2 -HWYL-1-CUM// 4   (0784)

THAARA 1 THE 9 OF 3 WEALLE/ 5 WOOP 3 GE- 2 -HYYR-2-DON.// 5   (0785)

GRYRE- 4 -LEEOOH 8 GA-9-LAN/ 3 GODES 5 =AND- 0 -SACAN// 4   (0786)

SIGE- 3 -LEEAS-1-NE 5 SANG/ 8 SAAR 9 WAANIGEAN.// 6   (0787)

HELLE 4 HAEFTON/ 5 HEEOLD 4 HINE 9 FAESTE// 5   (0788)

SEE 0 THE 3 MANNA 4 WAES/ 4 MAEGE-3-NE 4 STREN-9-GEST// 5   (0789)

ON 2 THAEAEM 4 DAEGE/ 4 THYS-2-SES 5 LIIFES.// 9   (0790)

                    .XII.   (FITT)

$NOLDE 4 EORLA 5 HLEEO/ 3 AEAENIGE 4 THINGA// 4   (0791)

THONE 9 CWEALM- 3 -CUMAN/ 4 CWICNE 4 FOR- 2 -LAEAETAN.// 3   (0792)

                              28

NEE 9 HIS 3 LIIF- 3 -DAGAS/ 6 LEEODA 4 AEAENIGUM// 5   (0793)

NYTTE 9 TEAL-1-DE/ 6 THAEAER 0 GE- 3 -NEHOST 4 BRAEGD// 4   (0794)

EORL 4 BEEO- 9 -WUL-1-FES/ 5 EAL-1-DE 4 LAAFE// 7   (0795)

WOL-1-DE 4 FREEA- 3 -DRIHT-9-NES/ 4 FEORH 8 EALGIAN// 6   (0796)

MAEAER-1-ES 4 THEEOD-9-NES/ 5 DHAEAER 3 HIIE 3 MEAHTON 3 SWAA.// 6   (0797)

HIIE 3 TH= 0 NE 3 WISTON/ 9 THAA 1 HIIE 4 GE- 1 -WIN 3 DRUGON// 5   (0798)

HEARD- 3 -HICGEN-1-DE/ 9 HIL-1-DE- 3 -MECGAS.// 5   (0799)

=AND 0 ON 1 HEAL-1-FA 4 GE- 3 -HWONE/ 5 HEEA-9-WAN 3 THOOHTON// 4   (0800)

SAAWLE 4 SEECAN/ 4 THONE 3 SYN- 2 -SCADHAN.// 9   (0801)

AEAENIG 3 OFER 3 EOR-1-THAN/ 4 IIREN-1-NA 4 CYST// 4   (0802)

GUUDH- 3 -BIL-9-LA 3 NAAN/ 4 GREETAN 3 NOLDE.// 7   (0803)

AC 0 4EE 4 SIGE- 2 -WAEÀEPNU=/ 9 FOR- 2 -SWOREN 4 HAEFDE// 6   (0804)

                END FOLIO 150R +

ECGA 4 GE- 1 -HWYLC-1-RE/ 4 SCOLDE 9 HIS 2 ALDOR- 4 -GE- 2 -DAAL// 5   (0805)

ON 0 DH-1-AEAEM 3 DAEGE/ 5 THYS-3-SES 9 LIIFES// 5   (0806)

EARM- 1 -LIIC 3 WURDHAN/ 4 =AND 0 SE 4 ELLOR- 4 -GAAST// 9   (0807)

ON 8 FEEONDA 4 GE- 2 -WEALD/ 4 FEOR 4 SIIDHIAN.// 7   (0808)

DHAA 3 THAET 9 ON- 8 -FUNDE/ 5 SEE 0 THE 4 FELA 4 AEAEROR// 5   (0809)

MOODES 4 MYRDHE/ 9 MAN-1-NA 4 CYNNE// 6   (0810)

FYRE-1-NE 6 GE- 0 -FREME-3-DE./ 4 HEE 9 *WAES 8 FAAG 3 WIDH 3 GOD// 6 (0811)

TH= 0 HIM 2 SE 1 LIIC- 2 -HOMA/ 4 LAEAESTAN 9 NOL-1-DE// 6   (0812)

AC 2 HINE 4 SE 0 MOODEGA/ 4 MAEAEG 4 HYGE- 3 -LAA-9-CES// 5   (0813)

HAEF-1-DE 3 BE 2 HONDA/ 4 WAES 2 GE- 2 -HWAE-1-THER 3 OODHRUM// 9   (0814)

LIFIGENDE 5 LAADH/ 5 LIIC- 3 -SAAR 2 GE- 2 -BAAD// 5   (0815)

ATOL 3 AEAEG- 0 -LAEAECA/ 9 HIM 3 ON 2 EAXLE 4 WEARDH// 5   (0816)

SYN- 0 -DOLH 4 SWEOTOL/ 4 SEO-9-NOWE 4 ON- 1 -SPRUN-1-GON// 5   (0817)

BUR-1-STON 3 BAAN- 3 -LOCAN/ 9 BEEO- 0 -WUL-1-FE 3 WEARDH// 5   (0818)

GUUDH- 4 -HR-1-EEDH 3 GYFE-1-THE/ 5 SCOLDE 9 GRENDEL 5 THONAN// 3   (0819)

FEORH- 4 -SEEOC 4 FLEEON/ 3 UN-1-DER 9 FEN- 3 -HL-1-EODHU// 4   (0820)

SEECEAN 3 WYN- 2 -LEEAS 4 +WIIC/ 4 WISTE 4 THEE 9 GEORNOR// 7   (0821)

TH= 0 HIS 2 ALDRES 4 WAES/ 4 ENDE 4 GE- 1 -GONGEN.// 9   (0822)

DOOGERA 4 DAEG- 3 -RIIM/ 4 DENUM 3 EALLUM 3 WEARDH// 3   (0823)

                                  29

AEFTER 9 THAAM 4 WAEL- 0 -RAEAESE/ 5 WILLA 4 GE- 2 -LUMPEN.// 5   (0824)

HAEFDE 4 THAA 0 GE- 9 -FAEAELSOD/ 4   (0825)

   SEE 1 THE 4 AEAER 3 FEOR-2-RAN 4 COOM// 4   (0825)

SNOTOR 4 =AND 9 SWYYDH- 4 -FERHDH/ 5 SELE 6 HROODH- 3 -GAARES// 4   (0826)

GE- 2 -NERED 2 WIDH 9 NIIDHE/ 5 NIHT- 3 -WEORCE 5 GE- 2 -FEH// 4   (0827)

    ✝ END FOLIO 150V

ELLEN- 2 -MAEAER-3-THUM/ 9 HAEF-1-DE 5 EEAST- 3 -DENUM// 4   (0828)

GEEAT- 3 -MECGA 3 LEEDD/ 2 GILP 9 GE- 2 -LAEAESTED.// 5   (0829)

$SWYLCE 4 ON- 1 -CYYTHDHE/ 5 EALLE 3 GE- 8 -BEETTE// 9   (0830)

IN-1-WID- 3 -SORGE/ 5 THE 3 HIIE 5 AEAER 3 DRU-1-GON// 5   (0831)

=AND 0 FOR 8 THREEA- 9 -NYYDUM/ 4 THOLIAN 4 SCOL-1-DON// 4   (0832)

TORN 3 UN- 1 -LYYTEL/ 9 TH= 0 WAES 4 TAACEN 3 SWEOTOL// 5   (0833)

SYTHDHAN 4 HILDE- 4 -DEEOR/ 9 HOND 3 AA- 0 -LEGDE// 5   (0834)

EARM 3 =AND 1 EAXLE/ 5 THAEAER 3 WAES 3 EAL 9 GEA-2-DOR// 4   (0835)

GRENDLES 4 GRAAPE/ 4 UNDER 3 GEEAPNE 2 HR*OOF.// 9   (0836)

   .XIII   (FITT)

$$DHAA 3 WAES 3 ON 1 MOR-2-GEN/ 3 MIINE 3 GE- 1 -FRAEAEGE// 5   (0837)

YMB 9 THAA 2 GIF- 2 -HEALLE/ 6 GUUDH- 2 -RINC 4 MONIG// 4   (0838)

FEER-1-DON 9 FOLC- 2 -TOGAN/ 4 FEOR-2-RAN 3 =AND 0 NEEAN// 4   (0839)

GEOND 2 WIID- 9 -WEGAS/ 4 WUN-1-DOR 4 SCEEA-1-WIAN// 5   (0840)

LAATHES 4 LAASTAS/ 9 NOO 2 HIS 5 LIIF- 2 -GE- 3 -DAAL// 5   (0841)

SAAR- 1 -LIIC 3 THUUHTE/ 6 SECGA 9 AEAENEGUM// 5   (0842)

THAARA 4 THE 4 TIIR- 3 -LEEASES/ 4 TRODE 9 SCEEAWODE// 6   (0843)

HUU 2 HEE 4 WEERIG- 4 -MOOD/ 3 ON 2 WEG 3 THANON// 9   (0844)

NIIDHA 3 OFER- 3 -CUMEN/ 4 ON 1 NICERA 4 MERE// 5   (0845)

FAEAEGE 9 =AND 1 GE- 3 -FLYYMED/ 4 FEORH- 4 -LAASTAS 4 BAER.// 6   (0846)

DHAEAER 9 WAES 3 ON 1 BLOODE/ 5 BRIM 3 WEALLENDE// 5   (0847)

ATOL 4 YYDHA 9 GE- 3 -SWING/ 4 EAL 4 GE- 3 -MENGED.// 6   (0848)

HAAT-3-ON 2 HEOLFRE/ 9 HEORO- 4 -DREEORE 4 WEEOL// 5   (0849)

    ✝ END FOLIO 151R

     30

DEEAD+- 2 -FAEAEGE 3 DEEOG./ 4 SIDHDHAN 9 DREEAMA 4 LEEAS.// 5   (0850)

IN 1 FEN- 2 -FREODHO/ 4 FEORH 2 AA- 0 -LEGDE.// 9   (0851)

$HAEAETHENE 5 SAAWLE/ 5 THAEAER 2 HIM 3 HEL 3 ON- 1 -FEENG.// 7   (0852)

THANON 9 EFT 8 GE- 0 -WITON/ 3 EALD- 3 -GE- 1 -SIIDHAS// 5   (0853)

SWYL-1-CE 4 GEONG 9 MANIG/ 3 OF 1 GOMEN- 3 -WAATHE// 5   (0854)

FRAM 3 MERE 4 MOODGE/ 9 MEEARUM 2 RIIDAN// 5   (0855)

BEOR-2-NAS 4 ON 2 BLAN-2-CUM/ 3 DHAEAER 9 WAES 4 BEEO- 0 -WUL-1-FES// 4 (0856)

MAEAERDHO 3 MAEAE-1-NED/ 4 MONIG 3 OFT 9 GE- 2 -CWAEDH// 5   (0857)

THAET-1-TE 2 SUUDH 4 NE 2 NORDH/ 5 BE 0 SAEAEM 3 TWEEO-9-NUM// 4   (0858)

OFER 3 EORMEN- 3 -GRUND/ 4 OOTHER 3 NAEAENIG// 3   (0859)

UN-9-DER 3 SWEGLES 5 BE- 0 -GONG/ 5 SEEL-1-RA 3 NAEAERE// 4   (0860)

ROND- 3 -HAEB-9-BEN-1-DRA/ 4 RIICES 3 WYRDH-1-RA.// 7   (0861)

NEE 2 HIIE 4 HUURU 3 WINE- 9 -DRIHTEN/ 4 WIHT 3 NE 2 LOOGON// 4   (0862)

GLAEDNE 4 HROODH- 2 -GAAR/ 9 AC 2 TH= 0 WAES 3 GOOD 3 CYNING.// 7   (0863)

$HWIILUM 4 HEA-1-THO- 3 -ROOFE/ 9 HLEEAPAN 3 LEETON// 4   (0864)

ON 0 GE- 3 -FLIT 4 FAR-1-AN/ 3 FEAL-1-WE 9 MEEARAS// 4   (0865)

DHAEAER 3 HIM 3 FOLD- 3 -WEGAS/ 4 FAEGERE 4 THUUH-9-TON// 4   (0866)

CYSTUM 3 CUUDH-8-E/ 6 HWIILUM 3 CYNINGES 9 THEGN// 3   (0867)

GUMA 2 GILP- 3 -HLAEDEN/ 3 GIDDA 3 GE- 1 -MYNDIG// 9   (0868)

SEE 0 DHE 3 EAL- 3 -FELA/ 4 EALD- 3 -GE- 0 -SEGENA// 5   (0869)

WORN 2 GE- 9 -MUNDE/ 5 WORD 3 OOTHER 4 FAND// 4   (0870)

SOODHE 4 GE- 3 -BUNDEN/ 9 SECG 3 EFT 4 ON- 1 -GAN// 4   (0871)

SIIDH 4 BEEO- 2 -WUL-1-FES/ 4 SNYTTRUM 9 STYRIAN// 3   (0872)

ENO FOLIO 151V +

=AND 0 ON 2 SPEED 3 WRE-1-CAN/ 4 SPEL 3 GE- 1 -RAA-2-DE// 9   (0873)

WOR-2-DUM 3 WRIXLAN/ 4 WEEL- 3 -HWYLC 3 GE- 3 -CWAEDH// 6   (0874)

THAET 2 HEE 9 FRAM 3 SIGE- 4 -MUNDE*S/ 5 SECGAN 3 HYYR-1-DE// 4   (0875)

ELLEN- 8 -DAEAE-9-DUM/ 3 UN- 2 -CUUTHES 4 FELA// 5   (0876)

WAEL-1-SINGES 4 GE- 2 -WIN/ 8 WIIDE 9 SIIDHAS// 6   (0877)

THAARA 3 THE 1 GUMENA 3 BEARN/ 4 GEAR-2-WE 3 NE 9 WISTON.// 5   (0878)

FAEAEHDHE 5 =AND 0 FYRENA/ 5 BUUTON 3 FITELA 2 MID 9 HINE// 7   (0879)

THONNE 4 HEE 2 SWUL-1-CES 4 HWAET/ 4 SECGAN 3 HOLDE// 9   (0880)

31

EEAM 3 HIS 3 NEFAN/ 3 SWAA 2 HIIE 2 AA 0 WAEAERON// 4   (0881)

AET 2 NIIDHA 3 GE- 9 -HWAAM/ 4 NYYD- 3 -GE- 0 -STEALL-1-AN.// 7   (0882)

$HAEF-1-DON 3 EAL- 3 -FELA/ 9 EOTENA 3 CYNNES// 5   (0883)

SWEORDUM 2 GE- 2 -SAEAEGED/ 4 SIGE- 9 -MUNDE 4 GE- 2 -SPRONG// 4   (0884)

AEFTER 3 DEEADH- 3 -DAEGE/ 4 DOOM 9 UN- 2 -LYYTEL.// 7   (0885)

$SYTHDHAN 3 WIIGES 5 HEARD/ 3 WYRM 3 AA- 0 -CWEAL-9-DE// 6   (0886)

HORDES 4 HYR-1-DE/ 6 HEE 1 UNDER 3 HAAR-2-NE 3 STAAN// 9   (0887)

AETHE-2-LINGES 5 BEARN/ 3 AANA 1 GE- 2 -NEEDH-1-DE// 5   (0888)

FREECNE 9 DAEAE-1-DE/ 5 NE 2 WAES 3 HIM 3 FITELA 3 MID.// 6   (0889)

HWAETHRE 9 HIM 3 GE- 0 -SAEAELDE/ 6   (0890)

          DHAET 3 TH= 2 SWURD 4 THURH- 3 -WOOD// 3   (0890)

WRAEAET- 9 -LIICNE 3 WYRM/ 4 TH= 3 HIT 2 ON 0 WEALLE 4 AET- 2 -STOOD// 3   (0891)

DRYHT- 9 -LIIC 3 IIREN/ 3 DRACA 3 MORDHRE 4 SWEALT.// 7   (0892)

HAEFDE 9 AAG- 0 -LAEAECA/ 4 ELNE 2 GE- 2 -GONGEN// 3   (0893)

TH= 0 HEE 3 BEEAH- 4 -HOR-9-DES/ 5 BRUUCAN 3 MOOSTE// 8   (0894)

SELFES 3 DOOME/ 9 +SAEAE- 3 -BAAT 2 GE- 3 -HLEOOD// 5   (0895)

          ↑ END FOLIO 152R

BAER 3 ON 2 BEAR= 4 SCIPES/ 3 BEO-9-RHTE 4 FRAET-1-WA// 4   (0896)

WAEL-1-SES 3 EAFERA/ 4 WYRM 3 +HAAT 9 GE- 8 -MEALT.// 6   (0897)

$SEE 1 WAES 3 WRECCENA/ 4 WIIDE 3 MAEAEROST// 9   (0898)

OFER 3 WER- 1 -THEEODE/ 5 WIIGEN-1-DRA 3 HLEEO// 3   (0899)

ELLEN- 2 -DAEAEDU=/ 9 HEE 8 THAES 3 AEAER 2 ON- 0 -DHAAH// 4   (0900)

SIDHDHAN 4 HER-1-E- 3 -MOODES/ 5 HILD 9 SWEDHRODE// 4   (0901)

()EARFODH*EAFODH 3 =AND 0 ELLEN/ 4 HEE 2 MID 3 EEOTENUM 9 WEARDH// 4   (0902)

ON 0 FEEONDA 3 GE- 1 -WEALD/ 4 FORDH 3 FOR- 2 -LAACEN// 9   (0903)

SNUUDE 3 FOR- 2 -SENDED/ 4 HINE 3 SORH- 3 -WYL-1-MAS// 4   (0904)

LEME-9-DE 4 TOO 0 LANGE/ 6 HEE 3 HIS 4 LEEODUM 3 WEARDH// 3   (0905)

EALLU= 9 AETHELLINGUM/ 3 TOO 1 AL-1-DOR- 3 -CEARE.// 7   (0906)

$SWYLCE 2 OFT 9 BE- 3 -MEARN/ 4 AEAER-1-RAN 3 MAEAELUM// 4   (0907)

SWIIDH- 2 -FERHTHES 9 SIIDH/ 4 SNOTOR 3 CEORL 4 MONIG// 4   (0908)

SEE 0 THE 5 HIM 3 BEALWA 9 TOO/ 0 BOOTE 5 GE- 1 -LYYF-1-DE// 6   (0909)

TH= 1 TH= 2 DHEEOD-1-NES 3 BEARN/ 3 GE- 9 -THEEON 4 SCOLDE// 6   (0910)

```
FAEDER- 3 -AETHELUM 3 ON- 1 -+FOON/ 3 FOLC 9 GE- 3 -HEALDAN// 4          (0911)
HORD 3 =AND 0 HLEEO- 1 -BURH/ 4 HEAL-1-E-1-THA 3 RIICE// 9               (0912)
.=EETHEL. 8 SCYL-1-DINGA/ 4 HEE 1 THAEAER 2 EALLUM 3 WEARDH// 4          (0913)
MAEAEG 9 HIGE- 3 -LAACES/ 4 MANNA 3 CYNNE// 4                            (0914)
FREEONDUM 2 GE- 9 -FAEGRA/ 4 HINE 3 FYREN 3 ON- 1 -WOOD.// 6             (0915)
HWIILUM 3 FLII-9-TENDE/ 5 FEALWE 5 STRAEAETE// 4                         (0916)
MEEARJM 2 MAEAETON/ 9 DHAA 3 WAES 2 MORGEN- 4 -LEEOHT// 4                (0917)
SCOFEN 3 =AND 0 SCYN-1-DED/ 9 EEODE 4 SCEALC 3 MONIG// 5                 (0918)
              END FOLIO 152V +

SWIIDH- 5 -HICGENDE/ 5 TOO 0 SELE 9 THAAM 4 HEEAN// 5                    (0919)
SEARO- 3 -WUNDOR 4 SEEON/ 3 SWYLCE 3 SELF 9 CYNING// 4                   (0920)
OF 1 BRYYD- 3 -BUURE/ 7 BEEAH- 3 -HOR-1-DA 3 WEARD// 9                   (0921)
TRYDDJDE 6 TIIR- 2 -FAEST./ 6 GE- 0 -TRUME 5 MICLE// 9                   (0922)
CYSTUM 3 GE- 3 -CYYTHED/ 5 =AND 0 HIS 3 CWEEN 3 MID 3 HIM// 3            (0923)
MEDO- 9 -STIG-1-GE 5 MAET/ 2 MAEG-1-THA 4 HOOSE.// 9                     (0924)


                    .XIIII.                                             (FITT)
$HROODH- 2 -GAAR 5 MA-1-THE-1-LODE/ 7 HEE 0 TOO 3 HEALLE 5 GEEONG// 9    (0925)
STOOD 3 ON 1 STA-1-POLE/ 5 GE- 1 -SEAH 4 STEEAP-2-NE 5 HROOF// 9         (0926)
GOLDE 4 FAAHNE/ 5 =AND 0 GRENDLES 5 HOND.// 5                            (0927)
DHISSE 4 AN- 9 -SYYNE/ 5 AL- 0 -WEALDAN 3 THANC// 5                      (0928)
LUNGRE 4 GE- 1 -LIMPE/ 9 FELA 3 IC 1 LAATHES 4 GE- 1 -BAAD// 3           (0929)
GRYN-1-NA 4 AET 2 GRENDLE./ 9 AA 0 MAEG 3 GOD 3 WYRCAN// 4               (0930)
WUN-1-DER 3 AEFTER 3 WUN-1-DRE/ 9 WUL-1-DRES 4 HYRDE.// 6                (0931)
DHAET 3 WAES 3 UN- 1 -GEAARA/ 3 THAET 1 IC 9 AEAENIGRA 3 MEE// 4         (0932)
WEEANA 3 NE 2 WEENDE/ 5 TOO 0 WIIDAN 9 FEORE// 5                         (0933)
BOOTE 4 GE- 2 -BIIDAN/ 5 THONNE 5 BLOODE 2 FAAH// 9                      (0934)
HUUSA 3 SEELEST/ 5 HEORO- 3 -DREEORIG 3 STOOD// 4                        (0935)
WEEA 9 WIID- 3 -SCOFEN/ 3 WIT-1-ENA 4 GE- 2 -HWYL-1-C-1-()NE*UM.// 7     (0936)
DHAARA 9 THE 0 NE 3 WEENDON/ 4 TH= 1 HIIE 4 WIIDE- 6 -FERHDH// 5         (0937)
LEEODA 9 LAND- 3 -GE- 3 -WEORC/ 5 LAATHUM 4 BE- 3 -WERE-1-DON.// 9       (0938)
              END FOLIO 153R +
```

33

SCUC-1-CUM 3 =AND 0 SCIN-1-NUM/ 3 NUU 1 SCEALC 4 HAFADH// 4   (0939)

THURH 9 DRIH1-1-NES 3 MIHT/ 4 DAEAED 2 GE- 2 -FREMEDE.// 5   (0940)

DHE 0 WEE 2 EALLE/ 9 AEAER 8 NE 3 MEAHTON// 4   (0941)

SNYTTRUM 3 BE- 0 -SYR-1-WAN/ 5 HWAET 9 TH= 8 SECGAN 3 MAEG// 3   (0942)

EFNE 3 SWAA 2 HWYLC 4 MAEGTHA/ 4 SWAA 9 DHONE 4 MAGAN 3 CENDE.// 5 (0943)

AEFTER 2 GUM- 1 -CYNNU=/ 4 GYF 9 HEEO 1 GYYT 3 LYFADH// 5   (0944)

TH= 0 HYRE 4 EALD- 2 -METOD/ 3 EESTE 2 WAEAERE.// 9   (0945)

BEARN- 3 -GE- 0 -BYRDO/ 4 NUU 1 IC 2 BEED- 0 -WULF 5 THEC// 3   (0946)

SECG 3 BETSTA/ 9 MEE 4 FOR 2 SUNU 3 WYLLE// 5   (0947)

FREEOGAN 3 ON 0 FERHTHE/ 5 HEALD 9 FORDH 3 TELA.// 7   (0948)

NIIWE 3 SIBBE/ 4 NE 0 BIDH 3 THEE 4 ()AENIGRE*NAEAENIGRE 4 GAAD/.' 9 (0949)

WOROLDE 5 WIL-1-NA/ 4 THE 2 IC 0 GE- 3 -WEALD 4 HAEBBE// 5   (0950)

FUL 9 OFT 2 IC 1 FOR 3 LAEAES-3-SAN/ 5 LEEAN 3 TEOH-3-HODE// 6   (0951)

HORD- 9 -WEORTHUNGE/ 7 HNAAHRAN 3 RINCE// 5   (0952)

SAEAEMRAN 3 AET 9 SAECCE/ 5 THUU 2 THEE 3 SELF 4 HAFAST.// 7   (0953)

DAEAE-2-DUM 2 GE- 0 -FREMED/ 9 TH= 1 THIIN 8 *DOOM 8 LYFADH// 4   (0954)

AAWA 3 TOO 2 ALDRE/ 5 AL- 0 -WAL-1-DA 3 THEC// 3   (0955)

GOODE 9 FOR- 2 -GYLDE/ 5 SWAA 4 HEE 1 NUU 2 GYYT 3 DYDE.// 7   (0956)

BEED- 0 -WULF 9 MA-1-THE-1-LODE/ 5 BEARN 2 ()EC*ECG- 2 -THEEO-1-WES// 5 (0957)

WEE 3 TH= 1 ELLEN- 3 -WEORC/ 9 EESTUM 3 MIC-1-LUM// 3   (0958)

FEOHTAN 3 FREMEDON/ 4 FREECNE 9 GE- 3 -NEEDH-2-DON.// 3   (0959)

EAFODH 3 UN- 0 -CUUTHES/ 5 UUTHE 4 IC 1 SWIITHOR// 3   (0960)

TH= 9 DHUU 1 HINE 4 SELFNE/ 5 GE- 1 -SEEON 2 MOOSTE// 5   (0961)

FEEOND 3 ON 9 FRAETEWUM/ 4 FYL- 3 -WEERIGNE.// 5   (0962)

IC 1 ()HIM*HINE 3 HRAED- 0 -LIICE/ 9 HEAR-1-DAN 3 CLAM-1-MU=// 4 (0963)

                    END FOLIO 153V ✝

ON 1 WAEL- 5 -BEDDE/ 4 WRIITHAN 9 THOOHTE// 5   (0964)

TH= 1 HEE 2 FOR 3 ()HAND*MUND- 3 -GRIPE/ 4 MIINUM 2 SCOLDE// 9   (0965)

LICGEAN 4 LIIF- 3 -BYSIG/ 4 BUUTAN 5 HIS 4 LIIC 3 SWICE.// 4   (0966)

IC 9 HINE 4 NE 2 MIHTE/ 5 THAA 1 METOD 4 NOLDE// 6   (0967)

GANGES 9 GE- 3 -THWAEAEMAN/ 4   (0968)

NOO 2 IC 2 HIM 4 THAES 3 GEORNE 4 AET- 9 -FEALH// 4   (0968)

FEOR-1-H- 3 -GE- 3 -NIIDH-3-LAN/ 4 WAES 3 TOO 1 FORE- 3 -MIHTIG// 9   (0969)

FEEOND 4 ON 2 FEE-1-THE/ 7   (0970)

    HWAETHERE 5 HEE 2 HIS 3 FOLME 4 FOR- 9 -LEET// 3   (0970)

TOO 0 LIIF- 3 -WRATHE/ 6 LAAST 2 WEARDIAN// 4   (0971)

EARM 8 =AND 8 EAX-9-LE/ 5 NOO 2 THAEAER 4 AEAENIGE 5 SWAA 3 THEEAH// 3   (0972)

FEEA- 3 -SCEAFT 8 GU-9-MA/ 4 FROOFRE 5 GE- 1 -BOHTE.// 7   (0973)

NOO 1 THYY 2 LENG 3 LEOFADH/ 9 LAADH- 3 -GE- 1 -TEEO-1-NA// 5   (0974)

SYNNUM 3 GE- 1 -SWENCED/ 4 AC 2 HYNE 9 +SAAR 5 HAFADH// 5   (0975)

IN 1 ()MID*NIID- 3 -GRIPE/ 5 NEAR-2-WE 4 BE- 0 -FONGEN.// 9   (0976)

BAL-2-WON 4 BENDUM/ 3 DHAEAER 2 AA- 0 -BIIDAN 4 SCEAL// 4   (0977)

MAGA 9 MAANE 4 FAAH/ 3 MICLAN 3 DOOMES// 6   (0978)

HUU 2 HIM 3 SCIIR 3 ME-9-TOD/ 4 SCRIIFAN 3 WILLE.// 7   (0979)

$DHAA 0 WAES 5 SWIIGRA 3 SECG/ 3 SUNU 9 ()EC*ECG- 1 -LAAFES// 4   (0980)

ON 1 GYLP- 2 -SPRAEAECE/ 4 GUUDH- 3 -GE- 1 -WEOR-2-CA// 4   (0981)

SITH-9-DHAN 3 AETHE-1-LINGAS/ 4 EOR-1-LES 2 CRAEFTE// 5   (0982)

OFER 4 HEEAN-9-NE 4 HROOF/ 5 HAND 4 SCEEA-1-WE-1-DON// 3   (0983)

FEEONDES 4 FINGRAS/ 9 FORAN 3 AEAEG- 2 -HWYLC 3 WAES// 5   (0984)

()STEDA*STIIDHRA 4 NAEGLA 4 GE- 3 -HWYLC/ 9 STYYLE 4 GE- 3 -LIICOST// 6   (0985)

HAEAE-2-THENES 6 HAND- 3 -SPORU/ 3 ()HILDE 9 HILDE- 4 -RINCES// 4   (0986)

END FOLIO 154R +

EGL*U 3 UN- 1 -HEEORU/ 4 AEAEG- 1 -HWYLC 2 GE- 4 -CWAEDH// 9   (0987)

TH= 8 HIM 3 HEAR-1-DRA 4 NAAN/ 4 HRIINAN 3 WOLDE// 5   (0988)

IIREN 2 AEAER- 9 -GOOD/ 4 TH= 0 DHAES 4 AAH- 2 -LAEAECAN// 4   (0989)

BLOODGE 4 BEADU- 3 -FOLME/ 9 ON- 8 -BERAN 4 WOLDE.// 9   (0990)

.XV.   (FITT)

$$DHAA 4 WAES 4 HAATEN 4 HRETHE/ 5 HEORT 3 INNAN- 2 -HEARD// 9   (0991)

FOLMUM 3 GE- 1 -FRAET-1-WOD/ 4 FE-1-L-2-A 3 THAEAERA 3 WAES// 3   (0992)

WERA 9 =AND 0 WIIFA/ 4 THE 3 TH= 1 WIIN- 2 -RECED// 4   (0993)

GEST- 4 -SELE 4 GYRE-2-DON/ 9 GOLD- 3 -FAAG 3 SCINON// 4   (0994)

WEB 2 AEFTER 4 WAAGUM/ 3 WUNDOR- 9 -SIIONA 3 FELA// 4   (0995)

SECGA 3 GE- 2 -HWYLCUM/ 3 THAARA 3 THE 9 ON 2 SWYLC 4 STARADH.// 6   (0996)

WAES 4 TH= 0 BEORHTE 5 BOLD/ 2 TOO- 9 -BROCEN 3 SWIIDHE// 5   (0997)

EAL 3 INNE- 3 -WEARD/ 3 IIREN- 2 -BENDU= 9 FAEST// 6   (0998)

HEORRAS 4 TOO- 1 -HLIDENE/ 7 HROOF 3 AANA 1 GE- 9 -NAES// 5   (0999)

EALLES 3 ANSUND/ 4 THE 0 SE 3 AAG- 0 -LAEAECA// 4   (1000)

FYREN- 9 -DAEAE-1-DUM 3 FAAG/ 4 ON 1 FLEEAM 3 GE- 3 -WAND// 4   (1001)

ALDRES 3 OR- 9 -WEENA/ 5 NOO 1 TH= 1 YYDHE 4 BYDH// 3   (1002)

TOO 0 BE- 2 -FLEEON-1-NE/ 5 FREM-9-ME 2 SEE 0 THE 3 WILLE.// 7   (1003)

$AC 0 GE- 3 -()SACAN*SEECAN 3 SCEAL/ 4 SAAWL- 9 -BEREN-1-DRA// 4   (1004)

NYYDE 4 GE- 4 -NYYDDE/ 5 NITHDHA 4 BEAR-9-NA// 4   (1005)

GRUND- 4 -BUUEN-1-DRA/ 4 GEAR-2-WE 3 STOOWE.// 7   (1006)

THAEAER 9 HIS 4 LIIC- 3 -HOMA/ 4 LEGER- 4 -BEDDE 4 FAEST.// 5   (1007)

SWEFETH 9 AEFTER 3 SYMLE/ 5 THAA 0 WAES 3 SAEAEL 5 =AND 0 MAEAEL// 5   (1008)

TH= 0 TOO 2 HEALLE 9 GANG/ 4 HEALF- 2 -DENES 4 SUNU// 3   (1009)

        ✦ END FOLIO 154V

WOLDE 4 SELF 2 CYNING/ 9 SYMBEL 5 THICGAN// 4   (1010)

NE 0 GE- 4 -FRAEGEN 3 IC 1 THAA 2 MAEAEGTHE/ 9 MAARAN 3 WEORODE// 5   (1011)

YMB 2 HYRA 3 SINC- 2 -GYFAN/ 8 SEEL 9 GE- 0 -BAEAERAN.// 7   (1012)

BUGON 4 THAA 2 TOO 2 BENCE/ 6 BLAEAED- 8 -AAGAN-9-DE// 5   (1013)

FYLLE 4 GE- 0 -FAEAEGON/ 3 FAEGERE 4 GE- 1 -THAEAEGON// 8   (1014)

ME-9-DO- 3 -FUL 4 MANIG/ 4 MAAGAS 4 THAARA// 3   (1015)

SWIIDH- 3 -HICGENDE/ 9 ON 1 SELE 3 THAAM 4 HEEAN// 5   (1016)

HROODH- 0 -GAAR 4 =AND 1 HROOTHULF/ 8 HEO-9-ROT 3 INNAN 3 WAES// 5   (1017)

FREEONDU= 1 AA- 0 -FYLLED/ 3 NALLES 8 FAACEN- 9 -STAFAS// 5   (1018)

THEEOD- 3 -SCYLDINGAS/ 6 THENDEN 3 FREME-2-DON// 9   (1019)

FOR- 0 -GEAF 3 THAA 3 BEEO- 0 -WULFE/ 7   (1020)

      ()BRAND*BEARN 4 HEALF- 0 -DENES// 9   (1020)

SEGEN 2 GYLDENNE/ 6 SIGORES 4 TOO 1 LEEANE// 6   (1021)

HRODEN 9 ()HILTE*HILDE- 4 -CUMBOR/ 5 HELM 3 =AND 0 BYR-1-NAN// 4   (1022)

MAEAERE 4 MAADH-9-THU=- 4 -SWEORD/ 3 MANIGE 5 GE- 1 -SAAWON.// 6   (1023)

BE- 1 -FORAN 4 BEORN 9 BERAN/ 4 BEEO- 1 -WULF 5 GE- 2 -THAH// 4   (1024)

FUL 3 ON 1 FLETTE./ 6 NOO 8 HEE 9 THAEAERE 6 FEOH- 2 -GYFTE// 6   (1025)

FOR 3 ()SCOTENUM*SCEEOTENDUM/ 4 SCAMIGAN 9 DHORFTE// 7   (1026)

NE 0 GE- 3 -FRAEGN 2 IC 2 FREEOND- 1 -LIICOR/ 5 FEEOWER 9 MAADMAS// 4   (1027)

GOLDE 4 GE- 3 -GYREDE/ 5 GUM- 3 -MAN-2-NA 9 FELA// 4   (1028)

IN 1 EALO- 4 -BEN-1-CE/ 5 OODHRUM 3 GE- 2 -SELLAN.// 3   (1029)

YMB 9 THAES 4 HEL-2-MES 5 HROOF/ 5 HEEAFOD- 4 -BEORGE// 4   (1030)

HIIRUM 9 BE- 3 -WUNDEN/ 4 ()WALAN*WALA 3 UUTAN 3 HEEOLD// 3   (1031)

THAET 4 HIM 3 FEELA 9 LAAF/ 8 FREECNE 5 NE 2 ()MEAHTON*MEAHTE// 4   (1032)

                    + END FOLIO 155R

SCUUR- 3 -HEARD 4 SCETH-9-DHAN/ 5 THON= 3 SCYLD- 4 -FRECA// 5   (1033)

ON- 0 -GEEAN 3 GRAMUM/ 9 GANGAN 3 SCOLDE.// 7   (1034)

BHEHT 3 DHAA 2 EORLA 5 HLEEO/ 3 EAH-9-TA 8 MEEARAS// 4   (1035)

FAEAETED- 4 -HLEEORE/ 4 ON 1 FLET 4 TEEON.// 9   (1036)

KN 8 UNDER 5 EODERAS/ 5 THAARA 4 AANUM 3 STOOD// 3   (1037)

BADOL 9 SEARWUM 3 +FAAH/ 3 SINCE 3 GE- 3 -WUR-1-THAD// 4   (1038)

THAET 2 WAES 9 HILDE.- 6 -SETL/ 4 HEEAH- 3 -CYNINGES// 5   (1039)

DHON= 3 SWEOR-1-DA 9 GE- 1 -LAAC/ 4 SUNU 3 HEALF- 1 -DENES// 5   (1040)

EF-1-NAN 3 WOL-1-DE/ 9 NAEAEFRE 5 ON 1 OORE 3 LAEG// 4   (1041)

WIID- 3 -CUUTHES 3 WIIG/ 4 DHON-2-NE 9 WALU 2 FEEOLLON// 5   (1042)

=AND 0 DHAA 4 BEEO- 0 -WULFE/ 5 BEEGA 3 GE- 2 -HWAETH-9-RES// 4   (1043)

EODOR 4 ING- 3 -WINA/ 3 ON- 1 -WEALD 4 GE- 2 -TEEAH.// 4   (1044)

NIC-9-GA 4 =AND 0 WAEAEPNA/ 5 HEET 2 HINE 4 WEEL 4 BRUUCAN.// 5   (1045)

SWAA 9 MAN- 1 -LIICE/ 5 MAEAERE 4 THEEODEN// 4   (1046)

HORD- 2 -WEARD 3 HAELE-9-THA/ 5 HEATHO- 4 -RAEAESAS 4 GEALD// 3   (1047)

MEEARJM 3 =AND 1 MAAD-9-MUM./ 5 $SWAA 4 HYY 2 NAEAEFRE 5 MAN 3 LYYHDH// 3   (1048)

EE 1 THE 9 SECGAN 3 WILE/ 3 SOODH 3 AEFTER 4 RIHTE.// 9   (1049)

                    .XVI.   (FITT)

B$DHAA 2 GYYT 2 AEAEG- 0 -HWYL-2-CUM/ 3 EORLA 3 DRIHTEN// 3   (1050)

THAARA 9 THE 1 MID 4 BEEO- 0 -WULFE/ 5 BRIM- 2 -()LEADE*LAADE 4 TEEAH// 3   (1051)

DN 0 THAEAE-9-RE 4 MEDU- 3 -BENCE/ 6 MAATHDHUM 3 GE- 3 -SEALDE// 3   (1052)

WR-9-FE- 3 -LAAFE/ 4 =AND 0 THONE 3 AEAENE 5 HEHT// 3   (1053)

    + END FOLIO 155V

GOLDE 5 FOR- 0 -GYL-9-DAN/ 4 THONE 4 OHE 1 GRENDEL 4 AEAER// 3   (1054)

MAANE 3 AA- 0 -CWEALDE/ 9 SWAA 4 HEE 2 HYRA 3 MAA 2 WOLDE// 5   (1055)

NEF-2-NE 4 HIM 3 WIITIG 9 GOD/ 4 WYRD 3 FOR- 0 -STOODE// 6   (1056)

=AND 0 DHAES 4 MAN-1-NES 3 MOOD/ 8 ME-9-TOD 3 EALLUM 3 WEEOLD// 4   (1057)

GUME-2-NA 3 CYN-1-NES/ 4 SWAA 1 HEE 9 NUU 1 GIIT 5 DEEDH// 4   (1058)

FOR- 2 -THAN 4 BIOH 2 AND- 1 -GIT/ 4 AEAEG- 3 -HWAEAER 9 SEELEST// 5   (1059)

FERHO1ES 5 FORE- 4 -THANC/ 4 FE-1-LA 3 SCEAL 3 GE- 9 -BIIDAN// 4   (1060)

LEEOFES 4 =AND 0 LAATHES/ 5 SEE 0 THE 4 LONGE 4 HEER// 3   (1061)

ON 9 DHYS-2-SU= 4 WIN- 2 -DAGUM/ 4 WOROLDE 4 BRUUCEDH.// 4   (1062)

THAEAER 9 WAES 3 SANG 4 =AND 0 SWEEG/ 4 SAMOD 2 AET- 2 -GAEDERE// 4   (1063)

FORE 9 HEALF- 1 -DENES/ 5 HILDE- 3 -WII-8-SAN// 4   (1064)

GOMEN- 3 -WUDU 9 GREETED/ 4 GID 2 OFT 2 WRE-1-CEN.// 6   (1065)

$DHON= 3 HEAL- 3 -GAMEN/ 9 HROOTH- 3 -GAARES 4 SCOP// 4   (1066)

AEF-1-TER 3 ME-2-DO- 2 -BENCE/ 4 MAEAE-9-NAN 3 SCOL-2-DE// 5   (1067)

*BE 8 FINNES 3 EAFERUM/ 4 DHAA 3 HIIE 3 SE 9 FAEAER 4 BE- 1 -GEAT// 5   (1068)

HAELEDH 5 HEALF- 3 -DENA/ 4 HNAEF 9 SCYLDINGA// 4   (1069)

IN 0 FR-8-EES- 3 -WAELE/ 4 FEALLAN 2 SCOLDE// 9   (1070)

NEE 4 HUURU 3 HILDE- 5 -BURH/ 4 HERIAN 4 THORF-1-TE.// 9   (1071)

EEOTENA 4 TREEOWE/ 5 UN- 1 -SYNNUM 4 WEARDH// 4   (1072)

BE- 9 -LOR-2-EN 4 LEEOFU=/ 3 AET 0 THAA= 3 ()HILD*LIND- 3 -PLEGAN// 5   (1073)

BEAR-1-NUM 9 =AND 0 BROODH-1-RUM/ 5 HIIE 4 ON 0 GE- 3 -BYRD 5 HRURON// 4   (1074)

GAARE 9 WUNDE/ 5 TH= 0 WAES 3 GEOOMURU 3 IDES// 4   (1075)

        ✦ END FOLIO 156R

NALLES 4 HOOLINGA/ 9 HOOCES 4 DOHTOR// 6   (1076)

MECTOD- 3 -SCEAFT 4 BE- 2 -MEARN/ 9 SYTHDHAN 3 MORGEN 2 COOM.// 7   (1077)

$DHAA 2 HEEO 2 UNDER 3 SWEGLE/ 9 GE- 8 -SEEON 3 MEAHTE// 5   (1078)

MORTHOR- 4 -BEALO 3 MAAGA/ 9   (1079)

        THAEAER 3 ()HE*HEEO 3 AEAER 2 MAEAESTE 4 HEEOLD// 3   (1079)

WOROLDE 5 WYNNE/ 9 WIIG 2 EALLE 4 FOR- 1 -NAM// 3   (1080)

FIN-1-NES 4 THEGNAS/ 5 NEMNE 9 FEEAU= 8 AANUM// 4   (1081)

THAET 3 HEE 1 NE 3 MEHTE/ 4 ON 2 THAEAEM 3 ME-9-DHEL- 5 -STEDE.// 7   (1082)

WIIG 3 HENGESTE/ 5 WIHT 3 GE- 3 -FEOHTAN.// 9   (1083)

NEE 1 THAA 4 WEEA- 2 -LAAFE/ 4 WIIGE 3 FOR- 4 -THRINGAN// 4   (1084)

THEEODNES 9 DHEGNE./ 5 AC 3 HIG 4 HIM 2 GE- 1 -THINGO 3 BUDON// 5   (1085)

TH= 1 HIIE 9 HIM 3 OODHER 4 FLET/ 4 EAL 3 GE- 3 -RYYM-1-DON// 5   (1086)

HEALLE 3 =AND 9 HEEAH- 0 -SETL/ 5 TH= 3 HIIE 5 HEALFRE 4 GE- 1 -WEALD// 4 (1087)

WIDH 2 EEOTE-9-NA 4 BEARN/ 4 AAGAN 3 MOOSTON// 4   (1088)

=AND 0 AET 2 FEOH- 2 -GYF-9-TU=/ 5 FOLC- 4 -WALDAN 3 SUNU// 3   (1089)

DOOGRA 3 GE- 2 -HWYL-1-CE/ 9 DENE 4 WEOR-2-THODE// 7   (1090)

HENGESTES 5 HEEAP/ 4 HRIN-9-GU= 3 WENEDE// 5   (1091)

EFNE 5 SWAA 4 SWIIDHE/ 4 SINC- 2 -GE- 3 -STREEO-9-NUM// 4   (1092)

FAEAETTAN 4 GOL-1-DES/ 4 SWAA 2 HEE 4 FREESENA 2 CYN// 9   (1093)

ON 1 BEEOR- 4 -SELE/ 5 BYL-1-DAN 4 WOLDE.// 7   (1094)

DHAA 2 HIIE 3 GE- 9 -TRUWE-1-DON/ 4 ON 0 TWAA 5 HEALFA// 4   (1095)

FAESTE 4 FRIODHU- 9 -WAEAERE/ 6 FIN 3 HENGESTE// 5   (1096)

ELNE 4 UN- 0 -FLIT-2-ME/ 3 AADHU= 9 BE- 2 -NEMDE.// 7   (1097)

END FOLIO 156V ✦

TH= 2 HEE 3 THAA 4 WEEA- 1 -LAAFE// 6 WEOTENA 9 DOOME// 5   (1098)

AARUM 3 HEEOLDE/ 6 TH= 0 DHAEAER 3 AEAENIG 3 MON.// 9   (1099)

WOR-1-DU= 4 NEE 2 WORCUM/ 4 WAEAER-1-E 4 NE 3 BRAEAE-1-CE.// 4 (1100)

NEE 9 THURH 4 INWIT- 3 -SEARO/ 4 AEAEFRE 5 GE- 2 -MAEAENDEN// 3 (1101)

DHEEAH 9 HIIE 4 HIRA 4 BEEAG- 3 -GYFAN/ 4 BANAN 4 FOLGEDON.// 9 (1102)

DHEEODEN- 4 -LEEASE/ 5 THAA 1 HIM 2 SWAA 3 GE- 4 -THEARFOD 2 WAES// 9 (1103)

GYF 4 THONNE 4 FRYYSNA 5 HWYLC/ 4 ( )FRECNEN*FREECNAN 4 SPRAEAECE// 9 (1104)

DHAES 4 MORTHOR- 5 -HETES/ 4 MYND-3-GIEND 3 WAEAERE// 9   (1105)

THONNE 7 HIT 3 SWEORDES 4 ECG/ 4 ( )SYDHDHAN*SEEDHAN 4 SCOLDE// 9 (1106)

( )ADH*AAD 2 WAES 4 GE- 1 -AEFNED/ 4 =AND 1 ICGE 2 GOLD.// 5   (1107)

AA- 0 -HAEFEN 2 OF 9 HORDE/ 5 HERE- 4 -SCYLDINGA// 5   (1108)

BETST 4 BEADO- 2 -RINCA./ 9 WAES 3 ON 1 BAEAEL 3 GEARU// 4   (1109)

AET 2 THAEAEM 3 AADE 5 WAES/ 9 EETH- 2 -GE- 3 -SYYNE// 6   (1110)

SWAAT- 4 -FAAH 4 SYRCE/ 5 SWYYN 9 EAL- 3 -GYLDEN.// 6   (1111)

EOFER 4 IIREN- 3 -HEARD/ 4 AETHELING 3 MA-9-NIG// 5   (1112)

HUN-1-DUM 5 AA- 0 -WYRDED/ 4 SUME 3 ON 2 WAELE 9 CRUNGON.// 5 (1113)

HEET 4 DHAA 3 HILDE- 5 -BURH/ 3 AET 3 HNAEFES 9 AADE// 7   (1114)

HIRE 5 SELFRE 5 SUNU/ 4 SWEO-1-LODHE 6 BE- 9 -FAESTAN// 7   (1115)

+BAAN- 4 -FATU 3 BAER-2-NAN/ 4 =AND 0 ON 1 BAEAEL 9 +DOON// 4   (1116)

( )EARME*EEAME 5 ON 1 EAXLE/ 6 IDES 3 GNORNODE// 9   (1117)

GEOOHRODE 5 GIDDUM/ 4 GUUDH- 2 -RINC 4 AA- 0 -STAAH.// 3   (1118)

WAND 3 TOO 8 WOLCNUM/ 4 WAEL- 3 -FYYRA 3 MAEAEST// 6   (1119)

       ✝ END FOLIO 157R

HLYNODE 9 FOR 8 HLAAWE/ 6 HAFELAN 3 MULTON.// 5   (1120)

BEN- 0 -GEATO 9 BURSTON/ 4 DHONNE 6 +BLOOD 2 AET- 2 -SPRANC.// 4   (1121)

LAADH- 9 -BITE 4 LIICES/ 5 LIIG 2 EALLE 5 FOR- 2 -SWEALG// 4   (1122)

GAEAESTA 9 GIIFROST/ 5 THAARA 4 DHE 4 THAEAER 4 GUUDH 3 FOR- 2 -NAM// 9   (1123)

BEEGA 3 FOLCES/ 4 WAES 4 HIRA 5 BLAEAED 4 SCA-1-CEN.// 9   (1124)

          .XVII.   (FITT)

$$GE- 8 -WITON 4 HIM 4 DHAA 0 WIIGEND/ 5 WIICA 3 NEEOSIAN// 9   (1125)

FREEONDU= 5 BE- 1 -FEALLEN/ 3 FRYYS- 4 -LAND 2 GE- 2 -SEEON// 9   (1126)

HAAMAS 4 =AND 1 HEEA- 3 -BURH/ 6 HENGEST 5 DHAA 0 GYYT// 4   (1127)

WAEL- 9 -FAAGNE 4 WINTER/ 4 WUN-1-ODE 4 MID 2 FIN-1-NE( )L// 3   (1128)

*EAL 8 UN- 9 -HLITME/ 4 EARD 4 GE- 1 -MUNDE// 5   (1129)

THEEAH 2 THE 5 ( )HE*NE 1 MEAH-9-TE/ 5 ON 0 MERE 5 DRIIFAN// 5   (1130)

HRINGED- 3 -STEF-1-NAN/ 9 HOLM 2 STORME 5 WEEOL// 4   (1131)

WON 2 WIDH 3 WIN-1-DE/ 5 WINTER 9 YYTHE 3 BE- 1 -LEEAC// 5   (1132)

IIS- 2 -GE- 1 -BINDE/ 4 OTH 0 DHAET 3 OOTHER 3 COOM// 9   (1133)

GEEAR 3 IN 1 GEAR-2-DAS/ 5 SWAA 2 NUU 2 GYYT 4 DEEDH// 4   (1134)

THAA 1 DHE 9 SYN-1-GAALES/ 5 SEELE 3 BE- 2 -WITIADH// 5   (1135)

WULDOR- 4 -TORH-9-TAN 3 WEDER/ 5 DHAA 0 WAES 4 WINTER 4 SCA-1-CEN// 3   (1136)

FAEGER 9 FOL-1-DAN 4 BEARM/ 4 FUNDODE 4 WRECCA// 4   (1137)

GIST 9 OF 3 GEAR-2-DUM/ 6 HEE 0 TOO 3 GYRN- 3 -WRAECE// 4   (1138)

SWIID+OR 9 THOOHTE/ 6 THON= 2 TOO 2 SAEAE- 2 -LAADE// 6   (1139)

      ✝ END FOLIO 157V

GIF 2 HEE 3 TORN- 8 -GE- 9 -MOOT/ 5 THURH- 3 -TEEON 3 MIHTE// 7   (1140)

TH= 2 HEE 4 EEOTENA 9 BEARN/ 3 ()INNE*IIRNE 5 GE- 3 -MUNDE.// 7   (1141)

$SWAA 3 HEE 3 NE 2 FOR- 9 -WYRNDE/ 6   (1142)

      ()WOROLD*WEOROD- 2 -RAEAE-1-DEN-1-()NE*DE// 6   (1142)

THONNE 3 HIM 9 HUUN- 2 -LAAFING/ 5 HILDE- 4 -LEEOMAN// 4   (1143)

BILLA 3 SEELEST/ 9 ON 1 BEARM 3 DYDE// 5   (1144)

SWYLCE 3 FERHDH- 3 -FRECAN/ 4 FIN 9 EFT 4 BE- 2 -GEAT// 4   (1146)

THAES 2 WAEAERON 3 MID 2 EEOTENU=/ 9 ECGE 3 CUUDHE// 5   (1145)

SWEORD- 4 -BEALO 3 SLIIDHEN/ 8 AET 8 HIS 9 SELFES 5 +HAAM// 4   (1147)

SITHDHAN 4 GRIM-1-NE 5 GRIPE/ 9 GUUDH- 2 -LAAF 7 OND 1 OOS- 2 -LAAF// 5   (1148)

AEFTER 3 +SAEAE- 5 -SIIDHE/ 9 SORGE 4 MAEAENDON// 3   (1149)

AET- 1 -WITON 4 WEEANA 4 DAEAEL/ 9 NE 3 MEAHTE 5 WAEAEFRE 4 MOOD// 3   (1150)

FOR- 3 -HABBAN 9 IN 1 HRE-1-THRE/ 5   (1151)

      DHAA 1 WAES 5 HEAL 4 ()HR*R-1-O-1-DEN// 3   (1151)

FEEONDA 9 FEEORUM/ 2 SWILCE 4 FIN 1 SLAEGEN// 4   (1152)

CYNING 3 ON 9 CORTHRE/ 5 =AND 0 SEEO 1 CWEEN 3 NUMEN// 4   (1153)

SCEEOTEND 3 SCYL-9-DINGA/ 4 TOO 0 SCYPON 3 FERE-2-DON// 4   (1154)

EAL 3 IN- 1 -GE- 9 -STEALD/ 3 EORDH- 3 -CYNINGES// 4   (1155)

SWYLCE 5 HIIE 3 AET 9 FIN-1-NES 5 HAAM/ 2 FINDAN 3 MEAHTON// 4   (1156)

SIGLA 9 SEARO- 4 -GIMMA/ 5 HIIE 4 ON 0 SAEAE- 5 -LAADE// 5   (1157)

DRIHT- 9 -LIICE 4 WIIF/ 5 TOO 0 DENUM 3 FEREDON// 5   (1158)

LAEAEODON. 9 TOO 8 LEEODUM/ 5 LEEODH 4 WAES 4 AA- 0 SUNGEN// 4   (1159)

      + END FOLIO 158R

GLEEO- 0 -MAN-9-NES 8 GYD/ 4 GA-1-MEN 4 EFT 5 AA- 0 STAAH.// 6   (1160)

BEORHTODE 9 BENC- 4 -SWEEG/ 7 BYRE-1-LAS 5 SEALDON// 4   (1161)

+WIIN 1 OF 9 WUNDER- 5 -FATUM./ 6   (1162)

      THAA 2 CWOOM 3 WEALH- 0 -THEEO 3 FORDH// 9   (1162)

+GAAN 3 UNDER 4 GYLDNUM 4 BEEAGE/ 5   (1163)

      THAEAER 5 THAA 9 GOODAN 5 TWEEGEN// 4   (1163)

SAEAETON 2 SU-1-HTER- 2 -GE- 1 -FAE-1-DE-9-RAN/ 4   (1164)

      THAA 0 GYYT 3 WAES 5 HIERA 4 SIB 2 AET- 2 -GAE-1-DERE// 9   (1164)

AEAEG- 3 -HWYLC 4 OODHRUM 4 TRYYWE/ 5   (1165)

      SWYL-1-CE 3 THAEAER 9 ()HUN*UN- 1 -FER-1-TH 8 THYLE// 3   (1165)

AET 2 FOOTUM 3 SAET 3 FREEAN 9 SCYL-3-DINGA/ 5   (1166)

      GE- 3 -HWYLC 5 HIORA 4 HIS 4 FER-9-HTHE 6 TREEOW-2-DE.// 7   (1166)

THAET 4 HEE 3 HAEF-1-DE 5 +MODD 9 MIC-1-EL/ 7   (1167)

      THEEAH 3 THE 7 HEE 4 HIS 4 MAAGUM 4 NAEAERE// 9   (1167)

+AAR- 2 -FAEST 5 AET 2 ECGA 4 GE- 0 -LAACUM./ 7   (1168)

     $SPR-1-AEC 9 DHAA 5 IDES 5 SCYL-3-DINGA.// 5   (1168)

ON- 0 -FOOH 4 THIS-2-SUM 9 FULLE/ 6 FREED- 4 -DRIHTEN 3 MIIN// 4 (1169)

SIN-1-CES 3 BRYT-9-TA/ 5 THUU 0 ON 2 SAEAELUM 3 WES// 5   (1170)

GOLD- 2 -WINE 5 GUME-9-NA/ 4 =AND 0 TOO 1 GEEATUM 4 SPR-1-AEC// 5 (1171)

MIL-3-DUM 3 WOR-9-DUM/ 4 SWAA 1 SCEAL 3 MAN 2 DOON.// 6   (1172)

BEEO 1 WIDH 3 GEEATAS 9 GLAED/ 6 GEOFENA 4 GE- 2 -MYNDIG// 4 (1173)

NEEAN 3 =AND 0 FEOR-9-RAN/ 4 THUU 0 NUU 3 HAFAST// 5   (1174)

MEE 1 MAN 2 SAEGDE/ 5 THAET 9 THUU 0 DHEE 5 FOR 4 SUNU 2 WOLDE// 6 (1175)

       END FOLIO 158V +

HERE- 3 -()RIC*RINC 3 HABBAN/ 9 HEOROT 4 IS 2 GE- 5 -FAEAEL-1-SOD// 5 (1176)

BEEAH- 2 -SELE 5 BEORHTA/ 9 +BRUUC 4 THEN-2-DEN 5 THUU 0 MOOTE// 5 (1177)

MANIGRA 4 MEEDO/ 9 =AND 0 THIINUM 3 MAAGUM 4 LAEAEF// 4   (1178)

FOLC 3 =AND 0 RIICE/ 4 THON-2-NE 9 DHUU 1 FORDH 4 SCYLE// 6 (1179)

METOD- 3 -SCEAFT 4 SEEON/ 8 IC 9 MIINNE 4 CAN// 4   (1180)

GLAEDNE 4 HROOTHULF/ 4 TH= 1 HEE 3 THAA 0 GEO-9-GODHE 4 WILE// 5 (1181)

AARUM 3 HEALDAN/ 3 GYF 2 THUU 2 AEAER 3 THON= 9 HEE// 5   (1182)

WINE 4 SCIL-2-DINGA/ 5 WOROLD 3 OF- 2 -LAEAETEST// 9   (1183)

WEENE 4 IC 3 TH= 0 HEE 3 MID 2 GOODE/ 5 GYL-1-DAN 3 WILLE// 4 (1184)

UN-9-CRAN 3 EAFERAN/ 4 GIF 3 HEE 1 TH= 1 EAL 4 GE- 2 -MON// 3 (1185)

HWAET 9 WIT 2 TOO 1 WILLAN/ 4 =AND 1 TOO 1 WORDH- 3 -MYN-1-DUM// 4 (1186)

UM-1-BOR- 9 -WESEN-1-DUM 2 +AEAER/ 4 AARNA 3 GE- 2 -FREME-2-DON.// 4 (1187)

HWEA-9-RF 5 THAA 1 BII 2 BENCE/ 5 THAEAER 3 HYRE 5 BYRE 4 WAEAERON// 9 (1188)

HREEDH- 1 -RIIC 4 =AND 0 HROODH- 1 -MUND/ 4   (1189)

     =AND 0 HAELE-1-THA 4 BEARN// 9   (1189)

GIOGODH 4 AET- 3 -GAEDERE/ 5 THAEAER 0 SE 2 GOODA 5 SAET// 9 (1190)

BEEO- 0 -WULF 3 GEEATA/ 6   (1191)

    BE 2 THAEAE= 3 GE- 1 -BROODH-1-RUM 3 TWAEAEM.// 9   (1191)

SHIM 3 WAES 5 FUL 3 BOREN/ 5 =AND 0 FREEOND- 3 -L-1-A-1-THU// 3   (1192)

OR-9-DUM 3 GE- 2 -WAEGNED/ 4 =AND 0 WUNDEN 4 GOLD// 4   (1193)

ESTUM 9 GE- 3 -EEAWED/ 3 EARM- 2 -()READE*HREEADE 5 TWAA// 4   (1194)

RAEGL 4 =AND 0 HRIN-9-GAS/ 8 HEALS- 3 -BEEAGA 3 MAEAEST// 4   (1195)

✝ END FOLIO 159R

HAARA 3 THE 2 IC 1 ON 3 FOLDAN/ 9 GE- 8 -FRAEGEN 4 HAEBBE// 5   (1196)

AEAE-2-NIG-1-NE 5 IC 2 UNDER 3 SWEG-9-LE/ 8 SEELRAN 5 HYYRDE// 6   (1197)

ORD- 3 -()MAD-2-MUM*MAADHUM 4 HAELETHA/ 9   (1198)

SYTHDHAN 5 HAAMA 4 AET- 1 -WAEG// 4   (1198)

OO 2 ()HERE*THAEAERE 5 BYRHTAN 9 BYRIG/ 5 BROOSINGA 3 MENE// 5   (1199)

IG-1-LE 5 =AND 0 SINC- 4 -FAET/ 9 SEARO- 3 -NIIDHAS 5 ()FEALH*FLEEAH// 3 (1200)

ORMEN- 3 -RIIC-1-ES/ 4 GE- 1 -CEEAS 9 EECNE 3 +RAEAED// 5   (1201)

HONE 4 HRING 3 HAEF-1-DE/ 5 HIGE- 1 -LAAC 2 GEEA-9-TA// 5   (1202)

EFA 3 SWER-1-TINGES/ 4 NYYHSTAN 3 SIIDHE// 5   (1203)

IDH-1-THAN 9 HEE 2 UNDER 5 SEGNE/ 5 SINC 4 EAL-2-GODE.// 6   (1204)

AEL- 2 -REEAF 9 WERE-1-DE/ 7 HYNE 4 WYRD 3 FOR- 3 -NAM// 4   (1205)

YTHDHAN 1 HEE 9 FOR 3 WLENCO/ 4 WEEAN 2 AAHSODE// 5   (1206)

AEAE+DHE 4 TOO 1 FRYYSU=/ 9 HEE 1 THAA 3 FRAET-1-WE 4 WAEG// 4   (1207)

ORCLAN- 4 -STAANAS/ 3 OFER 9 YYDHA 4 FUL.// 4   (1208)

IICE 5 THEEODEN/ 3 HEE 8 UNDER 4 RANDE 5 GE- 9 -CRANC// 5   (1209)

E- 4 -HWEARF 5 THAA 3 IN 1 FRANC-1-NA 4 FAETHM/ 9 FEORH 3 CYNINGES// 6   (1210)

REEOST- 4 -GE- 3 -WAEAEDU/ 4 =AND 0 SE 3 BEEAH 9 SOMOD// 3   (1211)

YRSAN 4 WIIG- 2 -FRECAN/ 5 WAEL 4 REEAFE-2-()DEN*DON// 3   (1212)

EFTER 9 GUUDH- 3 -SCEARE/ 6 GEEATA 4 LEEODE// 6   (1213)

REEA- 2 -WIIC 5 HEEOLDON/ 9 HEAL 5 SWEEGE 5 ON- 1 -FEENG.// 7   (1214)

WEAL+- 0 -DHEEO 4 MATHELODE/ 9   (1215)

HEEO 3 FORE 5 THAEAEM 3 WERE-1-DE 6 SPRAEC// 6   (1215)

RUUC 5 DHISSES 9 BEEAGES/ 7 BEEO- 0 -WULF 5 LEEOFA// 5   (1216)

YSE 5 MID 3 HAEAELE/ 9 =AND 8 THISSES 5 HRAEGLES 4 NEEOT// 5   (1217)

✝ END FOLIO 159V

()THEO*THEEOO- 3 -GE- 3 -STREEONA/ 8 =AND 8 GE- 8 -THEEOH 9 TELA// 5   (1218)

CEN 3 THEC 2 MID 2 CRAEFTE/ 6 =AND 0 THYSSUM 3 CNYHTUM 9 WES// 5   (1219)

LAARA 3 LIIDHE/ 6 IC 2 THEE 4 THAES 5 LEEAN 0 GE- 2 -MAN// 5   (1220)

HAFAST 9 THUU 0 GE- 4 -FEERED/ 3 TH= 1 DHEE 2 FEOR 2 =AND 0 NEEAH// 4   (1221)

EALNE 3 WIIDE- 3 -FERHTH/ 9 WERAS 3 EHTIGADH// 5   (1222)

EFNE 4 SWAA 4 SIIDE/ 5 SWAA 2 +SAEAE 5 BE- 0 -BUUGEDH// 9   (1223)

WIND- 2 -GEARD 3 WEALLAS/ 5 WES 3 THENDEN 4 THUU 0 LIFIGE// 4   (1224)

AETHELING 9 EEADIG/ 4 IC 1 THEE 3 AN 0 TELA// 4   (1225)

SINC- 3 -GE- 0 -STREEONA/ 5 BEEO 2 THUU 3 SUNA 4 MIINU=// 5   (1226)

OAEAE-2-DUM 3 GE- 1 -DEEFE/ 6 OREEAM- 4 -HEAL-2-DEN-9-DE.// 7   (1227)

HEER 2 IS 4 AEAEG- 1 -HWYLC 4 EORL/ 4 OOTHRUM 3 GE- 2 -TRYYWE// 9   (1228)

MOODES 4 MILDE/ 5 MAN- 3 -DRIHTNE 5 ()HEOL*HOLD// 5   (1229)

THEGNAS 3 SYN-9-DON 3 GE- 3 -THWAEAERE/ 5 THEEOD 3 EAL- 2 -GEARO// 4   (1230)

DRUNC-1-NE 3 DRYHT- 9 -GUMAN/ 4 DOODH 3 SWAA 2 IC 3 BIDDE.// 5   (1231)

$EEODE 5 THAA 1 TOO 3 SETLE/ 9 THAEAER 3 WAES 4 SYMBLA 4 CYST// 5   (1232)

DRUNCON 4 +WIIN 3 WERAS/ 3 WYRD 9 NE 4 CUUTHON// 4   (1233)

GEOO- 1 -SCEAFT 4 ()GRIMNE*GRIMME/ 5   (1234)

          SWAA 2 HIT 3 AA- 0 -GAN-9-GEN 3 WEARDH// 4   (1234)

EORLA 4 MANEGU=/ 4 SYTHDHAN 3 AEAEFEN 3 CWOOM// 9   (1235)

=AND 0 HIM 3 HROOTH- 0 -GAAR 4 GE- 1 -WAAT/ 4 TOO 0 HOFE 3 SIINUM// 3   (1236)

RIICE 9 TOO 0 RAESTE/ 5 RECED 1 WEARDODE// 4   (1237)

UN- 0 -RIIM 3 EORLA/ 3 SWAA 9 HIIE 4 OFT 2 AEAER 3 DYDON// 5   (1238)

BENC- 4 -THELU 4 BERE-3-DON/ 4 HIT 9 GEOND- 4 -BRAEAEDED 3 WEARDH// 5   (1239)

BEDDUM 3 =AND 0 BOLSTRUM/ 9 BEEOR- 4 -SCEAL-1-CA 3 SUM// 2   (1240)

FUUS 3 =AND 0 FAEAEGE/ 5 FLET- 3 -RAESTE 4 GE- 9 -BEEAG// 8   (1241)

                    END FOLIO 160R +

SET-2-TON 3 HIM 2 TOO 1 HEEAFDON/ 5 HILDE- 3 -RANDAS// 9   (1242)

BORD- 3 -WUDU 4 BEORHTAN/ 5 THAEAER 3 ON 1 BENCE 4 WAES.// 4   (1243)

OFER 9 AETHELINGE/ 5 YYTH- 1 -GE- 4 -SEENE// 4   (1244)

HEATHO- 3 -STEEAPA 5 HELM/ 9 HRINGED 4 BYRNE// 5   (1245)

THREC- 3 -WUDU 4 THRYM- 1 -LIIC/ 4 WAES 3 THEEAW 4 HYRA// 5   (1246)

                              44

H= 1 HIIE 3 OFT 3 WAEAERON/ 3 AN 0 WIIG 3 GEARWE// 9   (1247)

EE 2 AET 2 HAAM 3 GEE 2 ON 0 HERGE/ 5 GEE 1 GE- 4 -HWAETHER 4 THAARA// 9 (1248)

FNE 3 SWYL-1-CE 4 MAEAELA/ 3 SWIL-1-CE 4 HIRA 4 MAN- 2 -DRYHT-9-NE// 5   (1249)

HEARF 3 GE- 1 -SAEAELDE/ 4 WAES 3 SEEO 2 THEEOD 3 TILU.// 9   (1250)

.XVIIII.   (FITT)

SIGON 4 THAA 0 TOO 2 SLAEAEPE/ 4 SUM 3 SAARE 5 AN- 0 -GEALD// 3   (1251)

EAEFEN- 9 -RAESTE/ 5 SWAA 3 HIM 2 FUL 3 OFT 4 GE- 1 -LAMP// 4   (1252)

ITHD1AN 2 GOLD- 9 -SELE/ 5 GRENDEL 4 WARODE// 6   (1253)

N- 0 -RIHT 3 AEFNDE/ 4 OTH 0 TH= 9 ENDE 3 BE- 1 -CWOOM// 4   (1254)

WYLT 3 AEFTER 3 SYNNUM/ 3 TH= 1 GE- 1 -SYYNE 9 WEARTH// 4   (1255)

IID- 1 -CUUTH 3 WERUM/ 5 TH=TE 3 WREC-1-END 3 THAA 0 GYYT// 4   (1256)

IF-9-DE 3 AEFTER 4 LAATHU=/ 5 LANGE 4 THRAAGE// 5   (1257)

EFTER 4 GUUDH- 9 -CEARE/ 5 GRENDLES 4 MOODOR// 5   (1258)

DES 3 AAG- 0 -LAEAEC- 3 -WIIF/ 2 YRM-9-THE 4 GE- 1 -MUNDE// 6   (1259)

EE 0 THE 4 WAETER- 4 -EGESAN/ 4 WUNIAN 9 SCOL-1-DE// 5   (1260)

EALDE 4 STREEAMAS/ 5 SITHDHAN 3 ()CAMP*GAAIN 1 WEARDH// 9   (1261)

OO 2 ECG- 0 -BANAN/ 3 AANGAN 4 BREETHER// 4   (1262)

AEDER-1-EN- 3 -MAEAEGE/ 9 HEE 0 THAA 4 FAAG 4 GE- 0 -WAAT// 5   (1263)

OR-1-THRE 5 GE- 1 -MEAR-1-COD/ 9 MAN- 8 -DREEAM 4 FLEEON// 4   (1264)

END FOLIO 160V +

EESTEN 3 WARODE/ 7 THANON 8 WOOC 9 FELA// 5   (1265)

EOO- 2 -SCEAFT- 3 -GAASTA/ 5 WAES 4 THAEAERA 4 GRENDEL 9 SUM// 6   (1266)

EORO- 2 -WEARH 5 HETE- 0 -LIIC/ 4 SEE 1 AET 3 HEOR-1-0-1-TE 9 FAND// 4   (1267)

AEC-1-CENDNE 4 WER/ 3 WIIGES 4 BIIDAN// 4   (1268)

HAEAER 3 HIM 9 AAG- 0 -LAEAECA/ 4 AET- 0 -GRAEAEPE 4 WEARDH// 5   (1269)

WAET1RE 5 HEE 1 GE- 9 -MUNDE/ 4 MAEGENES 4 STRENGE// 5   (1270)

IM- 1 -FAES-1-TE 3 GIFE/ 9 DHE 2 HIM 4 GOD 3 SEALDE// 5   (1271)

AND 0 HIM 2 TOO 2 AN- 0 -WALDAN/ 4 AARE 9 GE- 1 -LYYFDE// 5   (1272)

ROOFRE 4 =AND 0 FULTUM/ 3   (1273)

DHYY 3 HEE 3 THONE 4 FEEOND 9 OFER- 4 -CWOOM// 3   (1273)

E- 4 -HNAEAEGDE 5 HELLE 5 GAAST/ 5 THAA 0 HEE 9 HEEAN 2 GE- 3 -+WAAT// 5 (1274)

45

DREEAME 5 BE- 1 -DAEAEL-1-ED/ 4 DEEATH- 2 -+WIIC 9 SEEON// 4   (1275)

MAN- 1 -CYNNES 4 FEEOND/ 5 =AND 1 HIS 4 MOODOR 3 THAA 0 GYYT// 9   (1276)

GIIFRE 4 =AND 0 GALG- 0 -MOOD/ 4 GE- 1 -GAAN 3 WOLDE// 6   (1277)

SORH- 3 -FULNE 9 SIIDH/ 5 SUNU 3 ()THEOD*DEEODH 3 WRECAN// 5   (1278)

COOM 3 THAA 0 TOO 2 HEOROTE/ 9 DHAEAER 5 HRING- 3 -DENE// 6   (1279)

GEOND 2 TH= 1 SAELD 8 SWAEAEFUN/ 4 THAA 9 DHAEAER 3 SOONA 4 WEARDH// 5   (1280)

ED- 2 -HWYRFT 4 EORLUM/ 3 SITHDHAN 9 INNE 3 FEALH// 4   (1281)

GREND-1-LES 4 MOODOR/ 4 WAES 1 SE 4 GRY-3-RE 5 LAEAES-1-SA// 4   (1282)

EFNE 3 SWAA 3 MICLE/ 4 SWAA 2 BIDH 4 MAEGTHA 9 CRAEFT// 5   (1283)

WIIG- 2 -GRYRE 5 WIIFES/ 6 BE 1 WAEAEPNED- 3 -MEN// 9   (1284)

THON= 8 HEORU 4 BUNDEN/ 4 HAMERE 5 GE- 0 -()THUREN*THRUUEN// 9   (1285)

SWEORD 3 SWAATE 4 FAAH/ 5 SWIIN 1 OFER 5 HELME// 4   (1286)

ECGUM 9 DYHTIG/ 8 AND- 1 -WEARD 4 SCIREDH.// 5   (1287)

        ↑ END FOLIO 161R

THAA 1 WAES 3 ON 8 HEALLE/ 9 HEARD- 3 -ECG 4 TOGEN// 5   (1288)

SWEORD 4 OFER 4 SETLUM/ 2 SIID- 9 -RAND 4 MA-1-NIG// 7   (1289)

HAFEN 5 HAN-1-DA 4 FAEST/ 5 HELM 9 NE 0 GE- 4 -MUNDE// 7   (1290)

BYR-1-NAN 4 SIIDE/ 6 THAA 1 HINE 2 SE 9 BROOGA 4 AN- 0 -GEAT// 5   (1291)

HEEO 1 WAES 4 ON 2 OFSTE/ 5 WOLDE 9 UUT 1 THANON// 5   (1292)

FEEORE 4 BEOR-2-GAN/ 5 THAA 2 HEEO 2 ON- 1 -FUN-9-DEN 2 WAES// 6   (1293)

HRADHE 5 HEEO 3 AETHELINGA/ 4 AANNE 9 HAEFDE// 6   (1294)

FAESTE 5 BE- 2 -FANGEN/ 6 THAA 2 HEEO 2 TOO 1 FEN-9-NE 4 GANG// 4   (1295)

SEE 1 WAES 4 HROOTH- 0 -GAARE/ 7 HAELETHA 9 LEEOFOST// 6   (1296)

ON 0 GE- 3 -SIIDHES 5 +HAAD/ 5 BE 1 SAEAEM 4 TWEEONU=// 9   (1297)

RIICE 5 RAND- 3 -WIGA/ 6   (1298)

        THONE 5 DHE 4 HEEO 3 ON 0 RAESTE 9 AA- 0 -BREEAT// 7   (1298)

BLAEAED- 3 -FAESTNE 6 BEORN/ 3 NAES 3 BEEO- 9 -WULF 4 DHAEAER.// 6   (1299)

AC 2 WAES 5 OOTHER 3 IN/ 3 AEAER 0 GE- 4 -TEOHHOD// 9   (1300)

AEFTER 3 MAATHDHUM- 4 -GIFE./ 6 MAEAERUM 4 GEEATE// 9   (1301)

HREEAM 3 WEARDH 4 IN 2 HEOROTE/ 5   (1302)

        HEEO 1 UNDER 3 HEOLF-9-RE 3 GE- 2 -NAM// 5   (1302)

CUUTHE 3 FOL-1-ME/ 5 CEARU 1 WAES 2 GE- 9 -NIIWOD// 4   (1303)

                                46

E- 2 -WORDEN 2 IN 0 WIICUN/ 4 NE 0 WAES 4 TH= 0 GE- 9 -WRIXLE 5 TIL// 5   (1304)

H= 2 HIIE 4 ON 1 BAA 4 HEALFA/ 4 BICGAN 9 SCOL-1-DON.// 6   (1305)

REEONDA 5 FEEORU=/ 4 THAA 0 WAES 4 FROOJ 9 CYNING.// 5   (1306)

HAAR 3 HIL-1-DE- 5 -RINC/ 4 ON 2 HREEON 9 MOODE// 5   (1307)

END FOLIO 161V +

YDH-1-TH-1-AN 3 HEE 4 ALDOR- 5 -THEGN/ J UN- 0 -LYFIGENDNE// 9   (1308)

HONE 4 DEEORESTAN/ 4 DEEADNE 5 WISSE.// 7   (1309)

RATHE 8 WAES 9 TOO 1 BUURE/ 6 BEEO- 0 -WULF 4 FE-1-TOD// 4   (1310)

IGOR- 4 -EEADIG 3 SECG/ 9 SAMOD 1 AEAER- 3 -DAEGE// 5   (1311)

EODE 4 EORLA 3 SUM/ 4 AETHELE 9 CEM-1-PA// 5   (1312)

ELF 4 MID 2 GE- 4 -SIIDHUM/ 3 THAEAER 1 SE 4 SNOTE-9-RA 4 +BAAD.// 7   (1313)

)HWAETHRE*HWAETHER 4 HIM 1 ()ALF*AL- 2 -WALDA/ 4 AEAEFRE 9 WILLE// 5   (1314)

EFTER 3 WEEA- 2 -SPELLE/ 5 WYRPE 5 GE- 2 -FREM-9-MAN// 5   (1315)

ANG 3 DHAA 4 AEFTER 3 FLOORE/ 5 FYRD- 2 -WYR-9-DHE 4 MAN// 3   (1316)

ID 2 HIS 5 HAND- 3 -SCALE/ 5 HEAL- 3 -WUDU 9 DYNE-2-DE// 6   (1317)

H= 1 HEE 3 THONE 5 WIISAN/ 4 WORDUM 4 ()HNAEGDE*NAEAEGDE// 9   (1318)

REEAN 2 ING- 2 -WINA/ 4 FRAEGN 3 GIF 2 HIM 3 WAEAERE// 9   (1319)

EFTER 3 NEEOD- 2 -LADHU*M/ 5 NIHT 3 GE- 3 -TAEAESE.// 9   (1320)

.XX.   (FITT)

HROOJH- 3 -GAAR 5 MATHELODE/ 6 HELM 3 SCYLDINGA// 9   (1321)

E 3 FRIIN 3 THUU 2 AEFTER 5 SAEAELU=/ 5 SORH 0 IS 2 GE- 2 -NII-9-WOD// 4   (1322)

ENIGEA 4 LEEODUM/ 5 DEEAD 3 IS 2 AESC- 1 -HERE// 9   (1323)

R-1-MEN- 5 -LAAFES/ 4 YL-1-DRA 5 BROO-1-THOR// 4   (1324)

IIN 1 +RUUN- 9 -WITA/ 4 =AND 0 MIIN 1 RAEAED- 4 -BORA// 5   (1325)

AXL- 3 -GE- 2 -STEA-1-LLA/ 9 DHONNE 4 WEE 2 ON 2 OR- 0 -LEGE.// 6   (1326)

AFELAN 4 WEREDON/ 9 THON= 5 HNITON 3 FEETHAN// 3   (1327)

OFERAS 4 CNYSE-3-DAN/ 9 SWYLC 8 SCOLDE 4 EORL 3 WESAN// 4   (1328)

END FOLIO 162R +

AETHELING 8 AEAER- 1 -GOOD/ 2 SWYLC 8 AESC- 9 -HERE 9 WAES// 8   (1329)

EARDH 4 HIM 1 ON 2 HEOROTE/ 5 TOO 0 HAND- 3 -BANAN// 9   (1330)

```
WAEL- 2 -GAEAEST 5 WAEAEFRE/ 5 IC 0 NE 2 +WAAT 5 ()HWAETHER*HWAEDER//  4    (1331)

ATOL 3 AEAESE 9 WLANC/ 4 EFT- 2 -SIIDHAS 4 TEEAH// 3                        (1332)

FYLLE 3 GE- 1 -()FRAEGNOD*FAEGNOD/ 3 HEED 9 THAA 2 FAEAEHDHE 5 WRAEC// 5   (1333)

THE 3 THUU 2 GYSTRAN 3 NIHT/ 4 GREN-9-DEL 5 CWEAL-2-DEST// 5               (1334)

THURH 3 HAEAESTNE 5 HAAD/ 4 HEAR-2-DU= 9 CLAMMUM// 3                       (1335)

FOR- 3 -THAN 4 HEE 0 TOO 2 LANGE/ 4 LEEODE 3 MIINE// 9                     (1336)

WANODE 4 =AND 0 WYRDE/ 4 HEE 2 AET 1 WIIGE 4 GE- 1 -CRANG// 4             (1337)

EAL-9-DRES 5 SCYLDIG/ 4 =AND 0 NUU 2 OOTHER 2 CWOOM// 3                    (1338)

MIHTIG 3 MAAN- 9 -SCADHA/ 4 WOLDE 2 HYRE 3 MAEAEG 3 WRECAN.// 4           (1339)

GEE 2 FEOR 3 HAFADH/ 9 FAEAEHDHE 3 GE- 0 -STAEAELED// 4                    (1340)

THAES 3 THE 3 THINCEAN 3 MAEG/ 5 THEGNE 9 MONEGUM// 4                      (1341)

SEE 0 THE 3 AEFTER 4 SINC- 2 -GYFAN/ 3 ON 0 SEFAN 9 GREED-1-TE-1-TH// 5  (1342)

HRETHER- 3 -BEALO 5 HEARDE/ 4 NUU 0 SEEO 2 HAND 9 LIGEDH// 4             (1343)

SEE 0 THE 2 EEOW 3 WEEL- 4 -HWYLCRA/ 5 WILNA 3 DOHTE.// 9                  (1344)

IC 2 TH= 2 LOND- 3 -BUUEND/ 4 LEEODE 3 MIINE// 4                           (1345)

SELE- 2 -RAEAE-1-DEN-1-DE/ 9 SECGAN 5 HYYRDE// 5                          (1346)

TH= 1 HIIE 2 GE- 1 -SAAWON/ 4 SWYLCE 3 TWEEGEN// 9                         (1347)

MICLE 4 MEARC- 2 -STAPAN/ 3 MOORAS 4 HEAL-2-DAN// 3                        (1348)

ELLOR- 9 -GAEAESTAS/ 4 DHAEAERA 3 OODHER 2 WAES// 5                        (1349)

THAES 4 THE 4 HIIE 3 GE- 2 -WIS- 0 -LIICOST/ 9 GE- 1 -WITAN 3 MEAHTON// 3 (1350)

IDESE 4 ON- 0 -LIIC- 3 -()NAES*NES/ 2 OODHER 3 EAR-9-M- 3 -SCEAPEN// 4    (1351)

ON 0 WERES 5 WAESTMUM/ 3 WRAEC- 3 -LAAS-1-TAS 9 TRAED// 5                 (1352)
```

END FOLIO 162V ✝

```
NAEF-1-NE 4 HEE 3 WAES 3 MAARA/ 5 THON= 3 AEAENIG 8 MAN 9 OODHER// 5      (1353)

THONE 5 ON 0 GEEAR- 4 -DAGU=/ 4 GRENDEL 4 ()NEMDOD*NEMDON// 9            (1354)

FOLD- 3 -BUUENDE/ 5 NOO 2 HIIE 4 FAEDER 4 CUN-1-NON// 3                   (1355)

HWAETHER 9 HIM 3 AEAENIG 3 WAES/ 4 AEAER 2 AA- 0 -CEN-1-NED// 4          (1356)

DYRNA 4 GAASTA/ 9 HIIE 2 DYYGEL 4 LOND// 4                                (1357)

WARIGEADH 4 WULF- 3 -HLEOTHU/ 4 WINDIGE 9 NAESSAS// 4                     (1358)

FREECNE 4 FEN- 1 -GE- 2 -LAAD/ 5 DHAEAER 2 FYRGEN- 9 -STREEAM// 5        (1359)

UNDER 4 NAESSA 4 GE- 1 -NIPU/ 5 NITHER 1 GE- 0 -WIITEDH// 9              (1360)

FLOOD 3 UNDER 4 FOLDAN/ 4 NIS 4 TH= 1 FEOR 3 HEO-1-NON// 4                (1361)
```

```
IIL- 2 -GE- 9 -MEAR-1-CES/ 5 TH= 0 SE 3 MERE 4 ()STANDHEDH*STANDEDH// 4      (1362)

FER 2 THAEAEM 2 HON-9-GIADH/ 6 HRINDE 5 BEAR-1-WAS// 5                         (1363)

UDU 1 WYRTU= 4 FAEST/ 9 WAETER 3 OFER- 2 -HELMADH// 6                          (1364)

HAEAER 2 MAEG 2 NIHTA 3 GE- 2 -HWAEAEM/ 9 NIIDH- 2 -WUNDOR 5 SEEON// 5         (1365)

YYR 3 ON 1 FLOODE/ 5 NOO 1 THAES 4 FROOD 9 LEOFADH// 5                         (1366)

UME-2-NA 5 BEARNA/ 5 TH= 2 THONE 4 GRUND 1 WITE// 9                            (1367)

HEEAH 4 THE 3 HAEAEDH- 4 -STAPA/ 5 HUNDU= 2 GE- 0 -SWENCED// 7                 (1368)

EOROT 9 HOR-2-NU= 2 TRUM/ 6 HOLT- 3 -WUDU 2 SEECE// 5                          (1369)

EOR-2-RAN 2 GE- 9 -FLYYMED/ 3 AEAER 2 HEE 2 FEORH 2 SELEDH// 4                 (1370)

LOOR 3 ON 1 OOFRE/ 4 +AEAER 9 HEE 3 IN 1 WILLE// 6                             (1371)

AFELAN 8 *BEORGAN/ 8 NIS 3 TH= 1 HEEORU 2 STOOW.// 6                           (1372)

HANON 9 YYDH- 1 -GE- 2 -BLOND/ 4 UP 1 AA- 0 -STIIGEDH// 5                      (1373)

ON 1 TOO 3 WOLC-1-NUM/ 3 THON= 9 WIND 2 STYRETH// 5                            (1374)

AADH 1 GE- 4 -WIDRU/ 2 ODH 3 TH= 0 LYFT 3 DRYSMATH// 9                         (1375)

ODERAS 4 REEOTADH/ 5 NUU 0 IS 2 SE 2 RAEAED 2 GE- 1 -LANG// 4                  (1376)

FI 1 AET 9 THEE 8 AANU=/ 3 EARD 2 GIIT 2 NE 2 CONST// 4                        (1377)

          + END FOLIO 163R


REECNE 4 STOOWE/ 9 DHAEAER 8 THUU 1 FINDA-8-N 3 MIHT// 5                       (1378)

)FELA 3 SINNIGNE 4 SECG/ 9 SEEC 2 GIF 3 THUU 2 DYRRE// 6                       (1379)

C 2 THEE 4 THAA 0 FAEAEHDHE/ 5 FEEO 1 LEEA-9-NIGE// 5                          (1380)

ALD- 2 -GE- 2 -STREEONU=/ 3 SWAA 2 IC 0 AEAER 2 DYDE// 5                       (1381)

UN-9-()DINI*DNUM 3 GOLDE/ 5 GYF 3 THUU 1 ON 3 WEG 3 CYMEST.// 9                (1382)


                    .XXI.                                                      (FITT)

$BEEO- 0 -$$WULF 6 MATHELODE/ 6 BEARN 2 ECG- 1 -THEEO-9-WES// 4               (1383)

E 2 SORGA 4 SNOTOR 4 GUMA/ 5 SEELRE 3 BIDH 9 AEAEG- 3 -HWAEAEM// 4            (1384)

HAET 2 HEE 2 HIS 4 FREEOND 3 WRECE/ 5 THONNE 9 HEE 3 FELA 3 MURNE// 5         (1385)

URE 3 AEAEG- 1 -HWYLC 3 SCEAL/ 4 ENDE 9 GE- 2 -BIIDAN// 5                      (1386)

OROLDE 5 LIIFES/ 3 WYRCE 5 SEE 2 THE 3 MOOTE// 9                               (1387)

OOMES 3 +AEAER 4 DEEATHE/ 5 TH= 1 BIDH 3 DRIHT- 3 -GUMAN// 3                   (1388)

N- 0 -LIF-9-GENDUM/ 4 AEFTER 4 SEELEST// 4                                     (1389)

AA- 0 -RIIS 3 RIICES 2 WEARD/ 3 UTON 9 HRA-1-THE 4 FEERAN// 3                  (1390)
```

GRENDLES 4 MAAGAN/ 4 GANG 8 SCEEA-9-WIGAN.// 5   (1391)

$IC 1 HIT 3 THEE 0 GE- 4 -HAATE/ 5 NOO 1 HEE 4 ON 0 HELM 3 LOSATH.// 9   (1392)

NEE 3 ON 1 FULDAN 3 FAETHM/ 3 NEE 2 ON 0 FYRGEN- 3 -HOLT.// 4   (1393)

NEE 9 ON 1 GYFENES 4 GRUND/ 3 +GAA 3 THAEAER 3 HEE 2 WILLE// 4   (1394)

DHYYS 2 DOOGOR 9 THUU/ 0 GE- 5 -THYLD 4 HAFA// 4   (1395)

WEEANA 3 GE- 3 -HWYL-1-CES/ 4 SWAA 2 IC 1 THEE 9 WEENE 4 TOO.// 6 (1396)

AA- 0 -HLEEOP 3 DHAA 2 SE 2 GOMELA/ 4 GODE 3 THAN-9-CODE// 4   (1397)

MIHTIGAN 3 DRIHTNE/ 5 THAES 3 SE 3 MAN 2 GE- 9 -SPRAEC// 4   (1398)

END FOLIO 163V +

THAA 1 WAES 6 HROODH- 1 -GAARE/ 6 HORS 4 GE- 8 -BAEAETED// 9   (1399)

WICG 4 WUNDEN- 4 -FEAX/ 3 WIISA 4 FENGEL// 4   (1400)

GEATO- 8 -LIIC 9 GENDE/ 4 GUM- 2 -FEETHA 3 STOOP// 5   (1401)

LIND- 3 -HAEBBENDRA/ 3 LAASTAS 9 WAEAERON// 3   (1402)

AEFTER 4 WALD- 2 -SWA-2-THU=/ 4 WIIDE 3 GE- 2 -SYYNE// 9   (1403)

GANG 3 OFER 3 GRUNDAS/ 4 *SWAA 8 GEGNU= 3 FOOR// 4   (1404)

OFER 3 MYR-9-CAN 4 MOOR/ 5 MAGO- 3 -THEGNA 4 BAER// 4   (1405)

THONE 2 SEELESTAN/ 9 SAAWOL- 4 -LEEAS-2-NE// 6   (1406)

THAARA 4 THE 2 MID 4 HROODH- 2 -GAARE/ 9 +HAAM 3 EAHTODE// 6   (1407)

OFER- 3 -EEODE 3 THAA/ 2 AETHELINGA 9 BEARN// 5   (1408)

STEEAP 3 STAAN- 4 -HLIDHO/ 5 STIIGE 3 NEARWE// 9   (1409)

ENGE 4 AAN- 1 -PADHAS/ 5 UN- 0 -CUUDH 2 GE- 2 -LAAD// 4   (1410)

NEOWLE 3 NAES-9-SAS/ 4 NICOR- 5 -HUUSA 3 FELA.// 7   (1411)

HEE 2 FEEARA 4 SUM/ 3 BE- 9 -FORAN 3 GENGDE// 6   (1412)

WIISRA 3 MONNA/ 4 WONG 4 SCEEAWIAN// 9   (1413)

OTH 2 TH= 1 HEE 3 FAEAERINGA/ 5 FYRGEN- 3 -BEEAMAS// 5   (1414)

OFER 9 HAAR-2-NE 5 STAAN/ 5 HLEONIAN 2 FUNDE// 5   (1415)

WYN- 0 -LEEASNE 9 WUDU/ 4 WAETER 3 UNDER 4 STOOD// 4   (1416)

DREEORIG 3 =AND 0 GE- 3 -DREE-9-FED/ 4 DENUM 4 EALL-1-UM 4 WAES// 5 (1417)

WINUM 3 SCYL-1-DINGA/ 9 WEORCE 5 ON 1 MOODE// 4   (1418)

TOO 0 GE- 3 -THOLIAN-1-NE/ 6 DHEGNE 9 MONEGU=// 4   (1419)

ON- 1 -CYYDH 3 EORL-2-A 2 GE- 4 -HWAEAEM/ 3   (1420)

SYDH-3-THAN 9 AESC- 3 -HERES// 5   (1420)

50

ON 2 THAA= 4 HOLM- 3 -CLIFE/ 6 HAFE-1-LAN 9 MEET-3-TON// 5   (1421)

FLOOD 4 BLOODE 5 WEEOL/ 4 FOLG 2 TOO 2 SAEAEGON// 9   (1422)

END FOLIO 164R +

HAATAN 8 HEOL-2-FRE/ 5 HORN 3 STUNDUM 3 SONG// 4   (1423)

FUUS- 8 -LIIC 9 FYRD- 8 -LEEODH/ 4 FEETHA 3 EAL 3 GE- 2 -SAET.// 6 (1424)

GE- 0 -SAAWON 3 DHAA 3 AEFTER 9 WAETERE/ 4 WYRM- 1 -CYNNES 4 FELA// 4 (1425)

SEL- 0 -LICE 4 SAEAE- 4 -DRACAN/ 9 SUND 3 CUN-1-NIAN// 4   (1426)

SWYLCE 3 ON 1 NAES- 5 -HLEODHUM/ 3 NICRAS 9 LICGEAN.// 2   (1427)

DHAA 1 ON 1 UNDERN- 2 -MAEAEL/ 5 OFT 4 BE- 2 -WITIGADH// 4   (1428)

SORH- 9 -FULNE 4 SIIDH/ 3 ON 0 SEGL- 3 -RAADE// 6   (1429)

WYRMAS 5 =AND 0 WILDEEOR/ 4 HIIE 2 ON 9 WEG 3 HRURON// 4   (1430)

BITERE 4 =AND 0 GE- 0 -BOLGNE/ 7 BEARHTM 2 ON- 0 -GEEA-9-TON// 3   (1431)

GUUDH- 5 -HORN 2 GALAN/ 3 SUM-1-NE 4 GEEATA 2 LEEOD// 3   (1432)

OF 0 FLAAN- 9 -BOGAN/ 4 FEEORES 3 GE- 3 -TWAEAEF-1-DE// 5   (1433)

YYDH- 1 -GE- 1 -WINNES/ 5 TH= 1 HIM 2 ON 9 ALDRE 4 STOOD// 4   (1434)

HERE- 3 -STRAEAEL 5 HEARDA/ 5 HEE 1 ON 3 HOL-1-ME 9 WAES// 5   (1435)

SUNDES 4 THEE 1 SAEAENRA/ 5 DHEE 1 HYNE 4 SWYLT 3 FOR- 1 -NAM.// 4 (1436)

HRAE-9-THE 3 WEARDH 3 ON 0 YYDHUM/ 3 MID 2 EOFER- 1 -SPREEOTUM// 4 (1437)

HEORO- 3 -HOOC-9-YHTUM/ 4 HEAR-1-DE 4 GE- 8 -NEAR-2-WOD// 4   (1438)

NIIDHA 2 GE- 3 -NAEAEGED/ 3 =AND 0 ON 9 NAES 3 TOGEN// 4   (1439)

WUN-1-DOR- 3 -LIIC 5 WAEAEG- 4 -BORA/ 4 WERAS 4 SCEEAWE-9-DON// 4 (1440)

GRYRE- 2 -LIIC-1-NE 4 GIST/ 4 GYRE-1-DE 6 HINE 5 BEEO- 0 -WULF// 9 (1441)

EORL- 3 -GE- 1 -WAEAE-2-DUM/ 4 NALLES 4 FOR 3 EALDRE 4 MEARN// 2   (1442)

SCOLDE 9 HERE- 3 -BYRNE/ 6 HONDUM 3 GE- 2 -BROODEN// 4   (1443)

SIID 0 =AND 1 SEARO- 3 -FAAH/ 9 SUND 2 CUN-1-NIAN// 4   (1444)

SEEO 0 DHE 5 +BAAN- 2 -COFAN/ 6 BEORGAN 2 GUUTHE// 9   (1445)

TH= 1 HIM 3 HIL-1-DE- 4 -GRAAP/ 5 HRETHRE 4 NE 2 MIHTE// 5   (1446)

EORRES 3 IN-9-WIT- 3 -FENG/ 3 ALDRE 4 GE- 1 -SCETHDHAN.// 7   (1447)

AC 0 SE 4 HWIITA 4 HELM./ 9 HAFELAN 4 WEREDE// 5   (1448)

END FOLIO 164V +

SEE 0 THE 3 MERE- 2 -GRUNDAS/ 5 MENGAN 9 SCOLDE// 4   (1449)

51

SEECAN 3 SUND- 2 -GE- 2 -BLAND/ 4 SINCE 4 GE- 2 -WEORDHAD// 9   (1450)

BE- 2 -FONGEN 3 FREEA- 3 -WRAASNUM/ 5 SWAA 3 HINE 4 FYRN- 1 -DA-9-GUM// 4 (1451)

WORHTE 4 WAEAEPNA 4 SMIDH/ 4 WUNDRUM 3 TEEODE// 9   (1452)

BE- 3 -SETTE 4 SWIIN- 0 -LIICUM/ 5 TH= 1 HINE 4 SYDH-2-THAN 2 NOO// 4   (1453)

BROND 0 NEE 9 BEA-1-DO- 4 -MEECAS/ 6 BIITAN 2 NE 2 MEAHTON.// 6   (1454)

$NAES 4 THAET 9 THONNE 5 MAEAETOST/ 4 MAEGEN- 3 -FULTUMA// 5   (1455)

TH= 0 HIM 2 ON 9 DHEARFE 3 LAAH/ 4 DHYLE 5 HROODH- 2 -GAARES// 5   (1456)

WAES 4 THAEAEM 3 HAEFT- 9 -MEECE/ 6 HRUNTING 4 NAMA// 5   (1457)

TH= 0 WAES 3 AAN 0 FORAN/ 3 EALD- 9 -GE- 4 -STREEONA// 5   (1458)

ECG 3 WAES 4 IIREN/ 4 AATER- 1 -TAANUM 3 FAAH// 9   (1459)

AA- 2 -HYRDED 5 HEATHO- 2 -SWAATE/ 5   (1460)

          NAEAEFRE 3 HIT 3 AET 1 HILDE 9 NE 2 SWAAC// 5   (1460)

MANNA 4 AEAENGUM/ 5   (1461)

          THAARA 4 THE 2 HIT 3 MID 9 MUN-1-DUM 4 BE- 2 -WAND// 4   (1461)

SEE 0 DHE 3 GRYRE- 5 -SIIDHAS/ 4 GE- 1 -GAAN 9 DOR-1-STE// 5   (1462)

FOLC- 1 -STEDE 5 FAARA/ 3 NAES 3 TH= 2 FOR-1-MA 3 SIIDH// 9   (1463)

TH= 2 HIT 2 ELLEN- 3 -WEORC/ 5 AEFNAN 3 SCOLDE.// 7   (1464)

HUURU 1 NE 0 GE- 9 -MUNDE/ 5 MAGO 3 ECG- 0 -LAAFES// 5   (1465)

EAFOTHES 4 CRAEFTIG/ 3 TH= 9 HEE 3 AEAER 2 GE- 3 -SPRAEC// 4   (1466)

WIINE 4 DRUNCEN/ 5 THAA 0 HEE 4 THAES 3 WAEAEPNES 9 ON- 2 -LAAH.// 6   (1467)

SEELRAN 4 SWEORD- 1 -FRECAN/ 4 SELFA 4 NE 1 DOR-9-STE// 4   (1468)

UNDER 4 YYDHA 3 GE- 2 -WIN/ 4 ALDRE 4 GE- 1 -NEE-2-THAN// 3   (1469)

DRIHT- 9 -SCYPE 5 DREEO-1-GAN/ 5   (1470)

          THAEAER 4 HEE 2 DOOME 4 FOR- 3 -LEEAS// 4   (1470)

ELLEN- 9 -MAEAERDHUM/ 3 NE 2 WAES 4 THAEAEM 1 DODHRUM 4 SWAA// 4   (1471)

          ✝ END FOLIO 165R

SYDH-3-THAN 9 HEE 8 HINE 5 TOO 1 GUUDHE/ 5 GE- 2 -GYRED 4 HAEFDE.// 9   (1472)

                    .XXII.   (FITT)

$$BEED- 0 -$$WULF 5 MADHELODE/ 6 BEARN 2 ECG- 1 -THEEOWES// 9   (1473)

GE- 3 -THENC 4 NUU 1 SE 3 MAEAERA/ 4 MAGA 4 HEALF- 2 -DENES// 9   (1474)

SNOTTRA 5 FENGEL/ 4 NUU 0 IC 4 EOM 1 SIIDHES 4 FUUS// 3   (1475)

52

GOLD- 9 -WINE 5 GUME-3-NA/ 5 HWAET 3 WIT 3 GEOO 1 SPRAEAECON// 3   (1476)

GIF 9 IC 1 AET 4 THEARFE/ 5 THIINRE 4 SCOLDE// 5   (1477)

ALDRE 4 LINNAN/ 9 TH= 0 OHUU 0 MEE 3 AA 3 WAEAERE// 5   (1478)

FORDH- 4 -GE- 1 -WITENUM/ 3 ON 0 FAEDER 9 STAEAELE// 5   (1479)

WES 4 THUU 1 MUND- 3 -BORA/ 4 MIINUM 3 MAGO- 9 -THEGNUM// 6   (1480)

HOND- 2 -GE- 8 -SELLUM/ 4 GIF 1 MEC 3 HILD 3 NIME.// 9   (1481)

BSWYLCE 5 THUU 0 DHAA 4 MAAD-1-MAS/ 5 THE 3 THUU 0 MEE 4 SEALDEST// 9   (1482)

HROODH- 1 -GAAR 5 LEEOFA/ 5 HIGE- 2 -LAACE 4 ON- 0 -SEND.// 5   (1483)

MAEG 9 THONNE 4 ON 1 THAEAEM 2 GOLDE 4 ON- 0 -GITAN/ 5   (1484)

          GEEA-1-TA 3 DRI-9-HTEN// 3   (1484)

GE- 0 -SEEON 2 SUNU 4 HRAEAED-1-LES/ 5   (1485)

          THON= 2 HEE 3 ON 1 THAET 9 SINC 5 STARADH// 5   (1485)

TH= 0 IC 3 GU=- 2 -CYSTUM/ 4 GOODNE 4 FUNDE// 9   (1486)

BEEAGA 3 BRYT-1-TAN/ 5 BREEAC 5 THON= 4 MOOSTE.// 7   (1487)

=AND 0 THUU 9 ()HUN*UN- 0 -FERDH 5 LAEAET/ 4 EALDE 4 LAAFE// 5   (1488)

WRAEAET- 1 -LIIC 4 WAEAEG- 9 -SWEORD/ 5 WIID- 1 -CUUDH-1-NE 4 MAN// 5   (1489)

HEARD- 3 -ECG 3 HABBAN/ 9 IC 1 MEE 4 MID 5 HRUNTINGE// 5   (1490)

+DOOM 3 GE- 1 -WYRCE/ 9 OTHDHE 5 MEC 3 DEEADH 4 NIMEDH.// 6   (1491)
          END FOLIO 165V +

MEFTER 3 THAEAEM 8 WORDU=/ 9 WEDER- 4 -GEEATA 4 LEEOD// 4   (1492)

EFSTE 3 MID 3 ELNE/ 4 NALAS 8 =AND- 9 -SWARE// 6   (1493)

BIIDAN 2 WOL-1-DE/ 6 BRIM- 4 -WYLM 3 ON- 1 -FEENG// 8   (1494)

HIL-9-DE- 4 -RINCE/ 6 DHAA 0 WAES 5 HWIIL 4 DAEGES// 5   (1495)

AEAER 2 HEE 3 THONE 9 GRUND- 2 -WONG/ 4 ON- 0 -GYTAN 2 MEHTE.// 7   (1496)

BSOONA 4 TH= 1 ON- 9 -FUNDE/ 5 SEE 0 OHE 2 FLOODA 3 BE- 2 -GONG// 6   (1497)

HEORO- 3 -GIIF-1-RE 9 BE- 4 -HEEOLD/ 5 HUND 2 MIS-1-SEERA// 4   (1498)

GRIM 3 =AND 0 GRAEAEDIG/ 4 TH= 1 THAEAER 9 GUME-1-NA 5 SUM// 4   (1499)

AEL- 1 -WIHTA 3 EARD/ 4 UFAN 2 CUNNODE// 9   (1500)

GRAAP 4 THAA 0 TOO- 2 -GEEANES/ 5 GUUDH- 2 -RINC 4 GE- 1 -FEENG// 5   (1501)

ATOLAN 9 CLOM-2-MUM/ 4 NOO 1 THYY 2 AEAER 4 IN 0 GE- 2 -SCOOD// 5   (1502)

HAAL-1-AN 9 LIICE/ 6 HRING 4 UUTAN 4 YMB- 5 -BEARH// 6   (1503)

TH= 1 HEEO 4 THONE 9 FYRD- 4 -HOM/ 4 DHURH- 3 -FOON 3 NE 1 MIHTE// 6   (1504)

LO-1-3-1-ENE 4 LEODHO- 9 -SYRCAN/ 5 LAATHAN 2 FINGRUM// 5   (1505)

BAER 3 THAA 2 SEEO 3 BRIM- 9 -WYL*F/ 4   (1506)

        THAA 0 HEEO 1 TOO 3 BOTME 5 COOM// 4   (1506)

HRINGA 3 THENGEL/ 3 TOO 9 HOFE 5 SIINUM// 4   (1507)

SWAA 4 HEE 0 NE 4 MIHTE/ 5 NOO 1 HEE 4 ()THAEM*THAES 9 MOODIG 4 WAES// 5   (1508)

WAEAEPNA 3 GE- 1 -WEALDAN/ 4 AC 1 HINE 4 WUN-9-DRA 4 THAES 3 FELA// 4   (1509)

()SWECTE*SWENCTE 5 ON 0 SUNDE/ 6 SAEAE- 3 -DEEOR 9 MONIG// 5   (1510)

HILDE- 4 -TUUXUM/ 5 HERE- 5 -SYR-2-CAN 4 BRAEC// 9   (1511)

EEHTON 4 AAG- 0 -LAEAE-1-CAN/ 5 DHAA 0 SE 4 EORL 4 ON- 0 -GEAT// 4   (1512)

TH= 1 HEE 9 *IN 8 NIIDH- 3 -SELE/ 4 NAAT- 3 -HWYLCUM 4 WAES// 4   (1513)

THAEAER 4 HIM 1 NAEAENIG 9 WAETER/ 3 WIHTE 4 NE 0 SCETHEDE// 5   (1514)

NEE 1 HIM 2 FOR 3 HROOF- 9 -SELE/ 5 HRIINAN 3 NE 2 MEHTE// 6   (1515)

+FAEAER- 4 -GRIPE 4 FLOODES/ 9 FYYR- 8 -LEEOHT 4 GE- 2 -SEAH// 6   (1516)

        END FOLIO 166R +

BLAACNE 5 LEEOMAN/ 4 BEORHTE 9 SCIINAN.// 8   (1517)

$ON- 2 -GEAT 2 THAA 0 SE 2 GOODA/ 5 GRUND- 3 -WYR-1-GENNE// 9   (1518)

MERE- 8 -WIIF 3 MIHTIG/ 4 MAEGEN- 3 -RAEAES 4 FOR- 2 -GEAF// 5   (1519)

HILDE- 9 -BILLE/ 6 ()HORD*HOND 3 ()SWENGE*SWENG 4 NE 3 OF- 1 -TEEAH// 5   (1520)

TH= 1 HIRE 3 ON 0 HA-9-FELAN/ 5 HRING- 3 -MAEAEL 4 AA- 0 -GOOL// 5   (1521)

GRAEAEDIG 4 GUUDH- 4 -LEEODH/ 9 DHAA 8 SE 0 GIST 3 ON- 0 -FAND// 5   (1522)

TH= 0 SE 3 BEADO- 4 -LEEOMA/ 3 BIITAN 9 NOL-1-DE// 5   (1523)

ALDRE 3 SCETHDHAN./ 6 AC 0 SEEO 2 ECG 3 GE- 1 -SWAAC// 9   (1524)

DHEEODNE 5 AET 2 THEARFE/ 6 DHOLODE 4 AEAER 2 FELA// 4   (1525)

HOND- 9 -GE- 8 -MOOTA/ 5 HELM 3 OFT 3 GE- 0 -SCAER// 5   (1526)

FAEAEGES 4 FYRD- 9 -HRAEGL/ 6 DHAA 1 WAES 3 FOR-1-MA 4 SIIDH// 4   (1527)

DEEORUM 3 MAADME/ 9 TH= 8 HIS 3 +DOOM 3 AA- 0 -LAEG.// 6   (1528)

EFT 3 WAES 3 AN- 0 -RAEAED/ 3 NALAS 4 ELNES 9 LAET// 5   (1529)

MAEAERDHA 5 GE- 1 -MYNDIG/ 4 MAEAEG 2 HYY- 0 -LAACES// 4   (1530)

WEARP 9 DHAA 3 ()WUNDEL*WUNDEN- 4 -MAEAEL/ 5   (1531)

        WRAEAETTUM 3 GE- 1 -BUNDEN// 4   (1531)

YRRE 3 OORETTA/ 4 TH= 2 HIT 2 ON 1 EORDHAN 3 LAEG// 3   (1532)

STIIDH 4 =AND 0 STYYL- 2 -ECG/ 9 STRENGE 5 GE- 1 -TRUWODE// 5   (1533)

MUND- 3 -GRIPE 5 MAEGENES/ 9 SWAA 3 SCEAL 4 MAN 1 DOON// 4   (1534)

THON= 3 HEE 3 AET 1 GUUDHE/ 5 GE- 1 -GAAN 9 THENCEDH// 4   (1535)

LONG- 3 -SUMNE 4 LOF/ 5 NAA 1 YMB 2 HIS 3 LIIF 2 CEA-9-RADH.// 7   (1536)

BGE- 0 -FEENG 4 THAA 1 BE 4 EAXLE/ 5 NALAS 3 FOR 3 FAEAEHDHE 9 MEARN// 4   (1537)

GUUDH- 1 -GEEATA 4 LEEOD/ 4 GRENDLES 4 MOODOR// 9   (1538)

RAEGD 4 THAA 3 BEAD-1-WE 5 HEARD/ 4   (1539)

       THAA 1 HEE 0 GE- 4 -BOLGEN 2 WAES// 9   (1539)

EORH- 3 -GE- 3 -NIIDH-2-LAN/ 4 TH= 0 HEEO 3 ON 0 FLET 4 GE- 1 -BEEAH// 4 (1540)

NEEO 9 HIM 2 EFT 3 HRATHE/ 5 ()HAND*AND- 0 -LEEAN 3 FOR- 1 -GEALD// 4   (1541)

GRIM-9-MAN 3 GRAAPUM/ 5 =AND 0 HIM 1 TOO- 1 -GEEANES 4 FEENG// 4   (1542)

     ✝ END FOLIO 166V

IFER- 3 -WEARP 9 THAA 3 WEERIG- 2 -MOOD/ 4 WIGENA 4 STRENGEST// 4   (1543)

EETHE- 3 -CEMPA/ 9 TH= 0 HEE 2 ON 0 FYLLE 5 WEARDH.// 7   (1544)

BOF- 1 -SAET 2 THAA 3 THONE 4 SELE- 1 -GYST/ 9   (1545)

       =AND 0 HYRE 4 ()SEAXE*SEAX 4 GE- 2 -TEEAH// 4   (1545)

BRAAD 3 *=AND 8 +BRUUN- 3 -ECG/ 3 WOLDE 9 HIRE 5 BEARN 4 WRECAN// 3   (1546)

AANGAN 4 EAFERAN/ 4 HIM 1 ON 9 EAXLE 5 LAEG// 4   (1547)

REEOST- 3 -NET 2 BROODEN/ 4 TH= 0 GE- 2 -BEARH 9 FEEORE// 5   (1548)

WIDH 2 ORD 3 =AND 0 WIDH 2 ECGE/ 4 IN- 0 -GANG 2 FOR- 3 -STOOD.// 9 (1549)

SHAEFJE 5 DHAA 1 FOR- 3 -SIIDHOD/ 4 SUNU 3 ECG- 0 -THEEOWES// 5   (1550)

UNDER 9 GYNNE 4 GRUND/ 3 GEEATA 3 CEMPA// 6   (1551)

MEMNE 9 HIM 4 HEADHO- 5 -BYRNE/ 7 HELPE 5 GE- 0 -FREME-2-DE// 9   (1552)

MERE- 4 -NET 3 HEAR-1-DE/ 4 =AND 0 HAALIG 3 GOD// 3   (1553)

GE- 1 -WEEOLD 3 WIIG- 9 -SIGOR/ 4 WIITIG 4 DRIHTEN// 4   (1554)

RODE-1-RA 4 RAEAEDEND/ 4 HIT 9 ON 1 RYHT 0 GE- 1 -SCEED// 4   (1555)

YDHE- 0 -LIICE/ 4 SYTHDHAN 3 HEE 1 EFT 3 AA- 0 -STOOD.// 9   (1556)

          .XXIII.   (FITT)

BSGE- 4 -SEAH 3 DHAA 3 ON 0 SEAR-2-WUM/ 5 SIGE- 2 -EEADIG 3 BIL// 4 (1557)

ALD- 9 -SWEORD 4 EOTENISC/ 4 ECGUM 5 THYYHTIG// 4   (1558)

IGENA 9 WEORDH- 3 -MYND/ 5 TH= 0 *WAES 8 WAEAEP-1-NA 4 CYST// 6   (1559)

UUTON 3 HIT 2 WAES 9 MAARE/ 5 DHON= 3 AEAENIG 3 MON 4 OODHER// 4   (1560)

TOO 1 BEADU- 3 -LAACE/ 9 AET- 2 -BERAN 2 MEA-1-HTE// 6   (1561)

+GOOD 3 =AND 1 GEATO- 0 -LIIC/ 5 GIIGAN-3-TA 3 GE- 2 -WEORC.// 6   (1562)

HEE 0 GE- 3 -FEENG 5 THAA 3 FETEL- 4 -HILT/ 9 FRECA 4 SCYLDINGA// 6   (1563)

HREEOH 4 =AND 0 HEORO- 4 -GRIM/ 3 HRING- 9 -MAEAEL 5 GE- 3 -BRAEGD// 4   (1564)

ALORES 4 OR- 0 -WEENA/ 5 YRRINGA 9 SLOOH// 3   (1565)

                END FOLIO 167R +

TH= 0 HIRE 4 WIOH 3 HALSE/ 6 HEARD 3 GRAAPODE// 5   (1566)

BAAN- 9 -HRINGAS 5 BRAEC/ 3 BIL 2 EAL 4 OHURH- 2 -WOOD// 4   (1567)

FAEAEGNE 4 FLAEAESC- 9 -HOMAN/ 5 HEEO 2 ON 2 FLET 3 GE- 2 -CRONG// 5   (1568)

SWEORD 2 WAES 3 SWAA-9-TIG/ 3 SECG 2 WEORCE 5 GE- 1 -FEH// 5   (1569)

LIIXTE 4 SE 1 LEEOMA/ 9 LEEOHT 3 IN-1-NE 1 STOOD// 5   (1570)

EFNE 3 SWAA 3 OF 2 HEFENE/ 6 HAADRE 9 SCIINEOH// 4   (1571)

RODORES 3 CAN-1-DEL/ 6 HEE 2 AEFTER 4 RECEDE 9 WLAAT.// 6   (1572)

$HWEARF 5 THAA 1 BE 3 WEALLE/ 5 WAEAEPEN 3 HAFENA-9-DE// 8   (1573)

HEARD 2 BE 2 HIL-1-TUM/ 4 HIGE- 4 -LAACES 4 OHEGN// 3   (1574)

YRRE 3 =AND 8 AN- 0 -RAEAED./ 8 NAES 4 SEEO 1 ECG 2 FRACOD// 6   (1575)

HILDE- 2 -RINCE/ 4 AC 1 HEE 9 HRATHE 4 WOLDE// 5   (1576)

GRENDLE 3 FOR- 1 -GYL-2-DAN/ 4 GUUOH- 1 -RAEAESA 9 FELA// 5   (1577)

OHAARA 4 THE 2 HEE 1 GE- 1 -WORHTE/ 5 TOO 0 WEST- 3 -DENUM// 9   (1578)

OFTOR 3 MICLE/ 5 OHONNE 3 ON 1 AEAENNE 4 SIIOH// 5   (1579)

THON= 3 HEE 9 HROOOH- 3 -GAARES/ 5 HEORDH- 3 -GE- 2 -NEEATAS// 6   (1580)

SLOOH 2 ON 0 SWEO-9-FOTE/ 5 SLAEAEPENDE 4 FRAEAET// 2   (1581)

FOLCES 3 DENIGEA/ 4 FYYF- 0 -TYY-9-NE 4 MEN// 3   (1582)

=AND 0 OODHER 2 SWYLC/ 3 UUT 0 OF- 2 -FEREDE// 4   (1583)

LAADH- 2 -LICU 9 LAAC/ 4 HEE 2 HIM 3 THAES 4 LEEAN 3 FOR- 3 -GEALD// 4   (1584)

REETHE 3 CEMPA/ 9   (1585)

        TOO 0 OHAES. 5 THE 1 HEE 4 ON 3 RAESTE 5 GE- 2 -SEAH// 3   (1585)

GUUOH- 2 -WEERIGNE/ 9 GRENDEL 3 LICGAN// 5   (1586)

ALDOR- 3 -LEEAS-1-NE/ 6 SWAA 3 HIM 3 +AEAER 9 GE- 1 -SCOOD// 5   (1587)

HILD 3 AET 1 HEOROTE/ 6 HRAA 1 WIIDE 4 SPRONG// 9   (1588)

SYTHOHAN 5 HEE 2 AEFTER 3 DEEAOHE/ 5 OREPE 4 THROOWADE// 9   (1589)

HEORO- 4 -SWENG 4 HEARDNE/ 5   (1590)

```
=AND 0 HINE 5 THAA 3 HEEAFOE 9 BE- 3 -CEARF.// 7                    (1590)

SOONA 3 TH= 2 GE- 2 -SAAWON/ 4 SNOTTRE 9 CEORLAS// 5                (1591)

               END FOLIO 167V +


HAA 0 DHE 3 MID 3 HROODH- 1 -GAARE/ 5 ON 1 HOLM 8 WLITON// 9        (1592)

H= 1 WAES 4 YYDH- 2 -GE- 3 -BLOND/ 4 EAL 2 GE- 3 -MENGED// 5        (1593)

RIM 8 BLOODE 9 FAAH/ 5 BLONDEN- 3 -FEAXE// 5                        (1594)

OMELE 4 YMB 3 GOODNE/ 9 ON- 3 -GEADOR 4 SPRAEAECON// 5              (1595)

H= 1 HIG 3 THAES 3 AEDHE-2-LINGES/ 9 EFT 3 NE 4 WEENDON// 5         (1596)

H= 1 HEE 3 SIGE- 5 -HREEDHIG/ 4 SEECEAN 9 COOME// 5                 (1597)

AEAER-1-NE 5 THEEODEN/ 5 THAA 1 DHAES 3 MONIGE 5 GE- 9 -WEARDH// 5  (1598)

H= 2 HINE 4 SEEO 4 BRIM- 4 -WYLF/ 4                                 (1599)

     AA- 0 -()BREOTEN*BROTEN 3 HAEF-9-DE.// 7                       (1599)

HAA 1 COOM 4 NOON 3 DAEGES/ 5 NAES 3 OF- 3 -GEEAFON// 3            (1600)

WATE 9 SCYL-1-DINGAS/ 4 GE- 2 -WAAT 3 HIM 3 HAAM 4 THONON// 4       (1601)

OLD- 8 -WINE 9 GUME-3-NA/ 5 GISTAS 5 ()SECAN*SEETAN// 3             (1602)

OODES 3 SEEOCE/ 4 =AND 0 ON 9 MERE 5 STARE-1-DON// 3               (1603)

IISTON 3 =AND 0 NE 2 WEEN-1-DON/ 5                                  (1604)

     TH= 1 HIIE 9 HEORA 4 WINE- 3 -ORI-1-HTEN// 1                   (1604)

ELFNE 6 GE- 1 -SAAWON/ 2 THAA 0 TH= 9 SWEORD 4 ON- 0 -GAN// 4       (1605)

EFTER 5 HEA-2-THO- 3 -SWAATE/ 4 HIL-1-DE- 9 -GI-1-C-1-ELUM// 4      (1606)

IIG- 1 -BIL 4 WANIAN/ 5 THAET 3 WAES 4 WUN-1-DRA 9 SUM.// 5         (1607)

H= 1 HIT 3 EAL 2 GE- 1 -MEALT/ 4 IISE 1 GE- 2 -LIICOST// 4          (1608)

HON= 9 FORSTES 5 BEND/ 3 FAEDER 2 ON- 1 -LAEAETEDH// 5              (1609)

N- 0 -WINDEDH 3 WAEAEL- 9 -RAAPAS/ 4 SEE 0 GE- 4 -WEALD 4 HAFADH// 4 (1610)

AEAELA 3 =AND 0 MAEAELA/ 4 THAET 9 IS 4 SOODH 3 METOD.// 6          (1611)

E 1 NOOM 4 HEE 4 IN 1 THAEAEM 3 WIICU=/ 4 WEDER- 9 -GEEATA 4 LEEOD// 4 (1612)

AADH-1-M- 5 -AEAEHTA 3 MAA/ 4                                       (1613)

     THEEH 2 HEE 4 THAEAER 9 MONIGE 4 GE- 3 -SEAH// 5               (1613)

UUTON 4 THONE 4 HAFELAN/ 9 =AND 0 THAA 3 HILT 3 SOMOD// 4          (1614)

INCE 2 FAAGE/ 4 SWEORD 3 AEAER 1 GE- 9 -MEALT// 5                   (1615)

OR- 3 -BARN 4 BROU-2-DEN- 3 -MAEAEL/ 5                              (1616)

     WAES 3 TH= 3 BLOOD 9 TOO 8 THAES 5 HAAT// 5                    (1616)
```

```
AET-1-TREN 3 ELLOR- 3 -GAEAEST/ 4 SEE 3 THAEAER 9 INNE 3 SWEALT.// 7        (1617)
$SOONA 3 WAES 3 ON 1 SUNDE/ 5                                                (1618)
        SEE 0 THE 9 AEAER 2 AET 3 SAECCE 4 GE- 3 -BAAD// 3                   (1618)
WIIG- 3 -HRYRE 5 WRAADHRA/ 9 WAETER 3 UP 2 THURH- 3 -DEEAF// 4              (1619)
WAEAERON 3 YYDH- 1 -GE- 3 -BLAND/ 9 EAL 3 GE- 4 -FAEAELSOD// 4              (1620)
EEAC-1-NE 5 EAR-1-DAS/ 5 THAA 0 SE 2 ELLOR- 9 -GAAST// 4                    (1621)
OF- 0 -LEET 3 LIIF- 2 -DAGAS/ 6                                             (1622)
        =AND 0 THAAS 4 LAEAENAN 2 GE- 2 -SCEAFT.// 9                        (1622)
$COOM 3 THAA 0 TOO 3 LANDE/ 6 LID- 2 -MANNA 5 HELM// 3                      (1623)
SWIIDH- 9 -MOOD 4 SWYMMAN/ 4 SAEAE- 2 -LAACE 3 GE- 1 -FEAH// 4              (1624)
MAEGEN- 9 -BYR-1-THENNE/ 5 THAARA 3 THE 1 HEE 5 HIM 2 MID 3 HAEFDE.// 9     (1625)
$EEODON 4 HIM 1 THAA 0 TOO- 1 -GEEANES/ 5 GODE 3 THANCODON// 9              (1626)
DHRYYDH- 4 -LIIC 4 THEGNA 4 HEEAP/ 4 THEEOD-1-NES 4 GE- 3 -FEEGON// 9       (1627)
THAES 4 THE 2 HII 1 HYNE 5 GE- 2 -SUND-1-NE/ 4                              (1628)
        GE- 0 -SEEON 2 MOOSTON.// 9                                         (1628)
DHAA 1 WAES 5 OF 1 THAEAEM 5 HROORAN/ 4 HELM 4 =AND 0 BYRNE// 9             (1629)
LUNGRE 5 AA- 0 -LYYSED/ 4 LAGU 2 DRUUSADE// 5                               (1630)
WAETER 9 UNDER 3 WOLCNUM/ 4 WAEL- 1 -DREEO-1-RE 3 FAAG.// 4                 (1631)
FEERDON 9 FORDH 4 THONON/ 4 FEE-1-THE- 5 -LAASTUM// 3                       (1632)
FER-1-H-1-THUM 9 FAEGNE/ 5 FOLD- 1 -WEG 3 MAEAETON// 4                      (1633)
CUUTHE 3 STRAEAETE/ 9 CYNING- 4 -BALDE 4 MEN// 3                            (1634)
FROM 3 THAEAEM 3 HOLM- 9 -CLIFE/ 5 HAFELAN 4 BAEAERON// 3                   (1635)
EARFODH- 2 -LIICE/ 4 HEEORA 9 AEAEG- 3 -HWAE-1-THRU=// 4                    (1636)
FELA- 5 -MOODIGRA/ 4 FEEOWER 1 SCO-1-L-1-DON// 9                            (1637)
ON 1 THAEAEM 4 WAEL- 2 -STENGE/ 4 WEORCUM 3 GE- 1 -FERIAN// 3               (1638)
TOO 9 THAEAEM 3 GOLD- 2 -SELE/ 5 GRENDLES 5 HEEAFOD// 3                     (1639)
OTH 0 DHAET 9 SEM-1-NINGA/ 4 TOO 0 SELE 5 COOMON// 4                        (1640)
```

```
FROME 4 FYRD- 9 -HWATE/ 5 FEEOWER- 1 -TYYNE// 5                            (1641)
GEEATA 3 GONGAN/ 3 GUM- 9 -DRYHTEN 3 MID// 3                               (1642)
```

```
MOODIG 3 ON 1 GE- 3 -MONGE/ 5 MEODO- 9 -WONGAS 5 TRAED.// 6          (1643)

$DHAA 0 COOM 3 IN 1 GAAN/ 4 EALDOR 9 DHEGNA// 5                      (1644)

DAEAEJ- 2 -CEENE 5 MON/ 3 DOOME 5 GE- 2 -WUR-2-THAD// 9             (1645)

HAELE 4 HILDE- 3 -DEEOR/ 6 HROODH- 1 -GAAR 5 GREETAN.// 5           (1646)

THAA 9 WAES 5 BE 1 FEAXE/ 5 ON 1 FLET 3 BOREN// 4                   (1647)

GREND-2-LES 9 HEEAFOO/ 4 THAEAER 2 GUMAN 3 DRUNCON// 4              (1648)

EGES- 3 -LIIC 2 FOR 9 EORLUM/ 5 =AND 0 THAEAERE 4 IDESE 4 MID// 3   (1649)

WLITE- 5 -SEEON 3 WRAEAET- 9 -LIIC/ 4 WERAS 5 ON 0 SAAWON.// 9      (1650)


                    .XXIIII                                          (FITT)

$$BEED- 0 -WULF 4 MATHELODE/ 7 BEARN 4 ECG- 2 -THEEOWES// 9         (1651)

HWAET 2 WEE 4 THEE 5 THAAS 4 +SAEAE- 0 -LAAC/ 4                     (1652)

            SUNU 4 HEALF- 1 -DENES// 9                              (1652)

LEEOD 3 SCYL-1-DINGA/ 5 LUSTU= 5 BROOHTON// 4                       (1653)

TIIRES 9 TOO 2 TAACNE/ 6 THE 3 THUU 2 HEER 4 TOO 0 LOOCAST.// 7     (1654)

IC 2 TH= 1 UN- 9 -SOOFTE/ 5 EALDRE 4 GE- 3 -DIIGDE// 5             (1655)

WIGGE 4 UNDER 9 WAETERE/ 5 WEORC 3 GE- 1 -NEETH-1-DE// 5           (1656)

EAR-1-FODH- 3 -LIICE/ 9 AET- 1 -RIHTE 6 WAES// 3                   (1657)

GUUDH 3 GE- 2 -TWAEAEFED/ 4 NYMDHE 9 MEC 3 GOD 3 SCYLDE.// 7       (1658)

$NE 1 MEAHTE 4 IC 3 AET 1 HIL-9-DE/ 5 MID 3 HRUNTINGE// 6          (1659)

WIHT 3 GE- 2 -WYRCAN/ 9 THEEAH 2 TH= 2 WAEAEPEN 4 DUGE.// 7        (1660)

AC 1 MEE 4 GE- 3 -UUDHE/ 9 YLDA 5 WALDEND// 4                      (1661)

TH= 1 IC 2 ON 1 WAAGE 5 GE- 0 -SEAH/ 3 WLITIG 9 HANGIAN// 4        (1662)

                    END FOLIO 169R +


EALD- 3 -SWEORD 4 EEACEN/ 4 OFTOST 4 WIISODE// 9                   (1663)

WINIGEA 4 LEEASUM/ 6 TH= 0 IC 2 DHYY 2 WAEAEPNE 4 GE- 1 -BRAEAED.// 9   (1664)

OF- 8 -SLOOH 3 DHAA 5 AET 1 THAEAERE 5 SAEGCE/ 7                   (1665)

            THAA 1 MEE 4 SAEAEL 9 AA- 8 -GEALD// 5                 (1665)

HUUSES 4 HYRDAS/ 6 THAA 2 TH= 3 HILDE- 5 -BIL// 5                  (1666)

FOR- 9 -BARN 5 BROGDEN- 3 -MAEAEL./ 6                              (1667)

            SWAA 3 TH= 2 BLOOD 3 GE- 2 -SPRANG// 9                 (1667)

HAATOST 5 HEATHO- 3 -SWAATA/ 5 IC 1 TH= 3 HILT 3 THANAN// 3        (1668)
```

FEEON-9-DUM 4 AET- 2 -FERE-2-DE/ 5 FYR-1-EN- 4 -DAEAE-3-DA 3 WRAEC// 4   (1669)

DEEADH- 9 -CWEALM 4 DENIGEA/ 4 SWAA 2 HIT 3 GE- 2 -DEEFE 4 WAES.// 5   (1670)

IC 9 HIT 3 THEE 2 THON= 3 GE- 3 -HAATE/ 5   (1671)

        TH= 1 THUU 2 ON 3 HEOROTE 4 MOOST// 9   (1671)

SORH- 2 -LEEAS 5 SWEFAN/ 4 MID 2 THIINRA 4 SECGA 3 GE- 1 -DRYHT// 9   (1672)

=AND 8 THEGNA 4 GE- 3 -HWYLC/ 5 THIINRA 5 LEEODA// 4   (1673)

DUGUDHE 4 =AND 0 IO-9-GOTHE/ 6   (1674)

        TH= 2 THUU 1 HIM 3 ON- 2 -DRAEAE-1-DAN 4 NE 2 THEARFT// 4   (1674)

THEEO-9-DEN 2 SCYLDINGA/ 5 ON 1 THAA 3 HEALFE// 5   (1675)

ALDOR- 3 -BEALU 9 EORLUM/ 4 SWAA 2 THUU 2 AEAER 2 DYDEST.// 7   (1676)

DHAA 3 WAES 3 GYLDEN 9 HILT/ 5 GAMELUM 3 RINCE// 6   (1677)

HAARUM 4 HILD- 2 -FRU-9-MAN/ 4 ON 2 HAND 3 GYFEN// 4   (1678)

ENTA 4 AEAER- 2 -GE- 1 -WEORC/ 9 HIT 1 ON 3 AEAEHT 4 GE- 3 -HWEARF// 5   (1679)

AEFTER 4 DEEOFLA 3 HRY-9-RE/ 5 DENIGEA 4 FREEAN// 5   (1680)

WUNDOR- 2 -SMITHA 3 GE- 9 -WEORC/ 5   (1681)

        =AND 0 THAA 3 THAAS 4 WOROLD 3 OF- 1 -GEAF// 4   (1681)

GROM- 9 -HEORT 4 GUMA/ 4 GODES 4 =AND- 0 -SACA// 4   (1682)

MORDH-1-RES 3 SCYL-9-DIG/ 5 =AND 0 HIS 4 MOODOR 4 EEAC// 4   (1683)

ON 0 GE- 4 -WEALD 3 GE- 2 -HWE-9-ARF/ 5 WOROLD- 4 -CYNINGA// 5   (1684)

DHAEAEM 3 SEELESTAN/ 3 BE 9 +SAEAEM 4 TWEEONU=// 4   (1685)

        END FOLIO 169V +

DHAARA 2 THE 3 ON 2 SCE-2-DENIGGE/ 8 SCEAT-9-TAS 4 DAEAEL-1-DE.// 5   (1686)

HROODH- 2 -GAAR 4 MADHELO-1-DE/ 6 HYLT 9 SCEEAWODE// 6   (1687)

EALDE 5 LAAFE/ 5 ON 0 DHAEAEM 3 WAES 4 OOR 8 WRI-9-TEN// 5   (1688)

FYRN- 3 -GE- 3 -WIN-1-NES./ 6 SYDH-3-THAN 3 FLOOD 4 OF- 2 -SLOOH// 9   (1689)

GIFEN 3 GEEOTENDE/ 4 GIIGANTA 4 CYN// 4   (1690)

FREEC-1-NE 8 GE- 9 -FEERDON/ 4 TH= 1 WAES 4 FREM-2-DE 4 THEEOD// 4   (1691)

EECEAN 4 DRYHTNE/ 9 HIM 3 THAES 3 ENDE- 4 -LEEAN// 5   (1692)

THURH 4 WAETERES 4 WYLM/ 9 WALDEND 4 SEALDE.// 7   (1693)

$SWAA 3 WAES 4 ON 0 DHAEAEM 4 SCENNU=/ 9 SCIIRAN 4 GOLDES// 5   (1694)

THURH 3 RUUN- 2 -STAFAS/ 4 RIHTE 8 GE- 9 -MEARCOD// 4   (1695)

GE- 0 -SETED 4 =AND 0 GE- 2 -SAEAED/ 5   (1696)

```
        HWAAM 4 TH= 2 SWEORD 9 GE- 3 -WORHT// 5                    (1696)

IIRENA 4 CYST/ 4 AEAEREST 4 WAEAERE// 5                            (1697)

WREO-9-THEN- 5 -HILT 5 =AND 0 WYRM- 3 -FAAH/ 4                     (1698)

        DHAA 0 SE 3 WIISA 4 SPRAEC// 3                             (1698)

SU-9-NU 5 HEALF- 2 -DENES/ 6 SWIIGEDON 4 EALLE.// 7               (1699)

TH= 2 LAA 9 MAEG 3 SECGAN/ 5 SEE 0 THE 3 SOODH 4 =AND 0 RIHT// 5  (1700)

FREMEDH 9 ON 2 FOLCE/ 6 FEOR 4 EAL 3 GE- 2 -MON// 4              (1701)

EALD 3 .=EETHEL.- 2 -WEARD/ 9 TH= 0 DHES 4 EORL 4 WAEAERE// 6    (1702)

GE- 2 -BOREN 5 BETERA/ 4 BLAEAED 8 IS 9 AA- 0 -RAEAERED// 6      (1703)

GEOND 4 WIID- 3 -WEGAS/ 6 WINE 4 MIIN 4 3EEO- 0 -WULF// 9        (1704)

DHIIN 1 OFER 5 THEEODA 4 GE- 2 -HWYLCE/ 5                        (1705)

        EAL 4 THUU 1 HIT 3 GE- 9 -THYLDUM 6 HEALDEST// 5         (1705)

MAEGEN 3 MID 1 MOODES 3 SNYT-9-TRUM/ 4                           (1706)

        IC 1 THEE 2 SCEAL 6 MIINE 5 GE- 1 -LAEAESTAN// 4         (1706)

FREEODE 9 SWAA 3 WIT 2 FUR-1-DHUM 3 SPRAEAECON/ 4               (1707)

        DHUU 1 SCEALT 4 TOO 1 FROO-9-FRE 7 WEOR-8-THAN// 3       (1707)

EAL 0 LANG- 4 -TWIIDIG/ 5 LEEODU= 2 THIINU=// 9                  (1708)

                    END FOLIO 170R ↑


HAELEDHUM 4 TOO 2 HELPE/ 5 NE 2 WEARDH 5 HERE- 2 -MOOD 9 SWAA// 8  (1709)

EAFORUM 3 ECG- 2 -WELAN/ 4 AAR- 3 -SCYL-1-DINGUM.// 9             (1710)

$NE 8 GE- 8 -WEEOX 6 HEE 2 HIM 3 TOO 0 WILLAN/ 4                 (1711)

        AC 1 TOO 2 WAEL- 3 -FEAL-9-LE// 8                        (1711)

=AND 0 TOO 0 DEEADH- 3 -CWALUM/ 4 DENIGA 4 LEEODU=// 3           (1712)

BREEAT 9 BOLGEN- 4 -MOOD/ 6 BEEOD- 2 -GE- 8 -NEEATAS// 4         (1713)

EAXL- 3 -GE- 9 -STEALLAN/ 4 OTH 2 TH= 2 HEE 3 AANA 5 HWEARF// 4  (1714)

MAEAER-2-E 2 THEEO-9-DEN./ 4 MON- 1 -DREEAMU= 4 FROM// 4         (1715)

DHEEA4 3 THE 3 HINE 9 MIHTIG 4 GOD/ 4 MAEGENES 4 WYNNU=// 3      (1716)

EAFETHUM 9 STEEPTE/ 5 OFER 3 EALLE 5 MEN// 4                     (1717)

FORDH 3 GE- 1 -FREME-9-DE/ 6                                     (1718)

        HWAETHERE 6 HIM 3 ON 1 FERH-8-THE 5 GREEOW// 4           (1718)

BREEOST- 9 -HORD 6 BLOOD- 3 -REEOW/ 5 NALLAS 5 BEEAGAS 5 GEAF.// 3  (1719)

DE-9-NUM 4 AEFTER 4 DOOME/ 5 DREEAM- 3 -LEEAS 4 GE- 2 -+BAAD// 3   (1720)
```

TH= 9 HEE 1 THAES 3 GE- 3 -WIN-1-NES/ 5 WEORC 3 THROO-2-WADE// 5   (1721)

LEEOD- 2 -BEA-9-LO 4 LONGSUM/ 4 DHUU 1 THEE 4 LAEAER 5 BE 2 THON// 5   (1722)

GU=- 2 -CYSTE 9 ON- 1 -GIT./ 6 IC 2 THIS 3 GID 3 BE 1 THEE// 5   (1723)

AA- 0 -WRAEC 3 WIN-1-TRUM 9 FROOD/ 3 WUNDOR 4 IS 2 TOO 2 SECGAN-1-NE// 6   (1724)

HUU 0 MIHTIG 9 GOD/ 4 MAN-2-NA 3 CYNNE// 7   (1725)

THURH 4 SIIDNE 4 SEFAN/ 9 SNYTTRU 5 BRYT-2-TADH// 4   (1726)

EARD 4 =AND 0 EORL- 4 -SCIPE/ 4 HEE 9 AAH 3 EALRA 3 GE- 4 -WEALD.// 7   (1727)

HWIILU= 4 HEE 1 ON 1 LUFAN/ 3 LAEAE-9-TEDH 6 HWORFAN// 4   (1728)

MONNES 4 MOOD- 3 -GE- 3 -THONC/ 3 MAEAE-3-RAN 3 CYNNES.// 6   (1729)

$SELEDH 5 HIM 3 ON 2 EETHLE/ 5 EORTHAN 9 WYNNE// 6   (1730)

TOO 2 HEAL-3-DAN-1-NE/ 6 HLEEO- 4 -BURH 3 WERA// 9   (1731)

END FOLIO 170V +

GE- 3 -DEEDH 4 HIM 2 SWAA 2 GE- 3 -WEAL-2-DENE/ 5   (1732)

          WOROLDE 8 DAEAE-9-LAS// 5   (1732)

SIIDE 4 RIICE/ 6 TH= 2 HEE 4 HIS 3 SELFA 5 NE 3 MAEG// 9   (1733)

HIS 8 UN- 8 -SNYTTRUM/ 5 EN-1-DE 4 GE- 3 -THEN-1-CEAN.// 5   (1734)

WUNADH 9 HEE 3 ON 2 WISTE/ 6 NOO 2 HINE 6 WIHT 4 DHELEDH// 4   (1735)

AADL 9 NEE 3 YLDO/ 5 NEE 3 HIM 4 IN-1-WIT- 3 -SORH// 5   (1736)

ON 0 ()SEFADH*SEFAN 9 SWEOR-2-CEDH/ 4   (1737)

          NEE 0 GE- 5 -SACU 4 OO- 0 -HWAEAER// 5   (1737)

ECG- 3 -HETE 9 EEOWEDH/ 5 AC 2 HIM 3 EAL 3 WOROLD// 5   (1738)

WEN-2-DEDH 3 ON 1 WIL-9-LAN/ 5 HEE 2 THAET 4 WYRSE 5 NE 2 CON.// 9   (1739)

                    .XXV.   (FITT)

$ODH 3 TH= 2 HIM 3 ON 0 IN-1-NAN/ 3 OFER- 4 -HYGDA 5 DAEAEL// 4   (1740)

WEAXEDH 9 =AND 0 WRIIDADH/ 6 THON= 3 SE 2 WEARD 4 SWEFEDH// 4   (1741)

SAAWELE 1 HYRDE/ 9 BIDH 4 SE 3 SLAEAEP 3 TOO 1 FAEST// 5   (1742)

BIS-1-GUM 3 GE- 2 -BUNDEN/ 9 BONA 5 SWIIDHE 4 NEEAH// 4   (1743)

SEE 0 THE 5 OF 1 FLAAN- 5 -BOGAN/ 9 FYRENUM 4 SCEEO-1-TEDH// 5   (1744)

THON= 3 BIDH 4 ON 2 HRETHRE/ 9 UNDER 5 HELM 4 DREPEN// 5   (1745)

BITERAN 4 STRAEAELE/ 9 HIM 3 BE- 4 -BEOR-2-GAN 4 NE 3 CON// 4   (1746)

WOOM 3 WUN-2-DOR- 9 -BE- 2 -BODUM/ 5 WER-2-GAN 3 GAASTES// 5   (1747)

THINCEOH 4 HIM 9 TOO 0 LYYTEL/ 5 TH= 2 HEE 8 LANGE 6 HEEO-1-LO// 4   (1748)

GYYT-9-SAOH 5 GROM- 4 -HYYOIG/ 5 NALL-1-AS 5 ON 1 GYLP 9 SELEDH// 5   (1749)

()FAEDDE*FAEAETTE 4 BEEAGAS/ 6   (1750)

     =AND 0 HEE 2 THAA 4 FORDH- 9 -GE- 1 -SCEAFT// 5   (1750)

FOR- 3 -GYTEDH 5 =AND 0 FOR- 3 -GYYMEDH/ 9   (1751)

     THAES 5 THE 4 HIM 3 AEAER 2 GOO 2 SEALDE// 7   (1751)

WULDRES 9 WALDEND/ 5 WEORDH- 4 -MYNDA 3 OAEAEL.// 7   (1752)

    + END FOLIO 171R

HIT 3 ON 2 ENDE- 9 -STAEF/ 5 EFT 3 GE- 3 -LIMPEDH// 5   (1753)

TH= 0 SE 3 LIIC- 3 -HOMA/ 9 LAEAENE 8 GE- 2 -DREEOSEDH// 5   (1754)

FAEAEGE 4 GE- 2 -FEALLEDH/ 5 FEEHDH 8 OOTHER 9 TOO// 8   (1755)

SEE 0 THE 3 UN- 1 -MURN- 1 -LIICE/ 6 MAAO-2-MAS 3 OAEAEL-2-ETH// 9   (1756)

EORLES 3 AEAER- 3 -GE- 4 -STREEON/ 5 EGESAN 3 NE 3 GYYMEDH.// 9   (1757)

BE- 8 -BEOR-1-H 1 THEE 4 DHONE 3 BEALO- 2 -NIIDH/ 6   (1758)

     BEEO- 0 -WULF 3 LEEOFA// 9   (1758)

SECG 3 BETSTA/ 5 =AND 0 THEE 2 TH= 1 SEELRE 4 GE- 1 -CEEOS// 4   (1759)

EECE 3 RAEAE-1-OAS/ 9 OFER- 4 -HYYDA 3 NE 1 GYYM// 5   (1760)

MAEAERE 4 CEMPA/ 4 NUU 1 IS 3 THIINES 9 MAEGNES 5 BLAEO// 4   (1761)

AANE 4 HWIILE/ 5 EFT 3 SOONA 4 BIDH// 4   (1762)

TH= 9 THEC 8 AADL 3 OOHDHE 4 ECG/ 4 EOFOTHES 4 GE- 2 -TWAEAEFEDH// 4   (1763)

OOHDHE 9 FYYRES 5 FENG/ 4 OOHDHE 3 FLOODES 4 WYLM// 4   (1764)

OOHDHE 3 GRIPE 9 MEECES/ 5 OOHDHE 3 GAARES 4 FLIHT// 5   (1765)

OOHDHE 3 ATOL 4 YLDO/ 9 OOHDHE 3 EEAGENA 4 BEARHTM// 4   (1766)

FOR- 0 -SITEDH 4 =AND 0 FOR- 3 -SWOR-9-CEDH/ 5 SEM-1-NINGA 4 BIDH.// 5   (1767)

TH= 1 DHEC 3 ORYHT- 4 -GUMA/ 3 DEEADH 9 OFER- 4 -SWYYDHEDH// 4   (1768)

SWAA 2 IC 3 HRING- 2 -DENA/ 5 HUND 2 MISSEE-9-RA// 6   (1769)

WEEOLD 2 UNDER 5 WOLC-1-NUM/ 4 =AND 0 HIG 3 WIG-1-GE 4 BE- 9 -LEEAC// 5   (1770)

MANIGU= 4 MAEAEGTHA/ 4 GEOND 4 THYSNE 4 MID-9-DAN- 3 -GEARD.// 6   (1771)

AESCU= 3 =AND 1 ECGUM/ 4 TH= 0 IC 2 MEE 4 AEAENIG-9-NE// 5   (1772)

UNDER 3 SWEGLES 5 BE- 1 -GONG/ 1 GE- 5 -SACAN 2 NE 9 TEALDE.// 7   (1773)

HWAET 4 MEE 3 THAES 3 ON 0 EETHLE/ 5 ED- 1 -()WENDAN*WENDEN 9 CWOOM// 3   (1774)

GYRN 3 AEFTER 4 GOMENE/ 4 SEOTH-1-DHAN 4 GREN-9-DEL 4 WEARDH// 4   (1775)

EALD- 2 -GE- 4 -WINNA/ 3 IN- 0 -GENGA 4 MIIN.// 9   (1776)

END FOLIO 171V +

$IC 1 THAEAERE 4 SOOGNE/ 5 SIN- 1 -GAALES 4 WAEG// 5   (1777)

MOOD- 3 -CEARE 9 MICLE/ 6 THAES 1 SIG 4 METODE 6 THANC// 3   (1778)

EECEAN 2 DRYHT-9-NE/ 5 THAES 2 DHE 2 IC 1 ON 1 ALDRE 4 GE- 2 -BAAD// 4   (1779)

TH= 1 IC 2 ON 2 THONE 9 HAFELAN/ 5 HEORO- 4 -DREEORIGNE// 5   (1780)

OFER 2 EALD 8 GE- 9 -WIN/ 3 EEAGUM 3 STARIGE.// 7   (1781)

GAA 0 NUU 1 TOO 0 SETLE/ 8 SYM-9-BEL- 4 -WYNNE 5 DREEOH// 4   (1782)

WIIG- 0 -GE- 5 -WEORTHAD/ 4 UNC 8 SCEAL 9 WORN 2 FELA// 5   (1783)

MAATH-1-MA 4 GE- 2 -MAEAENRA/ 5 SITHDHAN 2 MOR-9-GEN 4 BIDH.// 6   (1784)

GEEAT 3 WAES 2 GLAED- 2 -MOOD/ 4 GEEONG 3 SOONA 8 TOO// 9   (1785)

SETLES 4 NEEOSAN/ 4 SWAA 3 SE 3 SNOT-1-TRA 4 HEHT.// 4   (1786)

THAA 8 WAES 9 EFT 2 SWAA 2 AEAER/ 4 ELLEN- 3 -ROOFUM// 4   (1787)

FLET- 1 -SITTEN-1-DUM/ 9 FAEAEGERE 5 GE- 2 -REORDED// 4   (1788)

NIIOWAN 3 STEFNE/ 5 NIHT- 9 -HELM 4 GE- 2 -SWEARC// 5   (1789)

DEORC 4 OFER 4 DRYHT- 4 -GUMU=/ 9 DUGUDH 3 EAL 4 AA- 0 -RAAS// 5   (1790)

WOLDE 4 BLONDEN- 3 -FEAX/ 4 BED-9-DES 4 NEEOSAN// 4   (1791)

GAMELA 3 SCYL-1-DING/ 2 GEEAT 2 UN- 0 -IG- 9 -METES 4 WEEL.// 7   (1792)

ROCFNE 4 RAND- 2 -WIGAN/ 4 RESTAN 2 LYSTE// 9   (1793)

SOONA 2 HIM 2 SELE- 5 -THEGN/ 3 SIIDHES 3 WEERGU=// 4   (1794)

FEORRAN- 9 -CUNDUM/ 4 FORDH 2 WIISADE// 5   (1795)

SEE 0 FOR 3 AND- 0 -RYSNUM/ 9 EALLE 4 BE- 1 -()WEOTENE*WEOTEDE// 6 (1796)

THEGNES 4 THEARFE/ 5 SWYLCE 9 THYY 2 DOOGORE// 6   (1797)

HEATHO- 3 -LIIDHENDE/ 6 HABBAN 3 SCOLDON.// 9   (1798)

RESTE 5 HINE 4 THAA 2 RUUM- 3 -HEORT/ 6 RECED 4 HLIIUADE// 9   (1799)

GEEAP 4 =AND 0 GOLD- 2 -FAAH/ 3 GAEST 3 INNE 4 SWAEF// 4   (1800)

OTH 3 TH= 3 HREFN 9 BLACA/ 5 HEOFONES 4 WYNNE// 4   (1801)

BLIIDH- 4 -HEORT 3 BODODE/ 9 DHAA 8 COOM 8 BEORHT 3 SCACAN// 8   (1802)

END FOLIO 172R +

*SCIIMA 8 *OFER 8 *SCEADWA/ 8 SCA-1-THAN 3 OONET-1-TON// 9   (1803)

WAEAERON 3 AETHELINGAS/ 5 EFT 3 TOO 2 LEEODUM// 4   (1804)

FUUSE 3 TOO 9 ()FARENE*FARENNE/ 5 ()NE 1 WOLDE 5 FEOR 4 THANON// 4   (1805)

CUMA 3 COL-9-LEN- 8 -FERHDH/ 5 CEEOLES 4 NEEOSAN.// 7   (1806)

$HEHT 4 THAA 2 SE 1 HEAR-9-DA/ 8 HRUNTING 5 BERAN// 3   (1807)

SUNU 3 ECG- 0 -LAAFES/ 4 HEHT 9 HIS 8 SWEORD 2 NIMAN// 4   (1808)

LEEOF- 0 -LIIC 4 IIREN/ 3 SAEGDE 3 HIM 9 THAES 5 LEEANES 5 THANC// 4   (1809)

CWAED4 4 HEE 2 THONE 4 GUUDH- 2 -WINE/ 9 GOODNE 4 TEAL-1-DE.// 5   (1810)

WIIG- 2 -CRAEFTIGNE/ 5 NALES 9 WORDUM 1 LOOG// 4   (1811)

MEECES 3 ECGE/ 5 TH= 1 WAES 3 MOODIG 4 SECG// 9   (1812)

=AND 8 THAA 1 SIIDH- 3 -FROME/ 5 SEARWU= 1 GEARWE// 4   (1813)

WIIGEND 3 WAEAERON./ 9 $EEODE 5 WEORDH 4 DENUM// 4   (1814)

AETHELING 8 TOO 2 YPPAN/ 9 THAEAER 2 SE 3 OOTHER 4 WAES// 6   (1815)

()HELLE*HAELE 5 HIL-1-DE- 3 -DEEOR/ 4 HRJODH- 9 -GAAR 5 GREETTE.// 9   (1816)

XXVI.   (FITT)

$BEEO- 8 -WULF 5 MATHELODE/ 5 BEARN 3 ECG- 2 -THEEOWES// 4   (1817)

NUU 9 WEE 4 SAEAE- 1 -LIIDHEND/ 4 SECGAN 3 WYLLADH// 4   (1818)

FEOR-1-RAN 2 CU-9-MENE/ 5 TH= 1 WEE 2 FUNDIADH// 6   (1819)

HIGE- 3 -LAAC 3 SEECAN/ 4 WAEAERON 9 HEER 2 TELA// 5   (1820)

WILLU= 3 BE- 1 -WENEDE/ 6 THUU 0 UUS 3 WEEL 1 DOHTEST.// 9   (1821)

$GIF 3 IC 2 THON-1-NE 5 ON 1 EOR-1-THAN/ 4 OO- 0 -WIHTE 3 MAEG// 3   (1822)

THIIN-9-RE 4 MOOD- 3 -LUFAN/ 4 MAARAN 2 TILIAN.// 5   (1823)

GUMENA 9 DRYHTEN/ 4 DHON-1-NE 4 IC 1 GYYT 4 DYDE// 5   (1824)

GUUDH- 3 -GE- 9 -WEORCA/ 5 IC 2 BEEO 3 GEARO 2 SOONA.// 7   (1825)

GIF 3 IC 4 THAET 0 GE- 9 -FRICGE/ 5 OFER 4 FLOODA 4 BE- 0 -GANG// 5   (1826)

        END FOLIO 172V +

TH= 1 THEC 3 YMB- 9 -SIT-1-TEND/ 4 EGESAN 5 THYYWADH// 5   (1827)

SWAA 3 THEC 4 HETENDE/ 9 HWIILUM 2 DYDON.// 5   (1828)

$IC 1 THEE 3 THUUSENDA/ 6 THEGNA 3 BRIN-3-GE// 7   (1829)

HAELETHA 3 TOO 1 HELPE/ 5 IC 0 ON 3 HIGE- 3 -LAACE 9 WAAT// 2   (1830)

GEEATA 3 DRYHTEN/ 5 THEEAH 2 DHE 1 HEE 3 GEONG 9 SYY// 4   (1831)

FOLCES 4 HYR-1-DE/ 5 TH= 1 HEE 1 MEC 5 FREM-1-MAN 9 WILE// 6   (1832)

()WEORDUM*WORDUM 4 =AND 0 ()WOR*WEOR-1-CUM/ 5   (1833)

                              65

TH= 1 IC 3 THEE 3 WEEL 2 HERIGE// 9   (1833)

=AND 0 THEE 1 TOO 2 GEEOCE/ 4 GAAR- 2 -HOLT 4 BERE// 5   (1834)

MAEGENES 9 FULTUM/ 5 THAEAER 2 OHEE 5 BIOH 3 MAN-1-NA 5 THEARF// 4   (1835)

GIF 9 HIM 3 THONNE 6 HREETH- 0 -()RINC*RIIC/ 5 TOO 1 HOFUM 3 GEEATA// 9 (1836)

GE- 1 -()THINGED*THINGEDH 3 THEEODNES 5 BEARN/ 4   (1837)

      HEE 2 MAEG 1 THAEAER 3 FE-9-LA.// 4   (1837)

FREEONDA 4 FINDAN/ 5 FEOR- 3 -CYYTHDHE 5 BEEODH// 9   (1838)

SEELRAN 3 GE- 0 -SOOHTE/ 6 THAEAEM 3 THE 1 HIM 3 SELFA 3 DEEAH.// 9 (1839)

$HROODH- 2 -GAAR 5 MATHELODE/ 6 HIM 2 ON 1 =AND- 0 -SWARE// 4   (1840)

THEE 9 THAA 3 WORD- 2 -CWYDAS/ 5 WIG-1-TIG 3 DRIHTEN// 5   (1841)

ON 0 SEFAN 9 SENDE/ 5 NE 2 HYYRDE 5 IC 1 SNOTOR- 4 -LIICOR// 5   (1842)

ON 1 SWAA 9 GEONGUM 4 FEORE/ 5 GUMAN 4 THINGIAN// 5   (1843)

THUU 1 EART 9 MAEGENES 4 STRANG/ 5 =AND 0 ON 1 MOODE 5 FROOD// 4 (1844)

WIIS 2 WORD- 9 -CWIDA/ 5 WEEN 1 IC 3 TALIGE// 5   (1845)

GIF 1 TH= 1 GE- 2 -GANGEDH/ 4 THAET 9 DHE 1 GAAR 2 NYMEDH// 7   (1846)

HILD 2 HEORU- 3 -GRIM-2-ME/ 2 HREETH-9-LES 4 EAFERAN// 4   (1847)

AAOL 3 OTHDHE 4 IIREN/ 4 EALDOR 4 DHIINNE// 9   (1848)

FOLCES 5 HYRDE/ 6 =AND 0 THUU 1 THIIN 2 FEORH 5 HAFAST.// 4   (1849)

TH= 1 THE 9 +SAEAE- 3 -GEEATAS/ 5 SEELR-1-AN 3 NAEBBEN// 4   (1850)

      + END FOLIO 173R

TOO 0 GE- 1 -CEEOSEN-3-NE/ 8 CYNING 2 AEAENIGNE// 5   (1851)

HORD- 2 -WEARD 4 HAEL-1-E-1-THA/ 9 GYF 1 THUU 2 HEALDAN 5 WYLT// 5 (1852)

MAAGA 2 RIICE/ 6 MEE 2 THIIN 9 MOOD- 4 -SEFA// 4   (1853)

LIICAJH 4 LENG 5 SWAA 4 WEEL/ 4 LEEOFA 3 BEEO- 9 -WULF// 6   (1854)

HAFAST 3 THUU 0 GE- 3 -FEERED/ 4 TH= 1 THAAM 3 FOLCUM 9 SCEAL// 5 (1855)

GEEA-1-TA 3 LEEODUM/ 4 =AND 0 GAAR- 3 -DENUM// 4   (1856)

SIB 9 GE- 4 -()MAENUM*MAEAENE/ 6 =AND 0 SACU 3 RESTAN// 4   (1857)

INWIT- 3 -NIITHAS/ 9 THE 8 HIIE 5 AEAER 2 DRUGON// 5   (1858)

WESAN 4 THEN-1-DEN 3 IC 4 WEAL-9-DE/ 8 WIIDAN 2 RIICES// 7   (1859)

MAATHMAS 4 GE- 2 -MAEAENE/ 4 MA-9-NIG 4 OOTHERNE// 6   (1860)

GOODUM 4 GE- 0 -GREETTAN/ 4 OFER 9 GANOTES 7 BAEDH// 4   (1861)

SCEAL 8 HRING- 3 INACA/ 4 OFER 9 HEA-3-()THU*FU 4 BRINGAN// 5 (1862)

+LAAC 4 =AND 0 LUF- 3 -TAACEN/ 4 IC 0 THAA 9 LEEODE 4 +WAAT// 5   (1863)

GEE 1 WIDH 4 FEEOND 4 GEE 0 WIDH 4 FREEOND/ 9 FAESTE 5 GE- 2 -WORHTE// 7   (1864)

AEAEG- 1 -HWAES 4 UN- 1 -TAEAELE/ 5 EAL-9-DE 4 WIISAN.// 6   (1865)

DHAA 0 GIIT 4 HIM 2 EORLA 3 HLEEO/ 5 INNE 9 GE- 4 -SEALDE// 6   (1866)

MAGO 4 HEALF- 2 -DE-2-NES/ 6 MAATHMAS 9 ().XII.*TWELFE// 5   (1867)

HEET 1 ()IN-1-()NE*HINE 5 MID 1 THAEAEM 5 LAACUM/ 4 LEEODE 9 SWAEAESE// 6 (1868)

SEECEAN 4 ON 0 GE- 2 -SYNTUM/ 3 SNUUDE 5 EFT 9 CUMAN// 2   (1869)

GE- 5 -CYSTE 5 THAA/ 2 CYNING 3 AETHELUM 2 +GOOD// 9   (1870)

THEEODEN 4 SCYLDINGA/ 5 DHEGN 4 BETSTAN// 4   (1871)

=AND 0 BE 8 HEALSE 9 GE- 2 -NAM/ 5 HRURON 3 HIM 3 TEEARAS// 4   (1872)

BLON-1-DEN- 9 -FEAXUM/ 5 HIM 3 WAES 5 BEEGA 4 WEEN// 3   (1873)

EALDUM 3 IN- 9 -FRO-1-DUM/ 4 OOTHRES 4 SWIIDHOR// 4   (1874)

            + END FOLIO 173V

TH= 1 ()HE*HIIE 2 SEODHDHAN 8 *NOO/ 9 GE- 1 -SEEON 4 MOOSTON// 3   (1875)

MOODIGE 4 ON 1 METHLE/ 8 WAES 9 HIM 3 SE 1 MAN 4 TOO 1 THON 3 LEEOF// 5   (1876)

TH= 1 HEE 2 THONE 4 BREEOST- 9 -WYLM/ 3 FOR- 3 -BERAN 3 NE 3 MEHTE.// 6   (1877)

AC 1 HIM 8 ON 9 HRETHRE/ 6 HYGE- 3 -BENDUM 3 FAEST// 4   (1878)

AEFTER 1 DEEO-9-RUM 4 MEN/ 2 DYRNE 4 LANGADH.// 5   (1879)

BEORN 2 WIDH 2 BLOO-9-DE/ 6 HIM 1 BEEO- 3 -WULF 5 THANAN// 4   (1880)

GUUDH- 1 -RINC 4 GOLD- 9 -WLANC/ 5 GRAES- 4 -MOLDAN 4 TRAED// 4   (1881)

SINCE 3 HREE-9-MIG/ 1 +SAEAE- 4 -GENGA 3 BAAD// 1   (1882)

()AGE)*AAGEND- 1 -FREEAN/ 3 SEE 1 THE 9 ON 2 AN-1-CRE 5 +RAAD// 4   (1883)

THAA 2 WAES 3 ON 1 GANGE/ 5 GIFU 9 HROODH- 3 -GAARES// 5   (1884)

OFT 1 GE- 4 -AEHTED/ 3 TH= 1 WAES 3 AAN 9 CYNING// 5   (1885)

AEAEG- 2 -HWAES 4 OR- 0 -LEAHTRE/ 5   (1886)

            OTH 2 TH= 1 HINE 9 YLDO 5 BE- 3 -NAM// 5   (1886)

MAEGENES 5 WYNNUM/ 3 SEE 9 THE 3 OFT 4 MA-2-NEGUM 5 SCOOD.// 9   (1887)

                .XXVII.   (FITT)

$$CWOOM 7 THAA 1 TOO 2 FLOODE/ 5 FELA- 4 -MOODIGRA// 9   (1888)

HAEG- 3 -STEAL-1-DRA 8 *HEEAP/ 8 HRING- 4 -NET 3 BAEAERON// 3   (1889)

LO-9-CENE 6 LEODHO- 4 -SYRCAN/ 4 LAND- 3 -WEARD 3 ON- 9 -FAND// 4   (1890)

                67

EFT- 2 -SIIDH 4 EORLA/ 5 SWAA 2 HEE 3 AEAER 3 DYDE// 9   (1891)

NOO 3 HEE 3 MID 4 HEAR-1-ME/ 6 OF 4 HLIIDHES 4 NOSAN// 9   (1892)

END FOLIO 174R +

GAESTAS 8 GREETTE/ 5 AC 1 HIM 1 TOO- 2 -GEEANES 4 RAAD// 9   (1893)

CWAEDH 4 TH= 2 WIL- 2 -CUMAN/ 3 WE-1-DERA 5 LEEODUM// 4   (1894)

SCA-9-THAN 8 +SCIIR- 4 -HAME/ 5 TOO 1 SCIPE 5 FOORON.// 7   (1895)

THAA 1 WAES 9 ON 8 SANDE/ 5 +SAEAE- 5 -GEEAP 3 NACA// 6   (1896)

HLADEN 4 HERE- 9 -WAEAEDUM/ 5 HRINGED- 3 -STEFNA// 5   (1897)

MEEARUM 4 =AND 0 MAADH-9-MUM/ 4 MAEST 4 HLIIFADE// 5   (1898)

OFER 4 HROODH- 3 -GAARES/ 9 HORD- 2 -GE- 2 -STREEONUM// 7   (1899)

HEE 2 THAEAEM 4 BAAT- 1 -WEARDE/ 9 BUNDEN 4 GOLDE// 5   (1900)

SWURD 3 GE- 1 -SEAL-1-DE/ 5 TH= 1 HEE 2 SYDH-9-THAN 8 WAES// 5   (1901)

ON 1 MEDDU- 4 -BENCE/ 5   (1902)

    ()MATHMA*MAATHME 4 THYY 2 WEO-3-RTHRE*RTHRA// 6   (1902)

YRFE- 3 -LAAFE/ 5 GE- 2 -WAAT 4 HIM 3 ON 1 ()NACAN*NACA// 9   (1903)

DREEFAN 4 DEEOP 2 WAETER/ 4 DENA 4 LAND 3 OF- 1 -GEAF.// 9   (1904)

THAA 1 WAES 5 BE 2 MAESTE/ 6 MERE- 5 -HRAEGLA 5 SUM// 9   (1905)

SEGL 4 SAALE 5 FAEST/ 5 SUND- 2 -WUDU 4 THUNEDE// 9   (1906)

NOO 0 THAEAER 4 WEEG- 2 -FLOTAN/ 4 WIND 3 OFER 2 YYDHUM// 9   (1907)

SIIDHES 4 GE- 1 -TWAEAEFDE/ 6 SAEAE- 2 -GENGA 4 FOOR// 0   (1908)

FLEEAT 9 FAAMIG- 4 -HEALS/ 4 FORDH 3 OFER 2 YYDHE// 4   (1909)

BUNDEN- 9 -STEFNA/ 4 OFER 2 BRIM- 3 -STREEAMAS// 5   (1910)

TH= 2 HIIE 2 GEEATA 9 CLIFU/ 4 ON- 0 -GITAN 4 MEAHTON// 4   (1911)

CUUTHE 2 NAES-9-SAS/ 5 CEEOL 4 UP 1 GE- 4 -THRANG// 5   (1912)

LYFT- 4 -GE- 4 -SWEN-9-CED/ 3 ON 2 LANDE 5 STOOD.// 7   (1913)

HRATHE 5 WAES 2 AET 9 HOLME/ 6 HYYDH- 3 -WEARD 3 GEARA// 5   (1914)

+ END FOLIO 174V

SEE 0 THE 3 AEAER 1 LANGE 9 TIID/ 4 LEEOFRA 4 MAN-1-NA// 4   (1915)

FUUS 4 AET 2 FARODHE/ 8 FEOR 9 WLAATODE// 5   (1916)

SAEAELDE 3 TOO 0 SANDE/ 5 SIID- 1 -FAETHME 3 SCIP// 9   (1917)

()ONCEAR*ONCER- 4 -BENDUM 2 FAEST/ 4   (1918)

THYY 0 LAEAES 5 HYM 3 YYTHA 9 DHRYM// 4   (1918)

WUDU 3 WYN- 0 -SUMAN/ 4 FOR- 4 -WRECAN 8 MEAH-9-TE// 6   (1919)

HEET 2 THAA 2 UP 1 BERAN/ 4 AETHELINGA 4 GE- 0 -STREEON// 9   (1920)

FRAETWE 4 =AND 0 FAEAET- 3 -GOLD/ 3 NAES 3 HIM 3 FEOR 3 THANON// 9   (1921)

TOO 2 GE- 3 -SEE-1-CAN-1-NE/ 5 SINCES 5 BRYTTAN.// 4   (1922)

HIGE- 9 -LAAC 5 HREETHLING/ 4 THAEAER 2 AET 1 HAAM 2 WUNADH// 4   (1923)

SELFA 9 MID 2 GE- 2 -SIIDHUM/ 4 +SAEAE- 4 -WEALLE 4 NEEAH// 5   (1924)

BOLD 2 WAES 9 BET- 2 -LIIC/ 5 BREGO- 3 -ROOF 2 CYNING// 4   (1925)

(}HEA*HEEAH 8 *ON 8 HEALL-1-E/ 9 HYGD 3 SWIIDHE 4 GEONG// 4   (1926)

WIIS 2 WEEL- 4 -THUNGEN/ 4 THEEAH 1 DHE 9 WINTRA 5 LYYT// 4   (1927)

UNDER 4 BURH- 2 -LOCAN/ 3 GE- 1 -BIDEN 9 HABBE// 7   (1928)

HAERE-1-THES 4 DOHTOR/ 4 NAES 4 HIIE 4 HNAAH 9 SWAA 3 THEEAH// 4   (1929)

NEE 2 TOO 2 GNEEADH 4 GIFA/ 3 GEEA-1-TA 4 LEEO-9-DUM// 4   (1930)

MAATHM- 3 -GE- 2 -STREEONA/ 4 MOOD- 3 -THRYYDHO 3 WAEG// 9   (1931)

FRE-1-MU 4 FOL-2-CES 4 CWEEN/ 3 FIREN 3 ON- 1 -DRYSNE// 9   (1932)

NAEAE-2-NIG 5 TH= 1 DORSTE/ 4 DEEOR 1 GE- 2 -NEETHAN// 4   (1933)

SWAEAESRA 9 GE- 2 -SIIDHA/ 5 NEFNE 4 SIN- 1 -FREEA// 4   (1934)

TH= 0 HIRE 4 AN 1 DAEG-1-ES/ 9 EEAGUM 4 STAREDE// 4   (1935)

AC 2 HIM 4 WAEL- 4 -BENDE./ 9 WEOTODE 5 TEALDE// 6   (1936)

          END FOLIO 175R ✝

HAND- 3 -GE- 1 -WRITHENE/ 5 HRATHE 9 SEOTHDHAN 4 WAES// 4   (1937)

AEFTER 4 MUND- 3 -GRIPE/ 5 MEECE 9 GE- 8 -THINGED// 5   (1938)

TH= 1 HIT 4 SCEAADEN- 4 -MAEAEL/ 4 SCYYRAN 9 MOOSTE// 4   (1939)

CWEALM- 3 -BEALU 3 CYYDHAN/ 4   (1940)

          NE 1 BIDH 2 SWYLC 9 CWEEN- 2 -LIIC 3 THEEAW// 3   (1940)

IDESE 4 TOO 1 EFNANNE/ 3 THEEAH 1 DHE 9 HIIO 8 AEAENLICU 3 SYY// 3   (1941)

TH=-2-TE 3 FREODHU- 4 -WEBBE/ 3 FEEORES 9 ON- 8 -SAEAECE// 3   (1942)

AEFTER 4 LIGE- 3 -TORNE/ 2 LEEOF-1-NE 2 MANNAN// 9   (1943)

HUURU 3 TH= 2 ON- 2 -HOOHSNOD*E/ 3   (1944)

          HEM-2-()NINGES*MINGES 3 MAEAEG// 9   (1944)

EALO- 3 -DRINCENDE/ 4 OODHER 4 SAEAEDAN// 2   (1945)

TH= 1 HIIO 1 LEEOD- 9 -BEALEWA/ 3 LAEAES 2 GE- 1 -FREMEDE// 3   (1946)

                              69

INWIT- 3 -NIIDHA/ 9 SYDHDHAN 3 AEAEREST 4 WEARDH// 3   (1947)

GYFEN 2 GOLD- 2 -HRO-9-DEN/ 3 GEON-1-GU= 3 CEMPAN// 3   (1948)

AEDHELUM 4 DIIORE/ 9 SYDHDHAN 3 HIIO 4 OFFAN 3 FLET// 4   (1949)

OFER 4 FEALONE 4 FLOOD/ 3 BE 0 FAEDER 5 LAARE// 5   (1950)

SIIDHE 3 GE- 0 -SOOHTE/ 9 DHAEAER 4 HIIO 3 SYDHDHAN 8 WELL// 5   (1951)

IN 0 SUM- 2 -STOOLE/ 9 GOODE 4 MAEAERE// 3   (1952)

LIIF- 1 -GE- 2 -SCEAFTA/ 4 LIFIGENDE 9 BREEAC.// 4   (1953)

HIIOLD 3 HEEAH- 4 -LUFAN/ 4 WIDH 4 HAELE-9-THA 4 BREGO// 3   (1954)

EALLES 3 MON- 3 -CYNNES/ 3 MIINE 9 GE- 1 -FRAEAEGE// 4   (1955)

()THAESSE 3 ()LESTAN*THONE 8 *SEELESTAN/ 2 BII 2 SAEAEM 3 TWEEO-9-NU=// 5 (1956)

EORMEN- 3 -CYNNES/ 4 FOR- 2 -DHAAM 1 OFFA 9 WAES// 3   (1957)

                         END FOLIO 175V +

GEO-1-FU= 3 =AND 0 GUUDHU=/ 3 GAAR- 3 -CEENE 2 MAN// 3   (1958)

+WIIDE 8 GE- 9 -WEURDHOD/ 4 WIIS- 2 -DOOME 4 HEEOLD// 8   (1959)

EEDHEL 9 SIINNE/ 4 THONON 3 ()GEOMOR*EEOMEER 5 WOOC// 4   (1960)

HAELEDHU= 9 TOO 1 HELPE/ 5 HEM-1-()INGES*MINGES 5 MAEAEG// 4   (1961)

NEFA 3 +GAAR- 9 -MUNDES/ 4 NIIDHA 3 CRAEFTIG..-// 9   (1962)

                              XXVIII   (FITT)

$$GE- 2 -WAAT 3 HIM 2 DHAA 4 SE 3 HEARDA/ 4   (1963)

            MID 1 HIS 9 HOND- 3 -SCOLE// 3   (1963)

SYLF 3 AEFTER 3 SANDE/ 9 SAEAE- 4 -WONG 4 TREDAN// 3   (1964)

WIIDE 2 WARODHAS/ 9 WORULD- 1 -CANDEL 3 SCAAN// 4   (1965)

SIGEL 5 SUUDHAN 2 +FUUS/ 9 HII 1 SIIDH 4 DRUGON// 4   (1966)

ELNE 3 GE- 3 -EEODON/ 5 TOO 0 DHAES 8 DHE 9 EORLA 4 HLEEO// 5   (1967)

BONAN 5 ON-2-GEN- 3 -THEEO-1-ES./ 2 BURGU= 9 IN 2 INNAN.// 4   (1968)

GEONGNE 4 GUUDH- 3 -CYNING/ 2 GOODNE 9 GE- 2 -FRUUNON// 5   (1969)

HRINGAS 3 DAEAELAN/ 4 HIGE- 0 -LAACE 9 WAES// 2   (1970)

SIIDH 4 BEEO- 2 -WULFES/ 3 SNUUDE 4 GE- 0 -CYYDHED// 3   (1971)

TH= 2 DHAEAER 9 ON 1 WORDHIG/ 4 WIIGENDRA 4 HLEEO// 4   (1972)

LIND- 3 -GE- 1 -STEALLA/ 9 LIFIGENDE 4 CWOOM// 3   (1973)

HEADHO- 2 -LAACES. 5 HAAL/ 3 TOO 9 HOFE 3 GONGAN// 5   (1974)

HRADHE 3 WAES 2 GE- 3 -RYYMED/ 9 SWAA 2 SE 3 RIICA 3 BE- 1 -BEEAD// 4   (1975)

FEEDHE- 3 -GESTU=/ 5 FLET 9 INNAN- 2 -WEARD// 4   (1976)

GE- 0 -SAET 3 THAA 4 WIDH 3 SYLFNE/ 9   (1977)

       SEE 1 DHAA 4 SAECCE 3 GE- 2 -NAES// 4   (1977)

MAEAEG 2 WIDH 3 MAEAEGE/ 9 SYDHDHAN 4 MAN- 4 -DRYHTEN// 4   (1978)

       END FOLIO 176R +

THURH 2 HLEEODHOR- 9 -CWYDE/ 3 HOLDNE 3 GE- 3 -GREETTE// 6   (1979)

MEEAGLUM 9 WORDU=/ 3 MEODU- 3 -SCENCU= 4 HWEARF.// 4   (1980)

GEOND 9 THAET 8 ()SIDE*HEAL- 8 -RECED/ 4 HAEREDHES 3 DOHTOR// 4   (1981)

LUFODE 9 DHAA 1 LEEODE/ 5 LIIDH- 3 -WAEAEGE 3 BAER// 4   (1982)

()HAE-d-()NU=*HAELEDHU= 2 TOO 0 HANDA/ 9 HIGE- 2 -LAAC 3 ON- 0 -GAN// 3   (1983)

SIINNE 3 GE- 1 -SELDAN/ 4 IN 9 SELE 3 THAA= 3 HEEAN// 4   (1984)

FAEGRE 4 FRIGGCEAN/ 5 HYNE 9 FYR- 3 -WET 1 BRAEC// 4   (1985)

HWYLCE 4 SAEAE- 2 -GEEATA/ 3 SIIDHAS 9 WAEAERON// 3   (1986)

HUU 1 LOMP 3 EEOW 3 ON 1 LAADE/ 4 LEEOFA 3 BIIO- 9 -WULF// 4   (1987)

THAA 0 DHUU 2 FAEAERINGA/ 4 FEORR 4 GE- 1 -HOGODEST.// 9   (1988)

SAECCE 4 SEECEAN/ 4 OFER 4 SEALT 4 WAETER// 4   (1989)

HILDE 9 TOO 0 HIOROTE/ 4 AC 0 DHUU 3 HROODH- 3 -GAARE// 5   (1990)

()WIDH*WIID- 2 -CUUDHNE 9 WEEAN/ 4 WIHTE 3 GE- 0 -BEETTEST// 5   (1991)

MAEAERU= 3 DHEEODNE/ 9 IC 0 DHAES 4 MOOD- 3 -CEARE// 4   (1992)

SORH- 2 -WYLMU= 4 SEEADH/ 9 SIIDHE 4 NE 0 TRUWODE// 4   (1993)

LEEOFES 4 MANNES/ 2 IC 0 DHEE 9 LANGE 3 BAED// 3   (1994)

TH= 1 DHUU 2 THONE 4 WAEL- 1 -GAEAEST/ 3 WIHTE 9 NE 0 GREETTE// 3   (1995)

LEETE 3 SUUDH- 3 -DENE/ 5 SYLFE 3 GE- 1 -WEORDHAN// 9   (1996)

GUUDHE 3 WIDH 2 GRENDEL/ 4 GODE 4 IC 1 THANC 4 SECGE// 9   (1997)

THAES 0 DHE 4 IC 0 DHEE 2 GE- 0 -SUNDNE/ 4 GE- 1 -SEEON 3 MOOSTE.// 9   (1998)

$BIIO- 2 -WULF 4 MADHELODE/ 4 BEARN 4 ECG- 3 -DHIIOES// 9   (1999)

       END FOLIO 176V +

TH= 3 IS 2 UN- 2 -DYRNE/ 4 DRYHTEN 2 HIGE- 8 -LAAC// 8   (2000)

()M++++*MICEL 9 GE- 0 -MEETING/ 5 MONEGU= 4 FIIRA// 5   (2001)

HWYLC 8 ()+++++*OR- 8 -*LEG- 9 -HWIIL/ 4 UNCER 4 GRENDLES// 4   (2002)

```
WEARD1 3 ON 8 DHAA= 9 WANGE/ 4 THAEAER 2 HEE 4 WORNA 4 FELA// 4                    (2003)

SIGE- 8 -SCYL-9-DI-8-NGU=/ 5 SORGE 3 GE- 1 -FREMEDE// 3                            (2004)

YRMDHE 9 TOO 3 ALDRE/ 5 IC O DHAET 4 EALL 3 GE- 2 -WRAEC// 4                       (2005)

SWAA 8 BE- 9 -GYLPAN 4 *NE 8 THEARF/ 3 GRENDELES 4 MAAGA// 8                       (2006)

()EN++*AEAENIG 9 OFER 4 EORDHAN/ 5 UUHT- 4 -HLEM 4 THONE.// 5                      (2007)

SEE 8 DHE 9 LENGEST 4 LEOFADH/ 5 LAADHAN 4 CYNNES// 8                              (2008)

()F++++*FAACNE 9 BI- O -FONGEN/ 4 IC O DHAEAER 5 FURDHUM 3 CWOOM.// 9              (2009)

TOO 1 DHAA= 4 HRING- 3 -SELE/ 4 HROODH- 1 -GAAR 4 GREETAN.// 9                     (2010)

SOONA 4 MEE O SE 3 MAEAERA/ 5 MAGO 3 HEALF- O -DE-9-NES// 3                        (2011)

SYDHDHAN 3 HEE O MOOD- 3 -SEFAN/ 4 MIINNE 9 CUUDHE// 4                             (2012)

WIDH 3 HIS O SYLFES 3 SUNU/ 3 SETL 3 GE- O -TAEAEHTE.// 9                          (2013)

WEOROD 3 WAES 3 ON 2 WYNNE/ 5 NE O SEAH 2 IC 2 WII-9-DAN 3 FEORH// 4               (2014)

UNDER 3 HEOFONES 2 HWEALF/ 9 HEAL- 4 -SITTEN-1-DRA// 5                             (2015)

MEDU- 4 -DREEAM 4 MAARAN/ 9 HWIILU= 4 MAEAERU 4 CWEEN// 4                          (2016)

FRIDHU- 4 -SIBB 3 FOLCA/ 9 FLET 3 EALL 4 GEOND- 4 -HWEARF// 3                      (2017)

BAEAEDDE 2 BYRE 9 GEONGE/ 4 OFT 1 HIIO 3 BEEA-2-H- 4 -WRIDHAN// 4                  (2018)

SECGE 9 ()++++++*SEALDE/ 8 AEAER 1 HIIE 3 TOO 3 SETLE 1 GEEONG.// 5                (2019)

        + END FOLIO 177R


HWIILU= 3 FOR 9 ()+UGUDHE*DUGUDHE/ 4 DOHTOR 4 HROODH- 2 -GAARES// 3                (2020)

EORLUM 9 ON 8 ENDE/ 3 EALU- 3 -WAEAEGE 3 BAER// 5                                  (2021)

THAA O IC 2 FREEA- 4 -WARE/ 9 FLET- 8 -SITTENDE.// 5                               (2022)

NEM-1-NAN 2 HYYRDE/ 4 THAEAER 2 HIIO 9 ()++GLED*NAEGLED 2 SINC// 2                 (2023)

HAELEDHU= 4 SEALDE/ 4 SIIO 1 GE- 2 -HAATEN 9 ()+ES*IS// 8                          (2024)

GEONG 2 GOLD- 2 -HRODEN/ 4 GLADU= 3 SUNA 2 FROODAN.// 9                            (2025)

()+AFADH*HAFADH 3 THAES 1 GE- 1 -WORDEN/ 4 WINE 3 SCYLDINGA// 4                    (2026)

RII-9-CES 8 HYRDE/ 3 =AND O THAET 1 RAEAED 2 TALADH// 3                            (2027)

TH= 2 HEE 3 MID 1 DHYY 9 WIIFE/ 4 WAEL- 1 -FAEAEHDHA 4 DAEAEL// 4                  (2028)

SAECCA 5 GE- O -SETTE/ 2 OFT 9 SELDAN 2 HWAEAER.// 6                               (2029)

AEFTER 4 LEEOD- 3 -HRYRE/ 3 LYYTLE 9 HWIILE// 3                                    (2030)

BON- 1 -GAAR 4 BUUGEDH/ 4 THEEAH 3 SEEO 2 BRYYD 1 DUGE// 9                         (2031)

MAEG 1 THAES 2 THON= 4 OF- 2 -THYNCAN/ 3                                           (2032)

        ()DHEODEN*DHEEODNE 4 HEADHO- 9 -BEARDNA// 5                                (2032)
```

72

=AND 1 THEGNA 2 GE- 1 -HWAAM/ 4 THAARA 2 LEEODA// 9   (2033)

THONNE 2 HEE 1 MID 2 FAEAEM-1-NAN/ 4 ON 2 FLETT 2 GAEAEDH.// 9   (2034)

ORYHT- 2 -BEARN 4 DENA/ 5 DUGUDHA 4 BI- 0 -WENEDE.// 9   (2035)

ON 1 HIM 1 GLADIADH/ 3 GOMELRA 3 LAAFE// 5   (2036)

HEARD 9 =AND 0 HRING- 3 -MAEAEL/ 5   (2037)

          HEADHA- 4 -()BEARNA*BEARDNA 3 GE- 1 -STREEON// 9   (2037)

THEN-1-DEN 2 HIIE 4 DHAA= 4 WAEAEPNU=/ 5 WEALDAN 4 MOOSTON.// 9   (2038)

                    *XXVIIII   (FITT)

$ODH 0 DHAET 3 HIIE 3 FOR- 3 -LAEAEDDAN/ 3   (2039)

          TOO 0 DHAAM 4 LIND- 9 -PLEGAN// 5   (2039)

SWAEAESE 4 GE- 0 -SIIDHAS/ 4 OND 3 HYRA 2 SYLF-9-RA 4 FEORH// 3   (2040)

THON= 3 CWIDH 2 AET 1 BEEORE/ 5 SEE 0 DHE 2 BEEAH 9 GE- 1 -SYHDH// 4   (2041)

                    END FOLIO 177V +

EALD 3 AESC- 3 -WIGA/ 5 SEE 0 DHE 5 EALL 2 GE- 8 -()+++*MAN// 9   (2042)

GAAR- 5 -CWEALM 4 GUMENA/ 5 HI= 2 BIDH 4 GRIM 8 ()++*SE-9-FA// 6   (2043)

ON- 2 -GINNEDH 4 GEOO-1-MOR- 4 -MOOD/ 2 GEONG()++*UM 9 CEM-1-PAN// 5   (2044)

THUR-2-H 5 HREDHRA 4 GE- 2 -HYGO/ 8 HIGES 9 CUNNIAN// 3   (2045)

WIIG- 3 -BEALU 4 WECCEAN/ 4 =AND 2 TH= 2 WORD 9 AA- 0 -CWYDH.// 5   (2046)

MEAHT 2 DHUU 4 MIIN 3 WINE/ 5 MEECE 9 GE- 0 -CNAAWAN// 4   (2047)

THONE 3 THIIN 3 FAEDER/ 4 TOO 0 GE- 0 -FEOHTE 9 BAER.// 6   (2048)

UNDER 5 HERE- 3 -GRIIMAN/ 4 HINDEMAN 9 SIIDHE.// 7   (2049)

DYYRE 4 IIREN/ 3 THAEAER 3 HYNE 4 DENE 9 SLOOGON// 4   (2050)

WEEOLDON 4 WAEL- 2 -STOOWE/ 4 SYDHDHAN 9 WIDHER- 3 -GYLD 3 LAEG.// 6   (2051)

AEFTER 4 HAELETHA 3 HRYRE/ 9 HWATE 4 SCYLDUNGAS// 5   (2052)

NUU 1 HEER 3 THAARA 4 BA-9-NENA/ 2 BYRE 3 NAAT- 4 -HWYLCES.// 6   (2053)

FRAETHU= 9 HREEMIG/ 5 ON 1 FLET 1 GAEAEDH// 4   (2054)

MORDHRES 3 ()GYLPEO*GYLPEDH/ 9 =AND 0 THONE 4 MAADHTHU= 4 BYREDH// 4   (2055)

THONE 2 THE 0 DHUU 2 MID 9 RIHTE/ 5 RAEAEDAN 4 SCEOLDEST// 4   (2056)

MANADH 3 SWAA 9 =AND 0 MYNDGADH/ 4 MAEAELA 3 GE- 1 -HWYLCE.// 6   (2057)

SAARUM 9 WORDUM/ 5 ODH 0 DHAET 3 SAEAEL 3 CYMEDH// 4   (2058)

TH= 2 SE 3 FAEAEM-9-NAN 3 THEGN/ 5 FORE 4 FAEDER 3 DAEAEDUM.// 5   (2059)

AEFT= 9 BILLES 3 BITE/ 3 BLOOD- 3 -FAAG 3 SWEFEDH.// 5   (2060)

EALDRES 9 SCYLDIG/ 5 HIM 2 SE 3 OODHER 3 THONAN// 3   (2061)

LOSADH 9 ()++FIGENDE*LIFIGENDE/ 3 CON 2 HIM 4 LAND 2 GEARE// 4   (2062)

         + END FOLIO 178R

THON= 2 BIIODH 9 ()+*AA- 8 -BROCENE/ 5 ON 0 BAA 2 HEALFE// 4   (2063)

AADH- 2 -()SWEORDH*SWEORD 3 EORLA/ 9 ()+++DHAN*SYDHDHAN 4 INGELDE// 4   (2064)

WEALLADH 3 WAEL- 4 -NIIDHAS/ 3 =AND 0 HI= 9 WIIF- 8 -LUFAN// 3   (2065)

AEFTER 3 CEAR- 4 -WAELMU=/ 4 COOLRAN 9 WEORDHADH// 4   (2066)

THYY 2 IC 1 HEADHO- 2 -()BEARNA*BEARDNA/ 4 HYLDO 3 NE 9 TELGE.// 6   (2067)

DRYHT- 3 -SIBBE 3 DAEAEL/ 4 DENU= 4 UN- 1 -FAEAECNE// 9   (2068)

FREEOND- 3 -SCIPE 4 FAESTNE/ 5 IC 1 SCEAL 4 FORDH 9 SPRECAN.// 6   (2069)

GEEN 1 YMBE 2 GRENDEL./ 5 TH= 1 DHUU 2 GEARE 9 CUNNE// 4   (2070)

SINCES 2 BRYTTA/ 5 TOO 2 HWAN 3 SYDHDHAN 9 WEARDH.// 5   (2071)

HOND- 1 -RAEAES 3 HAELEDHA/ 5 SYDHDHAN 3 HEOFONES 9 GIM.// 5   (2072)

GLAAD 3 OFER 3 GRUNDAS/ 3 GAEAEST 3 YRRE 1 CWOO=// 9   (2073)

EATOL 5 AEAEFEN- 2 -GROM/ 5 UUSER 3 NEEOSAN.// 6   (2074)

DHAEAER 2 WEE 9 GE- 0 -SUNDE/ 4 SAEL 2 WEARDODON// 3   (2075)

THAEAER 4 WAES 1 HOND- 9 -SCIOO/ 3 ()HILDE*HILD 4 ON- 1 -SAEAEGE// 5   (2076)

FEOR-2-H- 4 -BEALU 3 FAEAEGUM/ 9 HEE 1 FYR-2-MEST 2 LAEG// 4   (2077)

GYRDED 3 CEMPA/ 5 HIM 9 GRENDEL 5 WEARDH// 4   (2078)

MAEAERU= 5 ()MAGU=*MAGU- 4 -THEGNE/ 9 TOO 2 MUUDH- 3 -BONAN.// 6   (2079)

LEEOFES 2 MAN-1-NES/ 6 +LIIC 9 EALL 3 FOR- 4 -SWEALG.// 7   (2080)

NOO 0 DHYY 1 AEAER 5 UUT 2 DHAA 1 GEEN/ 9 IIDEL- 2 -HENDE.// 7   (2081)

BONA 3 BLOODIG- 3 -TOODH/ 4 BEALEWA 9 GE- 1 -MYNDIG// 5   (2082)

OF 0 DHAA= 4 GOLD- 3 -SELE/ 3 GON-1-GAN 9 WOLDE.// 7   (2083)

AC 1 HEE 2 MAEGNES 4 +ROOF/ 5 MIIN 2 COSTODE// 9   (2084)

                END FOLIO 178V +

GRAAPODE 3 ()GEAREO*GEARO- 3 -FOLM/ 3 GLOOF 8 HANGODE// 9   (2085)

SIID 2 =AND 0 SYL- 0 -LIIC/ 3 SEARO- 3 -BENDU= 4 FAEST.// 8   (2086)

SIIO 9 WAES 4 OR- 0 -DHON-1-CU=/ 4 EALL 3 GE- 2 -GYRWED// 3   (2087)

DEEOFLES 9 CRAEFTUM/ 4 =AND 1 DRACAN 4 FELLU=// 4   (2088)

```
EE 0 MEG 8 THAEAER 9 ON 2 IN-1-NAN/ 4 UN- 1 -SYNNIGNE// 4                    (2089)

IIOR 2 OAEAED- 9 -FRUMA/ 3 GE- 1 -+DOON 3 WOLDE// 9                          (2090)

ANIGRA 3 SUM-2-NE/ 5 HYT 2 NE 3 MIHTE 9 SWAA// 5                             (2091)

Y-1-OHDHAN 3 IC 2 ON 0 YRRE/ 4 UPP- 1 -RIHTE 9 AA- 0 -STOOD.// 7            (2092)

TOO 2 LANG 3 YS 2 TOO 1 RECCENNE/ 4                                         (2093)

        HUU 0 ()I+*IC 8 ()++*OHAA= 9 LEEOD- 3 -SCEADHAN// 2                 (2093)

FLA 3 GE- 1 -HWYLCES/ 3 ()HOND*OND- 8 -LEEAN 9 FOR- 3 -GEALD// 4           (2094)

HAEAER 3 IC 2 THEEOOEN 4 MIIN/ 3 THIINE 9 LEEODE// 6                        (2095)

EORD+0-1-DE 4 WEOR-1-CU=/ 4 HEE 1 ON 8 WEG 9 LOSADE.// 7                    (2096)

YYTLE 4 HWIILE/ 4 LIIF- 2 -WYNNA 1 BREAC// 9                                (2097)

WAETHRE 5 HIM 2 SIIO 3 SWIIDHRE/ 5 SWADHE 4 WEAR-9-DADE.// 7                (2098)

AND 3 ON 1 HIORTE/ 5 =AND 0 HEE 2 HEEAN 9 DHONAN// 5                        (2099)

OODES 4 GEOOMOR/ 5 MER-1-E- 1 -GRUND 9 GE- 1 -FEEOLL// 5                    (2100)

EE 0 THONE 4 WAEL- 3 -RAEAES/ 3 WINE 9 SCILDUNGA.// 6                       (2101)

AEAETTAN 3 GOLDE/ 4 FELA 3 LEEANO-9-DE// 5                                  (2102)

ANEGU= 5 MAADHMU=/ 3 SYDHDHAN 3 MER-9-GEN 4 +COOM.// 6                      (2103)

AND 1 WEE 3 TOO 0 SYMBLE/ 4 GE- 0 -SETEN 9 HAEFDON.// 6                     (2104)

HAEAER 3 WAES 2 GIDD 2 =AND 0 GLEEO/ 2 GOMELA 9 SCILDING// 8                (2105)
                            END FOLIO 179R +

ELA- 2 -FRICGENDE/ 8 FEORRAN 3 REHTE// 9                                    (2106)

WIILU= 8 HILDE- 3 -DEEOR/ 4 HEARPAN 4 WYNNE// 4                             (2107)

O-9-()MEL*MEN- 8 -WUDU 3 GREEITE/ 4 HWIILU= 3 GYD 3 AA- 0 -WRAEC.// 3       (2108)

OODH 9 =AND 8 SAAR- 1 -+LIIC/ 3 HWIILU= 4 SYL- 0 -LIIC 3 SPELL.// 5         (2109)

EHTE 2 AEFTER 9 RIHTE/ 4 RUUM- 3 -HEORT 3 CYNING.// 6                       (2110)

WIILU= 4 EFT 9 ON- 8 -GAN/ 4 ELDO 2 GE- 0 -BUNDEN// 4                       (2111)

OMEL 3 GUUDH- 3 -WIGA/ 9 GIOGUDHE 3 CWIIDHAN// 4                            (2112)

ILDE- 4 -STRENGO/ 4 HREDHER 9 INNE 3 WEEOLL.// 6                            (2113)

HON- 2 HEE 3 WINTRU= 4 FROOD/ 4 WORN 9 GE- 8 -MUNDE// 5                     (2114)

WAA 1 WEE 1 THAEAER 3 INNE/ 5 =AND- 0 -LANGNE 9 DAEG.// 8                   (2115)

IIODE 3 NAAMAN/ 5 ODH 0 DHAET 3 NIHT 2 BE- 0 -CWOOM.// 9                    (2116)

OODHER 8 TOO 1 YLDUM/ 3 THAA 0 WAES 3 EFT 3 HRADHE// 4                      (2117)

EARO 9 GYRN- 4 -WRAECE./ 5 GRENDELES 4 MOODOR// 5                          (2118)
```

75

$SIID-ODE 9 SORH- 2 -FULL/ 4 SUNU 2 DEEADH 3 FOR- 1 -NAM// 3   (2119)

WIIG- 2 -HETE 9 WEDRA/ 3 WIIF 8 UN- 1 -HYYRE// 6   (2120)

HYRE 3 BEARN 2 GE- 1 -WRAEC/ 9 BEORN 3 AA- 0 -CWEALDE// 4   (2121)

ELLEN- 1 -LIICE/ 4 THAEAER 3 WAES 2 AESC- 9 -HERE// 5   (2122)

FROO-1-DAN 3 FYRN- 3 -WITAN/ 5 FEORH 4 UUDH- 9 -GENGE.// 6   (2123)

NOODHER 3 HYY 1 HINE 5 NE 0 MOOSTON/ 3 SYDHDHAN 9 MER-3-GEN 3 CWOOM// 4   (2124)

DEEADH- 4 -WEERIG-1-NE/ 4 DENIA 9 LEEODE.// 8   (2125)

BRONDE 4 FOR- 3 -BAERNAN/ 9 NEE 1 ON 2 BAEAEL 4 HLADAN.// 5   (2126)

LEEOFNE 4 MAN-1-NAN/ 9 HIIO 1 TH= 1 LIIC 4 AET- 2 -BAER// 5   (2127)

⊹ END FOLIO 179V

FEEONDES 4 ()FAEDHRUNG*FAEDHMUM/ 8   (2128)

       ()⊹⊹*UN-9-DER 5 FIRGEN- 4 -STREEAM.// 6   (2128)

TH= 2 WAES 3 HROODH- 0 -GAARE/ 9 HREEOWA 4 TORNOST// 4   (2129)

THAARA 3 THE 1 LEEOD- 3 -FRU-9-MAN/ 2 LANGE 3 BE- 0 -GEEATE.// 7   (2130)

THAA 2 SE 2 DHEEO-1-DEN 8 MEC/ 9 DHIINE 3 LIIFE// 4   (2131)

HEAL-1-SODE 6 HREEOH- 4 -MOOD/ 8   (2132)

       TH= 8 IC 9 ON 2 HOLMA 4 GE- 1 -THRING// 3   (2132)

EORL- 3 -SCIPE 4 EFNDE/ 9 EALDRE 4 GE- 1 -NEEDH-3-DE.// 5   (2133)

MAEAER-1-DHO 3 FREMEDE/ 9 HEE 0 MEE 6 MEEDE 3 GE- 1 -HEET// 3   (2134)

IC 0 DHAA 2 DHAES 4 WAELMES/ 9 THE 1 IS 2 WIIDE 3 CUUDH// 4   (2135)

GRIM-1-()ME*NE 3 GRYRE- 2 -LIICNE/ 9 GRUND- 4 -HYRDE 4 FOND// 4   (2136)

THAEAER 4 UNC 3 HWIILE 9 WAES/ 4 HAND 2 GE- 1 -MAEAENE.// 3   (2137)

HOLM 2 HEOLFKE 9 WEEOLL/ 5 =AND 1 IC 1 HEEAFDE 3 BE- 1 -CEARF// 6   (2138)

IN 1 DHAAM 2 *GUUDH- 8 -SELE/ 9 GRENDELES 4 MOODOR.// 7   (2139)

EEACNUM 5 ECGUM/ 9 UN- 2 -SOOFTE 4 THONAN// 5   (2140)

FEORH 4 ODH- 3 -FEREDE./ 9 NAES 3 IC 2 FAEAEGE 4 THAA 0 GYYT.// 7   (2141)

AC 1 MEE 3 EORLA 2 HLEEO/ 9 EFT 3 GE- 0 -SEALDE// 5   (2142)

MAADH-1-MA 4 MENIGEO/ 4 MAGA 9 HEALF- 2 -DENES.// 9   (2143)

          XXXI   (FITT)

$SWAA 3 SE 1 DHEEOD- 4 -KYNING/ 4 THEEAWU= 4 LYFDE// 9   (2144)

NEALLES 4 IC 0 DHAA= 4 LEEANU=/ 4 FOR- 2 -LOREN 9 HAEFDE// 4   (2145)

AEGNES 6 NEEDE/ 5 AC 2 HEE 0 MEE 9 ()↓↓↓↓↓S*MAADHMAS 8 GEAF// 3   (2146)

END FOLIO 180R ✦

UNU 3 HEALF- 1 -DENES/ 3 ON 9 ()↓↓↓NE*MIINNE 4 SYLFES 2 DOOM.// 6   (2147)

HAA 2 IC 0 DHEE 3 BEORN- 9 -CYNING/ 3 BRINGAN 3 WYLLE.// 6   (2148)

ESTUM 2 GE- 9 -YYWAN/ 3 GEEN 3 IS 2 EALL 4 AET 1 DHEE.// 5   (2149)

ISSA 3 GE- 0 -LONG/ 9 IC 8 LYYT 3 HAFO.// 5   (2150)

EEAFOD- 4 -MAAGA/ 4 NEFNE 9 HYGE- 0 -LAAC 1 DHEC.// 5   (2151)

EET 2 DHAA 4 IN 1 BERAN/ 3 EAFOR 9 HEEAFOD- 2 -SEGN.// 6   (2152)

EADHO- 4 -STEEAPNE 5 HELM/ 9 HAARE 4 BYRNAN// 4   (2153)

JUDH- 3 -SWEORD 3 GEATO- 1 -LIIC/ 9 GYD 2 AEFTER 4 WRAEC.// 7   (2154)

EE 1 DHIS 4 HILDE- 3 -SCEORP/ 9 HROODH- 1 -↓GAAR 5 SEALDE// 5   (2155)

NOTRA 5 FENGEL/ 4 SUME 9 WORDE 3 HEET// 3   (2156)

H= 1 IC 3 HIS 2 AEAEREST 4 DHEE/ 4 EEST 2 GE- 1 -SAEGDE// 9   (2157)

WAEDH 4 TH= 1 HYT 3 HAEFDE/ 4 HIOR-1-O- 1 -GAAR 4 CYNING// 9   (2158)

EEOD 3 SCYLDUNGA/ 4 LANGE 3 HWIILE.// 7   (2159)

OO 0 DHYY 9 AEAER 4 SUNA 4 SIINU=/ 4 SYLLAN 3 WOL-2-DE// 4   (2160)

WATU= 9 HEORO- 3 -WEARDE/ 5 THEEAH 3 HEE 0 HI= 5 HOLD 3 WAEAERE.// 9   (2161)

REEOST- 4 -GE- 0 -WAEAEDU/ 3 BRUUC 3 EALLES 4 WELL.// 9   (2162)

YYR-1-DE 4 IC 1 TH= 2 THAAM 4 FRAETWUM/ 3 FEEOWER 9 MEEARAS.// 5   (2163)

UNGRE 4 GE- 0 -LIICE/ 4 LAAST 3 WEAR-9-DODE.// 7   (2164)

EPPEL- 4 -FEALUWE/ 4 HEE 0 HI= 3 EEST 2 GE- 9 -TEEAH// 4   (2165)

EEARA 4 =AND 0 MAADH-1-MA/ 4 SWAA 2 SCEAL 9 MAEAEG 2 ↓DOON.// 6   (2166)

END FOLIO 180V ✦

EALLES 4 IN-1-WIT- 3 -NET/ 4 OODHRUM 9 BREGDON// 4   (2167)

YRNU= 3 CRAEFTE/ 3 DEEADH 1 ()REN↓↓↓*REENIAN// 9   (2168)

OND- 3 -GE- 1 -STEALLAN/ 3 HYGE- 0 -LAACE 3 WAES// 8   (2169)

IIDHA 9 HEARDU=./ 7 NEFA 3 SWYYDHE 2 HOLD// 4   (2170)

AND 1 GE- 1 -HWAEDHER 9 OODHRU=/ 5 HROO-1-THRA 4 GE- 1 -MYNDIG.// 6   (2171)

YYRDE 9 IC 1 TH= 1 HEE 2 DHONE 5 HEALS- 3 -BEEAH/ 3   (2172)

        HYGDE 8 GE- 9 -SEALDE// 5   (2172)

RAEAETLICNE 5 WUNDUR- 4 -MAADHDHU=/ 9   (2173)

77

DHONE 4 THE 2 HIM 4 WEALH- 1 -DHEEO 5 GEAF// 3   (2173)

()DHEDD*DHEEODNES 9 DOHTOR/ 4 THRIIO 2 WICG 4 SOMOD// 3   (2174)

SWANCOR 9 =AND 0 SADOL- 3 -BEORHT/ 4 HYRE 4 SYDHDHAN 4 WAES// 8   (2175)

AEFT= 9 BEEAH- 1 -DHEGE/ 4 ()BROST*BREEOST 3 GE- 1 -WEOR-2-DHOD.// 5   (2176)

SWAA 1 BEAL-9-DODE/ 4 BEARN 3 ECG- 2 -DHEEOWES.// 6   (2177)

GUMA 2 GUUDHU= 9 CUUDH/ 3 GOODU= 4 DAEAEDU=// 4   (2178)

DREEAH 3 AEFTER 3 DOCME/ 9 NEALLES 4 DRUNCNE 4 SLOOG.// 5   (2179)

HEORDH- 3 -GE- 0 -NEEA-9-TAS/ 3 NAES 2 HI= 4 HREEOH 3 SEFA.// 7   (2180)

AC 1 HEE 1 MAN- 9 -CYNNES/ 5 MAEAESTE 4 CRAEFTE.// 6   (2181)

GIN- 2 -FAESTAN 9 GIFE/ 5 THE 0 HIM 2 GOD 3 SEALDE// 5   (2182)

HEEOLD 2 HILDE- 9 -DEEOR/ 2 HEEAN 3 WAES 3 LANGE// 3   (2183)

SWAA 1 HYNE 3 GEEATA 9 BEARN/ 4 GOODNE 4 NE 0 TEALDON.// 7   (2184)

NEE 1 HYNE 9 ON 3 MEDO- 2 -BENCE/ 4 MICLES 4 WYRDHNE.// 9   (2185)

END FOLIO 181R +

DRIHTEN 4 ()WEREDA*WEDERA/ 3 GE- 1 -DOON 3 WOLDE// 4   (2186)

SWYYDHE 9 ()+++DON*WEENDON/ 4 TH= 0 HEE 3 SLEEAC 3 WAEAERE// 5   (2187)

AEDHELING 3 UN- 9 -FROM/ 4 ED- 1 -WEN-2-DEN 3 CWOOM// 4   (2188)

TIIR- 3 -EEADIGU= 9 MENN/ 3 TORNA 2 GE- 0 -HWYLCES.// 5   (2189)

HEET 1 DHAA 3 EORLA 9 HLEEO/ 4 IN 1 GE- 3 -FETIAN.// 6   (2190)

HEADHO- 3 -ROOF 2 CYNING/ 9 HREEDH-2-LES 3 LAAFE.// 5   (2191)

GOLDE 2 GE- 2 -GYREDE/ 3 NAES 9 MID 8 GEEATU= 2 DHAA// 5   (2192)

SINC- 3 -MAADH-4-THU= 3 SEEL-1-RA/ 9 ON 8 SWEORDES 3 HAAD.// 5   (2193)

TH= 0 HEE 3 ON 0 BIIO- 2 -WULFES/ 9 BEARM 2 AA- 0 -LEGDE.// 5   (2194)

=AND 0 HI= 3 GE- 2 -SEALDE/ 4 SEOFAN 9 THUUSENDO.// 5   (2195)

BOLD 3 =AND 0 BREGO- 3 -STOOL/ 5 HI= 3 WAES 9 BAAM 3 SAMOD// 4   (2196)

ON 1 DHAAM 3 LEEOD- 3 -SCIPE/ 9 LOND 2 GE- 0 -CYNDE// 4   (2197)

EARD 2 EEDHEL- 4 -RIHT/ 3 OODHRU= 9 SWIIDHOR.// 7   (2198)

SIIDE 2 RIICE/ 4 THAA= 3 DHAEAER 4 SEELRA 3 WAES.// 9   (2199)

EFT 2 TH= 1 GE- 3 -IIODE/ 4 UFARAN 4 DOOGRU=.// 5   (2200)

HILDE- 9 -HLAEM-2-MU=/ 6 SYDHDHAN 4 HYGE- 0 -LAAC 2 LAEG.// 3   (2201)

=AND 9 ()HEAREDE*HEARD- 8 -*REEDE/ 4 HILDE- 3 -MEECEAS// 4   (2202)

UNDER 2 BORD- 9 -HREEODHAN/ 4 TOO 0 BONAN 2 WURDON.// 6   (2203)

78

HAA 2 HYNE 9 GE- 1 -SOOHTAN/ 4 ON 1 SIGE- 4 -THEEODE// 4   (2204)

EARDE 3 ()HILDE*HILD- 9 -FRECAN/ 3 HEADHO- 4 -SCILFINGAS.// 5   (2205)

KIDHA 1 GE- 9 -NAEAEGDAN./ 5 NEFAN 3 HERE- 3 -RIICES// 3   (2206)

WDHDHAN 9 BEEO- 1 -WULFE/ 3 BRAADE 3 RIICE// 4   (2207)

     + END FOLIO 181V

W 0 HAND 2 GE- 8 -HWEARF/ 9 HEE 0 GE- 3 -HEEOLD 4 TELA// 3   (2208)

KIFTIG 3 WINTRA/ 4 WAES 8 DHAA 9 FROOD 3 CYNING// 4   (2209)

ALD 2 EETHEL- 4 -WEARD/ 4 ODH 0 DHAET 9 +AAN 4 ON- 0 -GAN// 4   (2210)

CORCJ= 3 NIHTU=/ 4 DRACA 9 ()RICSAN*RIICSIAN// 9   (2211)

EE 0 DHE 5 ON 2 ()HEA++*HEEAUM 8 ()H++E*HAEAETHE/ 8   (2212)

     HORD 1 BE- 3 -WEOTODE// 9   (2212)

TAAN- 3 -BEORH 4 ()STEARNE*STEEAPNE/ 5 STIIG 3 UNDER 4 LAEG// 9 (2213)

LDU= 4 UN- 0 -CUUDH/ 4 THAEAER 3 ON 1 INNAN 1 GIIONG.// 5   (2214)

NIDHA*NIDHDHA 9 NAAT- 2 -HWYLC/ 8   (2215)

     SEE 8 ()++*DHE 8 ()+EH*NEEH 8 GE- 8 -()FENG*FEALG// 3   (2215)

AEAEDHNU= 4 HORDE/ 9 HOND 8 ()+++++++*WAEAEGE 8 *NAM// 8   (2216)

+++*SIID 8 SINCE 4 FAAH/ 5   (2217)

     NEE 8 HEE 8 TH= 9 SYDHDHAN 8 ()+++++*BE- 8 -*MAADH// 8   (2217)

TH++*THEEAH 8 ()DH+*DHE 8 ()++*HEE 8 SLAEAEPENDE/ 5   (2218)

     BE- 9 -()SYRE+*SYRED 8 ()+++DE*WURDE// 7   (2218)

HEEOFES 3 CRAEFTE/ 4 TH= 3 SIIE 9 DHIIOD 8 ON- 8 -()+++D*FAND// 8 (2219)

BU*BIG- 8 -FOLC 3 BEORNA/ 4   (2220)

     TH= 0 HEE 0 GE- 9 -()BOLGE+*BOLGEN 8 WAES.// 9   (2220)

          XXXII   (FITT)

NEALLES 8 MID 8 GE- 3 -WEALDU=/ 4   (2221)

     WYRM- 2 -()HORDA*HORD 9 ()CRAEFT*AA- 8 -*BRAEC// 5   (2221)

YLFES 4 WILLU=/ 4 SEE 0 DHE 2 HI= 4 SAARE 8 GE- 9 -SCEOOD// 5   (2222)

C 2 FOR 4 THREEA- 4 -NEEDLAN/ 4 ()TH+++*THEEOW 8 NAAT- 9 -HWYLCES// 8 (2223)

AELEDHA 3 BEARNA/ 4 HETE- 4 -SWENGEAS 9 FLEEAH// 8   (2224)

AERN+S*AERNES 8 THEARFA/ 8   (2225)

     =AND 1 DHAEAER 5 IN-1-NE 4 ()FEAL*FEALH// 9   (2225)

SECG 3 SYN- 8 -BYSIG/ 6 SOONA 6 MWATIDE// 4   (2226)

TH= 8 ++++++ 9 DHAA= 4 ()GYST++*GYSTE/ 8   (2227)

       ()++++++*GRYRE- 8 -BROOGA 8 STOOD// 3   (2227)

HWAEDHRE 9 ()++++*EARM- 8 -SCEAPEN/ 8 ++++++++++++++// 8   (2228)

+++ 9 ++++++++++++/ 8 ++++++++++ 8 SCEAPEN// 9   (2229)

    + END FOLIO 182R

++++++++++/ 8 ()++*THAA 8 ()++++*HYNE 8 SE 3 +FAEAER 5 BE- 0 -GEAT// 4   (2230)

SINC- 3 -FAET 8 +++ 9 ++/ 8 THAEAER 4 WAES 1 SWYLCRA 4 FELA// 4   (2231)

IN 0 DHAA= 4 EORDH- 9 -()++SE*HUUSE/ 8 AEAER- 4 -GE- 3 -STREEONA// 7   (2232)

SWAA 3 HYY 4 ON 2 GEEAR- 1 -DA-9-GU=/ 8 GUMENA 5 NAAT- 0 -HWYLC// 4   (2233)

EORMEN- 4 -LAAFE/ 9 AEDHELAN 2 CYNNES// 3   (2234)

THANC- 3 -HYCGENDE/ 5 THAEAER 0 GE- 9 -HYYDDE.// 5   (2235)

DEEORE 4 MAADH-1-MAS/ 3 EALLE 3 HIIE 3 DEEADH 9 FOR- 4 -NAM// 4   (2236)

AEAERRAN 3 MAEAELU=/ 5 =AND 1 ()SI*SEE 0 AAN 2 DHAA 2 GEEN// 9   (2237)

LEEODA 4 DUGUDHE/ 4 SEE 0 DHAEAER 5 LENGEST 3 HWEARF// 9   (2238)

WEARD 3 WINE- 4 -GEOO-1-MOR/ 5 ()RENDE*WEENDE 3 THAES 4 YLCAN// 9   (2239)

TH= 8 HEE 3 LYYTEL 3 FAEC/ 4 LONG- 2 -GE- 2 -STREEONA// 5   (2240)

BRUUCAN 9 MOOSTE/ 4 BEORH 4 EALL- 3 -GEARO// 4   (2241)

WUNODE 4 ON 1 WONGE/ 9 WAETER- 5 -YYTHU= 5 NEEAH// 4   (2242)

NIIWE 3 BE 1 NAESSE/ 5 NEARO- 9 -CRAEFTU= 4 FAEST// 5   (2243)

THAEAER 4 ON 5 INNAN 2 BAER/ 4 EORL- 9 -GE- 8 -STREEONA// 6   (2244)

HRINGA 4 HYRDE/ 4 ()HARD*HORD- 2 -WYRDHNE 9 DAEAEL// 4   (2245)

FAEAETTAN 2 GOLDES/ 3 FEEA 3 WORDA 2 CWAEDH.// 4   (2246)

HEALD 9 THUU 8 NUU 2 HRUUSE/ 5 NUU 1 HAELEDH 4 NE 2 ()MAESTON*MOOSTAN// 3 (2247)

EORLA 9 AEAEHTE/ 5 HWAET 2 HYT 4 AEAER 5 ON 0 DHEE// 5   (2248)

GOODE 2 BE- 0 -GEEATON/ 9 GUUDH- 4 -DEEADH 4 FOR- 3 -NAM.// 6   (2249)

FECRH- 4 -()BEALC*BEALO 3 FREECNE/ 9   (2250)

        ()FYRENA*FYYRA 2 GE- 1 -HWYLCNE.// 5   (2250)

LEEODA 3 MIINRA/ 3 ()THANA*THAARA 9 DHE 1 THIS 4 *LIIF 8 OF- 1 -GEAF// 1 (2251)

GE- 1 -SAAWON 4 SELE- 3 -DREEAM/ 9 NAAH 2 HWAA 4 SWEORD 3 WEGE// 4   (2252)

        END FOLIO 182V +

OHOHE 4 ()FE+R+++*FEORMIE/ 9 FAEAETED 3 WAEAEGE.// 5   (2253)

RYNC- 3 -FAET 1 DEEORE/ 5 ()DUG++*DUGUDH 9 ELLOR 3 ()SEOC*SCEOOC// 4   (2254)

CEAL 0 SE 4 HEARDA 4 HELM/ 8 ()+++*HYR-9-STED- 2 -GOLDE// 5   (2255)

AEAETU= 4 BE- 2 -FEALLEN/ 4 FEOR- 2 -MYND 9 SWEFADH.// 5   (2256)

HAA 1 OHE 3 BEADO- 3 -GRIIMAN/ 3 BYYWAN 9 SCEOLDON.// 6   (2257)

EE 1 SWYLCE 3 SEEO 2 HERE- 4 -+PAAD/ 2   (2258)

          SIIO 9 AET 0 HILDE 3 GE- 1 -BAAD// 5   (2258)

FER 4 BORDA 4 GE- 1 -BRAED/ 9 BITE 1 IIRENA// 5   (2259)

ROSNADH 4 AEFTER 3 BEOR-3-NE/ 9 NE 1 MAEG 3 BYRNAN 4 HRING// 4   (2260)

EFTER 4 WIIG- 8 -FRU-9-MAN/ 3 WIIDE 2 FEERAN// 4   (2261)

AELEDHU= 4 BE 2 HEALFE/ 9 NAES 2 HEAR-4-PAN 4 WYN.// 5   (2262)

OMEN 3 GLEEO- 2 -BEEAMES/ 9 NEE 0 GOOD 3 HAFOC// 4   (2263)

EOND 4 SAEL 3 SWINGEDH/ 3 NEE 1 SE 9 SWIFTA 4 MEARH// 4   (2264)

URH- 3 -STEDE 3 BEEATEDH/ 3 BEALO- 9 -CWEALM 3 HAFADH// 3   (2265)

ELA 3 FEOR-1-H- 4 -CYNNA/ 5 FORDH 9 ON- 1 -SENDED.// 5   (2266)

WAA 1 GIOO-1-MOR- 5 -MOOD/ 2 GIOHDHO 9 MAEAENDE.// 6   (2267)

AN 2 AEFTER 4 EALLU=/ 5 UN- 1 -BLIIDHE 2 ()HWE+++*HWEARF// 9   (2268)

AEGES 3 =AND 0 NIHTES/ 3 ODH 0 DHAET 4 DEEADHES 3 WYLM// 1   (2269)

HRAAN 9 AET 1 HEORTAN/ 3 HORD- 3 -WYNNE 4 FOND// 3   (2270)

ALD 1 UUHT- 9 -SCEADHA/ 5 OPENE 4 STANDAN// 4   (2271)

EE 0 DHE 0 BYR-1-NENDE/ 9 BIOR-2-GAS 2 SEECEDH.// 6   (2272)

ACOD 2 NIIDH- 2 -DRACA/ 3 NIHTES 9 FLEEO-1-GEDH// 4   (2273)

YYRE 2 BE- 2 -FANGEN/ 2 HYNE 3 FOLD- 1 -BUUEND.// 9   (2274)

                        END FOLIO 183R +

)+++++*SWIIDHE 8 ()++*ON- 8 -()+++DA+*DRAEAEDADH/ 8   (2275)

          HEE 0 GE- 4 -SEECEAN 4 SCEALL// 4   (2275)

)++R+*HORD 9 ()++*ON 8 HRUUSAN/ 5 THAEAER 3 HEE 4 HAEAEDHEN 4 GOLD// 4   (2276)

ARADH 9 WINTRUM 5 FROOD/ 4 NE 0 BYDH 4 HI= 4 WIHTE 2 DHYY 1 SEEL.// 9   (2277)

WAA 1 SE 3 DHEEOD- 3 -SCEADHA/ 5 THREEO 1 HUND 4 WINTRA.// 9   (2278)

EEOLD 4 ON 1 ()HRUSAM*HRUUSAN/ 4 HORD- 4 -AERNA 1 SU=// 3   (2279)

EACEN- 9 -CRAEFTIG/ 5 ODH 0 DHAET 2 HYNE 3 +AAN 4 AA- 0 -BEALCH// 4   (2280)

ON 9 ON 0 MOODE/ 5 MAN- 3 -DRYHTNE 3 BAER.// 6   (2281)

                              81

```
FAEAETED 9 WAEAEGE/ 5 FRIODHO- 3 -WAEAERE 3 BAED// 4                              (2282)

HLAAFORD 2 SIINNE/ 9 DHAA 8 WAES 3 HORD 3 RAASOD// 4                             (2283)

ON- 1 -BOREN 4 BEEAGA 9 HORD/ 5 BEENE 4 GE- 0 -TIIDHAD// 4                       (2284)

FEEA- 2 -SCEAFTU= 3 MEN/ 9 FREEA 3 SCEEAWODE.// 7                                (2285)

FIIRA 4 FYRN- 3 -GE- 1 -WEORC/ 9 FORMAN 3 SIIDHE.// 5                            (2286)

THAA 0 SE 3 WYRM 3 ON- 1 -+WOOC/ 3 WROOHT 9 WAES 3 GE- 1 -NIIWAD.// 5            (2287)

STONC 0 DHAA 4 AEFTER 5 STAANE/ 9 STEARC- 4 -HEORT 4 ON- 0 -FAND// 4            (2288)

FEEONDES 3 FOOT- 9 -LAAST/ 4 HEE 0 TOO 3 FORDH 3 GE- 0 -STOOP.// 6              (2289)

DYRNAN 2 CRAEFTE/ 9 DRACAN 3 HEEAFDE 5 NEEAH.// 5                                (2290)

SWAA 2 MAEG 4 UN- 0 -FAEAEGE/ 9 EEADHE 3 GE- 0 -DIIGAN// 4                       (2291)

WEEAN 3 =AND 0 WRAEAEC- 2 -SIIDH/ 3 SEE 0 DHE 4 WAL-9-DEN-1-DES// 3             (2292)

HYLDO 3 GE- 0 -HEALDETH/ 3 HORD- 4 -WEARD 9 SOOHTE// 5                           (2293)

GEORNE 5 AEFTER 5 GRUNDE/ 5 WOLDE 9 GUMAN 4 FINDAN.// 7                          (2294)

THONE 3 THE 1 HI= 3 ON 1 SWEO-9-FOTE/ 5 SAARE 3 GE- 0 -TEEODE.// 6              (2295)

HAAT 1 =AND 0 HREEOH- 3 -MOOD/ 9                                                 (2296)

                 END FOLIO 183V +


        ()HLAEWU=*HLAEAEW 3 OFT 1 YMBE- 7 -HWEARF// 3                            (2296)

EALNE 8 UUTAN- 9 -WEARD-1-NE/ 5 NEE 0 DHAEAER 4 AEAENIG 2 MON// 4               (2297)

ON 8 THAEAERE 9 WEESTENNE/ 4 HWAEDHRE 4 ()HILDE*WIIGES 3 GE- 2 -FEH// 2         (2298)

()BEA+*BEADUWE 9 WEORCES/ 4 HWII-1-LU= 4 ON 0 BEORH 3 AET- 1 -HWEARF// 9        (2299)

SINC- 4 -FAET 3 SOOHTE/ 4 HEE 1 TH= 2 SOONA 3 ON- 1 -FAND// 9                   (2300)

DHAET 1 HAEFDE 3 GUMENA 3 SU=/ 4 GOLDES 3 GE- 9 -FAN-1-DOD// 3                  (2301)

HEEAH- 3 -GE- 0 -STREEONA/ 4 HORD- 1 -WEARD 9 ON- 1 -+BAAD// 5                  (2302)

EARFODH- 5 -LIICE/ 5 ODH 0 DHAET 3 AEAEFEN 1 CWOO=// 9                          (2303)

WAES 0 DHAA 2 GE- 2 -BOL-1-GEN/ 5 BEORGES 3 HYRDE.// 9                          (2304)

WOLDE 4 ()FELA 3 ()DHA*SE 0 *LAADHA/ 4 LIIGE 4 FOR- 4 -GYLDAN// 2               (2305)

DRINC- 9 -FAET 5 DYYRE./ 7 THAA 0 WAES 4 DAEG 3 SCEACEN// 3                     (2306)

WYR-9-ME 4 ON 1 WILLAN/ 5 NOO 3 ON 2 WEALLE 4 ()LAEG*LAENG// 8                  (2307)

BII-9-DAN 4 WOLDE/ 5 AC 2 MID 2 BAEAELE 3 +FOOR// 5                             (2308)

FYYRE 9 GE- 1 -FYYSED/ 3 WAES 0 SE 3 FRUMA 4 EGES- 0 -LIIC// 9                  (2309)

LEEODU= 5 ON 1 LANDE/ 6 SWAA 1 HYT 4 LUNGRE 9 WEARDH// 4                        (2310)

ON 1 HYRA 3 SINC- 2 -GIFAN/ 4 SAARE 9 GE- 1 -ENDOD..-// 9                       (2311)
```

§$ÐHAA 2 SE 1 GAEST 3 ON- 0 -GAN/ 3 GLEEÐU= 3 SPIIWAN// 9   (2312)

EORHT 4 HOFU 3 BAERNAN/ 5 BRYNE- 9 -LEEÐMA 4 STOÐÐ// 4   (2313)

LÐUM 4 ON 2 ANÐAN/ 4 NOÐ 0 ÐHAEAER 9 AAHT 3 CWICES.// 6   (2314)

AAÐH 3 LYFT- 3 -FLOGA/ 4 LAEAEFAN 9 WOLÐE.// 8   (2315)

END FOLIO 184R ✝

WAES 2 THAES 3 WYRMES 3 WIIG/ 3 WIIÐE 2 GE- 1 -SYYNE// 9   (2316)

EARO- 2 -FAAGES 3 NIIÐH/ 4 NEEAN 3 =ANÐ 1 FEORRAN// 3   (2317)

WUU 9 SE 1 GUUÐH- 4 -SCEADHA/ 5 GEEATA 3 LEEOÐE// 4   (2318)

WATODE 3 =ANÐ 0 HYYN-9-ÐE/ 8 HORÐ 2 EFT 2 GE- 1 -SCEEAT.// 5   (2319)

ÐRYHT- 3 -SELE 4 ÐYRN-9-NE/ 8 AEAER 3 ÐAEGES 4 HWIILE.// 6   (2320)

WAEFÐE 3 LANÐ- 4 -WARA/ 9 LIIGE 1 BE- 1 -FANGEN// 6   (2321)

BAEAELE 3 =ANÐ 0 BRONÐE/ 4 BEORGES 9 GE- 1 -TRUWOÐE// 5   (2322)

WIIGES 3 =ANÐ 0 WEALLES/ 3 HI= 1 SEEO 3 WEEN 9 GE- 1 -LEEAH// 4   (2323)

'HAA 1 WAES 3 BIIO- 2 -WULFE/ 3 BROOGA 3 GE- 0 -CYY-9-ÐHEÐ// 3   (2324)

NUU-1-ÐE 3 TOO 0 SOOÐHE/ 6 TH= 1 HIS 1 SYLFES 3 ()HIM*HAAM// 9   (2325)

WOLÐA 3 SEELEST/ 4 BRYNE- 4 -WYLMU= 5 MEALT.// 9   (2326)

IF- 3 -STOOL 3 GEEATA/ 3 TH= 2 ÐHAA= 2 GOOÐAN 2 WAES.// 4   (2327)

WREEOW 9 ON 1 HREÐHRE/ 5 HYGE- 4 -SORGA 4 MAEAEST// 4   (2328)

WEENÐE 9 SE 2 WIISA/ 2 TH= 1 HEE 3 WEALDENÐE// 4   (2329)

WFER 4 EALÐE 9 RIHT/ 4 EECEAN 4 ÐRYHTNE// 4   (2330)

WITRE 3 GE- 0 -BULGE/ 9 BREEOST 2 INNAN 3 WEEOLL// 4   (2331)

HEEOSTRU= 3 GE- 1 -THONCUM/ 9   (2332)

        SWAA 2 HI= 1 GE- 0 -THYYWE 5 NE 1 WAES.// 5   (2332)

WAEF-1-ÐE 1 LIIG- 3 -ÐRACA/ 9 LEEOÐA 4 FAESTEN.// 5   (2333)

EALONÐ 4 UUTAN/ 4 EORÐH- 4 -WEARÐ 9 ÐHONE// 4   (2334)

LEEÐU= 4 FOR- 2 -GRUNDEN/ 5 HI= 2 ÐHAES 2 GUUÐH- 9 -KYNING// 4   (2335)

EÐERA 3 THIIOÐEN/ 4 WRAECE 3 LEORNOÐE// 9   (2336)

EHT 2 HI= 4 THAA 1 GE- 3 -WYRCEAN/ 4 WIIGENÐRA 4 HLEEO// 1   (2337)

ALL- 9 -IIRENNE/ 5 EORLA 4 ÐRYHTEN// 4   (2338)

IIG- 2 -BORÐ 2 WRAEAET- 0 -LIIC/ 9 WISSE 4 HEE 0 GEARWE// 3   (2339)

TH= 1 HI= 3 HOLT- 3 -WUDU/ 2 ()HE++++*HELPAN 9 NE 3 MEAHTE// 4   (2340)

LIND 3 WIDH 4 LIIGE/ 5 SCEOLDE 8 ()++ 9 ()THEND*LAEAEN- 3 -DAGA// 5   (2341)

AETHELING 3 AEAER- 3 -GOOD/ 3 ENDE 8 GE- 9 -BIIDAN// 4   (2342)

WORULDE 3 LIIFES/ 4 =AND 0 SE 2 WYRM 3 SO-9-MOD// 3   (2343)

THEEAH 1 DHE 3 HORD- 4 -WELAN/ 4 HEEOLDE 3 LANGE// 9   (2344)

OFER- 1 -HOGODE 2 DHAA/ 4 HRINGA 3 FENGEL// 4   (2345)

TH= 0 HEE 9 IHONE 3 +WIID- 3 -FLOGAN/ 5 WEORODE 4 GE- 1 -SOOHTE// 9   (2346)

SIIDA\ 3 HERGE/ 4   (2347)

        NOO 1 HEE 2 HI= 3 ()THA=*THAA 3 SAECCE 4 ON- 9 -DREED.// 6   (2347)

NEE 0 HIM 3 THAES 3 WYRMES 3 WIIG/ 4 FOR 9 WIHT 3 DYDE.// 6   (2348)

EAFOD+ 3 =AND 0 ELLEN/ 3 FOR- 0 -DHON 3 HEE 9 AEAER 4 FELA// 4   (2349)

NEARO 4 NEEDHENDE/ 4 NIIDHA 2 GE- 0 -DIIGDE.// 9   (2350)

HILDE- 5 -HLEM-1-MA/ 5 SYDHDHAN 3 HEE 1 HROODH- 3 -GAARES// 9   (2351)

SIGOR- 4 -EEADIG 2 SECG/ 3 SELE 3 FAEAELSODE.// 6   (2352)

=AND 0 AET 0 GUUDHE 9 FOR- 3 -GRAAP/ 3 GRENDELES 4 MAEAEGU=// 3   (2353)

LAADHAN 9 CYNNES/ 4 NOO 1 THAET 2 LAEAESEST 3 WAES// 3   (2354)

HOND- 1 -GE- 0 -()MOT*MOOTA/ 9 THAEAER 3 MON 3 HYGE- 0 -LAAC 3 SLOOH.// 6 (2355)

SYDHDHAN 1 GEEATA 9 CYNING/ 2 GUUDHE 4 RAEAESUM// 5   (2356)

FREEA- 1 -WINE 3 FOLCA/ 9 FREES- 2 -LONDUM 5 ON// 4   (2357)

HREEDH-2-LES 3 EAFORA/ 9 HIORO- 3 -DRYNCUM 4 SWEALT// 3   (2358)

BILLE 4 GE- 0 -BEEATEN/ 9 THONAN 1 BIIO- 1 -WULF 2 COOM// 4   (2359)

SYLFES 3 CRAEFTE/ 9 SUND- 3 -NYTTE 4 DREEAH// 4   (2360)

HAEFDE 3 HI= 3 ON 1 EARME/ 9 ()+++*AANA 8 ()XXX.*THRIITIG// 8   (2361)

HILDE- 3 -GEAT-2-WA/ 3 THAA 0 HEE 1 TOO 3 HOLME 9 ()++AG*STAAG// 4   (2362)

NEALLES 3 HET- 2 -WARE/ 4 HREEM-1-GE 2 THORF-9-()+ON*TON// 8   (2363)

FEEDHE- 4 -WIIGES/ 3 THE 0 HI= 4 FORAN 4 ON- 1 -GEEAN.// 9   (2364)

LINDE 4 BAEAERON/ 3 LYYT 1 EFT 3 BE- 1 -CWOOM// 4   (2365)

FRA= 2 THAA= 9 HILD- 3 -FRECAN/ 4 HAAMES 4 NIIOSAN// 4   (2366)

OFER- 9 -SWAM 1 DHAA 4 SIOLEDHA 2 BI- 0 -GONG/ 3   (2367)

```
       SUNU 3 ECG- 2 -DHEEOWES// 9                              (2367)

EARM 3 AAN- 2 -HAGA/ 3 EFT 1 TOO 1 LEEODU=// 4                  (2368)

THAEAER 3 HIM 9 HYGD 2 GE- 0 -BEEAD/ 4 HORD 3 =AND 0 RIICE// 4  (2369)

BEEAGAS 3 =AND 0 BREGO- 9 -STOOL/ 3 BEARNE 5 NE 0 TRUWODE// 5   (2370)

TH= 2 HEE 2 WIDH 2 AEL- 0 -FYL-9-CU=/ 4 EETHEL- 2 -STOOLAS// 4  (2371)

HEALDAN 3 CUUDHE./ 6 DHAA 2 WAES 9 HYGE- 1 -LAAC 3 DEEAD.// 6   (2372)

NOO 0 DHYY 2 AEAER 2 FEEA- 3 -SCEAFTE/ 9 FIN-1-DAN 4 MEAHTON// 3 (2373)

AET 0 DHAA= 4 AEDHELINGE/ 9 AEAENIGE 1 DHINGA// 4               (2374)

TH= 1 HEE 2 HEARD- 0 -REEDE/ 4 HLAAFORD 9 WAEAERE// 6           (2375)

ODHDHE 2 THONE 3 CYNE- 2 -+DOOM/ 3 CIIOSAN 1 WOL-9-DE.// 8      (2376)

HWAEDHRE 5 HEE 0 ()HI=*HINE 4 ON 1 FOLCE/ 4                     (2377)

       FREEON-1-D- 1 -LAARU= 9 HEEOLD.// 5                      (2377)

EESTU= 4 MID 1 AARE/ 4 ODH 0 DHAET 3 HEE 3 YLDRA 9 WEARDH.// 7  (2378)

WEDER- 3 -GEEATU= 3 WEEOLD/ 3 HYNE 4 WRAEC- 9 -MAECGAS// 3      (2379)

OFER 3 SAEAE 3 SOOHTAN/ 4 SUNA 4 OOHTERES// 9                   (2380)

HAEFDON 3 HYY 1 FOR- 8 -HEALDEN/ 4 HELM 3 SCYLFINGA// 9         (2381)

THONE 4 SEELESTAN/ 4 SAEAE- 0 -CYNINGA// 4                      (2382)

THAARA 3 DHE 9 ()DHE 3 IN 1 SWIIO- 3 -RIICE/ 4 SINC 3 BRYTNADE.// 5 (2383)

MAEAERNE 9 THEEODEN/ 4 HI= 2 TH= 2 TOO 1 MEARCE 5 WEARDH// 4    (2384)

       + END FOLIO 185V


HEE 8 THAEAER 9 ()OR*FOR 0 FEORME/ 5 FEORH- 3 -WUNDE 4 HLEEAT// 3 (2385)

SWEOR-9-DES 3 SWENGUM/ 5 SUNU 3 HYGE- 1 -LAACES.// 4            (2386)

=AND 0 HI= 9 EFT 1 GE- 1 -WAAT/ 4 ONGEN- 2 -DHIIOES 5 BEARN// 3 (2387)

HAAMES 9 NIIOSAN/ 5 SYDHDHAN 5 HEARD- 0 -REED 4 LAEG.// 4       (2388)

LEET 9 DHONE 4 BREGO- 3 -STOOL/ 5 BIIO- 2 -WULF 4 HEALDAN// 9   (2389)

GEEATU= 3 WEALDAN/ 3 TH= 2 WAES 3 GOOD 4 CYNING.// 9            (2390)


              XXXIIII.                                          (FITT)

B$SEE 2 DHAES 2 LEEOD- 3 -HRYRES/ 3 LEEAN 2 GE- 0 -MUNDE// 9    (2391)

UFERAN 4 DOOGRU=/ 5 EEAD- 1 -GILSE 5 WEARDH// 2                 (2392)

FEEA- 9 -SCEAFTU= 4 FREEOND/ 4 FOLCE 4 GE- 0 -STEEPTE.// 5      (2393)

OFER 9 SAEAE 3 SIIDE/ 4 SUNU 3 OOHTERES// 4                     (2394)
```

85

WIGU= 4 =AND 0 WAEAEPNU=/ 9 HEE 0 GE- 2 -WRAEC 3 SYDHDHAN// 5   (2395)

CEALDU= 3 CEAR- 3 -SIIDHUM/ 9 CYNING 3 EALDRE 4 BI- 0 -NEEAT.// 6   (2396)

SWAA 2 HEE 2 NIIDHA 3 GE- 9 -HWANE/ 5 GE- 0 -NESEN 3 HAEFDE// 5   (2397)

SLIIDHRA 4 GE- 1 -SLYHTA/ 9 SUNU 4 ECG- 2 -DHIIOWES.// 7   (2398)

ELLEN- 3 -WEORCA/ 4 ODH 0 DHONE 9 AANNE 4 DAEG// 3   (2399)

THE 1 HEE 4 WIDH 2 THAA= 4 WYRME/ 3 GE- 0 -WEGAN 9 SCEOLDE.// 5   (2400)

GE- 3 -WAAT 2 THAA 5 ().XIIA.*TWELFA 5 SU=/ 3 TORNE 4 GE- 9 -BOLGEN// 4 (2401)

DRYHTEN 2 GEEATA/ 5 DRACAN 3 SCEEAWIAN// 9   (2402)

HAEFDE 3 THAA 1 GE- 3 -FRUU-1-NEN/ 3   (2403)

        HWANAN 3 SIIO 2 FAEAEHDH 9 AA- 0 -RAAS.// 4   (2403)

BEALO- 3 -NIIDH 4 BIORNA/ 3 HI= 2 TOO 0 BEAR-2-ME 9 CWOOM// 8   (2404)

END FOLIO 186R +

MAADH-1-THUM- 3 -FAET 3 MAEAERE/ 5 THURH 2 DHAES 3 MEL-9-DAN 2 HOND// 3 (2405)

SEE 1 WAES 3 ON 0 DHAA= 4 DHREEATE/ 3 THREOTTEEO-9-DHA 8 SECG// 3   (2406)

SEE 0 DHAES 5 OR- 0 -LEGES/ 4 OOR 3 ON- 1 -STEALDE// 3   (2407)

HAEFT 9 HYGE- 3 -GIOOMOR/ 4 SCEOLDE 3 HEEAN 2 DHONON.// 4   (2408)

WONG 9 WIISIAN/ 4 HEE 2 OFER 4 WILLAN 2 GIIONG.// 5   (2409)

TOO 0 DHAES 0 DHE 9 HEE 3 EORDH- 3 -SELE/ 3 AANNE 5 WISSE.// 6   (2410)

HLAEAEW 3 UNDER 9 HRUUSAN/ 3 HOLM- 3 -WYLME 5 NEEH.// 3   (2411)

YYDH- 1 -GE- 1 -WINNE/ 9 SEE 1 WAES 4 INNAN 3 FULL// 4   (2412)

WRAEAETTA 4 =AND 0 WIIRA/ 3 WEARD 9 UN- 2 -HIIORE// 4   (2413)

GEARO 3 GUUDH- 3 -FRECA/ 3 GOLD- 3 -MAADH-9-MAS 3 HEEOLD.// 5   (2414)

EALD 3 UNDER 4 EORDHAN/ 3 NAES 0 TH= 9 YYDHE 2 CEEAP// 4   (2415)

TOO 0 GE- 1 -GAN-1-GENNE/ 4 GUMENA 3 AEAENIGU=// 9   (2416)

GE- 1 -SAET 0 DHAA 4 ON 1 NAESSE/ 5 NIIDH- 4 -HEARD 3 CYNING.// 9 (2417)

THENDEN 3 HAEAELO 3 AA- 0 -BEEAD/ 4 HEORDH- 3 -GE- 0 -NEEATU=// 3 (2418)

GOLD- 9 -WINE 3 GEEATA/ 3 HIM 1 WAES 3 GEOOMOR 3 SEFA// 2   (2419)

WAEAEFRE 9 =AND 0 WAEL- 0 -FUUS/ 3 WYRD 2 UN- 0 -GE- 4 -METE 4 NEEAH.// 4 (2420)

SEE 0 DHONE 9 GOMELAN/ 4 GREETAN 3 SCEOLDE// 5   (2421)

SEECEAN 3 SAAWLE 9 HORD/ 3 SUNDUR 4 GE- 0 -DAEAELAN// 3   (2422)

LIIF 1 WIDH 3 LIICE/ 4 NOO 9 THON 3 LANGE 4 WAES.// 5   (2423)

FEORH 2 AETHELINGES/ 2 FLAEAESCE 9 BE- 1 -WUNDEN.// 7   (2424)

BIIO- 2 -WULF 3 MATHELADE/ 2 BEARN 9 ECG- 2 -DHEEOWES// 5   (2425)

FELA 3 IC 1 ON 0 GIOGODHE/ 4 GUUDH- 0 -RAEAESA 9 GE- 1 -NAES// 4   (2426)

OR- 1 -LEG- 4 -HWIILA/ 3 IC 2 TH= 2 EALL 2 GE- 2 -MON.// 9   (2427)

END FOLIO 186V ✝

KC 0 WAES 3 SYFAN- 3 -WINTRE/ 5 THAA 2 MEC 2 SINCA 8 BAL-9-DOR// 4   (2428)

REEA- 2 -WINE 5 FOLCA/ 5 AET 0 MIINU= 4 FAEDER 9 GE- 0 -NAM// 5   (2429)

HEEOLD 2 MEC 3 =AND 0 HAEFDE/ 4 HREEDHEL 3 CYNING// 9   (2430)

EAF 0 MEE 5 SINC 4 =AND 0 SYMBEL/ 5 SIBBE 3 GE- 0 -MUNDE// 9   (2431)

WAES 1 IC 1 HI= 3 TOO 0 LIIFE/ 4 LAADHRA 3 OO- 0 -WIHTE// 5   (2432)

BEORN 8 IN 9 BURGU=/ 4 THON= 3 HIS 3 BEARNA 3 HWYLC.// 5   (2433)

HERE- 1 -BEALD 9 =AND 0 HAEDH- 2 -CYN./ 6   (2434)

          ODHDHE 3 HYGE- 0 -LAAC 4 MIIN// 3   (2434)

WAES 1 THAAM 9 YLDESTAN/ 5 UN- 0 -GE- 5 -DEEFE- 0 -LIICE// 5   (2435)

MAEAEGES 3 DAEAEDU=/ 9 MORTHOR- 4 -BED 1 STREED// 4   (2436)

SYDHDHAN 3 HYNE 3 HAEDH- 1 -CYN/ 9 OF 2 HORN- 3 -BOGAN.// 6   (2437)

HIS 3 FREEA- 4 -WINE/ 4 FLAANE 2 GE- 9 -SWENC-1-TE// 5   (2438)

MISTE 4 MER-1-CELSES/ 5 =AND 0 HIS 2 MAEAEG 2 OF- 9 -SCEET// 3   (2439)

HROODHOR 5 ODOHERNE/ 4 BLOODIGAN 4 GAARE// 4   (2440)

TH= 0 WAES 9 FEOH- 2 -LEEAS 2 GE- 1 -FEOHT/ 3   (2441)

          FYRENU= 3 GE- 1 -SYNGAD.// 4   (2441)

HREDHRE 9 HYGE- 3 -MEEDHE/ 4 SCEOLDE 4 HWAEDHRE 4 SWAA 1 THEEAH// 2   (2442)

EDHE-9-LING 3 UN- 1 -WRECEN/ 4 EALDRES 3 LINNAN// 4   (2443)

SWAA 1 BIDH 9 GEOOMOR- 3 -LIIC/ 3 GOMELU= 4 CEORLE// 4   (2444)

TOO 0 GE- 1 -BIIDANNE/ 9 TH= 2 HIS 2 BYRE 4 RIIDE// 4   (2445)

IONG 4 ON 1 GALGAN/ 4 THON= 1 HEE 9 GYD 3 WRECE// 4   (2446)

SAARIGNE 4 SANG/ 4 THON= 3 HIS 0 SUNU 9 HANGADH// 5   (2447)

HREFNE 4 TOO 0 HROODHRE/ 5   (2448)

          =AND 0 HEE 1 HI= 3 ()HELPAN*HELPE 9 NE 1 MAEG// 4   (2448)

CALD 3 =AND 0 IN- 1 -FRODO/ 5 AEAENIGE 3 GE- 1 -FREMMAN// 9   (2449)

SYMBLE 4 BIDH 3 GE- 2 -MYNDGAD/ 5 MORNA 4 GE- 0 -HWYLCE// 9   (2450)

END FOLIO 187R ✝

```
EAFORAN 4 ELLOR- 4 -SIIOH/ 3 OOOHRES 4 NE 0 GYYMEOH.// 9          (2451)

TOO 8 GE- 0 -BIIOANNE/ 3 BURGU= 4 IN 0 INNAN// 4                  (2452)

YRFE- 9 -WEAROAS/ 4 THON= 3 SE 3 AAN 1 HAFAOH// 5                 (2453)

THURH 1 DEEA-9-OHES 3 NYYO/ 3 DAEAEOA 2 GE- 1 -FONDAO.// 4       (2454)

GE- 0 -SYHOH 4 SORH- 9 -CEARIG/ 4 ON 1 HIS 1 SUNA 3 BUURE// 5    (2455)

WIIN- 0 -SELE 3 WEEST-9-NE/ 4 WIND-2-GE 1 RESTE.// 7             (2456)

REEOTE 2 BE- 3 -ROFENE/ 9 RIIDEND 3 SWEFAOH// 4                  (2457)

HAELEOH 3 IN 0 HOOH-2-MAN/ 2 NIS 9 THAEAER 3 HEARPAN 3 SWEEG// 3 (2458)

GOMEN 3 IN 0 GEAR-2-OU=/ 9 SWYLCE 3 OHAEAER 3 IUU 0 WAEAERON.// 9 (2459)


                    XXXV.                                         (FITT)

$$GE- 2 -WIITEOH 4 THON= 3 ON 1 SEAL-1-MAN/ 3                    (2460)

          SORH- 2 -LEEOOH 9 GAELEOH// 3                          (2460)

AAN 2 AEFTER 4 AANU=/ 4 THUUHTE 3 HIM 2 EALL 9 TOO 0 RUU=// 4    (2461)

WONGAS 3 =ANO 0 WIIC- 2 -STEOE/ 4 SWAA 4 WEORA 2 HELM// 9        (2462)

AEFTER 5 HERE- 3 -BEALOE/ 4 HEORTAN 3 SORGE// 3                  (2463)

WEAL-9-LINOE 5 WAEG/ 4 WIHTE 5 NE 1 MEAHTE.// 4                  (2464)

ON 1 OHAAM 2 FEORH- 9 -BONAN/ 4 FAEAEGHOHE 5 GE- 0 -BEETAN// 5   (2465)

NOO 0 OHYY 2 AEAER 3 HEE 3 THONE 9 HEADHO- 2 -RINC/ 3           (2466)

          HATIAN 4 NE 1 MEAHTE// 5                               (2466)

LAAOHUM 9 OAEAEOU=/ 4 THEEAH 2 HI= 3 LEEOF 2 NE 1 WAES.// 7      (2467)

HEE 1 OHAA 2 MIO 9 THAEAERE 4 SORHGE/ 4                         (2468)

          THE 1 HI= 2 ()SIO*TOO 3 +SAAR 4 BE- 2 -LAMP// 1       (2468)

GU=- 9 -OREEAM 5 OF- 1 -GEAF/ 4 GODES 3 LEEOHT 2 GE- 0 -CEEAS// 3 (2469)

EA-9-FERU= 5 LAEAEF-1-OE/ 3 SWAA 2 OEEOH 4 EEAOIG 4 MON// 3      (2470)

LOND 9 =ANO 0 LEEOO- 3 -BYRIG/ 4                                 (2471)

          THAA 1 HEE 4 OF 0 LIIFE 4 GE- 1 -WAAT// 4             (2471)

THAA 9 WAES 8 SYNN 2 =ANO 1 SACU/ 4 SWEEONA 4 =ANO 0 GEEATA// 4  (2472)

     + ENO FOLIO 187V


OFER 8 WIIO 9 WAETER/ 5 WROOHT 3 GE- 1 -MAEAENE.// 6            (2473)

HERE- 3 -NIIOH 3 HEAROA/ 9 SYOHOHAN 5 HREEOHEL 4 SWEALT// 4     (2474)

OOHOHE 3 HI= 3 ONGEN- 9 -OHEOWES/ 3 EAFERAN 4 WAEAERAN// 4      (2475)

                         88
```

ROME 4 FYRD- 9 -HWATE/ 5 FREEODE 4 NE 1 WOLDON// 4   (2476)

OFER 5 HEAFO 9 HEALDAN/ 4 AC 1 YMB 4 HREEOSNA- 4 -BEORH// 3   (2477)

CATOLNE 9 INWIT- 4 -SCEAR/ 5 OFT 1 GE- 2 -FREMEDON.// 5   (2478)

TH= 2 MAEAEG- 9 -WINE/ 5 MIINE 3 GE- 3 -WRAEAECAN// 4   (2479)

TAEAEHDHE 4 =AND 0 FYRENE/ 9 SWAA 1 HYT 3 GE- 1 -FRAEAEGE 4 WAES// 3   (2480)

THEEAH 0 DHE 4 OODHER 4 HIS/ 9 EALDRE 4 GE- 3 -BOHTE// 5   (2481)

HEARDAN 3 CEEAPE/ 5 HAEDH- 9 -CYNNE 4 WEARDH// 4   (2482)

EEATA 4 DRYHTNE/ 4 GUUDH 2 ON- 0 -SAEAEGE// 9   (2483)

THAA 2 IC 1 ON 1 MORGNE 4 GE- 1 -FRAEGN/ 4 MAEAEG 3 OODHERNE// 9   (2484)

BILLES 4 ECGU=/ 4 ON 0 BONAN 3 STAEAELAN.// 5   (2485)

THAEAER 3 ONGEN- 9 -THEEOW/ 3 EOFORES 3 NIIOSADH.// 5   (2486)

GUUDH- 4 -HELM 3 TOO- 0 -GLAAD/ 9 GOMELA 5 SCYLFING// 4   (2487)

HREEAS 3 *HEORO- 8 -BLAAC/ 2 HOND 2 GE- 9 -MUNDE..// 7   (2488)

TAEAEHDHO 4 GE- 0 -NODGE/ 4 FEORH- 2 -SWENG 3 NE 1 OF- 9 -TEEAH.// 5   (2489)

C 0 HI= 4 THAA 3 MAADH-3-MAS/ 1 THE 0 HEE 0 MEE 3 SEALDE// 9   (2490)

EALD 2 AET 1 GUUDHE/ 4 SWAA 0 MEE 2 GIFEDHE 3 WAES.// 5   (2491)

EEOHTAN 9 SWEORDE/ 5 HEE 0 MEE 2 LOND 2 FOR- 2 -GEAF// 3   (2492)

ARD 3 EEDHEL- 0 -WYN/ 9 NAES 1 HIM 3 AEAENIG 3 THEARF// 4   (2493)

TH= 1 HEE 0 TOO 2 GIFDHU=/ 4 ODHDHE 9 TOO 2 GAAR- 2 -DENU=// 4   (2494)

ODHDHE 3 IN 1 SWIIO- 2 -RIICE/ 5 SEECEAN 1 THURFE// 9   (2495)

END FOLIO 188R +

YRSAN 4 WIIG- 3 -FRECAN/ 5 WEORDHE 3 GE- 0 -CYYPAN// 8   (2496)

GY=LE 9 IC 0 HI= 3 ON 2 FEEDHAN/ 4 BE- 0 -FORAN 3 WOLDE// 4   (2497)

AANA 2 ON 9 ORDE/ 5 =AND 0 SWAA 2 TOO 3 ALDRE 4 SCEALL// 5   (2498)

SAECCE 4 FREM-9-MAN/ 4 THENDEN 3 THIS 3 SWEORD 3 THOLADH// 4   (2499)

TH= 2 MEC 2 AEAER 9 =AND 0 SIIDH/ 3 OFT 1 GE- 1 -LAEAESTE// 5   (2500)

GYOHDHAN 4 IC 1 FOR 2 DUGEDHU=/ 9 DAEG- 3 -HREFNE 4 WEARDH// 5   (2501)

TOO 1 HAND- C -BONAN/ 3 HUUGA 9 CEMPAN// 4   (2502)

WALLES 3 HEE 0 DHAA 3 FRAETHE/ 4 FREES- 0 -()CYNING*CYNINGE// 9   (2503)

BREEOST- 5 -WEORDHUNGE/ 4 BRINGAN 5 MOOSTE// 5   (2504)

AC 9 IN 0 ()CEM*CAM-1-()PAN*PE 4 GE- 0 -CRONG/ 4 CUMBLES 3 HYRDE// 9   (2505)

AETHELING 3 ON 1 ELNE/ 5 NE 1 WAES 3 ECG 1 BONA// 4   (2506)

89

AC 0 HI= 9 HILDE- 3 -GRAAP/ 3 HEORTAN 5 WYLMAS// 4   (2507)

BAAN- 1 -HUUS 9 GE- 0 -BRAEC/ 3 NUU 1 SCEALL 5 BILLES 3 ECG// 3   (2508)

HOND 1 =AND 0 HEARD 9 SWEORD/ 2 YMB 2 HORD 3 WIIGAN.// 7   (2509)

BEEO- 0 -WULF 2 MA-9-DHELODE/ 5 BEEOT- 1 -WORDU= 3 SPRAEC// 4   (2510)

NIIEHSTAN 1 SIIDHE/ 9 IC 0 GE- 2 -NEEDHDE 5 FELA// 4   (2511)

GUUDHA 4 ON 0 GEOGODHE/ 4 GYYT 1 IC 9 WYLLE// 5   (2512)

FROOD 2 FOLCES 3 WEARD/ 3 FAEAEHDHE 4 SEECAN// 9   (2513)

()MAERDHU=*MAEAERDHU 4 FREM-1-MAN/ 3   (2514)

        GIF 1 MEC 2 SE 4 +MAAN- 3 -SCEADHA// 9   (2514)

OF 3 EORDH- 3 -SELE/ 4 UUT 1 GE- 3 -SEECEDH// 4   (2515)

GE- 0 -GREETTE 4 DHAA/ 9 GUMENA 4 GE- 3 -HWYLCNE// 5   (2516)

HWATE 4 HELM- 4 -BE-9-REND/ 4 HINDEMAN 4 SIIDHE// 5   (2517)

SWAEAESE 3 GE- 1 -SIIDHAS/ 9 NOLDE 3 IC 3 SWEORD 3 BERAN// 4   (2518)

WAEAEPEN 2 TOO 1 WYRME/ 9 GIF 0 IC 0 WISTE 1 HUU// 4   (2519)

      END FOLIO 188V +

WIDH 0 DHAAM 4 AAG- 0 -LAEAECEAN/ 4 ELLES 9 MEAHTE.// 5   (2520)

GYLPE 4 WIDH- 1 -GRIIPAN/ 4 SWAA 1 IC 1 GIOO 1 WIDH 9 GRENDLE 3 DYDE// 4   (2521)

AC 8 IC 8 DHAEAER 4 HEADHU- 3 -FYYRES/ 2 HAATES 9 WEENE// 4   (2522)

()REDHES*OREDHES 3 =AND 1 ()HATTRES*ATTRES/ 4   (2523)

        FOR- 0 -DHON 2 IC 1 MEE 2 ON 9 HAFU// 3   (2523)

BORD 3 =AND 0 BYRNAN/ 4 NELLE 3 IC 1 BEORGES 9 WEARD// 3   (2524)

OFER- 4 -FLEEON 3 FOOTES 2 TREM/ 4 AC 1 UNC 8 *FURDHUR 8 SCEAL// 9   (2525)

WEORDHAN 4 AET 1 WEALLE/ 5 SWAA 1 UNC 2 WYRD 2 GE- 0 -TEEODH// 9   (2526)

METOD 3 MANNA 3 GE- 1 -HWAES/ 4 IC 1 EOM 3 ON 1 MOODE 9 FROM.// 6   (2527)

TH= 2 IC 2 WIDH 1 THONE 3 GUUDH- 2 -FLOGAN/ 3 GYLP 1 OFER- 9 -SITTE// 4   (2528)

GE- 0 -BIIDE 0 GEE 4 ON 1 BEORGE/ 4 BYRNU= 3 WEREDE// 9   (2529)

SECGAS 3 ON 1 SEAR-1-WU=/ 4 HWAEDHER 4 SEEL 5 MAEGE// 3   (2530)

AEFT= 9 WAEL- 2 -RAEAESE/ 4 WUNDE 3 GE- 2 -DYYGAN.// 5   (2531)

UNCER 4 TWEEGA/ 9 NIS 3 THAET 3 EEOWER 3 SIIDH// 4   (2532)

NEE 0 GE- 2 -MET 2 MANNES/ 2 NEFNE 9 MIIN 1 AANES// 3   (2533)

()WAT*THAET 2 HEE 3 WIDH 3 AAG- 0 -LAEAECEAN/ 4 EOFODHO 9 DAEAELE// 4   (2534)

EORL- 4 -SCYPE 4 EFNE/ 4 IC 1 MID 3 ELNE 4 SCEALL// 9   (2535)

GOLD 2 GE- 1 -GANGAN/ 4 OOHOHE 3 GUUOH 3 NIMEOH// 4   (2536)

FEORH- 9 -BEALU 4 FREECNE/ 4 FREEAN 3 EEOWERNE.// 6   (2537)

AA- 0 -RAAS 0 OHAA 9 BII 0 RONDE/ 3 ROOF 2 OORETTA// 3   (2538)

HEARD 4 UNDER 3 HELME/ 9 HIORO- 3 -SERCEAN 2 BAER// 4   (2539)

UNDER 4 STAAN- 4 -CLEOFU/ 9 STRENGO 3 GE- 3 -TRUWODE// 4   (2540)

AANES 4 MANNES/ 3 NE 0 BIDH 9 SWYLC 3 EARGES 2 SIIDH// 4   (2541)

GE- 1 -SEAH. 6 OHAA 2 BE 3 WEALLE/ 9 SEE 8 DHE 3 WORNA 3 FELA// 3   (2542)

                    END FOLIO 189R ✝

GU=- 2 -CYSTU= 2 +GOOD/ 2 GUUDHA 2 GE- 9 -DIIGDE// 3   (2543)

HILDE- 4 -HLEM-2-MA/ 3 THON= 3 HNITAN 2 FEEDHAN.// 9   (2544)

()STODAN*STONOAN 3 STAAN- 2 -BOGAN/ 3 STREEA= 4 UUT 1 THONAN.// 4   (2545)

BRECAN 9 OF 0 BEORGE/ 4 WAES 3 THAEAERE 4 BURNAN 3 WAELM// 2   (2546)

HEADHO- 9 -FYYRU= 4 HAAT./ 6 NE 1 MEAHTE 3 HORDE 3 NEEAH// 3   (2547)

UN- 9 -BYRNENDE/ 4 AEAENIGE 3 HWIILE// 4   (2548)

DEEOP 1 GE- 2 -OYYGAN/ 9 FOR 1 ORACAN 1 LEEGE.// 6   (2549)

LEET 0 OHAA 3 OF 0 BREEOSTU=/ 3 DHAA 0 HEE 9 GE- 1 -BOLGEN 3 WAES// 4   (2550)

WEDER- 3 -GEEATA 5 LEEOD/ 4 WORD 2 UUT 9 FARAN// 4   (2551)

STEARC- 3 -HEORT 3 STYRM-1-DE/ 4 STEFN 3 IN 9 BE- 1 -COOM// 2   (2552)

HEADHO- 2 -TORHT 3 HLYNNAN/ 4 UNDER 9 +HAARNE 4 +STAAN// 5   (2553)

HETE 3 WAES 3 ON- 2 -HREE-2-RED/ 3 HORD- 9 -WEARD 3 ON- 0 -CNIIOW// 5   (2554)

MANNES 4 REORDE/ 4 NAES 9 DHAEAER 5 MAARA 4 FYRST// 4   (2555)

FREEODE 3 TOO 2 FRICLAN/ 9 FRO= 3 AEAEREST 3 CWOOM// 4   (2556)

ORUDH 2 AAG- 0 -LAEAECEAN/ 3 UUT 9 OF 0 STAANE// 4   (2557)

HAAT 3 HILDE- 3 -+SWAAT/ 4 HRUUSE 3 DYNEOE// 9   (2558)

BIORN 4 UNDER 3 BEORGE/ 4 BORD- 1 -RAND 3 ON- 2 -+SWAAF// 9   (2559)

WIDH 0 OHAAM 3 GRYRE- 3 -GIESTE/ 4 GEEATA 4 ORYHTEN// 9   (2560)

OHAA 1 WAES 3 HRING- 3 -BOGAN/ 2 HEORTE 4 GE- 1 -FYYSED// 9   (2561)

SAECGE 3 TOO 1 SEECEANNE/ 4 SWEORD 2 AEAER 3 GE- 1 -BRAEAED// 9   (2562)

GOOD 2 GUUDH- 3 -CYNING/ 4 GOMELE 2 LAAFE// 5   (2563)

ECGU= 3 UN- 9 -()GLAW*SLAAW/ 4 AEAEG- 0 -HWAEDHRU= 4 WAES// 4   (2564)

BEALO- 3 -HYCGENDRA/ 9 BROOGA 5 FRA= 4 OODHRU=// 5   (2565)

                    ✝ END FOLIO 189V

STIIDH- 2 -MOOD 3 GE- 1 -STOOD/ 3 WIDH 9 STEEAPNE 4 ROND// 4   (2566)

WINIA 3 BEALDOR/ 4 DHAA 1 SE 1 WYRM 9 GE- 0 -BEEAH// 4   (2567)

SNUUDE 4 TOO- 0 -SOMNE/ 4 HEE 1 ON 2 SEARWUM 9 +BAAD// 3   (2568)

GE- 2 -WAAT 1 DHAA 2 BYRNENDE/ 4 GE- 1 -BOGEN 3 SCRIIDHAN// 9   (2569)

TOO 0 G=- 3 -SCIPE 4 SCYNDAN/ 4 SCYLD 3 WEEL 2 GE- 1 -BEARG// 3   (2570)

LIIFE 9 =AND 0 LIICE/ 4 LAEAESSAN 4 HWIILE// 5   (2571)

MAEAERU= 4 THEEOD-1-NE/ 5 THONNE 9 HIS 2 MYNE 4 SOOHTE// 4   (2572)

DHAEAER 3 HEE 4 THYY 1 FYRSTE/ 4 FOR-9-MAN 3 DOOGORE// 6   (2573)

WEALDAN 3 MOOSTE/ 4 SWAA 2 HIM 9 WYRD 4 NE 0 GE- 4 -SCRAAF// 5   (2574)

HREEDH 1 AET 0 HILDE/ 5 HOND 2 UP 9 AA- 0 -BRAEAED.// 5   (2575)

GEEATA 4 DRYHTEN/ 4 GRYRE- 3 -FAAH-1-NE 2 SLOOH.// 9   (2576)

INC-1-GE- 1 -LAAFE/ 3 TH= 0 SIIO 3 ECG 3 GE- 1 -+WAAC// 5   (2577)

BRUUN 2 ON 1 BAANE/ 9 BAAT 2 UN- 0 -SWIIDHOR.// 7   (2578)

THON= 2 HIS 2 DHIIOD- 3 -CYNING/ 3 THEARFE 9 HAEFDE// 4   (2579)

BYSIGU= 3 GE- 1 -BAEAEDED/ 3 THAA 1 WAES 3 BEORGES 9 WEARD// 5   (2580)

AEFTER 5 HEADHU- 3 -SWENGE/ 4 ON 1 HREEOUM 9 MOODE// 5   (2581)

WEARP 4 WAEL- 3 -FYYRE/ 4 WIIDE 3 SPRUNGON// 9   (2582)

HILDE- 3 -LEEOMAN/ 5 HREEDH- 2 -SIGORA 5 NE 0 GEALP// 3   (2583)

GOLD- 9 -WINE 3 GEEATA/ 4 GUUDH- 2 -BILL 3 GE- 2 -+SWAAC// 4   (2584)

NACOD 2 AET 0 NIIDHE/ 9 SWAA 2 HYT 3 NOO 1 SCEOLDE// 5   (2585)

IIREN 3 AEAER- 2 -+GOOD/ 4 NE 1 WAES 9 TH= 3 EEDHE 5 SIIDH.// 6   (2586)

TH= 0 SE 2 MAEAER-1-A/ 5 MAGA 4 ECG- 1 -DHEEOWES// 9   (2587)

GRUND- 3 -WONG 3 THONE/ 4 OF- 0 -GYFAN 4 WOLDE// 5   (2588)

SCEOLDE 9 *OFER 8 WILLAN/ 3 WIIC 3 EARDIAN.// 6   (2589)

ELLES 3 HWERGEN/ 5 SWAA 9 SCEAL 8 AEAEG- 1 -HWYLC 2 MON.// 5   (2590)

        END FOLIO 190R *

AA- 0 -LAEAETAN 3 LAEAEN- 2 -DAGAS/ 9 NAES 0 DHAA 3 LONG 3 TOO 0 DHON// 3 (2591)

TH= 0 DHAA 3 AAG- 0 -LAEAECEAN/ 5 HYY 9 EFT 2 GE- 0 -MEETTON// 4   (2592)

HYRTE 3 HYNE 3 HORD- 3 -WEARD/ 9 HREDHER 4 AEAEDHME 3 WEEOLL// 4   (2593)

NIIWAN 2 STEFNE/ 4 NEARO 9 DHROOWODE// 3   (2594)

FYYRE 3 BE- 0 -FONGEN/ 4 SEE 0 DHE 3 AEAER 2 FOLCE 9 WEEOLD.// 5   (2595)

                            32

```
NEALLES 3 HI= 3 ON 1 HEEAPE/ 4 ()HEAND*HAND- 2 -GE- 2 -STEALLAN// 9          (2596)

AEDHELINGA 4 BEARN/ 4 YMBE 2 GE- 2 -STOODON// 3                               (2597)

HILDE- 9 -CYSTU=/ 4 AC 0 HYY 3 ON 1 HOLT 3 BUGON// 5                          (2598)

EALDRE 2 BUR-9-GAN/ 3 HIORA 4 IN 0 AANU= 3 WEEOLL// 3                         (2599)

SEFA 3 WIDH 3 SORGU=/ 9 SIBB 3 AEAEFRE 4 NE 0 MAEG// 4                        (2600)

WIHT 4 ON- 1 -WENDAN/ 3 THAA= 9 DHE 2 WEEL 3 THENCEDH..-// 9                  (2601)


                    XXXVI.                                          (FITT)

$$WIIG- 2 -LAAF 3 WAES 4 HAATEN/ 4 WEEOX- 1 -STAANES 0 SUNU// 2              (2602)

LEEOF- 9 -LIIC 5 LIND- 3 -WIGA/ 4 LEEOD 2 SCYLFINGA.// 7                      (2603)

MAEAEj 1 AELF- 9 -HERES/ 4 GE- 0 -SEAH 2 HIS 3 MON- 2 -DRYHTEN// 3           (2604)

UNDER 9 HERE- 3 -GRIIMAN/ 4 HAAT 2 THROOWIAN.// 5                             (2605)

GE- 2 -MUNDE 9 DHAA 0 DHAA 4 AARE/ 4                                          (2606)

          THE 0 HEE 0 HIM 3 AEAER 3 FOR- 3 -GEAF.// 5                         (2606)

+WIIC- 9 -STEDE 5 WELIGNE/ 4 WAEAEG- 2 -MUNDINGA// 5                          (2607)

FOL-1-C- 1 -RIHTA 9 GE- 1 -HWYLC/ 4 SWAA 3 HIS 4 FAEDER 5 AAHTE// 4          (2608)

NE 1 MIHTE 9 DHAA 3 FOR- 3 -HABBAN/ 2 HOND 1 ROND 2 GE- 1 -FEENG// 9         (2609)

GEOLWE 4 LINDE/ 3 GOMEL 4 SWYRD 2 GE- 0 -TEEAH// 4                           (2610)

THAET 9 WAES 4 MID 3 ELDUM/ 4 EEAN- 3 -MUN-1-DES 4 LAAF.// 9                 (2611)
                              END FOLIO 190V +


SUNA 4 ()OHTERE*OOHTERES/ 3 THAA= 3 AET 1 SAECCE 5 WEARDH// 3                (2612)

()WRAECCA+*WRAECCAN 9 WINE- 3 -LEEASU=/ 4                                    (2613)

          WEEOH- 2 -()STANES*STAAN 3 BANA// 5                                (2613)

MEECES 0 ECGU=/ 9 =AND 0 HIS 4 MAAGU= 4 AET- 0 -BAER// 4                     (2614)

BRUUN- 3 -FAAGNE 4 HELM/ 9 HRINGDE 4 BYRNAN// 5                              (2615)

EALD- 2 -SWEORD 4 ETONISC/ 2 TH= 9 HI= 3 ONELA 4 FOR- 2 -GEAF// 4           (2616)

HIS 2 GAEDELINGES/ 2 GUUDH- 9 -GE- 2 -WAEAEDU// 5                            (2617)

FYRD- 3 -SEARO 3 FUUS- 0 -LIIC/ 4                                            (2618)

          NOO 2 YMBE 9 DHAA 2 FAEAEHDHE 5 SPRAEC// 3                         (2618)

THEEA+ 1 DHE 1 HEE 3 HIS 3 BROODHOR 9 BEARN/ 4 AA- 0 -BRED-2-WADE.// 7      (2619)

HEE 1 *DHAA 8 FRAETWE 3 GE- 0 -HEEOLD/ 9 FELA 4 MISSEERA// 4                (2620)

BILL 3 =AND 0 BYRNAN/ 4 ODH 0 DHAET 9 HIS 2 BYRE 4 MIHTE// 4                (2621)
```
93

EORL- 3 -SCIPE 4 EFNAN/ 4 SWAA 9 HIS 3 AEAER- 3 -FAEDER// 3   (2622)

GEAF 3 HI= 1 DHAA 3 MID 2 GEEATU=/ 3 GUUDH- 9 -GE- 3 -WAEAE-2-DA// 5   (2623)

AEAEG- 0 -HWAES 3 UN- 0 -RIIM/ 4   (2624)

      THAA 1 HEE 2 OF 9 EALDRE 4 GE- 2 -WAAT// 4   (2624)

FROOD 3 ON 2 FOROH- 4 -WEG/ 3 THAA 9 WAES 4 FOR-2-MA 4 SIIDH// 5   (2625)

GEONGAN 2 CEMPAN/ 1 THAET 9 HEE 2 GUUDHE 4 RAEAES// 5   (2626)

MID 3 HIS 4 FREEO- 3 -DRYHTNE/ 9 FREM-1-MAN 4 SCEOLDE// 5   (2627)

NE 0 GE- 2 -HEALT 2 HI= 0 SE 9 MOOD- 2 -SEFA/ 6   (2628)

      NEE 1 HIS 5 ()MAEGENES*MAEAEGES 2 LAAF// 2   (2628)

GE- 2 -WAAC 9 AET 1 WIIGE/ 5 ()THA*THAET 1 SE 3 WYRM 4 ON- 0 -FAND// 3 (2629)

SYDHDHAN 9 HIIE 4 TOO- 1 -GAEDRE/ 4 GE- 2 -GAAN 3 HAEFDON// 4   (2630)

WIIG- 3 -+LAAF 9 MADHE-1-LODE/ 4 WORD- 3 -RIHTA 4 FELA// 3   (2631)

SAEGDE 9 GE- 0 -SIIDHU=/ 5 HI= 3 WAES 2 SEFA 4 GEOOMOR.// 5   (2632)

IC 2 DHAET 9 MAEAEL 8 GE- 8 -MAN/ 3 THAEAER 3 WEE 4 MEDU 2 THEEGUN// 3 (2633)

    + END FOLIO 191R

THONNE 9 WEE 8 GE- 1 -HEETON/ 3 UUSU= 3 HLAAFORDE// 5   (2634)

IN 1 BIIOR- 3 -SELE/ 9 DHE 1 UUS 1 DHAAS 3 BEEAGAS 2 GEAF// 3   (2635)

TH= 1 WEE 3 HI= 3 DHAA 2 GUUDH- 2 -GE- 9 -TAAWA/ 4 GYLDAN 4 WOLDON// 5 (2636)

GIF 2 HI= 3 THYS-1-LICU/ 9 THEARF 2 G=- 1 -LU=-1-PE// 5   (2637)

HEL-1-MAS 3 =AND 1 HEARD 3 SWEORD/ 9   (2638)

      DHEE 1 HEE 2 UUSIC 4 ON 1 HERGE 4 GE- 1 -CEEAS.// 5   (2638)

TOO 1 DHYSSU= 4 SIIDH- 9 -FATE/ 4 SYLFES 3 WILLU=// 4   (2639)

ON- 1 -MUNDE 3 UUSIC 2 MAEAERDHA/ 9   (2640)

      =AND 0 MEE 2 THAAS 2 MAADH-2-MAS 3 GEAF// 4   (2640)

THE 1 HEE 3 UUSIC 3 +GAAR- 9 -WIIGEND/ 3 GOODE 4 TEALDE// 4   (2641)

HWATE 3 HELM- 3 -BEREND/ 9 THEEAH 0 DHE 4 HLAAFORD 3 UUS// 3   (2642)

THIS 2 ELLEN- 4 -WEORC/ 3 AANA 9 AA- 0 -DHOOHTE// 5   (2643)

TOO 0 GE- 2 -FREM-2-MAN-1-NE/ 5 FOLCES 2 HYRDE// 9   (2644)

FOR- 0 -DHAA= 4 HEE 2 MANNA 4 MAEAEST/ 3   (2645)

      MAEAERDHA 4 GE- 3 -FRE-9-MEDE// 4   (2645)

DAEAEDA 3 DOLLIICRA/ 4 NUU 1 IS 0 SE 8 DAEG 8 CUMEN// 3   (2646)

TH= 1 UURE 9 MAN- 3 -DRYHTEN/ 3 MAEGENES 2 BE- 2 -HOOFADH// 3   (2647)

GOODRA 9 GUUDH- 2 -RINGA/ 4 WUTUN 1 GON-1-GAN 2 TOO// 3   (2648)

HELPAN 9 HILD- 3 -FRUMAN/ 3 THENDEN 4 HYT 1 SYY// 3   (2649)

GLEED- 2 -EGESA 9 GRIM/ 4 GOD 2 WAAT 2 ON 1 MEC// 3   (2650)

TH= 2 MEE 3 IS 3 MICLE 9 LEEOFRE/ 4 TH= 2 MIINNE 3 LIIC- 2 -HAMAN// 4   (2651)

MID 2 MIINNE 9 GOLD- 3 -GYFAN/ 4 GLEED 2 FAEDH-2-MIE// 5   (2652)

NE 0 THYNCEDH 2 MEE 9 GE- 1 -RYSNE/ 3   (2653)

        TH= 1 WEE 2 RON-1-DAS 3 BER-1-EN// 3   (2653)

EFT 3 TOO 2 EARDE/ 9 NEMNE 3 WEE 4 AEAERDR 4 MAEGEN// 3   (2654)

+FAANE 3 GE- 0 -FYLLAN./ 9 FEDRH 4 EALGIAN// 4   (2655)

        END FOLIO 191V +

WEDRA 3 DHEEOD-1-NES/ 3 IC 0 WAAT 2 GEARE// 9   (2656)

TH= 2 NAEAERON 4 EALD- 3 -GE- 2 -WYRHT/ 3 TH= 2 HEE 3 AANA 2 SCYLE// 2   (2657)

GEEATA 9 DUGUDHE/ 3 GNORN 3 THROOWIAN// 4   (2658)

GE- 0 -SIIGAN 2 AET 1 SAECCE/ 9 UURU= 8 SCEAL 8 SWEORD 4 =AND 0 HELM// 4 (2659)

BYRNE 3 =AND 1 ()BRYDU*BEADU- 2 -SCRUUD/ 8 BAA= 9 GE- 0 -MAEAENE.// 5   (2660)

WOOD 1 THAA 3 THURH 2 THONE 3 WAEL- 1 -+REEC/ 3   (2661)

        WIIG- 8 -HEA-9-FOLAN 3 BAER// 4   (2661)

FREEAN 3 ON 2 FULTU=/ 4 FEEA 2 WORDA 8 CWAEDH// 9   (2662)

LEEOFA 3 BIIO- 1 -WULF/ 4 LAEAEST 3 EALL 2 TELA// 5   (2663)

SWAA 0 DHUU 2 ON 0 GEO-9-GUDH- 3 -FEEORE/ 5 GEAARA 4 GE- 1 -CWAEAEDE// 3 (2664)

TH= 1 DHUU 3 NE 1 AA- 0 -LAEAETE/ 9 BE 0 DHEE 4 LIFIGENDU=.// 7   (2665)

DOOM 3 GE- 2 -DREEDSAN/ 3 SCEALT 1 NUU 9 DAEAEDU= 4 ROOF// 5   (2666)

AEDHELING 3 AN- 2 -HYYDIG/ 4 EALLE 3 MAEGENE// 9   (2667)

FEORH 2 EALGIAN/ 4 IC 0 DHEE 2 FUL- 0 -LAEAESTU.// 5   (2668)

AEFTER 1 DHAAM 9 WORDU=/ 3 WYRM 3 YRRE 3 CWOOM// 4   (2669)

ATOL 2 IN-1-WIT- 1 -GAEST/ 9 OODHRE 3 SIIDHE// 4   (2670)

FYYR- 3 -WY-8-LMU= 3 FAAH/ 3 FIIONDA 3 NIIOSIAN// 9   (2671)

LAADHRA 4 MANNA/ 3 LIIG- 3 -YYDHU= 4 FOR- 5 -BORN// 2   (2672)

BORD 3 WIDH 9 ROND/ 2 BYRNE 4 NE 1 MEAHTE// 4   (2673)

GEONGU= 4 GAAR- 3 -WIGAN/ 9 GEEOCE 4 GE- 2 -FREM-1-MAN// 5 (2674)

AC 0 SE 3 MAGA 3 GEONGA/ 3 UNDER 9 HIS 3 MAEAEGES 2 SCYLD// 4 (2675)

ELNE 2 GE- 2 -EEODE/ 5 THAA 2 HIS 1 AAGEN 8 ()W+++*WAES// 9   (2676)

GLEEDU= 3 FOR- 1 -GRUNDEN/ 4 THAA 2 GEEN 2 GUUDH- 3 -CYNING// 3   (2677)

()M↓↓↓↓*MAEAERDHA 9 GE- 1 -MUNDE/ 4 MAEGEN- 3 -STRENGO 3 SLOOH// 3   (2678)

HILDE- 3 -BILLE/ 8 TH= 9 HYT 3 ON 1 HEAFOLAN 4 STOOD// 3   (2679)

NII-1-THE 3 GE- 1 -NYYDED/ 1 NAEGLING 9 FOR- 2 -BAERST// 3   (2680)

GE- 1 -SWAAC 3 AET 0 SAECCE/ 3 SWEORD 8 BIIO- 1 -WULFES// 9   (2681)

END FOLIO 192R ✝

GOMOL 4 =AND 0 GRAEAEG- 3 -MAEAEL/ 4 HI= 3 TH= 1 GIFEDHE 4 NE 2 WAES// 8   (2682)

TH= 9 HI= 2 IIRENNA/ 5 ECGE 4 MIHTON// 3   (2683)

HELPAN 3 AET 1 HILDE/ 9 WAES 0 SIIO 2 HOND 4 TOO 1 STRONG// 4   (2684)

SEE 0 DHE 3 MEECA 2 GE- 1 -HWANE/ 9 MIINE 3 GE- 1 -FRAEAEGE// 4   (2685)

SWENGE 3 OFER- 4 -SOOHTE/ 4 THON= 3 HEE 0 TOO 9 SAECCE 4 BAER// 4   (2686)

WAEAEPEN 3 ()WUNDU=*WUNDRU= 4 HEARD/ 3   (2687)

NAES 2 HIM 9 WIHTE 2 DHEE 1 SEEL.// 5   (2687)

THAA 2 WAES 2 THEEOD- 3 -SCEADHA/ 3 THRIDDAN 9 SIIDHE// 4   (2688)

FREECNE 4 +FYYR- 4 -DRACA/ 4 FAEAEHDHA 4 GE- 0 -MYNDIG// 9   (2689)

RAEAESDE 3 ON 0 DHONE 3 ROOFAN/ 3 THAA 1 HI= 1 RUU= 3 AA- 0 -GEALD// 9   (2690)

HAAT 3 =AND 1 HEADHO- 2 -GRIM/ 2 HEALS 3 EALNE 3 YMBE- 3 -FEENG// 9   (2691)

BITERAN 3 BAANU=/ 5 HEE 0 GE- 1 -BLOODEGOD 3 WEARDH// 3   (2692)

SAAWUL- 9 -DRIIORE/ 3 SWAAT 3 YYDHU= 3 WEEDLL.// 9   (2693)

XXXVII.   (FITT)

$$DHAA 0 IC 2 AET 1 THEARFE 8 *GE- 8 -*FRAEGN/ 8 THEEOD- 2 -CYNINGES// 3   (2694)

AND- 0 -LONGNE 9 EORL/ 5 ELLEN 3 CYYDHAN// 3   (2695)

CRAEFT 3 =AND 0 CEENDHU/ 4 SWAA 2 HIM 9 GE- 8 -CYNDE 3 WAES// 4   (2696)

NE 0 HEEDDE 3 HEE 3 THAES 3 HEAFOLAN/ 2   (2697)

AC 9 SIIO 2 HAND 3 GE- 1 -BARN// 3   (2697)

MOODIGES 4 MANNES/ 2   (2698)

THAEAER 1 HEE 9 HIS 1 ()MAEGENES*MAEAEGES 3 HEALP// 3   (2698)

TH= 1 HEE 2 THONE 3 NIIDH- 2 -GAEST/ 4 NIODHOR 9 HWEENE 2 SLOOH.// 5   (2699)

SECG 3 ON 1 SEARWU=/ 4 TH= 1 DHAET 4 SWEORD 2 GE- 9 -DEEAF// 3   (2700)

FAAH 3 =AND 0 FAEAETED/ 3 TH= 1 DHAET 2 +FYYR 3 ON- 1 -GON// 3   (2701)

SWEDHRIAN 9 SYDHDHAN/ 4 THAA 0 GEEN 3 SYLF 4 CYNING.// 5   (2702)

96

GE- 2 -WEEOLD 2 HIS 9 GE- 1 -WITTE/ 5   (2703)

          WAELL- 3 -SEAXE 3 GE- 0 -BRAEAED// 3   (2703)

BITER 4 =AND 0 BEADU- 9 -SCEARP/ 5 TH= 0 HEE 2 ON 2 BYRNAN 2 WAEG// 3   (2704)

FOR- 4 -WRAAT 2 WEDRA 9 HELM/ 3 WYRM 3 ON 2 MIDDAN// 4   (2705)

          • END FOLIO 192V

FEEONJ 3 GE- 2 -FYLDAN/ 9 FERH 3 ELLEN 4 WRAEC// 4   (2706)

=AND 1 HII 1 HYNE 3 THAA 1 BEEGEN/ 3 AA- 0 -BRO-9-TEN 2 HAEFDON// 4   (2707)

SIB- 2 -AEDHELINGAS/ 3 SWYLC 3 SCEOLDE 9 SECG 3 WESAN.// 2   (2708)

THEGN 2 AET 1 DHEARFE/ 5 TH= 1 DHAA= 3 THEEODNE 9 WAES// 4   (2709)

() SIDHAS*SIIDHAST 2 SIGE- 4 -HWIILE/ 4 SYLFES 3 DAEAEDU=// 3   (2710)

WORLDE 9 GE- 2 -WEORCES./ 3 DHAA 1 SIIO 3 MUND 4 ON- 1 -GON// 3   (2711)

THE 0 HI= 1 SE 1 EORDH- 9 -DRACA/ 4 AEAER 1 GE- 1 -WORHTE// 5   (2712)

SWELAN 4 =AND 0 SWELLAN/ 8 HEE 9 TH= 1 SOONA 4 ON- 1 -FAND// 3   (2713)

TH= 0 HI= 3 ON 1 BREEOSTU=/ 5 BEALO- 8 -NIIDHE 9 WEEOLL// 3   (2714)

ATTOR 4 ON 2 IN-1-NAN/ 3 DHAA 2 SE 2 AEDHELING 3 GIIONG// 9   (2715)

TH= 0 HEE 2 BII 1 WEALLE/ 4 WIIS- 3 -HYCGENDE// 4   (2716)

GE- 0 -SAET 3 ON 0 SESSE/ 9 SEAH 2 ON 2 ENTA 2 GE- 1 -WEORC// 5   (2717)

HUU 0 DHAA 4 STAAN- 2 -BOGAN/ 9 STAPULU= 3 FAESTE// 4   (2718)

EECE 3 EORDH- 2 -RECED/ 3 INNAN 1 HEALDE// 9   (2719)

HYNE 3 THAA 1 MID 2 HANDA/ 5 HEORO- 3 -DREEORIGNE// 8   (2720)

THEEO-9-DEN 3 MAEAERNE/ 4 THEGN 3 UN- 1 -GE- 0 -METE 4 TILL// 3   (2721)

WINE- 1 -DRYHTEN 9 HIS/ 4 WAETERE 3 GE- 1 -LAFEDE// 4   (2722)

HILDE 3 SAEDNE/ 4 =AND 1 HIS 1 () HEL+*HELM 9 ON- 1 -SPEEON.// 6   (2723)

BIIO- 1 -WULF 4 MATHELODE/ 5 HEE 1 OFER 4 BENNE 9 SPRAEC// 4   (2724)

WUNDE 5 WAEL- 3 -BLEEATE/ 4 WISSE 3 HEE 3 GEARWE// 9   (2725)

TH= 2 HEE 1 DAEG- 3 -HWIILA/ 3 G=- 2 -DROGEN 4 HAEFDE// 4   (2726)

EORDHAN 1 () WYNN+*WYNNE/ 9 DHAA 1 WAES 3 EALL 3 SCEACEN// 3   (2727)

DOOGOR- 3 -GE- 1 -RIIMES/ 4 DEEADH 2 UN- 0 -GE- 9 -METE 4 NEEAH// 2   (2728)

NUU 1 IC 2 SUNA 3 MIINU=/ 4 SYLLAN 4 WOLDE// 9   (2729)

GUUDH- 2 -GE- 1 -WAEAEDU/ 3 THAEAER 2 MEE 3 GIFEDHE 3 SWAA// 4   (2730)

AEAENIG 2 YRFE- 9 -WEARD/ 2 AEFTER 3 WURDE// 3   (2731)

          • END FOLIO 193R

LIICE 3 GE- 1 -LENGE/ 4 IC 0 DHAAS 1 LEEODE 9 HEEOLD.// 3   (2732)

FIIFTIG 3 WINTRA/ 5 NAES 0 SE 4 FOLC- 3 -CYNING// 9   (2733)

YMBE- 4 -SITTENDRA/ 5 AEAENIG 2 DHAARA// 5   (2734)

THE 0 MEC 2 GUUDH- 2 -WINU=/ 9 GREETAN 2 DORSTE// 4   (2735)

EGESAN 3 DHEEON/ 3 IC 1 ON 3 EARDE 2 +BAAD// 9   (2736)

MAEAEL- 2 -GE- 2 -SCEAFTA/ 4 HEEOLD 2 MIIN 2 TELA// 4   (2737)

NE 3 SOOHTE 9 SEARO- 4 -NIIDHAS/ 3 NEE 1 MEE 4 SWOOR 3 FELA// 4   (2738)

AADHA 3 ON 1 UN- 9 -RIHT/ 2 IC 0 DHAES 3 EALLES 2 MAEG// 3   (2739)

FEORH- 2 -BENNU= 4 SEEOC/ 3 GE- 9 -FEEAN 2 HAB-1-BAN// 4   (2740)

FOR- 0 -DHAA= 4 MEE 1 WIITAN 4 NE 0 DHEARF/ 9 WALDEND 3 FIIRA// 4   (2741)

MORDHOR- 4 -BEALO 3 MAAGA/ 4 THONNE 9 MIIN 2 SCEACEDH// 5   (2742)

+LIIF 2 OF 2 LIICE/ 4 NUU 0 DHUU 4 LUN-1-GRE 2 GEONG// 9   (2743)

HORD 3 SCEEAWIAN/ 3 UNDER 4 HAARNE 3 STAAN.// 4   (2744)

WIIG- 2 -LAAF 9 LEEOFA/ 4 NUU 1 SE 4 WYRM 2 LIGEDH// 3   (2745)

SWEFEDH 3 SAARE 3 WUND/ 9 SINCE 3 BE- 0 -REEAFOD// 3   (2746)

BIIO 2 NUU 2 ON 2 OFOSTE/ 4 TH= 1 IC 2 AEAER- 3 -WELAN// 9   (2747)

GOLD- 2 -AEAEHT 3 ON- 1 -GITE/ 3 GEARO 4 SCEEAWIGE// 4   (2748)

SWEGLE 3 SEARO- 9 -GI=MAS/ 3 TH= 1 IC 0 DHYY 2 SEEFT 2 MAEGE// 4   (2749)

AEFTER 5 MAADHDHU=- 3 -WELAN/ 9 MIIN 3 AA- 0 -LAEAETAN// 3   (2750)

+LIIF 4 =AND 0 LEEOD- 3 -SCIPE/ 3 THONE 4 IC 1 LONGE 1 HEEOLD..-// 9   (2751)

XXXVIII.   (FITT)

$$DHAA 0 IC 2 SNUUDE 3 GE- 0 -FRAEGN/ 4 SUNU 3 WIIH- 9 -STAANES// 3   (2752)

AEFT= 3 WORD- 3 -CWYDU=/ 3 WUNDU= 3 DRYHTNE.// 9   (2753)

HYYRAN 3 HEADHO- 3 -SIIOCU=/ 5 HRING- 1 -NET 2 BERAN// 2   (2754)

BROGDNE 9 BEADU- 4 -SER-2-CEAN/ 4 ()URDER*UNDER 3 BEORGES 3 HROOF.// 5   (2755)

GE- 1 -SEAH 0 DHAA 9 SIGE- 3 -HREEDHIG/ 4   (2756)

       THAA 1 HEE 2 BII 0 SESSE 3 GEEONG.// 5   (2756)

MAGO- 3 -THEGN 9 MOODIG/ 4 MAADHDHU=- 4 -SIGLA 4 FEALO// 2   (2757)

      + END FOLIO 193V

GOLD 4 GLITINIAN/ 9 GRUNDE 4 GE- 2 -TENGE// 5   (2758)

```
WUNDUR 4 ON 2 WEALLE/ 4 =AND 9 THAES 3 WYRMES 4 DENN// 4              (2759)

EALDES 3 UUHT- 4 -FLOGAN/ 9 ORCAS 2 STONDAN// 3                       (2760)

FYRN- 2 -MANNA 3 FATU/ 4 FEOR-9-MEND- 2 -LEEASE// 4                   (2761)

HYRSTU= 4 BE- 1 -HRORENE/ 4 THAEAER 3 WAES 9 HELM 3 MONIG// 3         (2762)

EALD 3 =AND 1 OOMIG/ 3 EARM- 2 -BEEAGA 3 FELA// 9                     (2763)

SEARWU= 3 GE- 0 -SAEAELED/ 3 SINC 3 EEADHE 4 MAEG// 3                 (2764)

GOLD 2 ON 0 ()GRUND+*GRUNDE/ 9 GU=- 2 -CYNNES 3 GE- 1 -HWONE// 4      (2765)

OFER- 3 -HIIGIAN/ 4 HYYDE 2 SEE 0 DHE 9 WYLLE// 4                     (2766)

SWYLCE 4 HEE 1 SIOMIAN 2 GE- 1 -SEAH/ 2 SEGN 4 EALL- 9 -GYLDEN// 5    (2767)

HEEAH 2 OFER 3 HORDE/ 5 HOND- 3 -WUNDRA 9 MAEAEST// 4                 (2768)

GE- 0 -LOCEN 3 LEODHO- 3 -CRAEFTU=/ 4                                 (2769)

          OF 0 DHAA= 3 ()LEOMAN*LEEOMA 9 STOOD// 2                    (2769)

TH= 0 HEE 2 THONE 3 GRUND- 3 -WONG/ 4 ON- 0 -GITAN 3 MEAHTE// 9       (2770)

()WRAECE*WRAEAETE 3 GIOND- 3 -WLIITAN/ 3                              (2771)

          NAES 2 DHAES 3 WYRMES 3 THAEAER// 9                         (2771)

ON- 1 -SYYN 3 AEAENIG/ 3 AC 0 HYNE 4 ECG 3 FOR- 4 -NA=// 4            (2772)

DHAA 1 IC 8 ON 9 HLAEAEWE 3 GE- 1 -FRAEGN/ 4 HORD 3 REEAFIAN// 4      (2773)

EALD 2 ENTA 9 GE- 1 -WEORC/ 3 AANNE 4 MANNAN// 3                      (2774)

HI= 2 ON 1 BEARM 2 ()HLODON*HLADON/ 9 BUNAN 4 =AND 0 DISCAS// 3       (2775)

SYLFES 3 DOOME/ 4 SEGN 3 EEAC 2 GE- 0 -NOOM// 9                       (2776)

BEEACNA 3 BEORHTOST/ 4 BILL 8 AEAER 1 GE- 2 -SCOOD// 3                (2777)

ECG 2 WAES 8 IIREN/ 9 EALD- 3 -HLAAFORDES// 4                         (2778)

THAA= 3 DHAARA 3 MAADHMA/ 4 MUND- 0 -BORA 9 WAES// 4                  (2779)

LONGE 3 HWIILE/ 5 LIIG- 3 -EGESAN 3 WAEG// 2                          (2780)

HAATNE 3 FOR 9 HO-8-RDE/ 5 HIORO- 4 -WEALLENDE// 4                    (2781)

MIDDEL- 3 -NIHTUM/ 9 ODH 3 TH= 0 HEE 2 MORDHRE 4 SWEALT// 5           (2782)

              + END FOLIO 194R


AAR 3 WAES 2 ON 2 OFOSTE/ 9 EFT- 2 -SIIDHES 3 GEORN// 4              (2783)

FRAETWU= 3 GE- 1 -FYRDH-1-RED/ 2 HYNE 9 FYR- 1 -WET 2 BRAEC// 3      (2784)

HWAEDHER 3 COLLEN- 3 -FERDH/ 2 CWICNE 9 GE- 0 -MEETTE// 5            (2785)

IN 1 DHAA= 3 WONG- 2 -STEDE/ 3 WEDRA 2 THEEO-2-DEN// 9               (2786)

ELLEN- 3 -SIIOCNE/ 5 THAEAER 2 HEE 2 HINE 4 AEAER 2 FOR- 2 -LEET.// 3 (2787)
```

HEE 0 DHAA 9 MID 1 THAA= 4 MAADH-2-MU=/ 5 MAEAER-1-NE 3 THIIODEN// 4   (2788)
DRYHTEN 9 SIINNE/ 4 DRIIORIGNE 3 FAND// 3   (2789)
EALDRES 3 AET 2 ENDE/ 9 HEE 1 HINE 3 EFT 3 ON- 1 -GON// 4   (2790)
WAETERES 3 WEORPAN/ 3 ODH 3 TH= 9 WORDES 3 ORD// 2   (2791)
BREEOST- 2 -HORD 3 THURH- 2 -BRAEC./ 4 *BIORN- 8 -*CYNING 8 *SPRAEC// 8   (2792)
GOMEL 9 ON 0 ()GIOGODHE*GIOHDHE/ 3 GOLD 2 SCEEAWODE.// 4   (2793)
$IC 0 DHAARA 4 FRAETWA/ 9 FREEAN 3 EALLES 3 DHANC// 3   (2794)
WULDUR- 4 -CYNINGE/ 3 WORDU= 9 SECGE.// 6   (2795)
EECU= 3 DRYHTNE/ 4 THE 1 IC 0 HEER 3 ON 1 STARIE// 4   (2796)
THAES 0 DHE 9 IC 8 MOOSTE/ 4 MIINU= 3 LEEODU=// 2   (2797)
AEAER 2 SWYLT- 2 -DAEGE/ 4 SWYLC 2 GE- 9 -STRYYNAN// 4   (2798)
NUU 1 IC 2 ON 1 MAADHMA 4 HORD/ 3 ()MINNE*MIINE 1 BE- 9 -BOHTE// 3   (2799)
FROODE 3 FEORH- 3 -LEGE/ 4 FREM-1-MADH 3 GEENA// 9   (2800)
LEEODA 3 THEARFE/ 4 NE 0 MAEG 2 IC 2 HEER 4 LENG 3 WESAN.// 5   (2801)
HAATADH 9 HEADHO- 3 -MAEAERE/ 4 HLAEAEW 3 GE- 2 -WYRCEAN.// 6   (2802)
BEOR-2-HTNE 9 AEFTER 4 BAEAELE/ 3 AET 1 BRIMES 4 NOSAN.// 5   (2803)
SEE 1 SCEL 3 TOO 0 GE- 9 -MYNDU=/ 4 MIINJ= 3 LEEODU=// 3   (2804)
HEEAH 3 HLIIFIAN/ 3 ON 1 HRO-9-NES- 3 -NAESSE// 4   (2805)
TH= 2 HIT 2 SAEAE- 1 -LIIDHEND/ 4 SYDHDHAN 3 HAATAN// 9   (2806)
BIIO- 1 -WULFES 4 BIORH/ 2 DHAA 1 DHE 3 BRENTINGAS// 4   (2807)
OFER 9 FLOODA 3 GE- 1 -NIPU/ 4 FEORRAN 3 DRIIFADH// 4   (2808)
        ✝ END FOLIO 194V

DYDE 0 HI= 9 OF 1 HEALSE/ 4 HRING 3 GYLDENNE// 4   (2809)
THIIODEN 3 THRIIST- 9 -HYYDIG/ 4 THEGNE 4 GE- 3 -SEALDE// 4   (2810)
GEO-1-N-1-GU= 3 GAAR- 1 -WIGAN/ 9 GOLD- 3 -FAAHNE 4 HELM// 4   (2811)
BEEAH 3 =AND 0 BYRNAN/ 3 HEET 0 HYNE 9 BRUUCAN 4 WELL.// 6   (2812)
THUU 2 EART 3 ENDE- 1 -LAAF/ 3 UUSSES 9 CYNNES// 8   (2813)
WAEAES- 2 -MUNDINGA/ 5 EALLE 4 WYRD 0 FOR- 9 -()SPEOF*SWEEOP// 8   (2814)
MIINE 3 MAAGAS/ 5 TOO 2 METOD- 2 -SCEAFTE// 9   (2815)
EORLAS 2 ON 1 ELNE/ 4 IC 0 HI= 3 AEFTER 3 SCEAL// 9   (2816)
TH= 2 WAES 4 THAA= 4 GOMELAN/ 4 GIN-3-GAESTE 4 WORD// 9   (2817)
BREEOST- 3 -GE- 1 -HYGDU=/ 4 AEAER 2 HEE 4 BAEAEL 4 CURE// 3   (2818)

```
HAATE 9 HEADHO- 3 -WYLMAS/ 3                                          (2819)

       HI= 2 OF 2 ()HWAEDHRE*HRAEDHRE 3 GE- 1 -+WAAT// 2              (2819)

SAA-9-WOL 3 SEECEAN/ 4 SOODH- 3 -FAESTRA 4 +DOOM.// 9                 (2820)


                  *XXXVIIII.                                          (FITT)

$DHAA 2 WAES 2 GE- 3 -GONGEN/ 4 ()GUMU=*GUMAN 4 UN- 1 -FROODU=// 3    (2821)

EAR-9-FODH- 4 -LIICE/ 4 TH= 2 HEE 3 ON 2 EORDHAN 5 GE- 2 -SEAH// 4    (2822)

THONE 9 LEEOFESTAN/ 3 LIIFES 3 AET 2 ENDE// 3                        (2823)

BLEEATE 3 GE- 0 -BAEAERAN/ 9 BONA 4 SWYLCE 3 LAEG// 3                (2824)

EGES- 0 -LIIC 3 EORDH- 3 -DRACA/ 3 EALDRE 9 BE- 1 -REEAFOD// 3       (2825)

BEALWE 3 GE- 1 -BAEAEDED/ 2 BEEAH- 4 -HORDU= 2 LENG// 9              (2826)

WYRM 4 WOOH- 2 -BOGEN/ 4 WEALDAN 4 NE 1 MOOSTE// 4                   (2827)

AC 1 +IM 9 IIRENNA/ 4 ECGA 4 FOR- 4 -NAAMON// 4                      (2828)

HEARDE 3 HEADHO- 2 -SCEAR-9-()DE*PE/ 4 HOMERA 6 LAAFE// 3            (2829)

TH= 0 SE 2 WIID- 2 -FLOGA/ 3 WUNDU= 2 STILLE// 9                     (2830)

HREEAS 3 ON 1 HRUUSAN/ 3 HORD- 3 -AERNE + NEEAH// 3                  (2831)

NALLES 9 AEFTER 3 LYFTE/ 3 LAACENDE. 4 H+EARF// 3                    (2832)

       + END FOLIO 195R


MIDDEL- 3 -NIHTU=/ 9 MAADHM- 4 -AEAEHTA 4 WLONC// 4                  (2833)

AN- 1 -SYYN 3 YYWDE/ 3 AC 1 HEE 2 EORDHAN 9 GE- 0 -FEEOLL// 4        (2834)

FOR 0 DHAES 2 HILD- 2 -FRUMAN/ 3 HOND- 2 -GE- 2 -WEORCE// 9          (2835)

HUURU 2 TH= 3 ON 0 LANDE/ 3 LYYT 2 MANNA 3 DHAAH// 3                 (2836)

MAEGEN- 9 -AAGENDRA/ 4 MIINE 2 GE- 3 -FRAEAEGE// 4                   (2837)

THEEAH 0 DHE 3 HEE 3 DAEAE-1-DA 2 GE- 9 -HWAES/ 3 DYRSTIG 3 WAEAERE// 4  (2838)

TH= 2 HEE 2 WIDH 2 ATTOR- 8 -SCEADHAN/ 9 OREDHE 3 GE- 1 -RAEAESDE// 3    (2839)

ODHDHE 4 HRING- 3 -SELE/ 9 HONDU= 4 STYREDE// 4                      (2840)

GIF 1 HEE 4 WAECCENDE/ 9 WEARD 3 ON- 1 -FUNDE// 3                    (2841)

BUUON 4 ON 1 BEORGE/ 3 BIIO- 2 -WULFE 9 WEARDH// 3                   (2842)

DRYHT- 2 -MAADHMA 4 DAEAEL/ 5 DEEADHE 4 FOR- 0 -GOLDEN// 9           (2843)

HAEFDE 4 AEAEG- 1 -()HWAEDHRE*HWAEDHER/ 4 ENDE 3 GE- 2 -FEERED// 2   (2844)

LAEAENAN 2 LIIFES/ 9 NAES 0 DHAA 3 LANG 3 TOO 0 DHON// 3             (2845)

TH= 0 DHAA 2 HILD- 3 -LATAN/ 2 HOLT 0 OF- 9 -GEEFAN// 3              (2846)
                              101
```

```
TYYORE 3 TREEOW- 4 -LOGAN/ 4 TYYNE 4 AET- 1 -SOMNE// 9                        (2847)

DHAA 0 NE 3 DORSTON 4 AEAER/ 5 DAREDHU= 4 LAACAN// 4                          (2848)

ON 1 HYRA 9 MAN- 1 -DRYHTNES/ 4 MICLAN 2 THEARFE// 3                          (2849)

AC 0 HYY 2 SCAMI-9-ENDE/ 4 SCYLDAS 2 BAEAERAN// 4                             (2850)

GUUDH- 2 -GE- 1 -WAEAEDU/ 2 THAEAER 2 SE 0 GO-9-MELA 3 LAEG/ 3               (2851)

WLITAY 3 ON 1 WII- 0 -LAAF/ 5 HEE 0 GE- 3 -WEERGAD 2 SAET// 9                 (2852)

FEEDHE- 2 -CEMPA/ 4 FREEAN 3 EAXLU= 4 NEEAH// 4                              (2853)

WEHTE 2 HYNE 9 WAETRE/ 4 HI= 2 WIHT 2 NE 3 ()SPEOP*SPEEOW// 3                (2854)

NE 1 MEAHTE 3 HEE 3 ON 2 EORDHAN/ 9 DHEEAH 1 HEE 3 UUDHE 3 WEEL// 4          (2855)

ON 0 DHAA= 3 FRU=- 2 -GAARE/ 4 FEORH 2 GE- 2 -HEALDAN// 9                    (2856)

NEE 0 DHAES 2 WEALDENDES/ 3 WIHT 2 ON- 1 -CIRRAN// 4                         (2857)

WOLDE 3 +DOOM 9 GODES/ 2 DAEAEDU= 3 RAEAEDAN// 3                             (2858)

            ✝ END FOLIO 195V


GUMENA 4 GE- 1 -HWYLCU=/ 3 SWAA 9 HEE 1 NUU 1 GEEN 2 DEEDH// 4               (2859)

THAA 1 WAES 2 AET 0 DHAA= 3 ()GEONGU=*GEONGAN/ 2                             (2860)

            GRI= 3 =AND- 0 -SWARU// 9                                        (2860)

EEDH- 2 -BEGEETE/ 3 THAA= 1 DHE 3 AEAER 3 HIS 3 ELNE 3 FOR- 2 -LEEAS.// 4   (2861)

WIIG- 0 -LAAF 9 MADHELODE/ 4 WEEDH- 0 -STAANES 2 SUNU// 3                    (2862)

()SEC*SECG 1 SAARIG- 0 -FERDH/ 9 SEAH 2 ON 2 UN- 1 -LEEOFE// 3              (2863)

TH= 2 LAA 1 MAEG 2 SECGAN/ 3 SEE 0 DHE 3 WYLE 9 SOODH 3 SPECAN// 4          (2864)

TH= 0 SE 2 MON- 3 -DRYHTEN/ 4 SEE 4 EEOW 1 DHAA 9 MAADH-1-MAS 2 GEAF// 4    (2865)

EEORED- 3 -GEATWE/ 3 THE 0 GEE 2 THAEAER 2 ON 9 STANDADH.// 5               (2866)

THON= 3 HEE 2 ON 3 EALU- 2 -BENCE/ 3 OFT 1 GE- 0 -SEALDE// 9                (2867)

HEAL- 3 -SITTENDU=/ 4 HELM 4 =AND 1 BYRNAN// 4                              (2868)

THEEODEN 3 HIS 9 THEGNU=/ 5 SWYLCE 3 HEE 4 THRYYD- 0 -LIICOST// 4           (2869)

OO- 0 -WER 3 FEOR 9 ODHDHE 4 NEEAH/ 4 FINDAN 5 MEAHTE// 4                   (2870)

TH= 1 HEE 3 GEENUNGA/ 9 GUUDH- 1 -GE- 1 -WAEAEDU// 3                        (2871)

WRAADHE 3 FOR- 2 -WURPE./ 6 DHAA 2 HYNE 3 WIIG 2 BE- 0 -GET// 4             (2872)

NEALLES 3 FOLC- 2 -CYNING/ 4 FYRD- 2 -GE- 1 -STEALLU=// 9                   (2873)

GYLPAN 3 THORFTE/ 4 HWAEDHRE 4 HI= 3 GOD 1 UUDHE// 4                        (2874)

SIGORA 9 WALDEND/ 4 TH= 1 HEE 2 HYNE 3 SYLFNE 3 GE- 2 -WRAEC// 3            (2875)

AANA 2 MID 9 ECGE/ 4 THAA 0 HI= 3 WAES 3 ELNES 3 THEARF.// 5                (2876)

                            102
```

$IC 1 HI= 3 LIIF- 3 -WRADHE/ 3 LYYTLE 9 MEAHTE// 5   (2877)

AET- 1 -GIFAN 3 AET 0 GUJDHE/ 6 =AND 1 ON- 1 -GAN 2 SWAA 3 THEEAH// 9   (2878)

OFER 2 MIIN 1 GE- 4 -MET/ 2 MAEAEGES 4 HELPAN.// 5   (2879)

$SYMLE 3 WAES 9 THYY 1 SAEAEM-1-RA/ 4 THON= 4 IC 3 SWEORDE 4 DREP// 3   (2880)

FERHDH- 3 -GE- 0 -NIIDH-9-LAN/ 3 FYYR 0 UN- 4 -SWIIDHOR// 5   (2881)

WEEOLL 4 OF 1 GE- 2 -WITTE/ 5 ()FERGEN*WERGEN-9-DRA 3 TOO 1 LYYT// 4   (2882)

THRONG 3 YMBE 4 THEEODEN/ 3   (2883)

    THAA 1 HYNE 3 SIIO 9 THRAAG 8 BE- 8 -CWOOM.// 6   (2883)

    END FOLIO 196R +

()HU*WUU 1 SCEAL 3 SINC- 2 -THEGO/ 4 =AND 0 SWYRD- 8 -GIFU// 9   (2884)

EALL 2 EEDHEL- 3 -WYN/ 8 EEOWRUM 8 CYNNE.// 8   (2885)

LUFEN 0 AA- 3 -LICGEAN/ 9 LOND- 2 -RIHTES 2 MOOT// 2   (2886)

THAEAERE 1 MAEAEG- 2 -BURGE/ 3 MONNA 9 AEAEG- 0 -HWYLC// 2   (2887)

IIDEL 2 HWEORFAN/ 3 SYDHOHAN 2 AEDHELINGAS// 9   (2888)

FEORRAN 3 GE- 2 -FRICGEAN/ 3 FLEEAM 3 EEOWERNE// 5   (2889)

DOO=- 9 -LEEASAN 1 DAEAED/ 8 DEEADH 3 BIOH 3 SEELLA// 5   (2890)

EORLA 3 GE- 0 -HWYLCU=/ 9 THONNE 4 EDWIIT- 2 -LIIF// 9   (2891)

        XL..-   (FITT)

$HEHT 1 DHAA 4 TH= 2 HEADHO- 4 -WEORC/ 4 TOO 1 HAGAN 4 BIIODAN// 9   (2892)

UP 2 OFER 4 ECG- 3 -CLIF/ 4 THAEAER 3 TH= 2 EORL- 4 -WEOROD// 2   (2893)

MOR-9-GEN- 3 -LONGNE 4 DAEG/ 3 MOOD- 2 -GIOOMOR 4 SAET// 3   (2894)

BORD- 9 -HAEBBENDE/ 4 BEEGA 5 ON 2 WEENU=// 4   (2895)

ENDE- 2 -DOOGORES/ 9 =AND 0 EFT- 2 -CYMES// 3   (2896)

LEEOFES 3 MONNES/ 3 LYYT 0 SWIIGODE// 9   (2897)

NIIWRA 4 SPELLA/ 5 SEE 0 DHE 4 NAES 2 GE- 1 -+RAAD// 4   (2898)

AC 1 +EE 1 SOODH- 9 -LIICE/ 4 SAEGDE 3 OFER 4 EALLE// 5   (2899)

NUU 1 IS 3 WIL- 2 -GEOFA/ 3 WEDRA 9 LEEODA// 4   (2900)

DRYHTEN 4 GEEATA/ 4 DEEADH- 3 -BEDDE 3 FAEST// 3   (2901)

WU-9-NADH 3 WAEL- 8 -RESTE/ 4 WYRMES 2 DAEAEDU=// 4   (2902)

HIM 9 ON 2 EFN 3 LIGEDH/ 4 EALDOR- 4 -GE- 1 -WINNA// 5   (2903)

()SIEX*SEX- 3 -BENNU= 9 SEEOC/ 3 SWEORDE 3 NE 1 MEAHTE// 5   (2904)

ON 0 DHAA= 4 AAG- 0 -LAEAECEAN/ 9 AEAENIGE 4 THINGA// 4   (2905)

WUNDE 4 GE- 0 -WYRCEAN/ 4 WIIG- 0 -LAAF 1 SITEDH// 9   (2906)

OFER 2 BIIO- 2 -WULFE/ 4 BYRE 4 WIIH- 1 -STAANES// 3   (2907)

EORL 4 OFER 9 OODHRU=/ 4 UN- 2 -LIFIGENDU=// 4   (2908)

HEALDEDH 4 HIGE- 3 -MAEAEDHUM/ 9 HEEAFOD- 8 -WEARDE// 5   (2909)

                    END FOLIO 196V ↑

LEEOFES 4 =AND 0 LAADHES/ 3 NUU 8 YS 8 LEEODU= 9 WEEN.// 5   (2910)

OR- 1 -LEG- 2 -HWIILE/ 5 SYDHDHAN 4 ()UNDER*UNDERNE// 4   (2911)

FRONCU= 9 =AND 0 FRYYSU=/ 4 FYLL 3 CYNINGES// 4   (2912)

WIIDE 3 WEORUHEDH/ 3 WAES 0 SIIO 9 WROOHT 3 SCEPEN// 2   (2913)

HEARD 3 WIDH 4 HUUGAS/ 3 SYDHDHAN 9 HIGE- 2 -LAAC 2 CWOOM// 3   (2914)

FARAN 3 FLOT- 2 -HERGE/ 3 ON 1 FREESNA 9 LAND// 3   (2915)

THAEAER 3 HYNE 3 HET- 2 -WARE/ 3 HILDE 3 GE- 2 -()HNAEGDON*NAEAEGDON// 9 (2916)

ELNE 3 GE- 2 -EEODON/ 4 MID 1 OFER- 4 -MAEGENE// 4   (2917)

TH= 1 SE 0 BYRN- 9 -WIGA/ 4 BUUGAN 3 SCEOLDE// 5   (2918)

FEEOLL 4 ON 1 FEEDHAN/ 5 NALLES 9 FRAETWE 4 GEAF// 4   (2919)

EALDOR 4 DUGODHE/ 4 UUS 1 WAES 3 AA 1 SYDHDHAN// 9   (2920)

MERE- 4 -WIIO-3-INGAS/ 0 MILTS 4 UN- 0 -GYFEDHE.// 5   (2921)

$NEE 2 IC 0 TE 0 SWEEO- 9 -DHEEODE/ 4 SIBBE 3 ODHDHE 4 TREEOWE// 5   (2922)

WIHTE 8 NE 0 WEENE/ 8 AC 0 WAES 2 WIIDE 9 CUUDH// 5   (2923)

TH=TE 3 ONGEN- 1 -DHIIO/ 3 EALDRE 4 BE- 2 -SNYDHEDE// 3   (2924)

HAEDH- 0 -CEN 9 HREETHLING/ 3 WIDH 4 HREF-1-NA- 3 -WUDU// 4   (2925)

THAA 2 FOR 4 ON- 1 -MEED-9-LAN/ 2 AEAEREST 2 GE- 0 -SOOHTON// 3   (2926)

GEEAT4 3 LEEODE/ 3 GUUDH- 3 -SCIL-9-FINGAS.// 5   (2927)

$SOONA 3 HI= 3 SE 0 FROODA/ 4 FAEDER 4 OOHTHERES// 9   (2928)

EALD 3 =AND U EGES- 3 -FULL/ 5 ()HOND*OND- 3 -SLYHT 2 AA- 0 -GEAF// 4   (2929)

AA- 0 -BREEOT 9 BRI=- 2 -WIISAN/ 5 BRYYD 0 AA- 4 -()HEORDE*HREDDE// 4   (2930)

GOMELA 4 IOO- 4 -MEEOWLAN/ 9 GOLDE 3 BE- 0 -ROFENE// 5   (2931)

ONELAN 4 MOODOR/ 4 =AND 0 OOHTHERES// 9   (2932)

=AND 0 DHAA 2 FOLGODE/ 3 FEORH- 2 -GE- 0 -NIIDH-2-LAN// 4   (2933)

ODH 0 DHAET 3 HII 3 ODH- 3 -EEODON/ 9 EARFODH- 4 -LIICE// 4   (2934)

IN 1 HREFNES- 3 -HOLT/ 3 HLAAFORD- 2 -LEEASE// 9   (2935)

                              104

BE- 0 -SAET 1 DHAA 4 SIN- 3 -HERGE/ 4 SWEORDA/ 3 LAAFE// 4   (2936)

WUNDU= 3 WEERGE/ 9 WEEAN 8 OFT 2 GE- 1 -HEET// 3   (2937)

        ↑ END FOLIO 197R

EARMRE 3 TEOHHE/ 3 OND- 8 -LONGE 9 NIHT// 3   (2938)

CWAEDH 2 HEE 3 ON 1 MERGENNE/ 4 MEECES 3 ECGUM// 9   (2939)

GEETAN 3 WOLDE/ 5 ()SUM*SUME 3 ON 1 GALG- 2 -()TREOWU*TREEOWU=// 4   (2940)

*FUGLUM 8 TOO 0 GAMENE/ 9 FROOFOR 3 EFT 1 GE- 0 -LAMP// 3   (2941)

SAARIG- 2 -MOODU=/ 3 SOMOD 9 AEAER- 2 -DAEGE// 4   (2942)

SYDHDHAN 3 HIIE 3 HYGE- 3 -LAACES/ 4 HORN 2 =AND 0 BYYMAN// 9   (2943)

GEALDOR 4 ON- 1 -GEEATON/ 3 THAA 0 SE 0 GOODA 3 +COOM// 3   (2944)

LEEODA 3 DUGODHE/ 9 ON 1 LAAST 3 FARAN.// 9   (2945)

                XLI.   (FITT)

$WAES 0 SIIO 3 SWAAT- 3 -SWADHU/ 4 ()SWONA*SWEEONA 3 =AND 0 GEEATA// 4   (2946)

WAEL- 2 -RAEAES 9 WEORA/ 4 WIIDE 2 GE- 0 -SYYNE// 5   (2947)

HUU 0 DHAA 3 FOLC 1 MID 3 HI=/ 3 FAEAEHDHE 9 TOO- 2 -WEHTON.// 4   (2948)

GE- 2 -WAAT 1 HI= 1 DHAA 2 SE 0 GOODA/ 5 MID 2 HIS 1 GAEDE-9-LINGU=// 4   (2949)

FROOD 3 FELA- 2 -GEOGMOR/ 4 FAESTEN 2 SEECEAN// 1   (2950)

EORL 9 ONGEN- 1 -THIIO/ 3 UFOR 5 ON- 1 -CIRDE// 5   (2951)

HAEFDE 3 HIGE- 2 -LAACES/ 9 HILDE 3 GE- 1 -FRUUNEN// 3   (2952)

WLONCES 3 WIIG- 1 -CRAEFT/ 3 WIDHRES 9 NE 8 TRUWODE// 4   (2953)

TH= 1 HEE 2 SAEAE- 1 -MANNU=/ 4 ON- 1 -SACAN 3 MIHTE// 9   (2954)

HEAOHO- 0 -LIIDHENDU=/ 4 HORO 2 FOR- 3 -STANDAN// 3   (2955)

BEARN 3 =AND 0 BRYY-9-DE/ 4 BEEAH 2 EFT 2 THONAN.// 6   (2956)

EALD 2 UNDER 4 EOROH- 2 -WEALL./ 9 THAA 2 WAES 2 AEAEHT 2 BODEN// 3   (2957)

SWEEONA 3 LEEODU=/ 3 SEGN 3 HIGE- 3 -()LACE*LAACES.// 9   (2958)

FREODHO- 3 -WONG 3 THONE/ 3 ()FORD*FORDH 3 OFER- 3 -EEODON// 4   (2959)

SYDHDHAN 9 HREEDH- 3 -LINGAS/ 3 TOO 1 HAGAN 3 THRUNGON// 4   (2960)

THAEAER 4 WEAROH 3 ON-9-GEN- 2 -DHIIOW/ 4 ECGU= 4 ()SWEORDU=*SWEORDA// 5   (2961)

BLONDEN- 3 -FEXA/ 5 ON 1 BID 2 WRE-9-CEN// 4   (2962)

TH= 1 SE 3 THEEOD- 3 -CYNING/ 4 DHAFIAN 2 SCEOLDE// 3   (2963)

EAFORES 9 AANNE 1 +DOOM/ 3 HYNE 4 YRRINGA// 4   (2964)

```
WULF 2 WON- 2 -REEDING/ 9 WAEAEPNE 3 GE- 1 -RAEAEHTE// 4          (2965)

TH= 1 HI= 3 FOR 3 SWENGE/ 4 SWAAT 1 AEAEDRU= 9 SPRONG// 3          (2966)

FORDH 3 UNDER 4 FEXE/ 5 NAES 3 HEE 1 FORHT 9 SWAA 2 DHEEH// 3      (2967)

GOMELA 4 SCILFING/ 4 AC 1 FOR- 1 -GEALD 3 HRADHE// 9              (2968)

WYRSAN 3 WRIXLE/ 4 WAEL- 3 -HLEM 2 THONE// 5                      (2969)

SYDHDHAN 2 DHEEOD- 9 -CYNING/ 3 THYDER 4 ON- 0 -CIRDE.// 5        (2970)

SNE 2 MEAHTE 3 SE 1 SNELLA/ 9 SUNU 4 WON- 1 -REEDES// 3           (2971)

EALDU= 3 CEORLE/ 4 ()HOND*OND- 1 -SLYHT 3 GIOFAN// 4              (2972)

AC 1 HEE 1 HI= 4 ON 2 HEEAFDE/ 3 HELM 3 AEAER 3 GE- 2 -SCER// 9   (2973)

TH= 1 HEE 2 BLOODE 2 FAAH/ 3 BUUGAN 4 SCEOLDE// 5                 (2974)

FEEOLL 3 ON 1 FOL-9-DAN/ 4 NAES 1 HEE 2 FAEAEGE 3 THAA 1 GIIT// 3 (2975)

AC 1 HEE 1 HYNE 2 GE- 2 -WYRPTE/ 9 THEEAH 0 DHE 1 HI= 3 WUND 3 HRINE// 5  (2976)

LEET 1 SE 2 HEARDA/ 3 HIGE- 9 -LAACES 3 THEGN// 5                 (2977)

()BRADE*BRAADNE 4 MEECE/ 5 THAA 1 HIS 3 BROODHOR 1 LAEG// 9       (2978)

EALD- 2 -SWEORD 3 EOTONISC/ 5 ENTISCNE 4 HELM// 3                 (2979)

BRECAN 9 OFER 3 BORD- 3 -WEAL/ 3 DHAA 1 GE- 1 -BEEAH 2 CYNING// 3 (2980)

FOLCES 0 HYRDE/ 9 WAES 2 IN 1 FEORH 4 DROPEN.// 5                 (2981)

DHAA 2 WAEAERON 4 MONIGE/ 3 THE 0 HIS 9 MAEAEG 3 WRIDHON// 4      (2982)

RICONE 4 AA- 0 -RAEAERDON/ 3 DHAA 2 HI= 2 GE- 1 -RYYMED 9 WEARDH// 5  (2983)

TH= 1 HIIE 4 WAEL- 2 -STOOWE/ 4 WEALDAN 4 MOOSTON// 3             (2984)

THEN-9-DEN 3 REEAFODE/ 4 RINC 2 OODHERNE// 4                      (2985)

NAM 0 ON 2 ONGEN- 1 -DHIIO/ 9 IIREN- 2 -BYRNAN// 4               (2986)

HEARD 1 SWYRD 2 HILTED/ 3 =AND 0 HIS 2 HELM 9 SOMOD// 3           (2987)

HAARES 3 HYRSTE/ 5 HIGE- 3 -LAACE 1 BAER// 5                      (2988)

HEE 8 ()DH♦♦*DHAAM 9 FRAETWU= 3 FEENG/ 3                          (2989)

          =AND 1 HI= 3 FAEGRE 4 GE- 1 -HEET// 3                   (2989)

LEEANA 8 ()♦♦♦♦*MID 9 LEEODU=/ 3                                  (2990)
```

```
          =AND 0 GE- 1 -()LAESTA*LAEAESTE 4 SWAA// 3              (2990)

GEALD 2 THONE 3 GUUDH- 2 -RAEAES/ 2 GEEATA 9 DRYHTEN// 4          (2991)
```

HREEDH-2-LES 3 EAFORA/ 3 THAA 1 HEE 1 TOO 0 HAA= 2 BE- 0 -+COOM// 9   (2992)

KOFORE 3 =AND 0 WULFE/ 4 MID 2 OFER- 2 -MAADHMUM// 4   (2993)

SEALDE 9 HIORA 3 GE- 2 -HWAEDHRU=/ 3 HUND 3 THUUSENDA// 4   (2994)

ANDES 2 =AND 9 LOCENRA 4 BEEAGA/ 5   (2995)

          NE 0 DHORFTE 4 HI= 3 DHAA 4 LEEAN 2 ODH- 9 -WIITAN// 4   (2995)

MON 3 ON 2 MIDDAN- 1 -GEARDE/ 4   (2996)

          SYDHDHA*N 2 HIIE 0 DHAA 9 MAEAERDHA 3 GE- 2 -SLOOGON.// 3   (2996)

*AND 1 DHAA 3 IOFORE 4 FOR- 4 -GEAF/ 9 AANGAN 3 DOHTOR// 4   (2997)

HAAM- 3 -WEORDHUNGE/ 4 HYLDO 2 TOO 0 WEDDE// 9   (2998)

TH= 0 YS 0 SIIO 4 FAEAEHDHO/ 4 =AND 1 SE 2 FEEOND- 2 -SCIPE// 5   (2999)

HAEL- 3 -NIIDH 3 WERA/ 9 DHAES 1 DHE 2 IC 2 *WEEN 8 HAFO// 4   (3000)

THE 1 UUS 2 SEECEADH 2 TOO/ 3 SWEEONA 3 LEEODA// 9   (3001)

SYDHDHAN 3 HIIE 3 GE- 1 -FRICGEADH/ 3 FREEAN 4 UUSERNE// 2   (3002)

ALDOR- 9 -LEEASNE/ 4 THONE 2 DHE 2 AEAER 3 GE- 1 -HEEOLD// 3   (3003)

WIDH 3 HETTENDU=/ 3 HORD 9 =AND 8 RIICE// 3   (3004)

EFTER 4 HAELEDHA 4 HRYRE/ 3 HWATE 3 ()SCILDINGAS*SCILD- 8 -*WIGAN// 9   (3005)

OLC- 0 -REED 4 FREMEDE./ 5 OOHDHE 3 FURDHUR 3 GEEN// 4   (3006)

ORL- 9 -SCIPE 4 EFNDE/ 4 ()ME*NUU 0 IS 3 OFOST 4 BETOST// 3   (3007)

H= 1 WEE 1 THEEOD- 9 -CYNING/ 4 THAEAER 4 SCEEAWIAN// 4   (3008)

AND 1 THONE 3 GE- 1 -BRINGAN/ 3 THE 9 UJS 3 BEEAGAS 3 GEAF// 4   (3009)

IN 2 +AAD- 2 -FAERE/ 5 NE 1 SCEL 3 AANES 9 HWAET// 3   (3010)

HELTAN 3 MID 2 THAA= 4 MOODIGAN/ 4 AC 1 THAEAER 4 IS 9 MAADHMA 4 HORD// 2 (3011)

OLD 3 UN- 0 -RIIME/ 4 GRI=-2-ME 2 GE- 0 -CEEA-9-()++D*POD// 8   (3012)

AND 1 NUU 2 AET 0 SIIDHESTAN/ 2 SYLFES 2 FEEORE// 4   (3013)

EEAGAS 9 ()+++++TE*GE- 8 -*BOHTE/ 5 THAA 3 SCEALL 4 BROND 2 FRETAN// 3   (3014)

EAELED 2 THECCEAN/ 9 NALLES 3 EORL 4 WEGAN// 4   (3015)

          + END FOLIO 198V

AADHDHU= 3 TOO 1 GE- 3 -MYNDUM/ 9 NEE 0 MAEGDH 3 SCYYNE// 5   (3016)

ABBAN 3 ON 1 HEALSE/ 4 HRING- 2 -WEOR-9-DHUNGE// 4   (3017)

C 2 SCEAL 4 GEOO-1-MOR- 5 -MOOD/ 3 GOLDE 3 BE- 1 -REEAFOD// 9   (3018)

FT 2 NALLES 3 AEAENE/ 4 EL- 0 -LAND 2 TREDAN// 3   (3019)

UU 1 SE 3 HERE- 9 -WIISA/ 4 HLEAHTOR 5 AA- 0 -LEGDE// 4   (3020)

107

GAMEN 4 =AND 0 GLEEO- 3 -DREEAM/ 9 (3021)

       FOR- 1 -DHON 3 SCEALL 4 GAAR 5 WESAN// 3 (3021)

MONIG 4 MORGEN- 9 -CEALD/ 4 MUNDU= 3 BE- 2 -WUNDEN// 4 (3022)

HAEFEN 3 ON 1 HANDA/ 9 NALLES 3 HEARPAN 3 SWEEG// 4 (3023)

WIIGEND 3 WECCEAN/ 4 AC 0 SE 9 WONNA 4 HREFN// 4 (3024)

+FUUS 2 OFER 4 FAEAEGU=/ 3 FELA 3 REOR-9-DIAN// 3 (3025)

EARNE 3 SECGAN/ 4 HUU 2 HI= 3 AET 1 AEAETE 3 SPEEOW// 3 (3026)

THENDEN 9 HEE 1 WIDH 2 WULF/ 3 WAEL 3 REEAFODE.// 4 (3027)

SWAA 2 SE 3 SECG 2 HWATA/ 9 SECG-1-GENDE 4 WAES// 3 (3028)

LAADHRA 4 SPELLA/ 5 HEE 0 NE 1 LEEAG 2 FELA// 9 (3029)

WYRDA 4 NEE 1 WORDA./ 5 WEOROD 2 EALL 4 AA- 0 -RAAS// 3 (3030)

EEODON 2 UN- 9 -BLIIDHE/ 4 UNDER 4 EARNA- 4 -NAES// 3 (3031)

WOLLEN- 2 -TEEARE/ 4 WUNDUR 9 SCEEAWIAN// 4 (3032)

FUNDON 2 DHAA 3 ON 1 SANDE/ 4 SAAWUL- 3 -LEEASNE// 9 (3033)

HLIM- 1 -BED 2 HEALDAN/ 4 THONE 2 THE 3 HI= 4 HRINGAS 3 GEAF// 9 (3034)

AEAERRAN 3 MAEAELU=/ 4 THAA 0 WAES 3 ENDE- 3 -DAEG// 3 (3035)

GOOUU= 3 GE- 1 -GONGEN/ 9 TH= 1 SE 0 GUUDH- 2 -CYNING// 4 (3036)

WEDRA 3 THEEODEN/ 4 WUNDOR- 3 -DEEADHE 9 SWEALT// 3 (3037)

AEAER 1 HII 2 THAEAER 2 GE- 2 -SEEGAN/ 4 SYL- 0 -LII-2-CRAN 4 WIHT// 9 (3038)

WYRM 3 ON 1 WONGE/ 4 WIDHER- 2 -RAEHTES 3 THAEAER// 4 (3039)

LAADHNE 9 LICGEAN/ 4 WAES 0 SE 3 LEEG- 3 -DRACA// 4 (3040)

GRIM- 0 -LIIC 2 ()GRY++++++*GRYRE- 8 -*FAAH/ 9 (3041)

               END FOLIO 139R +

      GLEEDU= 3 BE- 3 -SWAEAELED// 3 (3041)

SEE 2 WAES 3 FIIFTIGES/ 3 FOOT- 2 -GE- 2 -MEARCES// 9 (3042)

LANG 3 ON 1 LEGERE/ 4 LYFT- 2 -WYNNE 4 HEEOLD// 4 (3043)

NIHTES 9 HWIILU=/ 4 NYDHER 4 EFT 2 GE- 1 -WAAT// 3 (3044)

DENNES 3 NIIOSIAN/ 9 WAES 0 DHAA 3 DEEADHE 4 FAEST// 4 (3045)

HAEFDE 4 EORDH- 3 -SCRAFA/ 9 ENDE 3 GE- 0 -NYTTOD// 5 (3046)

HIM 2 BIG 3 STOODAN/ 4 BUNAN 2 =AND 9 ORCAS// 3 (3047)

DISCAS 3 LAAGON/ 4 =AND 0 DYYRE 4 SWYRD// 3 (3048)

OOMIGE 9 THURH- 4 -ETONE/ 4 SWAA 3 HIIE 3 WIDH 3 EORDHAN 4 FAEDHM// 1 (3049)

HUU-3-SEND 3 WINTRA/ 4 THAEAER 4 EARDODON.// 5   (3050)

HON= 3 WAES 2 TH= 2 YRFE/ 9 EEACEN- 2 -CRAEFTIG// 4   (3051)

UU- 1 -MONNA 4 GOLD/ 3 GALDRE 3 BE- 9 -WUNDEN// 4   (3052)

H= 2 DHAAM 4 HRING- 3 -SELE/ 5 HRIINAN 3 NE 1 MOOSTE// 9   (3053)

U-1-MENA 4 AEAENIG/ 5 NEFNE 4 GOD 3 SYLFA// 4   (3054)

IGORA 3 SOOOH- 9 -CYNING/ 3 SEALDE 5 THAA= 2 DHE 3 HEE 2 WOLDE// 4   (3055)

EE 2 IS 1 MANNA 9 GE- 2 -HYLD/ 3 HORD 3 OPENIAN// 3   (3056)

FNE 4 SWAA 3 HWYLCU= 9 MANNA/ 4 SWAA 2 HI= 2 GE- 2 -MET 2 DHUUHTE..-// 9 (3057)

XLII.   (FITT)

THAA 0 WAES 2 GE- 2 -SYYNE/ 5 TH= 1 SE 3 SIIDH 3 NE 0 DHAAH// 3   (3058)

HAA= 2 DHE 4 UN- 0 -RIHTE/ 9 INNE 3 GE- 2 -HYYDDE// 5   (3059)

)WRAECE*WRAEAETE 4 UNDER 5 WEALLE/ 4 WEARD 9 AEAER 3 OF- 1 -SLOOH// 4   (3060)

EEARA 3 SU=-2-NE/ 4 THAA 3 SIIO 4 FAEAEHDH 3 GE- 9 -WEARDH// 4   (3061)

E- 1 -WRECEN 4 WRAADH- 2 -LIICE/ 4 WUNDUR 5 HWAAR 9 THON=// 4   (3062)

ORL 3 ELLEN- 3 -+ROOF/ 3 ENDE 3 GE- 2 -FEERE.// 5   (3063)

IIF- 2 -GE- 9 -SCEAFTA/ 4 THON= 3 LENG 3 NE 2 MAEG// 4   (3064)

ON 4 MID 2 HIS 9 ()++GU=*MAAGU=/ 4 MEDU- 2 -SELD 3 BUUAN// 1   (3065)

WAA 3 WAES 2 BIIO- 1 -WULFE./ 9 THAA 0 HEE 3 BIORGES 2 WEARD// 3   (3066)

    END FOLIO 199V +

OOHTE 4 SEARO- 3 -NIIDHAS/ 2 SEOLFA 9 NE 0 CUUDHE// 4   (3067)

HURH 3 HWAET 2 HIS 3 WORULDE 3 GE- 0 -DAAL/ 3 WEOR-9-DHAN 3 SCEOLDE.// 5 (3068)

WAA 2 HIT 3 ODH 2 DOOMES 2 DAEG/ 3 DIIOPE 3 BE- 9 -NEM-1-DON// 4   (3069)

HEEOJ-1-NAS 3 MAEAERE/ 5 THAA 2 DHAET 2 THAEAER 3 DYDON// 9   (3070)

H= 0 SE 2 SECG 2 WAEAERE/ 5 SYNNU= 4 SCILDIG// 4   (3071)

ERGU= 2 GE- 1 -HEADHE-9-ROD/ 2 HELL- 3 -BENDU= 3 FAEST// 3   (3072)

O=-2-MU= 4 GE- 2 -WIITNAD/ 2 SEE 0 DHONE 9 WONG 2 ()STRADE*STRUDE// 5   (3073)

)NAESHE*NAEFNE 3 GOLD- 3 -HWAETE/ 3 GEAR-1-WOR 9 HAEFDE// 4   (3074)

AGEN-1-DES 3 EEST/ 3 AEAER 3 GE- 2 -SCEEAWOD.// 5   (3075)

IIG- 2 -+LAAF 9 MADHELODE/ 4 WIIH- 1 -STAANES 4 SUNU// 4   (3076)

FT 2 SCEALL 3 EORL 9 MONIG/ 3 AANES 2 WILLAN// 4   (3077)

RAEAEC 3 AA- 1 -()DREOGEDH*DREEOGAN/ 4   (3078)

SWAA 2 UUS 0 GE- 9 -WORDEN 2 IS// 3   (3078)

NE 1 MEAHTON 2 WEE 0 GE- 1 -LAEAERAN/ 3 LEEOFNE 9 THEEODEN// 3   (3079)

RIICES 3 HYRDE/ 4 RAEAED 2 AEAENIGNE// 4   (3080)

TH= 0 HEE 0 NE 0 GREETTE/ 9 GOLD- 3 -WEARD 3 THONE// 4   (3081)

LEETE 2 HYNE 4 LICGEAN/ 3 THAEAER 3 HEE 9 LONGE 4 WAES// 2   (3082)

WIICU= 4 WUNIAN/ 4 ODH 2 WORULD- 2 -ENDE// 9   (3083)

HEEOLD 0 ON 3 HEEAH- 2 -GE- 4 -SCEAP/ 3 HORD 2 YS 1 GE- 1 -SCEEAWOD// 2 (3084)

GRI=-9-ME 2 GE- 1 -GONGEN/ 4 WAES 1 TH= 2 GIFEDHE 5 TOO 1 SWIIDH// 3   (3085)

THE 0 DHONE 9 *THEEOD- 8 -*CYNING/ 8 THYJER 4 ON- 1 -TYHTE.// 5   (3086)

$IC 1 WAES 2 THAEAER 2 INNE/ 5 =AND 1 TH= 3 EALL 9 GEOND- 3 -SEH// 3   (3087)

RECEDES 3 GEATWA/ 5 THAA 0 MEE 2 GE- 1 -RYYMED 9 WAES// 3   (3088)

NEALLES 4 SWAEAES- 0 -LIICE/ 5 SIIDH 3 AA- 0 -LYYFED// 3   (3089)

INN 3 UNDER 9 EORDH- 2 -WEALL/ 4 IC 2 ON 2 OFOSTE 4 GE- 1 -FEENG// 4   (3090)

MICLE 3 MID 9 MUNDU=/ 4 MAEGEN- 3 -BYRDHENNE// 5   (3091)

HORD- 2 -GE- 1 -STREEONA/ 1 HIDER 9 UUT 2 AET- 0 -BAER// 3   (3092)

                    END FOLIO 200R +

CYNINGE 3 MIINU=/ 4 CWICO 1 WAES 2 THAA 0 GEENA// 9   (3093)

WIIS 2 =AND 0 GE- 1 -WITTIG/ 3 WORN 3 EALL 2 GE- 2 -SPRAEC// 3   (3094)

GOMOL 3 ON 1 GEHOHO/ 9 =AND 8 EEOW-2-IC 1 GREETAN 4 HEET// 2   (3095)

BAED 2 TH= 2 GEE 0 GE- 1 -WORHTON/ 3 AEFTER 9 WINES 2 DAEAEDU=// 3   (3096)

IN 0 BAEAEL- 3 -STEDE/ 3 BEORH 2 THONE 2 HEEAN// 1   (3097)

MICELNE 9 =AND 0 MAEAER-1-NE/ 4 SWAA 1 HEE 1 MAN-1-NA 3 WAES// 4   (3098)

WIIGEND 4 WEORDH- 9 -FULLOST/ 4 WIIDE 2 GEOND 3 EORDHAN// 3   (3099)

THENDEN 2 HEE 2 BURH- 9 -WELAN/ 2 BRUUCAN 4 MOOSTE.// 5   (3100)

$UTON 2 NUU 2 EFSTAN/ 2 OODHRE 9 *SIIDHE// 8   (3101)

SEEON 3 =AND 0 SEECEAN/ 2 SEARO- 3 -*GIMMA 8 GE- 2 -THRAEC/ 3   (3102)

WUNDUR 3 UNDER 9 WEALLE/ 4 IC 1 EEOW 2 WIISIGE// 4   (3103)

TH= 1 GEE 3 GE- 0 -NOOGE/ 4 NEEON 4 SCEEAWIADH// 9   (3104)

BEEAGAS 3 =AND 1 BRAAD 1 GOLD/ 3 SIIE 2 SIIO 3 BAEAER 4 GEARO// 4   (3105)

AEAEDRE 3 GE- 9 -AEFNED/ 2 THON= 3 WEE 4 UUT 1 CYMEN// 4   (3106)

=AND 1 THON= 3 GE- 2 -FERIAN/ 3 FREEAN 9 UUSERNE// 4   (3107)

LEEOFNE 3 MANNAN/ 3 THAEAER 3 HEE 2 LONGE 3 SCEAL// 9   (3108)

N 0 DHAES 2 WALDENDES/ 3 WAEAERE 3 GE- 1 -THO-2-LIAN.// 5   (3109)

EET 0 DHAA 2 GE- 0 -BEEODAN/ 9 BYRE 3 WIIH- 0 -STAANES// 3   (3110)

AELE 3 HILDE- 3 -DIIOR/ 4 HAELEDHA 2 MO-9-NEGU=// 4   (3111)

OLD- 3 -AAGENDRA/ 3 TH= 0 HIIE 4 BAEAEL- 4 -WUDU// 3   (3112)

EORRAN 9 FEREDON/ 4 FOLC- 3 -AAGENDE// 4   (3113)

OODU= 3 TOO- 1 -GEENES/ 3 NUU 1 SCEAL 3 GLEED 9 FRETAN// 4   (3114)

EAXAN 3 WONNA 3 LEEG/ 4 WIGENA 3 STRENGEL// 4   (3115)

HONE 9 DHE 3 OFT 2 GE- 0 -+BAAD/ 4 IISERN- 4 -SCUURE// 5   (3116)

HON= 3 STRAEAELA 3 STORM/ 9 STRENGU= 8 GE- 1 -BAEAEDED// 4   (3117)

COOC 2 OFER 3 SCILD- 2 -WEALL/ 4 SCEFT 2 NYTTE 9 HEEOLD// 4   (3118)

)FAEDER*FAEDHER- 4 -GEARWU= 3 FUUS/ 3 FLAANE 3 FULL- 3 -EEODE.// 4 (3119)

UURU 9 SE 3 SNOTRA/ 3 SUNU 3 WIIH- 0 -STAANES// 3   (3120)

A- 0 -CIISDE 3 OF 1 CORDHRE/ 9 CYNIGES 2 THEGNAS// 8   (3121)

                    END FOLIO 200V +

YFONE 8 ()++*TOO- 8 -SOMNE/ 4 THAA 0 SEELESTAN// 1   (3122)

EODE 9 EAHTA 3 SU=/ 3 UNDER 3 INWIT- 3 -+HROOF// 3   (3123)

ILDE- 3 -()RINC*RINCA/ 3 SU= 2 ON 9 HANJA 2 BAER// 4   (3124)

EAELED- 3 -LEEOMAN/ 3 SEE 0 DHE 3 ON 2 ORDE 3 GEEONG// 9   (3125)

AES 1 DHAA 2 ON 1 HLYTME/ 3 HWAA 2 TH= 1 HORD 3 STRUDE// 4   (3126)

YDHDHAN 9 OR- 2 -WEARDE/ 3 AEAENIGNE 3 DAEAEL// 3   (3127)

ECGAS 1 GE- 0 -SEEGON/ 3 ON 1 SELE 9 WUNIAN// 1   (3128)

AEAENE 3 LICGAN/ 2 LYYT 1 AEAENIG 2 MEARN// 3   (3129)

H= 2 HII 1 OFOST- 0 -()LIC+*LIICE/ 9 UUT 0 GE- 1 -FEREDON// 4   (3130)

YYRE 3 MAADHMAS/ 3 DRACAN 2 EEC 1 SCUFUN// 9   (3131)

YRM 2 OF= 2 WEALL- 1 -CLIF/ 3 LEE-2-TON 2 WEEG 2 NIMAN// 3   (3132)

LOOD 2 FAEDH-9-MIAN/ 4 FRAETWA 4 HYRDE// 8   (3133)

)TH=*THAA 2 WAES 3 WUN-1-DEN 1 GOLD/ 9 ON 1 WAEAEN 4 HLADEN// 3   (3134)

EAEG- 0 -HWAES 2 UN- 0 -RIIM/ 4 ()AETHELINGE*AETHELING 2 BOREN// 9 (3135)

AAR 2 HILDE- 8 -*RINC/ 8 TOO 1 HRONES- 3 -NAESSE..-// 9   (3136)

                    XLIII.   (FITT)

HIM 1 DHAA 2 GE- 1 -GIREDAN/ 2 GEEATA 2 LEEODE// 4   (3137)

                         111

+AAD 2 ON 2 EORDHAN/ 9 UN- 2 -WAAC- 1 -LIICNE// 3   (3138)

()HELM*HELMUM 2 BE- 0 -HONGEN/ 3 HILDE- 2 -BORDU=// 9   (3139)

BEORHTU= 3 BYRNU=/ 3 SWAA 2 HEE 1 BEENA 4 WAES// 2   (3140)

AA- 0 -LEGDON 2 DHAA 0 TOO- 9 -MIDDES/ 4 MAEAERNE 3 THEEODEN// 4   (3141)

HAELEDH 5 HIIOFENDE/ 3 HLAAFORD 9 LEEOFNE// 3   (3142)

ON- 0 -GUNNON 2 THAA 3 ON 1 BEORGE/ 2 BAEAEL- 3 -FYYRA 9 MAEAEST.// 4   (3143)

WIIGEND 3 WECCAN/ 3 ()WUD+*WUDU- 8 -+REEC 2 AA- 0 -STAAH// 3   (3144)

SWEART 9 OF= 2 ()SWICDHOLE*SWIODHOLE/ 4 SWOOGENDE 3 ()LET*LEEG// 8   (3145)

WOOPE 2 BE- 2 -WUNDEN/ 2 WIND- 9 -BLOND 1 G=- 1 -LAEG// 3   (3146)

ODH 3 TH= 1 HEE 0 DHAA 2 +BAAN- 3 -+HUUS/ 3 GE- 1 -BROCEN 3 HAEFDE// 9   (3147)

HAAT 1 ON 1 HREDHRE/ 4 HIGU= 4 UN- 0 -ROOTE// 3   (3148)

MOOD- 1 -CEARE 3 MAEAEN-9-DON/ 3 MON- 1 -DRYHTNES 8 ()CW+ALM*CWEALM// 3   (3149)

SWYLCE 3 GIOOMOR- 3 -GYD/ 9 ()+EAT+++*SIIO 8 *GEOO- 8 -MEEOWLE// 8   (3150)

     END FOLIO 201R +

()+++++++++++++++*AEFTER 8 *BIIO- 8 -*WULFE/ 8   (3151)

     ()+UNDEN*BUNDEN- 2 -HEORDE// 9   (3151)

()++NG*SONG 8 SORG- 2 -CEARIG/ 8 ()SEALDHE*SAEAEDE 8 GE- 8 -NEAHHE// 8   (3152)

TH= 1 HIIO 3 HYRE 9 ()++++G+NGAS*HEARM- 8 -*DAGAS/ 3   (3153)

     HEARDE 2 ON- 8 -()D+EDE*DREEDE// 4   (3153)

WAEL- 8 -FYLLA 3 WORN/ 9 ()+++UDES*WIIGENDES 8 EGESAN// 3   (3154)

()HYDHO*HYYNUHO 4 =AND 0 ()HAEF+*HAEFT- 8 -NYYD/ 3   (3155)

     HEOFON 2 REECE 9 ()SWE+LG*SWEALG// 8   (3155)

GE- 8 -WORHTON 1 DHAA/ 3 WEDRA 2 LEEODE// 4   (3156)

()HLEO*HLAEAEW 2 ON 1 ()HOE*HLIIDHE/ 3   (3157)

     SEE 9 ()+AES*WAES 2 HEEAH 3 =AND 0 BRAAD// 8   (3157)

WAEAEG- 1 -LIIDHENDU=/ 3 WIIDE 2 GE- 2 -SYYNE// 3   (3158)

=AND 0 BE- 0 -TIM-9-BREDON/ 3 ON 2 TYYN 2 DAGU=// 3   (3159)

BEADU- 1 -ROO-1-()FIS*FES 2 BEECN/ 2 BRONDA 9 ()L+++*LAAFE// 8   (3160)

WEALLE 2 BE- 2 -WORHTON/ 3 SWAA 1 HYT 0 WEORDH- 3 -LIICOST// 2   (3161)

()FO++*FORE- 9 -()+NOTRE*SNOTRE 2 M=/ 2 FINDAN 2 MIHTON// 2   (3162)

HII 2 ON 0 BEORG 2 DYDON/ 3 BEEG 2 =AND 9 SIGLU// 3   (3163)

EALL 1 SWYLCE 3 HYRSTA./ 3 SWYLCE 3 ON 1 HORDE 2 +AEAER// 4   (3164)

IIOH- 9 -HEEDIGE 2 M=/ 2 G=- 2 -NUM= 2 HAEFDON// 2   (3165)

OR- 1 -LEETON 3 EORLA 2 G=- 1 -STREEON/ 9   (3166)

        ()++RDHAN*EJRDHAN 2 HEALDAN// 1   (3166)

OLD 1 ON 1 GREEOTE/ 3 THAEAER 2 HIT 2 NJU 0 GEEN 1 LIFADH// 9   (3167)

LOU= 2 SWAA 2 UN- 1 -NYT/ 2   (3168)

        SWAA 0 ()HY++HYT 8 ()++OR*AEAEROR 3 WAES.// 4   (3168)

HAA 0 Y=BE 3 HLAEAEW 2 RIODON/ 9 HILDE- 2 -DEEORE// 3   (3169)

ETHELINGA 8 BEARN/ 2 EALRA 3 ()TWELFA*TWELFE// 3   (3170)

OLDON 9 ()++++*CARE 8 CWIIDHAN/ 4 *=AND 8 KYNING 3 MAEAENAN// 1   (3171)

ORD- 1 -GYD 1 WRECAN/ 3 =AND 0 Y=B 0 ()W+*WER 9 SPRECAN// 3   (3172)

AHTODAN 1 EORL- 2 -SCIPE/ 3 =AND 0 HIS 1 ELLEN- 2 -WEORC// 2   (3173)

UGUDHU= 9 DEEMDON/ 2 SWAA 1 HIT 2 G=- 0 -()D+++*DEEFE 8 BIDH// 3   (3174)

H= 1 MON 2 HIS 2 WINE- 2 -DRYH=/ 1 WORDJ= 9 HERG=// 3   (3175)

ERHDHU= 3 FREEOG=/ 2 THON= 8 HEE 1 FORDH 2 SCILE// 3   (3176)

F 1 LIIC- 0 -HAMAN/ 9 ()++++*LAEAEDED 8 WEORDHAN// 2   (3177)

WAA 1 BE- 0 -GNORNODON/ 2 GEEATA 2 LEEODE// 2   (3178)

LAAFORDES 9 ()+++RE*HRYRE/ 3 HEORDH- 1 -G=- 1 -NEEATAS// 1   (3179)

WAEAEDON 2 TH= 0 HEE 2 WAEAERE/ 3 WYRULD- 0 -()CYNING*CYNINGA// 9   (3180)

)+ANNU=*MANNA 3 MILDUST/ 3 =AND 0 MON- 3 -()++AERUST*DHWAEAERUST// 2   (3181)

EEODJ= 3 LIIDHOST/ 2 =AND 0 LOF- 9 -GEORNOST.// 9   (3182)

END FOLIO 201V +

Appendix I

Spacing at Other Than Morpheme Boundaries

This appendix concerns the scribes' habits in spacing strings of letters within words when the position of spacing does not coincide with onset of a root or prebase morpheme. Even a glance at the listing that follows will show that the incidence of spacing is neither arbitrary nor capricious; the regularity of phonological conditions forming the contexts of the spacings implies specifically linguistic habits underlying the leaving of space between letter strings making up words. In addition, the measure of the spaces is much more restricted in range than is the measure of spaces between words or their constituent root and prebase morphemes: seldom do the determinate spacings exceed 2-space.

For these data there is no need here for tabulation of features and other conventional abstracting of their characteristics. The lists are not too long to be scanned readily. Also, they are already ordered by the computer sort program by which they were produced. Each list follows the order of a double sort, represented by Set 1 and Set 2, displayed on the following page. The two sets operate together in this way: all items belonging to the first category in Set 1 appear first, in conjunction with all the categories (in sequence) contained in Set 2. Within each doubly-defined group, items appear in the order of their occurrence in the text.

The double phonological (strictly, graphemic) sort will illustrate the utility of having the text in machine-readable form, but its rationale may be of more interest. Any word can of course be located readily in the text with assistance of a

Set 1 (following spacing)	Set 2 (preceding spacing)
1. Nasal (m, n)	1. Vocalic nucleus--long (īo, īe, ēo, ēa, ǣ, ā, ē, ī, ō, ū, ȳ)
2. Liquid (l, r)	
3. Spirant (s, f) (þ/ð)	2. Vocalic nucleus--short (a, e, i, o, u, y, æ, io, ie, eo, ea)
4. Stop (b, p, d, t, c)	
5. Other (h, g, w, x)	3. Nasal (m, n)
	4. Liquid (l, r)
6. Vocalic nucleus (long or short)	5. Spirant (s, f) (þ/ð)
	6. Stop (b, p, d, t, c)
7. Nonalphabetic symbol	7. Other (h, g, w, x)
	8. Nonalphabetic symbol

Thus, for example, the order of any list is--

Long vocalic nucleus	+	Nasal
Short vocalic nucleus	+	Nasal
Nasal	+	Nasal
Liquid	+	Nasal
etc.;		

then

Long vocalic nucleus	+	Liquid
Short vocalic nucleus	+	Liquid
etc.;		

etc.

word index, such as that provided in Klaeber's Glossary, or
with assistance of A Concordance to Beowulf, by J. B. Bessinger,
Jr., and P. H. Smith, Jr. To locate words similar in structure,
though, only a sorting by spellings is practical. The listing
in this appendix places all forms of the kinds designated in
five major groupings on the basis of the class of sounds
following the spacing. On the other hand, to find, say, all
words in which spacing follows a long vowel, one need only turn
to the initial items in each group; or to find those in which
spacing follows a resonant consonant, one can turn to that
section of each group where all instances are listed together.
The sorting procedures for this appendix, then, will have
gathered data into linguistically defined classes for whatever
uses to which the information may be put.

Some few observations on the distribution of the spacings
will suggest the phonological conditionings of the writing
characteristics of these morphic strings. Taking the group for
lines 662-1320 as illustration, 401 morphemes have internal
spacing before a consonant; only 32 have internal spacing
before a vowel. Of the latter group, one is at a line-end
and two are indeterminate. Of the remaining 29, eight have
spacing both before and after the vowel; altogether twenty
have spacing between l or r and the vowel (see the section
"Measurement of Spacing," in the Introduction). One of the
spacings before vowels occurs after a long vowel (and at a
line-end), ostensibly at a syllable boundary: -bū-endum 768.
Only one has a 3-space, hāton 849, in hāton heolfre, implying
that the scribe may have construed the text as (nom. sg. neut.)
hāt followed by prepositional construction on heolfre, which
makes sense and is stylistically acceptable.

Of the approximately 400 spacings before consonants, about
a fourth (108 instances) occur between a resonant (m, n, l, r)
and a stop consonant. The greatest proportion of the full
list has a vowel or resonant consonant preceding the spacing
before a following consonant and subsequent vowel in what must

)e a new syllable.

The other groups of lines copied by S1 are similar in
respect to measure, frequency, and distribution of spacings.
The text copied by S2 has far less frequent spacing within
morpheme letter-strings, approximately 230 instances in the
nearly 1250 lines he copied. Roughly, S1 left spacing within
a morpheme in relation to number of verse lines in a ratio 2:3,
compared with S2's ratio of 1:5.

One conclusion may be warranted on the basis of the
positions and measures of spacings within words and not
preceding a prebase or root morpheme spelling: they reflect
syllable structure in the scribes' language. The exceptions
to the spacings occurring in contexts phonologically congruent
with those of syllable boundaries in Germanic languages are
remarkably few, being hardly more frequent than are patent
errors in copying the alphabetic text. Those apparent
exceptions that cannot be accounted for on nonphonological
grounds may, under closer analysis, yield some further phonetic
information. S2, for example, wrote

feor^{2}h	2077	þur^{2}h	2045
feor^{1}h	2266	beor^{2}htne	2803

and S1 wrote, among others like them,

beor^{1}hte	214	-for^{3}hte	444
beor^{1}hte	231	-fer^{1}hð	702
beor^{2}ht-	609	fer^{9}hþe	1166
sor^{2}h-	512	-bur^{1}h	522.

At the least, h appears to behave as does s in clustering
patterns of consonants, and the articulation of r and h may be
inferred commonly to have induced open transition between them
in succession.

117

SPACING WITHIN MORPHEME PRECEDES CONSQNANT-GRAPH

A. SPACING PRECEDES RESONANT
(0044) STREEO-9-NUM   [THEEOD-GE-STREEONUM]
(0297) STREEA-9-MAS   [LAGU-STREEAMAS]
(0559) TEEO-1-NAN   [LAAOH-GE-TEEONAN]
(0124) HREE-1-MIG   [HREEMIG]
(0218) FAA-9-MII-   [FAAMII-HEALS]
(0239) CWOO-1-MON   [CWOOMON]
(0324) CWOO-1-MON   [CWOOMON]
(0352) BEE-1-NA   [BEENA]
(0598) NAEAE-2-NEGU=   [NAEAENEGU=]
(0303) SCIO-1-NON   [SCIONON]
(0001) $$DE-9-NA   [GAAR-DENA]
(0003) FRE-2-ME-1-   [FREMEDON]
(0101) FYRE-1-NE   [FYRENE]
(0142) HY-9-NE   [HYNE]
(0165) FRE-1-MEDE.   [GE-FREMEDE]
(0177) FRE-2-ME-2-   [GE-FREMEDE]
(0269) LAARE-2-NA   [LAARENA]
(0297) MA-1-N-2-   [MANNAN]
(0399) MA-9-NIG   [MANIG]
(0424) GRA-9-MUM   [GRAMUM]
(0474) GUME-2-NA   [GUMENA]
(0500) SCYLDI-9-NGA.   [SCYLDINGA]
(0012) CEN-1-NED   [CENNED]
(0046) AEAEN-1-NE   [AEAENNE]
(0071) IN-1-NAN   [INNAN]
(0074) BAN-1-NAN   [GE-BANNAN]
(0094) SUN-1-NAN   [SUNNAN]
(0098) CYN-9-NA   [CYNNA]
(0101) FREM-9-MAN   [FREMMAN]
(0102) GRIM-2-MA   [GRIMMA]
(0104) CYN-9-NES   [FIIFEL-CYNNES]
(0107) CYN-1-NE   [CYNNE]
(0113) WUN-1-NON   [WUNNON]
(0118) IN-1-NE   [INNE]
(0155) MAN-1-NA   [MANNA]
(0162) CUN-1-NON   [CUNNON]
(0164) CYN-9-NES   [MAN-CYNNES]
(0174) FREM-2-MAN-1-   [GE-FREMMANNE]
(0174) MAN-1-N-1-   [GE-FREMMANNE]
(0196) CYN-2-NES   [MON-CYNNES]
(0201) MAN-2-NA   [MANNA]
(0216) DEN-1-NE.   [BUNDENNE]
(0235) THRYM-1-MUM   [THRYMMUM]
(0246) FREM-1-MEN-1-   [GUUDH-FREMMENDRA]
(0248) DHON-1-NE   [DHONNE]
(0257) CYYDHAN-1-NE   [GE-CYYDHANNE]
(0278) RUUM-1-NE   [RUUMNE]
(0297) N-2-NAN   [MANNAN]
(0299) FREM-3-MEN-1-   [GOOD-FREMMENDRA]
(0306) ()GRUMMON*GRIM-1-MON   [*GRIMMON]
(0307) SOM-1-NE   [AET-SOMNE]
(0329) MAN-2-NA   [SAEAE-MANNA]
(0339) THRYM-8-MUM   [HIGE-THRYMMUM]
(0346) UN-1-NAN   [GE-UNNAN]
(0353) THIIN-1-NE   [THIINNE]
(0364) NEM-1-NADH   [NEMNADH]
(0390) IN-9-NE   [INNE]

```
0409) GUN-1-NEN      [ON-GUNNEN]
0445) MAN-1-NA       [HREEDH-MANNA]
0445) MIIN-4-NE      [MIINNE]
0491) SOM-2-NE       [AET-SOMNE]
0508) CUN-1-NE-2-    [CUNNEDON]
0565) GEN-2-NE       [MERGENNE]
0573) THON-1-NE      [THONNE]
0580) FIN-1-NA       [FINNA]
0613) CYN-1-NA       [CYNNA]
0636) FREM-9-MAN     [GE-FREMMAN]
0642) IN-1-NE        [INNE]
0644) SEM-1-NINGA    [SEMNINGA]
0036) MAEAER-2-NE    [MAEAERNE]
0040) BYR-1-NUM      [BYRNUM]
0040) BEAR-9-ME      [BEARME]
0078) AER-9-NA       [HEAL-AERNA]
0201) MAEAER-9-NE    [MAEAERNE]
0271) DYR-2-NE       [DYRNE]
0353) MAEAER-9-NE    [MAEAERNE]
0366) WEAR-1-NE      [WEARNE]
0410) DYR-1-NE       [UN-DYRNE]
0429) WYR-2-NE       [FOR-WYRNE]
0512) FULL-1-NE      [SORH-FULLNE]
0513) EAR-2-MUM      [EARMUM]
0543) HOL-9-ME       [HOLME]
0075) THIS-2-NE      [THISNE]
0297) LEEOF-1-NE     [LEEOFNE]
0538) AEF-1-NOON     [GE-AEFNDON]
0302) TH-1-MED       [SIID-FAETHMED]
0039) WAEAEP-2-NUM   [HILDE-WAEAEPNUM]
0141) TAAC-1-NE      [TAACNE]
0238) BRONT-1-NE     [BRONTNE]
0295) WYD-2-NE       [NIIW-TYRWYDNE]
0360) DRIHT-2-NE     [WINE-DRIHTNE]
0385) MAAD-1-MAS     [MAADMAS]
0434) WAEAEP-1-NA    [WAEAEPNA]
0472) MAAD-1-MAS     [MAADMAS]
0480) DRUNC-1-NE     [DRUNCNE]
0568) BRONT-8-NE     [BRONTNE]
0314) GEG-1-NUM      [GEGNUM]

0480) BEEO-1-RE      [BEEORE]
0561) DEEO-1-RAN     [DEEORAN]
0154) GAA-9-LE       [SIN-GAALE]
0190) GAA-9-LA       [SIN-GAALA]
0285) SEE-2-LEST.    [SEELEST]
0281) BEA-1-LUWA     [BEALUWA]
0497) HEO-1-ROTE     [HEOROTE]
0593) HEO-1-ROTE     [HEOROTE]
0611) HAE-1-L-1-     [HAELETHA]
0003) AETHE-2-LINGAS [AETHELINGAS]
0053) SCY-1-L-1-2-   [SCYLDINGA]
0141) SWEOTO-9-LAN   [SWEOTOLAN]
0311) FE-1-LA.       [FELA]
0324) GRY-9-RE-      [GRYRE-GEATWUM]
0371) THE-1-LODE     [MATHELODE]
0446) HAFA-1-LAN     [HAFALAN]
0605) DOOGO-1-RES    [DOOGORES]
0410) MIIN-1-RE      [MIINRE]
0091) FEOR-1-RAN     [FEORRAN]
0156) FEOR-1-RAN     [FEORRAN]
0202) CEOR-1-LAS     [CEORLAS]
0430) FEOR-2-RAN     [FEORRAN]
0488) DEEOR-1-RE     [DEEORRE]
0637) EOR-2-LIIC     [EORLIIC]
```

119

(0280) AEAEF-1-RE   [AEAEFRE]
(0628) FROOF-1-RE   [FROOFRE]
(0587) BROODH-2-RUM   [BROODHRUM]
(0454) HRAEAED-1-LAN   [HRAEAEDLAN]
(0478) END-1-LES   [GRENDLES]
(0483) GREND-9-LES   [GRENDLES]
(0358) EAX-9-LUM   [EAXLUM]

B.   SPACING PRECEDES SPIRANT
(0049) GEEA-1-FON   [GEEAFON]
(0085) NII-9-DHE   [WAEL-NIIDHE]
(0094) HREE-2-THIG   [SIGE-HREETHIG]
(0163) SCRII-2-THADH   [SCRIITHADH]
(0325) MEE-1-THE   [SAEAE-MEETHE]
(0374) HREE-1-THEL   [HREETHEL]
(0440) LYY-9-FAN   [GE-LYYFAN]
(0182) HEO-2-FENA   [HEOFENA]
(0362) GEO-1-FENES   [GEOFENES]
(0381) HEA-1-THO-   [HEATHO-ROOF]
(0460) HEA-2-THO-   [HEATHO-LAAFE]
(0519) HEA-2-THO-   [HEATHO-RAEAEMES]
(0576) HEO-9-FONES   [HEOFONES]
(0287) HWAE-8-THRES   [AEAEG-HWAETHRES]
(0302) FAE-1-TH-1-   [SIID-FAETHMED]
(0584) HWAE-2-THER   [GE-HWAETHER]
(0046) WE-9-SENDE   [UMBOR-WESENDE]
(0160) GO-1-THE   [GEOGOTHE]
(0215) SCU-9-FON   [SCUFON]
(0226) HRY-1-SE-1-   [HRYSEDON]
(0299) GIFE-1-THE   [GIFETHE]
(0332) ()HAELE-9-THUM*AETHELUM   [*AETHELUM]
(0371) MA-2-THE-1-   [MATHELODE]
(0456) MA-1-THELODE   [MATHELODE]
(0543) HRA-2-THOR   [HRATHOR]
(0555) GYFE-1-THE   [GYFETHE]
(0611) E-1-THA   [HAELETHA]
(0621) DUGU-2-THE   [DUGUTHE]
(0621) GO-1-THE   [GEOGOTHE]
(0611) SWYN-1-SODE   [SWYNSODE]
(0086) EAR-9-FODH-   [EARFODH-LIICE]
(0176) WEOR-1-THUNGA   [WIIG-WEORTHUNGA]
(0254) FUR-1-THUR   [FURTHUR]
(0331) WUR-2-THAD   [GE-WURTHAD]
(0414) WEOR-1-THEDH.   [WEORTHEDH]
(0465) FUR-2-THUM   [FURTHUM]
(0504) MAEAER-1-DHA   [MAEAERDHA]
(0534) EAR-9-FETHO   [EARFETHO]
(0132) SYDH-3-THAN   [SYDHTHAN]
(0142) SYDH-2-THAN   [SYDHTHAN]
(0243) SCEDH-2-THAN   [SCEDHTHAN]
(0567) SYDH-2-THAN   [SYDHTHAN]
(0171) BREC-1-DHA   [BRECDHA]
(0276) EG-1-SAN   [EGSAN]

C.   SPACING PRECEDES STOP
(0035) BEEA-2-GA   [BEEAGA]
(0096) SCEEA-2-TAS   [SCEEATAS]
(0177) GEEO-1-CE   [GEEOCE]
(0205) GEEA-1-TA   [GEEATA]
(0353) THEEO-1-DEN   [THEEODEN]
(0374) GEEA-1-TA   [GEEATA]
(0378) GEEA-1-TA   [GEEATA]
(0385) BEEO-1-DAN   [BEEODAN]
(0417) THEEO-9-DEN   [THEEODEN]
(0443) GEEO-9-TENA   [GEEOTENA]

```
0513) EEA-9-GOR-     [EEAGOR-STREEAM]
0536) BEEO-1-TE-1-   [GE-BEEOTEDON]
0589) DREEO-1-GAN    [DREEOGAN]
0608) GEEO-1-CE      [GEEOCE]
0625) GEEA-1-TA      [GEEATA]
0051) RAEAE-1-DEN-1- [*SELE-RAEAEDENDE]
0055) FRAEAE-9-GE    [GE-FRAEAEGE]
0113) GII-9-GANTAS   [GIIGANTAS]
0121) GRAEAE-2-DIG   [GRAEAEDIG]
0175) HEE-9-TON      [GE-HEETON]
0181) DAEAE-1-DA     [DAEAEDA]
0194) LAA-9-CES      [HIGE-LAACES]
0195) DAEAE-1-DA     [DAEAEDA]
0227) WAEAE-2-DO     [GUUDH-GE-WAEAEDO]
0247) MEE-1-DU       [GE-MEEDU]
0292) WAEAE-1-DU     [GE-WAEAEDU]
0479) DAEAE-2-DA     [DAEAEDA]
0514) MAEAE-9-TON    [MAEAETON]
0514) STRAEAE-3-TA   [MERE-STRAEAETA]
0552) BROO-1-DEN     [BROODEN]
0649) NII-9-PEN-1-   [NIIPENDE]
0066) GEO-2-GODH     [GEOGODH]
0160) GEO-1-GO-1-    [GEOGOTHE]
0215) GEA-1-TOLIIC   [GEATOLIIC]
0421) EO-9-TENA      [EOTENA]
0428) EO-8-DOR       [EODOR]
0453) BEA-1-DU-      [BEADU-SCRUUDA]
0466) GEO-1-GODHE    [GEOGODHE]
0552) BEA-1-DO-      [BEADO-HRAEGL]
0621) GEO-1-GO-1-    [GEOGOTHE]
0245) HAE-1-BBENDE   [LIND-HAEBBENDE]
0321) GAE-1-DERE     [AET-GAEDERE]
0329) GAE-1-DERE     [AET-GAEDERE]
0373) FAE-2-DER      [EALD-FAEDER]
0385) THRAE-2-CE     [MOOD-THRAECE]
0459) FAE-1-DER      [FAEDER]
0003) ME-1-DON.      [FREMEDON]
0060) WEORO-2-DA     [WEORODA]
0076) STE-9-DE       [FOLC-STEDE]
0081) HLIIFA-2-DE.   [HLIIFADE]
0105) DO-1-DE        [WEARDODE]
0132) WE-1-DON       [SCEEAWEDON]
0161) SEOMA-1-DE     [SEOMADE]
0161) SYRE-2-DE      [SYREDE]
0162) MISTI-1-GE     [MISTIGE]
0169) METO-9-DE      [METODE]
0177) ME-2-DE.       [GE-FREMEDE]
0189) MA-1-GA        [MAGA]
0204) WE-2-DON       [SCEEAWEDON]
0225) WE-9-DERA      [WEDERA]
0226) SE-1-DON.      [HRYSEDON]
0238) WERE-9-DE      [WEREDE]
0285) STE-2-DE       [HEEAH-STEDE]
0304) HRO-1-DEN      [GE-HRODEN]
0310) RECE-1-DA      [RECEDA]
0326) RE-1-CE-1-     [RECEDES]
0326) CE-1-DES       [RECEDES]
0361) FERE-9-DE      [GE-FEREDE]
0378) FYRE-3-DON     [FYREDON]
0402) SNYRE-2-DON    [SNYREDON]
0403) HEORO-1-TES    [HEOROTES]
0470) THINGO-1-DE.   [THINGODE]
0498) WE-2-DERA.     [WEDERA]
0508) NE-2-DON       [CUNNEDON]
0515) GLI-2-DON      [GLIDON]
```

121

```
(0536) TE-1-DON    [GE-BEEOTEDON]
(0546) WE-1-DERA   [WEDERA]
(0551) FREME-2-DE  [GE-FREMEDE]
(0560) THREEATE-9-DON   [THREEATEDON]
(0560) THEENG-1-DE    [THEENODE]
(0570) GO-1-DES    [GODES]
(0591) FREME-2-DE  [GE-FREMEDE]
(0614) HRO-9-DEN   [GOLD-HRODEN]
(0624) ME-1-DO-    [MEDO-FUL]

(0009) SITTEN-1-DRA    [YMB-SITTENDRA]
(0057) THEN-1-DEN    [THENDEN]
(0095) BUUEN-9-DUM    [LAND-BUUENDUM]
(0102) GREN-1-DEL    [GRENDEL]
(0151) GREN-9-DEL    [GRENDEL]
(0179) MUN-9-DON    [GE-MUNDON]
(0206) CEM-2-PAN    [CEMPAN]
(0213) SAN-9-DE    [SANDE]
(0216) BUN-1-DEN-1-    [BUNDENNE]
(0217) WIN-1-DE    [WINDE]
(0227) THAN-9-CEDON    [THANCEDON]
(0246) MEN-1-DRA    [GUUDH-FREMMENDRA]
(0270) AEAEREN-2-DE    [AEAERENDE]
(0284) THEN-2-DEN    [THENDEN]
(0287) OM-1-BE-1-    [OMBEHT]
(0299) MEN-1-DRA    [GOOD-FREMMENDRA]
(0307) TIM-1-BRED.    [TIMBRED]
(0314) GAN-1-GAN    [GANGAN]
(0338) WLEN-1-CO    [WLENCO]
(0345) AEAEREN-1-DE.    [AEAERENDE]
(0355) THEN-1-CEDH.    [THENCEDH]
(0368) THIN-1-C-1-    [THINCEADH]
(0379) THAN-1-CE    [THANCE]
(0395) GAN-1-GAN    [GANGAN]
(0403) UN-4-DER    [UNDER]
(0424) GREN-2-DEL    [GRENDEL]
(0429) WIIGEN-2-DRA    [WIIGENDRA]
(0448) THEN-1-CEDH    [THENCEDH]
(0449) GEN-1-GA    [AN-GENGA]
(0505) UN-1-DER    [UNDER]
(0565) WUN-1-DE    [WUNDE]
(0581) WEALLEN-1-DU    [WEALLENDU]
(0591) ()GRE*GREN-8-DEL    [*GRENDEL]
(0595) FUN-1-DEN    [ON-FUNDEN]
(0649) PEN-1-DE    [NIIPENDE]
(0041) SCOL-9-DON    [SCOLDON]
(0047) ()GEL*GYL-9-DENNE    [*GYLDENNE]
(0053) L-2-DINGA    [SCYLDINGA]
(0056) EAR-2-DE    [EARDE]
(0058) SCYL-9-DINGAS    [SCYLDINGAS]
(0062) HYYR-2-DE    [HYYRDE]
(0066) HYYR-2-DON    [HYYRDON]
(0072) EAL-2-DUM    [EALDUM]
(0072) SEAL-2-DE    [SEALDE]
(0080) DAEAEL-1-DE    [DAEAELDE]
(0088) HYYR-9-DE.    [GE-HYYRDE]
(0089) HEAR-2-PAN    [HEARPAN]
(0105) WEAR-1-DO-1-    [WEARDODE]
(0166) EAR-2-DODE    [EARDODE]
(0167) SWEAR-2-TUM    [SWEARTUM]
(0170) SCYL-2-DINGA    [SCYLDINGA]
(0183) WUL-1-DRES    [WULDRES]
(0183) WAL-1-DEND    [WALDEND]
(0200) WOL-2-DE    [WOLDE]
(0209) MYR-9-CU    [LAND-GE-MYRCU]
```

122

```
(0228) WUR-3-DON.   [WURDON]
(0262) FOL-1-CUM    [FOLCUM]
(0265) GEAR-9-DUM   [GEARDUM]
(0275) DEOR-1-CUM   [DEORCUM]
(0280) SCOL-2-DE.   [SCOLDE]
(0289) WOR-2-DA     [WORDA]
(0289) WOR-2-CA     [WORCA]
(0291) SCYL-1-DINGA    [SCYLDINGA]
(0296) HEAL-9-DAN     [HEALDAN]
(0304) GOL-1-DE      [GOLDE]
(0305) WEAR-1-DE     [FERH-WEARDE]
(0317) HEAL-9-DE.     [GE-HEALDE]
(0319) WEAR-1-DE     [WEARDE]
(0319) HEAL-1-DAN.    [HEALDAN]
(0325) SCYL-1-DAS     [SCYLDAS]
(0334) SYR-1-CAN     [SYRCAN]
(0351) SCIL-2-DINGA    [SCILDINGA]
(0369) AL-1-DOR     [ALDOR]
(0371) SCYL-1-DINGA    [SCYLDINGA]
(0376) HOL-2-DNE     [HOLDNE]
(0401) HEEOL-1-DON    [HEEOLDON]
(0401) HEAR-2-DA     [HEARDA]
(0412) HWYL-1-CUM    [GE-HWYLCUM]
(0415) LAEAER-1-DON    [GE-LAEAERDON]
(0428) SCYL-3-DINGA    [SCYLDINGA]
(0430) FOL-1-CA     [FOLCA]
(0432) HEAR-9-DA     [HEARDA]
(0442) WEAL-3-DAN     [WEALDAN]
(0450) MEAR-1-CADH     [MEARCADH]
(0456) SCYL-2-DINGA    [SCYLDINGA]
(0464) SCYL-8-DINGA    [AAR-SCYLDINGA]
(0465) FOL-1-CE     [FOLCE]
(0482) WOL-2-DAN     [WOLDAN]
(0518) MOR-1-GEN-    [MORGEN-TIID]
(0546) CEAL-1-DOST    [CEALDOST]
(0561) SWEOR-9-DE     [SWEORDE]
(0565) MER-2-GEN-2-    [MERGENNE]
(0586) SWEOR-1-DUM    [SWEORDUM]
(0592) EAL-1-DRE     [EALDRE]
(0597) SCYL-1-DINGA    [SIGE-SCYLDINGA]
(0610) FOL-1-CES     [FOLCES]
(0626) WOR-2-DUM     [WORDUM]
(0644) FOL-2-CA     [SIGE-FOLCA]
(0645) WOL-1-DE     [WOLDE]
(0012) AEF-1-TER     [AEFTER]
(0036) MAES-1-TE     [MAESTE]
(0398) SCEAF-1-TAS     [WAEL-SCEAFTAS]
(0539) HAEF-1-DON    [HAEFDON]
(0608) LYYF-1-DE     [GE-LYYFDE]
(0646) RAES-1-TE.     [AEAEFEN-RAESTE]
(0421) YYDH-1-DE     [YYDHDE]
(0538) NEEDH-2-DON    [NEEDHDON]
(0094) SET-1-TE     [GE-SETTE]
(0151) THAET-1-TE     [THAETTE]
(0333) FAEAET-9-TE     [FAEAETTE]
(0352) BRYT-9-TAN     [BRYTTAN]
(0434) REC-2-CEDH.     [RECCEDH]
(0490) HWET-1-TE.     [HWETTE]
(0502) MOOD-1-GES     [MOODGES]
(0566) UP-1-PE     [UPPE]
(0569) LET-1-TON     [LETTON]
(0607) BRYT-1-TA     [BRYTTA]
(0652) GREET-1-TE     [*GE-GREETTE]
(0656) HEB-9-BAN     [HEBBAN]
(0158) ()BEOR*BEORH-2-TRE     [*BEORHTRE]
```

123

(0167) NIH-1-TUM   [NIHTUM]
(0233) HYG-1-DUM   [MOOD-GE-HYGDUM]
(0243) H-1-TE   [MEAHTE]
(0327) HRING-2-DON   [HRINGDON]
(0514) BRUG-9-DON   [BRUGDON]
(0379) ().XXX-9-()TIGES*THRIITIGES   [*THRIITIGES]

D.   SPACING PRECEDES W, X, OR H
(0132) SCEEA-9-WE-1-   [SCEEAWEDON]
(0204) SCEEA-2-WE-2-   [SCEEAWEDON]
(0253) SCEEA-2-WERAS   [LEEAS-SCEEAWERAS]
(0395) TAA-9-WUM   [*GUUDH-GE-TAAWUM]
(0243) MEA-1-H-1-   [MEAHTE]
(0287) BE-1-HT   [OMBEHT]
(0199) GYR-1-WAN   [GE-GYRWAN]
(0214) BEOR-1-HTE   [BEORHTE]
(0231) BEOR-1-HTE   [BEORHTE]
(0249) SEAR-1-WUM   [SEARWUM]
(0265) GEAR-3-WE   [GEARWE]
(0295) TYR-2-WYD-2-   [NIIW-TYRWYDNE]
(0323) SEAR-9-WUM   [SEARWUM]
(0419) SEAR-1-WUM   [SEARWUM]
(0444) FOR-3-HTE   [UN-FORHTE]
(0512) SOR-2-H-   [SORH-FULLNE]
(0522) BUR-1-H   [FREODHO-BURH]
(0553) GYR-9-WED   [GE-GYRWED]
(0609) BEOR-2-HT-   [BEORHT-DENA]
(0629) WEAL-1-H-   [WEALH-THEEON]
(0076) FRAET-1-WAN   [FRAETWAN]
(0096) FRAET-1-WADE   [GE-FRAETWADE]
(0324) GEAT-2-WUM   [GRYRE-GEATWUM]

SPACING WITHIN MORPHEME PRECEDES VOWEL-GRAPH

(0528) NEE-1-AN   [NEEAN]
(0451) SORGI-9-AN.   [SORGIAN]
(0499) BE-9-ARN   [BEARN]
(0174) N-1-E.   [GE-FREMMANNE]
(0281) CUM-1-AN   [CUMAN]
(0254) FEER-1-AN   [FEERAN]
(0478) GR-2-END-1-   [GRENDLES]
(0546) WEALL-1-ENDE   [WEALLENDE]
(0580) FAR-1-ODHE   [FARODHE]
(0611) L-1-E-1-   [HAELETHA]
(0612) WAEAER-1-ON   [WAEAERON]
(0458) UUS-2-IC   [UUSIC]
(0152) NIIDH-1-AS   [HETE-NIIDHAS]
(0042) FLOOD-1-ES   [FLOODES]
(0275) NIHT-1-UM   [NIHTUM]
(0368) C-1-EADH.   [THINCEADH]
(0397) BIID-8-AN   [ON-BIIDAN]
(0317) EEOW-3-IC   [EEOWIC]
(0062) ,,,-8-ELAN   [*ONELAN]

SPACING WITHIN MORPHEME PRECEDES EMENDED FORM
(0051) DEN-1-()NE*DE   [*SELE-RAEAEDENDE]
(0106) SCYP-1-()PEN*PEND   [*SCYPPEND]
(0207) ().XV.NA*FIIF-8-*TYYNA   [*FIIF-*TYYNA]
(0465) DE-9-()NINGA*NIGA   [*DENIGA]
(0466) ()GIM*GIN-2-()ME*NE   [*GINNE]

LINES 0662 - 1320 (FITS X - XIX)
SPACING WITHIN MORPHEME PRECEDES CONSONANT-GRAPH

A. SPACING PRECEDES RESONANT
```
(0721) DREEA-9-MUM    [DREEAMUM]
(0858) TWEEO-9-NUM    [TWEEONUM]
(0974) TEEO-1-NA      [LAADH-GE-TEEONA]
(1092) STREEO-9-NUM   [SINC-GE-STREEONUM]
(0857) MAEAE-1-NED    [MAEAENED]
(1067) MAEAE-9-NAN    [MAEAENAN]
(1197) NAEAE-2-NIG-1- [NAEAENIGNE]
(0817) SEO-9-NOWE     [SEONOWE]
(0711) GRE-9-NDEL     [GRENDEL]
(0715) GUME-9-NA      [GUMENA]
(0789) MAEGE-3-NE     [MAEGENE]
(0811) FYRE-1-NE      [FYRENE]
(0973) GU-9-MA        [GUMA]
(1058) GUME-2-NA      [GUMENA]
(1088) EEOTE-9-NA     [EEOTENA]
(1112) MA-9-NIG       [MANIG]
(1160) GA-1-MEN       [GAMEN]
(1171) GUME-9-NA      [GUMENA]
(1289) MA-1-NIG       [MANIG]
(0678) THON-2-NE      [THONNE]
(0712) MAN-2-NA       [MANNA]
(0712) CYN-1-NES      [CYNNES]
(0713) SUM-1-NE       [SUMNE]
(0735) MAN-1-NA       [MANNA]
(0735) CYN-1-NES      [CYNNES]
(0774) IN-1-NAN       [INNAN]
(0777) WUN-1-NON      [WUNNON]
(0779) MAN-1-NA       [MANNA]
(0802) IIREN-1-NA     [IIRENNA]
(0810) MAN-1-NA       [MANNA]
(0930) GRYN-1-NA      [GRYNNA]
(0939) SCIN-1-NUM     [SCINNUM]
(0963) CLAM-1-MU=     [CLAMMU=]
(0983) HEEAN-9-NE     [HEEANNE]
(1003) FLEEON-1-NE    [BE-FLEEONNE]
(1003) FREM-9-ME      [FREMME]
(1028) MAN-2-NA       [GUM-MANNA]
(1042) DHON-2-NE      [DHONNE]
(1057) MAN-1-NES      [MANNES]
(1058) CYN-1-NES      [CYNNES]
(1081) FIN-1-NES      [FINNES]
(1128) FIN-1-NE()L    [FINNE()L]
(1148) GRIM-1-NE      [GRIMNE]
(1156) FIN-1-NES      [FINNES]
(1160) MAN-9-NES      [GLEEO-MANNES]
(1179) THON-2-NE      [THONNE]
(1295) FEN-9-NE       [FENNE]
(1315) FREM-9-MAN     [GE-FREMMAN]
(0716) FOR-2-MA       [FORMA]
(0740) FOR-1-MAN      [FORMAN]
(0741) WEAR-1-NUM     [UN-WEARNUM]
(0856) BEOR-2-NAS     [BEORNAS]
(0887) HAAR-2-NE      [HAARNE]
(0904) WYL-1-MAS      [SORH-WYLMAS]
(0950) WIL-1-NA       [WILNA]
(1005) BEAR-9-NA      [BEARNA]
(1022) BYR-1-NAN      [BYRNAN]
(1030) HEL-2-MES      [HELMES]
(1074) BEAR-1-NUM     [BEARNUM]
(1116) BAER-2-NAN     [BAERNAN]
(1291) BYR-1-NAN      [BYRNAN]
```

(1303) FOL-1-ME   [FOLME]
(0787) LEEAS-1-NE   [SIGE-LEEASNE]
(1041) EF-1-NAN   [EFNAN]
(1056) NEF-2-NE   [NEFNE]
(1131) STEF-1-NAN   [HRINGED-STEFNAN]
(0714) WOLC-9-NUM   [WOLCNUM]
(0796) DRIHT-9-NES   [FREEA-DRIHTNES]
(0797) THEEOD-9-NES   [THEEODNES]
(0910) DHEEOD-1-NES   [DHEEODNES]
(0926) STEEAP-2-NE   [STEEAPNE]
(0940) DRIHT-1-NES   [DRIHTNES]
(1048) MAAD-9-MUM.   [MAADMUM]
(1097) FLIT-2-ME   [UN-FLITME]
(1198) ()MAD-2-MUM*MAADHUM   [*HORD-MAADHUM]
(1210) FRANC-1-NA   [FRANCNA]
(1231) DRUNC-1-NE   [DRUNCNE]
(1249) DRYHT-9-NE   [MAN-DRYHTNE]
(1197) NIG-1-NE   [NAEAENIGNE]

(1052) THAEAE-9-RE   [THAEAERE]
(0896) BEO-9-RHTE   [BEORHTE]
(1017) HEO-9-ROT   [HEOROT]
(1115) SWEO-1-LODHE   [SWEOLODHE]
(1188) HWEA-9-RF   [HWEARF]
(0662) HAE-9-LETHA   [HAELETHA]
(0672) HAFE-1-LAN   [HAFELAN]
(0690) SE-1-LE-   [SELE-RESTE]
(0782) THU-1-LE   [SWATHULE]
(0786) GA-9-LAN   [GALAN]
(0888) AETHE-2-LINGES   [AETHELINGES]
(0925) THE-1-LODE   [MATHELODE]
(0957) THE-1-LODE   [MATHELODE]
(0982) AETHE-1-LINGAS   [AETHELINGAS]
(0992) FE-1-L-2-   [FELA]
(1060) FE-1-LA   [FELA]
(1161) BYRE-1-LAS   [BYRELAS]
(1164) DE-9-RAN   [SUHTER-GE-FAEDERAN]
(1282) GRY-9-RE   [GRYRE]
(1313) SNOTE-9-RA   [SNOTERA]
(0702) WAN-1-RE   [WANRE]
(0752) EL-1-RAN   [ELRAN]
(0803) BIL-9-LA   [GUUDH-BILLA]
(0825) FEOR-2-RAN   [FEORRAN]
(0839) FEOR-2-RAN   [FEORRAN]
(0860) SEEL-1-RA   [SEELRA]
(0907) AEAER-1-RAN   [AEAERRAN]
(0982) EOR-1-LES   [EORLES]
(1174) FEOR-9-RAN   [FEORRAN]
(1302) HEOLF-9-RE   [HEOLFRE]
(0861) WYRDH-1-RA.   [WYRDHRA]
(0969) NIIDH-3-LAN   [FEORH-GE-NIIDHLAN]
(1043) HWAETH-9-RES   [GE-HWAETHRES]
(1074) BROODH-1-RUM   [BROODHRUM]
(1191) BROODH-1-RUM   [GE-BROODHRUM]
(0666) GREND-1-LE   [GRENDLE]
(0805) HWYLC-1-RE   [GE-HWYLCRE]
(0958) MIC-1-LUM   [MICLUM]
(1282) GREND-1-LES   [GRENDLES]
(1197) SWEG-9-LE   [SWEGLE]
(1200) SIG-1-LE   [SIGLE]
(0972) EAX-9-LE   [EAXLE]

B.   SPACING PRECEDES SPIRANT
(0700) CYY-9-THED   [GE-CYYTHED]
(0970) FEE-1-THE   [FEETHE]

```
(0986) HAEAE-2-THENES   [HAEAETHENES]
(1064) WII-8-SAN   [HILDE-WIISAN]
(0688) HEA-1-THO-    [HEATHO-DEEOR]
(0772) HEA-1-THO-    [HEATHO-DEEORUM]
(0864) HEA-1-THO-    [HEATHO-ROOFE]
(0814) HWAE-1-THER   [GE-HWAETHER]
(0740) HRA-1-DHE   [HRADHE]
(0748) HRA-1-THE   [HRATHE]
(0766) SCA-9-THA   [HEARM-SCATHA]
(0775) SMI-9-THOD   [BE-SMITHOD]
(0782) SWA-1-THU-1-   [SWATHULE]
(0819) GYFE-1-THE   [GYFETHE]
(0912) E-1-THA   [HEALETHA]
(0925) MA-1-THE-1-   [MATHELODE]
(0957) MA-1-THE-1-   [MATHELODE]
(1047) HAELE-9-THA   [HAELETHA]
(1082) ME-9-DHEL-   [MEDHEL-STEDE]
(1151) HRE-1-THRE   [HRETHRE]
(1189) HAELE-1-THA   [HAELETHA]
(1192) A-1-THU   [FREEOND-LATHU]
(0781) NYM-1-THE   [NYMTHE]
(1259) YRM-9-THE   [YRMTHE]
(0687) MAEAER-9-DHO   [MAEAERDHO]
(0700) SEL-2-FES   [SELFES]
(0752) EOR-2-THAN   [EORTHAN]
(0760) BUR-1-STON   [BURSTON]
(0761) FUR-1-THUR   [FURTHUR]
(0795) WUL-1-FES   [BEEO-WULFES]
(0800) HEAL-1-FA   [HEALFA]
(0802) EOR-1-THAN   [EORTHAN]
(0818) BUR-1-STON   [BURSTON]
(0818) WUL-1-FE   [BEEO-WULFE]
(0828) MAEAER-3-THUM   [ELLEN-MAEAERTHUM]
(0856) WUL-1-FES   [BEEO-WULFES]
(0872) WUL-1-FES   [BEEO-WULFES]
(0877) WAEL-1-SINGES   [WAELSINGES]
(0897) WAEL-1-SES   [WAELSES]
(1038) WUR-1-THAD   [GE-WURTHAD]
(1053) YR-9-FE-   [YRFE-LAAFE]
(1090) WEOR-2-THODE   [WEORTHODE]
(1165) FER-1-TH   [*UN-FERTH]
(1176) FAEAEL-1-SOD   [GE-FAEAELSOD]
(1264) MOR-1-THRE   [MORTHRE]
(1316) WYR-9-DHE   [FYRD-WYRDHE]
(0790) THYS-2-SES   [THYSSES]
(0806) THYS-3-SES   [THYSSES]
(0951) LAEAES-3-SAN   [LAEAESSAN]
(0982) SITH-9-DHAN   [SITHDHAN]
(1023) MAADH-9-THU=-    [MAADHTHU=-SWEORD]
(1033) SCETH-9-DHAN   [SCETHDHAN]
(1062) DHYS-2-SU=   [DHYSSU=]
(1169) THIS-2-SUM   [THISSUM]
(1204) SIDH-1-THAN   [SIDHTHAN]
(1282) LAEAES-1-SA   [LAEAESSA]
(1308) SYDH-1-TH-1-   [SYDHTHAN]
(0924) MAEG-1-THA   [MAEGTHA]

C.   SPACING PRECEDES STOP
(0680) NEEO-9-TAN   [BE-NEEOTAN]
(0697) LEEO-1-DUM   [LEEODUM]
(0703) SCEEO-1-TEND   [SCEEOTEND]
(0752) ()SCEAT*SCEEA-9-TA   [*SCEEATA]
(1202) GEEA-9-TA   [GEEATA]
(0664) SEE-9-CAN   [SEECAN]
(0677) HNAA-1-GRAN   [HNAAGRAN]
```

127

```
(0684) SEE-1-CEAN    [GE-SEECEAN]
(0813) LAA-9-CES     [HYGE-LAACES]
(0873) RAA-2-DE      [GE-RAADE]
(0876) DAEAE-9-DUM   [ELLEN-DAEAEDUM]
(0889) DAEAE-1-DE    [DAEAEDE]
(0916) FLII-9-TENDE  [FLIITENDE]
(0954) DAEAE-2-DUM   [DAEAEDUM]
(1001) DAEAE-1-DUM   [FYREN-DAEAEDUM]
(1100) BRAEAE-1-CE.  [BRAEAECE]
(1142) RAEAE-1-DEN-1- [*WEOROD-RAEAEDENDE]
(1227) DAEAE-2-DUM   [DAEAEDUM]
(0703) SCEA-9-DU-    [SCEADU-GENGA]
(0707) SCEA-2-DU     [SCEADU]
(0835) GEA-2-DOR     [GEADOR]
(1181) GEO-9-GODHE   [GEOGODHE]
(1164) FAE-1-DE-9-   [SUHTER-GE-FAEDERAN]
(1164) GAE-1-DERE    [AET-GAEDERE]
(0730) MA-1-GO-      [MAGO-RINCA]
(0780) BRE-9-CAN     [TOO-BRECAN]
(0811) FREME-3-DE.   [GE-FREMEDE]
(0831) DRU-1-GON     [DRUGON]
(0873) WRE-1-CAN     [WRECAN]
(0905) LEME-9-DE     [LEMEDE]
(0926) STA-1-POLE    [STAPOLE]
(0938) WERE-1-DON.   [BE-WEREDON]
(0979) ME-9-TOD      [METOD]
(0983) WE-1-DON      [SCEEAWEDON]
(0994) GYRE-2-DON    [GYREDON]
(1015) ME-9-DO-      [MEDO-FUL]
(1019) FREME-2-DON   [FREMEDON]
(1057) ME-9-TOD      [METOD]
(1065) WRE-1-CEN.    [WRECEN]
(1067) ME-2-DO-      [MEDO-BENCE]
(1095) TRUWE-1-DON   [GE-TRUWEDON]
(1124) SCA-1-GEN.    [SCAGEN]
(1136) SCA-1-GEN     [SCAGEN]
(1151) O-1-DEN       [*RODEN]
(1154) FERE-2-DON    [FEREDON]
(1187) FREME-2-DON.  [GE-FREMEDON]
(1205) WERE-1-DE     [WEREDE]
(1215) WERE-1-DE     [WEREDE]
(1239) BERE-3-DON    [BEREDON]
(1267) O-1-TE        [HEOROTE]
(1310) FE-1-TOD      [FETOD]
(1317) DYNE-2-DE     [DYNEDE]

(0673) OM-9-BIHT-    [OMBIHT-THEGNE]
(0730) RIN-9-CA      [MAGO-RINCA]
(0733) LUM-2-PEN     [AA-LUMPEN]
(0746) HAN-9-DA      [HANDA]
(0789) STREN-9-GEST  [STRENGEST]
(0799) HICGEN-1-DE   [HEARD-HICGENDE]
(0817) SPRUN-1-GON   [ON-SPRUNGON]
(0820) UN-1-DER      [UNDER]
(0840) WUN-1-DOR     [WUNDOR]
(0856) BLAN-2-CUM    [BLANCUM]
(0860) UN-9-DER      [UNDER]
(0861) BEN-1-DRA     [ROND-HAEBBENDRA]
(0899) WIIGEN-1-DRA  [WIIGENDRA]
(0918) SCYN-1-DED    [SCYNDED]
(0931) WUN-1-DER     [WUNDER]
(0931) WUN-1-DRE     [WUNDRE]
(1004) BEREN-1-DRA   [SAAWL-BERENDRA]
(1006) BUUEN-1-DRA   [GRUND-BUUENDRA]
(1013) AAGAN-9-DE    [BLAEAED-AAGANDE]
```

128

```
(1029) BEN-1-CE     [EALO-BENCE]
(1086) RYYM-1-DON   [GE-RYYMDON]
(1091) HRIN-9-GU=   [HRINGU=]
(1113) WUN-1-DUM    [ WUNDUM]
(1132) WIN-1-DE     [ WINDE]
(1135) SYN-1-GAALES   [SYNGAALES]
(1170) SIN-1-CES    [SINCES]
(1177) THEN-2-DEN   [THENDEN]
(1185) UN-9-CRAN    [ UNCRAN]
(1186) MYN-1-DUM    [ WORDH-MYNDUM]
(1187) UM-1-DOR-    [ UMBOR-WESENDUM]
(1187) WESEN-1-DUM  [UMBOR-WESENDUM]
(1195) HRIN-9-GAS   [HRINGAS]
(1227) DEN-9-DE.    [DREEAM-HEALDENDE]
(1230) SYN-9-DON    [ SYNDON]
(1234) GAN-9-GEN    [ AA-GANGEN]
(1290) HAN-1-DA     [HANDA]
(1293) FUN-9-DEN    [ ON-FUNDEN]
(1312) CEM-1-PA     [CEMPA]
(0664) WOL-1-DE     [WOLDE]
(0665) WUL-1-DOR    [ KYNING-WULDOR]
(0670) HYL-1-DO.    [HYLDO]
(0674) HEAL-2-DAN   [GE-HEALDAN]
(0704) HEAL-3-DAN   [HEALDAN]
(0704) SCOL-1-DON.  [SCOLDON]
(0719) HEAR-1-DRAN  [HEARDRAN]
(0738) WOL-9-DE.    [ WOLDE]
(0751) GEAR-1-DES   [MIDDAN-GEARDES]
(0770) WEAR-1-DAS   [REN-WEARDAS]
(0777) GOL-1-DE     [GOLDE]
(0778) SCYL-2-DINGA   [SCYLDINGA]
(0784) HWYL-1-CUM   [GE-HWYLCUM]
(0785) HYYR-2-DON.  [GE-HYYRDON]
(0794) TEAL-1-DE    [ TEALDE]
(0795) EAL-1-DE     [EALDE]
(0796) WOL-1-DE     [WOLDE]
(0799) HIL-1-DE-    [HILDE-MECGAS]
(0812) NOL-1-DE     [NOLDE]
(0832) SCOL-1-DON   [SCOLDON]
(0837) MOR-2-GEN    [ MORGEN]
(0839) FEER-1-DON   [FEERDON]
(0854) SWYL-1-CE    [ SWYLCE]
(0874) WOR-2-DUM    [ WORDUM]
(0875) HYYR-1-DE    [HYYRDE]
(0880) SWUL-1-CES   [SWULCES]
(0886) CWEAL-9-DE   [AA-CWEALDE]
(0887) HYR-1-DE     [HYRDE]
(0894) HOR-9-DES    [BEEAH-HORDES]
(0906) AL-1-DOR-    [ ALDOR-CEARE]
(0913) SCYL-1-DINGA   [SCYLDINGA]
(0921) HOR-1-DA     [BEEAH-HORDA]
(0931) WUL-1-DRES   [WULDRES]
(0936) HWYL-1-C-1-  [*GE-HWYLCUM]
(0955) WAL-1-DA     [ AL-WALDA]
(0963) HEAR-1-DAN   [HEARDAN]
(0981) WEOR-2-CA    [ GUUDH-GE-WEORCA]
(0988) HEAR-1-DRA   [HEARDRA]
(1040) SWEOR-1-DA   [SWEORDA]
(1041) WOL-1-DE     [ WOLDE]
(1050) HWYL-2-CUM   [AEAEG-HWYLCUM]
(1054) GYL-9-DAN    [FOR-GYLDAN]
(1067) SCOL-2-DE    [SCOLDE]
(1090) HWYL-1-CE    [GE-HWYLCE]
(1093) GOL-1-DES    [GOLDES]
(1094) BYL-1-DAN    [BYLDAN]
```

```
(1100)  WOR-1-DU=     [WORDU=]
(1134)  GEAR-2-DAS    [GEARDAS]
(1137)  FOL-1-DAN     [FOLDAN]
(1138)  GEAR-2-DUM    [GEARDUM]
(1154)  SCYL-9-DINGA    [SCYLDINGA]
(1165)  SWYL-1-CE     [SWYLCE]
(1166)  SCYL-3-DINGA    [SCYLDINGA]
(1168)  SCYL-3-DINGA.    [SCYLDINGA]
(1172)  MIL-3-DUM     [MILDUM]
(1172)  WOR-9-DUM     [WORDUM]
(1183)  SCIL-2-DINGA    [SCILDINGA]
(1184)  GYL-1-DAN     [GYLDAN]
(1193)  WOR-9-DUM     [WORDUM]
(1203)  SWER-1-TINGES    [SWERTINGES]
(1204)  EAL-2-GODE.    [EALGODE]
(1227)  HEAL-2-DEN-9-    [DREEAM-HEALDENDE]
(1240)  SCEAL-1-CA    [BEEOR-SCEALCA]
(1249)  SWYL-1-CE     [SWYLCE]
(1249)  SWIL-1-CE     [SWILCE]
(1260)  SCOL-1-DE     [SCOLDE]
(1264)  MEAR-1-COD    [GE-MEARCOD]
(1293)  BEOR-2-GAN    [BEORGAN]
(1305)  SCOL-1-DON.    [SCOLDON]
(1307)  HIL-1-DE-     [HILDE-RINC]
(0781)  LIS-1-TUM     [LISTUM]
(0814)  HAEF-1-DE     [HAEFDE]
(0828)  HAEF-1-DE     [HAEFDE]
(0883)  $HAEF-1-DON    [HAEFDON]
(0909)  LYYF-1-DE     [GE-LYYFDE]
(1067)  AEF-1-TER     [AEFTER]
(1071)  THORF-1-TE.    [THORFTE=]
(1089)  GYF-9-TU=     [FEOH-GYFTU=]
(1167)  HAEF-1-DE     [HAEFDE]
(1202)  HAEF-1-DE     [HAEFDE]
(1257)  LIF-9-DE     [LIFDE]
(1271)  FAES-1-TE     [GIM-FAESTE]
(0888)  NEEDH-1-DE    [GE-NEEDHDE]
(0959)  NEEDH-2-DON.    [GE-NEEDHDON]
(0667)  NYT-9-TE     [SUNDOR-NYTTE]
(0708)  WAEC-1-CENDE    [WAECCENDE]
(0716)  FAEAET-2-TUM    [FAEAETTUM]
(0725)  TRED-9-DODE    [TREDDODE]
(0729)  SIB-1-BE-     [SIBBE-GE-DRIHT]
(0858)  THAET-1-TE    [THAETTE]
(0861)  HAEB-9-BEN-1-    [ROND-HAEBBENDRA]
(0939)  SCUC-1-CUM    [SCUCCUM]
(1045)  WIC-9-GA     [WICGA]
(1105)  MYND-3-GIEND    [MYNDGIEND]
(1170)  BRYT-9-TA     [BRYTTA]
(1242)  SET-2-TON     [SETTON]
(1268)  WAEC-1-CENDNE    [WAECCENDNE]
(0707)  BREG-9-DAN.    [BREGDAN]
(0866)  THUUH-9-TON    [THUUHTON]
(0924)  STIG-1-GE     [MEDO-STIGGE]
(1035)  EAH-9-TA     [EAHTA]
(1130)  MEAH-9-TE     [MEAHTE]
(1136)  TORH-9-TAN    [WULDOR-TORHTAN]
(1166)  TREEOW-2-DE.    [TREEOWDE]


D.   SPACING PRECEDES W, X, OR H
(0800)  HEEA-9-WAN    [HEEAWAN]
(0840)  SCEEA-1-WIAN    [SCEEAWIAN]
(0957)  THEEO-1-WES    [*ECG-THEEOWES]
(0983)  SCEEA-1-WE-1-    [SCEEAWEDON]
(1164)  SU-1-HTER-    [SUHTER-GE-FAEDERAN]
```

130

```
(0749) IN-1-WIT-    [INWIT-THANCU=]
(0831) IN-1-WID-    [INWID-SORGE]
(0664) WEAL-1-H-    [WEALH-THEEO]
(0702) FER-1-HDH    [*WIIDE-FERHDH]
(0715) GEAR-1-WOST  [GEARWOST]
(0754) FOR-1-HT     [FORHT]
(0754) FER-1-HDHE   [FERHDHE]
(0865) FEAL-1-WE    [FEALWE]
(0878) GEAR-2-WE    [GEARWE]
(0942) SYR-1-WAN    [BE-SYRWAN]
(0969) FEOR-1-H-    [FEORH-GE-NIIDHLAN]
(0976) NEAR-2-WE    [NEARWE]
(0977) BAL-2-WON    [BALWON]
(1006) GEAR-2-WE    [GEARWE]
(1166) FER-9-HTHE   [FERHTHE]
(0896) FRAET-1-WA   [FRAETWA]
(0992) FRAET-1-WOD  [GE-FRAETWOD]
(1207) FRAET-1-WE   [FRAETWE]
(0783) NEAH-2-HE    [GE-NEAHHE]
(0951) TEOH-3-HODE  [TEOHHODE]
```

SPACING WITHIN MORPHEME PRECEDES VOWEL-GRAPH

```
(0768) BUU-9-ENOUM    [CEASTER-BUUENOUM]
(1128) WUN-1-ODE      [WUNODE]
(0764) FL-1-EEON      [FLEEON]
(0775) SEAR-1-O-      [SEARO-THONCUM]
(0797) MAEAER-1-ES    [MAEAERES]
(0819) HR-1-EEDH      [GUUDH-HREEDH]
(0820) HL-1-EODHU     [FEN-HLEODHU]
(0865) FAR-1-AN       [FARAN]
(0882) STEALL-1-AN.   [NYYD-GE-STEALLAN]
(0901) HER-1-E-       [HERE-MOODES]
(0912) HEAL-1-E-1-    [HEALETHA]
(0992) L-2-A          [FELA]
(1070) FR-8-EES-      [FREES-WAELE]
(1073) LOR-2-EN       [BE-LOREN]
(1100) WAEAER-1-E     [WAEAERE]
(1151) ()HR*R-1-O-1-  [*RODEN]
(1168) $SPR-1-AEC     [SPRAEC]
(1171) SPR-1-AEC      [SPRAEC]
(1192) L-1-A-1-       [FREEOND-LATHU]
(1263) FAEDER-1-EN-   [FAEDEREN-MAEAEGE]
(1267) HEOR-1-O-1-    [HEOROTE]
(1275) DAEAEL-1-ED    [BE-DAEAELED]
(0772) HRUUS-1-AN     [HRUUSAN]
(0806) DH-1-AEAEM     [DHAEAEM]
(0867) CUUDH-8-E      [CUUDHE]
(1308) TH-1-AN        [SYDHTHAN]
(0714) UND-1-ER       [UNDER]
(0849) HAAT-3-ON      [HAATON]
(0936) WIT-1-ENA      [WITENA]
(1167) MIC-1-EL       [MICEL]
(1201) RIIC-1-ES      [EORMEN-RIICES]
(1256) WREC-1-END     [WRECEND]
```

SPACING WITHIN MORPHEME PRECEDES EMENDED FORM

```
(0936) C-1-()NE*UM.          [*GE-HWYLCUM]
(1212) REEAFE-2-()DEN*DON    [*REEAFEDON]
(1142) DEN-1-()NE*DE         [*WEOROD-RAEAEDENDE]
```

131

APPENDIX I
LINES 1321 - 1939 (FIT XX - END OF
FIRST SCRIBE≠S COPY)

SPACING WITHIN MORPHEME PRECEDES CONSONANT-GRAPH

A.   SPACING PRECEDES RESONANT
(1380) LEEA-9-NIGE   [LEEANIGE]
(1582) TYY-9-NE   [FYYF-TYYNE]
(1882) HREE-9-MIG   [HREEMIG]
(1933) NAEAE-2-NIG   [NAEAENIG]
(1361) HEO-1-NON   [HEONON]
(1367) GUME-2-NA   [GUMENA]
(1378) FINDA-8-N   [FINDAN]
(1476) GUME-3-NA   [GUMENA]
(1499) GUME-1-NA   [GUMENA]
(1602) GUME-3-NA   [GUMENA]
(1678) FRU-9-MAN   [HILD-FRUMAN]
(1699) SU-9-NU   [SUNU]
(1720) DE-9-NUM   [DENUM]
(1819) CU-9-MENE   [CUMENE]
(1860) MA-9-NIG   [MANIG]
(1867) DE-2-NES   [HEALF-DENES]
(1887) MA-2-NEGUM   [MANEGUM]
(1932) FRE-1-MU   [FREMU]
(1355) CUN-1-NON   [CUNNON]
(1356) CEN-1-NED   [AA-CENNED]
(1419) THOLIAN-1-NE   [GE-THOLIANNE]
(1426) CUN-1-NIAN   [CUNNIAN]
(1432) SUM-1-NE   [SUMNE]
(1444) CUN-1-NIAN   [CUNNIAN]
(1502) CLOM-2-MUM   [CLOMMUM]
(1542) GRIM-9-MAN   [GRIMMAN]
(1570) IN-1-NE   [INNE]
(1640) SEM-1-NINGA   [SEMNINGA]
(1689) WIN-1-NES.   [FYRN-GE-WINNES]
(1721) WIN-1-NES   [GE-WINNES]
(1724) SECGAN-1-NE   [SECGANNE]
(1725) MAN-2-NA   [MANNA]
(1731) DAN-1-NE   [HEALDANNE]
(1740) IN-1-NAN   [INNAN]
(1767) SEM-1-NINGA   [SEMNINGA]
(1822) THON-1-NE   [THONNE]
(1824) DHON-1-NE   [DHONNE]
(1832) FREM-1-MAN   [FREMMAN]
(1835) MAN-1-NA   [MANNA]
(1847) GRIM-2-ME   [HEORU-GRIMME]
(1851) CEEOSEN-9-NE   [GE-CEEOSENNE]
(1915) MAN-1-NA   [MANNA]
(1922) CAN-1-NE   [GE-SEECANNE]
(1324) YR-1-MEN-   [YRMEN-LAAFES]
(1351) EAR-9-M-   [EARM-SCEAPEN]
(1369) HOR-2-NU=   [HORNU=]
(1415) HAAR-2-NE   [HAARNE]
(1435) HOL-1-ME   [HOLME]
(1463) FOR-1-MA   [FORMA]
(1527) FOR-1-MA   [FORMA]
(1598) MAEAER-1-NE   [MAEAERNE]
(1892) HEAR-1-ME   [HEARME]
(1353) NAEF-1-NE   [NAEFNE]
(1406) LEEAS-2-NE   [SAAWOL-LEEASNE]
(1587) LEEAS-1-NE   [ALDOR-LEEASNE]
(1489) CUUDH-1-NE   [WIID-CUUDHNE]
(1613) MAADH-1-M-   [MAADHM-AEAEHTA]
(1784) MAATH-1-MA   [MAATHMA]
(1898) MAADH-9-MUM   [MAADHMUM]

132

(1374) WOLC-1-NUM   [WOLCNUM]
(1441) LIIC-1-NE   [GRYRE-LIICNE]
(1482) MAAD-1-MAS   [MAADMAS]
(1559) WAEAEP-1-NA   [WAEAEPNA]
(1621) EEAC-1-NE   [EEACNE]
(1627) THEEOD-1-NES   [THEEODNES]
(1628) SUND-1-NE   [GE-SUNDNE]
(1691) FREEC-1-NE   [FREECNE]
(1756) MAAD-2-MAS   [MAADMAS]
(1770) WOLC-1-NUM   [WOLCNUM]
(1779) DRYHT-9-NE   [DRYHTNE]
(1772) AEAENIG-9-NE   [AEAENIGNE]

(1631) DREEO-1-RE   [WAEL-DREEORE]
(1748) HEEO-1-LD   [HEEOLD]
(1879) DEEO-9-RUM   [DEEORUM]
(1729) MAEAE-9-RAN   [MAEAERAN]
(1732) DAEAE-9-LAS   [DAEAELAS]
(1769) MISSEE-9-RA   [MISSEERA]
(1326) STEA-1-LLA   [EAXL-GE-STEALLA]
(1536) CEA-9-RADH.   [CEARADH]
(1722) BEA-9-LO   [LEEOD-BEALO]
(1421) HAFE-1-LAN   [HAFELAN]
(1555) RODE-1-RA   [RODERA]
(1596) AEDHE-2-LINGES   [AEDHELINGES]
(1637) SCO-1-L-1-   [SCOLDON]
(1680) HRY-9-RE   [HRYRE]
(1837) FE-9-LA.   [FELA]
(1823) THIIN-9-RE   [THIINRE]
(1370) FEOR-2-RAN   [FEORRAN]
(1711) FEAL-9-LE   [WAEL-FEALLE]
(1739) WIL-9-LAN   [WILLAN]
(1806) COL-9-LEN-   [COLLEN-FERHDH]
(1819) FEOR-1-RAN   [FEORRAN]
(1498) GIIF-1-RE   [HEORO-GIIFRE]
(1540) NIIDH-2-LAN   [FEORH-GE-NIIDHLAN]
(1683) MORDH-1-RES   [MORDHRES]
(1847) HREETH-9-LES   [HREETHLES]
(1485) HRAEAED-1-LES   [HRAEAEDLES]
(1648) GREND-2-LES   [GRENDLES]

B.   SPACING PRECEDES SPIRANT
(1324) BROO-1-THOR   [BROOTHOR]
(1417) DREE-9-FED   [GE-DREEFED]
(1469) NEE-2-THAN   [GE-NEETHAN]
(1632) FEE-1-THE-   [FEETHE-LAASTUM]
(1707) FROO-9-FRE   [FROOFRE]
(1581) SWEO-9-FOTE   [SWEOFOTE]
(1606) HEA-2-THO-   [HEATHO-SWAATE]
(1698) WREO-9-THEN-   [WREOTHEN-HILT]
(1862) HEA-3-()THU*FU   [*HEAFU]
(1437) HRAE-9-THE   [HRAETHE]
(1636) HWAE-1-THRU=   [AEAEG-HWAETHRU=]
(1342) TE-1-IH   [GREEOTETH]
(1390) HRA-1-THE   [HRATHE]
(1403) SWA-2-THU=   [WALD-SWATHU=]
(1521) HA-9-FELAN   [HAFELAN]
(1803) SCA-1-THAN   [SCATHAN]
(1852) E-1-THA   [HAELETHA]
(1895) SCA-9-THAN   [SCATHAN]
(1929) HAERE-1-THES   [HAERETHES]
(1423) HEOL-2-FRE   [HEOLFRE]
(1462) DOR-1-STE   [DORSTE]
(1468) DOR-9-STE   [DORSTE]
(1625) BYR-1-THENNE   [MAEGEN-BYRTHENNE]

```
(1645) WUR-2-THAD    [GE-WURTHAD]
(1657) EAR-1-FODH-   [EARFODH-LIICE]
(1707) FUR-1-DHUM    [FURDHUM]
(1707) WEOR-8-THAN   [WEORTHAN]
(1822) EOR-1-THAN    [EORTHAN]
(1411) NAES-9-SAS    [NAESSAS]
(1420) SYDH-3-THAN   [SYDHTHAN]
(1453) SYDH-2-THAN   [SYDHTHAN]
(1472) SYDH-3-THAN   [SYDHTHAN]
(1498) MIS-1-SEERA   [MISSEERA]
(1689) SYDH-3-THAN   [SYDHTHAN]
(1775) SEOTH-1-DHAN  [SEOTHDHAN]
(1901) SYDH-9-THAN   [SYDHTHAN]
(1912) NAES-9-SAS    [NAESSAS]
(1749) GYYT-9-SADH   [GYYTSADH]
(1633) H-1-THUM   [FERHTHUM]
(1718) FERH-8-THE    [FERHTHE]


C.  SPACING PRECEDES STOP
(1342) GREEO-1-TE-1-  [GREEOTETH]
(1431) GEEA-9-TON    [ON-GEEATON]
(1470) DREEO-1-GAN   [DREEOGAN]
(1484) GEEA-1-TA    [GEEATA]
(1675) THEEO-9-DEN    [THEEODEN]
(1715) THEEO-9-DEN.   [THEEODEN]
(1744) SCEEO-1-TEDH   [SCEEOTEDH]
(1856) GEEA-1-TA    [GEEATA]
(1930) GEEA-1-TA    [GEEATA]
(1930) LEEO-9-DUM    [LEEODUM]
(1346) RAEAE-1-DEN-1-  [SELE-RAEAEDENDE]
(1442) WAEAE-2-DUM    [EORL-GE-WAEAEDUM]
(1512) LAEAE-1-CAN    [AAG-LAEAECAN]
(1569) SWAA-9-TIG    [SWAATIG]
(1616) BROO-2-DEN-   [BROODEN-MAEAEL]
(1669) DAEAE-3-DA    [FYREN-DAEAEDA]
(1674) DRAEAE-1-DAN    [ON-DRAEAEDAN]
(1728) LAEAE-9-TEDH    [LAEAETEDH]
(1760) RAEAE-1-DAS    [RAEAEDAS]
(1880) BLOO-9-DE    [BLOODE]
(1922) SEE-1-CAN-1-   [GE-SEECANNE]
(1454) BEA-1-DO-    [BEADO-MEECAS]
(1328) CNYSE-3-DAN    [CNYSEDAN]
(1440) SCEEAWE-9-DON   [SCEEAWEDON]
(1441) GYRE-1-DE    [GYREDE]
(1451) DA-9-GUM    [FYRN-DAGUM]
(1505) LO-1-C-1-    [LOCENE]
(1552) FREME-2-DE    [GE-FREMEDE]
(1573) HAFENA-9-DE    [HAFENADE]
(1603) STARE-1-DON    [STAREDON]
(1606) GI-1-C-1-    [HILDE-GICELUM]
(1674) IO-9-GOTHE    [IOGOTHE]
(1669) FERE-2-DE    [AET-FEREDE]
(1686) SCE-2-DENIGGE   [SCEDENIGGE]
(1687) MADHELO-1-DE    [MADHELODE]
(1688) WRI-9-TEN    [WRITEN]
(1718) FREME-9-DE    [GE-FREMEDE]
(1874) FRO-1-DUM    [IN-FRODUM]
(1890) LO-9-CENE    [LOCENE]
(1894) WE-1-DERA    [WEDERA]


(1334) GREN-9-DEL    [GRENDEL]
(1346) DEN-1-DE    [SELE-RAEAEDENDE]
(1363) HON-9-GIADH    [HONGIADH]
(1397) THAN-9-CODE    [THANCODE]
(1440) WUN-1-DOR-    [WUNDOR-LIIC]
```

134

```
(1461) MUN-1-DUM    [MUNDUM]
(1509) WUN-9-DRA    [WUNDRA]
(1562) GIIGAN-9-TA    [GIIGANTA]
(1572) CAN-1-DEL    [CANDEL]
(1604) WEEN-1-DON    [WEENDON]
(1607) WUN-1-DRA    [WUNDRA]
(1669) FEEON-9-DUM    [FEEONDUM]
(1691) FREM-2-DE    [FREMDE]
(1724) WIN-1-TRUM    [WINTRUM]
(1734) EN-1-DE    [ENDE]
(1734) THEN-1-CEAN.    [GE-THENCEAN]
(1739) WEN-2-DEDH    [WENDEDH]
(1747) WUN-2-DOR-    [WUNDOR-BE-BODUM]
(1775) GREN-9-DEL    [GRENDEL]
(1782) SYM-9-BEL-    [SYMBEL-WYNNE]
(1788) SITTEN-1-DUM    [FLET-SITTENDUM]
(1829) BRIN-9-GE    [BRINGE]
(1859) THEN-1-DEN    [THENDEN]
(1873) BLON-1-DEN-    [BLONDEN-FEAXUM]
(1883) AN-1-CRE    [ANCRE]
(1913) SWEN-9-CED    [LYFT-GE-SWENCED]
(1324) YL-1-DRA    [YLDRA]
(1334) CWEAL-2-DEST    [CWEALDEST]
(1335) HEAR-2-DU=    [HEARDU=]
(1338) EAL-9-DRES    [EALDRES]
(1348) HEAL-2-DAN    [HEALDAN]
(1362) MEAR-1-CES    [MIIL-GE-MEARCES]
(1396) HWYL-1-CES    [GE-HWYLCES]
(1405) MYR-9-CAN    [MYRCAN]
(1418) SCYL-1-DINGA    [SCYLDINGA]
(1438) HEAR-1-DE    [HEARDE]
(1446) HIL-1-DE-    [HILDE-GRAAP]
(1494) WOL-1-DE    [WOLDE]
(1495) HIL-9-DE-    [HILDE-RINCE]
(1511) SYR-2-CAN    [HERE-SYRCAN]
(1518) WYR-1-GENNE    [GRUND-WYRGENNE]
(1523) NOL-1-DE    [NOLDE]
(1553) HEAR-1-DE    [HEARDE]
(1574) HIL-1-TUM    [HILTUM]
(1577) GYL-2-DAN    [FOR-GYLDAN]
(1601) SCYL-1-DINGAS    [SCYLDINGAS]
(1606) HIL-1-DE-    [HILDE-GICELUM]
(1621) EAR-1-DAS    [EARDAS]
(1637) L-1-DON    [SCOLDON]
(1653) SCYL-1-DINGA    [SCYLDINGA]
(1659) HIL-9-DE    [HILDE]
(1683) SCYL-9-DIG    [SCYLDIG]
(1686) DAEAEL-1-DE.    [DAEAELDE]
(1710) SCYL-1-DINGUM.    [AAR-SCYLDINGUM]
(1731) HEAL-3-DAN-1-    [HEALDANNE]
(1732) WEAL-2-DENE    [GE-WEALDENE]
(1737) SWEOR-2-CEDH    [SWEORCEDH]
(1746) BEOR-2-GAN    [BE-BEORGAN]
(1747) WER-2-GAN    [WERGAN]
(1767) SWOR-9-CEDH    [FOR-SWORCEDH]
(1784) MOR-9-GEN    [MORGEN]
(1792) SCYL-1-DING    [SCYLDING]
(1807) HEAR-9-DA    [HEARDA]
(1810) TEAL-1-DE.    [TEALDE]
(1816) HIL-1-DE-    [HILDE-DEEOR]
(1832) HYR-1-DE    [HYRDE]
(1833) ()WOR*WEOR-1-CUM    [*WEORCUM]
(1859) WEAL-9-DE    [WEALDE]
(1865) EAL-9-DE    [EALDE]
(1889) STEAL-1-DRA    [HAEG-STEALDRA]
```

135

```
(1901) SEAL-1-DE    [GE-SEALDE]
(1932) FOL-2-CES    [FOLCES]
(1352) LAAS-1-TAS   [WRAEC-LAASTAS]
(1389) LIF-9-GENDUM    [UN-LIFGENDUM]
(1433) TWAEAEF-1-DE    [GE-TWAEAEFDE]
(1599) HAEF-9-DE.   [HAEFDE]
(1656) NEETH-1-DE   [GE-NEETHDE]
(1743) BIS-1-GUM    [BISGUM]
(1421) MEET-3-TON   [MEETTON]
(1487) BRYT-1-TAN   [BRYTTAN]
(1617) AET-1-TREN   [AETTREN]
(1686) SCEAT-9-TAS    [SCEATTAS]
(1706) SNYT-9-TRUM    [SNYTTRUM]
(1726) BRYT-2-TADH    [BRYTTADH]
(1771) MID-9-DAN-   [MIDDAN-GEARD]
(1786) SNOT-1-TRA   [SNOTTRA]
(1791) BED-9-DES    [BEDDES]
(1803) OONET-1-TON    [OONETTON]
(1827) SIT-1-TEND   [YMB-SITTEND]
(1770) WIG-1-GE   [WIGGE]
(1841) WIG-1-TIG   [WIGTIG]
(1919) MEAH-9-TE   [MEAHTE]


D.   SPACING PRECEDES W, X, OR H
(1383) THEEO-9-WES   [ECG-THEEOWES]
(1391) SCEEA-9-WIGAN.   [SCEEAWIGAN]
(1322) NII-9-WOD   [GE-NIIWOD]
(1721) THROO-2-WADE   [THROOWADE]
(1561) MEA-1-HTE   [MEAHTE]
(1484) DRI-9-HTEN   [DRIHTEN]
(1604) DRI-1-HTEN   [WINE-DRIHTEN]
(1447) IN-9-WIT-   [INWIT-FENG]
(1736) IN-1-WIT-   [INWIT-SORH]
(1363) BEAR-1-WAS   [BEARWAS]
(1438) NEAR-2-WOD   [GE-NEARWOD]
(1557) SEAR-2-WUM   [SEARWUM]
(1633) FER-1-H-1-   [FERHTHUM]
(1758) BEOR-1-H   [BE-BEORH]
(1539) BEAD-1-WE   [BEADWE]


SPACING WITHIN MORPHEME PRECEDES VOWEL-GRAPH

(1684) HWE-9-ARF   [GE-HWEARF]
(1417) EALL-1-UM   [EALLUM]
(1420) EORL-2-A   [EORLA]
(1503) HAAL-1-AN   [HAALAN]
(1669) FYR-1-EN-   [FYREN-DAEAEDA]
(1715) MAEAER-2-E   [MAEAERE]
(1749) NALL-1-AS   [NALLAS]
(1756) DAEAEL-2-ETH   [DAEAELETH]
(1850) SEELR-1-AN   [SEELRAN]
(1852) HAEL-1-E-1-   [HAELETHA]
(1926) HEALL-1-E   [HEALLE]
(1438) HOOC-9-YHTUM   [HEORO-HOOCYHTUM]
(1505) C-1-ENE   [LOCENE]
(1606) C-1-ELUM   [HILDE-GICELUM]
(1935) DAEG-1-ES   [DAEGES]


SPACING WITHIN MORPHEME PRECEDES EMENDED FORM
(1382) WUN-9-()DINI*DNUM   [*WUNDNUM]
(1868) ()IN-1-()NE*HINE   [HINE]
(1902) WEO-9-()RTHRE*RTHRA   [*WEORTHRA]
```

SPACING WITHIN MORPHEME PRECEDES CONSONANT-GRAPH

A.   SPACING PRECEDES RESONANT
(1956) TWEEO-9-NU=   [TWEEONU=]
(2044) GEOO-1-MOR-   [GEOOMOR-MOOD]
(2239) GEOO-1-MOR   [WINE-GEOOMOR]
(2267) GIOO-1-MOR-   [GIOOMOR-MOOD]
(2403) FRUU-1-NEN   [GE-FRUUNEN]
(2811) GEO-1-N-1-   [GEONGU=]
(2004) DI-8-NGU=   [SIGE-SCYLDINGU=]
(2011) DE-9-NES   [HEALF-DENES]
(2053) BA-9-NENA   [BANENA]
(2130) FRU-9-MAN   [LEEOO-FRUMAN]
(2261) FRU-9-MAN   [WIIG-FRUMAN]
(2343) SO-9-MOD   [SOMOD]
(2645) FRE-9-MEOE   [GE-FREMEDE]
(2805) HRO-9-NES-   [HRONES-NAESSE]
(2851) GO-9-MELA   [GOMELA]
(2902) WU-9-NADH   [WUNADH]
(3054) GU-1-MENA   [GUMENA]
(3111) MO-9-NEGU=   [MONEGU=]
(2023) NEM-1-NAN   [NEMNAN]
(2034) FAEAEM-1-NAN   [FAEAEMNAN]
(2059) FAEAEM-9-NAN   [FAEAEMNAN]
(2080) MAN-1-NES   [MANNES]
(2089) IN-1-NAN   [INNAN]
(2091) SUM-2-NE   [SUMNE]
(2127) MAN-1-NAN   [MANNAN]
(2201) HLAEM-2-MU=   [HILOE-HLAEMMU=]
(2225) IN-1-NE   [INNE]
(2320) DYRN-9-NE   [DYRNNE]
(2351) HLEM-1-MA   [HILOE-HLEMMA]
(2499) FREM-9-MAN   [FREMMAN]
(2514) FREM-1-MAN   [FREMMAN]
(2544) HLEM-2-MA   [HILOE-HLEMMA]
(2627) FREM-1-MAN   [FREMMAN]
(2644) FREM-2-MAN-1- [GE-FREMMANNE]
(2644) MAN-1-NE   [GE-FREMMANNE]
(2674) FREM-1-MAN   [GE-FREMMAN]
(2715) IN-1-NAN   [INNAN]
(2800) FREM-1-MADH   [FREMMADH]
(3098) MAN-1-NA   [MANNA]
(2077) FYR-2-MEST   [FYRMEST]
(2260) BEOR-3-NE   [BEORNE]
(2272) BYR-1-NENDE   [BYRNENDE]
(2307) WYR-9-ME   [WYRME]
(2404) BEAR-2-ME   [BEARME]
(2460) SEAL-1-MAN   [SEALMAN]
(2573) FOR-9-MAN   [FORMAN]
(2625) FOR-2-MA   [FORMA]
(2638) HEL-1-MAS   [HELMAS]
(2761) FEOR-9-MEND-   [FEORMEND-LEEASE]
(2788) MAEAEK-1-NE   [MAEAERNE]
(3098) MAEAEK-1-NE   [MAEAERNE]
(1943) LEEOF-1-NE   [LEEOFNE]
(2143) MAAOH-1-MA   [MAADHMA]
(2166) MAAOH-1-MA   [MAADHMA]
(2236) MAAOH-1-MAS   [MAADHMAS]
(2414) MAAOH-9-MAS   [GOLD-MAADHMAS]
(2458) HODH-2-MAN   [HODHMAN]
(2490) MAAOH-3-MAS   [MAADHMAS]
(2640) MAAOH-2-MAS   [MAADHMAS]

137

(2652) FAEDH-2-MIE   [FAEDHMIE]
(2925) HREF-1-NA-   [HREFNA-WUDU]
(2788) MAADH-2-MU=   [MAADHMU=]
(2865) MAADH-1-MAS   [MAADHMAS]
(3133) FAEDH-9-MIAN   [FAEDHMIAN]
(2297) WEARD-1-NE   [UUTAN-WEARDNE]
(2456) WEEST-9-NE   [WEESTNE]
(2572) THEEOD-1-NE   [THEEODNE]
(2656) DHEEOD-1-NES   [DHEEODNES]
(3070) THEEOD-1-NAS   [THEEODNAS]
(2125) WEERIG-1-NE   [DEEADH-WEERIGNE]
(2576) FAAH-1-NE   [GRYRE-FAAHNE]
(3012) GRI=-2-ME   [GRI=ME]
(3061) SU=-2-NE   [SU=NE]
(3073) WO=-2-MU=   [WO=MU=]
(3085) GRI=-9-ME   [GRI=ME]

(2299) HWII-1-LU=   [HWIILU=]
(2554) HREE-2-RED   [ON-HREERED]
(2443) AEDHE-9-LING   [AEDHELING]
(2517) BE-9-REND   [HELM-BEREND]
(2631) MADHE-1-LODE   [MADHELODE]
(2671) WY-8-LMU=   [FYYR-WYLMU=]
(2781) HO-8-RDE   [HORDE]
(2949) GAEDE-9-LINGU=   [GAEDELINGU=]
(3072) HEADHE-9-ROD   [GE-HEADHEROD]
(3109) THO-2-LIAN.   [GE-THOLIAN]

(2880) SAEAEM-1-RA   [SAEAEMRA]
(2193) SEEL-1-RA   [SEELRA]
(2464) WEAL-9-LINDE   [WEALLINDE]
(2040) SYLF-9-RA   [SYLFRA]
(2191) HREEDH-2-LES   [HREEDHLES]
(2637) THYS-1-LICU   [THYSLICU]
(2358) HREEDH-2-LES   [HREEDHLES]
(2784) FYRDH-1-RED   [GE-FYRDHRED]
(2881) NIIDH-9-LAN   [FERHDH-GE-NIIDHLAN]
(2933) NIIDH-2-LAN   [FEORH-GE-NIIDHLAN]
(2992) HREEDH-2-LES   [HREEDHLES]
(2926) MEED-9-LAN   [ON-MEEDLAN]

8.   SPACING PRECEDES SPIRANT
(2406) THREOTTEEO-9-DHA   [THREOTTEEODHA]
(2454) DEEA-9-DHES   [DEEADHES]
(3050) THUU-9-SEND   [THUUSEND]
(2171) HROO-1-THRA   [HROOTHRA]
(2324) CYY-9-DHED   [GE-CYYDHED]
(2680) NII-1-THE   [NIITHE]
(1958) GEO-1-FU=   [GEOFU=]
(2295) SWEO-9-FOTE   [SWEOFOTE]
(2470) EA-9-FERU=   [EAFERU=]
(2661) HEA-9-FOLAN   [WIIG-HEAFOLAN]
(2043) ()++*SE-9-FA   [*SEFA]
(1954) HAELE-9-THA   [HAELETHA]
(2092) SY-1-DHDHAN   [SYDHDHAN]
(2510) MA-9-DHELODE   [MADHELODE]
(2132) HEAL-1-SODE   [HEALSODE]
(2255) ()++*HYR-9-STED-   [*HYRSTED-GOLDE]
(2822) EAR-9-FODH-   [EARFODH-LIICE]
(2927) SCIL-9-FINGAS.   [GUUDH-SCILFINGAS]
(2134) MAEAEK-1-DHO   [MAEAERDHO]
(2176) WEOR-2-DHOD.   [GE-WEORDHOD]
(3017) WEOR-9-DHUNGE   [HRING-WEORDHUNGE]
(3068) WEOR-9-DHAN   [WEORDHAN]
(2193) MAADH-4-THU=   [SINC-MAADHTHU=]

138

2405) MAADH-1-THUM-   [MAADHTHUM-FAET]

.   SPACING PRECEDES STOP
2131) DHEEO-1-DEN   [DHEEODEN]
2180) NEEA-9-TAS   [HEORDH-GE-NEEATAS]
2273) FLEEO-1-GEDH   [FLEEOGEDH]
2721) THEEO-9-DEN   [THEEODEN]
2786) THEEO-2-DEN   [THEEODEN]
2014) WII-9-DAN   [WIIDAN]
2027) RII-9-CES   [RIICES]
2123) FROO-1-DAN   [FROODAN]
2308) BII-9-DAN   [BIIDAN]
2325) SNUU-1-DE   [SNUUDE]
2623) WAEAE-2-DA   [GUUDH-GE-WAEAEDA]
2838) DAEAE-1-DA   [DAEAEDA]
2956) BRYY-9-DE   [BRYYDE]
3038) LII-2-CRAN   [SYL-LIICRAN]
3132) LEE-2-TON   [LEETON]
2664) GEO-9-GUDH-   [GEOGUDH-FEEORE]
1948) HRO-9-DEN   [GOLD-HRODEN]
2096) WEORDHO-1-DE   [WEORDHODE]
2102) LEEANU-9-DE   [LEEANODE]
2233) DA-9-GU=   [GEEAR-DAGU=]
2707) BRO-9-TEN   [AA-BROTEN]
2962) WRE-9-CEN   [WRECEN]
1948) GEON-1-GU=   [GEONGU=]
1968) ON-2-GEN-   [ONGEN-THEEOES]
2015) SITTEN-1-DRA   [HEAL-SITTENDRA]
2038) THEN-1-DEN   [THENDEN]
2044) CEM-1-PAN   [CEMPAN]
2083) GON-1-GAN   [GONGAN]
2087) DHON-1-CU=   [OR-DHONCU=]
2128) ()++*UN-9-DER [*UNDER]
2188) WEN-2-DEN   [ED-WENDEN]
2292) DEN-1-DES   [WALDENDES]
2301) FAN-1-DOO   [GE-FANDOO]
2319) HYYN-9-DE   [HYYNDE]
2363) HREEM-1-GE   [HREEMGE]
2373) FIN-1-DAN   [FINDAN]
2377) FREEON-1-D-   [FREEOND-LAARU=]
2416) GAN-1-GENNE   [GE-GANGENNE]
2552) STYRM-1-DE   [STYRMDE]
2611) MUN-1-DES   [EEAN-MUNDES]
2648) GON-1-GAN   [GONGAN]
2653) RON-1-DAS   [RONDAS]
2743) LUN-1-GRE   [LUNGRE]
2811) N-1-GU=   [GEONGU=]
2817) GIN-3-GAESTE   [GINGAESTE]
2882) ()FERGEN*WERGEN-9-DRA   [*WERGENDRA]
2961) ON-9-GEN-   [ONGEN-DHIIOW]
2985) THEN-9-DEN   [THENDEN]
3069) NEM-1-DON   [BE-NEMDON]
3075) AAGEN-1-DES   [AAGENDES]
3134) WUN-1-DEN   [WUNDEN]
3149) MAEAEN-9-DON   [MAEAENDON]
3159) TIM-9-BREDON   [BE-TIMBREDON]
2004) SCYL-9-DI-8-   [SIGE-SCYLDINGU=]
2096) WEOR-1-CU=   [WEORCU=]
2098) WEAR-9-DADE.   [WEARDADE]
2103) MER-9-GEN   [MERGEN]
2124) MER-3-GEN   [MERGEN]
2160) WOL-2-DE   [WOLDE]
2163) HYYR-1-DE   [HYYRDE]
2164) WEAR-9-DODE.   [WEARDODE]
2177) BEAL-9-DODE   [BEALDODE]

139

```
(2262) HEAR-4-PAN    [HEARPAN]
(2272) BIOR-2-GAS    [BIORGAS]
(2292) WAL-9-DEN-1-  [WALDENDES]
(2304) BOL-1-GEN     [GE-BOLGEN]
(2371) FYL-9-CU=     [ AEL-FYLCU=]
(2376) WOL-9-DE.     [ WOLDE]
(2386) SWEOR-9-DES   [SWEORDES]
(2405) MEL-9-DAN     [MELDAN]
(2428) BAL-9-DOR     [ BALDOR]
(2439) MER-1-CELSES  [MERCELSES]
(2459) GEAR-2-DU=    [GEARDU=]
(2599) BUR-9-GAN     [ BURGAN]
(2608) FOL-1-C-      [FOLC-RIHTA]
(2755) SER-2-CEAN    [BEADU-SERCEAN]
(2894) MOR-9-GEN-    [MORGEN-LONGNE]
(2975) FOL-9-DAN     [ FOLDAN]
(3025) REOR-9-DIAN   [REORDIAN]
(2333) HAEF-1-DE     [HAEFDE]
(2470) LAEAEF-1-DE   [LAEAEFDE]
(2133) NEEDH-3-DE.   [GE-NEEDHDE]
(2438) SWENC-1-TE    [GE-SWENCTE]
(2456) WIND-2-GE     [WINDGE]
(2577) INC-1-GE-     [ INCGE-LAAFE]
(2740) HAB-1-BAN     [ HABBAN]
(3028) SECG-1-GENDE  [SECGGENDE]
(1942) TH=-2-TE      [TH=TE]
(2637) LU=-1-PE      [G=-LU=PE]

D.  SPACING PRECEDES W, X, OR H
(2018) BEEA-2-H-     [ BEEAH-WRIDHAN]
(2820) SAA-9-WOL     [ SAAWOL]
(2167) IN-1-WIT-     [ INWIT-NET]
(2670) IN-1-WIT-     [ INWIT-GAEST]
(2045) THUR-2-H      [THURH]
(2077) FEOR-2-H-     [FEORH-BEALU]
(2266) FEOR-1-H-     [FEORH-CYNNA]
(2530) SEAR-1-WU=    [SEARWU=]
(2803) BEOR-2-HTNE   [BEORHTNE]
(3074) GEAR-1-WOR    [GEARWOR]
(2362) GEAT-2-WA     [HILDE-GEATWA]
(2619) BRED-2-WADE.  [ AA-BREDWADE]

SPACING WITHIN MORPHEME PRECEDES VOWEL-GRAPH

(1968) THEEO-1-ES.  [ONGEN-THEEOES]
(2921) WIIO-3-INGAS  [MERE-WIIOINGAS]
(2100) MER-1-E-     [MERE-GRUND]
(2850) SCAMI-9-ENDE  [SCAMIENDE]
(2158) HIOR-1-O-     [HIORO-GAAR]
(2587) MAEAER-1-A    [MAEAERA]
(2653) BER-1-EN     [ BEREN]
(3095) EEOW-2-IC     [EEOWIC]

SPACING WITHIN MORPHEME PRECEDES EMENDED FORM

(3012) CEEA-9-()++D*POD    [*GE-CEEAPOD]
(3160) ROO-1-()FIS*FES     [*BEADU-ROOFES]
(1983) ()HAE-8-()NU=*HAELEDHU=    [*HAELEDHU=]
(2108) GO-9-()MEL*MEN-     [*GOMEN-WUDU]
(1944) HEM-2-()NINGES*MINGES    [*HEMMINGES]
(1961) HEM-1-()INGES*MINGES     [*HEMMINGES]
(2136) GRIM-1-()ME*NE      [*GRIMNE]
(2505) ()CEM*CAM-1-()PAN*PE      [*CAMPE]
(2829) SCEAR-9-()DE*PE     [*HEADHO-SCEARPE]
(2363) THORF-9-()+ON*TON   [*THORFTON]
```

Appendix II

Spacing at Morpheme Boundaries:
Phonological Sort

he sorted lists making up this appendix consist of all pairs
f root or prebase morpheme sequences occurring within words.

The first principle of the sorting is phonological; within
ach phonological set the items are then listed seriatim as
hey occur in the text. The segment of the morpheme pair
erving as a basis for the phonological sort is the final
honemic element of the first of the two morphemes. The order
s as follows.

1. Long vocalic nucleus
    (a) diphthong (ᶦo, ᶦe, ĕo, or ĕa)
    (b) simple vowel (ǣ, ā, ē, ī, ō, ū, or ȳ)

2. Short vocalic nucleus (æ, a, e, i, o, u, y)
    (short diphthongs do not occur in this text in
    morpheme-final position)

3. Resonant consonant (m̲, n̲, l̲, or r̲)

4. Stop consonant (b̲, p̲, d̲, t̲, or c̲)

5. Spirant (s̲, f̲, or þ/ð)

6. Other consonant symbol (g̲, x̲, w̲, or h̲)

7. Nonalphabetic symbol

The sorting of forms containing root and prebase morpheme
equences within a word brings together in separate groupings
ll forms whose first morpheme terminates in one or another of
he various phonological classes. (Just as easily, the initial

sounds--or graphemes, strictly--of either morpheme can be
programmed as the key for sorting; or any other graphemically
definable key may be used.) The grouped listings in this
appendix, then, give all words having certain similarities of
structure. From these groups, in turn, can readily be drawn
all occurrences of root or prebase morphemes ending in a long
vowel, or in a spirant consonant, the spacing characteristics
within names (Beowulf, Hrothgar, etc.) or within gūþ- or sǣ-
compounds, the spacing characteristics of the prebase ge-, to
name but a few. Whether one is interested in meter, graphotactics, frequency of forms within a given run of text, or some
other matters, the sorting of forms here may prove useful. For
still different interests, these same forms are sorted by
spacing numeral in Appendix III.

Inevitably, a few words that may be expected, both in the
lists in this appendix and in Appendix III, will not appear.
The name Ēomēr 1960, presumably a compound of eoh + mǣre, is an
emendation of MS. geomor; it was written without internal
spacing. Hrōþulf is another name, compounded with the element
-wulf, but without the clear phonological markings of a compound, as in Hrōþ-gār and Hrōþ-mund; it too is written without
internal spacing between the etymologically defined root morphemes. It may be remarked parenthetically that the internal
spacing between the two parts of Beowulf's name characteris-
tically does not resemble that of spacing between root morphemes of compounds. In S1's copy, for instance, twenty-five
occurrences of the name have no spacing between Bēo- and -wulf,
only half a dozen occurrences have 1-space or 2-space, but none
has 3-space or larger; five times the division at line-end is
at the morpheme/syllable boundary. The range of spacing within
this name is essentially that of spacing at non-morpheme
boundaries, as displayed in Appendix I.

Likewise, wildēor 1430 will not appear in this appendix
and the one following, although etymologically it is a compound
of wild + dēor; it is not divided in the text, and it was

ritten by S1 without internal spacing. Derivations with -lic,
which are generally treated as spaceable morpheme sequences,
re listed (as explained in the Introduction), but with excep-
ions in eorl̄c 637, from eorl + l̄c, and atel̄c 784, from
tol + l̄c. Within atel̄c there is no scribal spacing. In
orl̄c there is, though, and the form transcribed EOR-2-LIIC
n the text will therefore be listed in Appendix I.

MORPHEME PAIRS GROUPED BY PHONOLOGICAL FEATURES

FIRST MORPHEME TERMINATES IN LONG VOCALIC UNIT

```
(0007) FEEA- 3 -SCEAFT 2    [FEEA-SCEAFT]
(0018) BEEO- 0 -WULF 3    [BEEO-WULF]
(0053) BEEO- 0 -WULF 3    [BEEO-WULF]
(0284) THREEA- 3 -NYYO 9    [THREEA-NYYO]
(0343) BEEO- 0 -WULF 3    [BEEO-WULF]
(0364) BEEO- 0 -WULF 5    [BEEO-WULF]
(0405) BEEO- 9 -WULF 2    [BEEO-WULF]
(0430) FREEO- 0 -WINE 9    [FREEO-WINE]
(0457) BEEO- 1 -WULF. 3    [BEEO-WULF]
(0501) BEEO- 2 -WULFES 5    [BEEO-WULFES]
(0506) BEEO- 2 -WULF 4    [BEEO-WULF]
(0529) BEEO- 1 -WULF 4    [BEEO-WULF]
(0609) BEEO- 9 -WULFE 5    [BEEO-WULFE]
(0615) FREEO- 0 -LIIC 9    [FREEO-LIIC]
(0623) BEEO- 0 -WULFE 5    [BEEO-WULFE]
(0631) BEEO- 0 -WULF 1    [BEEO-WULF]
(0641) FREEO- 1 -LICU 3    [FREEO-LICU]
(0653) BEEO- 0 -WULF 5    [BEEO-WULF]
(0034) AA- 0 -LEEDON 2    [AA-LEEDON]
(0047) AA- 0 -SETTON 4    [AA-SETTON]
(0080) AA- 0 -LEEH 5    [AA-LEEH]
(0128) AA- 0 -HAFEN 2    [AA-HAFEN]
(0218) FAA-9-MII- 4 -HEALS 3    [FAAMII-HEALS]
(0223) SAEAE- 2 -NAESSAS 4    [SAEAE-NAESSAS]
(0226) SAEAE- 2 -WUDU 2    [SAEAE-WUDU]
(0277) HRAA- 2 -FYL 5    [HRAA-FYL]
(0325) SAEAE- 0 -MEE-1-THE 4    [SAEAE-MEETHE]
(0329) SAEAE- 1 -MAN-2-NA 4    [SAEAE-MANNA]
(0344) AA- 0 -SECGAN 4    [AA-SECGAN]
(0355) AA- 0 -GIFAN 9    [AA-GIFAN]
(0377) SAEAE- 0 -LIITHENDE 6    [SAEAE-LIITHENDE]
(0390) AA- 0 -BEEAD. 5    [AA-BEEAD]
(0393) SAEAE- 4 -WYLMAS 9    [SAEAE-WYLMAS]
(0399) AA- 0 -RAAS 4    [AA-RAAS]
(0411) SAEAE- 1 -LIIDHEND 5    [SAEAE-LIIDHEND]
(0545) TOO- 1 -DRAAF 5    [TOO-DRAAF]
(0564) +SAEAE- 9 -GRUNDE 5    [SAEAE-GRUNDE]
(0567) AA- 0 -SWEFEDE 5    [AA-SWEFEDE]
(0571) SAEAE- 2 -NAESSAS 3    [SAEAE-NAESSAS]
(0633) SAEAE- 3 -BAAT 2    [SAEAE-BAAT]
(0622) AA- 0 -LAMP 3    [AA-LAMP]
(0651) AA- 0 -RAAS. 7    [AA-RAAS]
(0653) AA- 0 -BEEAD. 3    [AA-BEEAD]
(0654) AA- 0 -CWAEDH. 6    [AA-CWAEDH]
(0655) AA- 0 -LYYFDE 5    [AA-LYYFDE]
```

FIRST MORPHEME TERMINATES IN SHORT VOCALIC UNIT

```
(0005) MEODO- 3 -SETLA 9    [MEODO-SETLA]
(0019) SCEDE- 9 -LANDUM 3    [SCEDE-LANDUM]
(0027) FELA- 4 -HROOR 3    [FELA-HROOR]
(0039) HILDE- 3 -WAEAEP-2-NUM 9    [HILDE-WAEAEPNUM]
(0039) HEADHO- 3 -WAEAEDUM 3    [HEADHO-WAEAEDUM]
(0051) SELE- 4 -RAEAE-1-DEN-1-()NE*DE 4    [*SELE-RAEAEDENDE]
(0061) HEORO- 2 -GAAR. 3    [HEORO-GAAR]
(0063) HEADHO- 3 -SCILFINGAS 5    [HEADHO-SCILFINGAS]
```

```
)064) HERE- 3 -SPEED 2     [HERE-SPEED]
)065) WINE- 2 -MAAGAS 4    [WINE-MAAGAS]
)067) MAGO- 2 -DRIHT 4     [MAGO-DRIHT]
)067) BE- 1 -ARN 4     [BE-ARN]
)069) MEDO- 8 -AERN 4     [MEDO-AERN]
)082) HEADHO- 3 -WYLMA 9     [HEADHO-WYLMA]
)093) WLITE- 4 -BEORHTNE 5     [WLITE-BEORHTNE]
)093) BE- 9 -BUUGEDH 4     [BE-BUUGEDH]
)115) BE- 1 -COOM 9     [BE-COOM]
)152) HETE- 4 -NIIDH-1-AS 9     [HETE-NIIDHAS]
)184) BE- 0 -SCUUFAN 9     [BE-SCUUFAN]
)192) BE- 1 -COOM 3     [BE-COOM]
)209) LAGU- 2 -CRAEFTIG 2     [LAGU-CRAEFTIG]
)237) SEARO- 3 -HAEBBENDRA 4     [SEARO-HAEBBENDRA]
0239) LAGU- 2 -STRAEAETE 9     [LAGU-STRAEAETE]
0241) ENDE- 4 -SAEAETA 2     [ENDE-SAEAETA]
0255) MERE- 9 -LIIDHENDE 5     [MERE-LIIDHENDE]
0293) MAGU- 4 -THEGNAS 4     [MAGU-THEGNAS]
0297) LAGU- 3 -STREEA-9-MAS 8     [LAGU-STREEAMAS]
0300) HILDE- 4 -RAEAES 9     [HILDE-RAEAES]
0308) GEATO- 0 -LIIC 3     [GEATO-LIIC]
0309) FORE- 9 -MAEAEROST 5     [FORE-MAEAEROST]
0312) HILDE- 9 -DEEOR 3     [HILDE-DEEOR]
0324) GRY-9-RE- 3 -GEAT-2-WUM 4     [GRYRE-GEATWUM]
0335) HERE- 4 -SCEAFTA 5     [HERE-SCEAFTA]
0360) WINE- 3 -DRIHT-2-NE 6     [WINE-DRIHTNE]
0362) BE- 9 -GANG 4     [BE-GANG]
0370) HEADHO- 4 -RINCUM 9     [HEADHO-RINCUM]
0381) HEA-1-THO- 2 -ROOF 3     [HEATHO-ROOF]
0387) SIBBE- 4 -GE- 2     [SIBBE-GE-DRIHT]
0396) HERE- 4 -GRIIMAN 5     [HERE-GRIIMAN]
0397) HILDE- 4 -BORD 4     [HILDE-BORD]
0401) HEADHO- 3 -REEAF 5     [HEADHO-REEAF]
0401) BE- 3 -BEEAD. 5     [BE-BEEAD]
0403) *HEATHO- 8 -*RING 8     [*HEATHO-*RING]
0406) SEARO- 9 -NET 2     [SEARO-NET]
0408) MAGO- 9 -DHEGN. 5     [MAGO-DHEGN]
0414) BE- 9 -HOLEN 3     [BE-HOLEN]
0422) NEARO- 3 -THEARFE 3     [NEARO-THEARFE]
0438) GEOLO- 2 -RAND 3     [GEOLO-RAND]
0453) BEA-1-DU- 3 -SCRUUDA 5     [BEADU-SCRUUDA]
0460) HEA-2-THO- 2 -LAAFE 6     [HEATHO-LAAFE]
0462) HERE- 5 -BROOGAN 9     [HERE-BROOGAN]
0467) HERE- 2 -GAAR 9     [HERE-GAAR]
0475) HETE- 4 -THANCUM 4     [HETE-THANCUM]
0481) EALO- 3 -WAEAEGE 4     [EALO-WAEAEGE]
0484) MEDO- 8 -HEAL 4     [MEDO-HEAL]
0486) BE- 1 -STYYMED 4     [BE-STYYMED]
0487) HEORU- 9 -DREEORE 5     [HEORU-DREEORE]
0494) BE- 2 -HEEOLD 4     [BE-HEEOLD]
0495) EALO- 3 -WAEAEGE 4     [EALO-WAEAEGE]
0501) BEADU- 3 -RUUNE 5     [BEADU-RUUNE]
0502) MERE- 4 -FARAN 9     [MERE-FARAN]
0511) BE- 2 -LEEAN 2     [BE-LEEAN]
0514) MERE- 3 -STRAEAE-3-TA 4     [MERE-STRAEAETA]
0519) HEA-2-THO- 1 -RAEAEMES 9     [HEATHO-RAEAEMES]
0522) FREODHO- 3 -BUR-1-H 4     [FREODHO-BURH]
0526) HEADHO- 3 -RAEAESA 5     [HEADHO-RAEAESA]
0533) MERE- 4 -STRENGO 4     [MERE-STRENGO]
0548) HEADHO- 3 -GRIM 3     [HEADHO-GRIM]
0549) MERE- 3 -FIXA 3     [MERE-FIXA]
0552) BEA-1-DO- 4 -HRAEGL 9     [BEADO-HRAEGL]
0557) HILDE- 3 -BILLE 4     [HILDE-BILLE]
0557) HEATHO- 3 -RAEAES 9     [HEATHO-RAEAES]
0558) MERE- 3 -DEEOR 2     [MERE-DEEOR]
```

145

```
(0582)  SEARO- 3 -NIIDHA 3   [SEARO-NIIDHA]
(0584)  HEADHO- 9 -LAACE. 6   [HEADHO-LAACE]
(0594)  SEARO- 2 -GRIM 2   [SEARO-GRIM]
(0619)  SELE- 2 -FUL 4   [SELE-FUL]
(0624)  ME-1-DO- 2 -FUL 4   [MEDO-FUL]
(0637)  ENDE- 3 -DAEG 4   [ENDE-DAEG]
(0638)  MEODU- 3 -HEALLE 5   [MEODU-HEALLE]
(0650)  SCADU- 4 -HELMA 3   [SCADU-HELMA]
(0094)  SIGE- 6 -HREE-2-THIG 4   [SIGE-HREETHIG]
(0194)  HIGE- 1 -LAA-9-CES 4   [HIGE-LAACES]
(0204)  HIGE- 8 -ROOFNE 9   [HIGE-ROOFNE]
(0261)  HIGE- 2 -LAACES 5   [HIGE-LAACES]
(0339)  HIGE- 9 -THRYM-8-MUM 5   [HIGE-THRYMMUM]
(0342)  HIGE- 2 -LAACES. 5   [HIGE-LAACES]
(0391)  SIGE- 2 -DRIHTEN 9   [SIGE-DRIHTEN]
(0407)  HIGE- 4 -LAACES 4   [HIGE-LAACES]
(0435)  HIGE- 1 -LAAC 3   [HIGE-LAAC]
(0452)  HIGE- 1 -LAACE 5   [HIGE-LAACE]
(0490)  SIGE- 3 -HREEDH 2   [SIGE-HREEDH]
(0597)  SIGE- 9 -SCYL-1-DINGA 5   [SIGE-SCYLDINGA]
(0619)  SIGE- 2 -ROOF 9   [SIGE-ROOF]
(0644)  SIGE- 9 -FOL-2-CA 4   [SIGE-FOLCA]

(0002)  GE- 2 -FRUUNON 4   [GE-FRUUNON]
(0007)  GE- 1 -BAAD 9   [GE-BAAD]
(0020)  GE- 2 -WYRCEAN 3   [GE-WYRCEAN]
(0022)  GE- 3 -WUNIGEN 4   [GE-WUNIGEN]
(0024)  GE- 2 -LAEAESTEN 9   [GE-LAEAESTEN]
(0025)  GE- 2 -HWAEAERE 3   [GE-HWAEAERE]
(0025)  GE- 9 -THEEON. 6   [GE-THEEON]
(0026)  GE- 2 -WAAT 4   [GE-WAAT]
(0026)  GE- 3 -SCAEP- 2   [GE-SCAEP-HWIILE]
(0029)  GE- 0 -SIITHAS 9   [GE-SIITHAS]
(0037)  GE- 2 -LAEAEDED. 5   [GE-LAEAEDED]
(0038)  GE- 2 -GYRWAN 4   [GE-GYRWAN]
(0042)  GE- 2 -WIITAN. 5   [GE-WIITAN]
(0055)  GE- 0 -FRAEAE-9-GE 4   [GE-FRAEAEGE]
(0066)  GE- 0 -WEEOX 5   [GE-WEEOX]
(0069)  GE- 0 -WYRCEAN 5   [GE-WYRCEAN]
(0070)  GE- 2 -FRUUNON. 3   [GE-FRUUNON]
(0071)  GE- 2 -DAEAELAN 3   [GE-DAEAELAN]
(0074)  GE- 1 -FRAEGN 4   [GE-FRAEGN]
(0074)  GE- 1 -BAN-1-NAN 3   [GE-BANNAN]
(0076)  GE- 1 -LOMP 3   [GE-LOMP]
(0079)  GE- 1 -WEALD 3   [GE-WEALD]
(0087)  GE- 2 -THOLODE 4   [GE-THOLODE]
(0088)  GE- 2 -HWAAM 4   [GE-HWAAM]
(0088)  GE- 1 -HYYR-9-DE. 6   [GE-HYYRDE]
(0094)  GE- 0 -SET-1-TE 5   [GE-SETTE]
(0096)  GE- 4 -FRAET-1-WADE 5   [GE-FRAETWADE]
(0097)  GE- 1 -SCEOOP 4   [GE-SCEOOP]
(0098)  GE- 2 -HWYLCUM 3   [GE-HWYLCUM]
(0107)  GE- 2 -WRAEC 9   [GE-WRAEC]
(0109)  GE- 9 -FEAH 5   [GE-FEAH]
(0115)  $GE- 8 -WAAT 3   [GE-WAAT]
(0117)  GE- 1 -+BUUN 4   [GE-BUUN]
(0118)  GE- 1 -DRIHT 4   [GE-DRIHT]
(0122)  GE- 0 -NAM 3   [GE-NAM]
(0123)  GE- 1 -+WAAT 6   [GE-WAAT]
(0133)  GE- 3 -WIN 2   [GE-WIN]
(0135)  GE- 8 -FREMEDE 9   [GE-FREMEDE]
(0139)  GE- 0 -RUUM- 9   [GE-RUUM-LIICOR]
(0140)  GE- 2 -BEEACNOD 3   [GE-BEEACNOD]
(0141)  GE- 0 -SAEGD 4   [GE-SAEGD]
(0147)  GE- 9 -THOLODE 4   [GE-THOLODE]
```

1+6

```
0148)  GE- 2 -HWELCNE 9   [GE-HWELCNE]
0165)  GE- 1 -FRE-1-MEDE. 9   [GE-FREMEDE]
0171)  GE- 0 -SAET 4   [GE-SAET]
0174)  GE- 3 -FREM-2-MAN-1-N-1-E. 7   [GE-FREMMANNE]
0175)  GE- 1 -HEE-9-TON 3   [GE-HEETON]
0177)  GE- 1 -FRE-2-ME-2-DE. 5   [GE-FREMEDE]
0179)  GE- 1 -MUN-9-DON 4   [GE-MUNDON]
0186)  GE- 9 -WENDAN 3   [GE-WENDAN]
0191)  GE- 1 -WIN 2   [GE-WIN]
0194)  GE- 2 -FRAEGN 4   [GE-FRAEGN]
0199)  GE- 1 -GYR-1-WAN 3   [GE-GYRWAN]
0206)  GE- 1 -CORONE 5   [GE-CORONE]
0210)  GE- 1 -+WAAT 3   [GE-WAAT]
0217)  GE- 1 -WAAT 9   [GE-WAAT]
0217)  GE- 1 -FYYSED 4   [GE-FYYSED]
0218)  GE- 1 -LIICOST 3   [GE-LIICOST]
0220)  GE- 0 -WADEN 2   [GE-WADEN]
0221)  GE- 1 -SAAWON 5   [GE-SAAWON]
0229)  GE- 1 -SEAH 3   [GE-SEAH]
0234)  $GE- 0 -WAAT 3   [GE-WAAT]
0247)  GE- 9 -MEE-1-DJ 3   [GE-MEEDU]
0247)  GE- 0 -SEAH 3   [GE-SEAH]
0250)  GE- 1 -WEORDHAD 3   [GE-WEORDHAD]
0255)  GE- 1 -HYYRADH 5   [GE-HYYRADH]
0256)  GE- 9 -THOOHT 5   [GE-THOOHT]
0257)  GE- 3 -CYYDHAN-1-NE 9   [GE-CYYDHANNE]
0262)  GE- 2 -CYYTHED 3   [GE-CYYTHED]
0264)  GE- 1 -+BAAD 3   [GE-BAAD]
0265)  GE- 1 -MAN 3   [GE-MAN]
0278)  GE- 0 -LAEAERAN. 5   [GE-LAEAERAN]
0288)  GE- 0 -SCAAD 3   [GE-SCAAD]
0290)  GE- 2 -HYYRE 3   [GE-HYYRE]
0291)  GE- 0 -WIITATH 9   [GE-WIITATH]
0292)  GE- 1 -WAEAE-1-DU 3   [GE-WAEAEDU]
0294)  GE- 2 -HWONE 4   [GE-HWONE]
0300)  GE- 2 -DIIGEDH. 6   [GE-DIIGEDH]
0301)  GE- 1 -WITON 3   [GE-WITON]
0304)  GE- 3 -HRO-1-DEN 3   [GE-HRODEN]
0313)  GE- 1 -TAEAEHTE 4   [GE-TAEAEHTE]
0315)  GE- 2 -WENDE 5   [GE-WENDE]
0317)  GE- 3 -HEAL-9-DE. 6   [GE-HEALDE]
0318)  GE- 1 -SUNDE 5   [GE-SUNDE]
0331)  GE- 1 -WUR-2-THAD 4   [GE-WURTHAD]
0346)  GE- 2 -UN-1-NAN 3   [GE-UNNAN]
0349)  GE- 1 -CYYDHED. 9   [GE-CYYDHED]
0354)  GE- 2 -CYYDHAN 4   [GE-CYYDHAN]
0357)  GE- 2 -DRIHT. 5   [GE-DRIHT]
0358)  GE- 1 -STOOD 4   [GE-STOOD]
0361)  GE- 0 -FERE-9-DE 4   [GE-FEREDE]
0366)  GE- 2 -TEEOH 5   [GE-TEEOH]
0369)  GE- 3 -AEHTLAN 5   [GE-AEHTLAN]
0388)  GE- 0 -SAGA 3   [GE-SAGA]
0395)  -()GEA*GE- 8 -TAA-9-WUM 4   [*GUUDH-GE-TAAWUM]
0396)  GE- 9 -SEEON 4   [GE-SEEON]
0398)  GE- 1 -THINGES. 9   [GE-THINGES]
0404)  GE- 0 -STOOD. 5   [GE-STOOD]
0412)  GE- 2 -HWYL-1-CUM 5   [GE-HWYLCUM]
0415)  GE- 0 -LAEAER-1-DON 4   [GE-LAEAERDON]
0420)  GE- 0 -BAND 5   [GE-BAND]
0425)  GE- 3 -HEEGAN. 5   [GE-HEEGAN]
0431)  GE- 1 -DRYHT. 4   [GE-DRYHT]
0433)  GE- 0 -AAHSOD 5   [GE-AAHSOD]
0440)  GE- 0 -LYY-9-FAN 3   [GE-LYYFAN]
0455)  GE- 2 -WEORC 4   [GE-WEORC]
0457)  ()FYHTUM*GE- 8 -*WYRHTUM 4   [*GE-*WYRHTUM]
```

147

```
(0459)  GE- 2 -SLOOH 9    [GE-SLOOH]
(0463)  GE- 3 -SOOHTE 9   [GE-SOOHTE]
(0464)  GE- 2 -WEALC 5    [GE-WEALC]
(0476)  GE- 0 -FREMED 9   [GE-FREMED]
(0477)  GE- 0 -WANOD 3    [GE-WANOD]
(0479)  GE- 9 -TWAEAEFAN. 7    [GE-TWAEAEFAN]
(0480)  GE- 0 -BEEOTEDON 4    [GE-BEEOTEDON]
(0492)  GE- 1 -RYYMED 4    [GE-RYYMED]
(0505)  GE- 9 -()HEDDE*HEEDE 4    [*GE-HEEJE]
(0520)  GE- 4 -SOOHTE 9    [GE-SOOHTE]
(0524)  GE- 1 -LAEAESTE. 7    [GE-LAEAESTE]
(0525)  GE- 9 -THINGEA 6    [GE-THINGEA]
(0526)  GE- 3 -HWAEAER 9    [GE-HWAEAER]
(0535)  GE- 2 -CWAEAEDON 3    [GE-CWAEAEDON]
(0536)  GE- 9 -BEEO-1-TE-1-DON 3    [GE-BEEOTEDON]
(0538)  GE- 1 -AEF-1-NDON 3    [GE-AEFNDON]
(0551)  GE- 2 -FREME-2-DE 5    [GE-FREMEDE]
(0553)  GE- 2 -GYR-9-WED 3    [GE-GYRWED]
(0556)  GE- 0 -RAEAEHTE 6    [GE-RAEAEHTE]
(0559)  GE- 3 -LOOME 5    [GE-LOOME]
(0561)  GE- 2 -DEEFE 5    [GE-DEEFE]
(0562)  GE- 1 -FEEAN 3    [GE-FEEAN]
(0571)  GE- 2 -SEEON 3    [GE-SEEON]
(0574)  GE- 9 -SAEAELDE 5    [GE-SAEAELDE]
(0575)  GE- 0 -FRAEGN 4    [GE-FRAEGN]
(0578)  GE- 0 -DIIGDE 5    [GE-DIIGDE]
(0584)  GE- 3 -HWAE-2-THER 4    [GE-HWAETHER]
(0585)  GE- 0 -FREMEDE 4    [GE-FREMEDE]
(0591)  GE- 0 -FREME-2-DE 5    [GE-FREMEDE]
(0603)  GE- 9 -BEEODAN 4    [GE-BEEODAN]
(0608)  GE- 3 -LYYF-1-DE 9    [GE-LYYFDE]
(0609)  GE- 1 -HYYRDE 4    [GE-HYYRDE]
(0610)  GE- 3 -THOOHT 5    [GE-THOOHT]
(0613)  GE- 0 -MYNDIG 5    [GE-MYNDIG]
(0615)  GE- 1 -SEALDE 5    [GE-SEALDE]
(0618)  GE- 3 -THEAH 5    [GE-THEAH]
(0624)  GE- 2 -THUNGEN 4    [GE-THUNGEN]
(0626)  GE- 1 -LAMP 9    [GE-LAMP]
(0627)  GE- 0 -LYYFDE 5    [GE-LYYFDE]
(0628)  GE- 3 -THEAH 5    [GE-THEAH]
(0630)  GE- 8 -FYYSED. 9    [GE-FYYSED]
(0632)  GE- 1 -STAAH. 5    [GE-STAAH]
(0633)  GE- 9 -SAET 4    [GE-SAET]
(0633)  GE- 1 -DRIHT 5    [GE-DRIHT]
(0635)  GE- 1 -WORHTE 5    [GE-WORHTE]
(0636)  GE- 3 -FREM-9-MAN 3    [GE-FREMMAN]
(0638)  GE- 2 -BIIDAN. 5    [GE-BIIDAN]
(0647)  GE- 2 -THINGED. 6    [GE-THINGED]
(0648)  GE- 2 -SEEON 3    [GE-SEEON]
(0650)  GE- 9 -SCEAPU 4    [GE-SCEAPU]
(0652)  *GE- 8 -GREET-1-TE 3    [*GE-GREETTE]
(0654)  GE- 0 -WEALD 4    [GE-WEALD]
(0658)  GE- 3 -HEALD 5    [GE-HEALD]
(0659)  GE- 1 -MYNE 9    [GE-MYNE]
(0661)  GE- 2 -DIIGEST. 9    [GE-DIIGEST]
(0023)  -GE- 1 -SIITHAS 5    [WIL-GE-SIITHAS]
(0044)  -GE- 1 -STREEO-9-NUM 3    [THEEOD-GE-STREEONUM]
(0059)  -GE- 0 -RIIMED 2    [FORDH-GE-RIIMED]
(0063)  -GE- 1 -BEDDA 4    [HEALS-GE-BEDDA]
(0209)  -GE- 0 -MYR-9-CU 4    [LAND-GE-MYRCU]
(0227)  -GE- 1 -WAEAE-2-DO 3    [GUUDH-GE-WAEAEDO]
(0233)  -GE- 2 -HYG-1-DUM 2    [MOOD-GE-HYGDUM]
(0261)  -GE- 1 -NEEATAS. 9    [HEORDH-GE-NEEATAS]
(0269)  -GE- 2 -BYRGEAN 9    [LEEOD-GE-BYRGEAN]
(0343)  -GE- 1 -NEEATAS 5    [BEEOD-GE-NEEATAS]
```

148

(0368) -GE- 3 -TAAWUM 4   [WIIG-GE-TAAWUM]
(0387) -GE- 2 -DRIHT 3   [SIBBE-GE-DRIHT]
(0559) -GE- 3 -TEEO-1-NAN 4   [LAADH-GE-TEEONAN]

FIRST MORPHEME TERMINATES IN RESONANT CONSONANT

(0001) $$GAAR- 1 -$$DE-9-NA 3   [GAAR-DENA]
(0001) GEEAR- 3 -DAGUM. 6   [GEEAR-DAGUM]
(0010) HRON- 8 -RAADE 5   [HRON-RAADE]
(0014) FYREN- 2 -DHEARFE 3   [FYREN-DHEARFE]
(0014) ON- 9 -GEAT 4   [ON-GEAT]
(0015) ALDOR- 8 -()++ASE*LEEASE. 4   [*ALDOR-LEEASE]
(0017) FOR- 2 -GEAF. 6   [FOR-GEAF]
(0023) WIL- 9 -GE- 1   [WIL-GE-SIITHAS]
(0037) FEOR- 4 -WEGUM 3   [FEOR-WEGUM]
(0038) CYYM- 1 -LIICCR 4   [CYYM-LIICOR]
(0045) FRUM- 2 -SCEAFTE 9   [FRUM-SCEAFTE]
(0045) ON- 0 -SENDON 4   [ON-SENDON]
(0046) UMBOR- 3 -WE-9-SENDE 5   [UMBOR-WESENDE]
(0049) GAAR- 2 -SECG 4   [GAAR-SECG]
(0052) ON- 2 -FEENG. 9   [ON-FEENG]
(0056) ON- 1 -WOOC 4   [ON-WOOC]
(0068) HEAL- 3 -RECED 4   [HEAL-RECED]
(0075) MIDDAN- 3 -GEARD 3   [MIDDAN-GEARD]
(0077) EAL- 3 -GEARO 4   [EAL-GEARO]
(0078) HEAL- 4 -AER-9-NA 4   [HEAL-AERNA]
(0082) HORN- 3 -GEEAP 4   [HORN-GEEAP]
(0084) AATHUM- 2 -()SWERIAN*SWEEORAN 3   [*AATHUM-SWEEORAN]
(0085) WAEL- 2 -NII-9-DHE 4   [WAEL-NIIDHE]
(0086) ELLEN- 3 -GAEAEST 4   [ELLEN-GAEAEST]
(0091) FRUM- 3 -SCEAFT 4   [FRUM-SCEAFT]
(0092) AEL- 0 -MIHTIGA 4   [AEL-MIHTIGA]
(0100) ON- 1 -GAN 3   [ON-GAN]
(0104) FIIFEL- 2 -CYN-9-NES 3   [FIIFEL-CYNNES]
(0105) WON- 2 -SAEAELII 3   [WON-SAEAELII]
(0106) FOR- 2 -SCRIFEN 3   [FOR-SCRIFEN]
(0109) FOR- 2 -WRAEC 3   [FOR-WRAEC]
(0110) MAN- 1 -CYNNE 9   [MAN-CYNNE]
(0111) UN- 1 -TYYDRAS 3   [UN-TYYDRAS]
(0111) ON- 2 -WOOCON 9   [ON-WOOCON]
(0114) FOR- 4 -GEALD. 9   [FOR-GEALD]
(0117) BEEOR- 2 -THEGE 3   [BEEOR-THEGE]
(0120) WON- 0 -SCEAFT 3   [WON-SCEAFT]
(0120) UN- 2 -HAEAELO 3   [UN-HAEAELO]
(0125) WAEL- 2 -FYLLE 3   [WAEL-FYLLE]
(0126) AEAER- 2 -DAEGE 9   [AEAER-DAEGE]
(0127) UN- 1 -DYRNE 9   [UN-DYRNE]
(0129) MORGEN- 2 -SWEEG 3   [MORGEN-SWEEG]
(0130) AEAER- 0 -GOOD 9   [AEAER-GOOD]
(0130) UN- 2 -BLIIDHE 3   [UN-BLIIDHE]
(0131) THEGN- 1 -SORGE 9   [THEGN-SORGE]
(0139) -RUUM- 9 -LIICOR 3   [GE-RUUM-LIICOR]
(0142) HEAL- 4 -DHEGNES 5   [HEAL-DHEGNES]
(0149) FOR- 0 -DHAAM 8   [FOR-DHAAM]
(0150) UN- 0 -DYRNE 4   [UN-DYRNE]
(0154) SIN- 1 -GAA-9-LE 4   [SIN-GAALE]
(0161) SIN- 1 -NIHTE 3   [SIN-NIHTE]
(0163) HEL- 2 -RUUNAN 3   [HEL-RUUNAN]
(0164) MAN- 1 -CYN-9-NES 2   [MAN-CYNNES]
(0165) AAN- 0 -GENGEA 3   [AAN-GENGEA]
(0174) FAEAER- 2 -GRYRU= 9   [FAEAER-GRYRU=]
(0189) MAEAEL- 3 -CEARE 4   [MAEAEL-CEARE]
(0190) SIN- 0 -GAA-9-LA 4   [SIN-GAALA]
(0191) ON- 9 -WENDAN 3   [ON-WENDAN]
(0196) MON- 0 -CYN-2-NES 5   [MON-CYNNES]

149

```
(0200) SWAN- 3 -RAADE 4    [SWAN-RAADE]
(0216) WIL- 2 -SIIDH 3    [WIL-SIIDH]
(0219) AAN- 2 -TIID 9    [AAN-TIID]
(0220) WUNDEN- 2 -STEFNA 4    [WUNDEN-STEFNA]
(0222) BRIM- 3 -CLIFU 3    [BRIM-CLIFU]
(0230) HOLM- 9 -CLIFU 5    [HOLM-CLIFU]
(0232) FYR- 2 -WYT 3    [FYR-WYT]
(0236) MAEGEN- 9 -WUDU 2    [MAEGEN-WUDU]
(0236) METHEL- 3 -WORDUM 2    [METHEL-WORDUM]
(0244) ON- 2 -GUNNON. 9    [ON-GUNNON]
(0251) AEAEN- 2 -LIIC 3    [AEAEN-LIIC]
(0251) AN- 1 -SYYN 3    [AN-SYYN]
(0252) FRUM- 2 -CYN 2    [FRUM-CYN]
(0254) FEOR- 6 -BUUEND 3    [FEOR-BUUEND]
(0256) AAN- 3 -FEALDNE 3    [AAN-FEALDNE]
(0259) ON- 1 -LEEAC 4    [ON-LEEAC]
(0260) GUM- 1 -CYNNES 9    [GUM-CYNNES]
(0266) WEEL- 9 -HWYLC 4    [WEEL-HWYLC]
(0276) UN- 1 -CUUDHNE 4    [UN-CUUDHNE]
(0279) OFER- 3 -SWYYDHETH 4    [OFER-SWYYDHETH]
(0282) CEAR- 4 -WYLMAS 4    [CEAR-WYLMAS]
(0287) UN- 1 -FORHT 3    [UN-FORHT]
(0298) WUNDEN- 4 -HALS 9    [WUNDEN-HALS]
(0298) WEDER- 5 -MEARCE 6    [WEDER-MEARCE]
(0303) EOFOR- 3 -LIIC 3    [EOFOR-LIIC]
(0304) HLEEOR- 5 -( )BERAN*BERGAN 5    [*HLEEOR-BERGAN]
(0305) FYYR- 4 -HEARD 4    [FYYR-HEARD]
(0308) ON- 0 -GYTON 3    [ON-GYTON]
(0316) AL- 0 -WALDA 4    [AL-WALDA]
(0317) AAR- 2 -STAFUM 4    [AAR-STAFUM]
(0320) STAAN- 3 -FAAH 4    [STAAN-FAAH]
(0326) REGN- 2 -HEARDE 9    [REGN-HEARDE]
(0330) IIREN- 3 -THREEAT 4    [IIREN-THREEAT]
(0334) GRIIM- 3 -HELMAS 9    [GRIIM-HELMAS]
(0336) OM- 2 -BIHT. 5    [OM-BIHT]
(0336) EL- 1 -THEEODIGE 5    [EL-THEEODIGE]
(0340) ELLEN- 9 -ROOF 2    [ELLEN-ROOF]
(0357) ( )UN*AN- 2 -+HAAR 5    [*AN-HAAR]
(0358) ELLEN- 3 -ROOF 4    [ELLEN-ROOF]
(0367) GEGN- 3 -CWIDA 6    [GEGN-CWIDA]
(0374) FOR- 3 -GEAF 5    [FOR-GEAF]
(0380) MAEGEN- 2 -CRAEFT 3    [MAEGEN-CRAEFT]
(0382) AAR- 2 -STAFUM 3    [AAR-STAFUM]
(0382) ON- 1 -SENDE 4    [ON-SENDE]
(0388) WIL- 0 -CUMAN 4    [WIL-CUMAN]
(0394) WIL- 0 -CUMAN 4    [WIL-CUMAN]
(0397) ON- 1 -BIID-8-AN 9    [ON-BIIDAN]
(0398) WAEL- 4 -SCEAF-1-TAS 4    [WAEL-SCEAFTAS]
(0406) OR- 2 -THANCUM 1    [OR-THANCUM]
(0409) ON- 1 -GUN-1-NEN 9    [ON-GUNNEN]
(0410) EETHEL- 3 -TYRF 5    [EETHEL-TYRF]
(0410) UN- 0 -DYR-1-NE 4    [UN-DYRNE]
(0413) UN- 2 -NYT 4    [UN-NYT]
(0413) AEAEFEN- 4 -LEEOHT 4    [AEAEFEN-LEEOHT]
(0418) FOR- 3 -THAN 3    [FOR-THAN]
(0419) OFER- 9 -SAAWON 4    [OFER-SAAWON]
(0424) FOR- 3 -GRAND 8    [FOR-GRAND]
(0429) FOR- 1 -WYR-2-NE 7    [FOR-WYRNE]
(0434) WON- 4 -HYYDUM 9    [WON-HYYDUM]
(0435) FOR- 2 -HICGE 9    [FOR-HICGE]
(0436) MON- 3 -DRIHTEN 9    [MON-DRIHTEN]
(0444) UN- 0 -FOR-3-HTE 1    [UN-FORHTE]
(0449) +AN- 0 -GEN-1-GA 4    [AN-GENGA]
(0449) UN- 1 -MURN- 0    [UN-MURN-LIICE]
(0449) -MURN- 0 -LIICE 9    [UN-MURN-LIICE]
```

150

```
(0450) MOOR- 3 -HOPU 3    [MOOR-HOPU]
(0452) $ON- 1 -SEND 5    [ON-SEND]
(0458) AAR- 2 -STAFUM 4    [AAR-STAFUM]
(0464) AAR- 9 -SCYL-8-DINGA 6    [AAR-SCYLDINGA]
(0468) UN- 0 -LIFIGENDE 5    [UN-LIFIGENDE]
(0476) FAEAER- 4 -NIIDHA 1    [FAEAER-NIIDHA]
(0477) FOR- 3 -SWEEOP 4    [FOR-SWEEOP]
(0479) DOL- 4 -()SCADHAN*SCEADHAN 3    [*DOL-SCEADHAN]
(0482) BEEOR- 1 -SELE 7    [BEEOR-SELE]
(0484) MORGEN- 3 -TIID 3    [MORGEN-TIID]
(0485) DREEOR- 3 -FAAH 6    [DREEOR-FAAH]
(0488) FOR- 1 -NAM 4    [FOR-NAM]
(0489) ON- 2 -SAEAEL 3    [ON-SAEAEL]
(0492) BEEOR- 9 -SELE 7    [BEEOR-SELE]
(0498) UN- 2 -LYYTEL 9    [UN-LYYTEL]
(0499) ()$$HUN*$$UN- 2 -FERDH 4    [*UN-FERDH]
(0501) ON- 1 -BAND 3    [ON-BAND]
(0503) FOR- 3 -THON 3    [FOR-THON]
(0504) MIDDAN- 4 -GEARDES. 4    [MIDDAN-GEARDES]
(0509) DOL- 3 -GILPE 5    [DOL-GILPE]
(0513) EEA-9-GOR- 4 -STREEAM 3    [EEAGOR-STREEAM]
(0515) GAAR- 4 -SECG 4    [GAAR-SECG]
(0517) OFER- 2 -FLAAT. 5    [OFER-FLAAT]
(0518) MOR-1-GEN- 4 -TIID 3    [MORGEN-TIID]
(0524) BEEAN- 0 -STAANES 5    [BEEAN-STAANES]
(0530) ()HUN*UN- 2 -FERDH 9    [*UN-FERDH]
(0537) +GAAR- 0 -SECG 4    [GAAR-SECG]
(0540) HRON- 3 -FIXAS 4    [HRON-FIXAS]
(0547) NORTHAN- 9 -WIND 4    [NORTHAN-WIND]
(0549) ON- 3 -HREERED. 4    [ON-HREERED]
(0557) FOR- 2 -NAM 4    [FOR-NAM]
(0563) MAAN- 2 -FOR- 2    [MAAN-FOR-DAEAEDLAN]
(0563) -FOR- 2 -DAEAEDLAN 9    [MAAN-FOR-DAEAEDLAN]
(0568) BRIM- 3 -LIIDHENDE 5    [BRIM-LIIDHENDE]
(0573) UN- 0 -FAEAEGNE 9    [UN-FAEAEGNE]
(0585) DEEOR- 0 -LIICE 9    [DEEOR-LIICE]
(0595) ON- 1 -FUN-1-DEN 4    [ON-FUNDEN]
(0597) ON- 1 -SITTAN 4    [ON-SITTAN]
(0601) GAAR- 3 -DENUM 4    [GAAR-DENUM]
(0602) UN- 1 -GEAARA 4    [UN-GEAARA]
(0604) MORGEN- 3 -LEEOHT 4    [MORGEN-LEEOHT]
(0606) SWEGL- 5 -WERED 3    [SWEGL-WERED]
(0608) GAMOL- 9 -FEAX 4    [GAMOL-FEAX]
(0612) WYN- 0 -SUME 9    [WYN-SUME]
(0616) EETHEL- 3 -WEARDE 6    [EETHEL-WEARDE]
(0617) BEEOR- 3 -THEGE 7    [BEEOR-THEGE]
(0629) WAEL- 3 -REEOW 3    [WAEL-REEOW]
(0646) AEAEFEN- 2 -RAES-1-TE. 5    [AEAEFEN-RAESTE]
(0654) WIIN- 1 -AERNES 9    [WIIN-AERNES]
(0659) MAEGEN- 2 -ELLEN 2    [MAEGEN-ELLEN]
(0661) ELLEN- 2 -WEORC 3    [ELLEN-WEORC]
```

IRST MORPHEME TERMINATES IN STOP CONSONANT

```
0002) THEEOD- 2 -CYNINGA 9    [THEEOD-CYNINGA]
0009) YMB- 2 -SITTEN-1-DRA 9    [YMB-SITTENDRA]
0017) WOROLD- 2 -AARE 3    [WOROLD-AARE]
0026) -SCAEP- 2 -HWIILE 9    [GE-SCAEP-HWIILE]
0028) AET- 1 -BAEAERON 4    [AET-BAEAERON]
0031) LAND- 2 -FRUMA 5    [LAND-FRUMA]
0032) HRINGED- 2 -STEFNA 2    [HRINGED-STEFNA]
0033) +UUT- 3 -FUUS 3    [UUT-FUUS]
0044) THEEOD- 2 -GE- 1    [THEEOD-GE-STREEONUM]
0054) LEEOD- 2 -CYNING 4    [LEEOD-CYNING]
0073) FOLC- 3 -SCARE 4    [FOLC-SCARE]
```

```
(0076) FOLC- 3 -STE-9-DE 4    [FOLC-STEDE]
(0095) LAND- 2 -BUUEN-9-DUM 3    [LAND-BUUENDUM]
(0099) DRIHT- 3 -GUMAN 3    [DRIHT-GUMAN]
(0103) MEARC- 3 -STAPA 9    [MEARC-STAPA]
(0112) ORC- 0 -NEEAS 3    [ORC-NEEAS]
(0143) AET- 2 -WAND. 6    [AET-WAND]
(0167) SINC- 9 -FAAGE 4    [SINC-FAAGE]
(0177) GAAST- 4 -BONA 3    [GAAST-BONA]
(0178) THEEOD- 3 -THREEAUM 2    [THEEOD-THREEAUM]
(0180) MOOD- 2 -SEFAN 3    [MOOD-SEFAN]
(0193) NYYD- 2 -WRACU 3    [NYYD-WRACU]
(0193) NIHT- 9 -BEALWA 4    [NIHT-BEALWA]
(0203) LYYT- 3 -HWOON 2    [LYYT-HWOON]
(0208) SUND- 3 -WUDU 3    [SUND-WUDU]
(0209) LAND- 2 -GE- 0    [LAND-GE-MYRCU]
(0232) FYRD- 2 -SEARU 3    [FYRD-SEARU]
(0233) MOOD- 1 -GE- 2    [MOOD-GE-HYGDUM]
(0243) SCIP- 3 -HERGE 4    [SCIP-HERGE]
(0245) LIND- 4 -HAE-1-BBENDE 5    [LIND-HAEBBENDE]
(0249) SELD- 3 -GUMA 4    [SELD-GUMA]
(0258) =AND- 0 -SWARODE 5    [=AND-SWARODE]
(0259) WORD- 4 -HORD 2    [WORD-HORD]
(0263) ORD- 2 -FRUMA 5    [ORD-FRUMA]
(0269) LEEOD- 3 -GE- 2    [LEEOD-GE-BYRGEAN]
(0275) DAEAED- 3 -HATA 3    [DAEAED-HATA]
(0280) ED- 0 -()WENDAN*WENDEN 9    [*ED-WENDEN]
(0288) SCYLD- 3 -WIGA 3    [SCYLD-WIGA]
(0299) GOOD- 2 -FREM-3-MEN-1-DRA 9    [GOOD-FREMMENDRA]
(0302) SIID- 1 -FAE-1-TH-1-MED 9    [SIID-FAETHMED]
(0307) AET- 9 -SOM-1-NE 4    [AET-SOMNE]
(0308) GOLD- 2 -FAAH 3    [GOLD-FAAH]
(0309) FOLD- 3 -BUUENDUM 4    [FOLD-BUUENDUM]
(0321) AET- 1 -GAE-1-DERE 6    [AET-GAEDERE]
(0322) HOND- 3 -LOCEN 6    [HOND-LOCEN]
(0329) AET- 2 -GAE-1-DERE 5    [AET-GAEDERE]
(0330) AESC- 3 -HOLT 3    [AESC-HOLT]
(0332) OORET- 3 -MECGAS 4    [OORET-MECGAS]
(0338) WRAEC- 3 -SIIDHUM. 4    [WRAEC-SIIDHUM]
(0340) AND- 2 -SWARODE 4    [AND-SWARODE]
(0343) BEEOD- 3 -GE- 1    [BEEOD-GE-NEEATAS]
(0349) MOOD- 0 -SEFA 4    [MOOD-SEFA]
(0354) =AND- 0 -SWARE 9    [=AND-SWARE]
(0356) HRAED- 2 -LIICE 6    [HRAED-LIICE]
(0363) OORET- 9 -MECGAS. 7    [OORET-MECGAS]
(0367) GLAED- 0 -MAN 9    [GLAED-MAN]
(0372) CNIHT- 5 -WESENDE 6    [CNIHT-WESENDE]
(0373) EALD- 1 -FAE-2-DER 5    [EALD-FAEDER]
(0380) MUND- 9 -GRIPE 5    [MUND-GRIPE]
(0383) WEST- 3 -DENU= 9    [WEST-DENU=]
(0385) MOOD- 3 -THRAE-2-CE 9    [MOOD-THRAECE]
(0387) AET- 9 -GAEDERE. 6    [AET-GAEDERE]
(0390) *WIID- 8 -*CUUDH 8    [*WIID-*CUUDH]
(0392) EEAST- 2 -DENA 4    [EEAST-DENA]
(0394) HEARD- 2 -HICGENDE 6    [HEARD-HICGENDE]
(0402) AET- 2 -SOMNE 8    [AET-SOMNE]
(0427) BEORHT- 4 -DENA 4    [BEORHT-DENA]
(0460) HAND- 3 -BONAN 3    [HAND-BONAN]
(0467) HORD- 5 -BURH 4    [HORD-BURH]
(0476) FLET- 1 -WEROD 4    [FLET-WEROD]
(0481) OORET- 2 -MECGAS 9    [OORET-MECGAS]
(0485) DRIHT- 9 -SELE 5    [DRIHT-SELE]
(0486) BENC- 3 -THELU 4    [BENC-THELU]
(0491) GEEAT- 9 -MAECGUM 3    [GEEAT-MAECGUM]
(0491) AET- 0 -SOM-2-NE 5    [AET-SOMNE]
(0519) AET- 2 -BAER. 5    [AET-BAER]
```

152

```
(0528) NIHT- 3 -LONGNE 3    [NIHT-LONGNE]
(0535) CNIHT- 4 -WESENDE 5    [CNIHT-WESENDE]
(0542) FLOOD- 2 -YYTHU= 9    [FLOOD-YYTHU=]
(0544) AET- 9 -SOMNE 5    [AET-SOMNE]
(0548) =OND- 1 -HWEARF 5    [=OND-HWEARF]
(0550) LIIC- 3 -SYRCE 4    [LIIC-SYRCE]
(0551) HOND- 9 -LOCEN 4    [HOND-LOCEN]
(0554) FEEOND- 0 -SCADHA 9    [FEEOND-SCADHA]
(0564) YMB- 3 -SAEAETON 4    [YMB-SAEAETON]
(0588) HEEAFOD- 3 -MAEAEGUM 4    [HEEAFOD-MAEAEGUM]
(0598) NYYD- 3 -BAADE 4    [NYYD-BAADE]
(0609) BEOR-2-HT- 5 -DENA 4    [BEORHT-DENA]
(0610) FAEST- 4 -RAEAEDNE 9    [FAEST-RAEAEDNE]
(0614) GOLD- 2 -HRO-9-DEN 3    [GOLD-HRODEN]
(0616) EEAST- 3 -DENA 9    [EEAST-DENA]
(0620) YMB- 2 -EEODE 5    [YMB-EEODE]
(0622) SINC- 2 -FATO 3    [SINC-FATO]
(0624) AET- 2 -BAER. 7    [AET-BAER]
(0636) FEEOND- 3 -GRAAPUM 4    [FEEOND-GRAAPUM]
(0640) GILP- 2 -CWIDE 4    [GILP-CWIDE]
(0640) GOLD- 4 -HRODEN. 5    [GOLD-HRODEN]
(0641) FOLC- 3 -CWEEN 3    [FOLC-CWEEN]
```

FIRST MORPHEME TERMINATES IN SPIRANT

```
(0005) OF- 2 -TEEAH 3    [OF-TEEAH]
(0008) WEORDH- 3 -MYNDUM 3    [WEORDH-MYNDUM]
(0016) LIIF- 2 -FREEA 4    [LIIF-FREEA]
(0024) LOF- 2 -DAEAEDU= 3    [LOF-DAEAEDU=]
(0057) HEALF- 3 -DENE 4    [HEALF-DENE]
(0058) GUUTH- 2 -REEOUW 4    [GUUTH-REEOUW]
(0059) FORDH- 4 -GE- 0    [FORDH-GE-RIIMED]
(0061) HROODH- 3 -GAAR 4    [HROODH-GAAR]
(0063) HEALS- 2 -GE- 1    [HEALS-GE-BEDUA]
(0064) HROODH- 9 -GAARE 5    [HROODH-GAARE]
(0065) WEORDH- 3 -MYND. 3    [WEORDH-MYND]
(0086) EAR-9-FODH- 2 -LIICE 6    [EARFODH-LIICE]
(0127) GUUDH- 2 -CRAEFT 4    [GUUDH-CRAEFT]
(0131) DHRYYDH- 2 -SWYYDH 3    [DHRYYDH-SWYYDH]
(0136) MORDH- 4 -BEALA 3    [MORDH-BEALA]
(0138) EEADH- 2 -FYNDE 5    [EEADH-FYNDE]
(0141) SOODH- 3 -LIICE 5    [SOODH-LIICE]
(0152) HROOTH- 2 -GAAR 5    [HROOTH-GAAR]
(0160) DEEATH- 2 -SCUA 9    [DEEATH-SCUA]
(0168) GIF- 3 -STOOL 3    [GIF-STOOL]
(0173) SWIIDH- 3 -FERHDHUM 4    [SWIIDH-FERHDHUM]
(0187) DEEADH- 9 -DAEGE 3    [DEEADH-DAEGE]
(0189) HEALF- 1 -DENES 3    [HEALF-DENES]
(0193) NIITH- 1 -GRIM 3    [NIITH-GRIM]
(0198) YYDH- 2 -LIDAN 3    [YYDH-LIDAN]
(0199) GUUDH- 9 -CYNING 4    [GUUDH-CYNING]
(0202) SIIDH- 2 -FAET 2    [SIIDH-FAET]
(0215) GUUDH- 2 -SEARO 2    [GUUDH-SEARO]
(0227) GUUDH- 2 -GE- 1    [GUUDH-GE-WAEAEDO]
(0228) YYTH- 0 -LAADE 4    [YYTH-LAADE]
(0232) FUUS- 2 -LICU 1    [FUUS-LICU]
(0235) HROODH- 2 -GAARES 4    [HROODH-GAARES]
(0244) CUUDH- 2 -LIICOR 4    [CUUDH-LIICOR]
(0245) LEEAFNES- 3 -WORD 3    [LEEAFNES-WORD]
(0246) GUUDH- 9 -FREM-1-MEN-1-DRA 4    [GUUDH-FREMMENDRA]
(0253) LEEAS- 3 -SCEEA-2-WERAS 4    [LEEAS-SCEEAWERAS]
(0261) HEORDH- 2 -GE- 1    [HEORDH-GE-NEEATAS]
(0268) HEALF- 9 -DENES 4    [HEALF-DENES]
(0273) SOOTH- 1 -LIICE 9    [SOOTH-LIICE]
(0277) HROODH- 2 -GAAR 4    [HROODH-GAAR]
```

153

```
(0283) EARFODH- 4 -THRAAGE 5   [EARFODH-THRAAGE]
(0306) GUUTH- 0 -MOOD 9   [GUUTH-MOOD]
(0314) GUUDH- 3 -BEORNA 3   [GUUDH-BEORNA]
(0321) GUUDH- 4 -BYRNE 5   [GUUDH-BYRNE]
(0328) GUUDH- 3 -SEARO 3   [GUUDH-SEARO]
(0335) HROODH- 2 -GAARES 9   [HROODH-GAARES]
(0339) HROODH- 2 -GAAR 3   [HROODH-GAAR]
(0344) HEALF- 9 -DENES 4   [HEALF-DENES]
(0348) WULF- 1 -GAAR 5   [WULF-GAAR]
(0350) WIIS- 4 -DOOM 3   [WIIS-DOOM]
(0356) HROODH- 9 -GAAR 4   [HROODH-GAAR]
(0360) WULF- 0 -GAAR 5   [WULF-GAAR]
(0367) HROODH- 3 -GAAR 6   [HROODH-GAAR]
(0371) $HROODH- 2 -GAAR 5   [HROODH-GAAR]
(0378) GIF- 3 -SCEATTAS 5   [GIF-SCEATTAS]
(0395) GUUDH- 3 -()GEA*GE- 8   [*GUUDH-GE-TAAWUM]
(0396) HROODH- 2 -GAAR 3   [HROODH-GAAR]
(0400) THRYYDH- 1 -LIIC 4   [THRYYDH-LIIC]
(0407) HROODH- 9 -GAAR 3   [HROODH-GAAR]
(0417) HROODH- 3 -GAAR 5   [HROODH-GAAR]
(0443) GUUDH- 4 -SELE 5   [GUUDH-SELE]
(0445) HREEDH- 3 -MAN-1-NA 4   [HREEDH-MANNA]
(0456) $HROODH- 4 -GAAR 5   [HROODH-GAAR]
(0463) SUUDH- 3 -DENA 4   [SUUDH-DENA]
(0469) HEALF- 1 -DENES 5   [HEALF-DENES]
(0493) SWIIDH- 3 -FERHTHE 9   [SWIIDH-FERHTHE]
(0502) AEF- 1 -THUNCA. 5   [AEF-THUNCA]
(0537) GEOGODH- 9 -FEEORE 5   [GEOGODH-FEEORE]
(0559) LAADH- 2 -GE- 3   [LAADH-GE-TEEONAN]
(0566) YYDH- 2 -LAAFE 5   [YYDH-LAAFE]
(0574) OF- 2 -SLOOH 4   [OF-SLOOH]
(0579) OTH- 2 -BAER 4   [OTH-BAER]
(0608) GUUDH- 3 -ROOF 5   [GUUDH-ROOF]
(0613) HROODH- 2 -GAARES 9   [HROODH-GAARES]
(0626) WIIS- 3 -FAEST 9   [WIIS-FAEST]
(0643) THRYYDH- 3 -WORD 3   [THRYYDH-WORD]
(0645) HEALF- 3 -DENES 9   [HEALF-DENES]
(0653) HROODH- 2 -GAAR 4   [HROODH-GAAR]
(0657) DHRYYTH- 3 -AERN 3   [DHRYYTH-AERN]
```

FIRST MORPHEME TERMINATES IN G, X, W, OR H

```
(0009) AEAEG- 0 -HWYLC 4   [AEAEG-HWYLC]
(0021) FEOH- 2 -GIFTUM. 3   [FEOH-GIFTUM]
(0084) ()SECG*ECG- 3 -HETE 4   [*ECG-HETE]
(0100) EEADIG- 2 -LIICE 4   [EEADIG-LIICE]
(0116) HRING- 3 -DENE 3   [HRING-DENE]
(0134) LONG- 1 -SUM 3   [LONG-SUM]
(0156) FEORH- 3 -BEALO 3   [FEORH-BEALO]
(0159) AEAEG- 0 -LAEAECA 8   [AEAEG-LAEAECA]
(0175) ()HRAERG*HAERG- 3 -TRAFUM 2   [*HAERG-TRAFUM]
(0176) WIIG- 2 -WEOR-1-THUNGA 9   [WIIG-WEORTHUNGA]
(0192) LONG- 2 -SUM 2   [LONG-SUM]
(0217) WAEAEG- 3 -HOLM 3   [WAEAEG-HOLM]
(0241) AEAEG- 1 -WEARDE 4   [AEAEG-WEARDE]
(0263) ECG- 8 -THEEOW 3   [ECG-THEEOW]
(0285) HEEAH- 3 -STE-2-DE 9   [HEEAH-STEJE]
(0287) AEAEG- 2 -HWAE-8-THRES 3   [AEAEG-HWAETHRES]
(0295) NIIW- 9 -TYR-2-WYD-2-NE 5   [NIIW-TYRWYDNE]
(0305) FERH- 2 -WEAR-1-DE 5   [FERH-WEARDE]
(0322) HRING- 3 -IIREN 3   [HRING-IIREN]
(0337) MOODIG- 0 -LIICRAN. 4   [MOODIG-LIICRAN]
(0368) WIIG- 5 -GE- 3   [WIIG-GE-TAAWUM]
(0373) ECG- 3 -THEEO 3   [ECG-THEEO]
(0425) AAG- 0 -LAEAECAN 4   [AAG-LAEAECAN]
```

154

```
(0433) AEAEG- 0 -LAEAECA 4    [AEAEG-LAEAECA]
(0477) WIIG- 2 -HEEAP 4       [WIIG-HEEAP]
(0499) ECG- 0 -LAAFES 4       [ECG-LAAFES]
(0512) SOR-2-H- 1 -FULL-1-NE 9    [SORH-FULLNE]
(0529) ECG- 1 -THEEOWES 9     [ECG-THEEOWES]
(0556) AAG- 0 -LAEAECAN 9     [AAG-LAEAECAN]
(0577) EEG- 9 -STREEAMUM 3    [EEG-STREEAMUM]
(0590) ECG- 9 -LAAFES 6       [ECG-LAAFES]
(0592) AEAEG- 0 -LAEAECA 3    [AEAEG-LAEAECA]
(0596) ECG- 3 -THRAECE 9      [ECG-THRAECE]
(0612) WEALH- 1 -THEEOW 8     [WEALH-THEEOW]
(0621) AEAEG- 0 -HWYLCNE 9    [AEAEG-HWYLCNE]
(0623) BEEAG- 4 -HRODEN 3     [BEEAG-HRODEN]
(0629) WEAL-1-H- 0 -THEEON. 5    [WEALH-THEEON]
(0631) ECG- 2 -THEEOWES. 5    [ECG-THEEOWES]
(0646) AAH- 0 -LAEAECAN 9     [AAH-LAEAECAN]
(0647) HEEAH- 1 -SELE 5       [HEEAH-SELE]


                APPENDIX II
LINES 0662 - 1320  (FITS X - XIX)


MORPHEME PAIRS GROUPED BY PHONOLOGICAL FEATURES

FIRST MORPHEME TERMINATES IN LONG VOCALIC UNIT

(0676) BEEO- 0 -WULF 9        [BEEO-WULF]
(0693) FREEO- 1 -BURH 9       [FREEO-BURH]
(0795) BEEO- 9 -WUL-1-FES 5   [BEEO-WULFES]
(0796) FREEA- 3 -DRIHT-9-NES 4    [FREEA-DRIHTNES]
(0818) BEEO- 0 -WUL-1-FE 3    [BEEO-WULFE]
(0832) THREEA- 9 -NYYDUM 4    [THREEA-NYYDUM]
(0856) BEEO- 0 -WUL-1-FES 4   [BEEO-WULFES]
(0872) BEEO- 2 -WUL-1-FES 4   [BEEO-WULFES]
(0912) HLEEO- 1 -BURH 4       [HLEEO-BURH]
(0946) BEEO- 0 -WULF 5        [BEEO-WULF]
(0957) BEEO- 0 -WULF 9        [BEEO-WULF]
(0973) FEEA- 3 -SCEAFT 8      [FEEA-SCEAFT]
(1020) BEEO- 0 -WULFE 7       [BEEO-WULFE]
(1024) BEEO- 1 -WULF 5        [BEEO-WULF]
(1043) BEEO- 0 -WULFE 5       [BEEO-WULFE]
(1051) BEEO- 0 -WULFE 5       [BEEO-WULFE]
(1084) WEEA- 2 -LAAFE 4       [WEEA-LAAFE]
(1098) WEEA- 1 -LAAFE 6       [WEEA-LAAFE]
(1127) HEEA- 3 -BURH 6        [HEEA-BURH]
(1160) GLEEO- 0 -MAN-9-NES 8  [GLEEO-MANNES]
(1169) FREEO- 4 -DRIHTEN 3    [FREEO-DRIHTEN]
(1191) BEEO- 0 -WULF 3        [BEEO-WULF]
(1214) HREEA- 2 -WIIC 5       [HREEA-WIIC]
(1216) BEEO- 0 -WULF 5        [BEEO-WULF]
(1299) BEEO- 9 -WULF 4        [BEEO-WULF]
(1310) BEEO- 0 -WULF 4        [BEEO-WULF]
(1315) WEEA- 2 -SPELLE 5      [WEEA-SPELLE]
(0666) TOO- 3 -GEEANES 4      [TOO-GEEANES]
(0667) AA- 0 -SETED 3         [AA-SETED]
(0668) AA- 0 -BEEAD 4         [AA-BEEAD]
(0690) +SAEAE- 3 -RINC 4      [SAEAE-RINC]
(0693) AA- 0 -FEEDED 2        [AA-FEEDED]
(0730) AA- 0 -HLOOG. 5        [AA-HLOOG]
(0733) AA- 0 -LUM-2-PEN 2     [AA-LUMPEN]
(0759) AA- 0 -+STOOD 3        [AA-STOOD]
(0766) AA- 0 -TEEAH. 6        [AA-TEEAH]
(0775) +AA- 0 -BEEAG. 6       [AA-BEEAG]
```

```
(0780) TOO- 2 -BRE-9-CAN 3    [TOO-BRECAN]
(0781) TOO- 0 -LUUCAN 4       [TOO-LUUCAN]
(0782) AA- 0 -STAAG. 6        [AA-STAAG]
(0834) AA- 0 -LEGDE 5         [AA-LEGDE]
(0851) AA- 0 -LEGDE. 9        [AA-LEGDE]
(0886) AA- 0 -CWEAL-9-DE 6    [AA-CWEALDE]
(0895) +SAEAE- 3 -BAAT 2      [SAEAE-BAAT]
(0977) AA- 0 -BIIDAN 4        [AA-BIIDAN]
(0997) TOO- 9 -BROCEN 3       [TOO-BROCEN]
(0999) TOO- 1 -HLIDENE 7      [TOO-HLIDENE]
(1018) AA- 0 -FYLLED 3        [AA-FYLLED]
(1055) AA- 0 -CWEALDE 9       [AA-CWEALDE]
(1108) AA- 0 -HAEFEN 2        [AA-HAEFEN]
(1113) AA- 0 -WYRDED 4        [AA-WYRDED]
(1118) AA- 0 -STAAH. 3        [AA-STAAH]
(1139) SAEAE- 2 -LAADE 6      [SAEAE-LAADE]
(1149) +SAEAE- 5 -SIIDHE 9    [SAEAE-SIIDHE]
(1157) SAEAE- 5 -LAADE 5      [SAEAE-LAADE]
(1159) AA- 0 SUNGEN 4         [AA-SUNGEN]
(1160) AA- 0 STAAH. 6         [AA-STAAH]
(1234) AA- 0 -GAN-9-GEN 3     [AA-GANGEN]
(1298) AA- 0 -BREEAT 7        [AA-BREEAT]
(1234) GEOO- 1 -SCEAFT 4      [GEOO-SCEAFT]
(1266) GEOO- 2 -SCEAFT- 3     [GEOO-SCEAFT-GAASTA]
```

FIRST MORPHEME TERMINATES IN SHORT VOCALIC UNIT

```
(0667) SELE- 3 -WEARD 3       [SELE-WEARD]
(0667) BE- 1 -HEEOLD 4        [BE-HEEOLD]
(0674) HILDE- 3 -GEATWE 9     [HILDE-GEATWE]
(0677) HERE- 3 -WAESMUM 5     [HERE-WAESMUM]
(0680) BE- 2 -NEEO-9-TAN 3    [BE-NEEOTAN]
(0688) HEA-1-THO- 4 -DEEOR 5  [HEATHO-DEEOR]
(0690) SE-1-LE- 3 -RESTE 2    [SELE-RESTE]
(0702) ()RIDE*WIIDE- 9 -FER-1-HDH 4    [*WIIDE-FERHDH]
(0703) SCEA-9-DU- 4 -GENGA 5  [SCEADU-GENGA]
(0713) BE- 9 -SYRWAN 4        [BE-SYRWAN]
(0721) BE- 0 -DAEAELED 4      [BE-DAEAELED]
(0723) BEALO- 4 -HYYDIG 4     [BEALO-HYYDIG]
(0726) YRRE- 4 -MOOD 3        [YRRE-MOOD]
(0729) SIB-1-BE- 9 -GE- 2     [SIBBE-GE-DRIHT]
(0730) MA-1-GO- 2 -RIN-9-CA 3 [MAGO-RINCA]
(0736) BE- 3 -HEEOLD 5        [BE-HEEOLD]
(0769) EALU- 9 -SCERWEN 3     [EALU-SCERWEN]
(0772) HEA-1-THO- 9 -DEEORUM 4    [HEATHO-DEEORUM]
(0775) SEAR-1-O- 3 -THONCUM 3 [SEARO-THONCUM]
(0775) BE- 0 -SMI-9-THOD 4    [BE-SMITHOD]
(0776) MEDU- 3 -BENC 9        [MEDU-BENC]
(0786) GRYRE- 4 -LEEODH 8     [GRYRE-LEEODH]
(0799) HIL-1-DE- 3 -MECGAS. 5 [HILDE-MECGAS]
(0834) HILDE- 4 -DEEOR 9      [HILDE-DEEOR]
(0849) HEORO- 4 -DREEORE 4    [HEORO-DREEORE]
(0860) BE- 0 -GONG 5          [BE-GONG]
(0862) WINE- 9 -DRIHTEN 4     [WINE-DRIHTEN]
(0864) HEA-1-THO- 3 -ROOFE 9  [HEATHO-ROOFE]
(0901) HER-1-E- 3 -MOODES 5   [HERE-MOODES]
(0907) BE- 3 -MEARN 4         [BE-MEARN]
(0920) SEARO- 3 -WUNDOR 4     [SEARO-WUNDOR]
(0924) MEDO- 9 -STIG-1-GE 5   [MEDO-STIGGE]
(0935) HEORO- 3 -DREEORIG 3   [HEORO-DREEORIG]
(0937) WIIDE- 6 -FERHDH 5     [WIIDE-FERHDH]
(0938) BE- 3 -WERE-1-DON. 9   [BE-WEREDON]
(0942) BE- 0 -SYR-1-WAN 5     [BE-SYRWAN]
(0969) FORE- 3 -MIHTIG 9      [FORE-MIHTIG]
```

156

```
(0976)  BE- 0 -FONGEN. 9    [BE-FONGEN]
(0986)  HILDE- 4 -RINCES 4    [HILDE-RINCES]
(0990)  BEADU- 3 -FOLME 9    [BEADU-FOLME]
(0998)  INNE- 3 -WEARD 3    [INNE-WEARD]
(1003)  BE- 2 -FLEEON-1-NE 5    [BE-FLEEONNE]
(1015)  ME-9-DO- 3 -FUL 4    [MEDO-FUL]
(1022)  ()HILTE*HILDE- 4 -CUMBOR 5    [*HILDE-CUMBOR]
(1024)  BE- 1 -FORAN 4    [BE-FORAN]
(1029)  EALO- 4 -BEN-1-CE 5    [EALO-BENCE]
(1031)  BE- 3 -WUNDEN 4    [BE-WUNDEN]
(1047)  HEATHO- 4 -RAEAESAS 4    [HEATHO-RAEAESAS]
(1052)  MEDU- 3 -BENCE 6    [MEDU-BENCE]
(1053)  YR-9-FE- 3 -LAAFE 4    [YRFE-LAAFE]
(1060)  FORE- 4 -THANC 4    [FORE-THANC]
(1064)  HILDE- 3 -WII-8-SAN 4    [HILDE-WIISAN]
(1067)  ME-2-DO- 2 -BENCE 4    [MEDO-BENCE]
(1068)  BE- 1 -GEAT 5    [BE-GEAT]
(1071)  HILDE- 5 -BURH 4    [HILDE-BURH]
(1073)  BE- 9 -LOR-2-EN 4    [BE-LOREN]
(1077)  BE- 2 -MEARN 9    [BE-MEARN]
(1096)  FRIODHU- 9 -WAEAERE 6    [FRIODHU-WAEAERE]
(1097)  BE- 2 -NEMDE. 7    [BE-NEMDE]
(1108)  HERE- 4 -SCYLDINGA 5    [HERE-SCYLDINGA]
(1109)  BEADO- 2 -RINCA. 9    [BEADO-RINCA]
(1114)  HILDE- 5 -BURH 3    [HILDE-BURH]
(1115)  BE- 9 -FAESTAN 7    [BE-FAESTAN]
(1126)  BE- 1 -FEALLEN 3    [BE-FEALLEN]
(1132)  BE- 1 -LEEAC 5    [BE-LEEAC]
(1135)  BE- 2 -WITIADH 5    [BE-WITIADH]
(1143)  HILDE- 4 -LEEOMAN 4    [HILDE-LEEOMAN]
(1146)  BE- 2 -GEAT 4    [BE-GEAT]
(1157)  SEARO- 4 -GIMMA 5    [SEARO-GIMMA]
(1176)  HERE- 3 -()RIC*RING 3    [*HERE-RINC]
(1193)  BE- 2 -WAEGNED 4    [BE-WAEGNED]
(1200)  SEARO- 3 -NIIDHAS 5    [SEARO-NIIDHAS]
(1222)  WIIDE- 3 -FERHTH 9    [WIIDE-FERHTH]
(1223)  BE- 0 -BUUGEDH 9    [BE-BUUGEDH]
(1242)  HILDE- 4 -RANDAS 9    [HILDE-RANDAS]
(1245)  HEATHO- 3 -STEEAPA 5    [HEATHO-STEEAPA]
(1254)  BE- 1 -CWOOM 4    [BE-CWOOM]
(1267)  HEORO- 2 -WEARH 5    [HEORO-WEARH]
(1267)  HETE- 0 -LIIC 4    [HETE-LIIC]
(1275)  BE- 1 -DAEAEL-1-ED 4    [BE-DAEAELED]
(1295)  BE- 2 -FANGEN 6    [BE-FANGEN]
(1307)  HIL-1-DE- 5 -RING 4    [HILDE-RING]
(0737)  HIGE- 3 -LAACES 6    [HIGE-LAACES]
(0746)  HIGE- 3 -THIIHTIGNE 4    [HIGE-THIIHTIGNE]
(0758)  HIGE- 2 -LAACES 4    [HIGE-LAACES]
(0787)  SIGE- 3 -LEEAS-1-NE 5    [SIGE-LEEASNE]
(0804)  SIGE- 2 -WAEAEPNU= 9    [SIGE-WAEAEPNU=]
(0813)  HYGE- 3 -LAA-9-CES 5    [HYGE-LAACES]
(0875)  SIGE- 4 -MUNDE*S 5    [SIGE-MUNDE*S]
(0884)  SIGE- 9 -MUNDE 4    [SIGE-MUNDE]
(0914)  HIGE- 3 -LAACES 4    [HIGE-LAACES]
(1202)  HIGE- 1 -LAAC 2    [HIGE-LAAC]

(0662)  GE- 0 -WAAT 5    [GE-WAAT]
(0662)  GE- 1 -DRYHT 5    [GE-DRYHT]
(0665)  GE- 2 -BEDDAN 5    [GE-BEDDAN]
(0666)  GE- 1 -FRUNGON 5    [GE-FRUNGON]
(0674)  GE- 2 -HEAL-2-DAN 3    [GE-HEALDAN]
(0675)  GE- 2 -SPRAEC 3    [GE-SPRAEC]
(0682)  GE- 1 -HEEAWE 3    [GE-HEEAWE]
(0684)  GE- 9 -SEE-1-CEAN 3    [GE-SEECEAN]
(0687)  GE- 2 -MET 3    [GE-MET]
```

157

```
(0690)  GE- 1 -BEEAH. 6     [GE-BEEAH]
(0692)  GE- 1 -SEECEAN 4    [GE-SEECEAN]
(0694)  GE- 0 -FRUUNEN 9    [GE-FRUUNEN]
(0697)  GE- 2 -WIOFU. 9     [GE-WIOFU]
(0700)  GE- 2 -CYY-9-THED 4     [GE-CYYTHED]
(0709)  GE- 1 -THINGES. 9     [GE-THINGES]
(0717)  GE- 1 -SOOHTE. 7     [GE-SOOHTE]
(0723)  GE- 8 -BOLGEN 3     [GE-BOLGEN]
(0727)  GE- 0 -LIICOST 4     [GE-LIICOST]
(0728)  GE- 0 -SEAH 2     [GE-SEAH]
(0731)  GE- 2 -DAEAELDE 5     [GE-DAEAELDE]
(0732)  GE- 2 -HWYLCES 5     [GE-HWYLCES]
(0738)  GE- 0 -FARAN 2     [GE-FARAN]
(0740)  GE- 9 -FEENG 4     [GE-FEENG]
(0744)  GE- 1 -FEORMOD. 4     [GE-FEORMOD]
(0749)  GE- 9 -SAET 5     [GE-SAET]
(0756)  GE- 2 -DRAEG 4     [GE-DRAEG]
(0757)  GE- 0 -MEETTE. 7     [GE-MEETTE]
(0758)  GE- 9 -MUNDE 4     [GE-MUNDE]
(0763)  GE- 2 -WINDAN 8     [GE-WINDAN]
(0764)  GE- 0 -WEALD 4     [GE-WEALD]
(0768)  GE- 1 -HWYLCUM 4     [GE-HWYLCUM]
(0776)  GE- 0 -FRAEAEGE 5     [GE-FRAEAEGE]
(0777)  GE- 1 -REGNAD 9     [GE-REGNAD]
(0779)  GE- 0 -METE 9     [GE-METE]
(0783)  GE- 0 -NEAH-2-HE 5     [GE-NEAHHE]
(0784)  GE- 2 -HWYL-1-CUM 4     [GE-HWYLCUM]
(0785)  GE- 2 -HYYR-2-DON. 5     [GE-HYYRDON]
(0794)  GE- 3 -NEHOST 4     [GE-NEHOST]
(0798)  GE- 1 -WIN 3     [GE-WIN]
(0800)  GE- 3 -HWONE 5     [GE-HWONE]
(0805)  GE- 1 -HWYLC-1-RE 4     [GE-HWYLCRE]
(0808)  GE- 2 -WEALD 4     [GE-WEALD]
(0811)  GE- 0 -FREME-3-DE. 4     [GE-FREMEDE]
(0814)  GE- 2 -HWAE-1-THER 3     [GE-HWAETHER]
(0815)  GE- 2 -BAAD 5     [GE-BAAD]
(0822)  GE- 1 -GONGEN. 9     [GE-GONGEN]
(0824)  GE- 2 -LUMPEN. 5     [GE-LUMPEN]
(0825)  GE- 9 -FAEAELSOD 4     [GE-FAEAELSOD]
(0827)  GE- 2 -NERED 2     [GE-NERED]
(0827)  GE- 2 -FEH 4     [GE-FEH]
(0829)  GE- 2 -LAEAESTED. 5     [GE-LAEAESTED]
(0830)  GE- 8 -BEETTE 9     [GE-BEETTE]
(0837)  GE- 1 -FRAEAEGE 5     [GE-FRAEAEGE]
(0846)  GE- 3 -FLYYMED 4     [GE-FLYYMED]
(0848)  GE- 3 -SWING 4     [GE-SWING]
(0848)  GE- 3 -MENGED. 6     [GE-MENGED]
(0853)  GE- 0 -WITON 3     [GE-WITON]
(0857)  GE- 2 -CWAEDH 5     [GE-CWAEDH]
(0865)  GE- 3 -FLIT 4     [GE-FLIT]
(0868)  GE- 1 -MYNDIG 9     [GE-MYNDIG]
(0870)  GE- 9 -MUNDE 5     [GE-MUNDE]
(0871)  GE- 3 -BUNDEN 9     [GE-BUNDEN]
(0873)  GE- 1 -RAA-2-DE 9     [GE-RAADE]
(0874)  GE- 3 -CWAEDH 6     [GE-CWAEDH]
(0877)  GE- 2 -WIN 8     [GE-WIN]
(0882)  GE- 9 -HWAAM 4     [GE-HWAAM]
(0884)  GE- 2 -SAEAEGED 4     [GE-SAEAEGED]
(0884)  GE- 2 -SPRONG 4     [GE-SPRONG]
(0888)  GE- 2 -NEEDH-1-DE 5     [GE-NEEDHDE]
(0890)  GE- 0 -SAEAELDE 6     [GE-SAEAELDE]
(0893)  GE- 2 -GONGEN 3     [GE-GONGEN]
(0895)  GE- 3 -HLEOOD 5     [GE-HLEOOD]
(0897)  GE- 8 -MEALT. 6     [GE-MEALT]
(0903)  GE- 1 -WEALD 4     [GE-WEALD]
```

158

```
(0909) GE- 1 -LYYF-1-DE 6   [GE-LYYFDE]
(0910) GE- 9 -THEEON 4   [GE-THEEON]
(0911) GE- 3 -HEALDAN 4   [GE-HEALDAN]
(0915) GE- 9 -FAEGRA 4   [GE-FAEGRA]
(0922) GE- 0 -TRUME 5   [GE-TRUME]
(0923) GE- 3 -CYYTHED 5   [GE-CYYTHED]
(0926) GE- 1 -SEAH 4   [GE-SEAH]
(0929) GE- 1 -LIMPE 9   [GE-LIMPE]
(0929) GE- 1 -BAAD 3   [GE-BAAD]
(0934) GE- 2 -BIIDAN 5   [GE-BIIDAN]
(0936) GE- 2 -HWYL-1-C-1-()NE*UM. 7   [*GE-HWYLCUM]
(0940) GE- 2 -FREMEDE. 5   [GE-FREMEDE]
(0950) GE- 3 -WEALD 4   [GE-WEALD]
(0954) GE- 0 -FREMED 9   [GE-FREMED]
(0959) GE- 3 -NEEDH-2-DON. 3   [GE-NEEDHJON]
(0961) GE- 1 -SEEON 2   [GE-SEEON]
(0968) GE- 3 -TWAEAEMAN 4   [GE-TWAEAEMAN]
(0973) GE- 1 -BOHTE. 7   [GE-BOHTE]
(0975) GE- 1 -SWENCED 4   [GE-SWENCED]
(0985) GE- 3 -HWYLC 9   [GE-HWYLC]
(0985) GE- 3 -LIICOST 6   [GE-LIICOST]
(0987) GE- 4 -CWAEDH 9   [GE-CWAEDH]
(0992) GE- 1 -FRAET-1-WOD 4   [GE-FRAETWOD]
(0996) GE- 2 -HWYLCUM 3   [GE-HWYLCUM]
(0999) GE- 9 -NAES 5   [GE-NAES]
(1001) GE- 3 -WAND 4   [GE-WAND]
(1004) GE- 3 -()SACAN*SEECAN 3   [*GE-SEECAN]
(1005) GE- 4 -NYYDDE 5   [GE-NYYDDE]
(1011) GE- 4 -FRAEGEN 3   [GE-FRAEGEN]
(1012) GE- 0 -BAEAERAN. 7   [GE-BAEAERAN]
(1014) GE- 0 -FAEAEGON 3   [GE-FAEAEGON]
(1014) GE- 1 -THAEAEGON 8   [GE-THAEAEGON]
(1023) GE- 1 -SAAWON. 6   [GE-SAAWON]
(1024) GE- 2 -THAH 4   [GE-THAH]
(1027) GE- 3 -FRAEGN 2   [GE-FRAEGN]
(1028) GE- 3 -GYREDE 5   [GE-GYREDE]
(1029) GE- 2 -SELLAN. 3   [GE-SELLAN]
(1038) GE- 3 -WUR-1-THAD 4   [GE-WURTHAD]
(1040) GE- 1 -LAAC 4   [GE-LAAC]
(1043) GE- 2 -HWAETH-9-RES 4   [GE-HWAETHRES]
(1044) GE- 2 -TEEAH. 4   [GE-TEEAH]
(1052) GE- 3 -SEALDE 3   [GE-SEALDE]
(1060) GE- 9 -BIIDAN 4   [GE-BIIDAN]
(1074) GE- 3 -BYRD 5   [GE-BYRD]
(1078) GE- 8 -SEEON 3   [GE-SEEON]
(1083) GE- 3 -FEOHTAN. 9   [GE-FEOHTAN]
(1085) GE- 1 -THINGO 3   [GE-THINGO]
(1086) GE- 3 -RYYM-1-DON 5   [GE-RYYMDON]
(1087) GE- 1 -WEALD 4   [GE-WEALD]
(1090) GE- 2 -HWYL-1-CE 9   [GE-HWYLCE]
(1095) GE- 9 -TRUWE-1-DON 4   [GE-TRUWEDON]
(1101) GE- 2 -MAEAENDEN 3   [GE-MAEAENDEN]
(1103) GE- 4 -THEARFOD 2   [GE-THEARFOD]
(1107) GE- 1 -AEFNED 4   [GE-AEFNED]
(1125) $$GE- 8 -WITON 4   [GE-WITON]
(1126) GE- 2 -SEEON 9   [GE-SEEON]
(1129) GE- 1 -MUNDE 5   [GE-MUNDE]
(1141) GE- 3 -MUNDE. 7   [GE-MUNDE]
(1166) GE- 3 -HWYLC 5   [GE-HWYLC]
(1168) GE- 0 -LAACUM. 7   [GE-LAACUM]
(1173) GE- 2 -MYNDIG 4   [GE-MYNDIG]
(1176) GE- 5 -FAEAEL-1-SOD 5   [GE-FAEAELSOD]
(1185) GE- 2 -MON 3   [GE-MON]
(1187) GE- 2 -FREME-2-DON. 4   [GE-FREMEDON]
(1191) GE- 1 -BROODH-1-RUM 3   [GE-BROODHRUM]
```

159

```
(1194) GE- 3 -EEAWED 3    [GE-EEAWED]
(1196) GE- 8 -FRAEGEN 4   [GE-FRAEGEN]
(1201) GE- 1 -CEEAS 9     [GE-CEEAS]
(1209) GE- 9 -CRANC 5     [GE-CRANC]
(1210) GE- 4 -HWEARF 5    [GE-HWEARF]
(1218) GE- 8 -THEEOH 9    [GE-THEEOH]
(1220) GE- 2 -MAN 5    [GE-MAN]
(1221) GE- 4 -FEERED 3    [GE-FEERED]
(1227) GE- 1 -DEEFE 6     [GE-DEEFE]
(1228) GE- 2 -TRYYWE 9    [GE-TRYYWE]
(1230) GE- 3 -THWAEAERE 5    [GE-THWAEAERE]
(1236) GE- 1 -WAAT 4    [GE-WAAT]
(1241) GE- 9 -BEEAG 8    [GE-BEEAG]
(1248) GE- 4 -HWAETHER 4    [GE-HWAETHER]
(1250) GE- 1 -SAEAELDE 4    [GE-SAEAELDE]
(1252) GE- 1 -LAMP 4    [GE-LAMP]
(1255) GE- 1 -SYYNE 9    [GE-SYYNE]
(1259) GE- 1 -MUNDE 6    [GE-MUNDE]
(1263) GE- 0 -WAAT 5    [GE-WAAT]
(1264) GE- 1 -MEAR-1-COD 9    [GE-MEARCOD]
(1270) GE- 9 -MUNDE 4    [GE-MUNDE]
(1272) GE- 1 -LYYFDE 5    [GE-LYYFDE]
(1274) GE- 4 -HNAEAEGDE 5    [GE-HNAEAEGDE]
(1274) GE- 3 -+WAAT 5    [GE-WAAT]
(1277) GE- 1 -GAAN 3    [GE-GAAN]
(1285) GE- 0 -()THUREN*THRUUEN 9    [*GE-THRUUEN]
(1290) GE- 4 -MUNDE 7    [GE-MUNDE]
(1297) GE- 3 -SIIDHES 5    [GE-SIIDHES]
(1300) GE- 4 -TEOHHOD 9    [GE-TEOHHOD]
(1302) GE- 2 -NAM 5    [GE-NAM]
(1303) GE- 9 -NIIWOD 4    [GE-NIIWOD]
(1304) GE- 2 -WORDEN 2    [GE-WORDEN]
(1304) GE- 9 -WRIXLE 5    [GE-WRIXLE]
(1313) GE- 4 -SIIDHUM 3    [GE-SIIDHUM]
(1315) GE- 2 -FREM-9-MAN 5    [GE-FREMMAN]
(1320) GE- 3 -TAEAESE. 9    [GE-TAEAESE]
(0678) -GE- 9 -WEORCA 4    [GUUTH-GE-WEORCA]
(0683) -GE- 1 -WEORCA 3    [NIITH-GE-WEORCA]
(0729) -GE- 2 -DRIHT 4    [SIBBE-GE-DRIHT]
(0805) -GE- 2 -DAAL 5    [ALDOR-GE-DAAL]
(0841) -GE- 3 -DAAL 5    [LIIF-GE-DAAL]
(0853) -GE- 1 -SIIDHAS 5    [EALD-GE-SIIDHAS]
(0869) -GE- 0 -SEGENA 5    [EALD-GE-SEGENA]
(0882) -GE- 0 -STEALL-1-AN. 7    [NYYD-GE-STEALLAN]
(0938) -GE- 3 -WEORC 5    [LAND-GE-WEORC]
(0946) -GE- 0 -BYRDO 4    [BEARN-GE-BYRDO]
(0969) -GE- 3 -NIIDH-3-LAN 4    [FEORH-GE-NIIDHLAN]
(0974) -GE- 1 -TEEO-1-NA 5    [LAADH-GE-TEEONA]
(0981) -GE- 1 -WEOR-2-CA 4    [GUUDH-GE-WEORCA]
(1092) -GE- 3 -STREEO-9-NUM 4    [SINC-GE-STREEONUM]
(1110) -GE- 3 -SYYNE 6    [EETH-GE-SYYNE]
(1133) -GE- 1 -BINDE 4    [IIS-GE-BINDE]
(1140) -GE- 9 -MOOT 5    [TORN-GE-MOOT]
(1155) -GE- 9 -STEALD 3    [IN-GE-STEALD]
(1164) -GE- 1 -FAE-1-DE-9-RAN 4    [SUHTER-GE-FAEDERAN]
(1211) -GE- 3 -WAEAEDU 4    [BREEOST-GE-WAEAEDU]
(1218) -GE- 3 -STREEONA 8    [*THEEOD-GE-STREEONA]
(1226) -GE- 0 -STREEONA 5    [SINC-GE-STREEONA]
(1244) -GE- 4 -SEENE 4    [YYTH-GE-SEENE]
```

FIRST MORPHEME TERMINATES IN RESONANT CONSONANT

```
(0667) SUNDOR- 3 -NYT-9-TE 5    [SUNDOR-NYTTE]
(0668) EOTON- 2 -WEARD 9    [EOTON-WEARD]
```

160

```
(0671) IISERN- 4 -BYRNAN 4   [IISERN-BYRNAN]
(0679) FOR- 2 -THAN 2   [FOR-THAN]
(0681) ON- 0 -GEEAN 3   [ON-GEEAN]
(0684) OFER- 3 -SITTAN 4   [OFER-SITTAN]
(0688) HLEEOR- 4 -BOLSTER 3   [HLEEOR-BOLSTER]
(0688) ON- 9 -FEENG 6   [ON-FEENG]
(0690) SNEL- 0 -LIIC 5   [SNEL-LIIC]
(0695) WIIN- 2 -SELE 9   [WIIN-SELE]
(0695) WAEL- 3 -DEEADH 3   [WAEL-DEEADH]
(0695) FOR- 1 -NAM 3   [FOR-NAM]
(0696) FOR- 3 -GEAF 4   [FOR-GEAF]
(0699) OFER- 4 -COOMON 4   [OFER-COOMON]
(0704) HORN- 9 -RECED 5   [HORN-RECED]
(0707) ()SYN*SCYN- 2 -SCATHA 5   [*SCYN-SCATHA]
(0709) BOLGEN- 3 -MOOD 4   [BOLGEN-MOOD]
(0712) MAAN- 3 -SCADHA 5   [MAAN-SCADHA]
(0714) WIIN- 1 -RECED 4   [WIIN-RECED]
(0718) ALDOR- 3 -DAGUM 2   [ALDOR-DAGUM]
(0719) HEAL- 3 -DHEGNAS 9   [HEAL-DHEGNAS]
(0721) ON- 1 -ARN 3   [ON-ARN]
(0722) FYYR- 9 -BENDUM 3   [FYYR-BENDUM]
(0723) $ON- 2 -BRAEAED 3   [ON-BRAEAED]
(0727) UN- 0 -FAEAEGER. 4   [UN-FAEAEGER]
(0737) MAAN- 9 -SCADHA 5   [MAAN-SCADHA]
(0738) FAEAER- 3 -GRIPUM 3   [FAEAER-GRIPUM]
(0741) UN- 1 -WEAR-1-NUM 5   [UN-WEARNUM]
(0742) BAAN- 1 -LOCAN 2   [BAAN-LOCAN]
(0743) SYN- 3 -SNAEAEDUM 3   [SYN-SNAEAEDUM]
(0744) UN- 1 -LYFIGENDES 4   [UN-LYFIGENDES]
(0747) ON- 1 -GEEAN 3   [ON-GEEAN]
(0748) ON- 9 -FEENG 3   [ON-FEENG]
(0750) ON- 0 -FUNDE 5   [ON-FUNDE]
(0751) MIDDAN- 4 -GEAR-1-DES 5   [MIDDAN-GEARDES]
(0755) HIN- 2 -FUUS 9   [HIN-FUUS]
(0757) EALDER- 4 -DAGUM 3   [EALDER-DAGUM]
(0759) AEAEFEN- 9 -SPRAEAECE 5   [AEAEFEN-SPRAEAECE]
(0764) FEN- 4 -HOPU 4   [FEN-HOPU]
(0766) HEARM- 3 -SCA-9-THA 4   [HEARM-SCATHA]
(0768) CEASTER- 3 -BUU-9-ENDUM 4   [CEASTER-BUUENDUM]
(0770) REN- 9 -WEAR-1-DAS 5   [REN-WEARDAS]
(0771) WIIN- 1 -SELE. 7   [WIIN-SELE]
(0774) IIREN- 2 -BENDUM 4   [IIREN-BENDUM]
(0780) +BAAN- 3 -FAAG 4   [BAAN-FAAG]
(0792) CWEALM- 3 -CUMAN 4   [CWEALM-CUMAN]
(0792) FOR- 2 -LAEAETAN. 3   [FOR-LAEAETAN]
(0801) SYN- 2 -SCADHAN. 9   [SYN-SCADHAN]
(0804) FOR- 2 -SWOREN 4   [FOR-SWOREN]
(0805) ALDOR- 4 -GE- 2   [ALDOR-GE-DAAL]
(0807) EARM- 1 -LIIC 3   [EARM-LIIC]
(0807) ELLOR- 4 -GAAST 9   [ELLOR-GAAST]
(0809) ON- 8 -FUNDE 5   [ON-FUNDE]
(0817) SYN- 0 -DOLH 4   [SYN-DOLH]
(0817) ON- 1 -SPRUN-1-GON 5   [ON-SPRUNGON]
(0818) BAAN- 3 -LOCAN 9   [BAAN-LOCAN]
(0820) FEN- 3 -HL-1-EODHU 4   [FEN-HLEODHU]
(0821) WYN- 2 -LEEAS 4   [WYN-LEEAS]
(0824) WAEL- 0 -RAEAESE 5   [WAEL-RAEAESE]
(0828) ELLEN- 2 -MAEAER-3-THUM 9   [ELLEN-MAEAERTHUM]
(0830) ON- 1 -CYYTHDHE 5   [ON-CYYTHDHE]
(0833) UN- 1 -LYYTEL 9   [UN-LYYTEL]
(0842) SAAR- 1 -LIIC 3   [SAAR-LIIC]
(0843) TIIR- 3 -LEEASES 4   [TIIR-LEEASES]
(0845) OFER- 3 -CUMEN 4   [OFER-CUMEN]
(0851) FEN- 2 -FREODHO 4   [FEN-FREODHO]
(0852) ON- 1 -FEENG. 7   [ON-FEENG]
```

161

```
(0854) GOMEN- 3 -WAATHE 5   [GOMEN-WAATHE]
(0859) EORMEN- 3 -GRUND 4   [EORMEN-GRUND]
(0869) EAL- 3 -FELA 4   [EAL-FELA]
(0871) ON- 1 -GAN 4   [ON-GAN]
(0874) WEEL- 3 -HWYLC 3   [WEEL-HWYLC]
(0876) ELLEN- 8 -DAEAE-9-DUM 3   [ELLEN-DAEAEDUM]
(0876) UN- 2 -CUUTHES 4   [UN-CUUTHES]
(0883) EAL- 3 -FELA 9   [EAL-FELA]
(0885) UN- 2 -LYYTEL. 7   [UN-LYYTEL]
(0899) WER- 1 -THEEODE 5   [WER-THEEODE]
(0900) ELLEN- 2 -DAEAEDU= 9   [ELLEN-DAEAEDU=]
(0900) ON- 0 -DHAAH 4   [ON-DHAAH]
(0903) FOR- 2 -LAACEN 9   [FOR-LAACEN]
(0904) FOR- 2 -SENDED 4   [FOR-SENDED]
(0906) AL-1-DOR- 3 -CEARE. 7   [ALDOR-CEARE]
(0911) FAEDER- 3 -AETHELUM 3   [FAEDER-AETHELUM]
(0911) ON- 1 -+FOON 3   [ON-FOON]
(0915) ON- 1 -WOOD. 6   [ON-WOOD]
(0917) MORGEN- 4 -LEEOHT 4   [MORGEN-LEEOHT]
(0922) TIIR- 2 -FAEST. 6   [TIIR-FAEST]
(0928) AN- 9 -SYYNE 5   [AN-SYYNE]
(0928) AL- 0 -WEALDAN 3   [AL-WEALDAN]
(0932) UN- 1 -GEAARA 3   [UN-GEAARA]
(0944) GUM- 1 -CYNNU= 4   [GUM-CYNNU=]
(0946) BEARN- 3 -GE- 0   [BEARN-GE-BYRDO]
(0955) AL- 0 -WAL-1-DA 3   [AL-WALDA]
(0956) FOR- 2 -GYLDE 5   [FOR-GYLDE]
(0958) ELLEN- 3 -WEORC 9   [ELLEN-WEORC]
(0960) UN- 0 -CUUTHES 5   [UN-CUUTHES]
(0962) FYL- 3 -WEERIGNE. 5   [FYL-WEERIGNE]
(0964) WAEL- 5 -BEDDE 4   [WAEL-BEDDE]
(0970) FOR- 9 -LEET 3   [FOR-LEET]
(0987) UN- 1 -HEEORU 4   [UN-HEEORU]
(0989) AEAER- 9 -GOOD 4   [AEAER-GOOD]
(0990) ON- 8 -BERAN 4   [ON-BERAN]
(0991) INNAN- 2 -WEARD 9   [INNAN-WEARD]
(0993) WIIN- 2 -RECED 4   [WIIN-RECED]
(0995) WUNDOR- 9 -SIIONA 3   [WUNDOR-SIIONA]
(0998) IIREN- 2 -BENDU= 9   [IIREN-BENDU=]
(1001) FYREN- 9 -DAEAE-1-DUM 3   [FYREN-DAEAEDUM]
(1002) OR- 9 -WEENA 5   [OR-WEENA]
(1004) SAAWL- 9 -BEREN-1-DRA 4   [SAAWL-BERENDRA]
(1007) LEGER- 4 -BEDDE 4   [LEGER-BEDDE]
(1018) FAACEN- 9 -STAFAS 5   [FAACEN-STAFAS]
(1020) FOR- 0 -GEAF 3   [FOR-GEAF]
(1028) GUM- 3 -MAN-2-NA 9   [GUM-MANNA]
(1033) SCUUR- 3 -HEARD 4   [SCUUR-HEARD]
(1034) ON- 0 -GEEAN 3   [ON-GEEAN]
(1044) ON- 1 -WEALD 4   [ON-WEALD]
(1046) MAN- 1 -LIICE 5   [MAN-LIICE]
(1051) BRIM- 2 -()LEADE*LAADE 4   [*BRIM-LAADE]
(1054) FOR- 0 -GYL-9-DAN 4   [FOR-GYLDAN]
(1056) FOR- 0 -STOODE 6   [FOR-STOODE]
(1059) FOR- 2 -THAN 4   [FOR-THAN]
(1062) WIN- 2 -DAGUM 4   [WIN-DAGUM]
(1065) GOMEN- 3 -WUDU 9   [GOMEN-WUDU]
(1066) HEAL- 3 -GAMEN 9   [HEAL-GAMEN]
(1072) UN- 1 -SYNNUM 4   [UN-SYNNUM]
(1079) MORTHOR- 4 -BEALO 3   [MORTHOR-BEALO]
(1080) FOR- 1 -NAM 3   [FOR-NAM]
(1082) ME-9-DHEL- 5 -STEDE. 7   [MEDHEL-STEDE]
(1084) FOR- 4 -THRINGAN 4   [FOR-THRINGAN]
(1094) BEEOR- 4 -SELE 5   [BEEOR-SELE]
(1097) UN- 0 -FLIT-2-ME 3   [UN-FLITME]
(1103) DHEEODEN- 4 -LEEASE 5   [DHEEODEN-LEEASE]
```

```
(1105) MORTHOR- 5 -HETES 4    [MORTHOR-HETES]
(1111) EAL- 3 -GYLDEN. 6    [EAL-GYLDEN]
(1112) IIREN- 3 -HEARD 4    [IIREN-HEARD]
(1116) +BAAN- 4 -FATU 3    [BAAN-FATU]
(1119) WAEL- 3 -FYYRA 3    [WAEL-FYYRA]
(1121) BEN- 0 -GEATO 9    [BEN-GEATO]
(1122) FOR- 2 -SWEALG 4    [FOR-SWEALG]
(1123) FOR- 2 -NAM 9    [FOR-NAM]
(1128) WAEL- 9 -FAAGNE 4    [WAEL-FAAGNE]
(1129) UN- 9 -HLITME 4    [UN-HLITME]
(1136) WULDOR- 4 -TORH-9-TAN 3    [WULDOR-TORHTAN]
(1138) GYRN- 3 -WRAECE 4    [GYRN-WRAECE]
(1140) TORN- 8 -GE- 9    [TORN-GE-MOOT]
(1142) FOR- 9 -WYRNDE 6    [FOR-WYRNDE]
(1143) HUUN- 2 -LAAFING 5    [HUUN-LAAFING]
(1151) FOR- 3 -HABBAN 9    [FOR-HABBAN]
(1155) IN- 1 -GE- 9    [IN-GE-STEALD]
(1162) WUNDER- 5 -FATUM. 6    [WUNDER-FATUM]
(1164) SU-1-HTER- 2 -GE- 1    [SUHTER-GE-FAEDERAN]
(1165) ()HUN*UN- 1 -FER-1-TH 8    [*UN-FERTH]
(1168) +AAR- 2 -FAEST 5    [AAR-FAEST]
(1169) ON- 0 -FOOH 4    [ON-FOOH]
(1187) UM-1-BOR- 9 -WESEN-1-DUM 2    [UMBOR-WESENDUM]
(1194) EARM- 2 -()READE*HREEADE 5    [*EARM-HREEADE]
(1201) EORMEN- 3 -RIIC-1-ES 4    [EORMEN-RIICES]
(1205) WAEL- 2 -REEAF 9    [WAEL-REEAF]
(1205) FOR- 3 -NAM 4    [FOR-NAM]
(1208) EORCLAN- 4 -STAANAS 3    [EORCLAN-STAANAS]
(1214) ON- 1 -FEENG. 7    [ON-FEENG]
(1227) DREEAM- 4 -HEAL-2-DEN-9-DE. 7    [DREEAM-HEALDENDE]
(1229) MAN- 3 -DRIHTNE 5    [MAN-DRIHTNE]
(1230) EAL- 2 -GEARO 4    [EAL-GEARO]
(1238) UN- 0 -RIIM 3    [UN-RIIM]
(1240) BEEOR- 4 -SCEAL-1-CA 3    [BEEOR-SCEALCA]
(1246) THRYM- 1 -LIIC 4    [THRYM-LIIC]
(1249) MAN- 2 -DRYHT-9-NE 5    [MAN-DRYHTNE]
(1251) AN- 0 -GEALD 3    [AN-GEALD]
(1252) AEAEFEN- 9 -RAESTE 5    [AEAEFEN-RAESTE]
(1254) UN- 0 -RIHT 3    [UN-RIHT]
(1260) WAETER- 4 -EGESAN 5    [WAETER-EGESAN]
(1263) FAEDER-1-EN- 3 -MAEAEGE 9    [FAEDEREN-MAEAEGE]
(1264) MAN- 6 -DREEAM 4    [MAN-DREEAM]
(1271) GIM- 1 -FAES-1-TE 3    [GIM-FAESTE]
(1272) AN- 0 -WALDAN 4    [AN-WALDAN]
(1273) OFER- 4 -CWOOM 3    [OFER-CWOOM]
(1276) MAN- 1 -CYNNES 4    [MAN-CYNNES]
(1291) AN- 0 -GEAT 5    [AN-GEAT]
(1293) ON- 1 -FUN-9-DEN 2    [ON-FUNDEN]
(1301) MAATHDHUM- 4 -GIFE. 6    [MAATHDHUM-GIFE]
(1308) ALDOR- 5 -THEGN 0    [ALDOR-THEGN]
(1308) UN- 0 -LYFIGENDNE 9    [UN-LYFIGENDNE]
(1311) SIGOR- 4 -EEADIG 3    [SIGOR-EEADIG]
(1311) AEAER- 3 -DAEGE 5    [AEAER-DAEGE]
(1314) ()ALF*AL- 2 -WALDA 4    [*AL-WALDA]
(1317) HEAL- 3 -WUDU 9    [HEAL-WUDU]
```

FIRST MORPHEME TERMINATES IN STOP CONSONANT

```
(0673) OM-9-BIHT- 5 -THEGNE 5    [OMBIHT-THEGNE]
(0675) GYLP- 3 -WORDA 4    [GYLP-WORDA]
(0689) AND- 1 -WLITAN 3    [AND-WLITAN]
(0692) EARD- 9 -LUFAN 4    [EARD-LUFAN]
(0710) MIST- 5 -HLEOTHUM 3    [MIST-HLEOTHUM]
(0715) GOLD- 2 -SELE 3    [GOLD-SELE]
```

```
(0722) AET- 8 -HRAAN. 7    [AET-HRAAN]
(0729) AET- 2 -GAEDERE 5    [AET-GAEDERE]
(0734) WIST- 3 -FYLLE 4    [WIST-FYLLE]
(0745) AET- 0 -STOOP 4    [AET-STOOP]
(0749) IN-1-WIT- 3 -THANCU= 5    [INWIT-THANCU=]
(0753) MUND- 3 -GRIPE 4    [MUND-GRIPE]
(0759) UP- 1 -LANG 3    [UP-LANG]
(0761) UUT- 9 -WEARD 3    [UUT-WEARD]
(0767) DRYHT- 3 -SELE 9    [DRYHT-SELE]
(0773) FOLD- 4 -BOLD 4    [FOLD-BOLD]
(0780) ()HET*BET- 0 -LIIC 3    [*BET-LIIC]
(0786) =AND- 0 -SACAN 4    [=AND-SACAN]
(0799) HEARD- 3 -HICGEN-1-DE 9    [HEARD-HICGENDE]
(0812) LIIC- 2 -HOMA 4    [LIIC-HOMA]
(0815) LIIC- 3 -SAAR 2    [LIIC-SAAR]
(0827) NIHT- 3 -WEORCE 5    [NIHT-WEORCE]
(0828) EEAST- 3 -DENUM 4    [EEAST-DENUM]
(0829) GEEAT- 3 -MECGA 3    [GEEAT-MECGA]
(0831) IN-1-WID- 3 -SORGE 5    [INWID-SORGE]
(0839) FOLC- 2 -TOGAN 4    [FOLC-TOGAN]
(0840) WIID- 9 -WEGAS 4    [WIID-WEGAS]
(0853) EALD- 3 -GE- 1    [EALD-GE-SIIDHAS]
(0861) ROND- 3 -HAEB-9-BEN-1-DRA 4    [ROND-HAEBBENDRA]
(0866) FOLD- 3 -WEGAS 4    [FOLD-WEGAS]
(0868) GILP- 3 -HLAEDEN 3    [GILP-HLAEDEN]
(0869) EALD- 3 -GE- 0    [EALD-GE-SEGENA]
(0882) NYYD- 3 -GE- 0    [NYYD-GE-STEALLAN]
(0891) WRAEAET- 9 -LIICNE 3    [WRAEAET-LIICNE]
(0891) AET- 2 -STOOD 3    [AET-STOOD]
(0892) DRYHT- 9 -LIIC 3    [DRYHT-LIIC]
(0921) BRYYD- 3 -BUURE 7    [BRYYD-BUURE]
(0936) WIID- 3 -SCOFEN 3    [WIID-SCOFEN]
(0938) LAND- 3 -GE- 3    [LAND-GE-WEORC]
(0945) EALD- 2 -METOD 3    [EALD-METOD]
(0952) HORD- 9 -WEORTHUNGE 7    [HORD-WEORTHUNGE]
(0963) HRAED- 0 -LIICE 9    [HRAED-LIICE]
(0965) ()HAND*MUND- 3 -GRIPE 4    [*MUND-GRIPE]
(0968) AET- 9 -FEALH 4    [AET-FEALH]
(0976) ()MID*NIID- 3 -GRIPE 5    [*NIID-GRIPE]
(0981) GYLP- 2 -SPRAEAECE 4    [GYLP-SPRAEAECE]
(0986) HAND- 3 -SPORU 3    [HAND-SPORU]
(0994) GEST- 4 -SELE 4    [GEST-SELE]
(0994) GOLD- 3 -FAAG 3    [GOLD-FAAG]
(1006) GRUND- 4 -BUUEN-1-DRA 4    [GRUND-BUUENDRA]
(1007) LIIC- 3 -HOMA 4    [LIIC-HOMA]
(1012) SINC- 2 -GYFAN 8    [SINC-GYFAN]
(1013) BLAEAED- 8 -AAGAN-9-DE 5    [BLAEAED-AAGANDE]
(1019) THEEOD- 3 -SCYLDINGAS 6    [THEEOD-SCYLDINGAS]
(1027) FREEOND- 1 -LIICOR 3    [FREEOND-LIICOR]
(1030) HEEAFOD- 4 -BEORGE 4    [HEEAFOD-BEORGE]
(1033) SCYLD- 4 -FRECA 5    [SCYLD-FRECA]
(1036) FAEAETED- 4 -HLEEORE 4    [FAEAETED-HLEEORE]
(1042) WIID- 3 -CUUTHES 3    [WIID-CUUTHES]
(1047) HORD- 2 -WEARD 3    [HORD-WEARD]
(1059) AND- 1 -GIT 4    [AND-GIT]
(1063) AET- 2 -GAEDERE 4    [AET-GAEDERE]
(1073) ()HILD*LIND- 3 -PLEGAN 5    [*LIND-PLEGAN]
(1077) MEOTOD- 3 -SCEAFT 4    [MEOTOD-SCEAFT]
(1089) FOLC- 4 -WALDAN 3    [FOLC-WALDAN]
(1092) SINC- 2 -GE- 3    [SINC-GE-STREEONUM]
(1101) INWIT- 3 -SEARO 4    [INWIT-SEARO]
(1111) SWAAT- 4 -FAAH 4    [SWAAT-FAAH]
(1121) AET- 2 -SPRANC. 4    [AET-SPRANC]
(1131) HRINGED- 3 -STEF-1-NAN 9    [HRINGED-STEFNAN]
(1142) ()WOROLD*WEOROD- 2 -RAEAE-1-DEN-1-()NE*DE 6    [*WEOROD-RAEAEDENDE]
```

```
(1147)  SWEORD- 4 -BEALO 3   [SWEORD-BEALO]
(1150)  AET- 1 -WITON 4   [AET-WITON]
(1158)  DRIHT- 9 -LIICE 4   [DRIHT-LIICE]
(1161)  BENC- 4 -SWEEG 7   [BENC-SWEEG]
(1164)  AET- 2 -GAE-1-DERE 9   [AET-GAEDERE]
(1171)  GOLD- 2 -WINE 5   [GOLD-WINE]
(1180)  METOD- 3 -SCEAFT 4   [METOD-SCEAFT]
(1190)  AET- 3 -GAEDERE 5   [AET-GAEDERE]
(1192)  FREEOND- 3 -L-1-A-1-THU 3   [FREEOND-LATHU]
(1198)  HORD- 3 -()MAD-2-MUM*MAADHUM 4   [*HORD-MAADHUM]
(1198)  AET- 1 -WAEG 4   [AET-WAEG]
(1200)  SINC- 4 -FAET 9   [SINC-FAET]
(1211)  BREEOST- 4 -GE- 3   [BREEOST-GE-WAEAEDU]
(1218)  ()THEO*THEEOD- 3 -GE- 3   [*THEEOD-GE-STREEONA]
(1224)  WIND- 2 -GEARD 3   [WIND-GEARD]
(1226)  SINC- 3 -GE- 0   [SINC-GE-STREEONA]
(1231)  DRYHT- 9 -GUMAN 4   [DRYHT-GUMAN]
(1239)  BENC- 4 -THELU 4   [BENC-THELU]
(1239)  GEOND- 4 -BRAEAEDED 3   [GEOND-BRAEAEDED]
(1241)  FLET- 3 -RAESTE 4   [FLET-RAESTE]
(1243)  BORD- 3 -WUDU 4   [BORD-WUDU]
(1246)  THREC- 3 -WUDU 4   [THREC-WUDU]
(1253)  GOLD- 9 -SELE 5   [GOLD-SELE]
(1256)  WIID- 1 -CUUTH 3   [WIID-CUUTH]
(1259)  -LAEAEC- 3 -WIIF 2   [AAG-LAEAEC-WIIF]
(1266)  -SCEAFT- 3 -GAASTA 5   [GEOO-SCEAFT-GAASTA]
(1269)  AET- 0 -GRAEAEPE 4   [AET-GRAEAEPE]
(1281)  ED- 2 -HWYRFT 4   [ED-HWYRFT]
(1284)  WAEAEPNED- 3 -MEN 9   [WAEAEPNED-MEN]
(1287)  AND- 1 -WEARD 4   [AND-WEARD]
(1288)  HEARD- 3 -ECG 4   [HEARD-ECG]
(1289)  SIID- 9 -RAND 4   [SIID-RAND]
(1298)  RAND- 3 -WIGA 6   [RAND-WIGA]
(1299)  BLAEAED- 3 -FAESTNE 6   [BLAEAED-FAESTNE]
(1316)  FYRU- 2 -WYR-9-DHE 4   [FYRD-WYRDHE]
(1317)  HAND- 3 -SCALE 5   [HAND-SCALE]
(1320)  NEEOD- 2 -LADHU*M 5   [NEEOD-LADHU*M]
```

FIRST MORPHEME TERMINATES IN SPIRANT

```
(0793)  LIIF- 3 -DAGAS 6   [LIIF-DAGAS]
(0838)  GIF- 2 -HEALLE 6   [GIF-HEALLE]
(0841)  LIIF- 2 -GE- 3   [LIIF-GE-DAAL]
(0966)  LIIF- 3 -BYSIG 4   [LIIF-BYSIG]
(0971)  LIIF- 3 -WRATHE 6   [LIIF-WRATHE]
(1009)  HEALF- 2 -DENES 4   [HEALF-DENES]
(1020)  HEALF- 0 -DENES 9   [HEALF-DENES]
(1040)  HEALF- 1 -DENES 5   [HEALF-DENES]
(1064)  HEALF- 1 -DENES 5   [HEALF-DENES]
(1069)  HEALF- 3 -DENA 4   [HEALF-DENA]
(1070)  FR-8-EES- 3 -WAELE 4   [FREES-WAELE]
(1126)  FRYYS- 4 -LAND 2   [FRYYS-LAND]
(1133)  IIS- 2 -GE- 1   [IIS-GE-BINDE]
(1148)  OOS- 2 -LAAF 5   [OOS-LAAF]
(1183)  OF- 2 -LAEAETEST 9   [OF-LAEAETEST]
(1195)  HEALS- 3 -BEEAGA 3   [HEALS-BEEAGA]
(0662)  HROOTH- 1 -GAAR 5   [HROOTH-GAAR]
(0678)  GUUTH- 3 -GE- 9   [GUUTH-GE-WEORCA]
(0683)  NIITH- 2 -GE- 1   [NIITH-GE-WEORCA]
(0717)  HROOTH- 0 -GAARES 4   [HROOTH-GAARES]
(0736)  THRYYDH- 2 -SWYYDH 9   [THRYYDH-SWYYDH]
(0760)  WIDH- 9 -FEENG 5   [WIDH-FEENG]
(0772)  WIDH- 3 -HAEFDE 5   [WIDH-HAEFDE]
(0783)  NORDH- 3 -DENU= 2   [NORDH-DENU=]
```

165

```
(0803) GUUDH- 3 -BIL-9-LA 3    [GUUDH-BILLA]
(0819) GUUDH- 4 -HR-1-EEDH 3    [GUUDH-HREEDH]
(0826) SWYYDH- 4 -FERHDH 5    [SWYYDH-FERHDH]
(0826) HROODH- 3 -GAARES 4    [HROODH-GAARES]
(0838) GUUDH- 2 -RINC 4    [GUUDH-RINC]
(0850) DEEADH- 2 -FAEAEGE 3    [DEEADH-FAEAEGE]
(0863) HROODH- 2 -GAAR 9    [HROODH-GAAR]
(0885) DEEADH- 3 -DAEGE 4    [DEEADH-DAEGE]
(0908) SWIIDH- 2 -FERHTHES 9    [SWIIDH-FERHTHES]
(0919) SWIIDH- 5 -HICGENDE 5    [SWIIDH-HICGENDE]
(0925) $HROODH- 2 -GAAR 5    [HROODH-GAAR]
(0974) LAADH- 3 -GE- 1    [LAADH-GE-TEEONA]
(0981) GUUDH- 3 -GE- 1    [GUUDH-GE-WEORCA]
(1016) SWIIDH- 3 -HICGENDE 9    [SWIIDH-HICGENDE]
(1017) HROODH- 0 -GAAR 4    [HROODH-GAAR]
(1066) HROOTH- 3 -GAARES 4    [HROOTH-GAARES]
(1110) EETH- 2 -GE- 3    [EETH-GE-SYYNE]
(1118) GUUDH- 2 -RINC 4    [GUUDH-RINC]
(1122) LAADH- 9 -BITE 4    [LAADH-BITE]
(1146) FERHDH- 3 -FRECAN 4    [FERHDH-FRECAN]
(1148) GUUDH- 2 -LAAF 7    [GUUDH-LAAF]
(1155) EORDH- 3 -CYNINGES 4    [EORDH-CYNINGES]
(1186) WORDH- 3 -MYN-1-DUM 4    [WORDH-MYNDUM]
(1189) HREEDH- 1 -RIIC 4    [HREEDH-RIIC]
(1189) HROODH- 1 -MUND 4    [HROODH-MUND]
(1213) GUUDH- 3 -SCEARE 6    [GUUDH-SCEARE]
(1236) HROOTH- 0 -GAAR 4    [HROOTH-GAAR]
(1244) YYTH- 1 -GE- 4    [YYTH-GE-SEENE]
(1258) GUUDH- 9 -CEARE 5    [GUUDH-CEARE]
(1275) DEEATH- 2 -+WIIC 9    [DEEATH-WIIC]
(1296) HROOTH- 0 -GAARE 7    [HROOTH-GAARE]
```

FIRST MORPHEME TERMINATES IN G, X, W, OR H

```
(0664) WIIG- 1 -FRUMA 4    [WIIG-FRUMA]
(0664) WEAL-1-H- 2 -THEEO 3    [WEALH-THEEO]
(0665) KYNING- 9 -WUL-1-DOR 4    [KYNING-WULDOR]
(0697) WIIG- 2 -SPEEDA 4    [WIIG-SPEEDA]
(0732) AAG- 0 -LAEAECA 5    [AAG-LAEAECA]
(0739) AAG- 0 -LAEAECA 5    [AAG-LAEAECA]
(0816) AEAEG- 0 -LAEAECA 9    [AEAEG-LAEAECA]
(0820) FEORH- 4 -SEEOC 4    [FEORH-SEEOC]
(0823) DAEG- 3 -RIIM 4    [DAEG-RIIM]
(0844) WEERIG- 4 -MOOD 3    [WEERIG-MOOD]
(0846) FEORH- 4 -LAASTAS 4    [FEORH-LAASTAS]
(0890) THURH- 3 -WOOD 3    [THURH-WOOD]
(0893) AAG- 0 -LAEAECA 4    [AAG-LAEAECA]
(0894) BEEAH- 4 -HOR-9-DES 5    [BEEAH-HORDES]
(0904) SORH- 3 -WYL-1-MAS 4    [SORH-WYLMAS]
(0921) BEEAH- 3 -HOR-1-DA 3    [BEEAH-HORDA]
(0957) ()EC*ECG- 2 -THEEO-1-WES 5    [*ECG-THEEOWES]
(0969) FEOR-1-H- 3 -GE- 3    [FEORH-GE-NIIDHLAN]
(0980) ()EC*ECG- 1 -LAAFES 4    [*ECG-LAAFES]
(0984) AEAEG- 2 -HWYLC 3    [AEAEG-HWYLC]
(0987) AEAEG- 1 -HWYLC 2    [AEAEG-HWYLC]
(0989) AAH- 2 -LAEAECAN 4    [AAH-LAEAECAN]
(1000) AAG- 0 -LAEAECA 4    [AAG-LAEAECA]
(1025) FEOH- 2 -GYFTE 6    [FEOH-GYFTE]
(1039) HEEAH- 3 -CYNINGES 5    [HEEAH-CYNINGES]
(1044) ING- 3 -WINA 3    [ING-WINA]
(1050) AEAEG- 0 -HWYL-2-CUM 3    [AEAEG-HWYLCUM]
(1059) AEAEG- 3 -HWAEAER 9    [AEAEG-HWAEAER]
(1087) HEEAH- 0 -SETL 5    [HEEAH-SETL]
(1089) FEOH- 2 -GYF-9-TU= 5    [FEOH-GYFTU=]
```

```
(1102)  BEEAG- 3 -GYFAN 4    [BEEAG-GYFAN]
(1140)  THURH- 3 -TEEON 3    [THURH-TEEON]
(1162)  WEALH- 0 -THEEO 3    [WEALH-THEEO]
(1165)  AEAEG- 3 -HWYLC 4    [AEAEG-HWYLC]
(1177)  BEEAH- 2 -SELE 5     [BEEAH-SELE]
(1212)  WIIG- 2 -FRECAN 5    [WIIG-FRECAN]
(1215)  $WEALH- 0 -DHEEO 4    [WEALH-DHEEO]
(1228)  AEAEG- 1 -HWYLC 4    [AEAEG-HWYLC]
(1259)  AAG- 0 -LAEAEC- 3    [AAG-LAEAEC-WIIF]
(1262)  ECG- 0 -BANAN 3      [ECG-BANAN]
(1269)  AAG- 0 -LAEAECA 4    [AAG-LAEAECA]
(1277)  GALG- 0 -MOOD 4      [GALG-MOOD]
(1278)  SORH- 3 -FULNE 9     [SORH-FULNE]
(1279)  HRING- 3 -DENE 6     [HRING-DENE]
(1284)  WIIG- 2 -GRYRE 5     [WIIG-GRYRE]
(1319)  ING- 2 -WINA 4    [ING-WINA]
```

FIRST MORPHEME TERMINATES IN NONALPHABETIC SYMBOL

```
(1023)  MAADH-9-THU=- 4 -SWEORD 3    [MAADHTHU=-SWEORD]
(1039)  HILDE.- 6 -SETL 4    [HILDE-SETL]
```


APPENDIX II
LINES 1321 - 1939 (FIT XX - END OF
    FIRST SCRIBE$S COPY)

MORPHEME PAIRS GROUPED BY PHONOLOGICAL FEATURES

FIRST MORPHEME TERMINATES IN LONG VOCALIC UNIT

```
(1383)  $$BEEO- 0 -$$WULF 6    [BEEO-WULF]
(1441)  BEEO- 0 -WULF 9    [BEEO-WULF]
(1451)  FREEA- 3 -WRAASNUM 5    [FREEA-WRAASNUM]
(1473)  $$BEEO- 0 -$$WULF 5    [BEEO-WULF]
(1651)  $$BEEO- 0 -WULF 4    [BEEO-WULF]
(1704)  BEEO- 0 -WULF 9    [BEEO-WULF]
(1731)  HLEEO- 4 -BURH 3    [HLEEO-BURH]
(1758)  BEEO- 0 -WULF 3    [BEEO-WULF]
(1817)  $BEEO- 8 -WULF 5    [BEEO-WULF]
(1854)  BEEO- 9 -WULF 6    [BEEO-WULF]
(1880)  BEEO- 0 -WULF 5    [BEEO-WULF]
(1356)  AA- 0 -CEN-1-NED 4    [AA-CENNED]
(1373)  AA- 0 -STIIGEDH 5    [AA-STIIGEDH]
(1390)  +AA- 0 -RIIS 3    [AA-RIIS]
(1397)  AA- 0 -HLEEOP 3    [AA-HLEEOP]
(1426)  SAEAE- 4 -DRACAN 9    [SAEAE-DRACAN]
(1460)  AA- 2 -HYRDED 5    [AA-HYRDED]
(1501)  TOO- 2 -GEEANES 5    [TOO-GEEANES]
(1510)  SAEAE- 3 -DEEOR 9    [SAEAE-DEEOR]
(1521)  AA- 0 -GOOL 5    [AA-GOOL]
(1528)  AA- 0 -LAEG. 6    [AA-LAEG]
(1530)  HYY- 0 -LAACES 4    [HYY-LAACES]
(1542)  TOO- 1 -GEEANES 4    [TOO-GEEANES]
(1556)  AA- 0 -STOOD. 9    [AA-STOOD]
(1599)  AA- 0 -()BREOTEN*BROTEN 3    [*AA-BROTEN]
(1624)  SAEAE- 2 -LAACE 3    [SAEAE-LAACE]
(1626)  TOO- 1 -GEEANES 5    [TOO-GEEANES]
(1630)  AA- 0 -LYYSED 4    [AA-LYYSED]
(1652)  +SAEAE- 0 -LAAC 4    [SAEAE-LAAC]
(1665)  AA- 8 -GEALD 5    [AA-GEALD]
```

(1703) AA- 0 -RAEAERED 6   [AA-RAEAERED]
(1724) AA- 0 -WRAEC 3   [AA-WRAEC]
(1737) OO- 0 -HWAEAER 5   [OO-HWAEAER]
(1790) AA- 0 -RAAS 5   [AA-RAAS]
(1818) SAEAE- 1 -LIIDHEND 4   [SAEAE-LIIDHEND]
(1822) OO- 0 -WIHTE 3   [OO-WIHTE]
(1850) +SAEAE- 3 -GEEATAS 5   [SAEAE-GEEATAS]
(1882) +SAEAE- 4 -GENGA 3   [SAEAE-GENGA]
(1893) TOO- 2 -GEEANES 4   [TOO-GEEANES]
(1896) +SAEAE- 5 -GEEAP 3   [SAEAE-GEEAP]
(1908) SAEAE- 2 -GENGA 4   [SAEAE-GENGA]
(1924) +SAEAE- 4 -WEALLE 4   [SAEAE-WEALLE]

FIRST MORPHEME TERMINATES IN SHORT VOCALIC UNIT

(1346) SELE- 2 -RAEAE-1-DEN-1-DE 9   [SELE-RAEAEDENDE]
(1401) GEATO- 8 -LIIC 9   [GEATO-LIIC]
(1405) MAGO- 3 -THEGNA 4   [MAGO-THEGNA]
(1412) BE- 9 -FORAN 3   [BE-FORAN]
(1428) BE- 2 -WITIGADH 4   [BE-WITIGADH]
(1435) HERE- 3 -STRAEAEL 5   [HERE-STRAEAEL]
(1438) HEORO- 3 -HOOC-9-YHTUM 4   [HEORO-HOOCYHTUM]
(1441) GRYRE- 2 -LIIC-1-NE 4   [GRYRE-LIICNE]
(1443) HERE- 3 -BYRNE 6   [HERE-BYRNE]
(1444) SEARO- 3 -FAAH 9   [SEARO-FAAH]
(1446) HIL-1-DE- 4 -GRAAP 5   [HILDE-GRAAP]
(1449) MERE- 2 -GRUNDAS 5   [MERE-GRUNDAS]
(1451) BE- 2 -FONGEN 3   [BE-FONGEN]
(1453) BE- 3 -SETTE 4   [BE-SETTE]
(1454) BEA-1-DO- 4 -MEECAS 6   [BEADO-MEECAS]
(1460) HEATHO- 2 -SWAATE 5   [HEATHO-SWAATE]
(1461) BE- 2 -WAND 4   [BE-WAND]
(1462) GRYRE- 5 -SIIDHAS 4   [GRYRE-SIIDHAS]
(1480) MAGO- 9 -THEGNUM 6   [MAGO-THEGNUM]
(1495) HIL-9-DE- 4 -RINCE 6   [HILDE-RINCE]
(1497) BE- 2 -GONG 6   [BE-GONG]
(1498) HEORO- 3 -GIIF-1-RE 9   [HEORO-GIIFRE]
(1498) BE- 4 -HEEOLD 5   [BE-HEEOLD]
(1505) LEODHO- 9 -SYRCAN 5   [LEODHO-SYRCAN]
(1511) HILDE- 4 -TUUXUM 5   [HILDE-TUUXUM]
(1511) HERE- 5 -SYR-2-CAN 4   [HERE-SYRCAN]
(1519) MERE- 8 -WIIF 3   [MERE-WIIF]
(1520) HILDE- 9 -BILLE 6   [HILDE-BILLE]
(1523) BEADO- 4 -LEEOMA 3   [BEADO-LEEOMA]
(1544) FEETHE- 3 -CEMPA 9   [FEETHE-CEMPA]
(1545) SELE- 1 -GYST 9   [SELE-GYST]
(1552) HEADHO- 5 -BYRNE 7   [HEADHO-BYRNE]
(1553) HERE- 4 -NET 3   [HERE-NET]
(1556) YYDHE- 0 -LIICE 4   [YYDHE-LIICE]
(1561) BEADU- 3 -LAACE 9   [BEADU-LAACE]
(1562) GEATO- 0 -LIIC 5   [GEATO-LIIC]
(1564) HEORO- 4 -GRIM 3   [HEORO-GRIM]
(1576) HILDE- 2 -RINCE 4   [HILDE-RINCE]
(1590) HEORO- 4 -SWENG 4   [HEORO-SWENG]
(1590) BE- 3 -CEARF. 7   [BE-CEARF]
(1604) WINE- 3 -DRI-1-HTEN 1   [WINE-DRIHTEN]
(1606) HEA-2-THO- 3 -SWAATE 4   [HEATHO-SWAATE]
(1606) HIL-1-DE- 9 -GI-1-C-1-ELUM 4   [HILDE-GICELUM]
(1632) FEE-1-THE- 5 -LAASTUM 3   [FEETHE-LAASTUM]
(1637) FELA- 5 -MOODIGRA 4   [FELA-MOODIGRA]
(1643) MEODO- 9 -WONGAS 5   [MEODO-WONGAS]
(1646) HILDE- 3 -DEEOR 6   [HILDE-DEEOR]
(1650) WLITE- 5 -SEEON 3   [WLITE-SEEON]
(1666) HILDE- 5 -BIL 5   [HILDE-BIL]

```
(1668) HEATHO- 3 -SWAATA 5    [HEATHO-SWAATA]
(1692) ENDE- 4 -LEEAN 5    [ENDE-LEEAN]
(1709) HERE- 2 -MOOD 9    [HERE-MOOD]
(1746) BE- 4 -BEOR-2-GAN 4    [BE-BEORGAN]
(1747) -BE- 2 -BODUM 5    [WUNDOR-BE-BODUM]
(1753) ENDE- 9 -STAEF 5    [ENDE-STAEF]
(1758) BE- 8 -BEOR-1-H 1    [BE-BEORH]
(1758) BEALO- 2 -NIIDH 6    [BEALO-NIIDH]
(1770) BE- 9 -LEEAC 5    [BE-LEEAC]
(1773) BE- 1 -GONG 1    [BE-GONG]
(1780) HEORO- 4 -DREEORIGNE 5    [HEORO-DREEORIGNE]
(1794) SELE- 5 -THEGN 3    [SELE-THEGN]
(1796) BE- 1 -()WEOTENE*WEOTEDE 6    [*BE-WEOTEDE]
(1798) HEATHO- 3 -LIIDHENDE 6    [HEATHO-LIIDHENDE]
(1816) HIL-1-DE- 3 -DEEOR 4    [HILDE-DEEOR]
(1821) BE- 1 -WENEDE 6    [BE-WENEDE]
(1826) BE- 0 -GANG 5    [BE-GANG]
(1847) HEORU- 3 -GRIM-2-ME 2    [HEORU-GRIMME]
(1886) BE- 3 -NAM 5    [BE-NAM]
(1888) FELA- 4 -MOODIGRA 9    [FELA-MOODIGRA]
(1890) LEODHO- 4 -SYRCAN 4    [LEODHO-SYRCAN]
(1897) HERE- 9 -WAEAEDUM 5    [HERE-WAEAEDUM]
(1902) MEODU- 4 -BENCE 5    [MEODU-BENCE]
(1903) YRFE- 3 -LAAFE 5    [YRFE-LAAFE]
(1905) MERE- 5 -HRAEGLA 5    [MERE-HRAEGLA]
(1925) BREGO- 3 -ROOF 2    [BREGO-ROOF]
(1483) HIGE- 2 -LAACE 4    [HIGE-LAACE]
(1557) SIGE- 2 -EEADIG 3    [SIGE-EEADIG]
(1574) HIGE- 4 -LAACES 4    [HIGE-LAACES]
(1597) SIGE- 5 -HREEDHIG 4    [SIGE-HREEDHIG]
(1820) HIGE- 3 -LAAC 3    [HIGE-LAAC]
(1830) HIGE- 3 -LAACE 9    [HIGE-LAACE]
(1878) HYGE- 3 -BENDUM 3    [HYGE-BENDUM]
(1923) HIGE- 9 -LAAC 5    [HIGE-LAAC]

(1322) GE- 2 -NII-9-WOD 4    [GE-NIIWOD]
(1333) GE- 1 -()FRAEGNOD*FAEGNOD 3    [*GE-FAEGNOD]
(1337) GE- 1 -CRANG 4    [GE-CRANG]
(1340) GE- 0 -STAEAELED 4    [GE-STAEAELED]
(1347) GE- 1 -SAAWON 4    [GE-SAAWON]
(1350) GE- 2 -WIS- 0    [GE-WIS-LIICOST]
(1350) GE- 1 -WITAN 3    [GE-WITAN]
(1360) GE- 1 -NIPU 5    [GE-NIPU]
(1360) GE- 0 -WIITEDH 9    [GE-WIITEDH]
(1365) GE- 2 -HWAEAEM 9    [GE-HWAEAEM]
(1368) GE- 0 -SWENCED 7    [GE-SWENCED]
(1370) GE- 9 -FLYYMED 3    [GE-FLYYMED]
(1375) GE- 4 -WIDRU 2    [GE-WIDRU]
(1376) GE- 1 -LANG 4    [GE-LANG]
(1386) GE- 2 -BIIDAN 5    [GE-BIIDAN]
(1392) GE- 4 -HAATE 5    [GE-HAATE]
(1395) GE- 5 -THYLD 4    [GE-THYLD]
(1396) GE- 3 -HWYL-1-CES 4    [GE-HWYLCES]
(1398) GE- 9 -SPRAEC 4    [GE-SPRAEC]
(1399) GE- 8 -BAEAETED 9    [GE-BAEAETED]
(1403) GE- 2 -SYYNE 9    [GE-SYYNE]
(1410) GE- 2 -LAAD 4    [GE-LAAD]
(1417) GE- 3 -DREE-9-FED 4    [GE-DREEFED]
(1419) GE- 3 -THOLIAN-1-NE 6    [GE-THOLIANNE]
(1420) GE- 4 -HWAEAEM 3    [GE-HWAEAEM]
(1424) GE- 2 -SAET. 6    [GE-SAET]
(1425) GE- 0 -SAAWON 3    [GE-SAAWON]
(1431) GE- 0 -BOLGNE 7    [GE-BOLGNE]
(1433) GE- 3 -TWAEAEF-1-DE 5    [GE-TWAEAEFDE]
(1438) GE- 8 -NEAR-2-WOD 4    [GE-NEARWOD]
```

169

```
(1439) GE- 3 -NAEAEGED 3   [GE-NAEAEGED]
(1443) GE- 2 -BROODEN 4   [GE-BROODEN]
(1447) GE- 1 -SCETHDHAN. 7   [GE-SCETHDHAN]
(1450) GE- 2 -WEORDHAD 9   [GE-WEORDHAD]
(1462) GE- 1 -GAAN 9   [GE-GAAN]
(1465) GE- 9 -MUNDE 5   [GE-MUNDE]
(1466) GE- 3 -SPRAEC 4   [GE-SPRAEC]
(1469) GE- 2 -WIN 4   [GE-WIN]
(1469) GE- 1 -NEE-2-THAN 3   [GE-NEETHAN]
(1472) GE- 2 -GYRED 4   [GE-GYRED]
(1474) GE- 3 -THENC 4   [GE-THENC]
(1485) GE- 0 -SEEON 2   [GE-SEEON]
(1491) GE- 1 -WYRCE 9   [GE-WYRCE]
(1501) GE- 1 -FEENG 5   [GE-FEENG]
(1502) GE- 2 -SCOOD 5   [GE-SCOOD]
(1509) GE- 1 -WEALDAN 4   [GE-WEALDAN]
(1516) GE- 2 -SEAH 6   [GE-SEAH]
(1524) GE- 1 -SWAAC 9   [GE-SWAAC]
(1526) GE- 0 -SCAER 5   [GE-SCAER]
(1530) GE- 1 -MYNDIG 4   [GE-MYNDIG]
(1531) GE- 1 -BUNDEN 4   [GE-BUNDEN]
(1533) GE- 1 -TRUWODE 5   [GE-TRUWODE]
(1535) GE- 1 -GAAN 9   [GE-GAAN]
(1537) $GE- 0 -FEENG 4   [GE-FEENG]
(1539) GE- 4 -BOLGEN 2   [GE-BOLGEN]
(1540) GE- 1 -BEEAH 4   [GE-BEEAH]
(1545) GE- 2 -TEEAH 4   [GE-TEEAH]
(1548) GE- 2 -BEARH 9   [GE-BEARH]
(1552) GE- 0 -FREME-2-DE 9   [GE-FREMEDE]
(1554) GE- 1 -WEEOLD 3   [GE-WEEOLD]
(1555) GE- 1 -SCEED 4   [GE-SCEED]
(1557) $$GE- 4 -SEAH 3   [GE-SEAH]
(1562) GE- 2 -WEORC. 6   [GE-WEORC]
(1563) GE- 3 -FEENG 5   [GE-FEENG]
(1564) GE- 3 -BRAEGD 4   [GE-BRAEGD]
(1568) GE- 2 -CRONG 5   [GE-CRONG]
(1569) GE- 1 -FEH 5   [GE-FEH]
(1578) GE- 1 -WORHTE 5   [GE-WORHTE]
(1585) GE- 2 -SEAH 3   [GE-SEAH]
(1587) GE- 1 -SCOOD 5   [GE-SCOOD]
(1591) GE- 2 -SAAWON 4   [GE-SAAWON]
(1593) GE- 3 -MENGED 5   [GE-MENGED]
(1598) GE- 9 -WEARDH 5   [GE-WEARDH]
(1601) GE- 2 -WAAT 3   [GE-WAAT]
(1605) GE- 1 -SAAWON 2   [GE-SAAWON]
(1608) GE- 1 -MEALT 4   [GE-MEALT]
(1608) GE- 2 -LIICOST 4   [GE-LIICOST]
(1610) GE- 4 -WEALD 4   [GE-WEALD]
(1613) GE- 3 -SEAH 5   [GE-SEAH]
(1615) GE- 9 -MEALT 5   [GE-MEALT]
(1618) GE- 3 -BAAD 3   [GE-BAAD]
(1620) GE- 4 -FAEAELSOD 4   [GE-FAEAELSOD]
(1622) GE- 2 -SCEAFT. 9   [GE-SCEAFT]
(1624) GE- 1 -FEAH 4   [GE-FEAH]
(1627) GE- 3 -FEEGON 9   [GE-FEEGON]
(1628) GE- 2 -SUND-1-NE 4   [GE-SUNDNE]
(1628) GE- 0 -SEEON 2   [GE-SEEON]
(1638) GE- 1 -FERIAN 3   [GE-FERIAN]
(1643) GE- 3 -MONGE 5   [GE-MONGE]
(1645) GE- 2 -WUR-2-THAD 9   [GE-WURTHAD]
(1655) GE- 3 -DIIGDE 5   [GE-DIIGDE]
(1656) GE- 1 -NEETH-1-DE 5   [GE-NEETHDE]
(1658) GE- 2 -THAEAEFED 4   [GE-THAEAEFED]
(1660) GE- 2 -WYRCAN 9   [GE-WYRCAN]
(1661) GE- 3 -UUDHE 9   [GE-UUDHE]
```

170

```
1662)  GE- 0 -SEAH 3     [GE-SEAH]
1664)  GE- 1 -BRAEAED. 9   [GE-BRAEAED]
1667)  GE- 2 -SPRANG 9    [GE-SPRANG]
1670)  GE- 2 -DEEFE 4     [GE-DEEFE]
1671)  GE- 3 -HAATE 5     [GE-HAATE]
1672)  GE- 1 -DRYHT 9     [GE-DRYHT]
1673)  GE- 3 -HWYLC 5     [GE-HWYLC]
1679)  GE- 3 -HWEARF 5    [GE-HWEARF]
1681)  GE- 9 -WEORC 5     [GE-WEORC]
1684)  GE- 4 -WEALD 7     [GE-WEALD]
1684)  GE- 2 -HWE-9-ARF 5    [GE-HWEARF]
1691)  GE- 9 -FEERDON 4    [GE-FEERDON]
1695)  GE- 9 -MEARCOD 4    [GE-MEARCOD]
1696)  GE- 0 -SETED 4     [GE-SETED]
1696)  GE- 2 -SAEAED 5    [GE-SAEAED]
1696)  GE- 3 -WORHT 5     [GE-WORHT]
1701)  GE- 2 -MON 4    [GE-MON]
1703)  GE- 2 -BOREN 5     [GE-BOREN]
1705)  GE- 2 -HWYLCE 5    [GE-HWYLCE]
1705)  GE- 9 -THYLDUM 6    [GE-THYLDUM]
1706)  GE- 1 -LAEAESTAN 4    [GE-LAEAESTAN]
1711)  GE- 8 -WEEOX 6     [GE-WEEOX]
1718)  GE- 1 -FREME-9-DE 6    [GE-FREMEDE]
1720)  GE- 2 -+BAAD 3     [GE-BAAD]
1721)  GE- 3 -WIN-1-NES 5    [GE-WINNES]
1727)  GE- 4 -WEALD. 7    [GE-WEALD]
1732)  GE- 3 -DEEDH 4     [GE-DEEDH]
1732)  GE- 3 -WEAL-2-DENE 5    [GE-WEALDENE]
1734)  GE- 3 -THEN-1-CEAN. 5    [GE-THENCEAN]
1737)  GE- 5 -SACU 4     [GE-SACU]
1743)  GE- 2 -BUNDEN 9    [GE-BUNDEN]
1753)  GE- 3 -LIMPEDH 5    [GE-LIMPEDH]
1754)  GE- 2 -DREEOSEDH 5    [GE-DREEOSEDH]
1755)  GE- 2 -FEALLEDH 5    [GE-FEALLEDH]
1759)  GE- 1 -CEEOS 4     [GE-CEEOS]
1763)  GE- 2 -THWAEAEFEDH 4    [GE-THWAEAEFEDH]
1773)  GE- 5 -SACAN 2     [GE-SACAN]
1779)  GE- 2 -BAAD 4     [GE-BAAD]
1781)  GE- 9 -WIN 3    [GE-WIN]
1784)  GE- 2 -MAEAENRA 5    [GE-MAEAENRA]
1788)  GE- 2 -REORDED 4    [GE-REORDED]
1789)  GE- 2 -SWEARC 5    [GE-SWEARC]
1826)  GE- 9 -FRICGE 5    [GE-FRICGE]
1837)  GE- 1 -()THINGED*THINGEDH 3    [*GE-THINGEDH]
1839)  GE- 0 -SOOHTE 6    [GE-SOOHTE]
1846)  GE- 2 -GANGEDH 4    [GE-GANGEDH]
1851)  GE- 1 -CEEOSEN-9-NE 8    [GE-CEEOSENNE]
1855)  GE- 3 -FEERED 4    [GE-FEERED]
1857)  GE- 4 -()MAENUM*MAEAENE 6    [*GE-MAEAENE]
1860)  GE- 2 -MAEAENE 4    [GE-MAEAENE]
1861)  GE- 0 -GREETTAN 4    [GE-GREETTAN]
1864)  GE- 2 -WORHTE 7    [GE-WORHTE]
1866)  GE- 4 -SEALDE 6    [GE-SEALDE]
1869)  GE- 2 -SYNTUM 3    [GE-SYNTUM]
1870)  GE- 5 -CYSTE 5    [GE-CYSTE]
1872)  GE- 2 -NAM 5    [GE-NAM]
1875)  GE- 1 -SEEON 4    [GE-SEEON]
1885)  GE- 4 -AEHTED 3    [GE-AEHTED]
1901)  GE- 1 -SEAL-1-DE 5    [GE-SEALDE]
1903)  GE- 2 -WAAT 4    [GE-WAAT]
1908)  GE- 1 -THWAEAEFDE 6    [GE-THWAEAEFDE]
1912)  GE- 4 -THRANG 5    [GE-THRANG]
1920)  GE- 0 -STREEON 9    [GE-STREEON]
1922)  GE- 3 -SEE-1-CAN-1-NE 5    [GE-SEECANNE]
1924)  GE- 2 -SIIDHUM 4    [GE-SIIDHUM]
```

```
(1928) GE- 1 -BIDEN 9   [GE-BIDEN]
(1933) GE- 2 -NEETHAN 4   [GE-NEETHAN]
(1934) GE- 2 -SIIDHA 5   [GE-SIIDHA]
(1938) GE- 8 -THINGED 5   [GE-THINGED]
(1326) -GE- 2 -STEA-1-LLA 9   [EAXL-GE-STEALLA]
(1359) -GE- 2 -LAAD 5   [FEN-GE-LAAD]
(1362) -GE- 9 -MEAR-1-CES 5   [MIIL-GE-MEARCES]
(1373) -GE- 2 -BLOND 4   [YYDH-GE-BLOND]
(1381) -GE- 2 -STREEONU= 3   [EALD-GE-STREEONU=]
(1434) -GE- 1 -WINNES 5   [YYDH-GE-WINNES]
(1442) -GE- 1 -WAEAE-2-DUM 4   [EORL-GE-WAEAEDUM]
(1450) -GE- 2 -BLAND 4   [SUND-GE-BLAND]
(1458) -GE- 4 -STREEONA 5   [EALD-GE-STREEONA]
(1479) -GE- 1 -WITENUM 3   [FORDH-GE-WITENUM]
(1481) -GE- 8 -SELLUM 4   [HOND-GE-SELLUM]
(1526) -GE- 8 -MOOTA 5   [HOND-GE-MOOTA]
(1540) -GE- 3 -NIIDH-2-LAN 4   [FEORH-GE-NIIDHLAN]
(1580) -GE- 2 -NEEATAS 6   [HEORDH-GE-NEEATAS]
(1593) -GE- 3 -BLOND 4   [YYDH-GE-BLOND]
(1620) -GE- 3 -BLAND 9   [YYDH-GE-BLAND]
(1679) -GE- 1 -WEORC 9   [AEAER-GE-WEORC]
(1689) -GE- 3 -WIN-1-NES. 6   [FYRN-GE-WINNES]
(1713) -GE- 8 -NEEATAS 4   [BEEOD-GE-NEEATAS]
(1714) -GE- 9 -STEALLAN 4   [EAXL-GE-STEALLAN]
(1729) -GE- 3 -THONC 3   [MOOD-GE-THONC]
(1750) -GE- 1 -SCEAFT 5   [FORDH-GE-SCEAFT]
(1757) -GE- 4 -STREEON 5   [AEAER-GE-STREEON]
(1776) -GE- 4 -WINNA 3   [EALD-GE-WINNA]
(1783) -GE- 5 -WEORTHAD 4   [WIIG-GE-WEORTHAD]
(1825) -GE- 9 -WEORCA 5   [GUUDH-GE-WEORCA]
(1899) -GE- 2 -STREEONUM 7   [HORD-GE-STREEONUM]
(1913) -GE- 4 -SWEN-9-CED 3   [LYFT-GE-SWENCED]
(1931) -GE- 2 -STREEONA 4   [MAATHM-GE-STREEONA]
(1937) -GE- 1 -WRITHENE 5   [HAND-GE-WRITHENE]


FIRST MORPHEME TERMINATES IN RESONANT CONSONANT

(1324) YR-1-MEN- 5 -LAAFES 4   [YRMEN-LAAFES]
(1325) +RUUN- 9 -WITA 4   [RUUN-WITA]
(1326) EAXL- 3 -GE- 2   [EAXL-GE-STEALLA]
(1326) OR- 0 -LEGE. 6   [OR-LEGE]
(1329) AEAER- 1 -GOOD 2   [AEAER-GOOD]
(1331) WAEL- 2 -GAEAEST 5   [WAEL-GAEAEST]
(1336) FOR- 3 -THAN 4   [FOR-THAN]
(1339) MAAN- 9 -SCADHA 4   [MAAN-SCADHA]
(1343) HRETHER- 3 -BEALO 5   [HRETHER-BEALO]
(1344) WEEL- 4 -HWYLCRA 5   [WEEL-HWYLCRA]
(1349) ELLOR- 9 -GAEAESTAS 4   [ELLOR-GAEAESTAS]
(1351) ON- 0 -LIIC- 3   [*ON-LIIC-NES]
(1351) EAR-9-M- 3 -SCEAPEN 4   [EARM-SCEAPEN]
(1354) GEEAR- 4 -DAGU= 4   [GEEAR-DAGU=]
(1359) FEN- 1 -GE- 2   [FEN-GE-LAAD]
(1359) FYRGEN- 9 -STREEAM 5   [FYRGEN-STREEAM]
(1362) MIIL- 2 -GE- 9   [MIIL-GE-MEARCES]
(1364) OFER- 2 -HELMADH 6   [OFER-HELMADH]
(1389) UN- 0 -LIF-9-GENDUM 4   [UN-LIFGENDUM]
(1393) FYRGEN- 3 -HOLT. 4   [FYRGEN-HOLT]
(1400) WUNDEN- 4 -FEAX 3   [WUNDEN-FEAX]
(1401) GUM- 2 -FEETHA 3   [GUM-FEETHA]
(1406) SAAWOL- 4 -LEEAS-2-NE 6   [SAAWOL-LEEASNE]
(1408) OFER- 3 -EEODE 3   [OFER-EEODE]
(1409) STAAN- 4 -HLIDHO 5   [STAAN-HLIDHO]
(1410) AAN- 1 -PADHAS 5   [AAN-PADHAS]
(1410) UN- 0 -CUUDH 2   [UN-CUUDH]
```

172

```
411) NICOR- 5 -HUUSA 3    [NICOR-HUUSA]
414) FYRGEN- 3 -BEEAMAS 5    [FYRGEN-BEEAMAS]
416) WYN- 0 -LEEASNE 9    [WYN-LEEASNE]
420) ON- 1 -CYYDH 3    [ON-CYYDH]
421) HOLM- 3 -CLIFE 6    [HOLM-CLIFE]
425) WYRM- 1 -CYNNES 4    [WYRM-CYNNES]
426) SEL- 0 -LICE 4    [SEL-LICE]
428) UNDERN- 2 -MAEAEL 5    [UNDERN-MAEAEL]
429) SEGL- 3 -RAADE 6    [SEGL-RAADE]
431) ON- 0 -GEEA-9-TON 3    [ON-GEEATON]
433) FLAAN- 9 -BOGAN 4    [FLAAN-BOGAN]
436) FOR- 1 -NAM. 4    [FOR-NAM]
437) EOFER- 1 -SPREEDTUM 4    [EOFER-SPREEDTUM]
440) WUN-1-DOR- 3 -LIIC 5    [WUNDOR-LIIC]
442) EORL- 3 -GE- 1    [EORL-GE-WAEAEDUM]
445) +BAAN- 2 -COFAN 6    [BAAN-COFAN]
451) FYRN- 1 -DA-9-GUM 4    [FYRN-DAGUM]
453) SWIIN- 0 -LIICUM 5    [SWIIN-LIICUM]
455) MAEGEN- 3 -FULTUMA 5    [MAEGEN-FULTUMA]
459) AATER- 1 -TAANUM 3    [AATER-TAANUM]
464) ELLEN- 3 -WEORC 5    [ELLEN-WEORC]
467) ON- 2 -LAAH. 6    [ON-LAAH]
470) FOR- 3 -LEEAS 4    [FOR-LEEAS]
471) ELLEN- 9 -MAEAERDHUM 3    [ELLEN-MAEAERDHUM]
483) ON- 0 -SEND. 5    [ON-SEND]
484) ON- 0 -GITAN 5    [ON-GITAN]
488) ()HUN*UN- 0 -FERDH 5    [*UN-FERDH]
492) WEDER- 4 -GEEATA 4    [WEDER-GEEATA]
494) BRIM- 4 -WYLM 3    [BRIM-WYLM]
494) ON- 1 -FEENG 8    [ON-FEENG]
496) ON- 0 -GYTAN 2    [ON-GYTAN]
497) ON- 9 -FUNDE 5    [ON-FUNDE]
500) AEL- 1 -WIHTA 3    [AEL-WIHTA]
506) BRIM- 9 -WYL*F 4    [BRIM-WYL*F]
512) ON- 0 -GEAT 4    [ON-GEAT]
516) +FAEAER- 4 -GRIPE 4    [FAEAER-GRIPE]
516) FYYR- 8 -LEEOHT 4    [FYYR-LEEOHT]
518) $ON- 2 -GEAT 2    [ON-GEAT]
519) MAEGEN- 3 -RAEAES 4    [MAEGEN-RAEAES]
519) FOR- 2 -GEAF 5    [FOR-GEAF]
522) ON- 0 -FAND 5    [ON-FAND]
529) AN- 0 -RAEAED 3    [AN-RAEAED]
531) ()WUNDEL*WUNDEN- 4 -MAEAEL 5    [*WUNDEN-MAEAEL]
533) STYYL- 2 -ECG 9    [STYYL-ECG]
541) FOR- 1 -GEALD 4    [FOR-GEALD]
543) OFER- 3 -WEARP 9    [OFER-WEARP]
546) +BRUUN- 3 -ECG 3    [BRUUN-ECG]
549) IN- 0 -GANG 2    [IN-GANG]
549) FOR- 3 -STOOD. 9    [FOR-STOOD]
550) FOR- 3 -SIIDHOD 4    [FOR-SIIDHOD]
563) FETEL- 4 -HILT 9    [FETEL-HILT]
565) OR- 0 -WEENA 5    [OR-WEENA]
567) BAAN- 9 -HRINGAS 5    [BAAN-HRINGAS]
575) AN- 0 -RAEAED. 8    [AN-RAEAED]
577) FOR- 1 -GYL-2-DAN 4    [FOR-GYLDAN]
584) FOR- 3 -GEALD 4    [FOR-GEALD]
587) ALDOR- 3 -LEEAS-1-NE 6    [ALDOR-LEEASNE]
594) BLONDEN- 3 -FEAXE 5    [BLONDEN-FEAXE]
595) ON- 3 -GEADOR 4    [ON-GEADOR]
599) BRIM- 4 -WYLF 4    [BRIM-WYLF]
605) ON- 0 -GAN 4    [ON-GAN]
609) ON- 1 -LAEAETEDH 5    [ON-LAEAETEDH]
610) ON- 0 -WINDEDH 3    [ON-WINDEDH]
610) WAEAEL- 9 -RAAPAS 4    [WAEAEL-RAAPAS]
612) WEDER- 9 -GEEATA 4    [WEDER-GEEATA]
```

173

```
(1613) MAADH-1-M- 5 -AEAEHTA 3    [MAADHM-AEAEHTA]
(1616) FOR- 3 -BARN 4    [FOR-BARN]
(1616) BROO-2-DEN- 3 -MAEAEL 5    [BROODEN-MAEAEL]
(1617) ELLOR- 3 -GAEAEST 4    [ELLOR-GAEAEST]
(1621) ELLOR- 9 -GAAST 4    [ELLOR-GAAST]
(1625) MAEGEN- 9 -BYR-1-THENNE 5    [MAEGEN-BYRTHENNE]
(1631) WAEL- 1 -DREEO-1-RE 3    [WAEL-DREEORE]
(1635) HOLM- 9 -CLIFE 5    [HOLM-CLIFE]
(1638) WAEL- 2 -STENGE 4    [WAEL-STENGE]
(1641) FEEOWER- 1 -TYYNE 5    [FEEOWER-TYYNE]
(1642) GUM- 9 -DRYHTEN 3    [GUM-DRYHTEN]
(1655) UN- 9 -SOOFTE 5    [UN-SOOFTE]
(1667) FOR- 9 -BARN 5    [FOR-BARN]
(1667) BROGDEN- 3 -MAEAEL. 6    [BROGDEN-MAEAEL]
(1669) FYR-1-EN- 4 -DAEAE-3-DA 3    [FYREN-DAEAEDA]
(1674) ON- 2 -DRAEAE-1-DAN 4    [ON-DRAEAEDAN]
(1676) ALDOR- 3 -BEALU 9    [ALDOR-BEALU]
(1679) AEAER- 2 -GE- 1    [AEAER-GE-WEORC]
(1681) WUNDOR- 2 -SMITHA 3    [WUNDOR-SMITHA]
(1682) GROM- 9 -HEORT 4    [GROM-HEORT]
(1689) FYRN- 3 -GE- 3    [FYRN-GE-WINNES]
(1695) RUUN- 2 -STAFAS 4    [RUUN-STAFAS]
(1698) WREO-9-THEN- 5 -HILT 5    [WREOTHEN-HILT]
(1698) WYRM- 3 -FAAH 4    [WYRM-FAAH]
(1710) AAR- 3 -SCYL-1-DINGUM. 9    [AAR-SCYLDINGUM]
(1711) WAEL- 3 -FEAL-9-LE 3    [WAEL-FEALLE]
(1713) BOLGEN- 4 -MOOD 6    [BOLGEN-MOOD]
(1714) EAXL- 3 -GE- 9    [EAXL-GE-STEALLAN]
(1715) MON- 1 -DREEAMU= 4    [MON-DREEAMU=]
(1720) DREEAM- 3 -LEEAS 4    [DREEAM-LEEAS]
(1723) ON- 1 -GIT. 6    [ON-GIT]
(1727) EORL- 4 -SCIPE 4    [EORL-SCIPE]
(1734) UN- 8 -SNYTTRUM 5    [UN-SNYTTRUM]
(1740) OFER- 4 -HYGDA 5    [OFER-HYGDA]
(1744) FLAAN- 5 -BOGAN 9    [FLAAN-BOGAN]
(1747) WUN-2-DOR- 9 -BE- 2    [WUNDOR-BE-BODUM]
(1749) GROM- 4 -HYYDIG 5    [GROM-HYYDIG]
(1751) FOR- 3 -GYTEDH 5    [FOR-GYTEDH]
(1751) FOR- 3 -GYYMEDH 9    [FOR-GYYMEDH]
(1756) UN- 1 -MURN- 1    [UN-MURN-LIICE]
(1756) -MURN- 1 -LIICE 6    [UN-MURN-LIICE]
(1757) AEAER- 3 -GE- 4    [AEAER-GE-STREEON]
(1760) OFER- 4 -HYYDA 3    [OFER-HYYDA]
(1767) FOR- 0 -SITEDH 4    [FOR-SITEDH]
(1767) FOR- 3 -SWOR-9-CEDH 5    [FOR-SWORCEDH]
(1768) OFER- 4 -SWYYDHEDH 4    [OFER-SWYYDHEDH]
(1771) MID-9-DAN- 3 -GEARD. 6    [MIDDAN-GEARD]
(1776) IN- 0 -GENGA 4    [IN-GENGA]
(1777) SIN- 1 -GAALES 4    [SIN-GAALES]
(1782) SYM-9-BEL- 4 -WYNNE 5    [SYMBEL-WYNNE]
(1787) ELLEN- 3 -ROOFUM 4    [ELLEN-ROOFUM]
(1791) BLONDEN- 3 -FEAX 4    [BLONDEN-FEAX]
(1792) UN- 0 -IG- 9    [UN-IG-METES]
(1795) FEORRAN- 9 -CUNDUM 4    [FEORRAN-CUNDUM]
(1799) RUUM- 3 -HEORT 6    [RUUM-HEORT]
(1806) COL-9-LEN- 8 -FERHDH 5    [COLLEN-FERHDH]
(1834) GAAR- 2 -HOLT 4    [GAAR-HOLT]
(1838) FEOR- 3 -CYYTHDHE 5    [FEOR-CYYTHDHE]
(1842) SNOTOR- 4 -LIICOR 5    [SNOTOR-LIICOR]
(1856) GAAR- 3 -DENUM 4    [GAAR-DENUM]
(1865) UN- 1 -TAEAELE 5    [UN-TAEAELE]
(1873) BLON-1-DEN- 9 -FEAXUM 5    [BLONDEN-FEAXUM]
(1874) IN- 9 -FRO-1-DUM 4    [IN-FRODUM]
(1877) FOR- 3 -BERAN 3    [FOR-BERAN]
(1886) OR- 0 -LEAHTRE 5    [OR-LEAHTRE]
```

1890) ON- 9 -FAND 4   [ON-FAND]
1894) WIL- 2 -CUMAN 3   [WIL-CUMAN]
1895) +SCIIR- 4 -HAME 5   [SCIIR-HAME]
1910) BUNDEN- 9 -STEFNA 4   [BUNDEN-STEFNA]
1910) BRIM- 3 -STREEAMAS 5   [BRIM-STREEAMAS]
1911) ON- 0 -GITAN 4   [ON-GITAN]
1918) ()ONCEAR*ONCER- 4 -BENDUM 2   [*ONCER-BENDUM]
1919) WYN- 0 -SUMAN 4   [WYN-SUMAN]
1919) FOR- 4 -WRECAN 8   [FOR-WRECAN]
1927) WEEL- 4 -THUNGEN 4   [WEEL-THUNGEN]
1931) MAATHM- 3 -GE- 2   [MAATHM-GE-STREEONA]
1932) ON- 1 -DRYSNE 9   [ON-DRYSNE]
1934) SIN- 1 -FREEA 4   [SIN-FREEA]
1936) WAEL- 4 -BENDE. 9   [WAEL-BENDE]
1939) SCEAADEN- 4 -MAEAEL 4   [SCEAADEN-MAEAEL]

FIRST MORPHEME TERMINATES IN STOP CONSONANT

1323) AESC- 1 -HERE 9   [AESC-HERE]
1325) RAEAED- 4 -BORA 5   [RAEAED-BORA]
1329) AESC- 9 -HERE 9   [AESC-HERE]
1330) HAND- 3 -BANAN 9   [HAND-BANAN]
1332) EFT- 2 -SIIDHAS 4   [EFT-SIIDHAS]
1342) SINC- 2 -GYFAN 3   [SINC-GYFAN]
1345) LOND- 3 -BUUEND 4   [LOND-BUUEND]
1348) MEARC- 2 -STAPAN 3   [MEARC-STAPAN]
1351) -LIIC- 3 -()NAES*NES 2   [*ON-LIIC-NES]
1352) WRAEC- 3 -LAAS-1-TAS 9   [WRAEC-LAASTAS]
1355) FOLD- 3 -BUUENDE 5   [FOLD-BUUENDE]
1369) HOLT- 3 -WUDU 2   [HOLT-WUDU]
1381) EALD- 2 -GE- 2   [EALD-GE-STREEONU=]
1388) ORIHT- 3 -GUMAN 3   [ORIHT-GUMAN]
1402) LIND- 3 -HAEBBENDRA 3   [LIND-HAEBBENDRA]
1403) WALD- 2 -SWA-2-THU= 4   [WALD-SWATHU=]
1420) AESC- 3 -HERES 5   [AESC-HERES]
1424) FYRD- 8 -LEEODH 4   [FYRD-LEEODH]
1447) IN-9-WIT- 3 -FENG 3   [INWIT-FENG]
1450) SUND- 2 -GE- 2   [SUND-GE-BLAND]
1457) HAEFT- 9 -MEECE 6   [HAEFT-MEECE]
1458) EALD- 9 -GE- 4   [EALD-GE-STREEONA]
1463) FOLC- 1 -STEDE 5   [FOLC-STEDE]
1468) SWEORD- 1 -FRECAN 4   [SWEORD-FRECAN]
1470) ORIHT- 9 -SCYPE 5   [ORIHT-SCYPE]
1476) GOLD- 9 -WINE 5   [GOLD-WINE]
1480) MUND- 3 -BORA 4   [MUND-BORA]
1481) HOND- 2 -GE- 8   [HOND-GE-SELLUM]
1489) WRAEAET- 1 -LIIC 4   [WRAEAET-LIIC]
1489) WIID- 1 -CUUDH-1-NE 4   [WIID-CUUDHNE]
1490) HEARD- 3 -ECG 3   [HEARD-ECG]
1493) =AND- 9 -SWARE 6   [=AND-SWARE]
1496) GRUND- 2 -WONG 4   [GRUND-WONG]
1503) YMB- 5 -BEARH 6   [YMB-BEARH]
1504) FYRD- 4 -HOM 4   [FYRD-HOM]
1513) NAAT- 3 -HWYLCUM 4   [NAAT-HWYLCUM]
1518) GRUND- 3 -WYR-1-GENNE 9   [GRUND-WYRGENNE]
1526) HOND- 9 -GE- 8   [HOND-GE-MOOTA]
1527) FYRD- 9 -HRAEGL 6   [FYRD-HRAEGL]
1534) MUND- 3 -GRIPE 5   [MUND-GRIPE]
1541) ()HAND*AND- 0 -LEEAN 3   [*AND-LEEAN]
1548) BREEOST- 3 -NET 2   [BREEOST-NET]
1558) EALD- 9 -SWEORD 4   [EALD-SWEORD]
1561) AET- 2 -BERAN 2   [AET-BERAN]
1568) FLAEAESC- 9 -HOMAN 5   [FLAEAESC-HOMAN]
1578) WEST- 3 -DENUM 9   [WEST-DENUM]

```
(1602)  GOLD- 8 -WINE 9      [GOLD-WINE]
(1623)  LID- 2 -MANNA 5      [LID-MANNA]
(1633)  FOLD- 1 -WEG 3       [FOLD-WEG]
(1639)  GOLD- 2 -SELE 5      [GOLD-SELE]
(1641)  FYRD- 9 -HWATE 5     [FYRD-HWATE]
(1645)  DAEAED- 2 -CEENE 5   [DAEAED-CEENE]
(1650)  WRAEAET- 9 -LIIC 4   [WRAEAET-LIIC]
(1657)  AET- 1 -RIHTE 6      [AET-RIHTE]
(1663)  EALD- 3 -SWEORD 4    [EALD-SWEORD]
(1669)  AET- 2 -FERE-2-DE 5  [AET-FEREDE]
(1678)  HILD- 2 -FRU-9-MAN 4 [HILD-FRUMAN]
(1682)  =AND- 0 -SACA 4      [=AND-SACA]
(1684)  WOROLD- 4 -CYNINGA 5 [WOROLD-CYNINGA]
(1704)  WIID- 3 -WEGAS 6     [WIID-WEGAS]
(1713)  BEEOD- 2 -GE- 8      [BEEOD-GE-NEEATAS]
(1719)  BREEOST- 9 -HORD 6   [BREEOST-HORD]
(1719)  BLOOD- 3 -REEOW 5    [BLOOD-REEOW]
(1722)  LEEOD- 2 -BEA-9-LO 4 [LEEOD-BEALO]
(1729)  MOOD- 3 -GE- 3       [MOOD-GE-THONC]
(1736)  IN-1-WIT- 3 -SORH 5  [INWIT-SORH]
(1754)  LIIC- 3 -HOMA 9      [LIIC-HOMA]
(1768)  DRYHT- 4 -GUMA 3     [DRYHT-GUMA]
(1774)  ED- 1 -()WENDAN*WENDEN 9  [*ED-WENDEN]
(1776)  EALD- 2 -GE- 4       [EALD-GE-WINNA]
(1778)  MOOD- 3 -CEARE 9     [MOOD-CEARE]
(1785)  GLAED- 2 -MOOD 4     [GLAED-MOOD]
(1788)  FLET- 1 -SITTEN-1-DUM 9   [FLET-SITTENDUM]
(1789)  NIHT- 9 -HELM 4      [NIHT-HELM]
(1790)  DRYHT- 4 -GUMU= 9    [DRYHT-GUMU=]
(1793)  RAND- 2 -WIGAN 4     [RAND-WIGAN]
(1796)  AND- 0 -RYSNUM 9     [AND-RYSNUM]
(1800)  GOLD- 2 -FAAH 3      [GOLD-FAAH]
(1823)  MOOD- 3 -LUFAN 4     [MOOD-LUFAN]
(1827)  YMB- 9 -SIT-1-TEND 4 [YMB-SITTEND]
(1840)  =AND- 0 -SWARE 4     [=AND-SWARE]
(1841)  WORD- 2 -CWYDAS 5    [WORD-CWYDAS]
(1845)  WORD- 9 -CWIDA 5     [WORD-CWIDA]
(1852)  HORD- 2 -WEARD 4     [HORD-WEARD]
(1853)  MOOD- 4 -SEFA 4      [MOOD-SEFA]
(1858)  INWIT- 3 -NIITHAS 9  [INWIT-NIITHAS]
(1877)  BREEOST- 9 -WYLM 3   [BREEOST-WYLM]
(1881)  GOLD- 9 -WLANC 5     [GOLD-WLANC]
(1883)  ()AGED*AAGEND- 1 -FREEAN 3   [*AAGEND-FREEAN]
(1890)  LAND- 3 -WEARD 3     [LAND-WEARD]
(1891)  EFT- 2 -SIIDH 4      [EFT-SIIDH]
(1897)  HRINGED- 3 -STEFNA 5 [HRINGED-STEFNA]
(1899)  HORD- 2 -GE- 2       [HORD-GE-STREEONUM]
(1900)  BAAT- 1 -WEARDE 9    [BAAT-WEARDE]
(1906)  SUND- 2 -WUDU 4      [SUND-WUDU]
(1913)  LYFT- 4 -GE- 4       [LYFT-GE-SWENCED]
(1917)  SIID- 1 -FAETHME 3   [SIID-FAETHME]
(1921)  FAEAET- 3 -GOLD 3    [FAEAET-GOLD]
(1925)  BET- 2 -LIIC 5       [BET-LIIC]
(1931)  MOOD- 3 -THRYYDHO 3  [MOOD-THRYYDHO]
(1937)  HAND- 3 -GE- 1       [HAND-GE-WRITHENE]
(1938)  MUND- 3 -GRIPE 5     [MUND-GRIPE]
```

FIRST MORPHEME TERMINATES IN SPIRANT

```
(1321)  $HROODH- 3 -GAAR 5   [HROODH-GAAR]
(1350)  -WIS- 0 -LIICOST 9   [GE-WIS-LIICOST]
(1358)  WULF- 3 -HLEOTHU 4   [WULF-HLEOTHU]
(1365)  NIIDH- 2 -WUNDOR 5   [NIIDH-WUNDOR]
(1368)  HAEAEDH- 4 -STAPA 5  [HAEAEDH-STAPA]
```

```
1373) YYDH- 1 -GE- 2   [YYDH-GE-BLOND]
1399) HROODH- 1 -GAARE 6   [HROODH-GAARE]
1407) HROODH- 2 -GAARE 9   [HROODH-GAARE]
1424) FUUS- 8 -LIIC 9   [FUUS-LIIC]
1427) NAES- 5 -HLEODHUM 3   [NAES-HLEODHUM]
1432) GUUDH- 5 -HORN 2   [GUUDH-HORN]
1434) YYDH- 1 -GE- 1   [YYDH-GE-WINNES]
1456) HROODH- 2 -GAARES 5   [HROODH-GAARES]
1474) HEALF- 2 -DENES 9   [HEALF-DENES]
1479) FORDH- 4 -GE- 1   [FORDH-GE-WITENUM]
1483) HROODH- 1 -GAAR 5   [HROODH-GAAR]
1501) GUUDH- 2 -RINC 4   [GUUDH-RINC]
1513) NIIDH- 3 -SELE 4   [NIIDH-SELE]
1515) HROOF- 9 -SELE 5   [HROOF-SELE]
1520) OF- 1 -TEEAH 5   [OF-TEEAH]
1522) GUUDH- 4 -LEEODH 9   [GUUDH-LEEODH]
1538) GUUDH- 1 -GEEATA 4   [GUUDH-GEEATA]
1545) $OF- 1 -SAET 2   [OF-SAET]
1559) WEORDH- 3 -MYND 5   [WEORDH-MYND]
1577) GUUDH- 1 -RAEAESA 9   [GUUDH-RAEAESA]
1580) HROODH- 3 -GAARES 5   [HROODH-GAARES]
1580) HEORDH- 3 -GE- 2   [HEORDH-GE-NEEATAS]
1582) FYYF- 0 -TYY-9-NE 4   [FYYF-TYYNE]
1583) OF- 2 -FEREDE 4   [OF-FEREDE]
1584) LAADH- 2 -LICU 9   [LAADH-LICU]
1586) GUUDH- 2 -WEERIGNE 9   [GUUDH-WEERIGNE]
1592) HROODH- 1 -GAARE 5   [HROODH-GAARE]
1593) YYDH- 2 -GE- 3   [YYDH-GE-BLOND]
1600) OF- 3 -GEEAFON 3   [OF-GEEAFON]
1620) YYDH- 1 -GE- 3   [YYDH-GE-BLAND]
1622) OF- 0 -LEET 3   [OF-LEET]
1622) LIIF- 2 -DAGAS 6   [LIIF-DAGAS]
1624) SWIIDH- 9 -MOOD 4   [SWIIDH-MOOD]
1627) DHRYYDH- 4 -LIIC 4   [DHRYYDH-LIIC]
1636) EARFODH- 2 -LIICE 4   [EARFODH-LIICE]
1646) HROODH- 1 -GAAR 5   [HROODH-GAAR]
1649) EGES- 3 -LIIC 2   [EGES-LIIC]
1652) HEALF- 1 -DENES 9   [HEALF-DENES]
1657) EAR-1-FODH- 3 -LIICE 9   [EARFODH-LIICE]
1665) OF- 8 -SLOOH 3   [OF-SLOOH]
1670) DEEADH- 9 -CWEALM 4   [DEEADH-CWEALM]
1681) OF- 1 -GEAF 4   [OF-GEAF]
1687) HROODH- 2 -GAAR 4   [HROODH-GAAR]
1689) OF- 2 -SLOOH 9   [OF-SLOOH]
1699) HEALF- 2 -DENES 6   [HEALF-DENES]
1712) DEEADH- 3 -CWALUM 4   [DEEADH-CWALUM]
1750) FORDH- 9 -GE- 1   [FORDH-GE-SCEAFT]
1752) WEORDH- 4 -MYNDA 4   [WEORDH-MYNDA]
1802) BLIIDH- 4 -HEORT 3   [BLIIDH-HEORT]
1809) LEEOF- 0 -LIIC 4   [LEEOF-LIIC]
1810) GUUDH- 2 -WINE 9   [GUUDH-WINE]
1813) SIIDH- 3 -FROME 5   [SIIDH-FROME]
1816) HROODH- 9 -GAAR 5   [HROODH-GAAR]
1825) GUUDH- 3 -GE- 9   [GUUDH-GE-WEORCA]
1836) HREETH- 0 -()RINC*RIIC 5   [*HREETH-RIIC]
1840) $HROODH- 2 -GAAR 5   [HROODH-GAAR]
1863) LUF- 3 -TAACEN 4   [LUF-TAACEN]
1867) HEALF- 2 -DE-2-NES 6   [HEALF-DENES]
1881) GUUDH- 1 -RINC 4   [GUUDH-RINC]
1881) GRAES- 4 -MOLDAN 4   [GRAES-MOLDAN]
1884) HROODH- 3 -GAARES 5   [HROODH-GAARES]
1899) HROODH- 3 -GAARES 9   [HROODH-GAARES]
1904) OF- 1 -GEAF. 9   [OF-GEAF]
1914) HYYDH- 3 -WEARD 3   [HYYDH-WEARD]
```

177

FIRST MORPHEME TERMINATES IN G, X, W, OR H

```
(1383) ECG- 1 -THEEO-9-WES 4   [ECG-THEEOWES]
(1384) AEAEG- 3 -HWAEAEM 4   [AEAEG-HWAEAEM]
(1386) AEAEG- 1 -HWYLC 3   [AEAEG-HWYLC]
(1429) SORH- 9 -FULNE 4   [SORH-FULNE]
(1440) WAEAEG- 4 -BORA 4   [WAEAEG-BORA]
(1465) ECG- 0 -LAAFES 5   [ECG-LAAFES]
(1473) ECG- 1 -THEEOWES 9   [ECG-THEEOWES]
(1489) WAEAEG- 9 -SWEORD 5   [WAEAEG-SWEORD]
(1504) DHURH- 3 -FOON 3   [DHURH-FOON]
(1512) AAG- 0 -LAEAE-1-CAN 5   [AAG-LAEAECAN]
(1521) HRING- 3 -MAEAEL 4   [HRING-MAEAEL]
(1536) LONG- 3 -SUMNE 4   [LONG-SUMNE]
(1540) FEORH- 3 -GE- 3   [FEORH-GE-NIIDHLAN]
(1543) WEERIG- 2 -MOOD 4   [WEERIG-MOOD]
(1550) ECG- 0 -THEEOWES 5   [ECG-THEEOWES]
(1554) WIIG- 9 -SIGOR 4   [WIIG-SIGOR]
(1564) HRING- 9 -MAEAEL 5   [HRING-MAEAEL]
(1567) DHURH- 2 -WOOD 4   [DHURH-WOOD]
(1607) WIIG- 1 -BIL 4   [WIIG-BIL]
(1619) WIIG- 3 -HRYRE 5   [WIIG-HRYRE]
(1619) THURH- 3 -DEEAF 4   [THURH-DEEAF]
(1634) CYNING- 4 -BALDE 4   [CYNING-BALDE]
(1636) AEAEG- 3 -HWAE-1-THRU= 4   [AEAEG-HWAETHRU=]
(1651) ECG- 2 -THEEOWES 9   [ECG-THEEOWES]
(1672) SORH- 2 -LEEAS 5   [SORH-LEEAS]
(1708) LANG- 4 -TWIIDIG 5   [LANG-TWIIDIG]
(1710) ECG- 2 -WELAN 4   [ECG-WELAN]
(1738) ECG- 3 -HETE 9   [ECG-HETE]
(1769) HRING- 2 -DENA 5   [HRING-DENA]
(1783) WIIG- 0 -GE- 5   [WIIG-GE-WEORTHAD]
(1792) -IG- 9 -METES 4   [UN-IG-METES]
(1808) ECG- 0 -LAAFES 4   [ECG-LAAFES]
(1811) WIIG- 2 -CRAEFTIGNE 5   [WIIG-CRAEFTIGNE]
(1817) ECG- 2 -THEEOWES 4   [ECG-THEEOWES]
(1862) HRING- 3 -NACA 4   [HRING-NACA]
(1865) AEAEG- 1 -HWAES 4   [AEAEG-HWAES]
(1886) AEAEG- 2 -HWAES 4   [AEAEG-HWAES]
(1889) HAEG- 3 -STEAL-1-DRA 8   [HAEG-STEALDRA]
(1889) HRING- 4 -NET 3   [HRING-NET]
(1907) WEEG- 2 -FLOTAN 4   [WEEG-FLOTAN]
(1909) FAAMIG- 4 -HEALS 4   [FAAMIG-HEALS]
(1928) BURH- 2 -LOCAN 3   [BURH-LOCAN]
```

FIRST MORPHEME TERMINATES IN NONALPHABETIC SYMBOL

```
(1486) GU=- 2 -CYSTUM 4   [GU=-CYSTUM]
(1702) .=EETHEL.- 2 -WEARD 9   [=EETHEL-WEARD]
(1723) GU=- 2 -CYSTE 9   [GU=-CYSTE]
```

APPENDIX II
LINES 1940 - 3182 (SECOND SCRIBE≠S COPY)

MORPHEME PAIRS GROUPED BY PHONOLOGICAL FEATURES

FIRST MORPHEME TERMINATES IN LONG VOCALIC UNIT

```
(1971) BEEO- 2 -WULFES 3   [BEEO-WULFES]
```

```
987) BIIO- 9 -WULF 4    [BIIO-WULF]
999) $BIIO- 2 -WULF 4   [BIIO-WULF]
022) FREEA- 4 -WARE 9   [FREEA-WARE]
194) BIIO- 2 -WULFES 9  [BIIO-WULFES]
207) BEEO- 1 -WULFE 3   [BEEO-WULFE]
223) THREEA- 4 -NEEDLAN 4   [THREEA-NEEDLAN]
263) GLEEO- 2 -BEEAMES 9    [GLEEO-BEEAMES]
285) FEEA- 2 -SCEAFTU= 3    [FEEA-SCEAFTU=]
324) BIIO- 2 -WULFE 3   [BIIO-WULFE]
357) FREEA- 1 -WINE 3   [FREEA-WINE]
359) BIIO- 1 -WULF 2    [BIIO-WULF]
373) FEEA- 3 -SCEAFTE 9     [FEEA-SCEAFTE]
383) SWIIO- 3 -RIICE 4  [SWIIO-RIICE]
389) BIIO- 2 -WULF 4    [BIIO-WULF]
393) FEEA- 9 -SCEAFTU= 4    [FEEA-SCEAFTU=]
425) BIIO- 2 -WULF 3    [BIIO-WULF]
429) FREEA- 2 -WINE 5   [FREEA-WINE]
438) FREEA- 4 -WINE 4   [FREEA-WINE]
495) SWIIO- 2 -RIICE 5  [SWIIO-RIICE]
510) BEEO- 0 -WULF 2    [BEEO-WULF]
627) FREEO- 3 -DRYHTNE 9    [FREEO-DRYHTNE]
663) BIIO- 1 -WULF 4    [BIIO-WULF]
681) BIIO- 1 -WULFES 9  [BIIO-WULFES]
724) BIIO- 1 -WULF 4    [BIIO-WULF]
807) BIIO- 1 -WULFES 4  [BIIO-WULFES]
842) BIIO- 2 -WULFE 9   [BIIO-WULFE]
907) BIIO- 2 -WULFE 4   [BIIO-WULFE]
922) SWEEO- 9 -DHEEODE 4     [SWEEO-DHEEODE]
021) GLEEO- 3 -DREEAM 9  [GLEEO-DREEAM]
066) BIIO- 1 -WULFE. 9  [BIIO-WULFE]
151) *BIIO- 8 -*WULFE 8     [*BIIO-*WULFE]
964) SAEAE- 4 -WONG 4   [SAEAE-WONG]
986) SAEAE- 2 -GEEATA 3     [SAEAE-GEEATA]
046) AA- 0 -CWYDH. 5    [AA-CWYDH]
063) ()+*AA- 8 -BROCENE 5    [*AA-BROCENE]
092) AA- 0 -STOOD. 7    [AA-STOOD]
108) AA- 0 -WRAEC. 3    [AA-WRAEC]
121) AA- 0 -CWEALDE 4   [AA-CWEALDE]
194) AA- 0 -LEGDE. 5    [AA-LEGDE]
221) ()CRAEFT*AA- 8 -*BRAEC 5   [*AA-*BRAEC]
280) AA- 0 -BEALCH 4    [AA-BEALCH]
382) SAEAE- 0 -CYNINGA 4     [SAEAE-CYNINGA]
403) AA- 0 -RAAS. 4     [AA-RAAS]
418) AA- 0 -BEEAD 4     [AA-BEEAD]
432) OO- 0 -WIHTE 5     [OO-WIHTE]
487) TOO- 0 -GLAAD 9    [TOO-GLAAD]
538) AA- 0 -RAAS 0  [AA-RAAS]
568) TOO- 0 -SOMNE 4    [TOO-SOMNE]
575) AA- 0 -BRAEAED. 5  [AA-BRAEAED]
591) AA- 0 -LAEAETAN 3  [AA-LAEAETAN]
619) AA- 0 -BRED-2-WADE. 7   [AA-BREDWADE]
630) TOO- 1 -GAEDRE 4   [TOO-GAEDRE]
643) AA- 0 -DHOOHTE 5   [AA-DHOOHTE]
665) AA- 0 -LAEAETE 9   [AA-LAEAETE]
690) AA- 0 -GEALD 9     [AA-GEALD]
707) AA- 0 -BRO-9-TEN 2  [AA-BROTEN]
750) AA- 0 -LAEAETAN 3  [AA-LAEAETAN]
806) SAEAE- 1 -LIIDHEND 4    [SAEAE-LIIDHEND]
852) WII- 0 -LAAF 5     [WII-LAAF]
870) OO- 0 -WER 3   [OO-WER]
886) AA- 3 -LICGEAN 9   [AA-LICGEAN]
929) AA- 0 -GEAF 4  [AA-GEAF]
930) AA- 0 -BREEOT 9    [AA-BREEOT]
930) AA- 4 -()HEORDE*HREDDE 4   [*AA-HREDDE]
948) TOO- 2 -WEHTON. 4  [TOO-WEHTON]
```

179

```
(2954) SAEAE- 1 -MANNU= 4   [SAEAE-MANNU=]
(2983) AA- 0 -RAEAERDON 3   [AA-RAEAERDON]
(3020) AA- 0 -LEGDE 4   [AA-LEGDE]
(3030) AA- 0 -RAAS 3   [AA-RAAS]
(3052) IUU- 1 -MONNA 4   [IUU-MONNA]
(3078) AA- 1 -()DREOGEDH*DREEOGAN 4   [*AA-DREEOGAN]
(3089) AA- 0 -LYYFED 3   [AA-LYYFED]
(3114) TOO- 1 -GEENES 3   [TOO-GEENES]
(3121) AA- 0 -CIIGDE 3   [AA-CIIGDE]
(3122) ()++*TOO- 8 -SOMNE 4   [*TOO-SOMNE]
(3141) AA- 0 -LEGDON 2   [AA-LEGDON]
(3141) TOO- 9 -MIDDES 4   [TOO-MIDDES]
(3144) AA- 0 -STAAH 3   [AA-STAAH]
(2931) IOO- 4 -MEEOWLAN 9   [IOO-MEEOWLAN]
(3150) *GEOO- 8 -MEEOWLE 8   [*GEOO-MEEOWLE]
```

FIRST MORPHEME TERMINATES IN SHORT VOCALIC UNIT

```
(1942) FREODHU- 4 -WEBBE 3   [FREODHU-WEBBE]
(1945) EALO- 3 -DRINCENDE 4   [EALO-DRINCENDE]
(1974) HEADHO- 2 -LAAGES. 5   [HEADHO-LAAGES]
(1975) BE- 1 -BEEAD 4   [BE-BEEAD]
(1976) FEEDHE- 3 -GESTU= 5   [FEEDHE-GESTU=]
(1980) MEODU- 3 -SCENCU= 4   [MEODU-SCENCU=]
(2006) BE- 9 -GYLPAN 4   [BE-GYLPAN]
(2009) BI- 0 -FONGEN 4   [BI-FONGEN]
(2016) MEDU- 4 -DREEAM 4   [MEDU-DREEAM]
(2017) FRIDHU- 4 -SIBB 3   [FRIDHU-SIBB]
(2021) EALU- 3 -WAEAEGE 3   [EALU-WAEAEGE]
(2032) HEADHO- 9 -BEARDNA 5   [HEADHO-BEARDNA]
(2035) BI- 0 -WENEDE. 9   [BI-WENEDE]
(2037) HEADHA- 4 -()BEARNA*BEARDNA 3   [*HEADHA-BEARDNA]
(2049) HERE- 3 -GRIIMAN 4   [HERE-GRIIMAN]
(2067) HEADHO- 2 -()BEARNA*BEARDNA 4   [*HEADHO-BEARDNA]
(2079) ()MAGU=*MAGU- 4 -THEGNE 9   [*MAGU-THEGNE]
(2085) ()GEAREO*GEARO- 3 -FOLM 3   [*GEARO-FOLM]
(2086) SEARO- 3 -BENDU= 4   [SEARO-BENDU=]
(2100) MER-1-E- 1 -GRUND 9   [MERE-GRUND]
(2106) FELA- 2 -FRICGENDE 8   [FELA-FRICGENDE]
(2107) HILDE- 3 -DEEOR 4   [HILDE-DEEOR]
(2113) HILDE- 4 -STRENGO 4   [HILDE-STRENGO]
(2116) BE- 0 -CWOOM. 9   [BE-CWOOM]
(2130) BE- 0 -GEEATE. 7   [BE-GEEATE]
(2136) GRYRE- 2 -LIICNE 9   [GRYRE-LIICNE]
(2138) BE- 1 -CEARF 6   [BE-CEARF]
(2153) HEADHO- 4 -STEEAPNE 5   [HEADHO-STEEAPNE]
(2154) GEATO- 1 -LIIC 9   [GEATO-LIIC]
(2155) HILDE- 3 -SCEORP 9   [HILDE-SCEORP]
(2158) HIOR-1-O- 1 -GAAR 4   [HIORO-GAAR]
(2161) HEORO- 3 -WEARDE 5   [HEORO-WEARDE]
(2183) HILDE- 9 -DEEOR 2   [HILDE-DEEOR]
(2185) MEDO- 2 -BENCE 4   [MEDO-BENCE]
(2191) HEADHO- 3 -ROOF 2   [HEADHO-ROOF]
(2196) BREGO- 3 -STOOL 5   [BREGO-STOOL]
(2201) HILDE- 9 -HLAEM-2-MU= 6   [HILDE-HLAEMMU=]
(2202) HILDE- 3 -MEECEAS 4   [HILDE-MEECEAS]
(2205) HEADHO- 4 -SCILFINGAS. 5   [HEADHO-SCILFINGAS]
(2206) HERE- 3 -RIICES 3   [HERE-RIICES]
(2212) BE- 3 -WEOTODE 9   [BE-WEOTODE]
(2217) ()+++++*BE- 8 -*MAADH 8   [*BE-*MAADH]
(2218) BE- 9 -()SYRE+*SYRED 8   [*BE-SYRED]
(2224) HETE- 4 -SWENGEAS 9   [HETE-SWENGEAS]
(2227) ()+++++*GRYRE- 8 -BROOGA 8   [*GRYRE-BROOGA]
(2230) BE- 0 -GEAT 4   [BE-GEAT]
```

```
2239) WINE- 4 -GEOO-1-MOR 5    [WINE-GECOMOR]
2243) NEARO- 9 -CRAEFTU= 4    [NEARO-CRAEFTU=]
2249) BE- 0 -GEEATON 9    [BE-GEEATON]
2252) SELE- 3 -DREEAM 9    [SELE-DREEAM]
2256) BE- 2 -FEALLEN 4    [BE-FEALLEN]
2257) BEADO- 3 -GRIIMAN 3    [BEADO-GRIIMAN]
2258) HERE- 4 -+PAAD 2    [HERE-PAAD]
2265) BEALO- 9 -CWEALM 3    [BEALO-CWEALM]
2274) BE- 2 -FANGEN 2    [BE-FANGEN]
2282) FRIODHO- 3 -WAEAERE 3    [FRIODHO-WAEAERE]
2296) YMBE- 7 -HWEARF 3    [YMBE-HWEARF]
2313) BRYNE- 9 -LEEOMA 4    [BRYNE-LEEOMA]
2317) NEARO- 2 -FAAGES 3    [NEARO-FAAGES]
2321) BE- 1 -FANGEN 6    [BE-FANGEN]
326) BRYNE- 4 -WYLMU= 5    [BRYNE-WYLMU=]
2351) HILDE- 5 -HLEM-1-MA 5    [HILDE-HLEMMA]
2358) HIORO- 3 -DRYNCUM 4    [HIORO-DRYNCUM]
2362) HILDE- 3 -GEAT-2-WA 3    [HILDE-GEATWA]
2364) FEEDHE- 4 -WIIGES 3    [FEEDHE-WIIGES]
365) BE- 1 -CWOOM 4    [BE-CWOOM]
2367) BI- 0 -GONG 3    [BI-GONG]
2370) BREGO- 9 -STOOL 3    [BREGO-STOOL]
2376) CYNE- 2 -+DOOM 3    [CYNE-DOOM]
2389) BREGO- 3 -STOOL 5    [BREGO-STOOL]
396) BI- 0 -NEEAT. 6    [BI-NEEAT]
2404) BEALO- 3 -NIIDH 4    [BEALO-NIIDH]
2424) BE- 1 -WUNDEN. 7    [BE-WUNDEN]
2434) HERE- 1 -BEALD 9    [HERE-BEALD]
2435) -DEEFE- 0 -LIICE 5    [UN-GE-DEEFE-LIICE]
2453) YRFE- 9 -WEARDAS 4    [YRFE-WEARDAS]
2457) BE- 3 -ROFENE 9    [BE-ROFENE]
2463) HERE- 3 -BEALDE 4    [HERE-BEALDE]
2466) HEADHO- 2 -RINC 3    [HEADHO-RINC]
2468) BE- 2 -LAMP 1    [BE-LAMP]
2474) HERE- 3 -NIIDH 3    [HERE-NIIDH]
2477) HREEOSNA- 4 -BEORH 3    [HREEOSNA-BEORH]
2488) *HEORO- 8 -BLAAC 2    [*HEORO-BLAAC]
2497) BE- 0 -FORAN 3    [BE-FORAN]
2507) HILDE- 3 -GRAAP 3    [HILDE-GRAAP]
2522) HEADHU- 3 -FYYRES 2    [HEADHU-FYYRES]
2539) HIORO- 3 -SERCEAN 2    [HIORO-SERCEAN]
2544) HILDE- 4 -HLEM-2-MA 3    [HILDE-HLEMMA]
2547) HEADHO- 9 -FYYRU= 4    [HEADHO-FYYRU=]
2552) BE- 1 -COOM 2    [BE-COOM]
2553) HEADHO- 2 -TORHT 3    [HEADHO-TORHT]
2558) HILDE- 3 -+SWAAT 4    [HILDE-SWAAT]
2560) GRYRE- 3 -GIESTE 4    [GRYRE-GIESTE]
2565) BEALO- 3 -HYCGENDRA 9    [BEALO-HYCGENDRA]
2576) GRYRE- 3 -FAAH-1-NE 2    [GRYRE-FAAHNE]
577) INC-1-GE- 1 -LAAFE 3    [INCGE-LAAFE]
2581) HEADHU- 3 -SWENGE 3    [HEADHU-SWENGE]
2583) HILDE- 3 -LEEOMAN 5    [HILDE-LEEOMAN]
2595) BE- 0 -FONGEN 4    [BE-FONGEN]
2598) HILDE- 9 -CYSTU= 4    [HILDE-CYSTU=]
2605) HERE- 3 -GRIIMAN 4    [HERE-GRIIMAN]
2613) WINE- 3 -LEEASU= 4    [WINE-LEEASU=]
2647) BE- 2 -HOOFADH 3    [BE-HOOFADH]
2660) ()BRYDU*BEADU- 2 -SCRUUD 8    [*BEADU-SCRUUD]
2679) HILDE- 3 -BILLE 8    [HILDE-BILLE]
2691) HEADHO- 2 -GRIM 3    [HEADHO-GRIM]
2691) YMBE- 3 -FEENG 9    [YMBE-FEENG]
2704) BEADU- 9 -SCEARP 5    [BEADU-SCEARP]
2714) BEALO- 8 -NIIDHE 9    [BEALO-NIIDHE]
2720) HEORO- 3 -DREEORIGNE 8    [HEORO-DREEORIGNE]
2722) WINE- 1 -DRYHTEN 9    [WINE-DRYHTEN]
```

181

```
(2731) YRFE- 9 -WEARD 2    [YRFE-WEARD]
(2734) YMBE- 4 -SITTENDRA 5    [YMBE-SITTENDRA]
(2738) SEARO- 4 -NIIDHAS 3    [SEARO-NIIDHAS]
(2746) BE- 0 -REEAFOD 3    [BE-REEAFOD]
(2749) SEARO- 9 -GI=MAS 3    [SEARO-GI=MAS]
(2754) HEADHO- 3 -SIIOCU= 5    [HEADHO-SIIOCU=]
(2755) BEADU- 4 -SER-2-CEAN 4    [BEADU-SERCEAN]
(2757) MAGO- 3 -THEGN 9    [MAGO-THEGN]
(2762) BE- 1 -HRORENE 4    [BE-HRORENE]
(2769) LEODHO- 3 -CRAEFTU= 4    [LEODHO-CRAEFTU=]
(2781) HIORO- 4 -WEALLENDE 4    [HIORO-WEALLENDE]
(2799) BE- 9 -BOHTE 3    [BE-BOHTE]
(2802) HEADHO- 3 -MAEAERE 4    [HEADHO-MAEAERE]
(2813) ENDE- 1 -LAAF 3    [ENDE-LAAF]
(2819) HEADHO- 3 -WYLMAS 3    [HEADHO-WYLMAS]
(2825) BE- 1 -REEAFOD 3    [BE-REEAFOD]
(2829) HEADHO- 2 -SCEAR-9-()DE*PE 4    [*HEADHO-SCEARPE]
(2853) FEEDHE- 2 -CEMPA 4    [FEEDHE-CEMPA]
(2867) EALU- 2 -BENCE 3    [EALU-BENCE]
(2872) BE- 0 -GET 4    [BE-GET]
(2883) BE- 8 -CWOOM. 6    [BE-CWOOM]
(2892) HEADHO- 4 -WEORC 4    [HEADHO-WEORC]
(2896) ENDE- 2 -DOOGORES 9    [ENDE-DOOGORES]
(2921) MERE- 4 -WIIO-3-INGAS 0    [MERE-WIIOINGAS]
(2924) BE- 2 -SNYDHEDE 3    [BE-SNYDHEDE]
(2925) HREF-1-NA- 3 -WUDU 4    [HREFNA-WUDU]
(2931) BE- 0 -ROFENE 5    [BE-ROFENE]
(2936) BE- 0 -SAET 1    [BE-SAET]
(2950) FELA- 2 -GEOOMOR 4    [FELA-GEOOMOR]
(2955) HEADHO- 0 -LIIDHENDU= 4    [HEADHO-LIIDHENDU=]
(2959) FREODHO- 3 -WONG 3    [FREODHO-WONG]
(2992) BE- 0 -+COOM 9    [BE-COOM]
(3018) BE- 1 -REEAFOD 9    [BE-REEAFOD]
(3020) HERE- 9 -WIISA 4    [HERE-WIISA]
(3022) BE- 2 -WUNDEN 4    [BE-WUNDEN]
(3031) EARNA- 4 -NAES 3    [EARNA-NAES]
(3035) ENDE- 3 -DAEG 3    [ENDE-DAEG]
(3041) ()GRY++++++*GRYRE- 8 -*FAAH 9    [*GRYRE-*FAAH]
(3041) BE- 3 -SWAEAELED 3    [BE-SWAEAELED]
(3052) BE- 9 -WUNDEN 4    [BE-WUNDEN]
(3065) MEDU- 2 -SELD 3    [MEDU-SELD]
(3067) SEARO- 3 -NIIDHAS 2    [SEARO-NIIDHAS]
(3069) BE- 9 -NEM-1-DON 4    [BE-NEMDON]
(3102) SEARO- 3 -*GIMMA 8    [SEARO-*GIMMA]
(3111) HILDE- 3 -DIIOR 4    [HILDE-DIIOR]
(3124) HILDE- 3 -()RINC*RINCA 3    [*HILDE-RINCA]
(3136) HILDE- 8 -*RINC 8    [HILDE-*RINC]
(3139) BE- 0 -HONGEN 3    [BE-HONGEN]
(3139) HILDE- 2 -BORDU= 9    [HILDE-BORDU=]
(3144) ()WUDU+*WUDU- 8 -+REEC 2    [*WUDU-REEC]
(3146) BE- 4 -WUNDEN 2    [BE-WUNDEN]
(3159) BE- 0 -TIM-9-BREDON 3    [BE-TIMBREDON]
(3160) BEADU- 1 -ROO-1-()FIS*FES 2    [*BEADU-ROOFES]
(3161) BE- 2 -WORHTON 3    [BE-WORHTON]
(3162) ()FO++*FORE- 9 -()+NOTRE*SNOTRE 2    [*FORE-SNOTRE]
(3169) HILDE- 2 -DEEORE 3    [HILDE-DEEORE]
(3175) WINE- 2 -DRYH= 1    [WINE-DRYH=]
(3178) BE- 0 -GNORNODON 2    [BE-GNORNODON]
(1943) LIGE- 3 -TORNE 2    [LIGE-TORNE]
(1970) HIGE- 0 -LAACE 9    [HIGE-LAACE]
(1983) HIGE- 2 -LAAC 3    [HIGE-LAAC]
(2000) HIGE- 8 -LAAC 8    [HIGE-LAAC]
(2004) SIGE- 8 -SCYL-9-DI-8-NGU= 5    [SIGE-SCYLDINGU=]
(2151) HYGE- 0 -LAAC 1    [HYGE-LAAC]
(2169) HYGE- 0 -LAACE 3    [HYGE-LAACE]
```

```
2201)  HYGE- 0 -LAAC 2    [HYGE-LAAC]
2204)  SIGE- 4 -THEEODE 4    [SIGE-THEEODE]
2328)  HYGE- 4 -SORGA 4    [HYGE-SORGA]
2355)  HYGE- 0 -LAAC 3    [HYGE-LAAC]
2372)  HYGE- 1 -LAAC 3    [HYGE-LAAC]
2386)  HYGE- 1 -LAACES. 4    [HYGE-LAACES]
2408)  HYGE- 3 -GIOOMOR 4    [HYGE-GIOOMOR]
2434)  HYGE- 0 -LAAC 4    [HYGE-LAAC]
2442)  HYGE- 3 -MEEDHE 4    [HYGE-MEEDHE]
2710)  SIGE- 4 -HWIILE 4    [SIGE-HWIILE]
2756)  SIGE- 3 -HREEDHIG 4    [SIGE-HREEDHIG]
2909)  HIGE- 3 -MAEAEDHUM 9    [HIGE-MAEAEDHUM]
2914)  HIGE- 2 -LAAC 2    [HIGE-LAAC]
2943)  HYGE- 3 -LAACES 4    [HYGE-LAACES]
2952)  HIGE- 2 -LAACES 9    [HIGE-LAACES]
2958)  HIGE- 3 -()LACE*LAACES. 9    [*HIGE-LAACES]
2977)  HIGE- 9 -LAACES 3    [HIGE-LAACES]
2988)  HIGE- 3 -LAACE 1    [HIGE-LAACE]

1946)  GE- 1 -FREMEDE 3    [GE-FREMEDE]
1951)  GE- 0 -SOOHTE 9    [GE-SOOHTE]
1955)  GE- 1 -FRAEAEGE 4    [GE-FRAEAEGE]
1959)  GE- 9 -WEORUHOD 4    [GE-WEORDHOD]
1963)  $$GE- 2 -WAAT 3    [GE-WAAT]
1967)  GE- 3 -EEODON 5    [GE-EEODON]
1969)  GE- 2 -FRUUNON 5    [GE-FRUUNON]
1971)  GE- 0 -CYYDHED 3    [GE-CYYDHED]
1975)  GE- 3 -RYYMED 9    [GE-RYYMED]
1977)  GE- 0 -SAET 3    [GE-SAET]
1977)  GE- 2 -NAES 4    [GE-NAES]
1979)  GE- 3 -GREETTE 6    [GE-GREETTE]
1984)  GE- 1 -SELDAN 4    [GE-SELDAN]
1988)  GE- 1 -HOGODEST. 9    [GE-HOGODEST]
1991)  GE- 0 -BEETTEST 5    [GE-BEETTEST]
1996)  GE- 1 -WEORDHAN 9    [GE-WEORDHAN]
1998)  GE- 0 -SUNDNE 4    [GE-SUNDNE]
1998)  GE- 1 -SEEON 3    [GE-SEEON]
2001)  GE- 0 -MEETING 5    [GE-MEETING]
2004)  GE- 1 -FREMEDE 3    [GE-FREMEDE]
2005)  GE- 2 -WRAEC 4    [GE-WRAEC]
2013)  GE- 0 -TAEAEHTE. 9    [GE-TAEAEHTE]
2024)  GE- 2 -HAATEN 9    [GE-HAATEN]
2026)  GE- 1 -WORDEN 4    [GE-WORDEN]
2029)  GE- 0 -SETTE 2    [GE-SETTE]
2033)  GE- 1 -HWAAM 4    [GE-HWAAM]
2037)  GE- 1 -STREEON 9    [GE-STREEON]
2040)  GE- 0 -SIIDHAS 4    [GE-SIIDHAS]
2041)  GE- 1 -SYHDH 4    [GE-SYHDH]
2042)  GE- 8 -()+++*MAN 9    [*GE-MAN]
2045)  GE- 2 -HYGD 8    [GE-HYGD]
2047)  GE- 0 -CNAAWAN 4    [GE-CNAAWAN]
2048)  GE- 0 -FEOHTE 9    [GE-FEOHTE]
2057)  GE- 1 -HWYLCE. 6    [GE-HWYLCE]
2075)  GE- 0 -SUNDE 4    [GE-SUNDE]
2082)  GE- 1 -MYNDIG 5    [GE-MYNDIG]
2087)  GE- 2 -GYRWED 3    [GE-GYRWED]
2090)  GE- 1 -+DOON 3    [GE-DOON]
2094)  GE- 1 -HWYLCES 3    [GE-HWYLCES]
2100)  GE- 1 -FEEOLL 5    [GE-FEEOLL]
2104)  GE- 0 -SETEN 9    [GE-SETEN]
2111)  GE- 0 -BUNDEN 4    [GE-BUNDEN]
2114)  GE- 8 -MUNDE 5    [GE-MUNDE]
2121)  GE- 1 -WRAEC 9    [GE-WRAEC]
2132)  GE- 1 -THRING 3    [GE-THRING]
2133)  GE- 1 -NEEDH-3-DE. 5    [GE-NEEDHDE]
```

133

```
(2134) GE- 1 -HEET 3    [GE-HEET]
(2137) GE- 1 -MAEAENE. 3    [GE-MAEAENE]
(2142) GE- 0 -SEALDE 5    [GE-SEALDE]
(2149) GE- 9 -YYWAN 3    [GE-YYWAN]
(2150) GE- 0 -LONG 9    [GE-LONG]
(2157) GE- 1 -SAEGDE 9    [GE-SAEGDE]
(2164) GE- 0 -LIICE 4    [GE-LIICE]
(2165) GE- 9 -TEEAH 4    [GE-TEEAH]
(2171) GE- 1 -HWAEDHER 9    [GE-HWAEDHER]
(2171) GE- 1 -MYNDIG. 6    [GE-MYNDIG]
(2172) GE- 9 -SEALDE 5    [GE-SEALDE]
(2176) GE- 1 -WEOR-2-DHOD. 5    [GE-WEORDHOD]
(2186) GE- 1 -DOON 3    [GE-DOON]
(2189) GE- 0 -HWYLCES. 5    [GE-HWYLCES]
(2190) GE- 3 -FETIAN. 6    [GE-FETIAN]
(2192) GE- 2 -GYREDE 3    [GE-GYREDE]
(2195) GE- 2 -SEALDE 4    [GE-SEALDE]
(2197) GE- 0 -CYNDE 4    [GE-CYNDE]
(2200) GE- 3 -IIODE 4    [GE-IIODE]
(2204) GE- 1 -SOOHTAN 4    [GE-SOOHTAN]
(2206) GE- 9 -NAEAEGDAN. 5    [GE-NAEAEGDAN]
(2208) GE- 8 -HWEARF 9    [GE-HWEARF]
(2208) GE- 3 -HEEOLD 4    [GE-HEEOLD]
(2215) GE- 8 -()FENG*FEALG 3    [*GE-FEALG]
(2220) GE- 9 -()BOLGE+*BOLGEN 8    [*GE-BOLGEN]
(2221) GE- 3 -WEALDU= 4    [GE-WEALDU=]
(2222) GE- 9 -SCEOOD 5    [GE-SCEOOD]
(2235) GE- 9 -HYYDDE. 5    [GE-HYYDDE]
(2250) GE- 1 -HWYLCNE. 5    [GE-HWYLCNE]
(2252) GE- 1 -SAAWON 4    [GE-SAAWON]
(2258) GE- 1 -BAAD 5    [GE-BAAD]
(2259) GE- 1 -BRAED 9    [GE-BRAED]
(2275) GE- 4 -SEECEAN 4    [GE-SEECEAN]
(2284) GE- 0 -TIIDHAD 4    [GE-TIIDHAD]
(2287) GE- 1 -NIIWAD. 5    [GE-NIIWAD]
(2289) GE- 0 -STOOP. 6    [GE-STOOP]
(2291) GE- 0 -DIIGAN 4    [GE-DIIGAN]
(2293) GE- 0 -HEALDETH 3    [GE-HEALDETH]
(2295) GE- 0 -TEEODE. 6    [GE-TEEODE]
(2298) GE- 2 -FEH 2    [GE-FEH]
(2301) GE- 9 -FAN-1-DOO 3    [GE-FANDOD]
(2304) GE- 2 -BOL-1-GEN 5    [GE-BOLGEN]
(2309) GE- 1 -FYYSED 3    [GE-FYYSED]
(2316) GE- 1 -SYYNE 9    [GE-SYYNE]
(2319) GE- 1 -SCEEAT. 5    [GE-SCEEAT]
(2322) GE- 1 -TRUWODE 5    [GE-TRUWODE]
(2323) GE- 1 -LEEAH 4    [GE-LEEAH]
(2324) GE- 0 -CYY-9-DHED 3    [GE-CYYDHED]
(2331) GE- 0 -BULGE 9    [GE-BULGE]
(2332) GE- 1 -THONCUM 9    [GE-THONCUM]
(2332) GE- 0 -THYYWE 5    [GE-THYYWE]
(2337) GE- 3 -WYRCEAN 4    [GE-WYRCEAN]
(2342) GE- 9 -BIIDAN 4    [GE-BIIDAN]
(2346) GE- 1 -SOOHTE 9    [GE-SOOHTE]
(2350) GE- 0 -DIIGDE. 9    [GE-DIIGDE]
(2359) GE- 0 -BEEATEN 9    [GE-BEEATEN]
(2369) GE- 0 -BEEAD 4    [GE-BEEAD]
(2387) GE- 1 -WAAT 4    [GE-WAAT]
(2391) GE- 0 -MUNDE 9    [GE-MUNDE]
(2393) GE- 0 -STEEPTE. 5    [GE-STEEPTE]
(2395) GE- 2 -WRAEC 3    [GE-WRAEC]
(2397) GE- 1 -HWANE 5    [GE-HWANE]
(2397) GE- 0 -NESEN 3    [GE-NESEN]
(2398) GE- 1 -SLYHTA 9    [GE-SLYHTA]
(2400) GE- 0 -WEGAN 9    [GE-WEGAN]
```

```
2401) GE- 3 -WAAT 2    [GE-WAAT]
2401) GE- 9 -BOLGEN 4   [GE-BOLGEN]
2403) GE- 3 -FRUU-1-NEN 3   [GE-FRUUNEN]
2416) GE- 1 -GAN-1-GENNE 4    [GE-GANGENNE]
2417) GE- 1 -SAET 0   [GE-SAET]
2422) GE- 0 -OAEAELAN 3   [GE-DAEAELAN]
2426) GE- 1 -NAES 4    [GE-NAES]
2427) GE- 2 -MON. 9    [GE-MON]
2429) GE- 0 -NAM 5    [GE-NAM]
2431) GE- 0 -MUNDE 9   [GE-MUNDE]
2438) GE- 9 -SWENC-1-TE 5   [GE-SWENCTE]
2441) GE- 1 -FEOHT 3    [GE-FEOHT]
2441) GE- 1 -SYNGAD. 4    [GE-SYNGAD]
2445) GE- 1 -BIIDANNE 9    [GE-BIIDANNE]
2449) GE- 1 -FREMMAN 9    [GE-FREMMAN]
2450) GE- 2 -MYNDGAD 5    [GE-MYNDGAD]
2450) GE- 0 -HWYLCE 9    [GE-HWYLCE]
2452) GE- 0 -BIIDANNE 3    [GE-BIIDANNE]
2454) GE- 1 -FONDAD. 4    [GE-FONDAD]
2455) GE- 0 -SYHDH 4    [GE-SYHDH]
2460) $$GE- 2 -WIITEDH 4    [GE-WIITEDH]
2465) GE- 0 -BEETAN 5    [GE-BEETAN]
2469) GE- 0 -CEEAS 3    [GE-CEEAS]
2471) GE- 1 -WAAT 4    [GE-WAAT]
2473) GE- 1 -MAEAENE. 6    [GE-MAEAENE]
2478) GE- 2 -FREMEDON. 5    [GE-FREMEDON]
2479) GE- 3 -WRAEAECAN 4    [GE-WRAEAECAN]
2480) GE- 1 -FRAEAEGE 4    [GE-FRAEAEGE]
2481) GE- 3 -BOHTE 5    [GE-BOHTE]
2484) GE- 1 -FRAEGN 4    [GE-FRAEGN]
2488) GE- 9 -MUNDE.. 7    [GE-MUNDE]
2489) GE- 0 -NOOGE 4    [GE-NOOGE]
2496) GE- 0 -CYYPAN 8    [GE-CYYPAN]
2500) GE- 1 -LAEAESTE 5    [GE-LAEAESTE]
2505) GE- 0 -CRONG 4    [GE-CRONG]
2508) GE- 0 -BRAEC 3    [GE-BRAEC]
2511) GE- 2 -NEEDHDE 5    [GE-NEEDHDE]
2515) GE- 3 -SEECEDH 4    [GE-SEECEDH]
2516) GE- 0 -GREETTE 4    [GE-GREETTE]
2516) GE- 3 -HWYLCNE 5    [GE-HWYLCNE]
2518) GE- 1 -SIIDHAS 9    [GE-SIIDHAS]
2526) GE- 0 -TEEODH 9    [GE-TEEODH]
2527) GE- 1 -HWAES 4    [GE-HWAES]
2529) GE- 0 -BIIDE 0    [GE-BIIDE]
2531) GE- 2 -DYYGAN. 5    [GE-DYYGAN]
2533) GE- 2 -MET 2    [GE-MET]
2536) GE- 1 -GANGAN 4    [GE-GANGAN]
2540) GE- 3 -TRUWODE 4    [GE-TRUWODE]
2542) GE- 1 -SEAH. 6    [GE-SEAH]
2543) GE- 9 -DIIGDE 3    [GE-DIIGDE]
2549) GE- 2 -DYYGAN 9    [GE-DYYGAN]
2550) GE- 1 -BOLGEN 3    [GE-BOLGEN]
2561) GE- 1 -FYYSED 9    [GE-FYYSED]
2562) GE- 1 -BRAEAED 9    [GE-BRAEAED]
2566) GE- 1 -STOOD 3    [GE-STOOD]
2567) GE- 0 -BEEAH 4    [GE-BEEAH]
2569) GE- 2 -WAAT 1    [GE-WAAT]
2569) GE- 1 -BOGEN 3    [GE-BOGEN]
2570) GE- 1 -BEARG 3    [GE-BEARG]
2574) GE- 4 -SCRAAF 5    [GE-SCRAAF]
2577) GE- 1 -+WAAC 5    [GE-WAAC]
2580) GE- 1 -BAEAEDED 3    [GE-BAEAEDED]
2584) GE- 2 -+SWAAC 4    [GE-SWAAC]
2592) GE- 0 -MEETTON 4    [GE-MEETTON]
2597) GE- 2 -STOODON 3    [GE-STOODON]
```

185

```
(2604)  GE- 0 -SEAH 2     [GE-SEAH]
(2606)  GE- 2 -MUNDE 9     [GE-MUNDE]
(2608)  GE- 1 -HWYLC 4     [GE-HWYLC]
(2609)  GE- 1 -FEENG 9     [GE-FEENG]
(2610)  GE- 0 -TEEAH 4     [GE-TEEAH]
(2620)  GE- 0 -HEEOLD 9    [GE-HEEOLD]
(2624)  GE- 2 -WAAT 4      [GE-WAAT]
(2628)  GE- 2 -MEALT 2     [GE-MEALT]
(2629)  GE- 2 -WAAC 9      [GE-WAAC]
(2630)  GE- 2 -GAAN 3      [GE-GAAN]
(2632)  GE- 0 -SIIDHU= 5   [GE-SIIDHU=]
(2633)  GE- 8 -MAN 3       [GE-MAN]
(2634)  GE- 1 -HEETON 3    [GE-HEETON]
(2638)  GE- 1 -CEEAS. 5    [GE-CEEAS]
(2644)  GE- 2 -FREM-2-MAN-1-NE 5    [GE-FREMMANNE]
(2645)  GE- 3 -FRE-9-MEDE 4    [GE-FREMEDE]
(2653)  GE- 1 -RYSNE 3     [GE-RYSNE]
(2655)  GE- 0 -FYLLAN. 9   [GE-FYLLAN]
(2659)  GE- 0 -SIIGAN 2    [GE-SIIGAN]
(2660)  GE- 0 -MAEAENE. 5    [GE-MAEAENE]
(2664)  GE- 1 -CWAEAEDE 3    [GE-CWAEAEDE]
(2666)  GE- 2 -DREEOSAN 3    [GE-DREEOSAN]
(2674)  GE- 2 -FREM-1-MAN 5    [GE-FREMMAN]
(2676)  GE- 2 -EEODE 5     [GE-EEODE]
(2678)  GE- 1 -MUNDE 4     [GE-MUNDE]
(2680)  GE- 1 -NYYDED 1    [GE-NYYDED]
(2681)  GE- 1 -SWAAC 3     [GE-SWAAC]
(2685)  GE- 1 -HWANE 9     [GE-HWANE]
(2685)  GE- 1 -FRAEAEGE 4    [GE-FRAEAEGE]
(2689)  GE- 0 -MYNDIG 9    [GE-MYNDIG]
(2692)  GE- 3 -BLOODEGOD 3    [GE-BLOODEGOD]
(2694) *GE- 8 -*FRAEGN 8    [*GE-*FRAEGN]
(2696)  GE- 8 -CYNDE 3     [GE-CYNDE]
(2697)  GE- 1 -BARN 3      [GE-BARN]
(2700)  GE- 9 -DEEAF 3     [GE-DEEAF]
(2703)  GE- 2 -WEEOLD 2    [GE-WEEOLD]
(2703)  GE- 1 -WITTE 5     [GE-WITTE]
(2703)  GE- 0 -BRAEAED 3    [GE-BRAEAED]
(2706)  GE- 2 -FYLDAN 9    [GE-FYLDAN]
(2711)  GE- 2 -WEORCES. 3    [GE-WEORCES]
(2712)  GE- 1 -WORHTE 5    [GE-WORHTE]
(2717)  GE- 0 -SAET 3      [GE-SAET]
(2717)  GE- 1 -WEORC 5     [GE-WEORC]
(2722)  GE- 1 -LAFEDE 4    [GE-LAFEDE]
(2732)  GE- 1 -LENGE 4     [GE-LENGE]
(2740)  GE- 9 -FEEAN 2     [GE-FEEAN]
(2752)  GE- 0 -FRAEGN 4    [GE-FRAEGN]
(2756)  GE- 1 -SEAH 0      [GE-SEAH]
(2758)  GE- 2 -TENGE 5     [GE-TENGE]
(2764)  GE- 0 -SAEAELED 3    [GE-SAEAELED]
(2765)  GE- 1 -HWONE 4     [GE-HWONE]
(2767)  GE- 1 -SEAH 2      [GE-SEAH]
(2769)  GE- 0 -LOCEN 3     [GE-LOCEN]
(2773)  GE- 1 -FRAEGN 4    [GE-FRAEGN]
(2774)  GE- 1 -WEORC 3     [GE-WEORC]
(2776)  GE- 0 -NOOM 9      [GE-NOOM]
(2777)  GE- 2 -SCOOD 3     [GE-SCOOD]
(2784)  GE- 1 -FYRDH-1-RED 2    [GE-FYRDHRED]
(2785)  GE- 0 -MEETTE 5    [GE-MEETTE]
(2798)  GE- 9 -STRYYNAN 4    [GE-STRYYNAN]
(2802)  GE- 2 -WYRCEAN. 6    [GE-WYRCEAN]
(2804)  GE- 9 -MYNDU= 4    [GE-MYNDU=]
(2808)  GE- 1 -NIPU 4      [GE-NIPU]
(2810)  GE- 3 -SEALDE 4    [GE-SEALDE]
(2819)  GE- 1 -+WAAT 2     [GE-WAAT]
```

186

```
2821)  GE- 3 -GONGEN 4    [GE-GONGEN]
2822)  GE- 2 -SEAH 4    [GE-SEAH]
2824)  GE- 0 -BAEAERAN 9    [GE-BAEAERAN]
2826)  GE- 1 -BAEAEDED 2    [GE-BAEAEDED]
2834)  GE- 0 -FEEOLL 4    [GE-FEEOLL]
2837)  GE- 3 -FRAEAEGE 4    [GE-FRAEAEGE]
2838)  GE- 9 -HWAES 3    [GE-HWAES]
2839)  GE- 1 -RAEAESDE 3    [GE-RAEAESDE]
2844)  GE- 2 -FEERED 2    [GE-FEERED]
2852)  GE- 3 -WEERGAD 2.    [GE-WEERGAD]
2856)  GE- 2 -HEALDAN 9    [GE-HEALDAN]
2859)  GE- 1 -HWYLCU= 3    [GE-HWYLCU=]
2867)  GE- 0 -SEALDE 9    [GE-SEALDE]
2875)  GE- 2 -WRAEC 3    [GE-WRAEC]
2879)  GE- 4 -MET 2    [GE-MET]
2882)  GE- 2 -WITTE 5    [GE-WITTE]
2889)  GE- 2 -FRICGEAN 3    [GE-FRICGEAN]
2891)  GE- 0 -HWYLCU= 9    [GE-HWYLCU=]
2898)  GE- 1 -+RAAD 4    [GE-RAAD]
2906)  GE- 0 -WYRCEAN 4    [GE-WYRCEAN]
2916)  GE- 2 -()HNAEGDON*NAEAEGDON 9    [*GE-NAEAEGDON]
2917)  GE- 2 -EEODON 4    [GE-EEODON]
2926)  GE- 0 -SOOHTON 3    [GE-SOOHTON]
2937)  GE- 1 -HEET 3    [GE-HEET]
2941)  GE- 0 -LAMP 3    [GE-LAMP]
2947)  GE- 0 -SYYNE 5    [GE-SYYNE]
2949)  GE- 2 -WAAT 1    [GE-WAAT]
2952)  GE- 1 -FRUUNEN 3    [GE-FRUUNEN]
2965)  GE- 1 -RAEAEHTE 4    [GE-RAEAEHTE]
2973)  GE- 2 -SCER 9    [GE-SCER]
2976)  GE- 2 -WYRPTE 9    [GE-WYRPTE]
2980)  GE- 1 -BEEAH 2    [GE-BEEAH]
2983)  GE- 1 -RYYMED 9    [GE-RYYMED]
2989)  GE- 1 -HEET 3    [GE-HEET]
2990)  GE- 1 -()LAESTA*LAEAESTE 4    [*GE-LAEAESTE]
2994)  GE- 2 -HWAEDHRU= 3    [GE-HWAEDHRU=]
2996)  GE- 2 -SLOOGON. 3    [GE-SLOOGON]
3002)  GE- 1 -FRICGEADH 3    [GE-FRICGEADH]
3003)  GE- 1 -HEEOLD 3    [GE-HEEOLD]
3009)  GE- 1 -BRINGAN 3    [GE-BRINGAN]
3012)  GE- 0 -CEEA-9-()++D*POO 8    [*GE-CEEAPOO]
3014)  ()++++TE*GE- 8 -*BOHTE 5    [*GE-*BOHTE]
3016)  GE- 3 -MYNDUM 9    [GE-MYNDUM]
3036)  GE- 1 -GONGEN 9    [GE-GONGEN]
3038)  GE- 2 -SEEGAN 4    [GE-SEEGAN]
3044)  GE- 1 -WAAT 3    [GE-WAAT]
3046)  GE- 0 -NYTTOD 5    [GE-NYTTOD]
3056)  GE- 2 -HYLD 3    [GE-HYLD]
3057)  GE- 2 -MET 2    [GE-MET]
3058)  GE- 2 -SYYNE 5    [GE-SYYNE]
3059)  GE- 2 -HYYDDE 5    [GE-HYYDDE]
3061)  GE- 9 -WEARDH 4    [GE-WEARDH]
3062)  GE- 1 -WRECEN 4    [GE-WRECEN]
3063)  GE- 2 -FEERE. 5    [GE-FEERE]
3068)  GE- 0 -DAAL 3    [GE-DAAL]
3072)  GE- 1 -HEADHE-9-ROD 2    [GE-HEADHEROD]
3073)  GE- 2 -WIITNAD 2    [GE-WIITNAD]
3075)  GE- 2 -SCEEAWOD. 5    [GE-SCEEAWOD]
3078)  GE- 9 -WORDEN 2    [GE-WORDEN]
3079)  GE- 1 -LAEAERAN 3    [GE-LAEAERAN]
3084)  GE- 1 -SCEEAWOD 2    [GE-SCEEAWOD]
3085)  GE- 1 -GONGEN 4    [GE-GONGEN]
3088)  GE- 1 -RYYMED 9    [GE-RYYMED]
3090)  GE- 1 -FEENG 4    [GE-FEENG]
3094)  GE- 1 -WITTIG 3    [GE-WITTIG]
```

187

```
(3094) GE- 2 -SPRAEC 3    [GE-SPRAEC]
(3096) GE- 1 -WORHTON 3    [GE-WORHTON]
(3102) GE- 2 -THRAEC 3    [GE-THRAEC]
(3104) GE- 0 -NOOGE 4    [GE-NOOGE]
(3106) GE- 9 -AEFNED 2    [GE-AEFNED]
(3107) GE- 2 -FERIAN 3    [GE-FERIAN]
(3109) GE- 1 -THO-2-LIAN. 5    [GE-THOLIAN]
(3110) GE- 0 -BEEODAN 9    [GE-BEEODAN]
(3116) GE- 0 -+BAAD 4    [GE-BAAD]
(3117) GE- 1 -BAEAEDED 4    [GE-BAEAEDED]
(3128) GE- 0 -SEEGON 3    [GE-SEEGON]
(3130) GE- 1 -FEREDON 4    [GE-FEREDON]
(3137) GE- 1 -GIREDAN 2    [GE-GIREDAN]
(3147) GE- 1 -BROCEN 3    [GE-BROCEN]
(3152) GE- 8 -NEAHHE 8    [GE-NEAHHE]
(3156) GE- 8 -WORHTON 1    [GE-WORHTON]
(3158) GE- 2 -SYYNE 3    [GE-SYYNE]
(1953) -GE- 2 -SCEAFTA 4    [LIIF-GE-SCEAFTA]
(1973) -GE- 1 -STEALLA 9    [LIND-GE-STEALLA]
(2162) -GE- 0 -WAEAEDU 3    [BREEOST-GE-WAEAEDU]
(2169) -GE- 1 -STEALLAN 3    [HOND-GE-STEALLAN]
(2180) -GE- 0 -NEEA-9-TAS 3    [HEORDH-GE-NEEATAS]
(2232) -GE- 3 -STREEONA 7    [AEAER-GE-STREEONA]
(2240) -GE- 2 -STREEONA 5    [LONG-GE-STREEONA]
(2244) -GE- 8 -STREEONA 6    [EORL-GE-STREEONA]
(2286) -GE- 1 -WEORC 9    [FYRN-GE-WEORC]
(2302) -GE- 0 -STREEONA 4    [HEEAH-GE-STREEONA]
(2355) -GE- 0 -()MOT*MOOTA 9    [*HOND-GE-MOOTA]
(2412) -GE- 1 -WINNE 2    [YYDH-GE-WINNE]
(2418) -GE- 0 -NEEATU= 3    [HEORDH-GE-NEEATU=]
(2420) -GE- 4 -METE 4    [UN-GE-METE]
(2435) -GE- 5 -DEEFE- 0    [UN-GE-DEEFE-LIICE]
(2596) -GE- 2 -STEALLAN 9    [*HAND-GE-STEALLAN]
(2617) -GE- 2 -WAEAEDU 5    [GUUDH-GE-WAEAEDU]
(2623) -GE- 3 -WAEAE-2-DA 5    [GUUDH-GE-WAEAEDA]
(2636) -GE- 9 -TAAWA 4    [GUUDH-GE-TAAWA]
(2657) -GE- 2 -WYRHT 3    [EALD-GE-WYRHT]
(2721) -GE- 0 -METE 4    [UN-GE-METE]
(2728) -GE- 1 -RIIMES 4    [DOOGOR-GE-RIIMES]
(2728) -GE- 9 -METE 4    [UN-GE-METE]
(2730) -GE- 1 -WAEAEDU 3    [GUUDH-GE-WAEAEDU]
(2737) -GE- 2 -SCEAFTA 4    [MAEAEL-GE-SCEAFTA]
(2818) -GE- 1 -HYGDU= 4    [BREEOST-GE-HYGDU=]
(2835) -GE- 2 -WEORCE 9    [HOND-GE-WEORCE]
(2851) -GE- 1 -WAEAEDU 2    [GUUDH-GE-WAEAEDU]
(2871) -GE- 1 -WAEAEDU 1    [GUUDH-GE-WAEAEDU]
(2873) -GE- 1 -STEALLU= 9    [FYRD-GE-STEALLU=]
(2881) -GE- 0 -NIIDH-9-LAN 3    [FERHDH-GE-NIIDHLAN]
(2903) -GE- 1 -WINNA 1    [EALDOR-GE-WINNA]
(2933) -GE- 0 -NIIDH-2-LAN 4    [FEORH-GE-NIIDHLAN]
(3042) -GE- 2 -MEARCES 9    [FOOT-GE-MEARCES]
(3064) -GE- 9 -SCEAFTA 4    [LIIF-GE-SCEAFTA]
(3084) -GE- 4 -SCEAP 3    [HEEAH-GE-SCEAP]
(3092) -GE- 1 -STREEONA 1    [HORD-GE-STREEONA]
```

FIRST MORPHEME TERMINATES IN RESONANT CONSONANT

```
(1940) CWEALM- 3 -BEALU 3    [CWEALM-BEALU]
(1940) CWEEN- 2 -LIIC 3    [CWEEN-LIIC]
(1942) ON- 8 -SAEAECE 3    [ON-SAEAECE]
(1944) ON- 2 -HOOHSNOD*E 3    [ON-HOOHSNOD*E]
(1952) GUM- 2 -STOOLE 9    [GUM-STOOLE]
(1955) MON- 3 -CYNNES 3    [MON-CYNNES]
(1957) EORMEN- 3 -CYNNES 4    [EORMEN-CYNNES]
```

```
1957) FOR-  2 -DHAAM 1    [FOR-DHAAM]
1958) GAAR-  3 -CEENE 2    [GAAR-CEENE]
1962) +GAAR-  9 -MUNDES 4    [GAAR-MUNDES]
1968) ON-2-GEN-  3 -THEEO-1-ES. 2    [ONGEN-THEEOES]
1976) INNAN-  2 -WEARD 4    [INNAN-WEARD]
1978) MAN-  4 -DRYHTEN 4    [MAN-DRYHTEN]
1979) HLEEODHOR-  9 -CWYDE 3    [HLEEODHOR-CWYDE]
1981) ()SIDE*HEAL-  8 -RECED 4    [*HEAL-RECED]
1983) ON-  0 -GAN 3    [ON-GAN]
1985) FYR-  3 -WET 1    [FYR-WET]
1995) WAEL-  1 -GAEAEST 3    [WAEL-GAEAEST]
2000) UN-  2 -DYRNE 4    [UN-DYRNE]
2002) ()++++++*OR-  8 -*LEG-  9    [*OR-*LEG-HWIIL]
2015) HEAL-  4 -SITTEN-1-DRA 5    [HEAL-SITTENDRA]
2028) WAEL-  1 -FAEAEHDHA 4    [WAEL-FAEAEHDHA]
2031) BON-  1 -GAAR 4    [BON-GAAR]
2039) FOR-  3 -LAEAEDDAN 3    [FOR-LAEAEDDAN]
2043) GAAR-  5 -CWEALM 4    [GAAR-CWEALM]
2044) ON-  2 -GINNEDH 4    [ON-GINNEDH]
2044) GEOO-1-MOR-  4 -MOOD 2    [GEOOMOR-MOOD]
2051) WAEL-  2 -STOOWE 4    [WAEL-STOOWE]
2051) WIDHER-  3 -GYLD 3    [WIDHER-GYLD]
2065) WAEL-  4 -NIIDHAS 3    [WAEL-NIIDHAS]
2066) CEAR-  4 -WAELMU= 4    [CEAR-WAELMU=]
2068) UN-  1 -FAEAECNE 9    [UN-FAEAECNE]
2074) AEAEFEN-  2 -GROM 4    [AEAEFEN-GROM]
2076) ON-  1 -SAEAEGE 5    [ON-SAEAEGE]
2080) FOR-  4 -SWEALG. 7    [FOR-SWEALG]
2081) IIDEL-  2 -HENDE. 7    [IIDEL-HENDE]
2086) SYL-  0 -LIIC 3    [SYL-LIIC]
2087) OR-  0 -DHON-1-CU= 4    [OR-DHONCU=]
2089) UN-  1 -SYNNIGNE 4    [UN-SYNNIGNE]
2094) FOR-  3 -GEALD 4    [FOR-GEALD]
2101) WAEL-  3 -RAEAES 3    [WAEL-RAEAES]
2108) GO-9-()MEL*MEN-  8 -WUDU 3    [*GOMEN-WUDU]
2109) SAAR-  1 -+LIIC 3    [SAAR-LIIC]
2109) SYL-  0 -LIIC 3    [SYL-LIIC]
2110) RUUM-  3 -HEORT 3    [RUUM-HEORT]
2111) ON-  8 -GAN 4    [ON-GAN]
2118) GYRN-  4 -WRAECE. 5    [GYRN-WRAECE]
2119) FOR-  1 -NAM 3    [FOR-NAM]
2120) UN-  1 -HYYRRE 6    [UN-HYYRE]
2122) ELLEN-  1 -LIICE 4    [ELLEN-LIICE]
2123) FYRN-  3 -WITAN 5    [FYRN-WITAN]
2126) FOR-  3 -BAERNAN 9    [FOR-BAERNAN]
2128) FIRGEN-  4 -STREEAM. 6    [FIRGEN-STREEAM]
2133) EORL-  2 -SCIPE 4    [EORL-SCIPE]
2140) UN-  2 -SOOFTE 4    [UN-SOOFTE]
2145) FOR-  2 -LOREN 9    [FOR-LOREN]
2148) BEORN-  9 -CYNING 3    [BEORN-CYNING]
2165) AEPPEL-  4 -FEALUWE 4    [AEPPEL-FEALUWE]
2173) WUNDUR-  4 -MAADHDHU= 9    [WUNDUR-MAADHDHU=]
2175) SADOL-  3 -BEORHT 4    [SADOL-BEORHT]
2181) MAN-  9 -CYNNES 5    [MAN-CYNNES]
2182) GIN-  2 -FAESTAN 9    [GIN-FAESTAN]
2188) UN-  9 -FROM 4    [UN-FROM]
2189) TIIR-  3 -EEADIGU= 9    [TIIR-EEADIGU=]
2198) EEDHEL-  4 -RIHT 3    [EEDHEL-RIHT]
2210) EETHEL-  4 -WEARD 4    [EETHEL-WEARD]
2210) ON-  0 -GAN 4    [ON-GAN]
2213) STAAN-  3 -BEORH 4    [STAAN-BEORH]
2214) UN-  0 -CUUDH 4    [UN-CUUDH]
2219) ON-  8 -()+++D*FAND 8    [*ON-FAND]
2221) WYRM-  2 -()HORDA*HORD 9    [*WYRM-HORD]
2226) SYN-  8 -BYSIG 6    [SYN-BYSIG]
```

189

```
(2228) ()++++*EARM- 8 -SCEAPEN 8    [*EARM-SCEAPEN]
(2232) AEAER- 4 -GE- 3    [AEAER-GE-STREEONA]
(2233) GEEAR- 1 -DA-9-GU= 8    [GEEAR-DAGU=]
(2234) EORMEN- 4 -LAAFE 9    [EORMEN-LAAFE]
(2236) FOR- 4 -NAM 4    [FOR-NAM]
(2241) EALL- 3 -GEARO 4    [EALL-GEARO]
(2242) WAETER- 5 -YYTHU= 5    [WAETER-YYTHU=]
(2244) EORL- 9 -GE- 8    [EORL-GE-STREEONA]
(2249) FOR- 3 -NAM. 6    [FOR-NAM]
(2256) FEOR- 2 -MYND 9    [FEOR-MYND]
(2266) ON- 1 -SENDED. 5    [ON-SENDED]
(2267) GIOO-1-MOR- 5 -MOOD 2    [GIOOMOR-MOOD]
(2268) UN- 1 -BLIIDHE 2    [UN-BLIIDHE]
(2275) ()++*ON- 8 -()+++DA+*DRAEAEDADH 8    [*ON-DRAEAEDADH]
(2280) EEACEN- 9 -CRAEFTIG 5    [EEACEN-CRAEFTIG]
(2281) MAN- 3 -DRYHTNE 3    [MAN-DRYHTNE]
(2284) ON- 1 -BOREN 4    [ON-BOREN]
(2286) FYRN- 3 -GE- 1    [FYRN-GE-WEORC]
(2287) ON- 1 -+WOOC 3    [ON-WOOC]
(2288) ON- 0 -FAND 4    [ON-FAND]
(2291) UN- 0 -FAEAEGE 9    [UN-FAEAEGE]
(2297) UUTAN- 9 -WEARD-1-NE 5    [UUTAN-WEARDNE]
(2300) ON- 1 -FAND 9    [ON-FAND]
(2302) ON- 1 -+BAAD 5    [ON-BAAD]
(2305) FOR- 4 -GYLDAN 2    [FOR-GYLDAN]
(2312) ON- 0 -GAN 3    [ON-GAN]
(2335) FOR- 2 -GRUNDEN 5    [FOR-GRUNDEN]
(2338) EALL- 9 -IIRENNE 5    [EALL-IIRENNE]
(2341) ()++-9-()THEND*LAEAEN- 3 -DAGA 5    [*LAEAEN-DAGA]
(2342) AEAER- 3 -GOOD 3    [AEAER-GOOD]
(2345) OFER- 1 -HOGODE 2    [OFER-HOGODE]
(2347) ON- 9 -DREED. 6    [ON-DREED]
(2349) FOR- 0 -DHON 3    [FOR-DHON]
(2352) SIGOR- 4 -EEADIG 2    [SIGOR-EEADIG]
(2353) FOR- 3 -GRAAP 3    [FOR-GRAAP]
(2364) ON- 1 -GEEAN. 9    [ON-GEEAN]
(2367) OFER- 9 -SWAM 1    [OFER-SWAM]
(2368) AAN- 2 -HAGA 3    [AAN-HAGA]
(2371) AEL- 0 -FYL-9-CU= 4    [AEL-FYLCU=]
(2371) EETHEL- 2 -STOOLAS 4    [EETHEL-STOOLAS]
(2379) WEDER- 3 -GEEATU= 3    [WEDER-GEEATU=]
(2381) FOR- 8 -HEALDEN 4    [FOR-HEALDEN]
(2387) ONGEN- 2 -DHIIDES 5    [ONGEN-DHIIDES]
(2396) CEAR- 3 -SIIDHUM 9    [CEAR-SIIDHUM]
(2399) ELLEN- 3 -WEORCA 4    [ELLEN-WEORCA]
(2405) MAADH-1-THUM- 3 -FAET 3    [MAADHTHUM-FAET]
(2407) OR- 0 -LEGES 4    [OR-LEGES]
(2407) ON- 1 -STEALDE 3    [ON-STEALDE]
(2411) HOLM- 3 -WYLME 5    [HOLM-WYLME]
(2413) UN- 2 -HIIORE 4    [UN-HIIORE]
(2420) WAEL- 0 -FUUS 3    [WAEL-FUUS]
(2420) UN- 0 -GE- 4    [UN-GE-METE]
(2427) OR- 1 -LEG- 4    [OR-LEG-HWIILA]
(2428) SYFAN- 3 -WINTRE 5    [SYFAN-WINTRE]
(2435) UN- 0 -GE- 5    [UN-GE-DEEFE-LIICE]
(2436) MORTHOR- 4 -BED 1    [MORTHOR-BED]
(2437) HORN- 3 -BOGAN. 6    [HORN-BOGAN]
(2443) UN- 1 -WRECEN 4    [UN-WRECEN]
(2444) GEOOMOR- 3 -LIIC 3    [GEOOMOR-LIIC]
(2449) IN- 1 -FROOD 5    [IN-FROOD]
(2451) ELLOR- 4 -SIIDH 3    [ELLOR-SIIDH]
(2456) WIIN- 0 -SELE 3    [WIIN-SELE]
(2475) ONGEN- 9 -DHEOWES 3    [ONGEN-DHEOWES]
(2483) ON- 0 -SAEAEGE 9    [ON-SAEAEGE]
(2486) ONGEN- 9 -THEEOW 3    [ONGEN-THEEOW]
```

```
(2492) FOR- 2 -GEAF 3    [FOR-GEAF]
(2493) EEDHEL- 0 -WYN 9    [EEDHEL-WYN]
(2494) GAAR- 2 -DENU= 4    [GAAR-DENU=]
(2508) BAAN- 1 -HUUS 9    [BAAN-HUUS]
(2514) +MAAN- 3 -SCEADHA 9    [MAAN-SCEADHA]
(2517) HELM- 4 -BE-9-REND 4    [HELM-BEREND]
(2523) FOR- 0 -DHON 2    [FOR-DHON]
(2525) OFER- 4 -FLEEON 3    [OFER-FLEEON]
(2528) OFER- 9 -SITTE 4    [OFER-SITTE]
(2531) WAEL- 2 -RAEAESE 4    [WAEL-RAEAESE]
(2535) EORL- 4 -SCYPE 4    [EORL-SCYPE]
(2540) STAAN- 4 -CLEOFU 9    [STAAN-CLEOFU]
(2545) STAAN- 2 -BOGAN 3    [STAAN-BOGAN]
(2548) UN- 9 -BYRNENDE 4    [UN-BYRNENDE]
(2551) WEDER- 3 -GEEATA 5    [WEDER-GEEATA]
(2554) ON- 2 -HREE-2-RED 3    [ON-HREERED]
(2554) ON- 0 -CNIIOW 5    [ON-CNIIOW]
(2559) ON- 2 -+SWAAF 9    [ON-SWAAF]
(2564) UN- 9 -()GLAW*SLAAW 4    [*UN-SLAAW]
(2578) UN- 0 -SWIIDHOR. 7    [UN-SWIIDHOR]
(2582) WAEL- 3 -FYYRE 4    [WAEL-FYYRE]
(2586) AEAER- 2 -+GOOD 4    [AEAER-GOOD]
(2591) LAEAEN- 2 -DAGAS 9    [LAEAEN-DAGAS]
(2601) ON- 1 -WENDAN 3    [ON-WENDAN]
(2604) MON- 2 -DRYHTEN 3    [MON-DRYHTEN]
(2606) FOR- 3 -GEAF. 5    [FOR-GEAF]
(2609) FOR- 3 -HABBAN 2    [FOR-HABBAN]
(2611) EEAN- 3 -MUN-1-DES 4    [EEAN-MUNDES]
(2615) BRUUN- 3 -FAAGNE 4    [BRUUN-FAAGNE]
(2616) FOR- 2 -GEAF 4    [FOR-GEAF]
(2622) EORL- 3 -SCIPE 4    [EORL-SCIPE]
(2622) AEAER- 3 -FAEDER 3    [AEAER-FAEDER]
(2624) UN- 0 -RIIM 4    [UN-RIIM]
(2629) ON- 0 -FAND 3    [ON-FAND]
(2635) BIIOR- 3 -SELE 9    [BIIOR-SELE]
(2640) ON- 1 -MUNDE 3    [ON-MUNDE]
(2641) +GAAR- 9 -WIIGEND 3    [GAAR-WIIGEND]
(2642) HELM- 3 -BEREND 9    [HELM-BEREND]
(2643) ELLEN- 4 -WEORC 3    [ELLEN-WEORC]
(2645) FOR- 0 -DHAA= 4    [FOR-DHAA=]
(2647) MAN- 3 -DRYHTEN 3    [MAN-DRYHTEN]
(2661) WAEL- 1 -+REEC 3    [WAEL-REEC]
(2667) AN- 2 -HYYDIG 4    [AN-HYYDIG]
(2668) FUL- 0 -LAEAESTU. 5    [FUL-LAEAESTU]
(2671) FYYR- 3 -WY-8-LMU= 3    [FYYR-WYLMU=]
(2672) FOR- 5 -BORN 2    [FOR-BORN]
(2674) GAAR- 3 -WIGAN 9    [GAAR-WIGAN]
(2677) FOR- 1 -GRUNDEN 4    [FOR-GRUNDEN]
(2678) MAEGEN- 3 -STRENGO 3    [MAEGEN-STRENGO]
(2680) FOR- 2 -BAERST 3    [FOR-BAERST]
(2686) OFER- 4 -SOOHTE 4    [OFER-SOOHTE]
(2689) +FYYR- 4 -DRACA 4    [FYYR-DRACA]
(2693) SAAWUL- 9 -DRIIORE 3    [SAAWUL-DRIIORE]
(2701) ON- 1 -GON 3    [ON-GON]
(2703) WAELL- 3 -SEAXE 3    [WAELL-SEAXE]
(2705) FOR- 4 -WRAAT 2    [FOR-WRAAT]
(2711) ON- 1 -GON 3    [ON-GON]
(2713) ON- 1 -FAND 3    [ON-FAND]
(2718) STAAN- 2 -BOGAN 9    [STAAN-BOGAN]
(2721) UN- 1 -GE- 0    [UN-GE-METE]
(2723) ON- 1 -SPEEON. 6    [ON-SPEEON]
(2725) WAEL- 3 -BLEEATE 4    [WAEL-BLEEATE]
(2728) DOOGOR- 3 -GE- 1    [DOOGOR-GE-RIIMES]
(2728) UN- 0 -GE- 9    [UN-GE-METE]
(2737) MAEAEL- 2 -GE- 2    [MAEAEL-GE-SCEAFTA]
```

191

```
(2739) UN- 9 -RIHT 2    [UN-RIHT]
(2741) FOR- 0 -DHAA= 4    [FOR-DHAA=]
(2742) MORDHOR- 4 -BEALO 3    [MORDHOR-BEALO]
(2747) AEAER- 3 -WELAN 9    [AEAER-WELAN]
(2748) ON- 1 -GITE 3    [ON-GITE]
(2761) FYRN- 2 -MANNA 3    [FYRN-MANNA]
(2763) EARM- 2 -BEEAGA 3    [EARM-BEEAGA]
(2766) OFER- 3 -HIIGIAN 4    [OFER-HIIGIAN]
(2767) EALL- 9 -GYLDEN 5    [EALL-GYLDEN]
(2770) ON- 0 -GITAN 3    [ON-GITAN]
(2772) ON- 1 -SYYN 3    [ON-SYYN]
(2772) FOR- 4 -NA= 4    [FOR-NA=]
(2782) MIDDEL- 3 -NIHTUM 9    [MIDDEL-NIHTUM]
(2784) FYR- 1 -WET 2    [FYR-WET]
(2785) COLLEN- 3 -FERDH 2    [COLLEN-FERDH]
(2787) ELLEN- 3 -SIICCNE 5    [ELLEN-SIIOGNE]
(2787) FOR- 2 -LEET. 3    [FOR-LEET]
(2790) ON- 1 -GON 4    [ON-GON]
(2792) *BIORN- 8 -*CYNING 8    [*BIORN-*CYNING]
(2795) WULDUR- 4 -CYNINGE 3    [WULDUR-CYNINGE]
(2811) GAAR- 1 -WIGAN 9    [GAAR-WIGAN]
(2814) FOR- 9 -()SPEOF*SWEEOP 8    [*FOR-SWEEOP]
(2821) UN- 1 -FROODU= 3    [UN-FROODU=]
(2828) FOR- 4 -NAAMON 4    [FOR-NAAMON]
(2833) MIDDEL- 3 -NIHTU= 9    [MIDDEL-NIHTU=]
(2833) MAADHM- 4 -AEAEHTA 4    [MAADHM-AEAEHTA]
(2834) AN- 1 -SYYN 3    [AN-SYYN]
(2837) MAEGEN- 9 -AAGENDRA 4    [MAEGEN-AAGENDRA]
(2839) ATTOR- 8 -SCEADHAN 9    [ATTOR-SCEADHAN]
(2841) ON- 1 -FUNDE 3    [ON-FUNDE]
(2843) FOR- 0 -GOLDEN 9    [FOR-GOLDEN]
(2849) MAN- 1 -DRYHTNES 4    [MAN-DRYHTNES]
(2857) ON- 1 -CIRRAN 4    [ON-CIRRAN]
(2861) FOR- 2 -LEEAS. 4    [FOR-LEEAS]
(2863) UN- 1 -LEEOFE 3    [UN-LEEOFE]
(2865) MON- 3 -DRYHTEN 4    [MON-DRYHTEN]
(2868) HEAL- 3 -SITTENDU= 4    [HEAL-SITTENDU=]
(2872) FOR- 2 -WURPE. 6    [FOR-WURPE]
(2878) ON- 1 -GAN 2    [ON-GAN]
(2881) UN- 4 -SWIIDHOR 5    [UN-SWIIDHOR]
(2885) EEDHEL- 3 -WYN 8    [EEDHEL-WYN]
(2893) EORL- 4 -WEOROD 2    [EORL-WEOROD]
(2894) MOR-9-GEN- 3 -LONGNE 4    [MORGEN-LONGNE]
(2900) WIL- 2 -GEOFA 3    [WIL-GEOFA]
(2902) WAEL- 8 -RESTE 4    [WAEL-RESTE]
(2903) EALDOR- 4 -GE- 1    [EALDOR-GE-WINNA]
(2908) UN- 2 -LIFIGENDU= 4    [UN-LIFIGENDU=]
(2911) OR- 1 -LEG- 2    [OR-LEG-HWIILE]
(2917) OFER- 4 -MAEGENE 4    [OFER-MAEGENE]
(2918) BYRN- 9 -WIGA 4    [BYRN-WIGA]
(2921) UN- 0 -GYFEDHE. 5    [UN-GYFEDHE]
(2924) ONGEN- 1 -DHIIO 3    [ONGEN-DHIIO]
(2926) ON- 1 -MEED-9-LAN 2    [ON-MEEDLAN]
(2936) SIN- 3 -HERGE 4    [SIN-HERGE]
(2942) AEAER- 2 -DAEGE 4    [AEAER-DAEGE]
(2944) ON- 1 -GEEATON 3    [ON-GEEATON]
(2947) WAEL- 2 -RAEAES 9    [WAEL-RAEAES]
(2951) ONGEN- 1 -THIIO 3    [ONGEN-THIIO]
(2951) ON- 1 -CIRDE 5    [ON-CIRDE]
(2954) ON- 1 -SACAN 3    [ON-SACAN]
(2955) FOR- 1 -STANDAN 3    [FOR-STANDAN]
(2959) OFER- 3 -EEODON 4    [OFER-EEODON]
(2961) ON-9-GEN- 2 -DHIIOW 4    [ONGEN-DHIIOW]
(2962) BLONDEN- 3 -FEXA 5    [BLONDEN-FEXA]
(2965) WON- 2 -REEDING 9    [WON-REEDING]
```

```
(2968) FOR- 1 -GEALD 0   [FOR-GEALD]
(2969) WAEL- 3 -HLEM 2   [WAEL-HLEM]
(2970) ON- 0 -CIRDE. 5   [ON-CIRDE]
(2971) WON- 1 -REEDES 3   [WON-REEDES]
(2984) WAEL- 2 -STOOWE 4   [WAEL-STOOWE]
(2986) ONGEN- 1 -DHIID 9   [ONGEN-DHIID]
(2986) IIREN- 2 -BYRNAN 4   [IIREN-BYRNAN]
(2993) OFER- 2 -MAADHMUM 4   [OFER-MAADHMUM]
(2996) MIDDAN- 1 -GEARDE 4   [MIDDAN-GEARDE]
(2997) FOR- 4 -GEAF 9   [FOR-GEAF]
(2998) HAAM- 3 -WEORDHUNGE 4   [HAAM-WEORDHUNGE]
(3000) WAEL- 3 -NIIDH 3   [WAEL-NIIDH]
(3003) EALDOR- 9 -LEEASNE 4   [EALDOR-LEEASNE]
(3007) EORL- 9 -SCIPE 4   [EORL-SCIPE]
(3012) UN- 0 -RIIME 4   [UN-RIIME]
(3018) GEOO-1-MOR- 5 -MOOD 3   [GEOOMOR-MOOD]
(3019) EL- 0 -LAND 2   [EL-LAND]
(3021) FOR- 1 -DHON 3   [FOR-DHON]
(3022) MORGEN- 9 -CEALD 4   [MORGEN-CEALD]
(3031) UN- 9 -BLIIDHE 4   [UN-BLIIDHE]
(3032) WOLLEN- 2 -TEEARE 4   [WOLLEN-TEEARE]
(3033) SAAWUL- 3 -LEEASNE 9   [SAAWUL-LEEASNE]
(3034) HLIM- 1 -BED 2   [HLIM-BED]
(3037) WUNDOR- 3 -DEEADHE 9   [WUNDOR-DEEADHE]
(3038) SYL- 0 -LII-2-CRAN 4   [SYL-LIICRAN]
(3039) WIDHER- 2 -RAEHTES 3   [WIDHER-RAEHTES]
(3041) GRIM- 0 -LIIC 2   [GRIM-LIIC]
(3051) EEACEN- 2 -CRAEFTIG 4   [EEACEN-CRAEFTIG]
(3059) UN- 0 -RIHTE 9   [UN-RIHTE]
(3063) ELLEN- 3 -+ROOF 3   [ELLEN-ROOF]
(3072) HELL- 3 -BENDU= 3   [HELL-BENDU=]
(3086) ON- 1 -TYHTE. 5   [ON-TYHTE]
(3091) MAEGEN- 3 -BYRDHENNE 5   [MAEGEN-BYRDHENNE]
(3097) BAEAEL- 3 -STEDE 3   [BAEAEL-STEDE]
(3112) BAEAEL- 4 -WUDU 3   [BAEAEL-WUDU]
(3116) IISERN- 4 -SCUURE 5   [IISERN-SCUURE]
(3119) ()FAEDER*FAEDHER- 4 -GEARWU= 3   [*FAEDHER-GEARWU=]
(3119) FULL- 3 -EEODE. 4   [FULL-EEODE]
(3127) OR- 2 -WEARDE 3   [OR-WEARDE]
(3132) WEALL- 1 -CLIF 3   [WEALL-CLIF]
(3135) UN- 0 -RIIM 4   [UN-RIIM]
(3138) UN- 2 -WAAC- 1   [UN-WAAC-LIICNE]
(3143) ON- 0 -GUNNON 2   [ON-GUNNON]
(3143) BAEAEL- 3 -FYYRA 9   [BAEAEL-FYYRA]
(3147) +BAAN- 3 -+HUUS 3   [BAAN-HUUS]
(3148) UN- 0 -ROOTE 3   [UN-ROOTE]
(3149) MON- 1 -DRYHTNES 8   [MON-DRYHTNES]
(3150) GIOOMOR- 3 -GYD 9   [GIOOMOR-GYD]
(3151) ()+UNDEN*BUNDEN- 2 -HEORDE 9   [*BUNDEN-HEORDE]
(3153) ()++++G+NGAS*HEARM- 8 -*DAGAS 3   [*HEARM-*DAGAS]
(3153) ON- 8 -()D+EDE*DREEDE 4   [*ON-DREEDE]
(3154) WAEL- 8 -FYLLA 3   [WAEL-FYLLA]
(3166) FOR- 1 -LEETON 3   [FOR-LEETON]
(3168) UN- 1 -NYT 2   [UN-NYT]
(3173) EORL- 2 -SCIPE 3   [EORL-SCIPE]
(3173) ELLEN- 2 -WEORC 2   [ELLEN-WEORC]
(3181) MON- 8 -()++AERUST*DHWAEAERUST 2   [*MON-DHWAEAERUST]
```

FIRST MORPHEME TERMINATES IN STOP CONSONANT

```
(1946) LEEOD- 9 -BEALEWA 3   [LEEOD-BEALEWA]
(1947) INWIT- 3 -NIIDHA 9   [INWIT-NIIDHA]
(1948) GOLD- 2 -HRO-9-DEN 3   [GOLD-HRODEN]
(1963) HOND- 3 -SCOLE 3   [HOND-SCOLE]
```

```
(1965)  WORULD- 1 -CANDEL 3    [WORULD-CANDEL]
(1973)  LIND- 3 -GE- 1    [LIND-GE-STEALLA]
(1991)  ()WIDH*WIID- 2 -CUUDHNE 9    [*WIID-CUUDHNE]
(1992)  MOOD- 3 -CEARE 4    [MOOD-CEARE]
(2007)  UUHT- 4 -HLEM 4    [UUHT-HLEM]
(2012)  MOOD- 3 -SEFAN 4    [MOOD-SEFAN]
(2017)  GEOND- 4 -HWEARF 3    [GEOND-HWEARF]
(2022)  FLET- 8 -SITTENDE. 5    [FLET-SITTENDE]
(2025)  GOLD- 2 -HRODEN 4    [GOLD-HRODEN]
(2030)  LEEOD- 3 -HRYRE 3    [LEEOD-HRYRE]
(2035)  DRYHT- 2 -BEARN 4    [DRYHT-BEARN]
(2039)  LIND- 9 -PLEGAN 5    [LIND-PLEGAN]
(2042)  AESC- 3 -WIGA 5    [AESC-WIGA]
(2053)  NAAT- 4 -HWYLCES. 6    [NAAT-HWYLCES]
(2060)  BLOOD- 3 -FAAG 3    [BLOOD-FAAG]
(2068)  DRYHT- 3 -SIBBE 3    [DRYHT-SIBBE]
(2069)  FREEOND- 3 -SCIPE 4    [FREEOND-SCIPE]
(2072)  HOND- 1 -RAEAES 3    [HOND-RAEAES]
(2076)  HOND- 9 -SCIOO 3    [HOND-SCIOO]
(2083)  GOLD- 3 -SELE 3    [GOLD-SELE]
(2090)  DAEAED- 9 -FRUMA 3    [DAEAED-FRUMA]
(2092)  UPP- 1 -RIHTE 9    [UPP-RIHTE]
(2093)  LEEOD- 3 -SCEADHAN 2    [LEEOD-SCEADHAN]
(2094)  ()HOND*OND- 8 -LEEAN 9    [*OND-LEEAN]
(2115)  =AND- 0 -LANGNE 9    [=AND-LANGNE]
(2122)  AESC- 9 -HERE 5    [AESC-HERE]
(2127)  AET- 2 -BAER 5    [AET-BAER]
(2130)  LEEOD- 3 -FRU-9-MAN 2    [LEEOD-FRUMAN]
(2136)  GRUND- 4 -HYRDE 4    [GRUND-HYRDE]
(2144)  DHEEOD- 4 -KYNING 4    [DHEEOD-KYNING]
(2151)  HEEAFOD- 4 -MAAGA 4    [HEEAFOD-MAAGA]
(2152)  HEEAFOD- 2 -SEGN. 6    [HEEAFOD-SEGN]
(2162)  BREEOST- 4 -GE- 0    [BREEOST-GE-WAEAEDU]
(2167)  IN-1-WIT- 3 -NET 4    [INWIT-NET]
(2169)  HOND- 3 -GE- 1    [HOND-GE-STEALLAN]
(2188)  ED- 1 -WEN-2-DEN 3    [ED-WENDEN]
(2193)  SINC- 3 -MAADH-4-THU= 3    [SINC-MAADHTHU=]
(2197)  LEEOD- 3 -SCIPE 9    [LEEOD-SCIPE]
(2202)  ()HEAREDE*HEARD- 8 -*REEDE 4    [*HEARD-*REEDE]
(2203)  BORD- 9 -HREEODHAN 4    [BORD-HREEODHAN]
(2205)  ()HILDE*HILD- 9 -FRECAN 3    [*HILD-FRECAN]
(2215)  NAAT- 2 -HWYLC 8    [NAAT-HWYLC]
(2223)  NAAT- 9 -HWYLCES 8    [NAAT-HWYLCES]
(2231)  SINC- 3 -FAET 8    [SINC-FAET]
(2233)  NAAT- 0 -HWYLC 4    [NAAT-HWYLC]
(2235)  THANC- 3 -HYCGENDE 5    [THANC-HYCGENDE]
(2245)  ()HARD*HORD- 2 -WYRDHNE 9    [*HORD-WYRDHNE]
(2254)  DRYNC- 3 -FAET 1    [DRYNC-FAET]
(2255)  ()+++*HYR-9-STED- 2 -GOLDE 5    [*HYRSTED-GOLDE]
(2270)  HORD- 3 -WYNNE 4    [HORD-WYNNE]
(2271)  UUHT- 9 -SCEADHA 5    [UUHT-SCEADHA]
(2274)  FOLD- 1 -BUUEND. 9    [FOLD-BUUEND]
(2278)  DHEEOD- 3 -SCEADHA 5    [DHEEOD-SCEADHA]
(2279)  HORD- 4 -AERNA 1    [HORD-AERNA]
(2288)  STEARC- 4 -HEORT 4    [STEARC-HEORT]
(2289)  FOOT- 9 -LAAST 4    [FOOT-LAAST]
(2292)  WRAEAEC- 2 -SIIDH 3    [WRAEAEC-SIIDH]
(2293)  HORD- 4 -WEARD 9    [HORD-WEARD]
(2299)  AET- 1 -HWEARF 9    [AET-HWEARF]
(2300)  SINC- 4 -FAET 3    [SINC-FAET]
(2302)  HORD- 1 -WEARD 9    [HORD-WEARD]
(2306)  DRINC- 9 -FAET 5    [DRINC-FAET]
(2311)  SINC- 2 -GIFAN 4    [SINC-GIFAN]
(2315)  LYFT- 3 -FLOGA 4    [LYFT-FLOGA]
(2320)  DRYHT- 3 -SELE 4    [DRYHT-SELE]
```

```
(2321) LAND- 4 -WARA 9    [LAND-WARA]
(2339) WRAEAET- 0 -LIIC 9    [WRAEAET-LIIC]
(2340) HOLT- 3 -WUDU 2    [HOLT-WUDU]
(2344) HORD- 4 -WELAN 4    [HORD-WELAN]
(2346) +WIID- 3 -FLOGAN 5    [WIID-FLOGAN]
(2355) HOND- 1 -GE- 0    [*HOND-GE-MOOTA]
(2360) SUND- 3 -NYTTE 4    [SUND-NYTTE]
(2363) HET- 2 -WARE 4    [HET-WARE]
(2366) HILD- 3 -FRECAN 4    [HILD-FRECAN]
(2375) HEARD- 0 -REEDE 4    [HEARD-REEDE]
(2377) FREEON-1-D- 1 -LAARU= 9    [FREEOND-LAARU=]
(2379) WRAEC- 9 -MAECGAS 3    [WRAEC-MAECGAS]
(2388) HEARD- 0 -REED 4    [HEARD-REED]
(2391) LEEOD- 3 -HRYRES 3    [LEEOD-HRYRES]
(2392) EEAD- 1 -GILSE 5    [EEAD-GILSE]
(2414) GOLD- 3 -MAADH-9-MAS 3    [GOLD-MAADHMAS]
(2419) GOLD- 9 -WINE 3    [GOLD-WINE]
(2462) WIIC- 2 -STEDE 4    [WIIC-STEDE]
(2471) LEEOD- 3 -BYRIG 4    [LEEOD-BYRIG]
(2476) FYRD- 9 -HWATE 5    [FYRD-HWATE]
(2478) INWIT- 4 -SCEAR 5    [INWIT-SCEAR]
(2502) HAND- 0 -BONAN 3    [HAND-BONAN]
(2504) BREEOST- 5 -WEORDHUNGE 4    [BREEOST-WEORDHUNGE]
(2510) BEEOT- 1 -WORDU= 3    [BEEOT-WORDU=]
(2552) STEARC- 3 -HEORT 3    [STEARC-HEORT]
(2554) HORD- 9 -WEARD 3    [HORD-WEARD]
(2559) BORD- 1 -RAND 3    [BORD-RAND]
(2579) DHIIOD- 3 -CYNING 3    [DHIIOD-CYNING]
(2584) GOLD- 9 -WINE 3    [GOLD-WINE]
(2588) GRUND- 3 -WONG 3    [GRUND-WONG]
(2593) HORD- 3 -WEARD 9    [HORD-WEARD]
(2596) ()HEAND*HAND- 2 -GE- 2    [*HAND-GE-STEALLAN]
(2603) LIND- 3 -WIGA 4    [LIND-WIGA]
(2607) +WIIC- 9 -STEDE 5    [WIIC-STEDE]
(2608) FOL-1-C- 1 -RIHTA 9    [FOLC-RIHTA]
(2614) AET- 0 -BAER 4    [AET-BAER]
(2616) EALD- 2 -SWEORD 4    [EALD-SWEORD]
(2618) FYRD- 3 -SEARO 3    [FYRD-SEARO]
(2628) MOOD- 2 -SEFA 6    [MOOD-SEFA]
(2631) WORD- 3 -RIHTA 4    [WORD-RIHTA]
(2649) HILD- 3 -FRUMAN 3    [HILD-FRUMAN]
(2650) GLEED- 2 -EGESA 9    [GLEED-EGESA]
(2651) LIIC- 2 -HAMAN 4    [LIIC-HAMAN]
(2652) GOLD- 3 -GYFAN 4    [GOLD-GYFAN]
(2657) EALD- 3 -GE- 2    [EALD-GE-WYRHT]
(2670) IN-1-WIT- 1 -GAEST 9    [INWIT-GAEST]
(2688) THEEOD- 3 -SCEADHA 3    [THEEOD-SCEADHA]
(2694) THEEOD- 2 -CYNINGES 3    [THEEOD-CYNINGES]
(2695) AND- 0 -LONGNE 9    [AND-LONGNE]
(2708) SIB- 2 -AEDHELINGAS 3    [SIB-AEDHELINGAS]
(2733) FOLC- 3 -CYNING 9    [FOLC-CYNING]
(2748) GOLD- 2 -AEAEHT 3    [GOLD-AEAEHT]
(2751) LEEOD- 3 -SCIPE 3    [LEEOD-SCIPE]
(2753) WORD- 3 -CWYDU= 3    [WORD-CWYDU=]
(2760) UUHT- 4 -FLOGAN 9    [UUHT-FLOGAN]
(2761) FEOR-9-MEND- 2 -LEEASE 4    [FEORMEND-LEEASE]
(2768) HOND- 3 -WUNDRA 9    [HOND-WUNDRA]
(2770) GRUND- 3 -WONG 4    [GRUND-WONG]
(2771) GIOND- 3 -WLIITAN 3    [GIOND-WLIITAN]
(2778) EALD- 3 -HLAAFORDES 4    [EALD-HLAAFORDES]
(2779) MUND- 0 -BORA 9    [MUND-BORA]
(2783) EFT- 2 -SIIDHES 3    [EFT-SIIDHES]
(2792) BREEOST- 2 -HORD 3    [BREEOST-HORD]
(2798) SWYLT- 2 -DAEGE 4    [SWYLT-DAEGE]
(2810) THRIIST- 9 -HYYDIG 4    [THRIIST-HYYDIG]
```

195

```
(2811) GOLD- 3 -FAAHNE 4    [GOLD-FAAHNE]
(2815) METOD- 2 -SCEAFTE 9    [METOD-SCEAFTE]
(2818) BREEOST- 3 -GE- 1    [BREEOST-GE-HYGDU=]
(2830) WIID- 2 -FLOGA 3    [WIID-FLOGA]
(2831) HORD- 3 -AERNE 4    [HORD-AERNE]
(2835) HILD- 2 -FRUMAN 3    [HILD-FRUMAN]
(2835) HOND- 2 -GE- 2    [HOND-GE-WEORCE]
(2843) DRYHT- 2 -MAADHMA 4    [DRYHT-MAADHMA]
(2846) HILD- 3 -LATAN 2    [HILD-LATAN]
(2847) AET- 1 -SOMNE 9    [AET-SOMNE]
(2860) =AND- 0 -SWARU 9    [=AND-SWARU]
(2866) EEORED- 3 -GEATWE 3    [EEORED-GEATWE]
(2869) THRYYD- 0 -LIICOST 4    [THRYYD-LIICOST]
(2873) FOLC- 2 -CYNING 4    [FOLC-CYNING]
(2873) FYRD- 2 -GE- 1    [FYRD-GE-STEALLU=]
(2878) AET- 1 -GIFAN 3    [AET-GIFAN]
(2884) SINC- 2 -THEGO 4    [SINC-THEGO]
(2884) SWYRD- 8 -GIFU 9    [SWYRD-GIFU]
(2886) LOND- 2 -RIHTES 2    [LOND-RIHTES]
(2891) EDWIIT- 2 -LIIF 9    [EDWIIT-LIIF]
(2894) MOOD- 2 -GIOOMOR 4    [MOOD-GIOOMOR]
(2895) BORD- 9 -HAEBBENDE 4    [BORD-HAEBЗENDE]
(2896) EFT- 2 -CYMES 3    [EFT-CYMES]
(2909) HEEAFOD- 8 -WEARDE 5    [HEEAFOD-WEARDE]
(2915) FLOT- 2 -HERGE 3    [FLOT-HERGE]
(2916) HET- 2 -WARE 3    [HET-WARE]
(2929) ()HOND*OND- 3 -SLYHT 2    [*OND-SLYHT]
(2935) HLAAFORD- 2 -LEEASE 3    [HLAAFORD-LEEASE]
(2938) OND- 8 -LONGE 9    [OND-LONGE]
(2946) SWAAT- 3 -SWADHU 4    [SWAAT-SWADHJ]
(2963) THEEOD- 3 -CYNING 4    [THEEOD-CYNING]
(2970) DHEEOD- 9 -CYNING 3    [DHEEOD-CYNING]
(2972) ()HOND*OND- 1 -SLYHT 9    [*OND-SLYHT]
(2979) EALD- 2 -SWEORD 3    [EALD-SWEORD]
(2980) BORD- 3 -WEAL 3    [BORD-WEAL]
(2999) FEEOND- 2 -SCIPE 5    [FEEOND-SCIPE]
(3005) ()SCILDINGAS*SCILD- 8 -*WIGAN 9    [*SCILD-*WIGAN]
(3006) FOLC- 0 -REED 4    [FOLC-REED]
(3008) THEEOD- 9 -CYNING 4    [THEEOD-CYNING]
(3010) +AAD- 2 -FAERE 5    [AAD-FAERE]
(3042) FOOT- 2 -GE- 2    [FOOT-GE-MEARCES]
(3043) LYFT- 2 -WYNNE 4    [LYFT-WYNNE]
(3074) GOLD- 3 -HWAETE 3    [GOLD-HWAETE]
(3081) GOLD- 3 -WEARD 3    [GOLD-WEARD]
(3083) WORULD- 2 -ENDE 9    [WORULD-ENDE]
(3086) *THEEOD- 8 -*CYNING 8    [*THEEOD-*CYNING]
(3087) GEOND- 3 -SEH 3    [GEOND-SEH]
(3092) HORD- 2 -GE- 1    [HORD-GE-STREEONA]
(3092) AET- 0 -BAER 3    [AET-BAER]
(3112) BOLD- 3 -AAGENDRA 3    [BOLD-AAGENDRA]
(3113) FOLC- 3 -AAGENDE 4    [FOLC-AAGENDE]
(3118) SCILD- 2 -WEALL 4    [SCILD-WEALL]
(3123) INWIT- 3 -+HROOF 3    [INWIT-HROOF]
(3125) AEAELED- 3 -LEEOMAN 3    [AEAELED-LEEOMAN]
(3130) OFOST- 0 -()LIC+*LIICE 9    [*OFOST-LIICE]
(3138) -WAAC- 1 -LIICNE 3    [UN-WAAC-LIICNE]
(3146) WIND- 9 -BLOND 1    [WIND-BLOND]
(3149) MOOD- 1 -CEARE 3    [MOOD-CEARE]
(3155) ()HAEF+*HAEFT- 8 -NYYD 3    [*HAEFT-NYYD]
(3172) WORD- 1 -GYD 1    [WORD-GYD]
(3177) LIIC- 0 -HAMAN 9    [LIIC-HAMAN]
(3180) WYRULD- 0 -()CYNING*CYNINGA 9    [*WYRULD-CYNINGA]
```

FIRST MORPHEME TERMINATES IN SPIRANT

```
1953) LIIF- 1 -GE- 2    [LIIF-GE-SCEAFTA]
1959) WIIS- 2 -DOOME 4    [WIIS-DOOME]
1969) GUUDH- 3 -CYNING 2    [GUUDH-CYNING]
1982) LIIDH- 3 -WAEAEGE 3    [LIIDH-WAEAEGE]
1990) HROODH- 3 -GAARE 5    [HROODH-GAARE]
1996) SUUDH- 3 -DENE 5    [SUUDH-DENE]
2010) HROODH- 1 -GAAR 4    [HROODH-GAAR]
2011) HEALF- 0 -DE-9-NES 3    [HEALF-DENES]
2020) HROODH- 2 -GAARES 3    [HROODH-GAARES]
2032) OF- 2 -THYNCAN 3    [OF-THYNCAN]
2064) AADH- 2 -()SWEORDH*SWEORD 3    [*AADH-SWEORD]
2065) WIIF- 8 -LUFAN 3    [WIIF-LUFAN]
2079) MUUDH- 3 -BONAN. 6    [MUUDH-BONAN]
2097) LIIF- 2 -WYNNA 1    [LIIF-WYNNA]
2112) GUUDH- 3 -WIGA 9    [GUUDH-WIGA]
2123) UUDH- 9 -GENGE. 6    [UUDH-GENGE]
2125) DEEADH- 4 -WEERIG-1-NE 4    [DEEADH-WEERIGNE]
2129) HROODH- 0 -GAARE 9    [HROODH-GAARE]
2139) *GUUDH- 8 -SELE 9    [*GUUDH-SELE]
2141) ODH- 3 -FEREDE. 9    [ODH-FEREDE]
2143) HEALF- 2 -DENES. 9    [HEALF-DENES]
2147) HEALF- 1 -DENES 3    [HEALF-DENES]
2154) GUUDH- 3 -SWEORD 3    [GUUDH-SWEORD]
2155) HROODH- 1 -+GAAR 5    [HROODH-GAAR]
2172) HEALS- 3 -BEEAH 3    [HEALS-BEEAH]
2180) HEORDH- 3 -GE- 0    [HEORDH-GE-NEEATAS]
2232) EORDH- 9 -()++SE*HUUSE 8    [*EORDH-HUUSE]
2249) GUUDH- 4 -DEEADH 4    [GUUDH-DEEADH]
2251) OF- 1 -GEAF 1    [OF-GEAF]
2273) NIIDH- 2 -DRACA 3    [NIIDH-DRACA]
2303) EARFOODH- 5 -LIICE 5    [EARFOODH-LIICE]
2309) EGES- 0 -LIIC 9    [EGES-LIIC]
2318) GUUDH- 4 -SCEADHA 5    [GUUDH-SCEADHA]
2327) GIF- 3 -STOOL 3    [GIF-STOOL]
2334) EORDH- 4 -WEARD 9    [EORDH-WEARD]
2335) GUUDH- 9 -KYNING 4    [GUUDH-KYNING]
2351) HROODH- 3 -GAARES 9    [HROODH-GAARES]
2357) FREES- 2 -LONDUM 5    [FREES-LONDUM]
2410) EORDH- 3 -SELE 3    [EORDH-SELE]
2412) YYDH- 1 -GE- 1    [YYDH-GE-WINNE]
2414) GUUDH- 3 -FRECA 3    [GUUDH-FRECA]
2417) NIIDH- 4 -HEARD 3    [NIIDH-HEARD]
2418) HEORDH- 3 -GE- 0    [HEORDH-GE-NEEATU=]
2426) GUUDH- 0 -RAEAESA 9    [GUUDH-RAEAESA]
2434) HAEDH- 2 -CYN. 6    [HAEDH-CYN]
2437) HAEDH- 1 -CYN 9    [HAEDH-CYN]
2439) OF- 9 -SCEET 3    [OF-SCEET]
2469) OF- 1 -GEAF 4    [OF-GEAF]
2482) HAEDH- 9 -CYNNE 4    [HAEDH-CYNNE]
2487) GUUDH- 4 -HELM 3    [GUUDH-HELM]
2489) OF- 9 -TEEAH. 5    [OF-TEEAH]
2503) FREES- 0 -()CYNING*CYNINGE 9    [*FREES-CYNINGE]
2515) EORDH- 3 -SELE 4    [EORDH-SELE]
2521) WIDH- 1 -GRIIPAN 4    [WIDH-GRIIPAN]
2528) GUUDH- 2 -FLOGAN 3    [GUUDH-FLOGAN]
2563) GUUDH- 3 -CYNING 4    [GUUDH-CYNING]
2566) STIIDH- 2 -MOOD 3    [STIIDH-MOOD]
2583) HREEDH- 2 -SIGORA 5    [HREEDH-SIGORA]
2584) GUUDH- 2 -BILL 3    [GUUDH-BILL]
2588) OF- 0 -GYFAN 4    [OF-GYFAN]
2603) LEEOF- 9 -LIIC 5    [LEEOF-LIIC]
2604) AELF- 9 -HERES 4    [AELF-HERES]
2617) GUUDH- 9 -GE- 2    [GUUDH-GE-WAEAEDU]
2618) FUUS- 0 -LIIC 4    [FUUS-LIIC]
```

197

```
(2623)  GUUDH-  9 -GE- 3    [GUUDH-GE-WAEAEDA]
(2625)  FORDH-  4 -WEG 3    [FORDH-WEG]
(2636)  GUUDH-  2 -GE- 9    [GUUDH-GE-TAAWA]
(2639)  SIIDH-  9 -FATE 4    [SIIDH-FATE]
(2648)  GUUDH-  2 -RINCA 4    [GUUDH-RINCA]
(2664)  GEO-9-GUDH- 3 -FEEORE 5    [GEOGUDH-FEEORE]
(2677)  GUUDH-  3 -CYNING 3    [GUUDH-CYNING]
(2699)  NIIDH-  2 -GAEST 4    [NIIDH-GAEST]
(2712)  EORDH-  9 -DRACA 4    [EORDH-DRACA]
(2716)  WIIS-  3 -HYGGENDE 4    [WIIS-HYGGENDE]
(2719)  EORDH-  2 -RECED 3    [EORDH-RECED]
(2730)  GUUDH-  2 -GE- 1    [GUUDH-GE-WAEAEDU]
(2735)  GUUDH-  2 -WINU= 9    [GUUDH-WINU=]
(2805)  HRO-9-NES- 3 -NAESSE 4    [HRONES-NAESSE]
(2820)  SOODH-  3 -FAESTRA 4    [SOODH-FAESTRA]
(2822)  EAR-9-FODH- 4 -LIICE 4    [EARFODH-LIICE]
(2825)  EGES-  0 -LIIC 3    [EGES-LIIC]
(2825)  EORDH-  3 -DRACA 3    [EORDH-DRACA]
(2846)  OF-  9 -GEEFAN 3    [OF-GEEFAN]
(2851)  GUUDH-  2 -GE- 1    [GUUDH-GE-WAEAEDU]
(2861)  EEDH-  2 -BEGEETE 3    [EEDH-BEGEETE]
(2871)  GUUDH-  1 -GE- 1    [GUUDH-GE-WAEAEDU]
(2877)  LIIF-  3 -WRADHE 3    [LIIF-WRADHE]
(2881)  FERHDH-  3 -GE- 0    [FERHDH-GE-NIIJHLAN]
(2899)  SOODH-  9 -LIICE 4    [SOODH-LIICE]
(2901)  DEEADH-  3 -BEDDE 3    [DEEADH-BEDDE]
(2925)  HAEDH-  0 -CEN 9    [HAEDH-CEN]
(2927)  GUUDH-  3 -SCIL-9-FINGAS. 5    [GUUDH-SCILFINGAS]
(2929)  EGES-  3 -FULL 5    [EGES-FULL]
(2934)  ODH-  3 -EEODON 9    [ODH-EEODON]
(2934)  EARFODH-  4 -LIICE 4    [EARFODH-LIICE]
(2935)  HREFNES-  3 -HOLT 3    [HREFNES-HOLT]
(2957)  EORDH-  2 -WEALL. 9    [EORDH-WEALL]
(2960)  HREEDH-  3 -LINGAS 3    [HREEDH-LINGAS]
(2991)  GUUDH-  2 -RAEAES 2    [GUUDH-RAEAES]
(2995)  ODH-  9 -WIITAN 4    [ODH-WIITAN]
(3036)  GUUDH-  2 -CYNING 4    [GUUDH-CYNING]
(3046)  EORDH-  3 -SCRAFA 9    [EORDH-SCRAFA]
(3055)  SOODH-  9 -CYNING 3    [SOODH-CYNING]
(3060)  OF-  1 -SLOOH 4    [OF-SLOOH]
(3062)  WRAADH-  2 -LIICE 4    [WRAADH-LIICE]
(3064)  LIIF-  2 -GE- 9    [LIIF-GE-SCEAFTA]
(3089)  SWAEAES-  0 -LIICE 5    [SWAEAES-LIICE]
(3090)  EORDH-  2 -WEALL 4    [EORDH-WEALL]
(3099)  WEORDH-  9 -FULLOST 4    [WEORDH-FULLOST]
(3161)  WEORDH-  3 -LIICOST 2    [WEORDH-LIICOST]
(3165)  NIIDH-  9 -HEEDIGE 2    [NIIDH-HEEDIGE]
(3179)  HEORDH-  1 -G=- 1    [HEORDH-G=-NEEATAS]
(3182)  LOF-  9 -GEORNOST. 9    [LOF-GEORNOST]
```

FIRST MORPHEME TERMINATES IN G, X, W, OR H

```
(1954)  HEEAH-  4 -LUFAN 4    [HEEAH-LUFAN]
(1993)  SORH-  2 -WYLMU= 4    [SORH-WYLMU=]
(1999)  ECG-  3 -DHIIOES 9    [ECG-DHIIOES]
(2002)  -*LEG-  9 -HWIIL 4    [*OR-*LEG-HWIIL]
(2010)  HRING-  3 -SELE 4    [HRING-SELE]
(2018)  BEEA-2-H-  4 -WRIDHAN 4    [BEEAH-WRIDHAN]
(2037)  HRING-  3 -MAEAEL 5    [HRING-MAEAEL]
(2046)  WIIG-  3 -BEALU 4    [WIIG-BEALU]
(2077)  FEOR-2-H-  4 -BEALU 3    [FEORH-BEALU]
(2082)  BLOODIG-  3 -TOODH 4    [BLOODIG-TOODH]
(2119)  SORH-  2 -FULL 4    [SORH-FULL]
(2120)  WIIG-  2 -HETE 9    [WIIG-HETE]
```

```
(2132)  HREEOH- 4 -MOOD 8     [HREEOH-MOOD]
(2173)  WEALH- 1 -DHEEO 5     [WEALH-DHEEO]
(2176)  BEEAH- 1 -DHEGE 4     [BEEAH-DHEGE]
(2177)  ECG- 2 -DHEEOWES. 6   [ECG-DHEEOWES]
(2220)  ()BU*BIG- 8 -FOLC 3   [*BIG-FOLC]
(2240)  LONG- 2 -GE- 2        [LONG-GE-STREEONA]
(2250)  FEORH- 4 -()BEALC*BEALO 3    [*FEORH-BEALO]
(2261)  WIIG- 8 -FRU-9-MAN 3  [WIIG-FRUMAN]
(2265)  BURH- 3 -STEDE 3      [BURH-STEDE]
(2266)  FEOR-1-H- 4 -CYNNA 5  [FEORH-CYNNA]
(2296)  HREEOH- 3 -MOOD 9     [HREEOH-MOOD]
(2302)  HEEAH- 3 -GE- 0       [HEEAH-GE-STREEONA]
(2333)  LIIG- 3 -DRACA 9      [LIIG-DRACA]
(2339)  WIIG- 2 -BORD 2       [WIIG-BORD]
(2367)  ECG- 2 -DHEEOWES 9    [ECG-DHEEOWES]
(2385)  FEORH- 3 -WUNDE 4     [FEORH-WUNDE]
(2398)  ECG- 2 -DHIIOWES. 7   [ECG-DHIIOWES]
(2425)  ECG- 2 -DHEEOWES 5    [ECG-DHEEOWES]
(2427)  -LEG- 4 -HWIILA 3     [OR-LEG-HWIILA]
(2441)  FEOH- 2 -LEEAS 2      [FEOH-LEEAS]
(2455)  SORH- 9 -CEARIG 4     [SORH-CEARIG]
(2460)  SORH- 2 -LEEODH 9     [SORH-LEEODH]
(2465)  FEORH- 9 -BONAN 4     [FEORH-BONAN]
(2479)  MAEAEG- 9 -WINE 5     [MAEAEG-WINE]
(2489)  FEORH- 2 -SWENG 3     [FEORH-SWENG]
(2496)  WIIG- 3 -FRECAN 5     [WIIG-FRECAN]
(2501)  DAEG- 3 -HREFNE 4     [DAEG-HREFNE]
(2520)  AAG- 0 -LAEAECEAN 4   [AAG-LAEAECEAN]
(2534)  AAG- 0 -LAEAECEAN 4   [AAG-LAEAECEAN]
(2537)  FEORH- 9 -BEALU 4     [FEORH-BEALU]
(2557)  AAG- 0 -LAEAECEAN 3   [AAG-LAEAECEAN]
(2561)  HRING- 3 -BOGAN 2     [HRING-BOGAN]
(2564)  AEAEG- 0 -HWAEDHRU= 4   [AEAEG-HWAEDHRU=]
(2587)  ECG- 1 -DHEEOWES 9    [ECG-DHEEOWES]
(2590)  AEAEG- 1 -HWYLC 2     [AEAEG-HWYLC]
(2592)  AAG- 0 -LAEAECEAN 5   [AAG-LAEAECEAN]
(2602)  $$WIIG- 2 -LAAF 3     [WIIG-LAAF]
(2602)  WEEOX- 1 -STAANES 0   [WEEOX-STAANES]
(2607)  WAEAEG- 2 -MUNDINGA 5   [WAEAEG-MUNDINGA]
(2613)  WEEOH- 2 -()STANES*STAAN 3   [*WEEOH-STAAN]
(2624)  AEAEG- 0 -HWAES 3     [AEAEG-HWAES]
(2631)  WIIG- 3 -+LAAF 9      [WIIG-LAAF]
(2661)  WIIG- 8 -HEA-9-FOLAN 3   [WIIG-HEAFOLAN]
(2672)  LIIG- 3 -YYDHU= 4     [LIIG-YYDHU=]
(2682)  GRAEAEG- 3 -MAEAEL 4   [GRAEAEG-MAEAEL]
(2726)  DAEG- 3 -HWIILA 3     [DAEG-HWIILA]
(2740)  FEORH- 2 -BENNU= 4    [FEORH-BENNU=]
(2745)  WIIG- 2 -LAAF 9       [WIIG-LAAF]
(2752)  WIIH- 9 -STAANES 3    [WIIH-STAANES]
(2754)  HRING- 1 -NET 2       [HRING-NET]
(2780)  LIIG- 3 -EGESAN 3     [LIIG-EGESAN]
(2786)  WONG- 2 -STEDE 3      [WONG-STEDE]
(2792)  THURH- 2 -BRAEC. 4    [THURH-BRAEC]
(2800)  FEORH- 3 -LEGE 4      [FEORH-LEGE]
(2814)  WAEAEG- 2 -MUNDINGA 5   [WAEAEG-MUNDINGA]
(2826)  BEEAH- 4 -HORDU= 2    [BEEAH-HORDU=]
(2827)  WOOH- 2 -BOGEN 4      [WOOH-BOGEN]
(2840)  HRING- 3 -SELE 9      [HRING-SELE]
(2844)  AEAEG- 1 -()HWAEDHRE*HWAEDHER 4   [*AEAEG-HWAEDHER]
(2847)  TREEOW- 4 -LOGAN 4    [TREEOW-LOGAN]
(2862)  WIIG- 0 -LAAF 9       [WIIG-LAAF]
(2862)  WEEOH- 0 -STAANES 2   [WEEOH-STAANES]
(2863)  SAARIG- 0 -FERDH 9    [SAARIG-FERDH]
(2887)  MAEAEG- 2 -BURGE 3    [MAEAEG-BURGE]
(2887)  AEAEG- 0 -HWYLC 2     [AEAEG-HWYLC]
```

```
(2893) ECG- 3 -CLIF 4   [ECG-CLIF]
(2904) ()SIEX*SEX- 3 -BENNU= 9   [*SEX-BENNU=]
(2905) AAG- 0 -LAEAECEAN 9   [AAG-LAEAECEAN]
(2906) WIIG- 0 -LAAF 1   [WIIG-LAAF]
(2907) WIIH- 1 -STAANES 3   [WIIH-STAANES]
(2911) -LEG- 2 -HWIILE 5   [OR-LEG-HWIILE]
(2933) FEORH- 2 -GE- 0   [FEORH-GE-NIIDHLAN]
(2940) GALG- 2 -()TREEOWU*TREEOWU= 4   [*GALG-TREEOWU=]
(2942) SAARIG- 2 -MOODU= 3   [SAARIG-MOODU=]
(2953) WIIG- 1 -CRAEFT 3   [WIIG-CRAEFT]
(3017) HRING- 2 -WEOR-9-DHUNGE 4   [HRING-WEORDHUNGE]
(3040) LEEG- 3 -DRACA 4   [LEEG-DRACA]
(3049) THURH- 4 -ETONE 4   [THURH-ETONE]
(3053) HRING- 3 -SELE 5   [HRING-SELE]
(3076) WIIG- 2 -+LAAF 9   [WIIG-LAAF]
(3076) WIIH- 1 -STAANES 4   [WIIH-STAANES]
(3084) HEEAH- 2 -GE- 4   [HEEAH-GE-SCEAP]
(3100) BURH- 9 -WELAN 2   [BURH-WELAN]
(3110) WIIH- 0 -STAANES 3   [WIIH-STAANES]
(3120) WIIH- 0 -STAANES 3   [WIIH-STAANES]
(3135) AEAEG- 0 -HWAES 2   [AEAEG-HWAES]
(3152) SORG- 2 -CEARIG 8   [SORG-CEARIG]
(3158) WAEAEG- 1 -LIIDHENDU= 3   [WAEAEG-LIIDHENDU=]
```

FIRST MORPHEME TERMINATES IN NONALPHABETIC SYMBOL

```
(2469) GU=- 9 -DREEAM 5   [GU=-DREEAM]
(2543) GU=- 2 -CYSTU= 2   [GU=-CYSTU=]
(2570) G=- 3 -SCIPE 4   [G=-SCIPE]
(2637) G=- 1 -LU=-1-PE 5   [G=-LU=PE]
(2726) G=- 2 -DROGEN 4   [G=-DROGEN]
(2750) MAADHDHU=- 3 -WELAN 9   [MAADHDHU=-WELAN]
(2757) MAADHDHU=- 4 -SIGLA 4   [MAADHDHU=-SIGLA]
(2765) GU=- 2 -CYNNES 3   [GU=-CYNNES]
(2856) FRU=- 2 -GAARE 4   [FRU=-GAARE]
(2890) DOO=- 9 -LEEASAN 1   [DOO=-LEEASAN]
(2930) BRI=- 2 -WIISAN 5   [BRI=-WIISAN]
(3146) G=- 1 -LAEG 3   [G=-LAEG]
(3165) G=- 2 -NUM= 2   [G=-NUM=]
(3166) G=- 1 -STREEON 9   [G=-STREEON]
(3174) G=- 0 -()D+++*DEEFE 8   [*G=-DEEFE]
(3179) -G=- 1 -NEEATAS 1   [HEORDH-G=-NEEATAS]
```

Appendix III

Spacing at Morpheme Boundaries:
Graphotactic Sort

The sorted lists making up most of this appendix contain the same items that make up the lists in Appendix II. But here the word-constitutent morpheme pairs are grouped according to the spacing numeral that separates them in the transcription of the text.

Some prominent distributional characteristics of the varied spacings have been abstracted and set forth in tabular form, as Tables 1-4. For each spacing numeral, except 5-7 which are treated collectively, the count of its occurrences has been made according to whether it follows a one-syllable morpheme or a two-syllable morpheme; because the form ge- is special in both its nature and frequency of occurrence, the one-syllable morpheme count is further divided into a count of ge- and a count of all others. Most conspicuous of the scribes' habits in writing a two-syllable morpheme as the first in a pair within a word is that 0-spacing is so rare as to be regarded probably as a slip or as resulting from a correction after writing at least part of the second morpheme: only five instances in 386 such morpheme sequences are found in S1's copy, fourteen in 263 sequences in S2's copy (nearly half of these consisting of the name Hygelac). Nearly as rare is 1-spacing following a two-syllable morpheme, and 2-spacing is only moderately frequent. This range of spacings, clearly, overlaps but very little the range of spacings within morphemic strings of letters. The range for most instances is 3- and 4-space.

Within each list based on the spacing numeral between

201

morphemes the order of items is that of the phonological
features of the final segmental element of the first morpheme;
the order of features is the same as that used in Appendix II:
vocalic element, consonantal element, and other graphic
symbols, with ordered subdivisions in the first two of these
groups.

Spacing notation	0	1	2	3	4	5-7	8	9	(Total)
Follows two-syllable morpheme	2	4	31	43	25	3	5	18	131
Follows one-syllable morpheme	106	113	151	113	28	7	8	49	575
Morpheme not ge-	70	60	109	92	26	7	3	34	401
Morpheme is ge-	36	53	42	21	2	0	5[a]	15	174
Total Incidence	108	117	182	156	53	10	13	67	706

[a]Includes MS. geata/wum, emended as ge-tāwum (395)

Table 1

First Scribe, lines 662-1320

Spacing Notation	0	1	2	3	4	5-7	8	9	(Total)
Follows two-syllable morpheme	1	1	14	50[b]	36	9	1	15	127
Follows one-syllable morpheme	111	112	136	150	38	7	13	55	622
Morpheme not ge-	87	63	90	111	26	6	6	35	424
Morpheme is ge-	24	49	46	39	12	1	7	20	198
Total Incidence	112	113	150	200	74	16	14	70	749

[b]Includes three-syllable fæderen- (1263)

Table 2

First Scribe, lines 1321-1939

Spacing notation	0	1	2	3	4	5-7	8	9	(Total)
Follows two-syllable morpheme	2	5	15[c]	44	28	13	3	18	128
Follows one-syllable morpheme	79	103	137	120	54	11	16	49	579
Morpheme not ge-	64	58	78	88	37	6	9	45	385
Morpheme is ge-	15	45	59	32	17	5	7	14	194
Total Incidence	81	108	152	164	82	24	19	77	707

[c]Includes ⚓, i.e., ēþel, transcribed EETHEL.

Table 3

Second Scribe, lines 1940-3182

Spacing notation	0	1	2	3	4	5-7	8	9	(Total)
Follows two-syllable morpheme	14	18	43	95	48	6	11[d]	28[e]	263
Follows one-syllable morpheme	215	258	240	195	63	4	46	99	1120
Morpheme not ge-	135	124	169	171	58	1	35	73	766
Morpheme is ge-	80	134	71	24	5	3	11	26	354
Total Incidence	229	276	283	290	111	10	57	127	1383

[d]Includes MS. side, emended heal- (1981)

[e]Includes MS. hilde, emended hild- (2205)

Table 4

MORPHEME PAIRS GROUPED BY MEASURE OF SPACING

```
(0018) BEEO- 0 -WULF 3    [BEEO-WULF]
(0053) BEEO- 0 -WULF 3    [BEEO-WULF]
(0343) BEEO- 0 -WULF 3    [BEEO-WULF]
(0364) BEEO- 0 -WULF 5    [BEEO-WULF]
(0430) FREEO- 0 -WINE 9   [FREEO-WINE]
(0615) FREEO- 0 -LIIC 9   [FREEO-LIIC]
(0623) BEEO- 0 -WULFE 5   [BEEO-WULFE]
(0631) BEEO- 0 -WULF 1    [BEEO-WULF]
(0653) BEEO- 0 -WULF 5    [BEEO-WULF]
(0034) AA- 0 -LEEDON 2    [AA-LEEDON]
(0047) AA- 0 -SETTON 4    [AA-SETTON]
(0080) AA- 0 -LEEH 5    [AA-LEEH]
(0128) AA- 0 -HAFEN 2    [AA-HAFEN]
(0325) SAEAE- 0 -MEE-1-THE 4    [SAEAE-MEETHE]
(0344) AA- 0 -SECGAN 4    [AA-SECGAN]
(0355) AA- 0 -GIFAN 9    [AA-GIFAN]
(0377) SAEAE- 0 -LIITHENDE 6    [SAEAE-LIITHENDE]
(0390) AA- 0 -BEEAD. 5    [AA-BEEAD]
(0399) AA- 0 -RAAS 4    [AA-RAAS]
(0567) AA- 0 -SWEFEDE 5    [AA-SWEFEDE]
(0622) AA- 0 -LAMP 3    [AA-LAMP]
(0651) AA- 0 -RAAS. 7    [AA-RAAS]
(0653) AA- 0 -BEEAD. 3    [AA-BEEAD]
(0654) AA- 0 -CWAEDH. 6    [AA-CWAEDH]
(0655) AA- 0 -LYYFDE 5    [AA-LYYFDE]
(0184) BE- 0 -SCUUFAN 9    [BE-SCUUFAN]
(0308) GEATO- 0 -LIIC 3    [GEATO-LIIC]
(0029) GE- 0 -SIITHAS 9    [GE-SIITHAS]
(0037) GE- 0 -LAEAEDED. 5    [GE-LAEAEDED]
(0055) GE- 0 -FRAEAE-9-GE 4    [GE-FRAEAEGE]
(0066) GE- 0 -WEEOX 5    [GE-WEEOX]
(0069) GE- 0 -WYRCEAN 5    [GE-WYRCEAN]
(0094) GE- 0 -SET-1-TE 5    [GE-SETTE]
(0122) GE- 0 -NAM 3    [GE-NAM]
(0139) GE- 0 -RUUM- 9    [GE-RUUM-LIICOR]
(0141) GE- 0 -SAEGD 4    [GE-SAEGD]
(0171) GE- 0 -SAET 4    [GE-SAET]
(0220) GE- 0 -WADEN 2    [GE-WADEN]
(0234) $GE- 0 -WAAT 3    [GE-WAAT]
(0247) GE- 0 -SEAH 3    [GE-SEAH]
(0278) GE- 0 -LAEAERAN. 5    [GE-LAEAERAN]
(0288) GE- 0 -SCAAD 3    [GE-SCAAD]
(0291) GE- 0 -WIITATH 9    [GE-WIITATH]
(0361) GE- 0 -FERE-9-DE 4    [GE-FEREDE]
(0388) GE- 0 -SAGA 3    [GE-SAGA]
(0404) GE- 0 -STOOD. 5    [GE-STOOD]
(0415) GE- 0 -LAEAER-1-DON 4    [GE-LAEAERDON]
(0420) GE- 0 -BAND 5    [GE-BAND]
(0433) GE- 0 -AAHSOD 5    [GE-AAHSOD]
(0440) GE- 0 -LYY-9-FAN 3    [GE-LYYFAN]
(0476) GE- 0 -FREMED 9    [GE-FREMED]
(0477) GE- 0 -WANOD 3    [GE-WANOD]
(0480) GE- 0 -BEEOTEDON 4    [GE-BEEOTEDON]
(0556) GE- 0 -RAEAEHTE 6    [GE-RAEAEHTE]
(0575) GE- 0 -FRAEGN 4    [GE-FRAEGN]
(0578) GE- 0 -DIIGDE 5    [GE-DIIGDE]
(0585) GE- 0 -FREMEDE 4    [GE-FREMEDE]
(0591) GE- 0 -FREME-2-DE 5    [GE-FREMEDE]
```

```
(0613)  GE-   0 -MYNDIG 5      [GE-MYNDIG]
(0627)  GE-   0 -LYYFDE 5      [GE-LYYFDE]
(0654)  GE-   0 -WEALD 4       [GE-WEALD]
(0059)  -GE-  0 -RIIMED 2      [FORDH-GE-RIIMED]
(0209)  -GE-  0 -MYR-9-CU 4    [LAND-GE-MYRCU]
(0045)  ON-   0 -SENDON 4      [ON-SENDON]
(0092)  AEL-  0 -MIHTIGA 4     [AEL-MIHTIGA]
(0120)  WON-  0 -SCEAFT 3      [WON-SCEAFT]
(0130)  AEAER- 0 -GOOD 9       [AEAER-GOOD]
(0149)  FOR-  0 -DHAAM 8       [FOR-DHAAM]
(0150)  UN-   0 -DYRNE 4       [UN-DYRNE]
(0165)  AAN-  0 -GENGEA 3      [AAN-GENGEA]
(0190)  SIN-  0 -GAA-9-LA 4    [SIN-GAALA]
(0196)  MON-  0 -CYN-2-NES 5   [MON-CYNNES]
(0308)  ON-   0 -GYTON 3       [ON-GYTON]
(0316)  AL-   0 -WALDA 4       [AL-WALDA]
(0388)  WIL-  0 -CUMAN 4       [WIL-CUMAN]
(0394)  WIL-  0 -CUMAN 4       [WIL-CUMAN]
(0410)  UN-   0 -DYR-1-NE 4    [UN-DYRNE]
(0444)  UN-   0 -FOR-3-HTE 1   [UN-FORHTE]
(0449)  +AN-  0 -GEN-1-GA 4    [AN-GENGA]
(0449)  -MURN- 0 -LIICE 9      [UN-MURN-LIICE]
(0468)  UN-   0 -LIFIGENDE 5   [UN-LIFIGENDE]
(0524)  BEEAN- 0 -STAANES 5    [BEEAN-STAANES]
(0537)  +GAAR- 0 -SECG 4       [GAAR-SECG]
(0573)  UN-   0 -FAEAEGNE 9    [UN-FAEAEGNE]
(0585)  DEEOR- 0 -LIICE 9      [DEEOR-LIICE]
(0612)  WYN-  0 -SUME 9        [WYN-SUME]
(0112)  ORC-  0 -NEEAS 3       [ORC-NEEAS]
(0258)  =AND- 0 -SWARODE 5     [=AND-SWARODE]
(0280)  ED-   0 -()WENDAN*WENDEN 9  [*ED-WENDEN]
(0349)  MOOD- 0 -SEFA 4        [MOOD-SEFA]
(0354)  =AND- 0 -SWARE 9       [=AND-SWARE]
(0367)  GLAED- 0 -MAN 9        [GLAED-MAN]
(0491)  AET-  0 -SOM-2-NE 5    [AET-SOMNE]
(0554)  FEEOND- 0 -SCADHA 9    [FEEOND-SCADHA]
(0228)  YYTH- 0 -LAADE 4       [YYTH-LAADE]
(0306)  GUUTH- 0 -MOOD 9       [GUUTH-MOOD]
(0360)  WULF- 0 -GAAR 5        [WULF-GAAR]
(0009)  AEAEG- 0 -HWYLC 4      [AEAEG-HWYLC]
(0159)  AEAEG- 0 -LAEAECA 8    [AEAEG-LAEAECA]
(0337)  MOODIG- 0 -LIICRAN. 4  [MOODIG-LIICRAN]
(0425)  AAG-  0 -LAEAECAN 4    [AAG-LAEAECAN]
(0433)  AEAEG- 0 -LAEAECA 4    [AEAEG-LAEAECA]
(0499)  ECG-  0 -LAAFES 4      [ECG-LAAFES]
(0556)  AAG-  0 -LAEAECAN 9    [AAG-LAEAECAN]
(0592)  AEAEG- 0 -LAEAECA 3    [AEAEG-LAEAECA]
(0621)  AEAEG- 0 -HWYLCNE 9    [AEAEG-HWYLCNE]
(0629)  WEAL-1-H- 0 -THEEON. 5 [WEALH-THEEON]
(0646)  AAH-  0 -LAEAECAN 9    [AAH-LAEAECAN]

(0457)  BEEO- 1 -WULF. 3       [BEEO-WULF]
(0529)  BEEO- 1 -WULF 4        [BEEO-WULF]
(0641)  FREEO- 1 -LICU 3       [FREEO-LICU]
(0329)  SAEAE- 1 -MAN-2-NA 4   [SAEAE-MANNA]
(0411)  SAEAE- 1 -LIIDHEND 5   [SAEAE-LIIDHEND]
(0545)  TOO-  1 -DRAAF 5       [TOO-DRAAF]
(0067)  BE-   1 -ARN 4         [BE-ARN]
(0115)  BE-   1 -COOM 9        [BE-COOM]
(0192)  BE-   1 -COOM 3        [BE-COOM]
(0486)  BE-   1 -STYYMED 4     [BE-STYYMED]
(0519)  HEA-2-THO- 1 -RAEAEMES 9  [HEATHO-RAEAEMES]
(0194)  HIGE- 1 -LAA-9-CES 4   [HIGE-LAACES]
(0435)  HIGE- 1 -LAAC 3        [HIGE-LAAC]
(0452)  HIGE- 1 -LAACE 5       [HIGE-LAACE]
```

206

```
(0007) GE- 1 -BAAD 9   [GE-BAAD]
(0074) GE- 1 -FRAEGN 4   [GE-FRAEGN]
(0074) GE- 1 -BAN-1-NAN 3   [GE-BANNAN]
(0076) GE- 1 -LOMP 3   [GE-LOMP]
(0079) GE- 1 -WEALD 3   [GE-WEALD]
(0088) GE- 1 -HYYR-9-DE. 6   [GE-HYYRDE]
(0097) GE- 1 -SCEOOP 4   [GE-SCEOOP]
(0117) GE- 1 -+BUUN 4   [GE-BUUN]
(0118) GE- 1 -DRIHT 4   [GE-DRIHT]
(0123) GE- 1 -+WAAT 6   [GE-WAAT]
(0165) GE- 1 -FRE-1-MEDE. 9   [GE-FREMEDE]
(0175) GE- 1 -HEE-9-TON 3   [GE-HEETON]
(0177) GE- 1 -FRE-2-ME-2-DE. 5   [GE-FREMEDE]
(0179) GE- 1 -MUN-9-DON 4   [GE-MUNDON]
(0191) GE- 1 -WIN 2   [GE-WIN]
(0199) GE- 1 -GYR-1-WAN 3   [GE-GYRWAN]
(0206) GE- 1 -CORONE 5   [GE-CORONE]
(0210) GE- 1 -+WAAT 3   [GE-WAAT]
(0217) GE- 1 -WAAT 9   [GE-WAAT]
(0217) GE- 1 -FYYSED 4   [GE-FYYSED]
(0218) GE- 1 -LIICOST 3   [GE-LIICOST]
(0221) GE- 1 -SAAWON 5   [GE-SAAWON]
(0229) GE- 1 -SEAH 3   [GE-SEAH]
(0250) GE- 1 -WEORDHAD 3   [GE-WEORDHAD]
(0255) GE- 1 -HYYRADH 5   [GE-HYYRADH]
(0264) GE- 1 -+BAAD 3   [GE-BAAD]
(0265) GE- 1 -MAN 3   [GE-MAN]
(0292) GE- 1 -WAEAE-1-DU 3   [GE-WAEAEDU]
(0301) GE- 1 -WITON 3   [GE-WITON]
(0313) GE- 1 -TAEAEHTE 4   [GE-TAEAEHTE]
(0318) GE- 1 -SUNDE 5   [GE-SUNDE]
(0331) GE- 1 -WUR-2-THAD 4   [GE-WURTHAD]
(0349) GE- 1 -CYYDHED. 9   [GE-CYYDHED]
(0358) GE- 1 -STOOD 4   [GE-STOOD]
(0398) GE- 1 -THINGES. 9   [GE-THINGES]
(0431) GE- 1 -DRYHT. 4   [GE-DRYHT]
(0492) GE- 1 -RYYMED 4   [GE-RYYMED]
(0524) GE- 1 -LAEAESTE. 7   [GE-LAEAESTE]
(0538) GE- 1 -AEF-1-NDON 3   [GE-AEFNDON]
(0562) GE- 1 -FEEAN 3   [GE-FEEAN]
(0609) GE- 1 -HYYRDE 4   [GE-HYYRDE]
(0615) GE- 1 -SEALDE 5   [GE-SEALDE]
(0626) GE- 1 -LAMP 9   [GE-LAMP]
(0632) GE- 1 -STAAH. 5   [GE-STAAH]
(0633) GE- 1 -DRIHT 5   [GE-DRIHT]
(0635) GE- 1 -WORHTE 5   [GE-WORHTE]
(0659) GE- 1 -MYNE 9   [GE-MYNE]
(0023) -GE- 1 -SIITHAS 5   [WIL-GE-SIITHAS]
(0044) -GE- 1 -STREEO-9-NUM 3   [THEEOD-GE-STREEONUM]
(0063) -GE- 1 -BEDDA 4   [HEALS-GE-BEDDA]
(0227) -GE- 1 -WAEAE-2-DO 3   [GUUDH-GE-WAEAEDO]
(0261) -GE- 1 -NEEATAS. 9   [HEORDH-GE-NEEATAS]
(0343) -GE- 1 -NEEATAS 5   [BEEOD-GE-NEEATAS]
(0001) $$GAAR- 1 -$$DE-9-NA 3   [GAAR-DENA]
(0038) CYYM- 1 -LIICOR 4   [CYYM-LIICOR]
(0056) ON- 1 -WOOC 4   [ON-WOOC]
(0100) ON- 1 -GAN 3   [ON-GAN]
(0110) MAN- 1 -CYNNE 9   [MAN-CYNNE]
(0111) UN- 1 -TYYDRAS 3   [UN-TYYDRAS]
(0127) UN- 1 -DYRNE 9   [UN-DYRNE]
(0131) THEGN- 1 -SORGE 9   [THEGN-SORGE]
(0154) SIN- 1 -GAA-9-LE 4   [SIN-GAALE]
(0161) SIN- 1 -NIHTE 3   [SIN-NIHTE]
(0164) MAN- 1 -CYN-9-NES 2   [MAN-CYNNES]
(0251) AN- 1 -SYYN 3   [AN-SYYN]
```

207

```
(0259) ON- 1 -LEEAC 4     [ON-LEEAC]
(0260) GUM- 1 -CYNNES 9    [GUM-CYNNES]
(0276) UN- 1 -CUUDHNE 4    [UN-CUUDHNE]
(0287) UN- 1 -FORHT 3      [UN-FORHT]
(0336) EL- 1 -THEEODIGE 5  [EL-THEEODIGE]
(0382) ON- 1 -SENDE 4      [ON-SENDE]
(0397) ON- 1 -BIID-8-AN 9  [ON-BIIDAN]
(0409) ON- 1 -GUN-1-NEN 9  [ON-GUNNEN]
(0429) FOR- 1 -WYR-2-NE 7  [FOR-WYRNE]
(0449) UN- 1 -MURN- 0      [UN-MURN-LIICE]
(0452) $ON- 1 -SEND 5      [ON-SEND]
(0482) BEEOR- 1 -SELE 7    [BEEOR-SELE]
(0488) FOR- 1 -NAM 4       [FOR-NAM]
(0501) ON- 1 -BAND 3       [ON-BAND]
(0595) ON- 1 -FUN-1-DEN 4  [ON-FUNDEN]
(0597) ON- 1 -SITTAN 4     [ON-SITTAN]
(0602) UN- 1 -GEAARA 4     [UN-GEAARA]
(0654) WIIN- 1 -AERNES 9   [WIIN-AERNES]
(0028) AET- 1 -BAEAERON 4  [AET-BAEAERON]
(0233) MOOD- 1 -GE- 2      [MOOD-GE-HYGDUM]
(0302) SIID- 1 -FAE-1-TH-1-MED 9   [SIID-FAETHMED]
(0321) AET- 1 -GAE-1-DERE 6 [AET-GAEDERE]
(0373) EALD- 1 -FAE-2-DER 5 [EALD-FAEDER]
(0476) FLET- 1 -WEROD 4    [FLET-WEROD]
(0548) =OND- 1 -HWEARF 5   [=OND-HWEARF]
(0189) HEALF- 1 -DENES 3   [HEALF-DENES]
(0193) NIITH- 1 -GRIM 3    [NIITH-GRIM]
(0273) SOOTH- 1 -LIICE 9   [SOOTH-LIICE]
(0348) WULF- 1 -GAAR 5     [WULF-GAAR]
(0400) THRYYDH- 1 -LIIC 4  [THRYYDH-LIIC]
(0469) HEALF- 1 -DENES 5   [HEALF-DENES]
(0502) AEF- 1 -THUNCA. 5   [AEF-THUNCA]
(0134) LONG- 1 -SUM 3      [LONG-SUM]
(0241) AEAEG- 1 -WEARDE 4  [AEAEG-WEARDE]
(0512) SOR-2-H- 1 -FULL-1-NE 9  [SORH-FULLNE]
(0529) ECG- 1 -THEEOWES 9  [ECG-THEEOWES]
(0612) WEALH- 1 -THEEOW 8  [WEALH-THEEOW]
(0647) HEEAH- 1 -SELE 5    [HEEAH-SELE]

(0501) BEEO- 2 -WULFES 5   [BEEO-WULFES]
(0506) BEEO- 2 -WULF 4     [BEEO-WULF]
(0223) SAEAE- 2 -NAESSAS 4 [SAEAE-NAESSAS]
(0226) SAEAE- 2 -WUDU 2    [SAEAE-WUDU]
(0277) HRAA- 2 -FYL 5      [HRAA-FYL]
(0571) SAEAE- 2 -NAESSAS 3 [SAEAE-NAESSAS]
(0061) HEORO- 2 -GAAR. 3   [HEORO-GAAR]
(0065) WINE- 2 -MAAGAS 4   [WINE-MAAGAS]
(0067) MAGO- 2 -DRIHT 4    [MAGO-DRIHT]
(0209) LAGU- 2 -CRAEFTIG 2 [LAGU-CRAEFTIG]
(0239) LAGU- 2 -STRAEAETE 9 [LAGU-STRAEAETE]
(0381) HEA-1-THO- 2 -ROOF 3 [HEATHO-ROOF]
(0438) GEOLO- 2 -RAND 3    [GEOLO-RAND]
(0460) HEA-2-THO- 2 -LAAFE 6 [HEATHO-LAAFE]
(0467) HERE- 2 -GAAR 9     [HERE-GAAR]
(0494) BE- 2 -HEEOLD 4     [BE-HEEOLD]
(0511) BE- 2 -LEEAN 2      [BE-LEEAN]
(0594) SEARO- 2 -GRIM 2    [SEARO-GRIM]
(0619) SELE- 2 -FUL 4      [SELE-FUL]
(0624) ME-1-DO- 2 -FUL 4   [MEDO-FUL]
(0261) HIGE- 2 -LAACES 5   [HIGE-LAACES]
(0342) HIGE- 2 -LAACES. 5  [HIGE-LAACES]
(0391) SIGE- 2 -DRIHTEN 9  [SIGE-DRIHTEN]
(0619) SIGE- 2 -ROOF 9     [SIGE-ROOF]
(0002) GE- 2 -FRUUNON 4    [GE-FRUUNON]
(0020) GE- 2 -WYRCEAN 3    [GE-WYRCEAN]
```

```
(0024) GE- 2 -LAEAESTEN 9   [GE-LAEAESTEN]
(0025) GE- 2 -HWAEAERE 3   [GE-HWAEAERE]
(0026) GE- 2 -WAAT 4   [GE-WAAT]
(0038) GE- 2 -GYRWAN 4   [GE-GYRWAN]
(0042) GE- 2 -WIITAN. 5   [GE-WIITAN]
(0070) GE- 2 -FRUUNON. 3   [GE-FRUUNON]
(0071) GE- 2 -DAEAELAN 3   [GE-DAEAELAN]
(0087) GE- 2 -THOLODE 4   [GE-THOLODE]
(0088) GE- 2 -HWAAM 4   [GE-HWAAM]
(0098) GE- 2 -HWYLCUM 3   [GE-HWYLCUM]
(0107) GE- 2 -WRAEC 9   [GE-WRAEC]
(0140) GE- 2 -BEEACNCD 3   [GE-BEEACNOD]
(0148) GE- 2 -HWELCNE 9   [GE-HWELCNE]
(0194) GE- 2 -FRAEGN 4   [GE-FRAEGN]
(0262) GE- 2 -CYYTHED 3   [GE-CYYTHED]
(0290) GE- 2 -HYYRE 3   [GE-HYYRE]
(0294) GE- 2 -HWONE 4   [GE-HWONE]
(0300) GE- 2 -DIIGEDH. 6   [GE-DIIGEDH]
(0315) GE- 2 -WENDE 5   [GE-WENDE]
(0346) GE- 2 -UN-1-NAN 3   [GE-UNNAN]
(0354) GE- 2 -CYYDHAN 4   [GE-CYYDHAN]
(0357) GE- 2 -DRIHT. 5   [GE-DRIHT]
(0366) GE- 2 -TEEOH 5   [GE-TEEOH]
(0412) GE- 2 -HWYL-1-CUM 5   [GE-HWYLCUM]
(0455) GE- 2 -WEORC 4   [GE-WEORC]
(0459) GE- 2 -SLOOH 9   [GE-SLOOH]
(0464) GE- 2 -WEALC 5   [GE-WEALC]
(0535) GE- 2 -CWAEAEDON 3   [GE-CWAEAEDON]
(0551) GE- 2 -FREME-2-DE 5   [GE-FREMEDE]
(0553) GE- 2 -GYR-9-WED 3   [GE-GYRWED]
(0561) GE- 2 -DEEFE 5   [GE-DEEFE]
(0571) GE- 2 -SEEON 3   [GE-SEEON]
(0624) GE- 2 -THUNGEN 4   [GE-THUNGEN]
(0638) GE- 2 -BIIDAN. 5   [GE-BIIDAN]
(0647) GE- 2 -THINGED. 6   [GE-THINGED]
(0648) GE- 2 -SEEON 3   [GE-SEEON]
(0661) GE- 2 -DIIGEST. 9   [GE-DIIGEST]
(0233) -GE- 2 -HYG-1-DUM 2   [MOOD-GE-HYGDUM]
(0269) -GE- 2 -BYRGEAN 9   [LEEOD-GE-BYRGEAN]
(0387) -GE- 2 -DRIHT 3   [SIBBE-GE-DRIHT]
(0014) FYREN- 2 -DHEARFE 4   [FYREN-DHEARFE]
(0017) FOR- 2 -GEAF. 6   [FOR-GEAF]
(0045) FRUM- 2 -SCEAFTE 9   [FRUM-SCEAFTE]
(0049) GAAR- 2 -SECG 4   [GAAR-SECG]
(0052) ON- 2 -FEENG. 9   [ON-FEENG]
(0084) AATHUM- 2 -()SWERIAN*SWEEORAN 3   [*AATHUM-SWEEORAN]
(0085) WAEL- 2 -NII-9-DHE 4   [WAEL-NIIDHE]
(0104) FIIFEL- 2 -CYN-9-NES 3   [FIIFEL-CYNNES]
(0105) WON- 2 -SAEAELII 3   [WON-SAEAELII]
(0106) FOR- 2 -SCRIFEN 3   [FOR-SCRIFEN]
(0109) FOR- 2 -WRAEC 3   [FOR-WRAEC]
(0111) ON- 2 -WOOCON 9   [ON-WOOCON]
(0117) BEEOR- 2 -THEGE 3   [BEEOR-THEGE]
(0120) UN- 2 -HAEAELO 3   [UN-HAEAELO]
(0125) WAEL- 2 -FYLLE 3   [WAEL-FYLLE]
(0126) AEAER- 2 -DAEGE 9   [AEAER-DAEGE]
(0129) MORGEN- 2 -SWEEG 3   [MORGEN-SWEEG]
(0130) UN- 2 -BLIIDHE 3   [UN-BLIIDHE]
(0163) HEL- 2 -RUUNAN 3   [HEL-RUUNAN]
(0174) FAEAER- 2 -GRYRU= 9   [FAEAER-GRYRU=]
(0216) WIL- 2 -SIIDH 3   [WIL-SIIDH]
(0219) AAN- 2 -TIID 9   [AAN-TIID]
(0220) WUNDEN- 2 -STEFNA 4   [WUNDEN-STEFNA]
(0232) FYR- 2 -WYT 3   [FYR-WYT]
(0244) ON- 2 -GUNNON. 9   [ON-GUNNON]
```

209

```
(0251)  AEAEN- 2 -LIIC 3   [AEAEN-LIIC]
(0252)  FRUM- 2 -CYN 2   [FRUM-CYN]
(0317)  AAR- 2 -STAFUM 4   [AAR-STAFUM]
(0326)  REGN- 2 -HEARDE 9   [REGN-HEARDE]
(0336)  OM- 2 -BIHT. 5   [OM-BIHT]
(0357)  ()UN*AN- 2 -+HAAR 5   [*AN-HAAR]
(0380)  MAEGEN- 2 -CRAEFT 3   [MAEGEN-CRAEFT]
(0382)  AAR- 2 -STAFUM 3   [AAR-STAFUM]
(0406)  OR- 2 -THANCUM 1   [OR-THANCUM]
(0413)  UN- 2 -NYT 4   [UN-NYT]
(0435)  FOR- 2 -HICGE 9   [FOR-HICGE]
(0458)  AAR- 2 -STAFUM 4   [AAR-STAFUM]
(0489)  ON- 2 -SAEAEL 3   [ON-SAEAEL]
(0498)  UN- 2 -LYYTEL 9   [UN-LYYTEL]
(0499)  ()$$HUN*$$UN- 2 -FERDH 4   [*UN-FERDH]
(0517)  OFER- 2 -FLAAT. 5   [OFER-FLAAT]
(0530)  ()HUN*UN- 2 -FERDH 9   [*UN-FERDH]
(0557)  FOR- 2 -NAM 4   [FOR-NAM]
(0563)  MAAN- 2 -FOR- 2   [MAAN-FOR-DAEAEDLAN]
(0563)  -FOR- 2 -DAEAEDLAN 9   [MAAN-FOR-DAEAEDLAN]
(0646)  AEAEFEN- 2 -RAES-1-TE. 5   [AEAEFEN-RAESTE]
(0659)  MAEGEN- 2 -ELLEN 2   [MAEGEN-ELLEN]
(0661)  ELLEN- 2 -WEORC 3   [ELLEN-WEORC]
(0002)  THEEOD- 2 -CYNINGA 9   [THEEOD-CYNINGA]
(0009)  YMB- 2 -SITTEN-1-DRA 9   [YMB-SITTENDRA]
(0017)  WOROLD- 2 -AARE 3   [WOROLD-AARE]
(0026)  -SCAEP- 2 -HWIILE 9   [GE-SCAEP-HWIILE]
(0031)  LAND- 2 -FRUMA 5   [LAND-FRUMA]
(0032)  HRINGED- 2 -STEFNA 2   [HRINGED-STEFNA]
(0044)  THEEOD- 2 -GE- 1   [THEEOD-GE-STREEONUM]
(0054)  LEEOD- 2 -CYNING 4   [LEEOD-CYNING]
(0095)  LAND- 2 -BUUEN-9-DUM 3   [LAND-BUUENDUM]
(0143)  AET- 2 -WAND. 6   [AET-WAND]
(0180)  MOOD- 2 -SEFAN 3   [MOOD-SEFAN]
(0193)  NYYD- 2 -WRACU 3   [NYYD-WRACU]
(0209)  LAND- 2 -GE- 0   [LAND-GE-MYRCU]
(0232)  FYRD- 2 -SEARU 3   [FYRD-SEARU]
(0263)  ORD- 2 -FRUMA 5   [ORD-FRUMA]
(0299)  GOOD- 2 -FREM-3-MEN-1-DRA 9   [GOOD-FREMMENDRA]
(0308)  GOLD- 2 -FAAH 3   [GOLD-FAAH]
(0329)  AET- 2 -GAE-1-DERE 5   [AET-GAEDERE]
(0340)  AND- 2 -SWARODE 4   [AND-SWARODE]
(0356)  HRAED- 2 -LIICE 6   [HRAED-LIICE]
(0392)  EEAST- 2 -DENA 4   [EEAST-DENA]
(0402)  AET- 2 -SOMNE 8   [AET-SOMNE]
(0481)  OORET- 2 -MECGAS 9   [OORET-MECGAS]
(0519)  AET- 2 -BAER. 5   [AET-BAER]
(0542)  FLOOD- 2 -YYTHU= 9   [FLOOD-YYTHU=]
(0614)  GOLD- 2 -HRO-9-DEN 3   [GOLD-HRODEN]
(0620)  YMB- 2 -EEODE 5   [YMB-EEODE]
(0622)  SINC- 2 -FATO 3   [SINC-FATO]
(0624)  AET- 2 -BAER. 7   [AET-BAER]
(0640)  GILP- 2 -CWIDE 4   [GILP-CWIDE]
(0005)  OF- 2 -TEEAH 3   [OF-TEEAH]
(0016)  LIIF- 2 -FREEA 4   [LIIF-FREEA]
(0024)  LOF- 2 -DAEAEDU= 3   [LOF-DAEAEDU=]
(0058)  GUUTH- 2 -REEOUW 4   [GUUTH-REEOUW]
(0063)  HEALS- 2 -GE- 1   [HEALS-GE-BEDDA]
(0086)  EAR-9-FODH- 2 -LIICE 6   [EARFODH-LIICE]
(0127)  GUUDH- 2 -CRAEFT 4   [GUUDH-CRAEFT]
(0131)  DHRYYDH- 2 -SWYYDH 3   [DHRYYDH-SWYYDH]
(0138)  EEADH- 2 -FYNDE 5   [EEADH-FYNDE]
(0152)  HROOTH- 2 -GAAR 5   [HROOTH-GAAR]
(0160)  DEEATH- 2 -SCUA 9   [DEEATH-SCUA]
(0198)  YYDH- 2 -LIDAN 3   [YYDH-LIDAN]
```

210

```
(0202) SIIDH- 2 -FAET 2    [SIIDH-FAET]
(0215) GUUDH- 2 -SEARO 2    [GUUDH-SEARO]
(0227) GUUDH- 2 -GE- 1    [GUUDH-GE-WAEAEDO]
(0232) FUUS- 2 -LICU 1    [FUUS-LICU]
(0235) HROODH- 2 -GAARES 4    [HROODH-GAARES]
(0244) GUUDH- 2 -LIICOR 4    [GUUDH-LIICOR]
(0261) HEORDH- 2 -GE- 1    [HEORDH-GE-NEEATAS]
(0277) HROODH- 2 -GAAR 4    [HROODH-GAAR]
(0335) HROODH- 2 -GAARES 9    [HROODH-GAARES]
(0339) HROODH- 2 -GAAR 3    [HROODH-GAAR]
(0371) $HROODH- 2 -GAAR 5    [HROODH-GAAR]
(0396) HROODH- 2 -GAAR 3    [HROODH-GAAR]
(0559) LAADH- 2 -GE- 3    [LAADH-GE-TEEONAN]
(0566) YYOH- 2 -LAAFE 5    [YYOH-LAAFE]
(0574) OF- 2 -SLOOH 4    [OF-SLOOH]
(0579) OTH- 2 -BAER 4    [OTH-BAER]
(0613) HROODH- 2 -GAARES 9    [HROODH-GAARES]
(0653) HROODH- 2 -GAAR 4    [HROODH-GAAR]
(0021) FEOH- 2 -GIFTUM. 3    [FEOH-GIFTUM]
(0100) EEADIG- 2 -LIICE 4    [EEADIG-LIICE]
(0176) WIIG- 2 -WEOR-1-THUNGA 9    [WIIG-WEORTHUNGA]
(0192) LONG- 2 -SUM 2    [LONG-SUM]
(0287) AEAEG- 2 -HWAE-8-THRES 3    [AEAEG-HWAETHRES]
(0305) FERH- 2 -WEAR-1-DE 5    [FERH-WEARDE]
(0477) WIIG- 2 -HEEAP 4    [WIIG-HEEAP]
(0631) ECG- 2 -THEEOWES. 5    [ECG-THEEOWES]

(0007) FEEA- 3 -SCEAFT 2    [FEEA-SCEAFT]
(0284) THREEA- 3 -NYYD 9    [THREEA-NYYD]
(0633) SAEAE- 3 -BAAT 2    [SAEAE-BAAT]
(0005) MEODO- 3 -SETLA 9    [MEODO-SETLA]
(0039) HILDE- 3 -WAEAEP-2-NUM 9    [HILDE-WAEAEPNUM]
(0039) HEADHO- 3 -WAEAEDUM 3    [HEADHO-WAEAEDUM]
(0063) HEADHO- 3 -SCILFINGAS 5    [HEADHO-SCILFINGAS]
(0064) HERE- 3 -SPEED 2    [HERE-SPEED]
(0082) HEADHO- 3 -WYLMA 9    [HEADHO-WYLMA]
(0237) SEARO- 3 -HAEBBENDRA 4    [SEARO-HAEBBENDRA]
(0297) LAGU- 3 -STREEA-9-MAS 8    [LAGU-STREEAMAS]
(0324) GRY-9-RE- 3 -GEAT-2-WUM 4    [GRYRE-GEATWUM]
(0360) WINE- 3 -DRIHT-2-NE 6    [WINE-DRIHTNE]
(0401) HEADHO- 3 -REEAF 5    [HEADHO-REEAF]
(0401) BE- 3 -BEEAD. 5    [BE-BEEAD]
(0422) NEARO- 3 -THEARFE 4    [NEARO-THEARFE]
(0453) BEA-1-DU- 3 -SCRUUDA 5    [BEADU-SCRUUDA]
(0481) EALO- 3 -WAEAEGE 4    [EALO-WAEAEGE]
(0495) EALO- 3 -WAEAEGE 4    [EALO-WAEAEGE]
(0501) BEADU- 3 -RUUNE 5    [BEADU-RUUNE]
(0514) MERE- 3 -STRAEAE-3-TA 4    [MERE-STRAEAETA]
(0522) FREODHO- 3 -BUR-1-H 4    [FREODHO-BURH]
(0526) HEADHO- 3 -RAEAESA 5    [HEADHO-RAEAESA]
(0548) HEADHO- 3 -GRIM 3    [HEADHO-GRIM]
(0549) MERE- 3 -FIXA 3    [MERE-FIXA]
(0557) HILDE- 3 -BILLE 4    [HILDE-BILLE]
(0557) HEATHO- 3 -RAEAES 9    [HEATHO-RAEAES]
(0558) MERE- 3 -DEEOR 2    [MERE-DEEOR]
(0582) SEARO- 3 -NIIDHA 3    [SEARO-NIIDHA]
(0637) ENDE- 3 -DAEG 4    [ENDE-DAEG]
(0638) MEODU- 3 -HEALLE 5    [MEODU-HEALLE]
(0490) SIGE- 3 -HREEDH 2    [SIGE-HREEDH]
(0022) GE- 3 -WUNIGEN 4    [GE-WUNIGEN]
(0026) GE- 3 -SCAEP- 2    [GE-SCAEP-HWIILE]
(0133) GE- 3 -WIN 2    [GE-WIN]
(0174) GE- 3 -FREM-2-MAN-1-N-1-E. 7    [GE-FREMMANNE]
(0257) GE- 3 -CYYDHAN-1-NE 9    [GE-CYYDHANNE]
(0304) GE- 3 -HRO-1-DEN 3    [GE-HRODEN]
```

211

```
(0317) GE- 3 -HEAL-9-DE. 6   [GE-HEALDE]
(0369) GE- 3 -AEHTLAN 5   [GE-AEHTLAN]
(0425) GE- 3 -HEEGAN. 5   [GE-HEEGAN]
(0463) GE- 3 -SOOHTE 9   [GE-SOOHTE]
(0526) GE- 3 -HWAEAER 9   [GE-HWAEAER]
(0559) GE- 3 -LOOME 5   [GE-LOOME]
(0584) GE- 3 -HWAE-2-THER 4   [GE-HWAETHER]
(0608) GE- 3 -LYYF-1-DE 9   [GE-LYYFDE]
(0610) GE- 3 -THOOHT 5   [GE-THOOHT]
(0618) GE- 3 -THEAH 5   [GE-THEAH]
(0628) GE- 3 -THEAH 5   [GE-THEAH]
(0636) GE- 3 -FREM-9-MAN 3   [GE-FREMMAN]
(0658) GE- 3 -HEALD 5   [GE-HEALD]
(0368) -GE- 3 -TAAHUM 4   [WIIG-GE-TAAHUM]
(0559) -GE- 3 -TEEO-1-NAN 4   [LAADH-GE-TEEONAN]
(0001) GEEAR- 3 -DAGUM. 6   [GEEAR-DAGUM]
(0046) UMBOR- 3 -WE-9-SENDE 5   [UMBOR-WESENDE]
(0068) HEAL- 3 -RECEO 4   [HEAL-RECEO]
(0075) MIDDAN- 3 -GEARO 3   [MIDDAN-GEARJ]
(0077) EAL- 3 -GEARO 4   [EAL-GEARO]
(0082) HORN- 3 -GEEAP 4   [HORN-GEEAP]
(0086) ELLEN- 3 -GAEAEST 4   [ELLEN-GAEAEST]
(0091) FRUM- 3 -SCEAFT 4   [FRUM-SCEAFT]
(0189) MAEAEL- 3 -CEARE 4   [MAEAEL-CEARE]
(0200) SWAN- 3 -RAADE 4   [SWAN-RAADE]
(0222) BRIM- 3 -CLIFU 3   [BRIM-CLIFU]
(0236) METHEL- 3 -WORDUM 2   [METHEL-WORDUM]
(0256) AAN- 3 -FEALDNE 3   [AAN-FEALDNE]
(0279) OFER- 3 -SWYYDHETH 4   [OFER-SWYYDHETH]
(0303) EOFOR- 3 -LIIC 3   [EOFOR-LIIC]
(0320) STAAN- 3 -FAAH 4   [STAAN-FAAH]
(0330) IIREN- 3 -THREEAT 4   [IIREN-THREEAT]
(0334) GRIIM- 3 -HELMAS 9   [GRIIM-HELMAS]
(0358) ELLEN- 3 -ROOF 4   [ELLEN-ROOF]
(0367) GEGN- 3 -CWIDA 6   [GEGN-CWIDA]
(0374) FOR- 3 -GEAF 5   [FOR-GEAF]
(0410) EETHEL- 3 -TYRF 5   [EETHEL-TYRF]
(0418) FOR- 3 -THAN 3   [FOR-THAN]
(0424) FOR- 3 -GRAND 8   [FOR-GRAND]
(0436) MON- 3 -DRIHTEN 9   [MON-DRIHTEN]
(0450) MOOR- 3 -HOPU 3   [MOOR-HOPU]
(0477) FOR- 3 -SWEEOP 4   [FOR-SWEEOP]
(0484) MORGEN- 3 -TIID 3   [MORGEN-TIID]
(0485) DREEOR- 3 -FAAH 6   [DREEOR-FAAH]
(0503) FOR- 3 -THON 3   [FOR-THON]
(0509) DOL- 3 -GILPE 5   [DOL-GILPE]
(0540) HRON- 3 -FIXAS 4   [HRON-FIXAS]
(0549) ON- 3 -HREERED. 4   [ON-HREERED]
(0568) BRIM- 3 -LIIDHENDE 5   [BRIM-LIIDHENDE]
(0601) GAAR- 3 -DENUM 4   [GAAR-DENUM]
(0604) MORGEN- 3 -LEEOHT 4   [MORGEN-LEEOHT]
(0616) EETHEL- 3 -WEARDE 6   [EETHEL-WEARDE]
(0617) BEEOR- 3 -THEGE 7   [BEEOR-THEGE]
(0629) WAEL- 3 -REEOW 3   [WAEL-REEOW]
(0033) +UUT- 3 -FUUS 3   [UUT-FUUS]
(0073) FOLC- 3 -SCARE 4   [FOLC-SCARE]
(0076) FOLC- 3 -STE-9-DE 4   [FOLC-STEDE]
(0099) DRIHT- 3 -GUMAN 3   [DRIHT-GUMAN]
(0103) MEARC- 3 -STAPA 9   [MEARC-STAPA]
(0178) THEEOU- 3 -THREEAUM 2   [THEEOD-THREEAUM]
(0203) LYYT- 3 -HWOON 2   [LYYT-HWOON]
(0208) SUND- 3 -WUDU 3   [SUND-WUDU]
(0243) SCIP- 3 -HERGE 4   [SCIP-HERGE]
(0249) SELD- 3 -GUMA 4   [SELD-GUMA]
(0269) LEEOD- 3 -GE- 2   [LEEOD-GE-BYRGEAN]
```

```
(0275) DAEAED- 3 -HATA 3      [DAEAED-HATA]
(0288) SCYLD- 3 -WIGA 3       [SCYLD-WIGA]
(0309) FOLD- 3 -BUUENDUM 4    [FOLD-BUUENDUM]
(0322) HOND- 3 -LOCEN 6       [HOND-LOCEN]
(0330) AESC- 3 -HOLT 3        [AESC-HOLT]
(0332) OORET- 3 -MECGAS 4     [OORET-MECGAS]
(0338) WRAEC- 3 -SIIDHUM. 4   [WRAEC-SIIDHUM]
(0343) BEEOD- 3 -GE- 1        [BEEOD-GE-NEEATAS]
(0383) WEST- 3 -DENU= 9       [WEST-DENU=]
(0385) MOOD- 3 -THRAE-2-CE 9  [MOOD-THRAECE]
(0394) HEARD- 3 -HICGENDE 6   [HEARD-HICGENDE]
(0460) HAND- 3 -BONAN 3       [HAND-BONAN]
(0486) BENC- 3 -THELU 4       [BENC-THELU]
(0528) NIHT- 3 -LONGNE 3      [NIHT-LONGNE]
(0550) LIIC- 3 -SYRCE 4       [LIIC-SYRCE]
(0564) YMB- 3 -SAEAETON 4     [YMB-SAEAETON]
(0588) HEEAFOD- 3 -MAEAEGUM 4 [HEEAFOD-MAEAEGUM]
(0598) NYYD- 3 -BAADE 4       [NYYD-BAADE]
(0616) EEAST- 3 -DENA 9       [EEAST-DENA]
(0636) FEEOND- 3 -GRAAPUM 4   [FEEOND-GRAAPUM]
(0641) FOLG- 3 -CWEEN 3       [FOLG-CWEEN]
(0008) WEORDH- 3 -MYNDUM 3    [WEORDH-MYNDUM]
(0057) HEALF- 3 -DENE 4       [HEALF-DENE]
(0061) HROODH- 3 -GAAR 4      [HROODH-GAAR]
(0065) WEORDH- 3 -MYND. 3     [WEORDH-MYND]
(0141) SOODH- 3 -LIICE 5      [SOODH-LIICE]
(0168) GIF- 3 -STOOL 3        [GIF-STOOL]
(0173) SWIIDH- 3 -FERHDHUM 4  [SWIIDH-FERHDHUM]
(0245) LEEAFNES- 3 -WORD 3    [LEEAFNES-WORD]
(0253) LEEAS- 3 -SCEEA-2-WERAS 4   [LEEAS-SCEEAWERAS]
(0314) GUUDH- 3 -BEORNA 3     [GUUDH-BEORNA]
(0328) GUUDH- 3 -SEARO 3      [GUUDH-SEARO]
(0367) HROODH- 3 -GAAR 6      [HROODH-GAAR]
(0378) GIF- 3 -SCEATTAS 5     [GIF-SCEATTAS]
(0395) GUUDH- 3 -()GEA*GE- 8  [*GUUDH-GE-TAAWUM]
(0417) HROODH- 3 -GAAR 5      [HROODH-GAAR]
(0445) HREEDH- 3 -MAN-1-NA 4  [HREEDH-MANNA]
(0463) SUUDH- 3 -DENA 4       [SUUDH-DENA]
(0493) SWIIDH- 3 -FERHTHE 9   [SWIIDH-FERHTHE]
(0608) GUUDH- 3 -ROOF 5       [GUUDH-ROOF]
(0626) WIIS- 3 -FAEST 9       [WIIS-FAEST]
(0643) THRYYDH- 3 -WORD 3     [THRYYDH-WORD]
(0645) HEALF- 3 -DENES 9      [HEALF-DENES]
(0657) DHRYYTH- 3 -AERN 3     [DHRYYTH-AERN]
(0084) ()SECG*ECG- 3 -HETE 4  [*ECG-HETE]
(0116) HRING- 3 -DENE 3       [HRING-DENE]
(0156) FEORH- 3 -BEALO 3      [FEORH-BEALO]
(0175) ()HRAERG*HAERG- 3 -TRAFUM 2   [*HAERG-TRAFUM]
(0217) WAEAEG- 3 -HOLM 3      [WAEAEG-HOLM]
(0285) HEEAH- 3 -STE-2-DE 9   [HEEAH-STEDE]
(0322) HRING- 3 -IIREN 3      [HRING-IIREN]
(0373) ECG- 3 -THEEO 3        [ECG-THEEO]
(0596) ECG- 3 -THRAECE 9      [ECG-THRAECE]

(0218) FAA-9-MII- 4 -HEALS 3  [FAAMII-HEALS]
(0393) SAEAE- 4 -WYLMAS 9     [SAEAE-WYLMAS]
(0027) FELA- 4 -HROOR 3       [FELA-HROOR]
(0051) SELE- 4 -RAEAE-1-DEN-1-()NE*DE 4   [*SELE-RAEAEDENDE]
(0093) WLITE- 4 -BEORHTNE 5   [WLITE-BEORHTNE]
(0152) HETE- 4 -NIIDH-1-AS 9  [HETE-NIIDHAS]
(0241) ENDE- 4 -SAEAETA 2     [ENDE-SAEAETA]
(0293) MAGU- 4 -THEGNAS 4     [MAGU-THEGNAS]
(0300) HILDE- 4 -RAEAES 9     [HILDE-RAEAES]
(0335) HERE- 4 -SCEAFTA 5     [HERE-SCEAFTA]
(0370) HEADHO- 4 -RINCUM 9    [HEADHO-RINCUM]
```

213

```
(0387) SIBBE- 4 -GE- 2    [SIBBE-GE-DRIHT]
(0396) HERE- 4 -GRIIMAN 5    [HERE-GRIIMAN]
(0397) HILDE- 4 -BORD 4    [HILDE-BORD]
(0475) HETE- 4 -THANCUM 4    [HETE-THANCUM]
(0502) MERE- 4 -FARAN 9    [MERE-FARAN]
(0533) MERE- 4 -STRENGO 4    [MERE-STRENGO]
(0552) BEA-1-DO- 4 -HRAEGL 9    [BEADO-HRAEGL]
(0650) SCADU- 4 -HELMA 3 *  [SCADU-HELMA]
(0407) HIGE- 4 -LAACES 4    [HIGE-LAACES]
(0096) GE- 4 -FRAE1-1-WADE 5    [GE-FRAETWADE]
(0520) GE- 4 -SOOHTE 9    [GE-SOOHTE]
(0037) FEOR- 4 -WEGUM 3    [FEOR-WEGUM]
(0078) HEAL- 4 -AER-9-NA 4    [HEAL-AERNA]
(0114) FOR- 4 -GEALD. 9    [FOR-GEALD]
(0142) HEAL- 4 -DHEGNES 5    [HEAL-DHEGNES]
(0282) CEAR- 4 -WYLMAS 4    [CEAR-WYLMAS]
(0298) WUNDEN- 4 -HALS 9    [WUNDEN-HALS]
(0305) FYYR- 4 -HEARD 4    [FYYR-HEARD]
(0398) WAEL- 4 -SCEAF-1-TAS 4    [WAEL-SCEAFTAS]
(0413) AEAEFEN- 4 -LEEOHT 4    [AEAEFEN-LEEOHT]
(0434) WON- 4 -HYYDUM 9    [WON-HYYDUM]
(0476) FAEAER- 4 -NIIDHA 1    [FAEAER-NIIDHA]
(0479) DOL- 4 -()SCADHAN*SCEADHAN 3    [*DOL-SCEADHAN]
(0504) MIDDAN- 4 -GEARDES. 4    [MIDDAN-GEARDES]
(0513) EEA-9-GOR- 4 -STREEAM 3    [EEAGOR-STREEAM]
(0515) GAAR- 4 -SECG 4    [GAAR-SECG]
(0518) MOR-1-GEN- 4 -TIID 3    [MORGEN-TIID]
(0177) GAAST- 4 -BONA 3    [GAAST-BONA]
(0245) LIND- 4 -HAE-1-BBENDE 5    [LIND-HAEBBENDE]
(0259) WORD- 4 -HORD 2    [WORD-HORD]
(0427) BEORHT- 4 -DENA 4    [BEORHT-DENA]
(0535) CNIHT- 4 -WESENDE 5    [CNIHT-WESENDE]
(0610) FAEST- 4 -RAEAEDNE 9    [FAEST-RAEAEDNE]
(0640) GOLD- 4 -HRODEN. 5    [GOLD-HRODEN]
(0059) FORDH- 4 -GE- 0    [FORDH-GE-RIIMED]
(0136) MORDH- 4 -BEALA 3    [MORDH-BEALA]
(0283) EARFODH- 4 -THRAAGE 5    [EARFODH-THRAAGE]
(0321) GUUDH- 4 -BYRNE 5    [GUUDH-BYRNE]
(0350) WIIS- 4 -DOOM 3    [WIIS-DOOM]
(0443) GUUDH- 4 -SELE 5    [GUUDH-SELE]
(0456) $HROOUH- 4 -GAAR 5    [HROODH-GAAR]
(0623) BEEAG- 4 -HRODEN 3    [BEEAG-HRODEN]

(0462) HERE- 5 -BROOGAN 9    [HERE-BROOGAN]
(0094) SIGE- 6 -HREE-2-THIG 4    [SIGE-HREETHIG]
(0254) FEOR- 6 -BUUEND 3    [FEOR-BUUEND]
(0298) WEDER- 5 -MEARCE 6    [WEDER-MEARCE]
(0304) HLEEOR- 5 -()BERAN*BERGAN 5    [*HLEEOR-BERGAN]
(0606) SWEGL- 5 -WERED 3    [SWEGL-WERED]
(0372) CNIHT- 5 -WESENDE 6    [CNIHT-WESENDE]
(0467) HORD- 5 -BURH 4    [HORD-BURH]
(0609) BEOR-2-HT- 5 -DENA 4    [BEORHT-DENA]
(0368) WIIG- 5 -GE- 3    [WIIG-GE-TAAWUM]

(0069) MEDO- 8 -AERN 4    [MEDO-AERN]
(0403) *HEATHO- 8 -*RINC 8    [*HEATHO-*RINC]
(0484) MEDO- 8 -HEAL 4    [MEDO-HEAL]
(0204) HIGE- 8 -ROOFNE 9    [HIGE-ROOFNE]
(0115) $GE- 8 -WAAT 3    [GE-WAAT]
(0135) GE- 8 -FREMEDE 9    [GE-FREMEDE]
(0395) -()GEA*GE- 8 -TAA-9-WUM 4    [*GUUDH-GE-TAAWUM]
(0457) ()FYHTUM*GE- 8 -*WYRHTUM 4    [*GE-*WYRHTUM]
(0630) GE- 8 -FYYSED. 9    [GE-FYYSED]
(0652) *GE- 8 -GREET-1-TE 3    [*GE-GREETTE]
(0010) HRON- 8 -RAADE 5    [HRON-RAADE]
```

214

```
0015) ALDOR- 8 -()++ASE*LEEASE. 4    [*ALDOR-LEEASE]
0390) *WIID- 8 -*CUUDH 8    [*WIID-*CUUDH]
0263) ECG- 8 -THEEOW 3    [ECG-THEEOW]

0405) BEEO- 9 -WULF 2    [BEEO-WULF]
0609) BEEO- 9 -WULFE 5    [BEEO-WULFE]
0564) +SAEAE- 9 -GRUNDE 5    [SAEAE-GRUNDE]
0019) SCEDE- 9 -LANDUM 3    [SCEDE-LANDUM]
0093) BE- 9 -BUUGEDH 4    [BE-BUUGEDH]
0255) MERE- 9 -LIIDHENDE 5    [MERE-LIIDHENDE]
0309) FORE- 9 -MAEAEROST 5    [FORE-MAEAEROST]
0312) HILDE- 9 -DEEOR 3    [HILDE-DEEOR]
0362) BE- 9 -GANG 4    [BE-GANG]
0406) SEARO- 9 -NET 2    [SEARO-NET]
0408) MAGO- 9 -DHEGN. 5    [MAGO-DHEGN]
0414) BE- 9 -HOLEN 3    [BE-HOLEN]
0487) HEORU- 9 -DREEORE 5    [HEORU-DREEORE]
0584) HEADHO- 9 -LAAGE. 6    [HEADHO-LAAGE]
0339) HIGE- 9 -THRYM-8-MUM 5    [HIGE-THRYMMUM]
0597) SIGE- 9 -SCYL-1-DINGA 5    [SIGE-SCYLDINGA]
0644) SIGE- 9 -FOL-2-CA 4    [SIGE-FOLCA]
0025) GE- 9 -THEEON. 6    [GE-THEEON]
0109) GE- 9 -FEAH 5    [GE-FEAH]
0147) GE- 9 -THOLODE 4    [GE-THOLODE]
0186) GE- 9 -WENDAN 3    [GE-WENDAN]
0247) GE- 9 -MEE-1-DU 3    [GE-MEEDU]
0256) GE- 9 -THOOHT 5    [GE-THOOHT]
0396) GE- 9 -SEEON 4    [GE-SEEON]
0479) GE- 9 -TWAEAEFAN. 7    [GE-TWAEAEFAN]
0505) GE- 9 -()HEDDE*HEEDE 4    [*GE-HEEJE]
0525) GE- 9 -THINGEA 6    [GE-THINGEA]
0536) GE- 9 -BEEO-1-TE-1-DON 3    [GE-BEEOTEDON]
0574) GE- 9 -SAEAELDE 5    [GE-SAEAELDE]
0603) GE- 9 -BEEODAN 4    [GE-BEEODAN]
0633) GE- 9 -SAET 4    [GE-SAET]
0650) GE- 9 -SCEAPU 4    [GE-SCEAPU]
0014) ON- 9 -GEAT 4    [ON-GEAT]
0023) WIL- 9 -GE- 1    [WIL-GE-SIITHAS]
0139) -RUUM- 9 -LIICOR 3    [GE-RUUM-LIICOR]
0191) ON- 9 -WENDAN 3    [ON-WENDAN]
0230) HOLM- 9 -CLIFU 5    [HOLM-CLIFU]
0236) MAEGEN- 9 -WUDU 2    [MAEGEN-WUDU]
0266) WEEL- 9 -HWYLC 4    [WEEL-HWYLC]
0340) ELLEN- 9 -ROOF 2    [ELLEN-ROOF]
0419) OFER- 9 -SAAWON 4    [OFER-SAAWON]
0464) AAR- 9 -SCYL-8-DINGA 6    [AAR-SCYLDINGA]
0492) BEEOR- 9 -SELE 7    [BEEOR-SELE]
0547) NORTHAN- 9 -WIND 4    [NORTHAN-WIND]
0608) GAMOL- 9 -FEAX 4    [GAMOL-FEAX]
0167) SINC- 9 -FAAGE 4    [SINC-FAAGE]
0193) NIHT- 9 -BEALWA 4    [NIHT-BEALWA]
0307) AET- 9 -SOM-1-NE 4    [AET-SOMNE]
0363) OORET- 9 -MECGAS. 7    [OORET-MECGAS]
0380) MUND- 9 -GRIPE 5    [MUND-GRIPE]
0387) AET- 9 -GAEDERE. 6    [AET-GAEDERE]
0485) DRIHT- 9 -SELE 5    [DRIHT-SELE]
0491) GEEAT- 9 -MAECGUM 3    [GEEAT-MAECGUM]
0544) AET- 9 -SOMNE 5    [AET-SOMNE]
0551) HOND- 9 -LOCEN 4    [HOND-LOCEN]
0064) HROODH- 9 -GAARE 5    [HROODH-GAARE]
0187) DEEADH- 9 -DAEGE 3    [DEEADH-DAEGE]
0199) GUUDH- 9 -CYNING 4    [GUUDH-CYNING]
0246) GUUDH- 9 -FREM-1-MEN-1-DRA 5    [GUUDH-FREMMENDRA]
0268) HEALF- 9 -DENES 4    [HEALF-DENES]
0344) HEALF- 9 -DENES 4    [HEALF-DENES]
```

215

```
(0356) HROODH- 9 -GAAR 4     [HROODH-GAAR]
(0407) HROODH- 9 -GAAR 3     [HROODH-GAAR]
(0537) GEOGOOH- 9 -FEEORE 5     [GEOGOOH-FEEORE]
(0295) NIIW- 9 -TYR-2-WYD-2-NE 5     [NIIW-TYRWYONE]
(0577) EEG- 9 -STREEAMUM 3     [EEG-STREEAMUM]
(0590) ECG- 9 -LAAFES 6     [ECG-LAAFES]
```

```
              APPENDIX  III
LINES 0662 - 1320  (FITS X - XIX)
```

MORPHEME PAIRS GROUPED BY MEASURE OF SPACING

```
(0676) BEEO- 0 -WULF 9     [BEEO-WULF]
(0818) BEEO- 0 -WUL-1-FE 3     [BEEO-WULFE]
(0856) BEEO- 0 -WUL-1-FES 4     [BEEO-WULFES]
(0946) BEEO- 0 -WULF 5     [BEEO-WULF]
(0957) BEEO- 0 -WULF 9     [BEEO-WULF]
(1020) BEEO- 0 -WULFE 7     [BEEO-WULFE]
(1043) BEEO- 0 -WULFE 5     [BEEO-WULFE]
(1051) BEEO- 0 -WULFE 5     [BEEO-WULFE]
(1160) GLEEO- 0 -MAN-9-NES 8     [GLEEO-MANNES]
(1191) BEEO- 0 -WULF 3     [BEEO-WULF]
(1216) BEEO- 0 -WULF 5     [BEEO-WULF]
(1310) BEEO- 0 -WULF 4     [BEEO-WULF]
(0667) AA- 0 -SETED 3     [AA-SETED]
(0668) AA- 0 -BEEAD 4     [AA-BEEAD]
(0693) AA- 0 -FEEDED 2     [AA-FEEDED]
(0730) AA- 0 -HLOOG. 5     [AA-HLOOG]
(0733) AA- 0 -LUM-2-PEN 2     [AA-LUMPEN]
(0759) AA- 0 -+STOOD 3     [AA-STOOD]
(0766) AA- 0 -TEEAH. 6     [AA-TEEAH]
(0775) +AA- 0 -BEEAG. 6     [AA-BEEAG]
(0781) TOO- 0 -LUUCAN 4     [TOO-LUUCAN]
(0782) AA- 0 -STAAG. 6     [AA-STAAG]
(0834) AA- 0 -LEGDE 5     [AA-LEGDE]
(0851) AA- 0 -LEGDE. 9     [AA-LEGDE]
(0886) AA- 0 -CWEAL-9-DE 6     [AA-CWEALDE]
(0977) AA- 0 -BIIDAN 4     [AA-BIIDAN]
(1018) AA- 0 -FYLLED 3     [AA-FYLLED]
(1055) AA- 0 -CWEALDE 9     [AA-CWEALDE]
(1108) AA- 0 -HAEFEN 2     [AA-HAEFEN]
(1113) AA- 0 -WYRDED 4     [AA-WYRDED]
(1118) AA- 0 -STAAH. 3     [AA-STAAH]
(1159) AA- 0 SUNGEN 4     [AA-SUNGEN]
(1160) AA- 0 STAAH. 6     [AA-STAAH]
(1234) AA- 0 -GAN-9-GEN 3     [AA-GANGEN]
(1298) AA- 0 -BREEAT 7     [AA-BREEAT]
(0721) BE- 0 -DAEAELED 4     [BE-DAEAELED]
(0775) BE- 0 -SMI-9-THOD 4     [BE-SMITHOD]
(0860) BE- 0 -GONG 5     [BE-GONG]
(0942) BE- 0 -SYR-1-WAN 5     [BE-SYRWAN]
(0976) BE- 0 -FONGEN. 9     [BE-FONGEN]
(1223) BE- 0 -BUUGEDH 9     [BE-BUUGEDH]
(1267) HETE- 0 -LIIC 4     [HETE-LIIC]
(0662) GE- 0 -WAAT 5     [GE-WAAT]
(0694) GE- 0 -FRUUNEN 9     [GE-FRUUNEN]
(0727) GE- 0 -LIICOST 4     [GE-LIICOST]
(0728) GE- 0 -SEAH 2     [GE-SEAH]
(0738) GE- 0 -FARAN 2     [GE-FARAN]
(0757) GE- 0 -MEETTE. 7     [GE-MEETTE]
(0764) GE- 0 -WEALD 4     [GE-WEALD]
(0776) GE- 0 -FRAEAEGE 5     [GE-FRAEAEGE]
```

216

```
0779)  GE-  0 -METE 9    [GE-METE]
0783)  GE-  0 -NEAH-2-HE 5    [GE-NEAHHE]
0811)  GE-  0 -FREME-3-DE. 4    [GE-FREMEDE]
0853)  GE-  0 -WITON 3    [GE-WITON]
0890)  GE-  0 -SAEAELDE 6    [GE-SAEAELDE]
0922)  GE-  0 -TRUME 5    [GE-TRUME]
0954)  GE-  0 -FREMED 9    [GE-FREMED]
1012)  GE-  0 -BAEAERAN. 7    [GE-BAEAERAN]
1014)  GE-  0 -FAEAEGON 3    [GE-FAEAEGON]
1168)  GE-  0 -LAACUM. 7    [GE-LAACUM]
1263)  GE-  0 -WAAT 5    [GE-WAAT]
1285)  GE-  0 -()THUREN*THRUUEN 9    [*GE-THRUUEN]
0869)  -GE-  0 -SEGENA 5    [EALD-GE-SEGENA]
0882)  -GE-  0 -STEALL-1-AN. 7    [NYYD-GE-STEALLAN]
0946)  -GE-  0 -BYRDO 4    [BEARN-GE-BYRDO]
1226)  -GE-  0 -STREEONA 5    [SINC-GE-STREEONA]
0681)  ON-  0 -GEEAN 3    [ON-GEEAN]
0690)  SNEL-  0 -LIIC 5    [SNEL-LIIC]
0727)  UN-  0 -FAEAEGER. 4    [UN-FAEAEGER]
0750)  ON-  0 -FUNDE 5    [ON-FUNDE]
0817)  SYN-  0 -DOLH 4    [SYN-DOLH]
0824)  WAEL-  0 -RAEAESE 5    [WAEL-RAEAESE]
0900)  ON-  0 -DHAAH 4    [ON-DHAAH]
0928)  AL-  0 -WEALDAN 3    [AL-WEALDAN]
0955)  AL-  0 -WAL-1-DA 3    [AL-WALDA]
0960)  UN-  0 -CUUTHES 5    [UN-CUUTHES]
1020)  FOR-  0 -GEAF 3    [FOR-GEAF]
1034)  ON-  0 -GEEAN 3    [ON-GEEAN]
1054)  FOR-  0 -GYL-9-DAN 4    [FOR-GYLDAN]
1056)  FOR-  0 -STOODE 6    [FOR-STOODE]
1097)  UN-  0 -FLIT-2-ME 3    [UN-FLITME]
1121)  BEN-  0 -GEATO 9    [BEN-GEATO]
1169)  ON-  0 -FOOH 4    [ON-FOOH]
1238)  UN-  0 -RIIM 3    [UN-RIIM]
1251)  AN-  0 -GEALD 3    [AN-GEALD]
1254)  UN-  0 -RIHT 3    [UN-RIHT]
1272)  AN-  0 -WALDAN 4    [AN-WALDAN]
1291)  AN-  0 -GEAT 5    [AN-GEAT]
1308)  UN-  0 -LYFIGENDNE 9    [UN-LYFIGENDNE]
0745)  AET-  0 -STOOP 4    [AET-STOOP]
0780)  ()HET*BET-  0 -LIIC 3    [*BET-LIIC]
0786)  =AND-  0 -SACAN 4    [=AND-SACAN]
0963)  HRAED-  0 -LIIICE 9    [HRAED-LIIICE]
1269)  AET-  0 -GRAEAEPE 4    [AET-GRAEAEPE]
0717)  HROOTH-  0 -GAARES 4    [HROOTH-GAARES]
1017)  HROODH-  0 -GAAR 4    [HROODH-GAAR]
1020)  HEALF-  0 -DENES 9    [HEALF-DENES]
1236)  HROOTH-  0 -GAAR 4    [HROOTH-GAAR]
1296)  HROOTH-  0 -GAARE 7    [HROOTH-GAARE]
0732)  AAG-  0 -LAEAECA 5    [AAG-LAEAECA]
0739)  AAG-  0 -LAEAECA 5    [AAG-LAEAECA]
0816)  AEAEG-  0 -LAEAECA 9    [AEAEG-LAEAECA]
0893)  AAG-  0 -LAEAECA 4    [AAG-LAEAECA]
1000)  AAG-  0 -LAEAECA 4    [AAG-LAEAECA]
1050)  AEAEG-  0 -HWYL-2-CUM 3    [AEAEG-HWYLCUM]
1087)  HEEAH-  0 -SETL 5    [HEEAH-SETL]
1162)  WEALH-  0 -THEEO 3    [WEALH-THEEO]
1215)  $WEALH-  0 -DHEEO 4    [WEALH-DHEEO]
1259)  AAG-  0 -LAEAEC- 3    [AAG-LAEAEC-WIIF]
1262)  ECG-  0 -BANAN 3    [ECG-BANAN]
1269)  AAG-  0 -LAEAECA 4    [AAG-LAEAECA]
1277)  GALG-  0 -MOOD 4    [GALG-MOOD]

0693)  FREEO-  1 -BURH 9    [FREEO-BURH]
0912)  HLEEO-  1 -BURH 4    [HLEEO-BURH]
```

217

```
(1024) BEEO- 1 -WULF 5   [BEEO-WULF]
(1098) WEEA- 1 -LAAFE 6   [WEEA-LAAFE]
(0999) TOO- 1 -HLIOENE 7   [TOO-HLIOENE]
(1234) GEOO- 1 -SCEAFT 4   [GEOO-SCEAFT]
(0667) BE- 1 -HEEOLD 4   [BE-HEEOLD]
(1024) BE- 1 -FORAN 4   [BE-FORAN]
(1068) BE- 1 -GEAT 5   [BE-GEAT]
(1126) BE- 1 -FEALLEN 3   [BE-FEALLEN]
(1132) BE- 1 -LEEAC 5   [BE-LEEAC]
(1254) BE- 1 -CWOOM 4   [BE-CWOOM]
(1275) BE- 1 -OAEAEL-1-EO 4   [BE-OAEAELEO]
(1202) HIGE- 1 -LAAC 2   [HIGE-LAAC]
(0662) GE- 1 -ORYHT 5   [GE-ORYHT]
(0666) GE- 1 -FRUNGON 5   [GE-FRUNGON]
(0682) GE- 1 -HEEAWE 3   [GE-HEEAWE]
(0690) GE- 1 -BEEAH. 6   [GE-BEEAH]
(0692) GE- 1 -SEECEAN 4   [GE-SEECEAN]
(0709) GE- 1 -THINGES. 9   [GE-THINGES]
(0717) GE- 1 -SOOHTE. 7   [GE-SOOHTE]
(0744) GE- 1 -FEORMOD. 4   [GE-FEORMOD]
(0768) GE- 1 -HWYLCUM 4   [GE-HWYLCUM]
(0777) GE- 1 -REGNAD 9   [GE-REGNAD]
(0798) GE- 1 -WIN 3   [GE-WIN]
(0805) GE- 1 -HWYLC-1-RE 4   [GE-HWYLCRE]
(0822) GE- 1 -GONGEN. 9   [GE-GONGEN]
(0837) GE- 1 -FRAEAEGE 5   [GE-FRAEAEGE]
(0868) GE- 1 -MYNOIG 9   [GE-MYNOIG]
(0873) GE- 1 -RAA-2-OE 9   [GE-RAADE]
(0903) GE- 1 -WEALD 4   [GE-WEALD]
(0909) GE- 1 -LYYF-1-OE 6   [GE-LYYFOE]
(0926) GE- 1 -SEAH 4   [GE-SEAH]
(0929) GE- 1 -LIMPE 9   [GE-LIMPE]
(0929) GE- 1 -BAAD 3   [GE-BAAD]
(0961) GE- 1 -SEEON 2   [GE-SEEON]
(0973) GE- 1 -BOHTE. 7   [GE-BOHTE]
(0975) GE- 1 -SWENCED 4   [GE-SWENCED]
(0992) GE- 1 -FRAET-1-WOD 4   [GE-FRAETWOD]
(1014) GE- 1 -THAEAEGON 8   [GE-THAEAEGON]
(1023) GE- 1 -SAAWON. 6   [GE-SAAWON]
(1040) GE- 1 -LAAC 4   [GE-LAAC]
(1085) GE- 1 -THINGO 3   [GE-THINGO]
(1087) GE- 1 -WEALD 4   [GE-WEALD]
(1107) GE- 1 -AEFNED 4   [GE-AEFNED]
(1129) GE- 1 -MUNDE 5   [GE-MUNDE]
(1191) GE- 1 -BROODH-1-RUM 3   [GE-BROODHRUM]
(1201) GE- 1 -CEEAS 9   [GE-CEEAS]
(1227) GE- 1 -DEEFE 6   [GE-DEEFE]
(1236) GE- 1 -WAAT 4   [GE-WAAT]
(1250) GE- 1 -SAEAELOE 4   [GE-SAEAELOE]
(1252) GE- 1 -LAMP 4   [GE-LAMP]
(1255) GE- 1 -SYYNE 9   [GE-SYYNE]
(1259) GE- 1 -MUNDE 6   [GE-MUNDE]
(1264) GE- 1 -MEAR-1-COD 9   [GE-MEARCOD]
(1272) GE- 1 -LYYFOE 5   [GE-LYYFOE]
(1277) GE- 1 -GAAN 3   [GE-GAAN]
(0683) -GE- 1 -WEORCA 3   [NIITH-GE-WEORCA]
(0853) -GE- 1 -SIIOHAS 5   [EALD-GE-SIIOHAS]
(0974) -GE- 1 -TEEO-1-NA 5   [LAADH-GE-TEEONA]
(0981) -GE- 1 -WEOR-2-CA 4   [GUUDH-GE-WEORCA]
(1133) -GE- 1 -BINDE 4   [IIS-GE-BINDE]
(1164) -GE- 1 -FAE-1-DE-9-RAN 4   [SUHTER-GE-FAEDERAN]
(0695) FOR- 1 -NAM 3   [FOR-NAM]
(0714) WIIN- 1 -RECEO 4   [WIIN-RECEO]
(0721) ON- 1 -ARN 3   [ON-ARN]
(0741) UN- 1 -WEAR-1-NUM 5   [UN-WEARNUM]
```

```
742) BAAN-  1 -LOCAN  2    [BAAN-LOCAN]
744) UN-  1 -LYFIGENDES  4    [UN-LYFIGENDES]
747) ON-  1 -GEEAN  3    [ON-GEEAN]
771) WIIN-  1 -SELE.  7    [WIIN-SELE]
807) EARM-  1 -LIIC  3    [EARM-LIIC]
817) ON-  1 -SPRUN-1-GON  5    [ON-SPRUNGON]
830) ON-  1 -CYYTHDHE  5    [ON-CYYTHDHE]
833) UN-  1 -LYYTEL  9    [UN-LYYTEL]
842) SAAR-  1 -LIIC  3    [SAAR-LIIC]
852) ON-  1 -FEENG.  7    [ON-FEENG]
871) ON-  1 -GAN  4    [ON-GAN]
899) WER-  1 -THEEODE  5    [WER-THEEODE]
911) ON-  1 -+FOON  3    [ON-FOON]
915) ON-  1 -WOOD.  6    [ON-WOOD]
932) UN-  1 -GEAARA  3    [UN-GEAARA]
944) GUM-  1 -CYNNU=  4    [GUM-CYNNU=]
987) UN-  1 -HEEORU  4    [UN-HEEORU]
044) ON-  1 -WEALD  4    [ON-WEALD]
046) MAN-  1 -LIICE  5    [MAN-LIICE]
072) UN-  1 -SYNNUM  4    [UN-SYNNUM]
080) FOR-  1 -NAM  3    [FOR-NAM]
155) IN-  1 -GE-  9    [IN-GE-STEALD]
165) ()HUN*UN-  1 -FER-1-TH  8    [*UN-FERTH]
214) ON-  1 -FEENG.  7    [ON-FEENG]
246) THRYM-  1 -LIIC  4    [THRYM-LIIC]
271) GIM-  1 -FAES-1-TE  3    [GIM-FAESTE]
276) MAN-  1 -CYNNES  4    [MAN-CYNNES]
293) ON-  1 -FUN-9-DEN  2    [ON-FUNDEN]
689) AND-  1 -WLITAN  3    [AND-WLITAN]
759) UP-  1 -LANG  3    [UP-LANG]
027) FREEOND-  1 -LIICOR  5    [FREEOND-LIICOR]
059) AND-  1 -GIT  4    [AND-GIT]
150) AET-  1 -WITON  4    [AET-WITON]
198) AET-  1 -WAEG  4    [AET-WAEG]
256) WIID-  1 -CUUTH  3    [WIID-CUUTH]
287) AND-  1 -WEARD  4    [AND-WEARD]
662) HROOTH-  1 -GAAR  5    [HROOTH-GAAR]
040) HEALF-  1 -DENES  5    [HEALF-DENES]
064) HEALF-  1 -DENES  5    [HEALF-DENES]
189) HREEDH-  1 -RIIC  4    [HREEDH-RIIC]
189) HROODH-  1 -MUND  4    [HROODH-MUND]
244) YYTH-  1 -GE-  4    [YYTH-GE-SEENE]
664) WIIG-  1 -FRUMA  4    [WIIG-FRUMA]
980) ()EC*ECG-  1 -LAAFES  4    [*ECG-LAAFES]
987) AEAEG-  1 -HWYLC  2    [AEAEG-HWYLC]
228) AEAEG-  1 -HWYLC  4    [AEAEG-HWYLC]

872) BEEO-  2 -WUL-1-FES  4    [BEEO-WULFES]
084) WEEA-  2 -LAAFE  4    [WEEA-LAAFE]
214) HREEA-  2 -WIIC  5    [HREEA-WIIC]
315) WEEA-  2 -SPELLE  5    [WEEA-SPELLE]
780) TOO-  2 -BRE-9-CAN  3    [TOO-BRECAN]
139) SAEAE-  2 -LAADE  6    [SAEAE-LAADE]
266) GEOO-  2 -SCEAFT-  3    [GEOO-SCEAFT-GAASTA]
680) BE-  2 -NEEO-9-TAN  3    [BE-NEEOTAN]
730) MA-1-GO-  2 -RIN-9-CA  3    [MAGO-RINCA]
003) BE-  2 -FLEEON-1-NE  5    [BE-FLEEONNE]
067) ME-2-DO-  2 -BENCE  4    [MEDO-BENCE]
077) BE-  2 -MEARN  9    [BE-MEARN]
097) BE-  2 -NEMDE.  7    [BE-NEMDE]
109) BEADO-  2 -RINCA.  9    [BEADO-RINCA]
135) BE-  2 -WITIADH  5    [BE-WITIADH]
146) BE-  2 -GEAT  4    [BE-GEAT]
193) BE-  2 -WAEGNED  4    [BE-WAEGNED]
267) HEORO-  2 -WEARH  5    [HEORO-WEARH]
```

219

```
(1295) BE- 2 -FANGEN 6   [BE-FANGEN]
(0758) HIGE- 2 -LAACES 4   [HIGE-LAACES]
(0804) SIGE- 2 -WAEAEPNU= 9   [SIGE-WAEAEPNU=]
(0665) GE- 2 -BEODAN 5   [GE-BEODAN]
(0674) GE- 2 -HEAL-2-DAN 3   [GE-HEALDAN]
(0675) GE- 2 -SPRAEC 3   [GE-SPRAEC]
(0687) GE- 2 -MET 3   [GE-MET]
(0697) GE- 2 -WIOFU. 9   [GE-WIOFU]
(0700) GE- 2 -CYY-9-THEO 4   [GE-CYYTHEO]
(0731) GE- 2 -OAEAELOE 5   [GE-OAEAELOE]
(0732) GE- 2 -HWYLCES 5   [GE-HWYLCES]
(0756) GE- 2 -ORAEG 4   [GE-ORAEG]
(0763) GE- 2 -WINOAN 8   [GE-WINOAN]
(0784) GE- 2 -HWYL-1-CUM 4   [GE-HWYLCUM]
(0785) GE- 2 -HYYR-2-DON. 5   [GE-HYYRDON]
(0808) GE- 2 -WEALD 4   [GE-WEALD]
(0814) GE- 2 -HWAE-1-THER 3   [GE-HWAETHER]
(0815) GE- 2 -BAAO 5   [GE-BAAO]
(0824) GE- 2 -LUMPEN. 5   [GE-LUMPEN]
(0827) GE- 2 -NEREO 2   [GE-NEREO]
(0827) GE- 2 -FEH 4   [GE-FEH]
(0829) GE- 2 -LAEAESTEO. 5   [GE-LAEAESTEO]
(0857) GE- 2 -CWAEDH 5   [GE-CWAEDH]
(0877) GE- 2 -WIN 8   [GE-WIN]
(0884) GE- 2 -SAEAEGED 4   [GE-SAEAEGED]
(0884) GE- 2 -SPRONG 4   [GE-SPRONG]
(0888) GE- 2 -NEEDH-1-DE 5   [GE-NEEDHDE]
(0893) GE- 2 -GONGEN 3   [GE-GONGEN]
(0934) GE- 2 -BIIOAN 5   [GE-BIIOAN]
(0936) GE- 2 -HWYL-1-C-1-()NE*UM. 7   [*GE-HWYLCUM]
(0940) GE- 2 -FREMEDE. 5   [GE-FREMEDE]
(0996) GE- 2 -HWYLCUM 3   [GE-HWYLCUM]
(1024) GE- 2 -THAH 4   [GE-THAH]
(1029) GE- 2 -SELLAN. 3   [GE-SELLAN]
(1043) GE- 2 -HWAETH-9-RES 4   [GE-HWAETHRES]
(1044) GE- 2 -TEEAH. 4   [GE-TEEAH]
(1090) GE- 2 -HWYL-1-CE 9   [GE-HWYLCE]
(1101) GE- 2 -MAEAENDEN 3   [GE-MAEAENDEN]
(1126) GE- 2 -SEEON 9   [GE-SEEON]
(1173) GE- 2 -MYNOIG 4   [GE-MYNOIG]
(1185) GE- 2 -MON 3   [GE-MON]
(1187) GE- 2 -FREME-2-DON. 4   [GE-FREMEDON]
(1220) GE- 2 -MAN 5   [GE-MAN]
(1228) GE- 2 -TRYYWE 9   [GE-TRYYWE]
(1302) GE- 2 -NAM 5   [GE-NAM]
(1304) GE- 2 -WORDEN 2   [GE-WORDEN]
(1315) GE- 2 -FREM-9-MAN 5   [GE-FREMMAN]
(0729) -GE- 2 -ORIHT 4   [SIBBE-GE-ORIHT]
(0805) -GE- 2 -DAAL 5   [ALOOR-GE-DAAL]
(0668) EOTON- 2 -WEARD 9   [EOTON-WEARD]
(0679) FOR- 2 -THAN 2   [FOR-THAN]
(0695) WIIN- 2 -SELE 9   [WIIN-SELE]
(0707) ()SYN*SCYN- 2 -SCATHA 5   [*SCYN-SCATHA]
(0723) SON- 2 -BRAEAED 3   [ON-BRAEAED]
(0755) HIN- 2 -FUUS 9   [HIN-FUUS]
(0774) IIREN- 2 -BENDUM 4   [IIREN-BENDUM]
(0792) FOR- 2 -LAEAETAN. 3   [FOR-LAEAETAN]
(0801) SYN- 2 -SCADHAN. 9   [SYN-SCADHAN]
(0804) FOR- 2 -SWOREN 4   [FOR-SWOREN]
(0821) WYN- 2 -LEEAS 4   [WYN-LEEAS]
(0828) ELLEN- 2 -MAEAER-3-THUM 9   [ELLEN-MAEAERTHUM]
(0851) FEN- 2 -FREODHO 4   [FEN-FREODHO]
(0876) UN- 2 -CUUTHES 4   [UN-CUUTHES]
(0885) UN- 2 -LYYTEL. 7   [UN-LYYTEL]
(0900) ELLEN- 2 -DAEAEDU= 9   [ELLEN-DAEAEDU=]
```

```
903) FOR- 2 -LAACEN 9      [FOR-LAACEN]
904) FOR- 2 -SENDED 4      [FOR-SENDED]
922) IIIR- 2 -FAEST. 6     [IIIR-FAEST]
956) FOR- 2 -GYLDE 5       [FOR-GYLDE]
991) INNAN- 2 -WEARD 9     [INNAN-WEARD]
993) WIIN- 2 -RECED 4      [WIIN-RECED]
998) IIREN- 2 -BENDU= 9    [IIREN-BENDU=]
051) BRIM- 2 -()LEADE*LAADE 4    [*BRIM-LAADE]
059) FOR- 2 -THAN 4        [FOR-THAN]
062) WIN- 2 -DAGUM 4       [WIN-DAGUM]
122) FOR- 2 -SWEALG 4      [FOR-SWEALG]
123) FOR- 2 -NAM 9         [FOR-NAM]
143) HUUN- 2 -LAAFING 5    [HUUN-LAAFING]
164) SU-1-HTER- 2 -GE- 1   [SUHTER-GE-FAEDERAN]
168) +AAR- 2 -FAEST 5      [AAR-FAEST]
194) EARM- 2 -()READE*HREEADE 5    [*EARM-HREEADE]
205) WAEL- 2 -REEAF 9      [WAEL-REEAF]
230) EAL- 2 -GEARO 4       [EAL-GEARO]
249) MAN- 2 -DRYHT-9-NE 5  [MAN-DRYHTNE]
314) ()ALF*AL- 2 -WALDA 4  [*AL-WALDA]
715) GOLD- 2 -SELE 3       [GOLD-SELE]
729) AET- 2 -GAEDERE 5     [AET-GAEDERE]
812) LIIC- 2 -HOMA 4       [LIIC-HOMA]
839) FOLC- 2 -TOGAN 4      [FOLC-TOGAN]
891) AET- 2 -STOOD 3       [AET-STOOD]
945) EALD- 2 -METOD 3      [EALD-METOD]
981) GYLP- 2 -SPRAEAECE 4  [GYLP-SPRAEAECE]
012) SINC- 2 -GYFAN 8      [SINC-GYFAN]
047) HORD- 2 -WEARD 3      [HORD-WEARD]
063) AET- 2 -GAEDERE 4     [AET-GAEDERE]
092) SINC- 2 -GE- 3        [SINC-GE-STREEONUM]
121) AET- 2 -SPRANC. 4     [AET-SPRANC]
142) ()WOROLD*WEOROD- 2 -RAEAE-1-DEN-1-()NE*DE 6    [*WEOROD-RAEAEDENDE]
164) AET- 2 -GAE-1-DERE 9  [AET-GAEDERE]
171) GOLD- 2 -WINE 5       [GOLD-WINE]
224) WIND- 2 -GEARD 3      [WIND-GEARD]
281) ED- 2 -HWYRFT 4       [ED-HWYRFT]
316) FYRD- 2 -WYR-9-DHE 4  [FYRD-WYRDHE]
320) NEEOD- 2 -LADHU*M 5   [NEEOD-LADHU*M]
683) NIITH- 2 -GE- 1       [NIITH-GE-WEORCA]
736) THRYYDH- 2 -SWYYDH 9  [THRYYDH-SWYYDH]
838) GIF- 2 -HEALLE 6      [GIF-HEALLE]
838) GUUDH- 2 -RINC 4      [GUUDH-RINC]
841) LIIF- 2 -GE- 3        [LIIF-GE-DAAL]
850) DEEADH- 2 -FAEAEGE 3  [DEEADH-FAEAEGE]
863) HROODH- 2 -GAAR 9     [HROODH-GAAR]
908) SWIIDH- 2 -FERHTHES 9 [SWIIDH-FERHTHES]
925) $HROODH- 2 -GAAR 5    [HROODH-GAAR]
009) HEALF- 2 -DENES 4     [HEALF-DENES]
110) EETH- 2 -GE- 3        [EETH-GE-SYYNE]
118) GUUDH- 2 -RINC 4      [GUUDH-RINC]
133) IIS- 2 -GE- 1         [IIS-GE-BINDE]
148) GUUDH- 2 -LAAF 7      [GUUDH-LAAF]
148) OOS- 2 -LAAF 5        [OOS-LAAF]
183) OF- 2 -LAEAETEST 9    [OF-LAEAETEST]
275) DEEEATH- 2 -+WIIC 9   [DEEEATH-WIIC]
664) WEAL-1-H- 2 -THEEO 3  [WEALH-THEEO]
697) WIIG- 2 -SPEEDA 4     [WIIG-SPEEDA]
957) ()EC*ECG- 2 -THEEO-1-WES 5    [*ECG-THEEOWES]
984) AEAEG- 2 -HWYLC 3     [AEAEG-HWYLC]
989) AAH- 2 -LAEAECAN 4    [AAH-LAEAECAN]
025) FEOH- 2 -GYFTE 6      [FEOH-GYFTE]
089) FEOH- 2 -GYF-9-TU= 5  [FEOH-GYFTU=]
177) BEEAH- 2 -SELE 5      [BEEAH-SELE]
212) WIIG- 2 -FRECAN 5     [WIIG-FRECAN]
```

221

```
(1284) WIIG- 2 -GRYRE 5   [WIIG-GRYRE]
(1319) ING- 2 -WINA 4   [ING-WINA]

(0796) FREEA- 3 -DRIHT-9-NES 4   [FREEA-DRIHTNES]
(0973) FEEA- 3 -SCEAFT 8   [FEEA-SCEAFT]
(1127) HEEA- 3 -BURH 6   [HEEA-BURH]
(0666) TOO- 3 -GEEANES 4   [TOO-GEEANES]
(0690) +SAEAE- 3 -RINC 4   [SAEAE-RINC]
(0895) +SAEAE- 3 -BAAT 2   [SAEAE-BAAT]
(0667) SELE- 3 -WEARD 3   [SELE-WEARD]
(0674) HILDE- 3 -GEATWE 9   [HILDE-GEATWE]
(0677) HERE- 3 -WAESMUM 5   [HERE-WAESMUM]
(0690) SE-1-LE- 3 -RESTE 2   [SELE-RESTE]
(0736) BE- 3 -HEEOLD 5   [BE-HEEOLD]
(0775) SEAR-1-O- 3 -THONCUM 3   [SEARO-THONCUM]
(0776) MEDU- 3 -BENC 9   [MEDU-BENC]
(0799) HIL-1-DE- 3 -MECGAS. 5   [HILDE-MECGAS]
(0864) HEA-1-THO- 3 -ROOFE 9   [HEATHO-ROOFE]
(0901) HER-1-E- 3 -MOODES 5   [HERE-MOODES]
(0907) BE- 3 -MEARN 4   [BE-MEARN]
(0920) SEARO- 3 -WUNDOR 4   [SEARO-WUNDOR]
(0935) HEORO- 3 -DREEORIG 3   [HEORO-DREEORIG]
(0938) BE- 3 -WERE-1-DON. 9   [BE-WEREDON]
(0969) FORE- 3 -MIHTIG 9   [FORE-MIHTIG]
(0990) BEADU- 3 -FOLME 9   [BEADU-FOLME]
(0998) INNE- 3 -WEARD 3   [INNE-WEARD]
(1015) ME-9-DO- 3 -FUL 4   [MEDO-FUL]
(1031) BE- 3 -WUNDEN 4   [BE-WUNDEN]
(1052) MEDU- 3 -BENCE 6   [MEDU-BENCE]
(1053) YR-9-FE- 3 -LAAFE 4   [YRFE-LAAFE]
(1064) HILDE- 3 -WII-8-SAN 4   [HILDE-WIISAN]
(1176) HERE- 3 -()RIC*RINC 3   [*HERE-RINC]
(1200) SEARO- 3 -NIIDHAS 5   [SEARO-NIIDHAS]
(1222) WIIDE- 3 -FERHTH 9   [WIIDE-FERHTH]
(1242) HILDE- 3 -RANDAS 9   [HILDE-RANDAS]
(1245) HEATHO- 3 -STEEAPA 5   [HEATHO-STEEAPA]
(0737) HIGE- 3 -LAACES 6   [HIGE-LAACES]
(0746) HIGE- 3 -THIIHTIGNE 4   [HIGE-THIIHTIGNE]
(0787) SIGE- 3 -LEEAS-1-NE 5   [SIGE-LEEASNE]
(0813) HYGE- 3 -LAA-9-CES 5   [HYGE-LAACES]
(0914) HIGE- 3 -LAACES 4   [HIGE-LAACES]
(0794) GE- 3 -NEHOST 4   [GE-NEHOST]
(0800) GE- 3 -HWONE 5   [GE-HWONE]
(0846) GE- 3 -FLYYMED 4   [GE-FLYYMED]
(0848) GE- 3 -SWING 4   [GE-SWING]
(0848) GE- 3 -MENGED. 6   [GE-MENGED]
(0865) GE- 3 -FLIT 4   [GE-FLIT]
(0871) GE- 3 -BUNDEN 9   [GE-BUNDEN]
(0874) GE- 3 -CWAEDH 6   [GE-CWAEDH]
(0895) GE- 3 -HLEOOD 5   [GE-HLEOOD]
(0911) GE- 3 -HEALDAN 4   [GE-HEALDAN]
(0923) GE- 3 -CYYTHED 5   [GE-CYYTHED]
(0950) GE- 3 -WEALD 4   [GE-WEALD]
(0959) GE- 3 -NEEDH-2-DON. 3   [GE-NEEDHDON]
(0968) GE- 3 -TWAEAEMAN 4   [GE-TWAEAEMAN]
(0985) GE- 3 -HWYLC 9   [GE-HWYLC]
(0985) GE- 3 -LIICOST 6   [GE-LIICOST]
(1001) GE- 3 -WAND 4   [GE-WAND]
(1004) GE- 3 -()SACAN*SEECAN 3   [*GE-SEECAN]
(1027) GE- 3 -FRAEGN 2   [GE-FRAEGN]
(1028) GE- 3 -GYREDE 5   [GE-GYREDE]
(1038) GE- 3 -WUR-1-THAD 4   [GE-WURTHAD]
(1052) GE- 3 -SEALDE 3   [GE-SEALDE]
(1074) GE- 3 -BYRD 5   [GE-BYRD]
(1083) GE- 3 -FEOHTAN. 9   [GE-FEOHTAN]
```

```
086) GE- 3 -RYYM-1-DON 5   [GE-RYYMDON]
141) GE- 3 -MUNDE. 7   [GE-MUNDE]
166) GE- 3 -HWYLC 5   [GE-HWYLC]
194) GE- 3 -EEAWED 3   [GE-EEAWED]
230) GE- 3 -THWAEAERE 5   [GE-THWAEAERE]
274) GE- 3 -+WAAT 5   [GE-WAAT]
297) GE- 3 -SIIDHES 5   [GE-SIIDHES]
320) GE- 3 -TAEAESE. 9   [GE-TAEAESE]
841) -GE- 3 -DAAL 5   [LIIF-GE-DAAL]
938) -GE- 3 -WEORC 5   [LAND-GE-WEORC]
969) -GE- 3 -NIIDH-3-LAN 4   [FEORH-GE-NIIDHLAN]
092) -GE- 3 -STREEO-9-NUM 4   [SINC-GE-STREEONUM]
110) -GE- 3 -SYYNE 6   [EETH-GE-SYYNE]
211) -GE- 3 -WAEAEDU 4   [BREEOST-GE-WAEAEDU]
218) -GE- 3 -STREEONA 8   [*THEEOD-GE-STREEONA]
667) SUNDOR- 3 -NYT-9-TE 5   [SUNDOR-NYTTE]
684) OFER- 3 -SITTAN 4   [OFER-SITTAN]
695) WAEL- 3 -DEEADH 3   [WAEL-DEEADH]
696) FOR- 3 -GEAF 4   [FOR-GEAF]
709) BOLGEN- 3 -MOOD 4   [BOLGEN-MOOD]
712) MAAN- 3 -SCADHA 5   [MAAN-SCADHA]
718) ALDOR- 3 -DAGUM 2   [ALDOR-DAGUM]
719) HEAL- 3 -DHEGNAS 9   [HEAL-DHEGNAS]
738) FAEAER- 3 -GRIPUM 3   [FAEAER-GRIPUM]
743) SYN- 3 -SNAEAEDUM 3   [SYN-SNAEAEDUM]
766) HEARM- 3 -SCA-9-THA 4   [HEARM-SCATHA]
768) CEASTER- 3 -BUU-9-ENDUM 4   [CEASTER-BUUENDUM]
780) +BAAN- 3 -FAAG 4   [BAAN-FAAG]
792) CWEALM- 3 -CUMAN 4   [CWEALM-CUMAN]
818) BAAN- 3 -LOGAN 9   [BAAN-LOGAN]
820) FEN- 3 -HL-1-EODHU 4   [FEN-HLEODHU]
843) TIIR- 3 -LEEASES 4   [TIIR-LEEASES]
845) OFER- 3 -CUMEN 4   [OFER-CUMEN]
854) GOMEN- 3 -WAATHE 5   [GOMEN-WAATHE]
859) EORMEN- 3 -GRUND 4   [EORMEN-GRUND]
869) EAL- 3 -FELA 4   [EAL-FELA]
874) WEEL- 3 -HWYLC 3   [WEEL-HWYLC]
883) EAL- 3 -FELA 9   [EAL-FELA]
906) AL-1-DOR- 3 -CEARE. 7   [ALDOR-CEARE]
911) FAEDER- 3 -AETHELUM 3   [FAEDER-AETHELUM]
946) BEARN- 3 -GE- 0   [BEARN-GE-BYRDO]
958) ELLEN- 3 -WEORC 9   [ELLEN-WEORC]
962) FYL- 3 -WEERIGNE. 5   [FYL-WEERIGNE]
028) GUM- 3 -MAN-2-NA 9   [GUM-MANNA]
033) SCUUR- 3 -HEARD 4   [SCUUR-HEARD]
065) GOMEN- 3 -WUDU 9   [GOMEN-WUDU]
066) HEAL- 3 -GAMEN 9   [HEAL-GAMEN]
111) EAL- 3 -GYLDEN. 6   [EAL-GYLDEN]
112) IIREN- 3 -HEARD 4   [IIREN-HEARD]
119) WAEL- 3 -FYYRA 3   [WAEL-FYYRA]
138) GYRN- 3 -WRAECE 4   [GYRN-WRAECE]
151) FOR- 3 -HABBAN 9   [FOR-HABBAN]
201) EORMEN- 3 -RIIC-1-ES 4   [EORMEN-RIICES]
205) FOR- 3 -NAM 4   [FOR-NAM]
229) MAN- 3 -DRIHTNE 5   [MAN-DRIHTNE]
263) FAEDER-1-EN- 3 -MAEAEGE 9   [FAEDEREN-MAEAEGE]
311) AEAER- 3 -DAEGE 5   [AEAER-DAEGE]
317) HEAL- 3 -WUDU 9   [HEAL-WUDU]
675) GYLP- 3 -WORDA 4   [GYLP-WORDA]
734) WIST- 3 -FYLLE 4   [WIST-FYLLE]
749) IN-1-WIT- 3 -THANCU= 5   [INWIT-THANCU=]
753) MUND- 3 -GRIPE 4   [MUND-GRIPE]
767) DRYHT- 3 -SELE 9   [DRYHT-SELE]
799) HEARD- 3 -HICGEN-1-DE 9   [HEARD-HICGENDE]
815) LIIC- 3 -SAAR 2   [LIIC-SAAR]
```

223

```
(0827) NIHT- 3 -WEORCE 5   [NIHT-WEORCE]
(0828) EEAST- 3 -DENUM 4   [EEAST-DENUM]
(0829) GEEAT- 3 -MECGA 3   [GEEAT-MECGA]
(0831) IN-1-WID- 3 -SORGE 5   [INWID-SORGE]
(0853) EALD- 3 -GE- 1   [EALD-GE-SIIDHAS]
(0861) ROND- 3 -HAEB-9-BEN-1-DRA 4   [ROND-HAEBBENDRA]
(0866) FOLD- 3 -WEGAS 4   [FOLD-WEGAS]
(0868) GILP- 3 -HLAEDEN 3   [GILP-HLAEDEN]
(0869) EALD- 3 -GE- 0   [EALD-GE-SEGENA]
(0882) NYYD- 3 -GE- 0   [NYYD-GE-STEALLAN]
(0921) BRYYD- 3 -BUURE 7   [BRYYD-BUURE]
(0936) WIID- 3 -SCOFEN 3   [WIID-SCOFEN]
(0938) LAND- 3 -GE- 3   [LAND-GE-WEORC]
(0965) ()HAND*MUND- 3 -GRIPE 4   [*MUND-GRIPE]
(0976) ()MID*NIID- 3 -GRIPE 5   [*NIID-GRIPE]
(0986) HAND- 3 -SPORU 3   [HAND-SPORU]
(0994) GOLD- 3 -FAAG 3   [GOLD-FAAG]
(1007) LIIC- 3 -HOMA 4   [LIIC-HOMA]
(1019) THEEOD- 3 -SCYLDINGAS 6   [THEEOD-SCYLOINGAS]
(1042) WIID- 3 -CUUTHES 3   [WIID-CUUTHES]
(1073) ()HILD*LIND- 3 -PLEGAN 5   [*LIND-PLEGAN]
(1077) MEOTOD- 3 -SCEAFT 4   [MEOTOD-SCEAFT]
(1101) INWIT- 3 -SEARO 4   [INWIT-SEARO]
(1131) HRINGED- 3 -STEF-1-NAN 9   [HRINGED-STEFNAN]
(1180) METOD- 3 -SCEAFT 4   [METOD-SCEAFT]
(1190) AET- 3 -GAEDERE 5   [AET-GAEDERE]
(1192) FREEOND- 3 -L-1-A-1-THU 3   [FREEOND-LATHU]
(1198) HORD- 3 -()MAD-2-MUM*MAADHUM 4   [*HORD-MAADHUM]
(1218) ()THEO*THEEOD- 3 -GE- 2   [*THEEOD-GE-STREEONA]
(1226) SINC- 3 -GE- 0   [SINC-GE-STREEONA]
(1241) FLET- 3 -RAESTE 4   [FLET-RAESTE]
(1243) BORD- 3 -WUDU 4   [BORD-WUDU]
(1246) THREC- 3 -WUDU 4   [THREC-WUDU]
(1259) -LAEAEC- 3 -WIIF 2   [AAG-LAEAEC-WIIF]
(1266) -SCEAFT- 3 -GAASTA 5   [GEOO-SCEAFT-GAASTA]
(1284) WAEAEPNED- 3 -MEN 9   [WAEAEPNED-MEN]
(1288) HEARD- 3 -ECG 4   [HEARD-ECG]
(1298) RAND- 3 -WIGA 6   [RAND-WIGA]
(1299) BLAEAED- 3 -FAESTNE 6   [BLAEAED-FAESTNE]
(1317) HAND- 3 -SCALE 5   [HAND-SCALE]
(0678) GUUTH- 3 -GE- 9   [GUUTH-GE-WEORCA]
(0772) WIDH- 3 -HAEFDE 5   [WIDH-HAEFDE]
(0783) NORDH- 3 -DENU= 2   [NORDH-DENU=]
(0793) LIIF- 3 -DAGAS 6   [LIIF-DAGAS]
(0803) GUUDH- 3 -BIL-9-LA 3   [GUUDH-BILLA]
(0826) HROODH- 3 -GAARES 4   [HROODH-GAARES]
(0885) DEEADH- 3 -DAEGE 4   [DEEADH-DAEGE]
(0966) LIIF- 3 -BYSIG 4   [LIIF-BYSIG]
(0971) LIIF- 3 -WRATHE 6   [LIIF-WRATHE]
(0974) LAADH- 3 -GE- 1   [LAADH-GE-TEEONA]
(0981) GUUDH- 3 -GE- 1   [GUUDH-GE-WEORCA]
(1016) SWIIDH- 3 -HICGENDE 9   [SWIIDH-HICGENDE]
(1066) HROOTH- 3 -GAARES 4   [HROOTH-GAARES]
(1069) HEALF- 3 -DENA 4   [HEALF-DENA]
(1070) FR-8-EES- 3 -WAELE 4   [FREES-WAELE]
(1146) FERHDH- 3 -FRECAN 4   [FERHDH-FRECAN]
(1155) EORDH- 3 -CYNINGES 4   [EORDH-CYNINGES]
(1186) WORDH- 3 -MYN-1-DUM 4   [WORDH-MYNDUM]
(1195) HEALS- 3 -BEEAGA 3   [HEALS-BEEAGA]
(1213) GUUDH- 3 -SCEARE 6   [GUUDH-SCEARE]
(0823) DAEG- 3 -RIIM 4   [DAEG-RIIM]
(0890) THURH- 3 -WOOD 3   [THURH-WOOD]
(0904) SORH- 3 -WYL-1-MAS 4   [SORH-WYLMAS]
(0921) BEEAH- 3 -HOR-1-DA 3   [BEEAH-HORDA]
(0969) FEOR-1-H- 3 -GE- 3   [FEORH-GE-NIIDHLAN]
```

224

```
.039) HEEAH-  3 -CYNINGES 5   [HEEAH-CYNINGES]
.044) ING-  3 -WINA 3   [ING-WINA]
.059) AEAEG-  3 -HWAEAER 9   [AEAEG-HWAEAER]
.102) BEEAG-  3 -GYFAN 4   [BEEAG-GYFAN]
.140) THURH-  3 -TEEON 3   [THURH-TEEON]
.165) AEAEG-  3 -HWYLC 4   [AEAEG-HWYLC]
.278) SORH-  3 -FULNE 9   [SORH-FULNE]
.279) HRING-  3 -DENE 6   [HRING-DENE]

169) FREEO-  4 -DRIHTEN 3   [FREEO-DRIHTEN]
688) HEA-1-THO-  4 -DEEOR 5   [HEATHO-DEEOR]
703) SCEA-9-DU-  4 -GENGA 5   [SCEADU-GENGA]
723) BEALO-  4 -HYYDIG 4   [BEALO-HYYDIG]
726) YRRE-  4 -MOOD 3   [YRRE-MOOD]
786) GRYRE-  4 -LEEODH 8   [GRYRE-LEEODH]
834) HILDE-  4 -DEEOR 9   [HILDE-DEEOR]
849) HEORO-  4 -DREEDRE 4   [HEORO-DREEDRE]
986) HILDE-  4 -RINCES 4   [HILDE-RINCES]
022) ()HILTE*HILDE-  4 -CUMBOR 5   [*HILDE-CUMBOR]
029) EALO-  4 -BEN-1-CE 5   [EALO-BENCE]
047) HEATHO-  4 -RAEAESAS 4   [HEATHO-RAEAESAS]
060) FORE-  4 -THANC 4   [FORE-THANC]
108) HERE-  4 -SCYLDINGA 5   [HERE-SCYLDINGA]
143) HILDE-  4 -LEEOMAN 4   [HILDE-LEEOMAN]
157) SEARO-  4 -GIMMA 5   [SEARO-GIMMA]
875) SIGE-  4 -MUNDE*S 5   [SIGE-MUNDE*S]
987) GE-  4 -CWAEDH 9   [GE-CWAEDH]
005) GE-  4 -NYYDDE 5   [GE-NYYDDE]
011) GE-  4 -FRAEGEN 3   [GE-FRAEGEN]
103) GE-  4 -THEARFOD 2   [GE-THEARFOD]
210) GE-  4 -HWEARF 5   [GE-HWEARF]
221) GE-  4 -FEERED 3   [GE-FEERED]
248) GE-  4 -HWAETHER 4   [GE-HWAETHER]
274) GE-  4 -HNAEAEGDE 5   [GE-HNAEAEGDE]
290) GE-  4 -MUNDE 7   [GE-MUNDE]
300) GE-  4 -TEOHHOD 9   [GE-TEOHHOD]
313) GE-  4 -SIIDHUM 3   [GE-SIIDHUM]
244) -GE-  4 -SEENE 4   [YYTH-GE-SEENE]
671) IISERN-  4 -BYRNAN 4   [IISERN-BYRNAN]
688) HLEEOR-  4 -BOLSTER 3   [HLEEOR-BOLSTER]
699) OFER-  4 -COOMON 4   [OFER-COOMON]
751) MIDDAN-  4 -GEAR-1-DES 5   [MIDDAN-GEARDES]
757) EALDER-  4 -DAGUM 3   [EALDER-DAGUM]
764) FEN-  4 -HOPU 4   [FEN-HOPU]
805) ALDOR-  4 -GE- 2   [ALDOR-GE-DAAL]
807) ELLOR-  4 -GAAST 9   [ELLOR-GAAST]
917) MORGEN-  4 -LEEOHT 4   [MORGEN-LEEOHT]
007) LEGER-  4 -BEDDE 4   [LEGER-BEDDE]
079) MORTHOR-  4 -BEALO 3   [MORTHOR-BEALO]
084) FOR-  4 -THRINGAN 4   [FOR-THRINGAN]
094) BEEOR-  4 -SELE 5   [BEEOR-SELE]
103) DHEEODEN-  4 -LEEASE 5   [DHEEODEN-LEEASE]
116) +BAAN-  4 -FATU 3   [BAAN-FATU]
136) WULDOR-  4 -TORH-9-TAN 3   [WULDOR-TORHTAN]
208) EORCLAN-  4 -STAANAS 3   [EORCLAN-STAANAS]
227) DREEAM-  4 -HEAL-2-DEN-9-DE. 7   [DREEAM-HEALDENDE]
240) BEEOR-  4 -SCEAL-1-CA 3   [BEEOR-SCEALCA]
260) WAETER-  4 -EGESAN 4   [WAETER-EGESAN]
273) OFER-  4 -CWOOM 3   [OFER-CWOOM]
301) MAATHDHUM-  4 -GIFE. 6   [MAATHDHUM-GIFE]
311) SIGOR-  4 -EEADIG 3   [SIGOR-EEADIG]
773) FOLD-  4 -BOLD 4   [FOLD-BOLD]
994) GEST-  4 -SELE 5   [GEST-SELE]
006) GRUND-  4 -BUUEN-1-ORA 4   [GRUND-BUUENDRA]
030) HEEAFOD-  4 -BEORGE 4   [HEEAFOD-BEORGE]
```

225

```
(1033)  SCYLO- 4 -FRECA 5    [SCYLO-FRECA]
(1036)  FAEAETED- 4 -HLEEORE 4    [FAEAETED-HLEEORE]
(1089)  FOLC- 4 -WALDAN 3    [FOLC-WALDAN]
(1111)  SWAAT- 4 -FAAH 4    [SWAAT-FAAH]
(1147)  SWEORD- 4 -BEALO 3    [SWEORD-BEALO]
(1161)  BENC- 4 -SWEEG 7    [BENC-SWEEG]
(1200)  SINC- 4 -FAET 9    [SINC-FAET]
(1211)  BREEOST- 4 -GE- 3    [BREEOST-GE-WAEAEDU]
(1239)  BENC- 4 -THELU 4    [BENC-THELU]
(1239)  GEOND- 4 -BRAEAEDED 3    [GEOND-BRAEAEDED]
(0819)  GUUDH- 4 -HR-1-EEDH 3    [GUUDH-HREEDH]
(0826)  SWYYDH- 4 -FERHDH 5    [SWYYDH-FERHDH]
(1126)  FRYYS- 4 -LAND 2    [FRYYS-LAND]
(0820)  FEORH- 4 -SEEOC 4    [FEORH-SEEOC]
(0844)  WEERIG- 4 -MOOD 3    [WEERIG-MOOD]
(0846)  FEORH- 4 -LAASTAS 4    [FEORH-LAASTAS]
(0891)  BEEAH- 4 -HOR-9-DES 5    [BEEAH-HORDES]
(1023)  MAADH-9-THU=- 4 -SWEORD 3    [MAADHTHU=-SWEORD]


(1149)  +SAEAE- 5 -SIIDHE 9    [SAEAE-SIIDHE]
(1157)  SAEAE- 5 -LAADE 5    [SAEAE-LAADE]
(0937)  WIIDE- 6 -FERHDH 5    [WIIDE-FERHDH]
(1071)  HILDE- 5 -BURH 4    [HILDE-BURH]
(1114)  HILDE- 5 -BURH 3    [HILDE-BURH]
(1307)  HIL-1-DE- 5 -RINC 4    [HILDE-RINC]
(1176)  GE- 5 -FAEAEL-1-SOD 5    [GE-FAEAELSOD]
(0964)  WAEL- 5 -BEDDE 4    [WAEL-BEDDE]
(1082)  ME-9-DHEL- 5 -STEDE. 7    [MEDHEL-STEDE]
(1105)  MORTHOR- 5 -HETES 4    [MORTHOR-HETES]
(1162)  WUNDER- 5 -FATUM. 6    [WUNDER-FATUM]
(1308)  ALDOR- 5 -THEGN 0    [ALDOR-THEGN]
(0673)  OM-9-BIHT- 5 -THEGNE 5    [OMBIHT-THEGNE]
(0710)  MIST- 5 -HLEOTHUM 3    [MIST-HLEOTHUM]
(0919)  SWIIDH- 5 -HICGENDE 5    [SWIIDH-HICGENDE]
(1039)  HILDE.- 6 -SETL 4    [HILDE-SETL]


(0723)  GE- 8 -BOLGEN 3    [GE-BOLGEN]
(0830)  GE- 8 -BEETTE 9    [GE-BEETTE]
(0897)  GE- 8 -MEALT. 6    [GE-MEALT]
(1078)  GE- 8 -SEEON 3    [GE-SEEON]
(1125)  $$GE- 8 -WITON 4    [GE-WITON]
(1196)  GE- 8 -FRAEGEN 4    [GE-FRAEGEN]
(1218)  GE- 8 -THEEOH 9    [GE-THEEOH]
(0809)  ON- 8 -FUNDE 5    [ON-FUNDE]
(0876)  ELLEN- 8 -DAEAE-9-DUM 3    [ELLEN-DAEAEDUM]
(0990)  ON- 8 -BERAN 4    [ON-BERAN]
(1140)  TORN- 8 -GE- 9    [TORN-GE-MOOT]
(1264)  MAN- 8 -DREEAM 4    [MAN-DREEAM]
(0722)  AET- 8 -HRAAN. 7    [AET-HRAAN]
(1013)  BLAEAED- 8 -AAGAN-9-DE 5    [BLAEAED-AAGANDE]


(0795)  BEED- 9 -WUL-1-FES 5    [BEEO-WULFES]
(0832)  THREEA- 9 -NYYDUM 4    [THREEA-NYYDUM]
(1299)  BEEO- 9 -WULF 4    [BEEO-WULF]
(0997)  TOO- 9 -BROCEN 3    [TOO-BROCEN]
(0702)  ()RIDE*WIIDE- 9 -FER-1-HDH 4    [*WIIDE-FERHDH]
(0713)  BE- 9 -SYRWAN 4    [BE-SYRWAN]
(0729)  SIB-1-BE- 9 -GE- 2    [SIBBE-GE-DRIHT]
(0769)  EALU- 9 -SCERWEN 3    [EALU-SCERWEN]
(0772)  HEA-1-THO- 9 -DEEORUM 4    [HEATHO-DEEORUM]
(0862)  WINE- 9 -DRIHTEN 4    [WINE-DRIHTEN]
(0924)  MEDO- 9 -STIG-1-GE 5    [MEDO-STIGGE]
(1073)  BE- 9 -LOR-2-EN 4    [BE-LOREN]
(1096)  FRIODHU- 9 -WAEAERE 6    [FRIODHU-WAEAERE]
(1115)  BE- 9 -FAESTAN 7    [BE-FAESTAN]
```

226

```
884)  SIGE-  9  -MUNDE   4    [SIGE-MUNDE]
684)  GE-  9  -SEE-1-CEAN 3   [GE-SEECEAN]
740)  GE-  9  -FEENG   4     [GE-FEENG]
749)  GE-  9  -SAET    5     [GE-SAET]
758)  GE-  9  -MUNDE   4     [GE-MUNDE]
825)  GE-  9  -FAEAELSOD 4    [GE-FAEAELSO]]
870)  GE-  9  -MUNDE   5     [GE-MUNDE]
882)  GE-  9  -HWAAM   4     [GE-HWAAM]
910)  GE-  9  -THEEON  4     [GE-THEEON]
915)  GE-  9  -FAEGRA  4     [GE-FAEGRA]
999)  GE-  9  -NAES    5     [GE-NAES]
060)  GE-  9  -BIIDAN  4     [GE-BIIDAN]
095)  GE-  9  -TRUWE-1-DON 4   [GE-TRUWEDON]
209)  GE-  9  -CRANC   5     [GE-CRANC]
241)  GE-  9  -BEEAG   8     [GE-BEEAG]
270)  GE-  9  -MUNDE   4     [GE-MUNDE]
303)  GE-  9  -NIIWOD  4     [GE-NIIWOD]
304)  GE-  9  -WRIXLE  5     [GE-WRIXLE]
678)  -GE-  9  -WEORCA  4     [GUUTH-GE-WEORCA]
140)  -GE-  9  -MOOT    5     [TORN-GE-MOOT]
155)  -GE-  9  -STEALD  3     [IN-GE-STEALD]
688)  ON-  9  -FEENG   6     [ON-FEENG]
704)  HORN-  9  -RECED  5     [HORN-RECED]
722)  FYYR-  9  -BENDUM  3     [FYYR-BENDUM]
737)  MAAN-  9  -SCADHA  5     [MAAN-SCADHA]
748)  ON-  9  -FEENG   3     [ON-FEENG]
759)  AEAEFEN-  9  -SPRAEAECE 5   [AEAEFEN-SPRAEAECE]
770)  REN-  9  -WEAR-1-DAS  5    [REN-WEARDAS]
928)  AN-  9  -SYYNE   5     [AN-SYYNE]
970)  FOR-  9  -LEET    3     [FOR-LEET]
989)  AEAER-  9  -GOOD   4     [AEAER-GOOD]
995)  WUNDOR-  9  -SIIONA 3    [WUNDOR-SIIONA]
001)  FYREN-  9  -DAEAE-1-DUM 3   [FYREN-DAEAEDUM]
002)  OR-  9  -WEENA   3     [OR-WEENA]
004)  SAAWL-  9  -BEREN-1-DRA 4    [SAAWL-BERENDRA]
018)  FAAGEN-  9  -STAFAS  5     [FAAGEN-STAFAS]
128)  WAEL-  9  -FAAGNE  4     [WAEL-FAAGNE]
129)  UN-  9  -HLITME  4     [UN-HLITME]
142)  FOR-  9  -WYRNDE  6     [FOR-WYRNDE]
187)  UM-1-BOR-  9  -WESEN-1-DUM 2    [UMBOR-WESENDUM]
252)  AEAEFEN-  9  -RAESTE  5     [AEAEFEN-RAESTE]
692)  EARD-  9  -LUFAN   4     [EARD-LUFAN]
761)  UUT-  9  -WEARD   3     [UUT-WEARD]
840)  WIID-  9  -WEGAS   4     [WIID-WEGAS]
891)  WRAEAET-  9  -LIICNE  3     [WRAEAET-LIICNE]
892)  DRYHT-  9  -LIIC   3     [DRYHT-LIIC]
952)  HORD-  9  -WEORTHUNGE 7    [HORD-WEORTHUNGE]
968)  AET-  9  -FEALH   4     [AET-FEALH]
158)  DRIHT-  9  -LIICE  4     [DRIHT-LIICE]
231)  DRYHT-  9  -GUMAN  4     [DRYHT-GUMAN]
253)  GOLD-  9  -SELE   5     [GOLD-SELE]
289)  SIID-  9  -RAND   4     [SIID-RAND]
760)  WIDH-  9  -FEENG   5     [WIDH-FEENG]
122)  LAADH-  9  -BITE   4     [LAADH-BITE]
258)  GUUDH-  9  -CEARE  5     [GUUDH-CEARE]
665)  KYNING-  9  -WUL-1-DOR 4    [KYNING-WULDOR]
```

APPENDIX III
NES 1321 - 1939 (FIT XX - END OF
FIRST SCRIBE≠S COPY)

227

```
(1383)  $$BEEO-  0 -$$WULF 6   [BEEO-WULF]
(1441)  BEEO-  0 -WULF 9    [BEEO-WULF]
(1473)  $$BEEO-  0 -$$WULF 5   [BEEO-WULF]
(1651)  $$BEEO-  0 -WULF 4    [BEEO-WULF]
(1704)  BEEO-  0 -WULF 9    [BEEO-WULF]
(1758)  BEEO-  0 -WULF 3    [BEEO-WULF]
(1880)  BEEO-  0 -WULF 5    [BEEO-WULF]
(1356)  AA-  0 -CEN-1-NED 4   [AA-CENNED]
(1373)  AA-  0 -STIIGEDH 5   [AA-STIIGEDH]
(1390)  +AA-  0 -RIIS 3   [AA-RIIS]
(1397)  AA-  0 -HLEEOP 3   [AA-HLEEOP]
(1521)  AA-  0 -GOOL 5   [AA-GOOL]
(1528)  AA-  0 -LAEG. 6   [AA-LAEG]
(1530)  HYY-  0 -LAACES 4   [HYY-LAACES]
(1556)  AA-  0 -STOOD. 9   [AA-STOOD]
(1599)  AA-  0 -()BREOTEN*BROTEN 3   [*AA-BROTEN]
(1630)  AA-  0 -LYYSED 4   [AA-LYYSED]
(1652)  +SAEAE-  0 -LAAC 4   [SAEAE-LAAC]
(1703)  AA-  0 -RAEAERED 6   [AA-RAEAERED]
(1724)  AA-  0 -WRAEC 3   [AA-WRAEC]
(1737)  OO-  0 -HWAEAER 5   [OO-HWAEAER]
(1790)  AA-  0 -RAAS 5   [AA-RAAS]
(1822)  OO-  0 -WIHTE 3   [OO-WIHTE]
(1556)  YYDHE-  0 -LIICE 4   [YYDHE-LIICE]
(1562)  GEATO-  0 -LIIC 5   [GEATO-LIIC]
(1826)  BE-  0 -GANG 5   [BE-GANG]
(1340)  GE-  0 -STAEAELED 4   [GE-STAEAELED]
(1360)  GE-  0 -WIITEDH 9   [GE-WIITEDH]
(1368)  GE-  0 -SWENCED 7   [GE-SWENCED]
(1425)  GE-  0 -SAAWON 3   [GE-SAAWON]
(1431)  GE-  0 -BOLGNE 7   [GE-BOLGNE]
(1485)  GE-  0 -SEEON 2   [GE-SEEON]
(1526)  GE-  0 -SCAER 5   [GE-SCAER]
(1537)  $GE-  0 -FEENG 4   [GE-FEENG]
(1552)  GE-  0 -FREME-2-DE 9   [GE-FREMEDE]
(1628)  GE-  0 -SEEON 2   [GE-SEEON]
(1662)  GE-  0 -SEAH 3   [GE-SEAH]
(1696)  GE-  0 -SETED 4   [GE-SETED]
(1839)  GE-  0 -SOOHTE 6   [GE-SOOHTE]
(1861)  GE-  0 -GREETTAN 4   [GE-GREETTAN]
(1920)  GE-  0 -STREEON 9   [GE-STREEON]
(1326)  OR-  0 -LEGE. 6   [OR-LEGE]
(1351)  ON-  0 -LIIC- 3   [*ON-LIIC-NES]
(1389)  UN-  0 -LIF-9-GENDUM 4   [UN-LIFGENDUM]
(1410)  UN-  0 -CUUDH 2   [UN-CUUDH]
(1416)  WYN-  0 -LEEASNE 9   [WYN-LEEASNE]
(1426)  SEL-  0 -LICE 4   [SEL-LICE]
(1431)  ON-  0 -GEEA-9-TON 3   [ON-GEEATON]
(1453)  SWIIN-  0 -LIICUM 5   [SWIIN-LIICUM]
(1483)  ON-  0 -SEND. 5   [ON-SEND]
(1484)  ON-  0 -GITAN 5   [ON-GITAN]
(1488)  ()HUN*UN-  0 -FERDH 5   [*UN-FERDH]
(1496)  ON-  0 -GYTAN 2   [ON-GYTAN]
(1512)  ON-  0 -GEAT 4   [ON-GEAT]
(1522)  ON-  0 -FAND 5   [ON-FAND]
(1529)  AN-  0 -RAEAED 3   [AN-RAEAED]
(1549)  IN-  0 -GANG 2   [IN-GANG]
(1565)  OR-  0 -WEENA 5   [OR-WEENA]
(1575)  AN-  0 -RAEAED. 8   [AN-RAEAED]
(1605)  ON-  0 -GAN 4   [ON-GAN]
(1610)  ON-  0 -WINDEDH 3   [ON-WINDEDH]
(1767)  FOR-  0 -SITEDH 4   [FOR-SITEDH]
(1776)  IN-  0 -GENGA 4   [IN-GENGA]
```

```
792) UN- 0 -IG- 9   [UN-IG-METES]
886) OR- 0 -LEAHTRE 5   [OR-LEAHTRE]
911) ON- 0 -GITAN 4   [ON-GITAN]
919) WYN- 0 -SUMAN 4   [WYN-SUMAN]
541) ()HAND*AND- 0 -LEEAN 3   [*AND-LEEAN]
682) =AND- 0 -SACA 4   [=AND-SACA]
796) AND- 0 -RYSNUM 9   [AND-RYSNUM]
840) =AND- 0 -SWARE 4   [=AND-SWARE]
350) -WIS- 0 -LIICOST 9   [GE-WIS-LIICOST]
582) FYYF- 0 -TYY-9-NE 4   [FYYF-TYYNE]
622) OF- 0 -LEET 3   [OF-LEET]
809) LEEOF- 0 -LIIC 4   [LEEOF-LIIC]
836) HREETH- 0 -()RINC*RIIC 5   [*HREETH-RIIC]
465) ECG- 0 -LAAFES 5   [ECG-LAAFES]
512) AAG- 0 -LAEAE-1-CAN 5   [AAG-LAEAECAN]
550) ECG- 0 -THEEOWES 5   [ECG-THEEOWES]
783) WIIG- 0 -GE- 5   [WIIG-GE-WEORTHAD]
808) ECG- 0 -LAAFES 4   [ECG-LAAFES]

542) TOO- 1 -GEEANES 4   [TOO-GEEANES]
626) TOO- 1 -GEEANES 5   [TOO-GEEANES]
818) SAEAE- 1 -LIIDHEND 4   [SAEAE-LIIDHEND]
545) SELE- 1 -GYST 9   [SELE-GYST]
773) BE- 1 -GONG 1   [BE-GONG]
796) BE- 1 -()WEOTENE*WEOTEDE 6   [*BE-WEOTEDE]
821) BE- 1 -WENEDE 6   [BE-WENEDE]
333) GE- 1 -()FRAEGNOD*FAEGNOD 3   [*GE-FAEGNOD]
337) GE- 1 -CRANG 4   [GE-CRANG]
347) GE- 1 -SAAWON 4   [GE-SAAWON]
350) GE- 1 -WITAN 3   [GE-WITAN]
360) GE- 1 -NIPU 5   [GE-NIPU]
376) GE- 1 -LANG 4   [GE-LANG]
447) GE- 1 -SCETHDHAN. 7   [GE-SCETHDHAN]
462) GE- 1 -GAAN 9   [GE-GAAN]
469) GE- 1 -NEE-2-THAN 3   [GE-NEETHAN]
491) GE- 1 -WYRCE 9   [GE-WYRCE]
501) GE- 1 -FEENG 5   [GE-FEENG]
509) GE- 1 -WEALDAN 4   [GE-WEALDAN]
524) GE- 1 -SWAAC 9   [GE-SWAAC]
530) GE- 1 -MYNDIG 4   [GE-MYNDIG]
531) GE- 1 -BUNDEN 4   [GE-BUNDEN]
533) GE- 1 -TRUWODE 5   [GE-TRUWODE]
535) GE- 1 -GAAN 9   [GE-GAAN]
540) GE- 1 -BEEAH 4   [GE-BEEAH]
554) GE- 1 -WEEOLD 3   [GE-WEEOLD]
555) GE- 1 -SCEED 4   [GE-SCEED]
569) GE- 1 -FEH 5   [GE-FEH]
578) GE- 1 -WORHTE 5   [GE-WORHTE]
587) GE- 1 -SCOOD 5   [GE-SCOOD]
605) GE- 1 -SAAWON 2   [GE-SAAWON]
608) GE- 1 -MEALT 4   [GE-MEALT]
624) GE- 1 -FEAH 4   [GE-FEAH]
638) GE- 1 -FERIAN 3   [GE-FERIAN]
656) GE- 1 -NEETH-1-DE 5   [GE-NEETHDE]
664) GE- 1 -BRAEAED. 9   [GE-BRAEAED]
672) GE- 1 -DRYHT 9   [GE-DRYHT]
706) GE- 1 -LAEAESTAN 4   [GE-LAEAESTAN]
718) GE- 1 -FREME-9-DE 6   [GE-FREMEDE]
759) GE- 1 -CEEOS 4   [GE-CEEOS]
837) GE- 1 -()THINGED*THINGEDH 3   [*GE-THINGEDH]
851) GE- 1 -CEEOSEN-9-NE 8   [GE-CEEOSENNE]
875) GE- 1 -SEEON 4   [GE-SEEON]
901) GE- 1 -SEAL-1-DE 5   [GE-SEALDE]
908) GE- 1 -TWAEAEFDE 6   [GE-TWAEAEFDE]
928) GE- 1 -BIDEN 9   [GE-BIDEN]
```

```
(1434) -GE- 1 -WINNES 5    [YYDH-GE-WINNES]
(1442) -GE- 1 -WAEAE-2-DUM 4    [EORL-GE-WAEAEDUM]
(1479) -GE- 1 -WITENUM 3    [FORDH-GE-WITENUM]
(1679) -GE- 1 -WEORC 9    [AEAER-GE-WEORC]
(1750) -GE- 1 -SCEAFT 5    [FORDH-GE-SCEAFT]
(1937) -GE- 1 -WRITHENE 5    [HAND-GE-WRITHENE]
(1329) AEAER- 1 -GOOD 2    [AEAER-GOOD]
(1359) FEN- 1 -GE- 2    [FEN-GE-LAAD]
(1410) AAN- 1 -PADHAS 5    [AAN-PADHAS]
(1420) ON- 1 -CYYDH 3    [ON-CYYDH]
(1425) WYRM- 1 -CYNNES 4    [WYRM-CYNNES]
(1436) FOR- 1 -NAM. 4    [FOR-NAM]
(1437) EOFER- 1 -SPREEOTUM 4    [EOFER-SPREEOTUM]
(1451) FYRN- 1 -DA-9-GUM 4    [FYRN-DAGUM]
(1459) AATER- 1 -TAANUM 3    [AATER-TAANUM]
(1494) ON- 1 -FEENG 8    [ON-FEENG]
(1500) AEL- 1 -WIHTA 3    [AEL-WIHTA]
(1541) FOR- 1 -GEALD 4    [FOR-GEALD]
(1577) FOR- 1 -GYL-2-DAN 4    [FOR-GYLDAN]
(1609) ON- 1 -LAEAETEDH 5    [ON-LAEAETEDH]
(1631) WAEL- 1 -DREEO-1-RE 3    [WAEL-DREEORE]
(1641) FEEOWER- 1 -TYYNE 5    [FEEOWER-TYYNE]
(1715) MON- 1 -DREEAMU= 4    [MON-DREEAMU=]
(1723) ON- 1 -GIT. 6    [ON-GIT]
(1756) UN- 1 -MURN- 1    [UN-MURN-LIICE]
(1756) -MURN- 1 -LIICE 6    [UN-MURN-LIICE]
(1777) SIN- 1 -GAALES 4    [SIN-GAALES]
(1865) UN- 1 -TAEAELE 5    [UN-TAEAELE]
(1932) ON- 1 -DRYSNE 9    [ON-DRYSNE]
(1934) SIN- 1 -FREEA 4    [SIN-FREEA]
(1323) AESC- 1 -HERE 9    [AESC-HERE]
(1463) FOLC- 1 -STEDE 5    [FOLC-STEDE]
(1468) SWEORD- 1 -FRECAN 4    [SWEORD-FRECAN]
(1489) WRAEAET- 1 -LIIC 4    [WRAEAET-LIIC]
(1489) WIID- 1 -CUUDH-1-NE 4    [WIID-CUUDHNE]
(1633) FOLD- 1 -WEG 3    [FOLD-WEG]
(1657) AET- 1 -RIHTE 6    [AET-RIHTE]
(1774) ED- 1 -()WENDAN*WENDEN 9    [*ED-WENDEN]
(1788) FLET- 1 -SITTEN-1-DUM 9    [FLET-SITTENDUM]
(1883) ()AGED*AAGEND- 1 -FREEAN 3    [*AAGEND-FREEAN]
(1900) BAAT- 1 -WEARDE 9    [BAAT-WEARDE]
(1917) SIID- 1 -FAETHME 3    [SIID-FAETHME]
(1373) YYDH- 1 -GE- 2    [YYDH-GE-BLOND]
(1399) HROODH- 1 -GAARE 6    [HROODH-GAARE]
(1434) YYDH- 1 -GE- 1    [YYDH-GE-WINNES]
(1483) HROODH- 1 -GAAR 5    [HROODH-GAAR]
(1520) OF- 1 -TEEAH 5    [OF-TEEAH]
(1538) GUUDH- 1 -GEEATA 4    [GUUDH-GEEATA]
(1545) $OF- 1 -SAET 2    [OF-SAET]
(1577) GUUDH- 1 -RAEAESA 9    [GUUDH-RAEAESA]
(1592) HROODH- 1 -GAARE 5    [HROODH-GAARE]
(1620) YYDH- 1 -GE- 3    [YYDH-GE-BLOND]
(1646) HROODH- 1 -GAAR 5    [HROODH-GAAR]
(1652) HEALF- 1 -DENES 9    [HEALF-DENES]
(1681) OF- 1 -GEAF 4    [OF-GEAF]
(1881) GUUDH- 1 -RINC 4    [GUUDH-RINC]
(1904) OF- 1 -GEAF. 9    [OF-GEAF]
(1383) ECG- 1 -THEEO-9-WES 4    [ECG-THEEOWES]
(1386) AEAEG- 1 -HWYLC 3    [AEAEG-HWYLC]
(1473) ECG- 1 -THEEOWES 9    [ECG-THEEOWES]
(1607) WIIG- 1 -BIL 4    [WIIG-BIL]
(1865) AEAEG- 1 -HWAES 4    [AEAEG-HWAES]

(1460) AA- 2 -HYRDED 5    [AA-HYRDED]
(1501) TOO- 2 -GEEANES 5    [TOO-GEEANES]
```

```
(1624)  SAEAE- 2 -LAACE 3    [SAEAE-LAACE]
(1893)  TOO- 2 -GEEANES 4    [TOO-GEEANES]
(1908)  SAEAE- 2 -GENGA 4    [SAEAE-GENGA]
(1346)  SELE- 2 -RAEAE-1-DEN-1-DE 9    [SELE-RAEAEDENDE]
(1428)  BE- 2 -WITIGADH 4    [BE-WITIGADH]
(1441)  GRYRE- 2 -LIIC-1-NE 4    [GRYRE-LIICNE]
(1449)  MERE- 2 -GRUNDAS 5    [MERE-GRUNDAS]
(1451)  BE- 2 -FONGEN 3    [BE-FONGEN]
(1460)  HEATHO- 2 -SWAATE 5    [HEATHO-SWAATE]
(1461)  BE- 2 -WAND 4    [BE-WAND]
(1497)  BE- 2 -GONG 6    [BE-GONG]
(1576)  HILDE- 2 -RINCE 4    [HILDE-RINCE]
(1709)  HERE- 2 -MOOD 9    [HERE-MOOD]
(1747)  -BE- 2 -BODUM 5    [WUNDOR-BE-BODUM]
(1758)  BEALO- 2 -NIIDH 6    [BEALO-NIIDH]
(1483)  HIGE- 2 -LAACE 4    [HIGE-LAACE]
(1557)  SIGE- 2 -EEADIG 3    [SIGE-EEADIG]
(1322)  GE- 2 -NII-9-WOD 4    [GE-NIIWOD]
(1350)  GE- 2 -WIS- 0    [GE-WIS-LIICOST]
(1365)  GE- 2 -HWAEAEM 9    [GE-HWAEAEM]
(1386)  GE- 2 -BIIDAN 5    [GE-BIIDAN]
(1403)  GE- 2 -SYYNE 9    [GE-SYYNE]
(1410)  GE- 2 -LAAD 4    [GE-LAAD]
(1424)  GE- 2 -SAET. 6    [GE-SAET]
(1443)  GE- 2 -BROODEN 4    [GE-BROODEN]
(1450)  GE- 2 -WEORDHAD 9    [GE-WEORDHAD]
(1469)  GE- 2 -WIN 4    [GE-WIN]
(1472)  GE- 2 -GYRED 4    [GE-GYRED]
(1502)  GE- 2 -SCOOD 5    [GE-SCOOD]
(1516)  GE- 2 -SEAH 6    [GE-SEAH]
(1545)  GE- 2 -TEEAH 4    [GE-TEEAH]
(1548)  GE- 2 -BEARH 9    [GE-BEARH]
(1562)  GE- 2 -WEORC. 6    [GE-WEORC]
(1568)  GE- 2 -CRONG 5    [GE-CRONG]
(1585)  GE- 2 -SEAH 3    [GE-SEAH]
(1591)  GE- 2 -SAAWON 4    [GE-SAAWON]
(1601)  GE- 2 -WAAT 3    [GE-WAAT]
(1608)  GE- 2 -LIICOST 4    [GE-LIICOST]
(1622)  GE- 2 -SCEAFT. 9    [GE-SCEAFT]
(1628)  GE- 2 -SUND-1-NE 4    [GE-SUNDNE]
(1645)  GE- 2 -WUR-2-THAD 9    [GE-WURTHAD]
(1658)  GE- 2 -TWAEAEFED 4    [GE-TWAEAEFED]
(1660)  GE- 2 -WYRCAN 9    [GE-WYRCAN]
(1667)  GE- 2 -SPRANG 9    [GE-SPRANG]
(1670)  GE- 2 -DEEFE 4    [GE-DEEFE]
(1684)  GE- 2 -HWE-9-ARF 5    [GE-HWEARF]
(1696)  GE- 2 -SAEAED 5    [GE-SAEAED]
(1701)  GE- 2 -MON 4    [GE-MON]
(1703)  GE- 2 -BOREN 5    [GE-BOREN]
(1705)  GE- 2 -HWYLCE 5    [GE-HWYLCE]
(1720)  GE- 2 -+BAAD 3    [GE-BAAD]
(1743)  GE- 2 -BUNDEN 9    [GE-BUNDEN]
(1754)  GE- 2 -DREEOSEDH 5    [GE-DREEOSEDH]
(1755)  GE- 2 -FEALLEDH 5    [GE-FEALLEDH]
(1763)  GE- 2 -TWAEAEFEDH 4    [GE-TWAEAEFEDH]
(1779)  GE- 2 -BAAD 4    [GE-BAAD]
(1784)  GE- 2 -MAEAENRA 5    [GE-MAEAENRA]
(1788)  GE- 2 -REORDED 4    [GE-REORDED]
(1789)  GE- 2 -SWEARC 5    [GE-SWEARC]
(1846)  GE- 2 -GANGEDH 4    [GE-GANGEDH]
(1860)  GE- 2 -MAEAENE 4    [GE-MAEAENE]
(1864)  GE- 2 -WORHTE 7    [GE-WORHTE]
(1869)  GE- 2 -SYNTUM 3    [GE-SYNTUM]
(1872)  GE- 2 -NAM 5    [GE-NAM]
(1903)  GE- 2 -WAAT 4    [GE-WAAT]
```

231

```
(1924)  GE- 2 -SIIDHUM 4    [GE-SIIDHUM]
(1933)  GE- 2 -NEETHAN 4    [GE-NEETHAN]
(1934)  GE- 2 -SIIDHA 5     [GE-SIIDHA]
(1326)  -GE- 2 -STEA-1-LLA 9   [EAXL-GE-STEALLA]
(1359)  -GE- 2 -LAAD 5   [FEN-GE-LAAD]
(1373)  -GE- 2 -BLOND 4   [YYDH-GE-BLOND]
(1381)  -GE- 2 -STREEONU= 3   [EALD-GE-STREEONU=]
(1450)  -GE- 2 -BLAND 4   [SUND-GE-BLAND]
(1580)  -GE- 2 -NEEATAS 6    [HEORDH-GE-NEEATAS]
(1899)  -GE- 2 -STREEONUM 7    [HORD-GE-STREEONUM]
(1931)  -GE- 2 -STREEONA 4    [MAATHM-GE-STREEONA]
(1331)  WAEL- 2 -GAEAEST 5    [WAEL-GAEAEST]
(1362)  MIIL- 2 -GE- 9   [MIIL-GE-MEARCES]
(1364)  OFER- 2 -HELMADH 6    [OFER-HELMADH]
(1401)  GUM- 2 -FEETHA 3    [GUM-FEETHA]
(1428)  UNDERN- 2 -MAEAEL 5    [UNDERN-MAEAEL]
(1445)  +BAAN- 2 -COFAN 6   [BAAN-COFAN]
(1467)  ON- 2 -LAAH. 6    [ON-LAAH]
(1518)  $ON- 2 -GEAT 2    [ON-GEAT]
(1519)  FOR- 2 -GEAF 5    [FOR-GEAF]
(1533)  STYYL- 2 -ECG 9    [STYYL-ECG]
(1638)  WAEL- 2 -STENGE 4    [WAEL-STENGE]
(1674)  ON- 2 -DRAEAE-1-DAN 4    [ON-DRAEAEDAN]
(1679)  AEAER- 2 -GE- 1    [AEAER-GE-WEORC]
(1681)  WUNDOR- 2 -SMITHA 3    [WUNDOR-SMITHA]
(1695)  RUUN- 2 -STAFAS 4    [RUUN-STAFAS]
(1834)  GAAR- 2 -HOLT 4    [GAAR-HOLT]
(1894)  WIL- 2 -CUMAN 3    [WIL-CUMAN]
(1332)  EFT- 2 -SIIDHAS 4    [EFT-SIIDHAS]
(1342)  SINC- 2 -GYFAN 3    [SINC-GYFAN]
(1348)  MEARC- 2 -STAPAN 3    [MEARC-STAPAN]
(1381)  EALD- 2 -GE- 2    [EALD-GE-STREEONU=]
(1403)  WALD- 2 -SWA-2-THU= 4    [WALD-SWATHU=]
(1450)  SUND- 2 -GE- 2    [SUND-GE-BLAND]
(1481)  HOND- 2 -GE- 8    [HOND-GE-SELLUM]
(1496)  GRUND- 2 -WONG 4    [GRUND-WONG]
(1561)  AET- 2 -BERAN 2    [AET-BERAN]
(1623)  LID- 2 -MANNA 5    [LID-MANNA]
(1639)  GOLD- 2 -SELE 5    [GOLD-SELE]
(1645)  DAEAED- 2 -CEENE 5    [DAEAED-CEENE]
(1669)  AET- 2 -FERE-2-DE 5    [AET-FEREDE]
(1678)  HILD- 2 -FRU-9-MAN 4    [HILD-FRUMAN]
(1713)  BEEOD- 2 -GE- 8    [BEEOD-GE-NEEATAS]
(1722)  LEEOD- 2 -BEA-9-LO 4    [LEEOD-BEALO]
(1776)  EALD- 2 -GE- 4    [EALD-GE-WINNA]
(1785)  GLAED- 2 -MOOD 4    [GLAED-MOOD]
(1793)  RAND- 2 -WIGAN 4    [RAND-WIGAN]
(1800)  GOLD- 2 -FAAH 3    [GOLD-FAAH]
(1841)  WORD- 2 -CWYDAS 5    [WORD-CWYDAS]
(1852)  HORD- 2 -WEARD 4    [HORD-WEARD]
(1891)  EFT- 2 -SIIDH 4    [EFT-SIIDH]
(1899)  HORD- 2 -GE- 2    [HORD-GE-STREEONUM]
(1906)  SUND- 2 -WUDU 4    [SUND-WUDU]
(1925)  BET- 2 -LIIC 5    [BET-LIIC]
(1365)  NIIDH- 2 -WUNDOR 5    [NIIDH-WUNDOR]
(1407)  HROODH- 2 -GAARE 9    [HROODH-GAARE]
(1456)  HROODH- 2 -GAARES 5    [HROODH-GAARES]
(1474)  HEALF- 2 -DENES 9    [HEALF-DENES]
(1501)  GUUDH- 2 -RINC 4    [GUUDH-RINC]
(1583)  OF- 2 -FEREDE 4    [OF-FEREDE]
(1584)  LAADH- 2 -LICU 9    [LAADH-LICU]
(1586)  GUUDH- 2 -WEERIGNE 9    [GUUDH-WEERIGNE]
(1593)  YYDH- 2 -GE- 3    [YYDH-GE-BLOND]
(1622)  LIIF- 2 -DAGAS 6    [LIIF-DAGAS]
(1636)  EARFODH- 2 -LIICE 4    [EARFODH-LIICE]
```

```
1687) HROODH- 2 -GAAR 4    [HROODH-GAAR]
1689) OF- 2 -SLOOH 9    [OF-SLOOH]
1699) HEALF- 2 -DENES 6    [HEALF-DENES]
1810) GUUDH- 2 -WINE 9    [GUUDH-WINE]
1840) $HROODH- 2 -GAAR 5    [HROODH-GAAR]
1867) HEALF- 2 -DE-2-NES 6    [HEALF-DENES]
1543) WEERIG- 2 -MOOD 4    [WEERIG-MOOD]
1567) DHURH- 2 -WOOD 4    [DHURH-WOOD]
1651) ECG- 2 -THEEOWES 9    [ECG-THEEOWES]
1672) SORH- 2 -LEEAS 5    [SORH-LEEAS]
1710) ECG- 2 -WELAN 4    [ECG-WELAN]
1769) HRING- 2 -DENA 5    [HRING-DENA]
1811) WIIG- 2 -CRAEFTIGNE 5    [WIIG-CRAEFTIGNE]
1817) ECG- 2 -THEEOWES 4    [ECG-THEEOWES]
1886) AEAEG- 2 -HWAES 4    [AEAEG-HWAES]
1907) WEEG- 2 -FLOTAN 4    [WEEG-FLOTAN]
1928) BURH- 2 -LOCAN 3    [BURH-LOCAN]
1486) GU=- 2 -CYSTUM 4    [GU=-CYSTUM]
1702) .=EETHEL.- 2 -WEARD 9    [=EETHEL-WEARD]
1723) GU=- 2 -CYSTE 9    [GU=-CYSTE]


1451) FREEA- 3 -WRAASNUM 5    [FREEA-WRAASNUM]
1510) SAEAE- 3 -DEEOR 9    [SAEAE-DEEOR]
1850) +SAEAE- 3 -GEEATAS 5    [SAEAE-GEEATAS]
1405) MAGO- 3 -THEGNA 4    [MAGO-THEGNA]
1435) HERE- 3 -STRAEAEL 5    [HERE-STRAEAEL]
1438) HEORO- 3 -HOOG-9-YHTUM 4    [HEORO-HOOGYHTUM]
1443) HERE- 3 -BYRNE 6    [HERE-BYRNE]
1444) SEARO- 3 -FAAH 9    [SEARO-FAAH]
1453) BE- 3 -SETTE 4    [BE-SETTE]
1498) HEORO- 3 -GIIF-1-RE 9    [HEORO-GIIFRE]
1544) FEETHE- 3 -CEMPA 9    [FEETHE-CEMPA]
1561) BEADU- 3 -LAACE 9    [BEADU-LAACE]
1590) BE- 3 -CEARF. 7    [BE-CEARF]
1604) WINE- 3 -DRI-1-HTEN 1    [WINE-DRIHTEN]
1606) HEA-2-THO- 3 -SWAATE 4    [HEATHO-SWAATE]
1646) HILDE- 3 -DEEOR 6    [HILDE-DEEOR]
1668) HEATHO- 3 -SWAATA 5    [HEATHO-SWAATA]
1798) HEATHO- 3 -LIIDHENDE 6    [HEATHO-LIIDHENDE]
1816) HIL-1-DE- 3 -DEEOR 4    [HILDE-DEEOR]
1847) HEORU- 3 -GRIM-2-ME 2    [HEORU-GRIMME]
1886) BE- 3 -NAM 5    [BE-NAM]
1903) YRFE- 3 -LAAFE 5    [YRFE-LAAFE]
1925) BREGO- 3 -ROOF 2    [BREGO-ROOF]
1820) HIGE- 3 -LAAC 3    [HIGE-LAAC]
1830) HIGE- 3 -LAACE 9    [HIGE-LAACE]
1878) HYGE- 3 -BENDUM 3    [HYGE-BENDUM]
1396) GE- 3 -HWYL-1-CES 4    [GE-HWYLCES]
1417) GE- 3 -DREE-9-FED 4    [GE-DREEFED]
1419) GE- 3 -THOLIAN-1-NE 6    [GE-THOLIANNE]
1433) GE- 3 -TWAEAEF-1-DE 5    [GE-TWAEAEFDE]
1439) GE- 3 -NAEAEGED 3    [GE-NAEAEGED]
1466) GE- 3 -SPRAEC 4    [GE-SPRAEC]
1474) GE- 3 -THENC 4    [GE-THENC]
1563) GE- 3 -FEENG 5    [GE-FEENG]
1564) GE- 3 -BRAEGD 4    [GE-BRAEGD]
1593) GE- 3 -MENGED 5    [GE-MENGED]
1613) GE- 3 -SEAH 5    [GE-SEAH]
1618) GE- 3 -BAAD 3    [GE-BAAD]
1627) GE- 3 -FEEGON 9    [GE-FEEGON]
1643) GE- 3 -MONGE 5    [GE-MONGE]
1655) GE- 3 -DIIGDE 5    [GE-DIIGDE]
1661) GE- 3 -UUDHE 9    [GE-UUDHE]
1671) GE- 3 -HAATE 5    [GE-HAATE]
```

233

```
(1673) GE- 3 -HWYLC 5    [GE-HWYLC]
(1679) GE- 3 -HWEARF 5   [GE-HWEARF]
(1696) GE- 3 -WORHT 5    [GE-WORHT]
(1721) GE- 3 -WIN-1-NES 5   [GE-WINNES]
(1732) GE- 3 -DEEDH 4    [GE-DEEDH]
(1732) GE- 3 -WEAL-2-DENE 5    [GE-WEALDENE]
(1734) GE- 3 -THEN-1-CEAN. 5   [GE-THENCEAN]
(1753) GE- 3 -LIMPEDH 5   [GE-LIMPEDH]
(1855) GE- 3 -FEERED 4   [GE-FEERED]
(1922) GE- 3 -SEE-1-CAN-1-NE 5   [GE-SEECANNE]
(1540) -GE- 3 -NIIDH-2-LAN 4   [FEORH-GE-NIIDHLAN]
(1593) -GE- 3 -BLOND 4   [YYDH-GE-BLOND]
(1620) -GE- 3 -BLAND 9   [YYDH-GE-BLAND]
(1689) -GE- 3 -WIN-1-NES. 6   [FYRN-GE-WINNES]
(1729) -GE- 3 -THONC 3   [MOOD-GE-THONC]
(1326) EAXL- 3 -GE- 2    [EAXL-GE-STEALLA]
(1336) FOR- 3 -THAN 4    [FOR-THAN]
(1343) HRETHER- 3 -BEALO 5    [HRETHER-BEALO]
(1351) EAR-9-M- 3 -SCEAPEN 4    [EARM-SCEAPEN]
(1393) FYRGEN- 3 -HOLT. 4    [FYRGEN-HOLT]
(1408) OFER- 3 -EEODE 3    [OFER-EEODE]
(1414) FYRGEN- 3 -BEEAMAS 5    [FYRGEN-BEEAMAS]
(1421) HOLM- 3 -CLIFE 6    [HOLM-CLIFE]
(1429) SEGL- 3 -RAADE 6    [SEGL-RAADE]
(1440) WUN-1-DOR- 3 -LIIC 3    [WUNDOR-LIIC]
(1442) EORL- 3 -GE- 1    [EORL-GE-WAEAEDUM]
(1455) MAEGEN- 3 -FULTUMA 5    [MAEGEN-FULTUMA]
(1464) ELLEN- 3 -WEORC 5    [ELLEN-WEORC]
(1470) FOR- 3 -LEEAS 4    [FOR-LEEAS]
(1519) MAEGEN- 3 -RAEAES 4    [MAEGEN-RAEAES]
(1543) OFER- 3 -WEARP 9    [OFER-WEARP]
(1546) +BRUUN- 3 -ECG 3    [BRUUN-ECG]
(1549) FOR- 3 -STOOD. 9    [FOR-STOOD]
(1550) FOR- 3 -SIIDHOD 4    [FOR-SIIDHOD]
(1584) FOR- 3 -GEALD 4    [FOR-GEALD]
(1587) ALDOR- 3 -LEEAS-1-NE 6    [ALDOR-LEEASNE]
(1594) BLONDEN- 3 -FEAXE 5    [BLONDEN-FEAXE]
(1595) ON- 3 -GEADOR 4    [ON-GEADOR]
(1616) FOR- 3 -BARN 4    [FOR-BARN]
(1616) BROO-2-DEN- 3 -MAEAEL 5    [BROODEN-MAEAEL]
(1617) ELLOR- 3 -GAEAEST 4    [ELLOR-GAEAEST]
(1667) BROGDEN- 3 -MAEAEL. 6    [BROGDEN-MAEAEL]
(1676) ALDOR- 3 -BEALU 9    [ALDOR-BEALU]
(1689) FYRN- 3 -GE- 3    [FYRN-GE-WINNES]
(1698) WYRM- 3 -FAAH 4    [WYRM-FAAH]
(1710) AAR- 3 -SCYL-1-DINGUM. 9    [AAR-SCYLDINGUM]
(1711) WAEL- 3 -FEAL-9-LE 8    [WAEL-FEALLE]
(1714) EAXL- 3 -GE- 9    [EAXL-GE-STEALLAN]
(1720) DREEAM- 3 -LEEAS 4    [DREEAM-LEEAS]
(1751) FOR- 3 -GYTEDH 5    [FOR-GYTEDH]
(1751) FOR- 3 -GYYMEDH 9    [FOR-GYYMEDH]
(1757) AEAER- 3 -GE- 4    [AEAER-GE-STREEON]
(1767) FOR- 3 -SWOR-9-CEDH 5    [FOR-SWORCEDH]
(1771) MID-9-DAN- 3 -GEARD. 6    [MIDDAN-GEARD]
(1787) ELLEN- 3 -ROOFUM 4    [ELLEN-ROOFUM]
(1791) BLONDEN- 3 -FEAX 4    [BLONDEN-FEAX]
(1799) RUUM- 3 -HEORT 6    [RUUM-HEORT]
(1838) FEOR- 3 -CYYTHDHE 5    [FEOR-CYYTHDHE]
(1856) GAAR- 3 -DENUM 4    [GAAR-DENUM]
(1877) FOR- 3 -BERAN 3    [FOR-BERAN]
(1910) BRIM- 3 -STREEAMAS 5    [BRIM-STREEAMAS]
(1931) MAATHM- 3 -GE- 2    [MAATHM-GE-STREEONA]
(1330) HAND- 3 -BANAN 9    [HAND-BANAN]
(1345) LOND- 3 -BUUEND 4    [LOND-BUUEND]
(1351) -LIIC- 3 -()NAES*NES 2    [*ON-LIIC-NES]
```

```
(1352)  WRAEC- 3 -LAAS-1-TAS 9     [WRAEC-LAASTAS]
(1355)  FOLD- 3 -BUUENDE 5    [FOLD-BUUENDE]
(1369)  HOLT- 3 -WUDU 2    [HOLT-WUDU]
(1388)  DRIHT- 3 -GUMAN 3    [DRIHT-GUMAN]
(1402)  LIND- 3 -HAEBBENDRA 3    [LIND-HAEBBENDRA]
(1420)  AESC- 3 -HERES 5    [AESC-HERES]
(1447)  IN-9-WIT- 3 -FENG 3    [INWIT-FENG]
(1480)  MUND- 3 -BORA 4    [MUND-BORA]
(1490)  HEARD- 3 -ECG 3    [HEARD-ECG]
(1513)  NAAT- 3 -HWYLCUM 4    [NAAT-HWYLCUM]
(1518)  GRUND- 3 -WYR-1-GENNE 9    [GRUND-WYRGENNE]
(1534)  MUND- 3 -GRIPE 5    [MUND-GRIPE]
(1548)  BREEOST- 3 -NET 2    [BREEOST-NET]
(1578)  WEST- 3 -DENUM 9    [WEST-DENUM]
(1663)  EALD- 3 -SWEORD 4    [EALD-SWEORD]
(1704)  WIID- 3 -WEGAS 6    [WIID-WEGAS]
(1719)  BLOOD- 3 -REEOW 5    [BLOOD-REEOW]
(1729)  MOOD- 3 -GE- 3    [MOOD-GE-THONC]
(1736)  IN-1-WIT- 3 -SORH 5    [INWIT-SORH]
(1754)  LIIC- 3 -HOMA 9    [LIIC-HOMA]
(1778)  MOOD- 3 -CEARE 9    [MOOD-CEARE]
(1823)  MOOD- 3 -LUFAN 4    [MOOD-LUFAN]
(1858)  INWIT- 3 -NIITHAS 9    [INWIT-NIITHAS]
(1890)  LAND- 3 -WEARD 3    [LAND-WEARD]
(1897)  HRINGED- 3 -STEFNA 5    [HRINGED-STEFNA]
(1921)  FAEAET- 3 -GOLD 3    [FAEAET-GOLD]
(1931)  MOOD- 3 -THRYYDHO 3    [MOOD-THRYYDHO]
(1937)  HAND- 3 -GE- 1    [HAND-GE-WRITHENE]
(1938)  MUND- 3 -GRIPE 5    [MUND-GRIPE]
(1321)  $HROODH- 3 -GAAR 5    [HROODH-GAAR]
(1358)  WULF- 3 -HLEOTHU 4    [WULF-HLEOTHU]
(1513)  NIIDH- 3 -SELE 4    [NIIDH-SELE]
(1559)  WEORDH- 3 -MYND 5    [WEORDH-MYND]
(1580)  HROODH- 3 -GAARES 5    [HROODH-GAARES]
(1580)  HEORDH- 3 -GE- 2    [HEORDH-GE-NEEATAS]
(1600)  OF- 3 -GEEAFON 3    [OF-GEEAFON]
(1649)  EGES- 3 -LIIC 2    [EGES-LIIC]
(1657)  EAR-1-FODH- 3 -LIICE 9    [EARFODH-LIICE]
(1712)  DEEADH- 3 -CWALUM 4    [DEEADH-CWALUM]
(1813)  SIIDH- 3 -FROME 5    [SIIDH-FROME]
(1825)  GUUDH- 3 -GE- 9    [GUUDH-GE-WEORCA]
(1863)  LUF- 3 -TAACEN 4    [LUF-TAACEN]
(1884)  HROODH- 3 -GAARES 5    [HROODH-GAARES]
(1899)  HROODH- 3 -GAARES 9    [HROODH-GAARES]
(1914)  HYYDH- 3 -WEARD 3    [HYYDH-WEARD]
(1384)  AEAEG- 3 -HWAEAEM 4    [AEAEG-HWAEAEM]
(1504)  DHURH- 3 -FOON 3    [DHURH-FOON]
(1521)  HRING- 3 -MAEAEL 4    [HRING-MAEAEL]
(1536)  LONG- 3 -SUMNE 4    [LONG-SUMNE]
(1540)  FEORH- 3 -GE- 3    [FEORH-GE-NIIDHLAN]
(1619)  WIIG- 3 -HRYRE 5    [WIIG-HRYRE]
(1619)  THURH- 3 -DEEAF 4    [THURH-DEEAF]
(1636)  AEAEG- 3 -HWAE-1-THRU= 4    [AEAEG-HWAETHRU=]
(1738)  ECG- 3 -HETE 9    [ECG-HETE]
(1862)  HRING- 3 -NACA 4    [HRING-NACA]
(1889)  HAEG- 3 -STEAL-1-DRA 8    [HAEG-STEALDRA]

(1731)  HLEEO- 4 -BURH 3    [HLEEO-BURH]
(1426)  SAEAE- 4 -DRACAN 9    [SAEAE-DRACAN]
(1882)  +SAEAE- 4 -GENGA 3    [SAEAE-GENGA]
(1924)  +SAEAE- 4 -WEALLE 4    [SAEAE-WEALLE]
(1446)  HIL-1-DE- 4 -GRAAP 5    [HILDE-GRAAP]
(1454)  BEA-1-DO- 4 -MEECAS 6    [BEADO-MEECAS]
(1495)  HIL-9-DE- 4 -RINCE 6    [HILDE-RINCE]
(1498)  BE- 4 -HEEOLD 5    [BE-HEEOLD]
```

```
(1511) HILDE- 4 -TUUXUM 5    [HILDE-TUUXUM]
(1523) BEADO- 4 -LEEOMA 3    [BEADO-LEEOMA]
(1553) HERE- 4 -NET 3    [HERE-NET]
(1564) HEORO- 4 -GRIM 3    [HEORO-GRIM]
(1590) HEORO- 4 -SWENG 4    [HEORO-SWENG]
(1692) ENDE- 4 -LEEAN 5    [ENDE-LEEAN]
(1746) BE- 4 -BEOR-2-GAN 4    [BE-BEORGAN]
(1780) HEORO- 4 -DREEORIGNE 5    [HEORO-DREEORIGNE]
(1888) FELA- 4 -MOODIGRA 9    [FELA-MOODIGRA]
(1890) LEODHO- 4 -SYRCAN 4    [LEODHO-SYRCAN]
(1902) MEODU- 4 -BENCE 5    [MEODU-BENCE]
(1574) HIGE- 4 -LAACES 4    [HIGE-LAACES]
(1375) GE- 4 -WIDRU 2    [GE-WIDRU]
(1392) GE- 4 -HAATE 5    [GE-HAATE]
(1420) GE- 4 -HWAEAEM 3    [GE-HWAEAEM]
(1539) GE- 4 -BOLGEN 2    [GE-BOLGEN]
(1557) $$GE- 4 -SEAH 3    [GE-SEAH]
(1610) GE- 4 -WEALD 4    [GE-WEALD]
(1620) GE- 4 -FAEAELSOD 4    [GE-FAEAELSOD]
(1684) GE- 4 -WEALD 3    [GE-WEALD]
(1727) GE- 4 -WEALD. 7    [GE-WEALD]
(1857) GE- 4 -()MAENUM*MAEAENE 6    [*GE-MAEAENE]
(1866) GE- 4 -SEALDE 6    [GE-SEALDE]
(1885) GE- 4 -AEHTED 3    [GE-AEHTED]
(1912) GE- 4 -THRANG 5    [GE-THRANG]
(1458) -GE- 4 -STREEONA 5    [EALD-GE-STREEONA]
(1757) -GE- 4 -STREEON 5    [AEAER-GE-STREEON]
(1776) -GE- 4 -WINNA 3    [EALD-GE-WINNA]
(1913) -GE- 4 -SWEN-9-CED 3    [LYFT-GE-SWENCED]
(1344) WEEL- 4 -HWYLCRA 5    [WEEL-HWYLCRA]
(1354) GEEAR- 4 -DAGU= 4    [GEEAR-DAGU=]
(1400) WUNDEN- 4 -FEAX 3    [WUNDEN-FEAX]
(1406) SAAWOL- 4 -LEEAS-2-NE 6    [SAAWOL-LEEASNE]
(1409) STAAN- 4 -HLIDHO 5    [STAAN-HLIDHO]
(1492) WEDER- 4 -GEEATA 4    [WEDER-GEEATA]
(1494) BRIM- 4 -WYLM 3    [BRIM-WYLM]
(1516) +FAEAER- 4 -GRIPE 4    [FAEAER-GRIPE]
(1531) ()WUNDEL*WUNDEN- 4 -MAEAEL 5    [*WUNDEN-MAEAEL]
(1563) FETEL- 4 -HILT 9    [FETEL-HILT]
(1599) BRIM- 4 -WYLF 4    [BRIM-WYLF]
(1669) FYR-1-EN- 4 -DAEAE-3-DA 3    [FYREN-DAEAEDA]
(1713) BOLGEN- 4 -MOOD 6    [BOLGEN-MOOD]
(1727) EORL- 4 -SCIPE 4    [EORL-SCIPE]
(1740) OFER- 4 -HYGDA 5    [OFER-HYGDA]
(1749) GROM- 4 -HYYDIG 5    [GROM-HYYDIG]
(1760) OFER- 4 -HYYDA 3    [OFER-HYYDA]
(1768) OFER- 4 -SWYYDHEDH 4    [OFER-SWYYDHEDH]
(1782) SYM-9-BEL- 4 -WYNNE 5    [SYMBEL-WYNNE]
(1842) SNOTOR- 4 -LIICOR 5    [SNOTOR-LIICOR]
(1895) +SCIIR- 4 -HAME 5    [SCIIR-HAME]
(1918) ()ONCEAR*ONCER- 4 -BENDUM 2    [*ONCER-BENDUM]
(1919) FOR- 4 -WRECAN 8    [FOR-WRECAN]
(1927) WEEL- 4 -THUNGEN 4    [WEEL-THUNGEN]
(1936) WAEL- 4 -BENDE. 9    [WAEL-BENDE]
(1939) SCEAADEN- 4 -MAEAEL 4    [SCEAADEN-MAEAEL]
(1325) RAEAED- 4 -BORA 5    [RAEAED-BORA]
(1504) FYRD- 4 -HOM 4    [FYRD-HOM]
(1684) WOROLD- 4 -CYNINGA 5    [WOROLD-CYNINGA]
(1768) DRYHT- 4 -GUMA 3    [DRYHT-GUMA]
(1790) DRYHT- 4 -GUMU= 9    [DRYHT-GUMU=]
(1853) MOOD- 4 -SEFA 4    [MOOD-SEFA]
(1913) LYFT- 4 -GE- 4    [LYFT-GE-SWENCED]
(1368) HAEAEDH- 4 -STAPA 5    [HAEAEDH-STAPA]
(1479) FORDH- 4 -GE- 1    [FORDH-GE-WITENUM]
(1522) GUUDH- 4 -LEEODH 9    [GUUDH-LEEODH]
```

236

```
(1627) DHRYYDH- 4 -LIIC 4     [DHRYYDH-LIIC]
(1752) WEORDH- 4 -MYNDA 3     [WEORDH-MYNDA]
(1802) BLIIDH- 4 -HEORT 3     [BLIIDH-HEORT]
(1881) GRAES- 4 -MOLDAN 4     [GRAES-MOLDAN]
(1440) WAEAEG- 4 -BORA 4      [WAEAEG-BORA]
(1634) CYNING- 4 -BALDE 4     [CYNING-BALDE]
(1708) LANG- 4 -TWIIDIG 5     [LANG-TWIIDIG]
(1889) HRING- 4 -NET 3        [HRING-NET]
(1909) FAAHIG- 4 -HEALS 4     [FAAHIG-HEALS]


(1896) +SAEAE- 5 -GEEAP 3     [SAEAE-GEEAP]
(1462) GRYRE- 5 -SIIDHAS 4    [GRYRE-SIIDHAS]
(1511) HERE- 5 -SYR-2-CAN 4   [HERE-SYRCAN]
(1552) HEADHO- 5 -BYRNE 7     [HEADHO-BYRNE]
(1632) FEE-1-THE- 5 -LAASTUM 3  [FEETHE-LAASTUM]
(1637) FELA- 5 -MOODIGRA 4    [FELA-MOODIGRA]
(1650) WLITE- 5 -SEEON 3      [WLITE-SEEON]
(1666) HILDE- 5 -BIL 5        [HILDE-BIL]
(1794) SELE- 5 -THEGN 3       [SELE-THEGN]
(1905) MERE- 5 -HRAEGLA 5     [MERE-HRAEGLA]
(1597) SIGE- 5 -HREEDHIG 4    [SIGE-HREEDHIG]
(1395) GE- 5 -THYLD 4         [GE-THYLD]
(1737) GE- 5 -SACU 4          [GE-SACU]
(1773) GE- 5 -SACAN 2         [GE-SACAN]
(1870) GE- 5 -CYSTE 5         [GE-CYSTE]
(1783) -GE- 5 -WEORTHAD 4     [WIIG-GE-WEORTHAD]
(1324) YR-1-MEN- 5 -LAAFES 4  [YRMEN-LAAFES]
(1411) NICOR- 5 -HUUSA 3      [NICOR-HUUSA]
(1613) MAADH-1-M- 5 -AEAEHTA 3  [MAADHM-AEAEHTA]
(1698) WREO-9-THEN- 5 -HILT 5  [WREOTHEN-HILT]
(1744) FLAAN- 5 -BOGAN 9      [FLAAN-BOGAN]
(1503) YMB- 5 -BEARH 6        [YMB-BEARH]
(1427) NAES- 5 -HLEODHUM 3    [NAES-HLEODHUM]
(1432) GUUDH- 5 -HORN 2       [GUUDH-HORN]


(1817) $BEEO- 8 -WULF 5       [BEEO-WULF]
(1665) AA- 8 -GEALD 5         [AA-GEALD]
(1401) GEATO- 8 -LIIC 9       [GEATO-LIIC]
(1519) MERE- 8 -WIIF 3        [MERE-WIIF]
(1758) BE- 8 -BEOR-1-H 1      [BE-BEORH]
(1399) GE- 8 -BAEAETED 9      [GE-BAEAETED]
(1438) GE- 8 -NEAR-2-WOD 4    [GE-NEARWOD]
(1711) GE- 8 -WEEOX 6         [GE-WEEOX]
(1938) GE- 8 -THINGED 5       [GE-THINGED]
(1481) -GE- 8 -SELLUM 4       [HOND-GE-SELLUM]
(1526) -GE- 8 -MOOTA 5        [HOND-GE-MOOTA]
(1713) -GE- 8 -NEEATAS 4      [BEEOD-GE-NEEATAS]
(1516) FYYR- 8 -LEEOHT 4      [FYYR-LEEOHT]
(1734) UN- 8 -SNYTTRUM 5      [UN-SNYTTRUM]
(1806) COL-9-LEN- 8 -FERHDH 5 [COLLEN-FERHDH]
(1424) FYRD- 8 -LEEODH 4      [FYRD-LEEODH]
(1602) GOLD- 8 -WINE 9        [GOLD-WINE]
(1424) FUUS- 8 -LIIC 9        [FUUS-LIIC]
(1665) OF- 8 -SLOOH 3         [OF-SLOOH]


(1854) BEEO- 9 -WULF 6        [BEEO-WULF]
(1412) BE- 9 -FORAN 3         [BE-FORAN]
(1480) MAGO- 9 -THEGNUM 6     [MAGO-THEGNUM]
(1505) LEODHO- 9 -SYRCAN 5    [LEODHO-SYRCAN]
(1520) HILDE- 9 -BILLE 6      [HILDE-BILLE]
(1606) HIL-1-DE- 9 -GI-1-C-1-ELUM 4  [HILDE-GICELUM]
(1643) MEODO- 9 -WONGAS 5     [MEODO-WONGAS]
(1753) ENDE- 9 -STAEF 5       [ENDE-STAEF]
(1770) BE- 9 -LEEAC 5         [BE-LEEAC]
(1897) HERE- 9 -WAEAEDUM 5    [HERE-WAEAEDUM]
```

237

```
(1923) HIGE-  9 -LAAC 5    [HIGE-LAAC]
(1370) GE-  9 -FLYYMED 3   [GE-FLYYMED]
(1398) GE-  9 -SPRAEC 4    [GE-SPRAEC]
(1465) GE-  9 -MUNDE 5     [GE-MUNDE]
(1598) GE-  9 -WEARDH 5    [GE-WEARDH]
(1615) GE-  9 -MEALT 5     [GE-MEALT]
(1681) GE-  9 -WEORC 5     [GE-WEORC]
(1691) GE-  9 -FEERDON 4   [GE-FEERDON]
(1695) GE-  9 -MEARCOD 4   [GE-MEARCOD]
(1705) GE-  9 -THYLDUM 6   [GE-THYLDUM]
(1781) GE-  9 -WIN 3    [GE-WIN]
(1826) GE-  9 -FRICGE 5    [GE-FRICGE]
(1362) -GE-  9 -MEAR-1-CES 5    [MIIL-GE-MEARCES]
(1714) -GE-  9 -STEALLAN 4    [EAXL-GE-STEALLAN]
(1825) -GE-  9 -WEORCA 5    [GUUDH-GE-WEORCA]
(1325) +RUUN-  9 -WITA 4    [RUUN-WITA]
(1339) MAAN-  9 -SCADHA 4    [MAAN-SCADHA]
(1349) ELLOR-  9 -GAEAESTAS 4    [ELLOR-GAEAESTAS]
(1359) FYRGEN-  9 -STREEAM 5   [FYRGEN-STREEAM]
(1433) FLAAN-  9 -BOGAN 4    [FLAAN-BOGAN]
(1471) ELLEN-  9 -MAEAERDHUM 3    [ELLEN-MAEAERDHUM]
(1497) ON-  9 -FUNDE 5    [ON-FUNDE]
(1506) BRIM-  9 -WYL*F 4    [BRIM-WYL*F]
(1567) BAAN-  9 -HRINGAS 5    [BAAN-HRINGAS]
(1610) WAEAEL-  9 -RAAPAS 4    [WAEAEL-RAAPAS]
(1612) WEDER-  9 -GEEATA 4    [WEDER-GEEATA]
(1621) ELLOR-  9 -GAAST 4    [ELLOR-GAAST]
(1625) MAEGEN-  9 -BYR-1-THENNE 5    [MAEGEN-BYRTHENNE]
(1635) HOLM-  9 -CLIFE 5    [HOLM-CLIFE]
(1642) GUM-  9 -DRYHTEN 3    [GUM-DRYHTEN]
(1655) UN-  9 -SOOFTE 5    [UN-SOOFTE]
(1667) FOR-  9 -BARN 5    [FOR-BARN]
(1682) GROM-  9 -HEORT 4    [GROM-HEORT]
(1747) WUN-2-DOR-  9 -BE- 2    [WUNDOR-BE-BODUM]
(1795) FEORRAN-  9 -CUNDUM 4    [FEORRAN-CUNDUM]
(1873) BLON-1-DEN-  9 -FEAXUM 5    [BLONDEN-FEAXUM]
(1874) IN-  9 -FRO-1-DUM 4    [IN-FRODUM]
(1890) ON-  9 -FAND 4    [ON-FAND]
(1910) BUNDEN-  9 -STEFNA 4    [BUNDEN-STEFNA]
(1329) AESC-  9 -HERE 9    [AESC-HERE]
(1457) HAEFT-  9 -MEECE 6    [HAEFT-MEECE]
(1458) EALD-  9 -GE- 4    [EALD-GE-STREEONA]
(1470) DRIHT-  9 -SCYPE 5    [DRIHT-SCYPE]
(1476) GOLD-  9 -WINE 5    [GOLD-WINE]
(1493) =AND-  9 -SWARE 6    [=AND-SWARE]
(1526) HOND-  9 -GE- 8    [HOND-GE-MOOTA]
(1527) FYRD-  9 -HRAEGL 5    [FYRD-HRAEGL]
(1558) EALD-  9 -SWEORD 4    [EALD-SWEORD]
(1568) FLAEAESC-  9 -HOMAN 5    [FLAEAESC-HOMAN]
(1641) FYRD-  9 -HWATE 5    [FYRD-HWATE]
(1650) WRAEAET-  9 -LIIC 4    [WRAEAET-LIIC]
(1719) BREEOST-  9 -HORD 6    [BREEOST-HORD]
(1789) NIHT-  9 -HELM 4    [NIHT-HELM]
(1827) YMB-  9 -SIT-1-TEND 4    [YMB-SITTEND]
(1845) WORD-  9 -CWIDA 5    [WORD-CWIDA]
(1877) BREEOST-  9 -WYLM 3    [BREEOST-WYLM]
(1881) GOLD-  9 -WLANC 4    [GOLD-WLANC]
(1515) HROOF-  9 -SELE 5    [HROOF-SELE]
(1624) SWIIDH-  9 -MOOD 4    [SWIIDH-MOOD]
(1670) DEEADH-  9 -CWEALM 4    [DEEADH-CWEALM]
(1750) FORDH-  9 -GE- 1    [FORDH-GE-SCEAFT]
(1816) HROODH-  9 -GAAR 5    [HROODH-GAAR]
(1429) SORH-  9 -FULNE 4    [SORH-FULNE]
(1489) WAEAEG-  9 -SWEORD 5    [WAEAEG-SWEORD]
(1554) WIIG-  9 -SIGOR 4    [WIIG-SIGOR]
```

APPENDIX III
LINES 1940 - 3182 (SECOND SCRIBE≠S COPY)

MORPHEME PAIRS GROUPED BY MEASURE OF SPACING

(2510) BEEO- 0 -WULF 2   [BEEO-WULF]
(2046) AA- 0 -CWYDH. 5   [AA-CWYDH]
(2092) AA- 0 -STOOD. 7   [AA-STOOD]
(2108) AA- 0 -WRAEC. 3   [AA-WRAEC]
(2121) AA- 0 -CWEALDE 4   [AA-CWEALDE]
(2194) AA- 0 -LEGDE. 5   [AA-LEGDE]
(2280) AA- 0 -BEALCH 4   [AA-BEALCH]
(2382) SAEAE- 0 -CYNINGA 4   [SAEAE-CYNINGA]
(2403) AA- 0 -RAAS. 4   [AA-RAAS]
(2418) AA- 0 -BEEAD 4   [AA-BEEAD]
(2432) OO- 0 -WIHTE 5   [OO-WIHTE]
(2487) TOO- 0 -GLAAD 9   [TOO-GLAAD]
(2538) AA- 0 -RAAS 0   [AA-RAAS]
(2568) TOO- 0 -SOMNE 4   [TOO-SOMNE]
(2575) AA- 0 -BRAEAED. 5   [AA-BRAEAED]
(2591) AA- 0 -LAEAETAN 3   [AA-LAEAETAN]
(2619) AA- 0 -BRED-2-WADE. 7   [AA-BREDWADE]
(2643) AA- 0 -DHOOHTE 5   [AA-DHOOHTE]
(2665) AA- 0 -LAEAETE 9   [AA-LAEAETE]
(2690) AA- 0 -GEALD 9   [AA-GEALD]
(2707) AA- 0 -BRO-9-TEN 2   [AA-BROTEN]
(2750) AA- 0 -LAEAETAN 3   [AA-LAEAETAN]
(2852) WII- 0 -LAAF 5   [WII-LAAF]
(2870) OO- 0 -WER 3   [OO-WER]
(2929) AA- 0 -GEAF 4   [AA-GEAF]
(2930) AA- 0 -BREEOT 9   [AA-BREEOT]
(2983) AA- 0 -RAEAERDON 3   [AA-RAEAERDON]
(3020) AA- 0 -LEGDE 4   [AA-LEGDE]
(3030) AA- 0 -RAAS 3   [AA-RAAS]
(3089) AA- 0 -LYYFED 3   [AA-LYYFED]
(3121) AA- 0 -CIIGDE 3   [AA-CIIGDE]
(3141) AA- 0 -LEGDON 2   [AA-LEGDON]
(3144) AA- 0 -STAAH 3   [AA-STAAH]
(2009) BI- 0 -FONGEN 4   [BI-FONGEN]
(2035) BI- 0 -WENEDE. 9   [BI-WENEDE]
(2116) BE- 0 -CWOOM. 9   [BE-CWOOM]
(2130) BE- 0 -GEEATE. 7   [BE-GEEATE]
(2230) BE- 0 -GEAT 4   [BE-GEAT]
(2249) BE- 0 -GEEATON 9   [BE-GEEATON]
(2367) BI- 0 -GONG 3   [BI-GONG]
(2396) BI- 0 -NEEAT. 6   [BI-NEEAT]
(2435) -DEEFE- 0 -LIICE 5   [UN-GE-DEEFE-LIICE]
(2497) BE- 0 -FORAN 3   [BE-FORAN]
(2595) BE- 0 -FONGEN 4   [BE-FONGEN]
(2746) BE- 0 -REEAFOD 3   [BE-REEAFOD]
(2872) BE- 0 -GET 4   [BE-GET]
(2931) BE- 0 -ROFENE 5   [BE-ROFENE]
(2936) BE- 0 -SAET 1   [BE-SAET]
(2955) HEADHO- 0 -LIIDHENDU= 4   [HEADHO-LIIDHENDU=]
(2992) BE- 0 -+COOM 9   [BE-COOM]
(3139) BE- 0 -HONGEN 3   [BE-HONGEN]
(3159) BE- 0 -TIM-9-BREDON 3   [BE-TIMBREDON]
(3178) BE- 0 -GNORNODON 2   [BE-GNORNODON]

239

```
(1970) HIGE- 0 -LAACE 9    [HIGE-LAACE]
(2151) HYGE- 0 -LAAC 1     [HYGE-LAAC]
(2169) HYGE- 0 -LAACE 3    [HYGE-LAACE]
(2201) HYGE- 0 -LAAC 2     [HYGE-LAAC]
(2355) HYGE- 0 -LAAC 3     [HYGE-LAAC]
(2434) HYGE- 0 -LAAC 4     [HYGE-LAAC]
(1951) GE- 0 -SOOHTE 9     [GE-SOOHTE]
(1971) GE- 0 -GYYDHED 3    [GE-CYYDHED]
(1977) GE- 0 -SAET 3    [GE-SAET]
(1991) GE- 0 -BEETTEST 5    [GE-BEETTEST]
(1998) GE- 0 -SUNDNE 4    [GE-SUNDNE]
(2001) GE- 0 -MEETING 5    [GE-MEETING]
(2013) GE- 0 -TAEAEHTE. 9    [GE-TAEAEHTE]
(2029) GE- 0 -SETTE 2    [GE-SETTE]
(2040) GE- 0 -SIIDHAS 4    [GE-SIIDHAS]
(2047) GE- 0 -CNAAWAN 4    [GE-CNAAWAN]
(2048) GE- 0 -FEOHTE 9    [GE-FEOHTE]
(2075) GE- 0 -SUNDE 4    [GE-SUNDE]
(2104) GE- 0 -SETEN 9    [GE-SETEN]
(2111) GE- 0 -BUNDEN 4    [GE-BUNDEN]
(2142) GE- 0 -SEALDE 5    [GE-SEALDE]
(2150) GE- 0 -LONG 9    [GE-LONG]
(2164) GE- 0 -LIICE 4    [GE-LIICE]
(2189) GE- 0 -HWYLCES. 5    [GE-HWYLCES]
(2197) GE- 0 -CYNDE 4    [GE-CYNDE]
(2284) GE- 0 -TIIDHAD 4    [GE-TIIDHAD]
(2289) GE- 0 -STOOP. 6    [GE-STOOP]
(2291) GE- 0 -DIIGAN 4    [GE-DIIGAN]
(2293) GE- 0 -HEALDETH 3    [GE-HEALDETH]
(2295) GE- 0 -TEEODE. 6    [GE-TEEODE]
(2324) GE- 0 -CYY-9-DHED 3    [GE-CYYDHED]
(2331) GE- 0 -BULGE 9    [GE-BULGE]
(2332) GE- 0 -THYYWE 5    [GE-THYYWE]
(2350) GE- 0 -DIIGDE. 9    [GE-DIIGDE]
(2359) GE- 0 -BEEATEN 9    [GE-BEEATEN]
(2369) GE- 0 -BEEAD 4    [GE-BEEAD]
(2391) GE- 0 -MUNDE 9    [GE-MUNDE]
(2393) GE- 0 -STEEPTE. 5    [GE-STEEPTE]
(2397) GE- 0 -NESEN 3    [GE-NESEN]
(2400) GE- 0 -WEGAN 9    [GE-WEGAN]
(2422) GE- 0 -DAEAELAN 3    [GE-DAEAELAN]
(2429) GE- 0 -NAM 5    [GE-NAM]
(2431) GE- 0 -MUNDE 9    [GE-MUNDE]
(2450) GE- 0 -HWYLCE 9    [GE-HWYLCE]
(2452) GE- 0 -BIIDANNE 3    [GE-BIIDANNE]
(2455) GE- 0 -SYHDH 4    [GE-SYHDH]
(2465) GE- 0 -BEETAN 5    [GE-BEETAN]
(2469) GE- 0 -CEEAS 3    [GE-CEEAS]
(2489) GE- 0 -NOOGE 4    [GE-NOOGE]
(2496) GE- 0 -CYYPAN 8    [GE-CYYPAN]
(2505) GE- 0 -CRONG 4    [GE-CRONG]
(2508) GE- 0 -BRAEC 3    [GE-BRAEC]
(2516) GE- 0 -GREETTE 4    [GE-GREETTE]
(2526) GE- 0 -TEEODH 9    [GE-TEEODH]
(2529) GE- 0 -BIIDE 0    [GE-BIIDE]
(2567) GE- 0 -BEEAH 4    [GE-BEEAH]
(2592) GE- 0 -MEETTON 4    [GE-MEETTON]
(2604) GE- 0 -SEAH 2    [GE-SEAH]
(2610) GE- 0 -TEEAH 4    [GE-TEEAH]
(2620) GE- 0 -HEEOLD 9    [GE-HEEOLD]
(2632) GE- 0 -SIIDHU= 5    [GE-SIIDHU=]
(2655) GE- 0 -FYLLAN. 9    [GE-FYLLAN]
(2659) GE- 0 -SIIGAN 2    [GE-SIIGAN]
(2660) GE- 0 -MAEAENE. 5    [GE-MAEAENE]
(2689) GE- 0 -MYNDIG 9    [GE-MYNDIG]
```

```
(2703) GE- 0 -BRAEAED 3   [GE-BRAEAED]
(2717) GE- 0 -SAET 3   [GE-SAET]
(2752) GE- 0 -FRAEGN 4   [GE-FRAEGN]
(2764) GE- 0 -SAEAELED 3   [GE-SAEAELED]
(2769) GE- 0 -LOCEN 3   [GE-LOCEN]
(2776) GE- 0 -NOOM 9   [GE-NOOM]
(2785) GE- 0 -MEETTE 5   [GE-MEETTE]
(2824) GE- 0 -BAEAERAN 9   [GE-BAEAERAN]
(2834) GE- 0 -FEEOLL 4   [GE-FEEOLL]
(2867) GE- 0 -SEALDE 9   [GE-SEALDE]
(2891) GE- 0 -HWYLCU= 9   [GE-HWYLCU=]
(2906) GE- 0 -WYRCEAN 4   [GE-WYRCEAN]
(2926) GE- 0 -SOOHTON 3   [GE-SOOHTON]
(2941) GE- 0 -LAMP 3   [GE-LAMP]
(2947) GE- 0 -SYYNE 5   [GE-SYYNE]
(3012) GE- 0 -CEEA-9-()++D*POD 8   [*GE-CEEAPOD]
(3046) GE- 0 -NYTTOD 5   [GE-NYTTOD]
(3068) GE- 0 -DAAL 3   [GE-DAAL]
(3104) GE- 0 -NOOGE 4   [GE-NOOGE]
(3110) GE- 0 -BEEODAN 9   [GE-BEEODAN]
(3116) GE- 0 -+BAAD 4   [GE-BAAD]
(3128) GE- 0 -SEEGON 3   [GE-SEEGON]
(2162) -GE- 0 -WAEAEDU 3   [BREEOST-GE-WAEAEDU]
(2180) -GE- 0 -NEEA-9-TAS 3   [HEOROH-GE-NEEATAS]
(2302) -GE- 0 -STREEONA 4   [HEEAH-GE-STREEONA]
(2355) -GE- 0 -()MOT*MOOTA 9   [*HOND-GE-MOOTA]
(2418) -GE- 0 -NEEATU= 3   [HEOROH-GE-NEEATU=]
(2721) -GE- 0 -METE 4   [UN-GE-METE]
(2881) -GE- 0 -NIIDH-9-LAN 3   [FERHDH-GE-NIIDHLAN]
(2933) -GE- 0 -NIIDH-2-LAN 4   [FEORH-GE-NIIDHLAN]
(1983) ON- 0 -GAN 3   [ON-GAN]
(2086) SYL- 0 -LIIC 3   [SYL-LIIC]
(2087) OR- 0 -DHON-1-CU= 4   [OR-DHONCU=]
(2109) SYL- 0 -LIIC 3   [SYL-LIIC]
(2210) ON- 0 -GAN 4   [ON-GAN]
(2214) UN- 0 -CUUDH 4   [UN-CUUDH]
(2288) ON- 0 -FAND 4   [ON-FAND]
(2291) UN- 0 -FAEAEGE 9   [UN-FAEAEGE]
(2312) ON- 0 -GAN 3   [ON-GAN]
(2349) FOR- 0 -DHON 3   [FOR-DHON]
(2371) AEL- 0 -FYL-9-CU= 4   [AEL-FYLCU=]
(2407) OR- 0 -LEGES 4   [OR-LEGES]
(2420) WAEL- 0 -FUUS 3   [WAEL-FUUS]
(2420) UN- 0 -GE- 4   [UN-GE-METE]
(2435) UN- 0 -GE- 5   [UN-GE-DEEFE-LIICE]
(2456) WIIN- 0 -SELE 3   [WIIN-SELE]
(2483) ON- 0 -SAEAEGE 9   [ON-SAEAEGE]
(2493) EEDHEL- 0 -WYN 9   [EEDHEL-WYN]
(2523) FOR- 0 -DHON 2   [FOR-DHON]
(2554) ON- 0 -CNIIOW 5   [ON-CNIIOW]
(2578) UN- 0 -SWIIDHOR. 7   [UN-SWIIDHOR]
(2624) UN- 0 -RIIM 4   [UN-RIIM]
(2629) ON- 0 -FAND 3   [ON-FAND]
(2645) FOR- 0 -DHAA= 4   [FOR-DHAA=]
(2668) FUL- 0 -LAEAESTU. 5   [FUL-LAEAESTU]
(2728) UN- 0 -GE- 9   [UN-GE-METE]
(2741) FOR- 0 -DHAA= 4   [FOR-DHAA=]
(2770) ON- 0 -GITAN 3   [ON-GITAN]
(2843) FOR- 0 -GOLDEN 9   [FOR-GOLDEN]
(2921) UN- 0 -GYFEDHE. 5   [UN-GYFEDHE]
(2970) ON- 0 -CIRDE. 5   [ON-CIRDE]
(3012) UN- 0 -RIIME 4   [UN-RIIME]
(3019) EL- 0 -LAND 2   [EL-LAND]
(3038) SYL- 0 -LII-2-CRAN 4   [SYL-LIICRAN]
(3041) GRIM- 0 -LIIC 2   [GRIM-LIIC]
```

241

```
(3059) UN- 0 -RIHTE 9   [UN-RIHTE]
(3135) UN- 0 -RIIM 4    [UN-RIIM]
(3143) ON- 0 -GUNNON 2  [ON-GUNNON]
(3148) UN- 0 -ROOTE 3   [UN-ROOTE]
(2115) =AND- 0 -LANGNE 9   [=AND-LANGNE]
(2233) NAAT- 0 -HWYLC 4    [NAAT-HWYLC]
(2339) WRAEAET- 0 -LIIC 9  [WRAEAET-LIIC]
(2375) HEARD- 0 -REEDE 4   [HEARD-REEDE]
(2388) HEARD- 0 -REED 4    [HEARD-REED]
(2502) HAND- 0 -BONAN 3    [HAND-BONAN]
(2614) AET- 0 -BAER 4      [AET-BAER]
(2695) AND- 0 -LONGNE 9    [AND-LONGNE]
(2779) MUND- 0 -BORA 9     [MUND-BORA]
(2860) =AND- 0 -SWARU 9    [=AND-SWARU]
(2869) THRYYD- 0 -LIICOST 4  [THRYYD-LIICOST]
(3006) FOLC- 0 -REED 4     [FOLC-REED]
(3092) AET- 0 -BAER 3      [AET-BAER]
(3130) OFOST- 0 -()LIIC+*LIICE 9   [*OFOST-LIICE]
(3177) LIIC- 0 -HAMAN 9    [LIIC-HAMAN]
(3180) WYRULD- 0 -()CYNING*CYNINGA 9   [*WYRULD-CYNINGA]
(2011) HEALF- 0 -DE-9-NES 3   [HEALF-DENES]
(2129) HROODH- 0 -GAARE 9   [HROODH-GAARE]
(2309) EGES- 0 -LIIC 9      [EGES-LIIC]
(2426) GUUDH- 0 -RAEAESA 9  [GUUDH-RAEAESA]
(2503) FREES- 0 -()CYNING*CYNINGE 9   [*FREES-CYNINGE]
(2588) OF- 0 -GYFAN 4       [OF-GYFAN]
(2618) FUUS- 0 -LIIC 4      [FUUS-LIIC]
(2825) EGES- 0 -LIIC 3      [EGES-LIIC]
(2925) HAEDH- 0 -CEN 9      [HAEDH-CEN]
(3089) SWAEAES- 0 -LIICE 5  [SWAEAES-LIICE]
(2520) AAG- 0 -LAEAECEAN 4   [AAG-LAEAECEAN]
(2534) AAG- 0 -LAEAECEAN 4   [AAG-LAEAECEAN]
(2557) AAG- 0 -LAEAECEAN 3   [AAG-LAEAECEAN]
(2564) AEAEG- 0 -HWAEDHRU= 4   [AEAEG-HWAEDHRU=]
(2592) AAG- 0 -LAEAECEAN 5   [AAG-LAEAECEAN]
(2624) AEAEG- 0 -HWAES 3    [AEAEG-HWAES]
(2862) WIIG- 0 -LAAF 9      [WIIG-LAAF]
(2862) WEEOH- 0 -STAANES 2   [WEEOH-STAANES]
(2863) SAARIG- 0 -FERDH 9   [SAARIG-FERDH]
(2887) AEAEG- 0 -HWYLC 2    [AEAEG-HWYLC]
(2905) AAG- 0 -LAEAECEAN 9   [AAG-LAEAECEAN]
(2906) WIIG- 0 -LAAF 1      [WIIG-LAAF]
(3110) WIIH- 0 -STAANES 3   [WIIH-STAANES]
(3120) WIIH- 0 -STAANES 3   [WIIH-STAANES]
(3135) AEAEG- 0 -HWAES 2    [AEAEG-HWAES]
(3174) G=- 0 -()D+++*DEEFE 8   [*G=-DEEFE]

(2207) BEEO- 1 -WULFE 3     [BEEO-WULFE]
(2357) FREEA- 1 -WINE 3     [FREEA-WINE]
(2359) BIIO- 1 -WULF 2      [BIIO-WULF]
(2663) BIIO- 1 -WULF 4      [BIIO-WULF]
(2681) BIIO- 1 -WULFES 9    [BIIO-WULFES]
(2724) BIIO- 1 -WULF 4      [BIIO-WULF]
(2807) BIIO- 1 -WULFES 4    [BIIO-WULFES]
(3066) BIIO- 1 -WULFE. 9    [BIIO-WULFE.]
(2630) TOO- 1 -GAEDRE 4     [TOO-GAEDRE]
(2806) SAEAE- 1 -LIIDHEND 4   [SAEAE-LIIDHEND]
(2954) SAEAE- 1 -MANNU= 4   [SAEAE-MANNU=]
(3052) IUU- 1 -MONNA 4      [IUU-MONNA]
(3078) AA- 1 -()DREOGEDH*DREEOGAN 4   [*AA-DREEOGAN]
(3114) TOO- 1 -GEENES 3     [TOO-GEENES]
(1975) BE- 1 -BEEAD 4       [BE-BEEAD]
(2100) MER-1-E- 1 -GRUND 9   [MERE-GRUND]
(2138) BE- 1 -CEARF 6       [BE-CEARF]
(2154) GEATO- 1 -LIIC 9     [GEATO-LIIC]
```

242

```
(2158) HIOR-1-O- 1 -GAAR 4    [HIORO-GAAR]
(2321) BE- 1 -FANGEN 6    [BE-FANGEN]
(2365) BE- 1 -CWOOM 4    [BE-CWOOM]
(2424) BE- 1 -WUNDEN. 7    [BE-WUNDEN]
(2434) HERE- 1 -BEALD 9    [HERE-BEALD]
(2552) BE- 1 -COOM 2    [BE-COOM]
(2577) INC-1-GE- 1 -LAAFE 3    [INCGE-LAAFE]
(2722) WINE- 1 -DRYHTEN 9    [WINE-DRYHTEN]
(2762) BE- 1 -HRORENE 4    [BE-HRORENE]
(2813) ENDE- 1 -LAAF 3    [ENDE-LAAF]
(2825) BE- 1 -REEAFOD 3    [BE-REEAFOD]
(3018) BE- 1 -REEAFOD 9    [BE-REEAFOD]
(3160) BEADU- 1 -ROO-1-()FIS*FES 2    [*BEADU-ROOFES]
(2372) HYGE- 1 -LAAC 3    [HYGE-LAAC]
(2386) HYGE- 1 -LAACES. 4    [HYGE-LAACES]
(1946) GE- 1 -FREMEDE 3    [GE-FREMEDE]
(1955) GE- 1 -FRAEAEGE 4    [GE-FRAEAEGE]
(1984) GE- 1 -SELDAN 4    [GE-SELDAN]
(1988) GE- 1 -HOGODEST. 9    [GE-HOGODEST]
(1996) GE- 1 -WEORDHAN 9    [GE-WEORDHAN]
(1998) GE- 1 -SEEON 3    [GE-SEEON]
(2004) GE- 1 -FREMEDE 3    [GE-FREMEDE]
(2026) GE- 1 -WORDEN 4    [GE-WORDEN]
(2033) GE- 1 -HWAAM 4    [GE-HWAAM]
(2037) GE- 1 -STREEON 9    [GE-STREEON]
(2041) GE- 1 -SYHDH 4    [GE-SYHDH]
(2057) GE- 1 -HWYLCE. 6    [GE-HWYLCE]
(2082) GE- 1 -MYNDIG 5    [GE-MYNDIG]
(2090) GE- 1 -+DOON 3    [GE-DOON]
(2094) GE- 1 -HWYLCES 3    [GE-HWYLCES]
(2100) GE- 1 -FEEOLL 5    [GE-FEEOLL]
(2121) GE- 1 -WRAEC 9    [GE-WRAEC]
(2132) GE- 1 -THRING 3    [GE-THRING]
(2133) GE- 1 -NEEDH-3-DE. 5    [GE-NEEDHDE]
(2134) GE- 1 -HEET 3    [GE-HEET]
(2137) GE- 1 -MAEAENE. 3    [GE-MAEAENE]
(2157) GE- 1 -SAEGDE 9    [GE-SAEGDE]
(2171) GE- 1 -HWAEDHER 9    [GE-HWAEDHER]
(2171) GE- 1 -MYNDIG. 6    [GE-MYNDIG]
(2176) GE- 1 -WEOR-2-DHOD. 5    [GE-WEORDHOD]
(2186) GE- 1 -DOON 3    [GE-DOON]
(2204) GE- 1 -SOOHTAN 4    [GE-SOOHTAN]
(2250) GE- 1 -HWYLCNE. 5    [GE-HWYLCNE]
(2252) GE- 1 -SAAWON 4    [GE-SAAWON]
(2258) GE- 1 -BAAD 5    [GE-BAAD]
(2259) GE- 1 -BRAED 9    [GE-BRAED]
(2287) GE- 1 -NIIWAD. 5    [GE-NIIWAD]
(2309) GE- 1 -FYYSED 3    [GE-FYYSED]
(2316) GE- 1 -SYYNE 9    [GE-SYYNE]
(2319) GE- 1 -SCEEAT. 5    [GE-SCEEAT]
(2322) GE- 1 -TRUWODE 5    [GE-TRUWODE]
(2323) GE- 1 -LEEAH 4    [GE-LEEAH]
(2332) GE- 1 -THONCUM 9    [GE-THONCUM]
(2346) GE- 1 -SOOHTE 9    [GE-SOOHTE]
(2387) GE- 1 -WAAT 4    [GE-WAAT]
(2398) GE- 1 -SLYHTA 9    [GE-SLYHTA]
(2416) GE- 1 -GAN-1-GENNE 4    [GE-GANGENNE]
(2417) GE- 1 -SAET 0    [GE-SAET]
(2426) GE- 1 -NAES 4    [GE-NAES]
(2441) GE- 1 -FEOHT 3    [GE-FEOHT]
(2441) GE- 1 -SYNGAD. 4    [GE-SYNGAD]
(2445) GE- 1 -BIIDANNE 9    [GE-BIIDANNE]
(2449) GE- 1 -FREMMAN 9    [GE-FREMMAN]
(2454) GE- 1 -FONDAD. 4    [GE-FONDAD]
(2471) GE- 1 -WAAT 4    [GE-WAAT]
```

243

```
(2473) GE- 1 -MAEAENE. 6   [GE-MAEAENE]
(2480) GE- 1 -FRAEAEGE 4   [GE-FRAEAEGE]
(2484) GE- 1 -FRAEGN 4   [GE-FRAEGN]
(2500) GE- 1 -LAEAESTE 5   [GE-LAEAESTE]
(2518) GE- 1 -SIIDHAS 9   [GE-SIIDHAS]
(2527) GE- 1 -HWAES 4   [GE-HWAES]
(2536) GE- 1 -GANGAN 4   [GE-GANGAN]
(2542) GE- 1 -SEAH. 6   [GE-SEAH]
(2550) GE- 1 -BOLGEN 3   [GE-BOLGEN]
(2561) GE- 1 -FYYSED 9   [GE-FYYSED]
(2562) GE- 1 -BRAEAED 9   [GE-BRAEAED]
(2566) GE- 1 -STOOD 3   [GE-STOOD]
(2569) GE- 1 -BOGEN 3   [GE-BOGEN]
(2570) GE- 1 -BEARG 3   [GE-BEARG]
(2577) GE- 1 -+WAAC 5   [GE-WAAC]
(2580) GE- 1 -BAEAEDED 3   [GE-BAEAEDED]
(2608) GE- 1 -HWYLC 4   [GE-HWYLC]
(2609) GE- 1 -FEENG 9   [GE-FEENG]
(2634) GE- 1 -HEETON 3   [GE-HEETON]
(2638) GE- 1 -CEEAS. 5   [GE-CEEAS]
(2653) GE- 1 -RYSNE 3   [GE-RYSNE]
(2664) GE- 1 -CWAEAEDE 3   [GE-CWAEAEDE]
(2678) GE- 1 -MUNDE 4   [GE-MUNDE]
(2680) GE- 1 -NYYDED 1   [GE-NYYDED]
(2681) GE- 1 -SWAAC 3   [GE-SWAAC]
(2685) GE- 1 -HWANE 9   [GE-HWANE]
(2685) GE- 1 -FRAEAEGE 4   [GE-FRAEAEGE]
(2697) GE- 1 -BARN 3   [GE-BARN]
(2703) GE- 1 -WITTE 5   [GE-WITTE]
(2712) GE- 1 -WORHTE 5   [GE-WORHTE]
(2717) GE- 1 -WEORC 5   [GE-WEORC]
(2722) GE- 1 -LAFEDE 4   [GE-LAFEDE]
(2732) GE- 1 -LENGE 4   [GE-LENGE]
(2756) GE- 1 -SEAH 0   [GE-SEAH]
(2765) GE- 1 -HWONE 4   [GE-HWONE]
(2767) GE- 1 -SEAH 2   [GE-SEAH]
(2773) GE- 1 -FRAEGN 4   [GE-FRAEGN]
(2774) GE- 1 -WEORC 3   [GE-WEORC]
(2784) GE- 1 -FYRDH-1-RED 2   [GE-FYRDHRED]
(2808) GE- 1 -NIPU 4   [GE-NIPU]
(2819) GE- 1 -+WAAT 2   [GE-WAAT]
(2826) GE- 1 -BAEAEDED 2   [GE-BAEAEDED]
(2839) GE- 1 -RAEAESDE 3   [GE-RAEAESDE]
(2859) GE- 1 -HWYLCU= 3   [GE-HWYLCU=]
(2898) GE- 1 -+RAAD 4   [GE-RAAD]
(2937) GE- 1 -HEET 3   [GE-HEET]
(2952) GE- 1 -FRUUNEN 3   [GE-FRUUNEN]
(2965) GE- 1 -RAEAEHTE 4   [GE-RAEAEHTE]
(2980) GE- 1 -BEEAH 2   [GE-BEEAH]
(2983) GE- 1 -RYYMED 9   [GE-RYYMED]
(2989) GE- 1 -HEET 3   [GE-HEET]
(2990) GE- 1 -()LAESTA*LAEAESTE 4   [*GE-LAEAESTE]
(3002) GE- 1 -FRICGEADH 3   [GE-FRICGEADH]
(3003) GE- 1 -HEEOLD 3   [GE-HEEOLD]
(3009) GE- 1 -BRINGAN 3   [GE-BRINGAN]
(3036) GE- 1 -GONGEN 9   [GE-GONGEN]
(3044) GE- 1 -WAAT 3   [GE-WAAT]
(3062) GE- 1 -WRECEN 4   [GE-WRECEN]
(3072) GE- 1 -HEADHE-9-ROD 2   [GE-HEADHEROD]
(3079) GE- 1 -LAEAERAN 3   [GE-LAEAERAN]
(3084) GE- 1 -SCEEAWOD 2   [GE-SCEEAWOD]
(3085) GE- 1 -GONGEN 4   [GE-GONGEN]
(3088) GE- 1 -RYYMED 9   [GE-RYYMED]
(3090) GE- 1 -FEENG 4   [GE-FEENG]
(3094) GE- 1 -WITTIG 3   [GE-WITTIG]
```

```
(3096) GE- 1 -WORHTON 3   [GE-WORHTON]
(3109) GE- 1 -THO-2-LIAN. 5   [GE-THOLIAN]
(3117) GE- 1 -BAEAEDED 4   [GE-BAEAEDED]
(3130) GE- 1 -FEREDON 4   [GE-FEREDON]
(3137) GE- 1 -GIREDAN 2   [GE-GIREDAN]
(3147) GE- 1 -BROCEN 3   [GE-BROCEN]
(1973) -GE- 1 -STEALLA 9   [LIND-GE-STEALLA]
(2169) -GE- 1 -STEALLAN 3   [HOND-GE-STEALLAN]
(2286) -GE- 1 -WEORC 9   [FYRN-GE-WEORC]
(2412) -GE- 1 -WINNE 9   [YYDH-GE-WINNE]
(2728) -GE- 1 -RIIMES 4   [DOOGOR-GE-RIIMES]
(2730) -GE- 1 -WAEAEDU 3   [GUUDH-GE-WAEAEDU]
(2818) -GE- 1 -HYGDU= 4   [BREEOST-GE-HYGDU=]
(2851) -GE- 1 -WAEAEDU 2   [GUUDH-GE-WAEAEDU]
(2871) -GE- 1 -WAEAEDU 3   [GUUDH-GE-WAEAEDU]
(2873) -GE- 1 -STEALLU= 9   [FYRD-GE-STEALLU=]
(2903) -GE- 1 -WINNA 5   [EALDOR-GE-WINNA]
(3092) -GE- 1 -STREEONA 1   [HORD-GE-STREEONA]
(1995) WAEL- 1 -GAEAEST 3   [WAEL-GAEAEST]
(2028) WAEL- 1 -FAEAEHDHA 4   [WAEL-FAEAEHDHA]
(2031) BON- 1 -GAAR 4   [BON-GAAR]
(2068) UN- 1 -FAEAECNE 9   [UN-FAEAECNE]
(2076) ON- 1 -SAEAEGE 5   [ON-SAEAEGE]
(2089) UN- 1 -SYNNIGNE 4   [UN-SYNNIGNE]
(2109) SAAR- 1 -+LIIC 3   [SAAR-LIIC]
(2119) FOR- 1 -NAM 3   [FOR-NAM]
(2120) UN- 1 -HYYRE 6   [UN-HYYRE]
(2122) ELLEN- 1 -LIICE 4   [ELLEN-LIICE]
(2233) GEEAR- 1 -DA-9-GU= 8   [GEEAR-DAGU=]
(2266) ON- 1 -SENDED. 5   [ON-SENDED]
(2268) UN- 1 -BLIIDHE 2   [UN-BLIIDHE]
(2284) ON- 1 -BOREN 4   [ON-BOREN]
(2287) ON- 1 -+WOOC 3   [ON-WOOC]
(2300) ON- 1 -FAND 9   [ON-FAND]
(2302) ON- 1 -+BAAD 5   [ON-BAAD]
(2345) OFER- 1 -HOGODE 2   [OFER-HOGODE]
(2364) ON- 1 -GEEAN. 9   [ON-GEEAN]
(2407) ON- 1 -STEALDE 3   [ON-STEALDE]
(2427) OR- 1 -LEG- 4   [OR-LEG-HWIILA]
(2443) UN- 1 -WRECEN 4   [UN-WRECEN]
(2449) IN- 1 -FROOD 5   [IN-FROOD]
(2508) BAAN- 1 -HUUS 9   [BAAN-HUUS]
(2601) ON- 1 -WENDAN 3   [ON-WENDAN]
(2640) ON- 1 -MUNDE 3   [ON-MUNDE]
(2661) WAEL- 1 -+REEC 3   [WAEL-REEC]
(2677) FOR- 1 -GRUNDEN 4   [FOR-GRUNDEN]
(2701) ON- 1 -GON 3   [ON-GON]
(2711) ON- 1 -GON 3   [ON-GON]
(2713) ON- 1 -FAND 3   [ON-FAND]
(2721) UN- 1 -GE- 0   [UN-GE-METE]
(2723) ON- 1 -SPEEON. 6   [ON-SPEEON]
(2748) ON- 1 -GITE 3   [ON-GITE]
(2772) ON- 1 -SYYN 3   [ON-SYYN]
(2784) FYR- 1 -WET 2   [FYR-WET]
(2790) ON- 1 -GON 4   [ON-GON]
(2811) GAAR- 1 -WIGAN 9   [GAAR-WIGAN]
(2821) UN- 1 -FROODU= 3   [UN-FROODU=]
(2834) AN- 1 -SYYN 3   [AN-SYYN]
(2841) ON- 1 -FUNDE 3   [ON-FUNDE]
(2849) MAN- 1 -DRYHTNES 4   [MAN-DRYHTNES]
(2857) ON- 1 -CIRRAN 4   [ON-CIRRAN]
(2863) UN- 1 -LEEOFE 3   [UN-LEEOFE]
(2878) ON- 1 -GAN 2   [ON-GAN]
(2911) OR- 1 -LEG- 2   [OR-LEG-HWIILE]
(2924) ONGEN- 1 -DHIIO 3   [ONGEN-DHIIO]
```

245

```
(2926) ON- 1 -MEED-9-LAN 2    [ON-MEEDLAN]
(2944) ON- 1 -GEEATON 3    [ON-GEEATON]
(2951) ONGEN- 1 -THIIO 3    [ONGEN-THIIO]
(2951) ON- 1 -CIRDE 5    [ON-CIRDE]
(2954) ON- 1 -SACAN 3    [ON-SACAN]
(2968) FOR- 1 -GEALD 0    [FOR-GEALD]
(2971) WON- 1 -REEDES 3    [WON-REEDES]
(2986) ONGEN- 1 -DHIIO 9    [ONGEN-DHIIO]
(2996) MIDDAN- 1 -GEARDE 4    [MIDDAN-GEARDE]
(3021) FOR- 1 -DHON 3    [FOR-DHON]
(3034) HLIM- 1 -BED 2    [HLIM-BED]
(3086) ON- 1 -TYHTE. 5    [ON-TYHTE]
(3132) WEALL- 1 -CLIF 3    [WEALL-CLIF]
(3149) MON- 1 -DRYHTNES 8    [MON-DRYHTNES]
(3166) FOR- 1 -LEETON 3    [FOR-LEETON]
(3168) UN- 1 -NYT 2    [UN-NYT]
(1965) WORULD- 1 -CANDEL 3    [WORULD-CANDEL]
(2072) HOND- 1 -RAEAES 3    [HOND-RAEAES]
(2092) UPP- 1 -RIHTE 9    [UPP-RIHTE]
(2188) ED- 1 -WEN-2-DEN 3    [ED-WENDEN]
(2274) FOLD- 1 -BUUEND. 9    [FOLD-BUUEND]
(2299) AET- 1 -HWEARF 9    [AET-HWEARF]
(2302) HORD- 1 -WEARD 9    [HORD-WEARD]
(2355) HOND- 1 -GE- 0    [*HOND-GE-MOOTA]
(2377) FREEON-1-D- 1 -LAARU= 9    [FREEOND-LAARU=]
(2392) EEAD- 1 -GILSE 5    [EEAD-GILSE]
(2510) BEEOT- 1 -WORDU= 3    [BEEOT-WORDU=]
(2559) BORD- 1 -RAND 3    [BORD-RAND]
(2608) FOL-1-C- 1 -RIHTA 9    [FOLC-RIHTA]
(2670) IN-1-WIT- 1 -GAEST 9    [INWIT-GAEST]
(2847) AET- 1 -SOMNE 9    [AET-SOMNE]
(2878) AET- 1 -GIFAN 3    [AET-GIFAN]
(2972) ()HONU*OND- 1 -SLYHT 9    [*OND-SLYHT]
(3138) -WAAC- 1 -LIICNE 3    [UN-WAAC-LIICNE]
(3149) MOOD- 1 -CEARE 3    [MOOD-CEARE]
(3172) WORD- 1 -GYD 1    [WORD-GYD]
(1953) LIIF- 1 -GE- 2    [LIIF-GE-SCEAFTA]
(2010) HROODH- 1 -GAAR 4    [HROODH-GAAR]
(2147) HEALF- 1 -DENES 3    [HEALF-DENES]
(2155) HROODH- 1 -+GAAR 5    [HROODH-GAAR]
(2251) OF- 1 -GEAF 1    [OF-GEAF]
(2412) YYDH- 1 -GE- 1    [YYDH-GE-WINNE]
(2437) HAEDH- 1 -CYN 9    [HAEDH-CYN]
(2469) OF- 1 -GEAF 4    [OF-GEAF]
(2521) WIDH- 1 -GRIIPAN 4    [WIDH-GRIIPAN]
(2871) GUUDH- 1 -GE- 1    [GUUDH-GE-WAEAEDU]
(3060) OF- 1 -SLOOH 4    [OF-SLOOH]
(3179) HEORDH- 1 -G=- 1    [HEORDH-G=-NEEATAS]
(2173) WEALH- 1 -DHEEO 5    [WEALH-DHEEO]
(2176) BEEAH- 1 -DHEGE 4    [BEEAH-DHEGE]
(2587) ECG- 1 -DHEEOWES 9    [ECG-DHEEOWES]
(2590) AEAEG- 1 -HWYLC 2    [AEAEG-HWYLC]
(2602) WEEOX- 1 -STAANES 0    [WEEOX-STAANES]
(2754) HRING- 1 -NET 2    [HRING-NET]
(2844) AEAEG- 1 -()HWAEDHRE*HWAEDHER 4    [*AEAEG-HWAEDHER]
(2907) WIIH- 1 -STAANES 3    [WIIH-STAANES]
(2953) WIIG- 1 -CRAEFT 3    [WIIG-CRAEFT]
(3076) WIIH- 1 -STAANES 4    [WIIH-STAANES]
(3158) WAEAEG- 1 -LIIDHENDU= 3    [WAEAEG-LIIDHENDU=]
(2637) G=- 1 -LU=-1-PE 5    [G=-LU=PE]
(3146) G=- 1 -LAEG 3    [G=-LAEG]
(3166) G=- 1 -STREEON 9    [G=-STREEON]
(3179) -G=- 1 -NEEATAS 1    [HEORDH-G=-NEEATAS]

(1971) BEEO- 2 -WULFES 3    [BEEO-WULFES]
```

```
(1999) $BIIO- 2 -WULF 4    [BIIO-WULF]
(2194) BIIO- 2 -WULFES 9   [BIIO-WULFES]
(2263) GLEEO- 2 -BEEAMES 9    [GLEEO-BEEAMES]
(2285) FEEA- 2 -SCEAFTU= 3    [FEEA-SCEAFTU=]
(2324) BIIO- 2 -WULFE 3    [BIIO-WULFE]
(2389) BIIO- 2 -WULF 4    [BIIO-WULF]
(2425) BIIO- 2 -WULF 3    [BIIO-WULF]
(2429) FREEA- 2 -WINE 5    [FREEA-WINE]
(2495) SWIIO- 2 -RIICE 5    [SWIIO-RIICE]
(2842) BIIO- 2 -WULFE 9    [BIIO-WULFE]
(2907) BIIO- 2 -WULFE 4    [BIIO-WULFE]
(1986) SAEAE- 2 -GEEATA 3    [SAEAE-GEEATA]
(2948) TOO- 2 -WEHTON. 4    [TOO-WEHTON]
(1974) HEADHO- 2 -LAACES. 5    [HEADHO-LAACES]
(2067) HEADHO- 2 -()BEARNA*BEARDNA 4    [*HEADHO-BEARDNA]
(2106) FELA- 2 -FRICGENDE 8    [FELA-FRICGENDE]
(2136) GRYRE- 2 -LIICNE 9    [GRYRE-LIICNE]
(2185) MEDO- 2 -BENCE 4    [MEDO-BENCE]
(2256) BE- 2 -FEALLEN 4    [BE-FEALLEN]
(2274) BE- 2 -FANGEN 2    [BE-FANGEN]
(2317) NEARO- 2 -FAAGES 3    [NEARO-FAAGES]
(2376) CYNE- 2 -+DOOM 3    [CYNE-DOOM]
(2466) HEADHO- 2 -RINC 3    [HEADHO-RINC]
(2468) BE- 2 -LAMP 1    [BE-LAMP]
(2553) HEADHO- 2 -TORHT 3    [HEADHO-TORHT]
(2647) BE- 2 -HOOFADH 3    [BE-HOOFADH]
(2660) ()BRYDU*BEADU- 2 -SCRUUD 8    [*BEADU-SCRUUD]
(2691) HEADHO- 2 -GRIM 2    [HEADHO-GRIM]
(2829) HEADHO- 2 -SCEAR-9-()DE*PE 4    [*HEADHO-SCEARPE]
(2853) FEEDHE- 2 -CEMPA 4    [FEEDHE-CEMPA]
(2867) EALU- 2 -BENCE 3    [EALU-BENCE]
(2896) ENDE- 2 -DOOGORES 9    [ENDE-DOOGORES]
(2924) BE- 2 -SNYDHEDE 3    [BE-SNYDHEDE]
(2950) FELA- 2 -GEOOMOR 4    [FELA-GEOOMOR]
(3022) BE- 2 -WUNDEN 4    [BE-WUNDEN]
(3065) MEDU- 2 -SELD 3    [MEDU-SELD]
(3139) HILDE- 2 -BORDU= 9    [HILDE-BORDU=]
(3146) BE- 2 -WUNDEN 2    [BE-WUNDEN]
(3161) BE- 2 -WORHTON 3    [BE-WORHTON]
(3169) HILDE- 2 -DEEORE 3    [HILDE-DEEORE]
(3175) WINE- 2 -DRYH= 1    [WINE-DRYH=]
(1983) HIGE- 2 -LAAC 3    [HIGE-LAAC]
(2914) HIGE- 2 -LAAC 2    [HIGE-LAAC]
(2952) HIGE- 2 -LAACES 9    [HIGE-LAACES]
(1963) $$GE- 2 -WAAT 3    [GE-WAAT]
(1969) GE- 2 -FRUUNON 5    [GE-FRUUNON]
(1977) GE- 2 -NAES 4    [GE-NAES]
(2005) GE- 2 -WRAEC 4    [GE-WRAEC]
(2024) GE- 2 -HAATEN 9    [GE-HAATEN]
(2045) GE- 2 -HYGD 8    [GE-HYGD]
(2087) GE- 2 -GYRWED 3    [GE-GYRWED]
(2192) GE- 2 -GYREDE 3    [GE-GYREDE]
(2195) GE- 2 -SEALDE 4    [GE-SEALDE]
(2298) GE- 2 -FEH 2    [GE-FEH]
(2304) GE- 2 -BOL-1-GEN 5    [GE-BOLGEN]
(2395) GE- 2 -WRAEC 3    [GE-WRAEC]
(2427) GE- 2 -MON. 9    [GE-MON]
(2450) GE- 2 -MYNDGAD 5    [GE-MYNDGAD]
(2460) $$GE- 2 -WIITEDH 4    [GE-WIITEDH]
(2478) GE- 2 -FREMEDON. 5    [GE-FREMEDON]
(2511) GE- 2 -NEEDHDE 5    [GE-NEEDHDE]
(2531) GE- 2 -DYYGAN. 5    [GE-DYYGAN]
(2533) GE- 2 -MET 2    [GE-MET]
(2549) GE- 2 -DYYGAN 9    [GE-DYYGAN]
(2569) GE- 2 -WAAT 1    [GE-WAAT]
```

247

```
(2584) GE- 2 -+SWAAC 4    [GE-SWAAC]
(2597) GE- 2 -STOODON 3    [GE-STOODON]
(2606) GE- 2 -MUNDE 9    [GE-MUNDE]
(2624) GE- 2 -WAAT 4    [GE-WAAT]
(2628) GE- 2 -MEALT 2    [GE-MEALT]
(2629) GE- 2 -WAAC 9    [GE-WAAC]
(2630) GE- 2 -GAAN 3    [GE-GAAN]
(2644) GE- 2 -FREM-2-MAN-1-NE 5    [GE-FREMMANNE]
(2666) GE- 2 -DREEOSAN 3    [GE-DREEOSAN]
(2674) GE- 2 -FREM-1-MAN 5    [GE-FREMMAN]
(2676) GE- 2 -EEODE 5    [GE-EEODE]
(2703) GE- 2 -WEEOLD 2    [GE-WEEOLD]
(2706) GE- 2 -FYLDAN 9    [GE-FYLDAN]
(2711) GE- 2 -WEORCES. 3    [GE-WEORCES]
(2758) GE- 2 -TENGE 5    [GE-TENGE]
(2777) GE- 2 -SCOOD 3    [GE-SCOOD]
(2802) GE- 2 -WYRCEAN. 6    [GE-WYRCEAN]
(2822) GE- 2 -SEAH 4    [GE-SEAH]
(2844) GE- 2 -FEERED 2    [GE-FEERED]
(2856) GE- 2 -HEALDAN 9    [GE-HEALDAN]
(2875) GE- 2 -WRAEC 3    [GE-WRAEC]
(2882) GE- 2 -WITTE 5    [GE-WITTE]
(2889) GE- 2 -FRICGEAN 3    [GE-FRICGEAN]
(2916) GE- 2 -()HNAEGDON*NAEAEGDON 9    [*GE-NAEAEGDON]
(2917) GE- 2 -EEODON 4    [GE-EEODON]
(2949) GE- 2 -WAAT 1    [GE-WAAT]
(2973) GE- 2 -SCER 9    [GE-SCER]
(2976) GE- 2 -WYRPTE 9    [GE-WYRPTE]
(2994) GE- 2 -HWAEDHRU= 3    [GE-HWAEDHRU=]
(2996) GE- 2 -SLOOGON. 3    [GE-SLOOGON]
(3038) GE- 2 -SEEGAN 4    [GE-SEEGAN]
(3056) GE- 2 -HYLD 3    [GE-HYLD]
(3057) GE- 2 -MET 2    [GE-MET]
(3058) GE- 2 -SYYNE 5    [GE-SYYNE]
(3059) GE- 2 -HYYDDE 5    [GE-HYYDDE]
(3063) GE- 2 -FEERE. 5    [GE-FEERE]
(3073) GE- 2 -WIITNAD 2    [GE-WIITNAD]
(3075) GE- 2 -SCEEAWOOD. 5    [GE-SCEEAWOOD]
(3094) GE- 2 -SPRAEC 3    [GE-SPRAEC]
(3102) GE- 2 -THRAEC 3    [GE-THRAEC]
(3107) GE- 2 -FERIAN 3    [GE-FERIAN]
(3158) GE- 2 -SYYNE 3    [GE-SYYNE]
(1953) -GE- 2 -SCEAFTA 4    [LIIF-GE-SCEAFTA]
(2240) -GE- 2 -STREEONA 5    [LONG-GE-STREEONA]
(2596) -GE- 2 -STEALLAN 9    [*HAND-GE-STEALLAN]
(2617) -GE- 2 -WAEAEDU 5    [GUUDH-GE-WAEAEDU]
(2657) -GE- 2 -WYRHT 3    [EALD-GE-WYRHT]
(2737) -GE- 2 -SCEAFTA 4    [MAEAEL-GE-SCEAFTA]
(2835) -GE- 2 -WEORCE 9    [HOND-GE-WEORCE]
(3042) -GE- 2 -MEARCES 9    [FOOT-GE-MEARCES]
(1940) CWEEN- 2 -LIIC 3    [CWEEN-LIIC]
(1944) ON- 2 -HOOHSNOD*E 3    [ON-HOOHSNOO*E]
(1952) GUM- 2 -STOOLE 9    [GUM-STOOLE]
(1957) FOR- 2 -DHAAM 1    [FOR-DHAAM]
(1976) INNAN- 2 -WEARD 4    [INNAN-WEARD]
(2000) UN- 2 -DYRNE 4    [UN-DYRNE]
(2044) ON- 2 -GINNEDH 4    [ON-GINNEDH]
(2051) WAEL- 2 -STOOWE 4    [WAEL-STOOWE]
(2074) AEAEFEN- 2 -GROM 5    [AEAEFEN-GROM]
(2081) IIDEL- 2 -HENDE. 7    [IIDEL-HENDE]
(2140) UN- 2 -SOOFTE 4    [UN-SOOFTE]
(2145) FOR- 2 -LOREN 9    [FOR-LOREN]
(2182) GIN- 2 -FAESTAN 9    [GIN-FAESTAN]
(2221) WYRM- 2 -()HORDA*HORD 9    [*WYRM-HORD]
(2256) FEOR- 2 -MYND 9    [FEOR-MYND]
```

248

```
(2335) FOR- 2 -GRUNDEN 5    [FOR-GRUNDEN]
(2368) AAN- 2 -HAGA 3    [AAN-HAGA]
(2371) EETHEL- 2 -STOOLAS 4    [EETHEL-STOOLAS]
(2387) ONGEN- 2 -DHIIOES 5    [ONGEN-DHIIOES]
(2413) UN- 2 -HIIORE 4    [UN-HIIORE]
(2492) FOR- 2 -GEAF 3    [FOR-GEAF]
(2494) GAAR- 2 -DENU= 4    [GAAR-DENU=]
(2531) WAEL- 2 -RAEAESE 4    [WAEL-RAEAESE]
(2545) STAAN- 2 -BOGAN 3    [STAAN-BOGAN]
(2554) ON- 2 -HREE-2-RED 3    [ON-HREERED]
(2559) ON- 2 -+SWAAF 9    [ON-SWAAF]
(2586) AEAER- 2 -+GOOD 4    [AEAER-GOOD]
(2591) LAEAEN- 2 -DAGAS 9    [LAEAEN-DAGAS]
(2604) MON- 2 -DRYHTEN 3    [MON-DRYHTEN]
(2616) FOR- 2 -GEAF 4    [FOR-GEAF]
(2667) AN- 2 -HYYDIG 4    [AN-HYYDIG]
(2680) FOR- 2 -BAERST 3    [FOR-BAERST]
(2718) STAAN- 2 -BOGAN 9    [STAAN-BOGAN]
(2737) MAEAEL- 2 -GE- 2    [MAEAEL-GE-SCEAFTA]
(2761) FYRN- 2 -MANNA 3    [FYRN-MANNA]
(2763) EARM- 2 -BEEAGA 3    [EARM-BEEAGA]
(2787) FOR- 2 -LEET. 3    [FOR-LEET]
(2861) FOR- 2 -LEEAS. 4    [FOR-LEEAS]
(2872) FOR- 2 -WURPE. 6    [FOR-WURPE]
(2900) WIL- 2 -GEOFA 3    [WIL-GEOFA]
(2908) UN- 2 -LIFIGENDU= 4    [UN-LIFIGENDU=]
(2942) AEAER- 2 -DAEGE 4    [AEAER-DAEGE]
(2947) WAEL- 2 -RAEAES 9    [WAEL-RAEAES]
(2961) ON-9-GEN- 2 -DHIIOW 4    [ONGEN-DHIIOW]
(2965) WON- 2 -REEDING 9    [WON-REEDING]
(2984) WAEL- 2 -STOOWE 4    [WAEL-STOOWE]
(2986) IIREN- 2 -BYRNAN 4    [IIREN-BYRNAN]
(2993) OFER- 2 -MAADHMUM 4    [OFER-MAADHMUM]
(3032) WOLLEN- 2 -TEEARE 4    [WOLLEN-TEEARE]
(3039) WIDHER- 2 -RAEHTES 3    [WIDHER-RAEHTES]
(3051) EEACEN- 2 -CRAEFTIG 4    [EEACEN-CRAEFTIG]
(3127) OR- 2 -WEARDE 3    [OR-WEARDE]
(3138) UN- 2 -WAAC- 1    [UN-WAAC-LIICNE]
(3151) ()+UNDEN*BUNDEN- 2 -HEORDE 9    [*BUNDEN-HEORDE]
(3173) EORL- 2 -SCIPE 3    [EORL-SCIPE]
(3173) ELLEN- 2 -WEORC 2    [ELLEN-WEORC]
(1948) GOLD- 2 -HRO-9-DEN 3    [GOLD-HRODEN]
(1991) ()WIDH*WIID- 2 -CUUDHNE 9    [*WIID-CUUDHNE]
(2025) GOLD- 2 -HRODEN 4    [GOLD-HRODEN]
(2035) DRYHT- 2 -BEARN 4    [DRYHT-BEARN]
(2127) AET- 2 -BAER 5    [AET-BAER]
(2152) HEEAFOD- 2 -SEGN. 6    [HEEAFOD-SEGN]
(2215) NAAT- 2 -HWYLC 8    [NAAT-HWYLC]
(2245) ()HARD*HORD- 2 -WYRDHNE 9    [*HORD-WYRDHNE]
(2255) ()+++*HYR-9-STED- 2 -GOLDE 5    [*HYRSTED-GOLDE]
(2292) WRAEAEC- 2 -SIIDH 3    [WRAEAEC-SIIDH]
(2311) SINC- 2 -GIFAN 4    [SINC-GIFAN]
(2363) HET- 2 -WARE 4    [HET-WARE]
(2462) WIIC- 2 -STEDE 4    [WIIC-STEDE]
(2596) ()HEAND*HAND- 2 -GE- 2    [*HAND-GE-STEALLAN]
(2616) EALD- 2 -SWEORD 4    [EALD-SWEORD]
(2628) MOOD- 2 -SEFA 6    [MOOD-SEFA]
(2650) GLEED- 2 -EGESA 9    [GLEED-EGESA]
(2651) LIIC- 2 -HAMAN 4    [LIIC-HAMAN]
(2694) THEEOD- 2 -CYNINGES 3    [THEEOD-CYNINGES]
(2708) SIB- 2 -AEDHELINGAS 3    [SIB-AEDHELINGAS]
(2748) GOLD- 2 -AEAEHT 3    [GOLD-AEAEHT]
(2761) FEOR-9-MEND- 2 -LEEASE 4    [FEORMEND-LEEASE]
(2783) EFT- 2 -SIIDHES 3    [EFT-SIIDHES]
(2792) BREEOST- 2 -HORD 3    [BREEOST-HORD]
```

249

```
(2798) SWYLT- 2 -DAEGE 4    [SWYLT-DAEGE]
(2815) METOD- 2 -SCEAFTE 9    [METOD-SCEAFTE]
(2830) WIID- 2 -FLOGA 3    [WIID-FLOGA]
(2835) HILD- 2 -FRUMAN 3    [HILD-FRUMAN]
(2835) HOND- 2 -GE- 2    [HOND-GE-WEORCE]
(2843) DRYHT- 2 -MAADHMA 4    [DRYHT-MAADHMA]
(2873) FOLC- 2 -CYNING 4    [FOLC-CYNING]
(2873) FYRD- 2 -GE- 1    [FYRD-GE-STEALLU=]
(2884) SINC- 2 -THEGO 4    [SINC-THEGO]
(2886) LOND- 2 -RIHTES 2    [LOND-RIHTES]
(2891) EDWIIT- 2 -LIIF 9    [EDWIIT-LIIF]
(2894) MOOD- 2 -GIOOMOR 4    [MOOD-GIOOMOR]
(2896) EFT- 2 -CYMES 3    [EFT-CYMES]
(2915) FLOT- 2 -HERGE 3    [FLOT-HERGE]
(2916) HET- 2 -WARE 3    [HET-WARE]
(2935) HLAAFORD- 2 -LEEASE 9    [HLAAFORD-LEEASE]
(2979) EALD- 2 -SWEORD 3    [EALD-SWEORD]
(2999) FEEONU- 2 -SCIPE 5    [FEEOND-SCIPE]
(3010) +AAD- 2 -FAERE 5    [AAD-FAERE]
(3042) FOOT- 2 -GE- 2    [FOOT-GE-MEARGES]
(3043) LYFT- 2 -WYNNE 4    [LYFT-WYNNE]
(3083) WORULD- 2 -ENDE 9    [WORULD-ENDE]
(3092) HORD- 2 -GE- 1    [HORD-GE-STREEONA]
(3118) SCILD- 2 -WEALL 4    [SCILD-WEALL]
(1959) WIIS- 2 -DOOME 4    [WIIS-DOOME]
(2020) HROODH- 2 -GAARES 3    [HROODH-GAARES]
(2032) OF- 2 -THYNCAN 3    [OF-THYNCAN]
(2064) AADH- 2 -()SWEORDH*SWEORD 3    [*AADH-SWEORD]
(2097) LIIF- 2 -WYNNA 1    [LIIF-WYNNA]
(2143) HEALF- 2 -DENES. 9    [HEALF-DENES]
(2273) NIIDH- 2 -DRACA 3    [NIIDH-DRACA]
(2357) FREES- 2 -LONDUM 5    [FREES-LONDUM]
(2434) HAEDH- 2 -CYN. 6    [HAEDH-CYN]
(2528) GUUDH- 2 -FLOGAN 3    [GUUDH-FLOGAN]
(2566) STIIDH- 2 -MOOD 3    [STIIDH-MOOD]
(2583) HREEDH- 2 -SIGORA 5    [HREEDH-SIGORA]
(2584) GUUDH- 2 -BILL 3    [GUUDH-BILL]
(2636) GUUDH- 2 -GE- 9    [GUUDH-GE-TAAWA]
(2648) GUUDH- 2 -RINCA 4    [GUUDH-RINCA]
(2699) NIIDH- 2 -GAEST 4    [NIIDH-GAEST]
(2719) EORDH- 2 -RECED 3    [EORDH-RECED]
(2730) GUUDH- 2 -GE- 1    [GUUDH-GE-WAEAEDU]
(2735) GUUDH- 2 -WINU= 9    [GUUDH-WINU=]
(2851) GUUDH- 2 -GE- 1    [GUUDH-GE-WAEAEDU]
(2861) EEDH- 2 -BEGEETE 3    [EEDH-BEGEETE]
(2957) EORDH- 2 -WEALL. 9    [EORDH-WEALL]
(2991) GUUDH- 2 -RAEAES 2    [GUUDH-RAEAES]
(3036) GUUDH- 2 -CYNING 4    [GUUDH-CYNING]
(3062) WRAADH- 2 -LIICE 4    [WRAADH-LIICE]
(3064) LIIF- 2 -GE- 9    [LIIF-GE-SCEAFTA]
(3090) EORDH- 2 -WEALL 4    [EORDH-WEALL]
(1993) SORH- 2 -WYLMU= 4    [SORH-WYLMU=]
(2119) SORH- 2 -FULL 4    [SORH-FULL]
(2120) WIIG- 2 -HETE 9    [WIIG-HETE]
(2177) ECG- 2 -DHEEOWES. 6    [ECG-DHEEOWES]
(2240) LONG- 2 -GE- 2    [LONG-GE-STREEONA]
(2339) WIIG- 2 -BORD 2    [WIIG-BORD]
(2367) ECG- 2 -DHEEOWES 9    [ECG-DHEEOWES]
(2398) ECG- 2 -DHIIOWES. 7    [ECG-DHIIOWES]
(2425) ECG- 2 -DHEEOWES 5    [ECG-DHEEOWES]
(2441) FEOH- 2 -LEEAS 2    [FEOH-LEEAS]
(2460) SORH- 2 -LEEODH 9    [SORH-LEEODH]
(2489) FEORH- 2 -SWENG 3    [FEORH-SWENG]
(2602) $$WIIG- 2 -LAAF 3    [WIIG-LAAF]
(2607) WAEAEG- 2 -MUNDINGA 5    [WAEAEG-MUNDINGA]
```

```
2613) WEEOH- 2 -()STANES*STAAN 3  [*WEEOH-STAAN]
2740) FEORH- 2 -BENNU= 4  [FEORH-BENNU=]
2745) WIIG- 2 -LAAF 9  [WIIG-LAAF]
2786) WONG- 2 -STEDE 3  [WONG-STEDE]
2792) THURH- 2 -BRAEC. 4  [THURH-BRAEC]
2814) WAEAEG- 2 -MUNDINGA 5  [WAEAEG-MUNDINGA]
2827) WOOH- 2 -BOGEN 4  [WOOH-BOGEN]
2887) MAEAEG- 2 -BURGE 3  [MAEAEG-BURGE]
2911) -LEG- 2 -HWIILE 5  [OR-LEG-HWIILE]
2933) FEORH- 2 -GE- 0  [FEORH-GE-NIIDHLAN]
2940) GALG- 2 -()TREOWU*TREEOWU= 4  [*GALG-TREEOWU=]
2942) SAARIG- 2 -MOODU= 3  [SAARIG-MOODU=]
3017) HRING- 2 -WEOR-9-DHUNGE 4  [HRING-WEORDHUNGE]
3076) WIIG- 2 -+LAAF 9  [WIIG-LAAF]
3084) HEEAH- 2 -GE- 4  [HEEAH-GE-SCEAP]
3152) SORG- 2 -CEARIG 8  [SORG-CEARIG]
2543) GU=- 2 -CYSTU= 2  [GU=-CYSTU=]
2726) G=- 2 -DROGEN 4  [G=-DROGEN]
2765) GU=- 2 -CYNNES 3  [GU=-CYNNES]
2856) FRU=- 2 -GAARE 4  [FRU=-GAARE]
2930) BRI=- 2 -WIISAN 5  [BRI=-WIISAN]
3165) G=- 2 -NUM= 2  [G=-NUM=]

2373) FEEA- 3 -SCEAFTE 9  [FEEA-SCEAFTE]
2383) SWIIO- 3 -RIICE 4  [SWIIO-RIICE]
2627) FREEO- 3 -DRYHTNE 9  [FREEO-DRYHTNE]
3021) GLEEO- 3 -DREEAM 9  [GLEEO-OREEAM]
2886) AA- 3 -LICGEAN 9  [AA-LICGEAN]
1945) EALO- 3 -DRINCENDE 4  [EALO-DRINCENDE]
1976) FEEDHE- 3 -GESTU= 5  [FEEDHE-GESTU=]
1980) MEODU- 3 -SCENCU= 4  [MEODU-SCENCU=]
2021) EALU- 3 -WAEAEGE 3  [EALU-WAEAEGE]
2049) HERE- 3 -GRIIMAN 4  [HERE-GRIIMAN]
2085) ()GEAREO*GEARO- 3 -FOLM 3  [*GEARO-FOLM]
2086) SEARO- 3 -BENOU= 4  [SEARO-BENOU=]
2107) HILDE- 3 -DEEOR 4  [HILDE-DEEOR]
2155) HILDE- 3 -SCEORP 9  [HILDE-SCEORP]
2161) HEORO- 3 -WEARDE 5  [HEORO-WEARDE]
2191) HEADHO- 3 -ROOF 2  [HEADHO-ROOF]
2196) BREGO- 3 -STOOL 5  [BREGO-STOOL]
2202) HILDE- 3 -MEECEAS 4  [HILDE-MEECEAS]
2206) HERE- 3 -RIICES 3  [HERE-RIICES]
2212) BE- 3 -WEOTODE 9  [BE-WEOTODE]
2252) SELE- 3 -DREEAM 9  [SELE-DREEAM]
2257) BEADO- 3 -GRIIMAN 3  [BEADO-GRIIMAN]
2282) FRIODHO- 3 -WAEAERE 3  [FRIODHO-WAEAERE]
2358) HIORO- 3 -DRYNCUM 4  [HIORO-DRYNCUM]
2362) HILDE- 3 -GEAT-2-WA 3  [HILDE-GEATWA]
2389) BREGO- 3 -STOOL 5  [BREGO-STOOL]
2404) BEALO- 3 -NIIDH 4  [BEALO-NIIDH]
2457) BE- 3 -ROFENE 9  [BE-ROFENE]
2463) HERE- 3 -BEALDE 4  [HERE-BEALDE]
2474) HERE- 3 -NIIDH 3  [HERE-NIIDH]
2507) HILDE- 3 -GRAAP 3  [HILDE-GRAAP]
2522) HEADHU- 3 -FYYRES 2  [HEADHU-FYYRES]
2539) HIORO- 3 -SERCEAN 2  [HIORO-SERCEAN]
2558) HILDE- 3 -+SWAAT 4  [HILDE-SWAAT]
2560) GRYRE- 3 -GIESTE 4  [GRYRE-GIESTE]
2565) BEALO- 3 -HYCGENDRA 9  [BEALO-HYCGENDRA]
2576) GRYRE- 3 -FAAH-1-NE 2  [GRYRE-FAAHNE]
2581) HEADHU- 3 -SWENGE 4  [HEADHU-SWENGE]
2583) HILDE- 3 -LEEOMAN 5  [HILDE-LEEOMAN]
2605) HERE- 3 -GRIIMAN 4  [HERE-GRIIMAN]
2613) WINE- 3 -LEEASU= 4  [WINE-LEEASU=]
2679) HILDE- 3 -BILLE 8  [HILDE-BILLE]
```

251

```
(2691) YMBE- 3 -FEENG 9    [YMBE-FEENG]
(2720) HEORO- 3 -DREEORIGNE 8    [HEORO-DREEORIGNE]
(2754) HEADHO- 3 -SIIOCU= 5    [HEADHO-SIIOCU=]
(2757) MAGO- 3 -THEGN 9    [MAGO-THEGN]
(2769) LEODHO- 3 -CRAEFTU= 4    [LEODHO-CRAEFTU=]
(2802) HEADHO- 3 -MAEAERE 4    [HEADHO-MAEAERE]
(2819) HEADHO- 3 -WYLMAS 3    [HEADHO-WYLMAS]
(2925) HREF-1-NA- 3 -WUDU 4    [HREFNA-WUDU]
(2959) FREODHO- 3 -WONG 3    [FREODHO-WONG]
(3035) ENDE- 3 -DAEG 3    [ENDE-DAEG]
(3041) BE- 3 -SWAEAELED 3    [BE-SWAEAELED]
(3067) SEARO- 3 -NIIDHAS 2    [SEARO-NIIDHAS]
(3102) SEARO- 3 -*GIMMA 8    [SEARO-*GIMMA]
(3111) HILDE- 3 -DIIOR 4    [HILDE-DIIOR]
(3124) HILDE- 3 -()RINC*RINCA 3    [*HILDE-RINCA]
(1943) LIGE- 3 -TORNE 2    [LIGE-TORNE]
(2408) HYGE- 3 -GIOOMOR 4    [HYGE-GIOOMOR]
(2442) HYGE- 3 -MEEDHE 4    [HYGE-MEEDHE]
(2756) SIGE- 3 -HREECHIG 4    [SIGE-HREEDHIG]
(2909) HIGE- 3 -MAEAEDHUM 9    [HIGE-MAEAEDHUM]
(2943) HYGE- 3 -LAACES 4    [HYGE-LAACES]
(2958) HIGE- 3 -()LACE*LAACES. 9    [*HIGE-LAACES]
(2988) HIGE- 3 -LAACE 1    [HIGE-LAACE]
(1967) GE- 3 -EEODON 5    [GE-EEODON]
(1975) GE- 3 -RYYMED 9    [GE-RYYMED]
(1979) GE- 3 -GREETTE 6    [GE-GREETTE]
(2190) GE- 3 -FETIAN. 6    [GE-FETIAN]
(2200) GE- 3 -IIODE 4    [GE-IIODE]
(2208) GE- 3 -HEEOLD 4    [GE-HEEOLD]
(2221) GE- 3 -WEALDU= 4    [GE-WEALDU=]
(2337) GE- 3 -WYRCEAN 4    [GE-WYRCEAN]
(2401) GE- 3 -WAAT 2    [GE-WAAT]
(2403) GE- 3 -FRUU-1-NEN 3    [GE-FRUUNEN]
(2479) GE- 3 -WRAEAECAN 4    [GE-WRAEAECAN]
(2481) GE- 3 -BOHTE 5    [GE-BOHTE]
(2515) GE- 3 -SEECEDH 4    [GE-SEECEDH]
(2516) GE- 3 -HWYLCNE 5    [GE-HWYLCNE]
(2540) GE- 3 -TRUWODE 4    [GE-TRUWODE]
(2645) GE- 3 -FRE-9-MEDE 4    [GE-FREMEDE]
(2692) GE- 3 -BLOODEGOD 3    [GE-BLOODEGOD]
(2810) GE- 3 -SEALDE 4    [GE-SEALDE]
(2821) GE- 3 -GONGEN 4    [GE-GONGEN]
(2837) GE- 3 -FRAEAEGE 4    [GE-FRAEAEGE]
(2852) GE- 3 -WEERGAD 2    [GE-WEERGAD]
(3016) GE- 3 -MYNDUM 9    [GE-MYNDUM]
(2232) -GE- 3 -STREEONA 7    [AEAER-GE-STREEONA]
(2623) -GE- 3 -WAEAE-2-DA 5    [GUUDH-GE-WAEAEDA]
(1940) CWEALM- 3 -BEALU 3    [CWEALM-BEALU]
(1955) MON- 3 -CYNNES 3    [MON-CYNNES]
(1957) EORMEN- 3 -CYNNES 4    [EORMEN-CYNNES]
(1958) GAAR- 3 -CEENE 2    [GAAR-CEENE]
(1968) ON-2-GEN- 3 -THEEO-1-ES. 2    [ONGEN-THEEOES]
(1985) FYR- 3 -WET 1    [FYR-WET]
(2039) FOR- 3 -LAEAEODDAN 3    [FOR-LAEAEODDAN]
(2051) WIDHER- 3 -GYLD 3    [WIDHER-GYLD]
(2094) FOR- 3 -GEALD 4    [FOR-GEALD]
(2101) WAEL- 3 -RAEAES 3    [WAEL-RAEAES]
(2110) RUUM- 3 -HEORT 3    [RUUM-HEORT]
(2123) FYRN- 3 -WITAN 5    [FYRN-WITAN]
(2126) FOR- 3 -BAERNAN 9    [FOR-BAERNAN]
(2133) EORL- 3 -SCIPE 4    [EORL-SCIPE]
(2175) SADOL- 3 -BEORHT 4    [SADOL-BEORHT]
(2189) TIIR- 3 -EEADIGU= 9    [TIIR-EEADIGU=]
(2213) STAAN- 3 -BEORH 4    [STAAN-BEORH]
(2241) EALL- 3 -GEARO 4    [EALL-GEARO]
```

```
2249) FOR- 3 -NAM. 6   [FOR-NAM]
2281) MAN- 3 -DRYHTNE 3   [MAN-DRYHTNE]
2286) FYRN- 3 -GE- 1   [FYRN-GE-WEORC]
2341) ()+4-9-()THEND*LAEAEN- 3 -DAGA 5   [*LAEAEN-DAGA]
2342) AEAER- 3 -GOOD 3   [AEAER-GOOD]
2353) FOR- 3 -GRAAP 3   [FOR-GRAAP]
2379) WEDER- 3 -GEEATU= 3   [WEDER-GEEATU=]
2396) CEAR- 3 -SIIDHUM 9   [CEAR-SIIDHUM]
2399) ELLEN- 3 -WEORCA 4   [ELLEN-WEORCA]
2405) MAADH-1-THUH- 3 -FAET 3   [MAADHTHUH-FAET]
2411) HOLM- 3 -WYLME 5   [HOLM-WYLME]
2428) SYFAN- 3 -WINTRE 5   [SYFAN-WINTRE]
2437) HORN- 3 -BOGAN. 6   [HORN-BOGAN]
2444) GEOOMOR- 3 -LIIC 3   [GEOOMOR-LIIC]
2514) +MAAN- 3 -SCEADHA 9   [MAAN-SCEADHA]
2551) WEDER- 3 -GEEATA 5   [WEDER-GEEATA]
2582) WAEL- 3 -FYYRE 4   [WAEL-FYYRE]
2606) FOR- 3 -GEAF. 5   [FOR-GEAF]
2609) FOR- 3 -HABBAN 2   [FOR-HABBAN]
2611) EEAN- 3 -MUN-1-DES 4   [EEAN-MUNDES]
2615) BRUUN- 3 -FAAGNE 4   [BRUUN-FAAGNE]
2622) EORL- 3 -SCIPE 4   [EORL-SCIPE]
2622) AEAER- 3 -FAEDER 3   [AEAER-FAEDER]
2635) BIIOR- 3 -SELE 9   [BIIOR-SELE]
2642) HELM- 3 -BEREND 9   [HELM-BEREND]
2647) MAN- 3 -DRYHTEN 3   [MAN-DRYHTEN]
2671) FYYR- 3 -WY-8-LMU= 3   [FYYR-WYLMU=]
2674) GAAR- 3 -WIGAN 9   [GAAR-WIGAN]
2678) MAEGEN- 3 -STRENGO 3   [MAEGEN-STRENGO]
2703) WAELL- 3 -SEAXE 3   [WAELL-SEAXE]
2725) WAEL- 3 -BLEEATE 4   [WAEL-BLEEATE]
2728) DOOGOR- 3 -GE- 1   [DOOGOR-GE-RIIMES]
2747) AEAER- 3 -WELAN 9   [AEAER-WELAN]
2766) OFER- 3 -HIIGIAN 4   [OFER-HIIGIAN]
2782) MIDDEL- 3 -NIHTUM 9   [MIDDEL-NIHTUM]
2785) COLLEN- 3 -FERDH 2   [COLLEN-FERDH]
2787) ELLEN- 3 -SIIOCNE 5   [ELLEN-SIIOCNE]
2833) MIDDEL- 3 -NIHTU= 9   [MIDDEL-NIHTU=]
2865) MON- 3 -DRYHTEN 4   [MON-DRYHTEN]
2868) HEAL- 3 -SITTENDU= 4   [HEAL-SITTENDU=]
2885) EEDHEL- 3 -WYN 8   [EEDHEL-WYN]
2894) MOR-9-GEN- 3 -LONGNE 4   [MORGEN-LONGNE]
2936) SIN- 3 -HERGE 4   [SIN-HERGE]
2955) FOR- 3 -STANDAN 3   [FOR-STANDAN]
2959) OFER- 3 -EEODON 4   [OFER-EEODON]
2962) BLONDEN- 3 -FEXA 5   [BLONDEN-FEXA]
2969) WAEL- 3 -HLEM 2   [WAEL-HLEM]
2998) HAAM- 3 -WEORDHUNGE 4   [HAAM-WEORDHUNGE]
3000) WAEL- 3 -NIIDH 3   [WAEL-NIIDH]
3033) SAAWUL- 3 -LEEASNE 9   [SAAWUL-LEEASNE]
3037) WUNDOR- 3 -DEEADHE 9   [WUNDOR-DEEADHE]
3063) ELLEN- 3 -+ROOF 3   [ELLEN-ROOF]
3072) HELL- 3 -BENDU= 3   [HELL-BENDU=]
3091) MAEGEN- 3 -BYRDHENNE 5   [MAEGEN-BYRDHENNE]
3097) BAEAEL- 3 -STEDE 3   [BAEAEL-STEDE]
3119) FULL- 3 -EEODE. 4   [FULL-EEODE]
3143) BAEAEL- 3 -FYYRA 9   [BAEAEL-FYYRA]
3147) +BAAN- 3 -+HUUS 3   [BAAN-HUUS]
3150) GIOOMOR- 3 -GYD 9   [GIOOMOR-GYD]
1947) INWIT- 3 -NIIDHA 9   [INWIT-NIIDHA]
1963) HOND- 3 -SCOLE 3   [HOND-SCOLE]
1973) LIND- 3 -GE- 1   [LIND-GE-STEALLA]
1992) MOOD- 3 -CEARE 4   [MOOD-CEARE]
2012) MOOD- 3 -SEFAN 4   [MOOD-SEFAN]
2030) LEEOD- 3 -HRYRE 3   [LEEOD-HRYRE]
```

253

```
(2042) AESC- 3 -WIGA 5   [AESC-WIGA]
(2060) BLOOD- 3 -FAAG 3   [BLOOD-FAAG]
(2068) DRYHT- 3 -SIBBE 3   [DRYHT-SIBBE]
(2069) FREEOND- 3 -SCIPE 4   [FREEOND-SCIPE]
(2083) GOLD- 3 -SELE 3   [GOLD-SELE]
(2093) LEEOD- 3 -SCEADHAN 2   [LEEOD-SCEADHAN]
(2130) LEEOD- 3 -FRU-9-MAN 2   [LEEOD-FRUMAN]
(2167) IN-1-WIT- 3 -NET 4   [INWIT-NET]
(2169) HOND- 3 -GE- 1   [HOND-GE-STEALLAN]
(2193) SINC- 3 -MAADH-4-THU= 3   [SINC-MAADHTHU=]
(2197) LEEOD- 3 -SCIPE 9   [LEEOD-SCIPE]
(2231) SINC- 3 -FAET 8   [SINC-FAET]
(2235) THANC- 3 -HYCGENDE 5   [THANC-HYCGENDE]
(2254) DRYNC- 3 -FAET 1   [DRYNC-FAET]
(2270) HORD- 3 -WYNNE 4   [HORD-WYNNE]
(2278) DHEEOU- 3 -SCEADHA 5   [DHEEOD-SCEADHA]
(2315) LYFT- 3 -FLOGA 4   [LYFT-FLOGA]
(2320) DRYHT- 3 -SELE 4   [DRYHT-SELE]
(2340) HOLT- 3 -WUDU 2   [HOLT-WUDU]
(2346) +WIID- 3 -FLOGAN 5   [WIID-FLOGAN]
(2360) SUND- 3 -NYTTE 4   [SUND-NYTTE]
(2366) HILD- 3 -FRECAN 4   [HILD-FRECAN]
(2391) LEEOD- 3 -HRYRES 3   [LEEOD-HRYRES]
(2414) GOLD- 3 -MAADH-9-MAS 3   [GOLD-MAADHMAS]
(2471) LEEOD- 3 -BYRIG 4   [LEEOD-BYRIG]
(2552) STEARC- 3 -HEORT 3   [STEARC-HEORT]
(2579) DHIIOD- 3 -CYNING 3   [DHIIOD-CYNING]
(2588) GRUND- 3 -WONG 3   [GRUND-WONG]
(2593) HORD- 3 -WEARD 9   [HORD-WEARD]
(2603) LIND- 3 -WIGA 4   [LIND-WIGA]
(2618) FYRD- 3 -SEARO 3   [FYRD-SEARO]
(2631) WORD- 3 -RIHTA 4   [WORD-RIHTA]
(2649) HILD- 3 -FRUMAN 3   [HILD-FRUMAN]
(2652) GOLD- 3 -GYFAN 4   [GOLD-GYFAN]
(2657) EALD- 3 -GE- 2   [EALD-GE-WYRHT]
(2688) THEEOD- 3 -SCEADHA 3   [THEEOD-SCEADHA]
(2733) FOLC- 3 -CYNING 9   [FOLC-CYNING]
(2751) LEEOD- 3 -SCIPE 3   [LEEOD-SCIPE]
(2753) WORD- 3 -CWYDU= 3   [WORD-CWYDU=]
(2768) HOND- 3 -WUNDRA 9   [HOND-WUNDRA]
(2770) GRUND- 3 -WONG 4   [GRUND-WONG]
(2771) GIOND- 3 -WLIITAN 3   [GIOND-WLIITAN]
(2778) EALD- 3 -HLAAFORDES 4   [EALD-HLAAFORDES]
(2811) GOLD- 3 -FAAHNE 4   [GOLD-FAAHNE]
(2818) BREEOST- 3 -GE- 1   [BREEOST-GE-HYGDU=]
(2831) HORD- 3 -AERNE 4   [HORD-AERNE]
(2846) HILD- 3 -LATAN 2   [HILD-LATAN]
(2866) EEORED- 3 -GEATWE 3   [EEORED-GEATWE]
(2929) ()HOND*OND- 3 -SLYHT 2   [*OND-SLYHT]
(2946) SWAAT- 3 -SWADHU 4   [SWAAT-SWADHU]
(2963) THEEOD- 3 -CYNING 4   [THEEOD-CYNING]
(2980) BORD- 3 -WEAL 3   [BORD-WEAL]
(3074) GOLD- 3 -HWAETE 3   [GOLD-HWAETE]
(3081) GOLD- 3 -WEARD 3   [GOLD-WEARD]
(3087) GEOND- 3 -SEH 3   [GEOND-SEH]
(3112) BOLD- 3 -AAGENDRA 3   [BOLD-AAGENDRA]
(3113) FOLC- 3 -AAGENDE 4   [FOLC-AAGENDE]
(3123) INWIT- 3 -+HROOF 3   [INWIT-HROOF]
(3125) AEAELED- 3 -LEEOMAN 3   [AEAELED-LEEOMAN]
(1969) GUUDH- 3 -CYNING 2   [GUUDH-CYNING]
(1982) LIIDH- 3 -WAEAEGE 3   [LIIDH-WAEAEGE]
(1990) HROODH- 3 -GAARE 5   [HROODH-GAARE]
(1996) SUUDH- 3 -DENE 5   [SUUDH-DENE]
(2079) MUUDH- 3 -BONAN. 6   [MUUDH-BONAN]
(2112) GUUDH- 3 -WIGA 9   [GUUDH-WIGA]
```

254

```
2141) OOH- 3 -FEREDE. 9    [OOH-FEREDE]
2154) GUUDH- 3 -SWEORD 3    [GUUDH-SWEORD]
2172) HEALS- 3 -BEEAH 3    [HEALS-BEEAH]
2180) HEORDH- 3 -GE- 0    [HEORDH-GE-NEEATAS]
2327) GIF- 3 -STOOL 3    [GIF-STOOL]
2351) HROODH- 3 -GAARES 9    [HROODH-GAARES]
2410) EORDH- 3 -SELE 3    [EORDH-SELE]
2414) GUUDH- 3 -FRECA 3    [GUUDH-FRECA]
2418) HEORDH- 3 -GE- 0    [HEORDH-GE-NEEATU=]
2515) EORDH- 3 -SELE 4    [EORDH-SELE]
2563) GUUDH- 3 -CYNING 4    [GUUDH-CYNING]
2664) GEO-9-GUDH- 3 -FEEORE 3    [GEOGUDH-FEEORE]
2677) GUUDH- 3 -CYNING 3    [GUUDH-CYNING]
2716) WIIS- 3 -HYGGENDE 4    [WIIS-HYGGENDE]
2805) HRO-9-NES- 3 -NAESSE 4    [HRONES-NAESSE]
2820) SOODH- 3 -FAESTRA 4    [SOODH-FAESTRA]
2825) EORDH- 3 -DRACA 3    [EORDH-DRACA]
2877) LIIF- 3 -WRADHE 3    [LIIF-WRADHE]
2881) FERHDH- 3 -GE- 0    [FERHDH-GE-NIIDHLAN]
2901) DEEADH- 3 -BEDDE 3    [DEEADH-BEDDE]
2927) GUUDH- 3 -SCIL-9-FINGAS. 5    [GUUDH-SCILFINGAS]
2929) EGES- 3 -FULL 5    [EGES-FULL]
2934) ODH- 3 -EEODON 9    [ODH-EEODON]
2935) HREFNES- 3 -HOLT 3    [HREFNES-HOLT]
2960) HREEDH- 3 -LINGAS 3    [HREEDH-LINGAS]
3046) EORDH- 3 -SCRAFA 9    [EORDH-SCRAFA]
3161) WEORDH- 3 -LIICOST 2    [WEORDH-LIICOST]
3999) ECG- 3 -DHIIOES 9    [ECG-DHIIOES]
2010) HRING- 3 -SELE 4    [HRING-SELE]
2037) HRING- 3 -MAEAEL 5    [HRING-MAEAEL]
2046) WIIG- 3 -BEALU 4    [WIIG-BEALU]
2082) BLOODIG- 3 -TOODH 4    [BLOODIG-TOODH]
2265) BURH- 3 -STEDE 3    [BURH-STEDE]
2296) HREEOH- 3 -MOOD 9    [HREEOH-MOOD]
2302) HEEAH- 3 -GE- 0    [HEEAH-GE-STREEONA]
2333) LIIG- 3 -DRACA 9    [LIIG-DRACA]
2385) FEORH- 3 -WUNDE 4    [FEORH-WUNDE]
2496) WIIG- 3 -FRECAN 5    [WIIG-FRECAN]
2501) DAEG- 3 -HREFNE 4    [DAEG-HREFNE]
2561) HRING- 3 -BOGAN 2    [HRING-BOGAN]
 631) WIIG- 3 -+LAAF 9    [WIIG-LAAF]
2672) LIIG- 3 -YYDHU= 4    [LIIG-YYDHU=]
2682) GRAEAEG- 3 -MAEAEL 4    [GRAEAEG-MAEAEL]
2726) DAEG- 3 -HWIILA 3    [DAEG-HWIILA]
2780) LIIG- 3 -EGESAN 3    [LIIG-EGESAN]
2800) FEORH- 3 -LEGE 4    [FEORH-LEGE]
2840) HRING- 3 -SELE 9    [HRING-SELE]
2893) ECG- 3 -CLIF 4    [ECG-CLIF]
2904) ()SIEX*SEX- 3 -BENNU= 9    [*SEX-BENNU=]
3040) LEEG- 3 -DRACA 4    [LEEG-DRACA]
3053) HRING- 3 -SELE 5    [HRING-SELE]
2570) G=- 3 -SCIPE 4    [G=-SCIPE]
2750) MAADHDHU=- 3 -WELAN 9    [MAADHDHU=-WELAN]

3022) FREEA- 4 -WARE 9    [FREEA-WARE]
2223) THREEA- 4 -NEEDLAN 4    [THREEA-NEEDLAN]
2438) FREEA- 4 -WINE 4    [FREEA-WINE]
1964) SAEAE- 4 -WONG 4    [SAEAE-WONG]
2930) AA- 4 -()HEORDE*HREDDE 4    [*AA-HREDDE]
 931) IOO- 4 -MEEOWLAN 9    [IOO-MEEOWLAN]
3942) FREODHU- 4 -WEBBE 3    [FREODHU-WEBBE]
3016) MEDU- 4 -DREEAM 4    [MEDU-DREEAM]
3017) FRIDHU- 4 -SIBB 3    [FRIDHU-SIBB]
3037) HEADHA- 4 -()BEARNA*BEARDNA 3    [*HEADHA-BEARDNA]
 079) ()MAGU=*MAGU- 4 -THEGNE 9    [*MAGU-THEGNE]
```

255

```
(2113) HILDE- 4 -STRENGO 4    [HILDE-STRENGO]
(2153) HEADHO- 4 -STEEAPNE 5    [HEADHO-STEEAPNE]
(2205) HEADHO- 4 -SCILFINGAS. 5    [HEADHO-SCILFINGAS]
(2224) HETE- 4 -SWENGEAS 9    [HETE-SWENGEAS]
(2239) WINE- 4 -GEOO-1-MOR 5    [WINE-GEOOMOR]
(2258) HERE- 4 -+PAAD 2    [HERE-PAAD]
(2326) BRYNE- 4 -WYLMU= 5    [BRYNE-WYLMU=]
(2364) FEEDHE- 4 -WIIGES 3    [FEEDHE-WIIGES]
(2477) HREEOSNA- 4 -BEORH 3    [HREEOSNA-BEORH]
(2544) HILDE- 4 -HLEM-2-MA 3    [HILDE-HLEMMA]
(2734) YMBE- 4 -SITTENDRA 5    [YMBE-SITTENDRA]
(2738) SEARO- 4 -NIIDHAS 3    [SEARO-NIIDHAS]
(2755) BEADU- 4 -SER-2-CEAN 4    [BEADU-SERCEAN]
(2781) HIORO- 4 -WEALLENDE 4    [HIORO-WEALLENDE]
(2892) HEADHO- 4 -WEORC 4    [HEADHO-WEORC]
(2921) MERE- 4 -WIIO-3-INGAS 0    [MERE-WIIOINGAS]
(3031) EARNA- 4 -NAES 3    [EARNA-NAES]
(2204) SIGE- 4 -THEEODE 4    [SIGE-THEEODE]
(2328) HYGE- 4 -SORGA 4    [HYGE-SORGA]
(2710) SIGE- 4 -HWIILE 4    [SIGE-HWIILE]
(2275) GE- 4 -SEECEAN 4    [GE-SEECEAN]
(2574) GE- 4 -SCRAAF 5    [GE-SCRAAF]
(2879) GE- 4 -MET 2    [GE-MET]
(2420) -GE- 4 -METE 4    [UN-GE-METE]
(3084) -GE- 4 -SCEAP 3    [HEEAH-GE-SCEAP]
(1978) MAN- 4 -DRYHTEN 4    [MAN-DRYHTEN]
(2015) HEAL- 4 -SITTEN-1-DRA 5    [HEAL-SITTENDRA]
(2044) GEOO-1-MOR- 4 -MOOD 2    [GEOOMOR-MOOD]
(2065) WAEL- 4 -NIIDHAS 3    [WAEL-NIIDHAS]
(2066) CEAR- 4 -WAELMU= 4    [CEAR-WAELMU=]
(2080) FOR- 4 -SWEALG. 7    [FOR-SWEALG]
(2118) GYRN- 4 -WRAECE. 5    [GYRN-WRAECE]
(2128) FIRGEN- 4 -STREEAM. 6    [FIRGEN-STREEAM]
(2165) AEPPEL- 4 -FEALUWE 4    [AEPPEL-FEALUWE]
(2173) WUNDUR- 4 -MAADHDHU= 9    [WUNDUR-MAADHDHU=]
(2198) EEDHEL- 4 -RIHT 3    [EEDHEL-RIHT]
(2210) EETHEL- 4 -WEARD 4    [EETHEL-WEARD]
(2232) AEAER- 4 -GE- 3    [AEAER-GE-STREEONA]
(2234) EORMEN- 4 -LAAFE 9    [EORMEN-LAAFE]
(2236) FOR- 4 -NAM 4    [FOR-NAM]
(2305) FOR- 4 -GYLDAN 2    [FOR-GYLDAN]
(2352) SIGOR- 4 -EEADIG 2    [SIGOR-EEADIG]
(2436) MORTHOR- 4 -BED 1    [MORTHOR-BED]
(2451) ELLOR- 4 -SIIDH 3    [ELLOR-SIIDH]
(2517) HELM- 4 -BE-9-REND 4    [HELM-BEREND]
(2525) OFER- 4 -FLEEON 3    [OFER-FLEEON]
(2535) EORL- 4 -SCYPE 4    [EORL-SCYPE]
(2540) STAAN- 4 -CLEOFU 9    [STAAN-CLEOFU]
(2643) ELLEN- 4 -WEORC 3    [ELLEN-WEORC]
(2686) OFER- 4 -SOOHTE 4    [OFER-SOOHTE]
(2689) +FYYR- 4 -DRACA 4    [FYYR-DRACA]
(2705) FOR- 4 -WRAAT 2    [FOR-WRAAT]
(2742) MORDHOR- 4 -BEALO 3    [MORDHOR-BEALO]
(2772) FOR- 4 -NA= 4    [FOR-NA=]
(2795) WULDUR- 4 -CYNINGE 3    [WULDUR-CYNINGE]
(2828) FOR- 4 -NAAMON 4    [FOR-NAAMON]
(2833) MAADHM- 4 -AEAEHTA 4    [MAADHM-AEAEHTA]
(2881) UN- 4 -SWIIDHCR 5    [UN-SWIIDHOR]
(2893) EORL- 4 -WEOROD 2    [EORL-WEOROD]
(2903) EALDOR- 4 -GE- 1    [EALDOR-GE-WINNA]
(2917) OFER- 4 -MAEGENE 4    [OFER-MAEGENE]
(2997) FOR- 4 -GEAF 9    [FOR-GEAF]
(3112) BAEAEL- 4 -WUDU 3    [BAEAEL-WUDU]
(3116) IISERN- 4 -SCUURE 5    [IISERN-SCUURE]
(3119) ()FAEDER*FAEDHER- 4 -GEARWU= 3    [*FAEDHER-GEARWU=]
```

```
007) UUHT- 4 -HLEM 4    [UUHT-HLEM]
017) GEOND- 4 -HWEARF 3   [GEOND-HWEARF]
053) NAAT- 4 -HWYLGES. 6   [NAAT-HWYLCES]
136) GRUND- 4 -HYRDE 4    [GRUND-HYRDE]
144) DHEEOD- 4 -KYNING 4   [DHEEOD-KYNING]
151) HEEAFOD- 4 -MAAGA 4   [HEEAFOD-MAAGA]
162) BREEOST- 4 -GE- 0    [BREEOST-GE-WAEAEDU]
279) HORD- 4 -AERNA 1    [HORD-AERNA]
288) STEARC- 4 -HEORT 4   [STEARC-HEORT]
293) HORD- 4 -WEARD 9    [HORD-WEARD]
300) SINC- 4 -FAET 3    [SINC-FAET]
321) LAND- 4 -WARA 9    [LAND-WARA]
344) HORD- 4 -WELAN 4    [HORD-WELAN]
478) INWIT- 4 -SCEAR 5   [INWIT-SCEAR]
760) UUHT- 4 -FLOGAN 9    [UUHT-FLOGAN]
125) DEEAOH- 4 -WEERIG-1-NE 4    [DEEAOH-WEERIGNE]
249) GUUDH- 4 -DEEADH 4    [GUUDH-DEEADH]
318) GUUDH- 4 -SCEADHA 5    [GUUDH-SCEADHA]
334) EORDH- 4 -WEARD 9    [EORDH-WEARD]
417) NIIDH- 4 -HEARD 3    [NIIDH-HEARD]
487) GUUDH- 4 -HELM 2    [GUUDH-HELM]
625) FORDH- 4 -WEG 3    [FORDH-WEG]
822) EAR-9-FODH- 4 -LIICE 4    [EARFODH-LIICE]
934) EARFODH- 4 -LIICE 4    [EARFODH-LIICE]
954) HEEAH- 4 -LUFAN 4    [HEEAH-LUFAN]
018) BEEA-2-H- 4 -WRIDHAN 4    [BEEAH-WRIDHAN]
077) FEOR-2-H- 4 -BEALU 3    [FEORH-BEALU]
132) HREEOH- 4 -MOOD 8    [HREEOH-MOOD]
250) FEORH- 4 -()BEALC*BEALO 3    [*FEORH-BEALO]
266) FEOR-1-H- 4 -CYNNA 5    [FEORH-CYNNA]
427) -LEG- 4 -HWIILA 3    [OR-LEG-HWIILA]
826) BEEAH- 4 -HORDU= 2    [BEEAH-HORDU=]
847) TREEOW- 4 -LOGAN 4    [TREEOW-LOGAN]
049) THURH- 4 -ETONE 4    [THURH-ETONE]
757) MAADHDHU=- 4 -SIGLA 4    [MAADHDHU=-SIGLA]

296) YMBE- 7 -HWEARF 3    [YMBE-HWEARF]
351) HILDE- 5 -HLEM-1-MA 5    [HILDE-HLEMMA]
435) -GE- 5 -DEEFE- 0    [UN-GE-DEEFE-LIICE]
043) GAAR- 5 -CWEALM 4    [GAAR-CWEALM]
242) WAETER- 5 -YYTHU= 5    [WAETER-YYTHU=]
267) GIOO-1-MOR- 5 -MOOD 2    [GIOOMOR-MOOD]
672) FOR- 5 -BORN 2    [FOR-BORN]
018) GEOO-1-MOR- 5 -MOOD 3    [GEOOMOR-MOOD]
504) BREEOST- 5 -WEORDHUNGE 4    [BREEOST-WEORDHUNGE]
303) EARFODH- 5 -LIICE 5    [EARFODH-LIICE]

151) *BIIO- 8 -*WULFE 8    [*BIIO-*WULFE]
063) ()+*AA- 8 -BROCENE 5    [*AA-BROCENE]
221) ()CRAEFI*AA- 8 -*BRAEC 5    [*AA-*BRAEC]
122) ()++*TOO- 8 -SOMNE 4    [*TOO-SOMNE]
150) *GEOO- 8 -MEEOWLE 8    [*GEOO-MEEOWLE]
217) ()++++*BE- 8 -*MAADH 8    [*BE-*MAADH]
227) ()++++*GRYRE- 8 -BROOGA 8    [*GRYRE-BROOGA]
488) *HEORO- 8 -BLAAC 2    [*HEORO-BLAAC]
714) BEALO- 8 -NIIDHE 9    [BEALO-NIIDHE]
883) BE- 8 -CWOOM. 6    [BE-CWOOM]
041) ()GRY++++*GRYRE- 8 -*FAAH 9    [*GRYRE-*FAAH]
136) HILDE- 8 -*RINC 8    [HILDE-*RINC]
144) ()WUD+*WUDU- 8 -+REEC 2    [*WUDU-REEC]
000) HIGE- 8 -LAAC 8    [HIGE-LAAC]
004) SIGE- 8 -SCYL-9-DI-8-NGU= 5    [SIGE-SCYLDINGU=]
042) GE- 8 -()+++*MAN 9    [*GE-MAN]
114) GE- 8 -MUNDE 5    [GE-MUNDE]
208) GE- 8 -HWEARF 9    [GE-HWEARF]
```

257

```
(2215) GE- 8 -()FENG*FEALG 3    [*GE-FEALG]
(2633) GE- 8 -MAN 3    [GE-MAN]
(2694) *GE- 8 -*FRAEGN 8    [*GE-*FRAEGN]
(2696) GE- 8 -CYNDE 3    [GE-CYNDE]
(3014) ()++++++TE*GE- 8 -*BOHTE 5    [*GE-*BOHTE]
(3152) GE- 8 -NEAHHE 8    [GE-NEAHHE]
(3156) GE- 8 -WORHTON 1    [GE-WORHTON]
(2244) -GE- 8 -STREEONA 6    [EORL-GE-STREEONA]
(1942) ON- 8 -SAEAECE 3    [ON-SAEAECE]
(1981) ()SIDE*HEAL- 8 -RECED 4    [*HEAL-RECED]
(2002) ()++++++*OR- 8 -*LEG- 9    [*OR-*LEG-HWIIL]
(2108) GO-9-()MEL*MEN- 8 -WUDU 3    [*GOMEN-WUDU]
(2111) ON- 8 -GAN 4    [ON-GAN]
(2219) ON- 8 -()+++D*FAND 8    [*ON-FAND]
(2226) SYN- 8 -BYSIG 6    [SYN-BYSIG]
(2228) ()++++*EARM- 8 -SCEAPEN 8    [*EARM-SCEAPEN]
(2275) ()++*ON- 8 -()+++DA+*DRAEAEDADH 8    [*ON-DRAEAEDADH]
(2381) FOR- 8 -HEALDEN 4    [FOR-HEALDEN]
(2792) *BIORN- 8 -*CYNING 8    [*BIORN-*CYNING]
(2839) ATTOR- 8 -SCEADHAN 9    [ATTOR-SCEADHAN]
(2902) WAEL- 8 -RESTE 4    [WAEL-RESTE]
(3153) ()++++G+NGAS*HEARM- 8 -*DAGAS 3    [*HEARM-*DAGAS]
(3153) ON- 8 -()D+EDE*DREEDE 4    [*ON-DREEDE]
(3154) WAEL- 8 -FYLLA 3    [WAEL-FYLLA]
(3181) MON- 8 -()++AERUST*DHWAEAERUST 2    [*MON-DHWAEAERUST]
(2022) FLET- 8 -SITTENDE. 5    [FLET-SITTENDE]
(2094) ()HOND*OND- 8 -LEEAN 9    [*OND-LEEAN]
(2202) ()HEAREDE*HEARD- 8 -*REEDE 4    [*HEARD-*REEDE]
(2884) SWYRD- 8 -GIFU 9    [SWYRD-GIFU]
(2909) HEEAFOD- 8 -WEARDE 5    [HEEAFOD-WEARDE]
(2938) OND- 8 -LONGE 9    [OND-LONGE]
(3005) ()SCILDINGAS*SCILD- 8 -*WIGAN 9    [*SCILD-*WIGAN]
(3086) *THEEOD- 8 -*CYNING 8    [*THEEOD-*CYNING]
(3155) ()HAEF+*HAEFT- 8 -NYYD 3    [*HAEFT-NYYD]
(2065) WIIF- 8 -LUFAN 3    [WIIF-LUFAN]
(2139) *GUUDH- 8 -SELE 9    [*GUUDH-SELE]
(2220) ()BU*BIG- 8 -FOLC 3    [*BIG-FOLC]
(2261) WIIG- 8 -FRU-9-MAN 3    [WIIG-FRUMAN]
(2661) WIIG- 8 -HEA-9-FOLAN 3    [WIIG-HEAFOLAN]

(1987) BIIO- 9 -WULF 4    [BIIO-WULF]
(2393) FEEA- 9 -SCEAFTU= 4    [FEEA-SCEAFTU=]
(2922) SWEEO- 9 -DHEEODE 4    [SWEEO-DHEEODE]
(3141) TOO- 9 -MIDDES 4    [TOO-MIDDES]
(2006) BE- 9 -GYLPAN 4    [BE-GYLPAN]
(2032) HEADHO- 9 -BEARDNA 5    [HEADHO-BEARDNA]
(2183) HILDE- 9 -DEEOR 2    [HILDE-DEEOR]
(2201) HILDE- 9 -HLAEM-2-MU= 6    [HILDE-HLAEMMU=]
(2218) BE- 9 -()SYRE+*SYRED 8    [*BE-SYRED]
(2243) NEARO- 9 -CRAEFTU= 4    [NEARO-CRAEFTU=]
(2265) BEALO- 9 -CWEALM 3    [BEALO-CWEALM]
(2313) BRYNE- 9 -LEEOMA 4    [BRYNE-LEEOMA]
(2370) BREGO- 9 -STOOL 3    [BREGO-STOOL]
(2453) YRFE- 9 -WEARDAS 4    [YRFE-WEARDAS]
(2547) HEADHO- 9 -FYYRU= 4    [HEADHO-FYYRU=]
(2598) HILDE- 9 -CYSTU= 4    [HILDE-CYSTU=]
(2704) BEADU- 9 -SCEARP 5    [BEADU-SCEARP]
(2731) YRFE- 9 -WEARD 2    [YRFE-WEARD]
(2749) SEARO- 9 -GI=MAS 3    [SEARO-GI=MAS]
(2799) BE- 9 -BOHTE 3    [BE-BOHTE]
(3020) HERE- 9 -WIISA 4    [HERE-WIISA]
(3052) BE- 9 -WUNDEN 4    [BE-WUNDEN]
(3069) BE- 9 -NEM-1-DON 4    [BE-NEMDON]
(3162) ()FO++*FORE- 9 -()+NOTRE*SNOTRE 2    [*FORE-SNOTRE]
(2977) HIGE- 9 -LAACES 3    [HIGE-LAACES]
```

258

```
1959) GE- 9 -WEORDHOD 4    [GE-WEORDHOD]
2149) GE- 9 -YYWAN 3    [GE-YYWAN]
2165) GE- 9 -TEEAH 4    [GE-TEEAH]
2172) GE- 9 -SEALDE 5    [GE-SEALDE]
2206) GE- 9 -NAEAEGDAN. 5    [GE-NAEAEGDAN]
2220) GE- 9 -()BOLGE+*BOLGEN 8    [*GE-BOLGEN]
2222) GE- 9 -SCEOOD 5    [GE-SCEOOD]
2235) GE- 9 -HYYDDE. 5    [GE-HYYDDE]
2301) GE- 9 -FAN-1-DOD 3    [GE-FANDOD]
2342) GE- 9 -BIIDAN 4    [GE-BIIDAN]
2397) GE- 9 -HWANE 5    [GE-HWANE]
2401) GE- 9 -BOLGEN 4    [GE-BOLGEN]
2438) GE- 9 -SWENC-1-TE 5    [ GE-SWENCTE]
2488) GE- 9 -MUNDE.. 7    [GE-MUNDE]
2543) GE- 9 -DIIGDE 3    [GE-DIIGDE]
2700) GE- 9 -DEEAF 3    [GE-DEEAF]
2740) GE- 9 -FEEAN 2    [GE-FEEAN]
2798) GE- 9 -STRYYNAN 4    [GE-STRYYNAN]
2804) GE- 9 -MYNDU= 4    [GE-MYNDU=]
2838) GE- 9 -HWAES 3    [GE-HWAES]
3061) GE- 9 -WEARDH 4    [GE-WEARDH]
3078) GE- 9 -WORDEN 2    [GE-WORDEN]
3106) GE- 9 -AEFNED 2    [GE-AEFNED]
2636) -GE- 9 -TAAWA 4    [GUUDH-GE-TAAWA]
2728) -GE- 9 -METE 4    [UN-GE-METE]
3064) -GE- 9 -SCEAFTA 4    [LIIF-GE-SCEAFTA]
1962) +GAAR- 9 -MUNDES 4    [GAAR-MUNDES]
1979) HLEEODHOR- 9 -CWYDE 3    [HLEEODHOR-CWYDE]
2148) BEORN- 9 -CYNING 3    [BEORN-CYNING]
2181) MAN- 9 -CYNNES 5    [MAN-CYNNES]
2188) UN- 9 -FROM 4    [UN-FROM]
2244) EORL- 9 -GE- 8    [EORL-GE-STREEONA]
2280) EEACEN- 9 -CRAEFTIG 5    [EEACEN-CRAEFTIG]
2297) UUTAN- 9 -WEARD-1-NE 5    [UUTAN-WEARDNE]
2338) EALL- 9 -IIRENNE 5    [EALL-IIRENNE]
2347) ON- 9 -DREED. 6    [ON-DREED]
2367) OFER- 9 -SWAM 1    [OFER-SWAM]
2475) ONGEN- 9 -DHEOWES 3    [ONGEN-DHEOWES]
2486) ONGEN- 9 -THEEOW 3    [ONGEN-THEEOW]
2528) OFER- 9 -SITTE 4    [OFER-SITTE]
2548) UN- 9 -BYRNENDE 4    [UN-BYRNENDE]
2564) UN- 9 -()GLAW*SLAAW 4    [*UN-SLAAW]
2641) +GAAR- 9 -WIIGEND 3    [GAAR-WIIGEND]
2693) SAAWUL- 9 -DRIIORE 3    [SAAWUL-DRIIORE]
2739) UN- 9 -RIHT 2    [UN-RIHT]
2767) EALL- 9 -GYLDEN 5    [EALL-GYLDEN]
2814) FOR- 9 -()SPEOF*SWEEOP 8    [*FOR-SWEEOP]
2837) MAEGEN- 9 -AAGENDRA 4    [MAEGEN-AAGENDRA]
2918) BYRN- 9 -WIGA 4    [BYRN-WIGA]
3003) EALDOR- 9 -LEEASNE 4    [EALDOR-LEEASNE]
3007) EORL- 9 -SCIPE 4    [EORL-SCIPE]
3022) MORGEN- 9 -CEALD 4    [MORGEN-CEALD]
3031) UN- 9 -BLIIDHE 4    [UN-BLIIDHE]
1946) LEEOD- 9 -BEALEWA 3    [LEEOD-BEALEWA]
2039) LIND- 9 -PLEGAN 5    [LIND-PLEGAN]
2076) HOND- 9 -SCIOO 3    [HOND-SCIOO]
2090) DAEAED- 9 -FRUMA 3    [DAEAED-FRUMA]
2122) AESC- 9 -HERE 5    [AESC-HERE]
2203) BORD- 9 -HREEODHAN 4    [BORD-HREEODHAN]
2205) ()HILDE*HILD- 9 -FRECAN 3    [*HILD-FRECAN]
2223) NAAT- 9 -HWYLCES 8    [NAAT-HWYLCES]
2271) UUHT- 9 -SCEADHA 5    [UUHT-SCEADHA]
2289) FOOT- 9 -LAAST 4    [FOOT-LAAST]
2306) DRINC- 9 -FAET 5    [DRINC-FAET]
2379) WRAEC- 9 -MAECGAS 3    [WRAEC-MAECGAS]
```

```
(2419) GOLD- 9 -WINE 3    [GOLD-WINE]
(2476) FYRD- 9 -HWATE 5   [FYRD-HWATE]
(2554) HORD- 9 -WEARD 3   [HORD-WEARD]
(2584) GOLD- 9 -WINE 3    [GOLD-WINE]
(2607) +WIIC- 9 -STEDE 5  [WIIC-STEDE]
(2810) THRIIST- 9 -HYYDIG 4    [THRIIST-HYYDIG]
(2895) BORD- 9 -HAEBBENDE 4    [BORD-HAEBBENDE]
(2970) DHEEOD- 9 -CYNING 3    [DHEEOD-CYNING]
(3008) THEEOD- 9 -CYNING 4    [THEEOD-CYNING]
(3146) WIND- 9 -BLOND 1    [WIND-BLOND]
(2123) UUDH- 9 -GENGE. 6    [UUDH-GENGE]
(2232) EORDH- 9 -()++SE*HUUSE 8    [*EORDH-HUUSE]
(2335) GUUDH- 9 -KYNING 4    [GUUDH-KYNING]
(2439) OF- 9 -SCEET 3    [OF-SCEET]
(2482) HAEDH- 9 -CYNNE 4    [HAEDH-CYNNE]
(2489) OF- 9 -TEEAH. 5    [OF-TEEAH]
(2603) LEEOF- 9 -LIIC 5    [LEEOF-LIIC]
(2604) AELF- 9 -HERES 4    [AELF-HERES]
(2617) GUUDH- 9 -GE- 2    [GUUDH-GE-WAEAEDU]
(2623) GUUDH- 9 -GE- 3    [GUUDH-GE-WAEAEJA]
(2639) SIIDH- 9 -FATE 4    [SIIDH-FATE]
(2712) EORDH- 9 -DRACA 4    [EORDH-DRACA]
(2846) OF- 9 -GEEFAN 3    [OF-GEEFAN]
(2899) SOODH- 9 -LIICE 4    [SOODH-LIICE]
(2995) ODH- 9 -WIITAN 4    [ODH-WIITAN]
(3055) SOODH- 9 -CYNING 3    [SOODH-CYNING]
(3099) WEORDH- 9 -FULLOST 4    [WEORDH-FULLOST]
(3165) NIIDH- 9 -HEEDIGE 2    [NIIDH-HEEDIGE]
(3182) LOF- 9 -GEORNOST. 9    [LOF-GEORNOST]
(2002) -*LEG- 9 -HWIIL 4    [*OR-*LEG-HWIIL]
(2455) SORH- 9 -CEARIG 4    [SORH-CEARIG]
(2465) FEORH- 9 -BONAN 4    [FEORH-BONAN]
(2479) MAEAEG- 9 -WINE 5    [MAEAEG-WINE]
(2537) FEORH- 9 -BEALU 4    [FEORH-BEALU]
(2752) WIIH- 9 -STAANES 3    [WIIH-STAANES]
(3100) BURH- 9 -WELAN 2    [BURH-WELAN]
(2469) GU=- 9 -DREEAM 5    [GU=-DREEAM]
(2890) DOO=- 9 -LEEASAN 1    [DOO=-LEEASAN]
```